THE BATTLE OF ZNAIM

THE BATTLE OF ZNAIM
Napoleon, the Habsburgs
and the
End of the War of 1809

John H. Gill

Greenhill Books

The Battle of Znaim
First published in 2020 by
Greenhill Books,
c/o Pen & Sword Books Ltd,
47 Church Street, Barnsley,
S. Yorkshire, S70 2AS

www.greenhillbooks.com
contact@greenhillbooks.com

ISBN: 978-1-78438-450-0

All rights reserved.
© John H. Gill, 2020

The right of John Gill to be identified as author of this work
has been asserted in accordance with Section 77 of the
Copyrights Designs and Patents Act 1988.

CIP data records for this title are available from the British Library

Designed and typeset by Donald Sommerville

Printed and bound in the UK by TJ International Ltd, Padstow

Typeset in 12/15.2 pt Arno Pro Regular & Arno Pro Display

Frontispiece: Battle of Znaim. Leiningen's grenadiers driving the French
back towards the Thaya bridges; the original artist visited the site
to prepare this work. *(Author)*

This volume is dedicated to
Herbert J. Gill
(1919–2012)

Contents

	Lists of Charts and Maps	ix
	List of Illustrations	xi
	Conventions	xxi
	Preface	xiii
	Acknowledgements	xvii
Chapter 1	A Minister, an Archduke and an Emperor	1
Chapter 2	Armies on the Edge of War	36
Chapter 3	From Regensburg to Wagram	66
Chapter 4	Every Night a March, Every Day an Attack	102
Intermezzo	The Other Theatres of War	173
Chapter 5	I Found Myself in the Rear of the Austrian Army	177
Chapter 6	Can't You Hear the Cannon?	241
Chapter 7	An Armistice Saved Us	282
	Epilogue	324
	Notes	335

APPENDICES

1	The Coalitions Against France	384
2	Key Habsburg Personalities	386
3	Outline Chronology	388
4	Headquarters Locations, 6–12 July	391

5	Orders of Battle		392
	A. The Battle of Wagram, 5–6 July 1809	395	
	B. French Pursuit Forces, 7–8 July 1809	419	
	C. Austrian IV Corps, 10 July 1809	423	
	D. Austrian V Corps, 10 July 1809	426	
	E. The Battle of Znaim, 10–11 July 1809	428	
6	The French Cuirassiers on 11 July		444
7	Tactical Notes		446
	Bibliography		449
	Index		475
	Gazetteer		482

Charts and Maps

Charts

1. French and Allied Forces on 10 April — 44
2. Austrian Forces on 10 April — 45
3. Misaligned Austrian Units, 7–10 July — 132
4. Rough Comparative Strengths on 10 and 11 July — 257
5. Major Forces in Other Theatres of War — 309

Maps

1. Central Europe in 1809 — 16
2. Austrian Invasions, April 1809 — 68
3. French Counteroffensives, May–June 1809 — 72
4. Strategic Situation, 4 July — 93
5. The Battle of Wagram, 5 July — 96
6. The Battle of Wagram, 6 July — 98
7. Situation on morning of 7 July & action at Korneuburg — 111
8. Two Roads to Znaim: The operational area, 8–10 July — 126
9. Action at Stockerau, 8 July — 129
10. Pursuit to Znaim, Situation on 9 July — 147
11. Engagement at Hollabrunn, 9 July — 151
12. Staatz/Neudorf Actions, 9 July — 157
13. Znaim Area Orientation Map — 181
14. The Battlefield at Znaim* — 183
15. The Battle of Znaim, 10 July, mid-afternoon* — 195
16. The Battle of Znaim, 10 July, evening* — 206
17. Schöngrabern to Guntersdorf, Rearguard Actions 10 July — 212

x *Charts and Maps*

18. Rosenberg's Retreat, 9–11 July — 235
19. The Battle of Znaim, 11 July, mid-afternoon* — 245
20. The Operational Situation at the Armistice, 12 July — 296
21. Raids & Expeditions in Germany, May–July — 312
22. Strategic Situation, 8–13 July — 315

Extensive effort has been made to use contemporary or near contemporary cartography (i.e. late-eighteenth/early-nineteenth century) as the bases for the maps in this volume.

* Most maps are oriented conventionally with north at the top. The Znaim battle maps, however, are angled to afford adequate space. These draw heavily on maps from the Austrian Kriegsarchiv (KA): 'Plan des Treffens bei Znaim am 10. und 11.7.1809', no date, KA KPS KS H IV a, 1284 and 'Plan der Schlacht bei Znaim 1809', no date, KA KPS KS H IV a, 1285.

Key to Map Symbols
John H. Gill © 2020, all rights reserved

Primary road: ———
Secondary road: = = = = = = =
International border: • • • • • • • •
Internal border: ⋯⋯⋯⋯⋯
Forests/large gardens: [shaded box]
Vineyards/orchards: [hatched box]

Outlines for towns/villages include gardens as well as structures as these contributed to the defensive value of the buildings.

Fortresses or forts: ★
Battles and engagements: ✹

Units types are indicated by the following symbols with nationality shown by colour: white for Austrians, black for French and grey for Napoleon's German allies.

	Austrian:	French:	German:
Cavalry units:	[white w/ diagonal]	[black w/ diagonal]	[grey w/ diagonal]
Infantry and mixed units:	[white box]	[black box]	[grey box]
Artillery (all sides):	⫞⫞⫞		

Examples:
Bavarian 2nd Division = [2]   **Austrian III Corps =** [III]

Austrian movements (advance and retreat) are shown with dashed lines, while those of the French and allied German troops are solid.

Austrian movement = ‐ ‐ ‐ ‐ ▶   **French/Allied movement =** ——▶

Russian units and movement = [R]   ▰ ▰ ▰ ▰ ▶

Illustrations

1. Napoleon in silhouette *(Laa)*; Napoleon at Eggmühl *(Author)*.
2. Marshal Massena at Wagram *(Alamy)*; GD Michel Marie Claparède *(La Sabretache)*; Oberstleutnant August Graf zu Leiningen-Westerburg *(Wikicommons)*.
3. Uniforms. a) Austrian grenadiers from 'German' companies; b) Austrian line infantry from a 'German' regiment; c) Austrian Grenzer; d) Austrian Uhlans *(a, b: Alfred Umhey; c, d: Author)*.
4. Uniforms. a) Baden Jäger; b) Baden line infantry; c) Hessian light infantry; d) French grenadier; e) French chasseur-à-cheval; f) French light infantry *(a, b, c: Napoleonic Uniforms, vol. III; d, e, f: Napoleonic Uniforms, vol. I)*.
5. Uniforms. a) French cuirassier; b) Bavarian line infantry; c) Bavarian chevauleger; d) Bavarian artillery; e) Bavarian light infantry *(a: Napoleonic Uniforms, vol. I; b, c, e: Napoleonic Uniforms, vol. III; d: Author)*.
6. Engagement at Hollabrunn *(Art Resource)*; the *Schloß* at Wolkersdorf *(A. Rieman)*.
7. French troops attacking the Rother Hof; the 5th Vienna Volunteers at the Znaim gate *(both South Moravian Museum)*.
8. The Battle of Znaim: the view from Massena's side of the field *(Art Resource)*; Napoleon on the heights above Klein-Tesswitz *(ASKB)*.
9. Archduke Charles *(Author)*; Archduke Charles at Aspern *(ASKB)*.
10. Kaiser Franz; Johann Philipp Graf Stadion; Clemens von Metternich *(all Author)*.

11. FML Franz von Rosenberg-Orsini *(Author)*; FML Friedrich Fürst von Hohenzollern-Hechingen *(Author)*; FZM Karl Graf Kolowrat-Krakowsky *(ASKB)*; GdK Heinrich Graf Bellegarde *(ASKB)*.
12. FML Johann Graf Klenau *(ASKB)*; GdK Johan Fürst von und zu Liechtenstein *(ASKB)*; GM Maximilian Freiherr von Wimpffen *(Author)*; FZM Heinrich Fürst zu Reuss-Plauen *(Author)*.
13. Austrian and Brunswick troops near Nuremberg in June 1809 *(ASKB)*; Bavarian light infantry storm a bridge, July 1809 *(ASKB)*.
14. Marshal André Massena *(ASKB)*; GD Gabriel Molitor *(ASKB)*; GD Claude Carra St Cyr *(Author)*; GD Claude Legrand *(ASKB)*.
15. Massena and his son Jacques Prosper along with GD Nicolas Fririon, the marshal's chief of staff *(La Sabretache)*; GD Louis Montbrun *(ASKB)*; GD (later Marshal) Auguste Marmont *(ASKB)*; GD Bertrand Clauzel *(Alamy)*.
16. Archduke Charles at Aspern *(ASKB)*; Napoleon and the mortally wounded Marshal Lannes at Aspern *(ASKB)*.
17. French bridges over the Danube before Wagram *(Author)*; Napoleon at Wagram *(Author)*.
18. Charles rallying his men at Wagram *(Author)*; Napoleon with Austrian prisoners after Wagram *(ASKB)*.
19. Oberstleutnant Karl von Francken, Baden chief of staff *(Author)*; Major Rudolph Graf Salis-Zizers of the 5th Vienna Volunteers *(Wikicommons)*; GB Jean Marie de Stabenrath *(De Stabenrath Family)*; GB Jean Pierre Bruyère *(La Sabretache)*.
20. Parlementaire at Hollabrunn *(Author)*; Znaim from the west *(Czech National Heritage Institute)*.
21. General Franz von Minucci at Znaim *(Czech National Heritage Institute)*; Znaim from the east *(South Moravian Museum)*.
22. French troops charge across the bridge over the Thaya *(Alamy)*; Napoleon meeting Austrian officers *(Alfred Umhey)*.
23. Marshal Alexander Berthier *(Author)*; Hödnitz Mill *(South Moravian Museum)*.
24. Napoleon reviewing troops at Schönbrunn Palace after the armistice *(Art Resource)*; Napoleon meets his new wife, Marie Louise *(ASKB)*.

Abbreviations and Additional Acknowledgements

ASKB = Anne S. K. Brown Military Collection
Czech National Heritage Institute (with thanks to Ms Rainisová)
De Stabenrath Family (with thanks to M. le général de Stabenrath)
Napoleonic Uniforms = John R. Elting, *Napoleonic Uniforms*
    Vols. I and II: London: Greenhill, 2007
    Vols. III and IV: Rosemont: Emperor's Press, 2000 (with thanks to Mr Todd Fisher)
Le Sabretache (with thanks to M. Martin)
Laa = Stadtarchiv Laa an der Thaya (with thanks to Dr Fürnkranz)
South Moravian Museum (with thanks to Dr Kacetl)

Conventions

I have adopted the conventions outlined below to retain something of the flavour of the age.

- French, German and Austrian ranks are preserved insofar as this is feasible and convenient; a table on the following pages relates these to current U.S. and British ranks and lists abbreviations. Similarly, Austrian and German noble titles are employed throughout (see table for English translations).

- 'Ligne' and 'Léger' refer respectively to French line and light infantry.

- I have followed contemporary practice in designating Austrian line infantry and cavalry regiments by the titles derived from their *Inhaber* ('patrons' or 'proprietors') rather than their numbers (*Kaiser* Cuirassiers No. 1, not the 1st Cuirassier Regiment), although numbers are included on first use. Note that 'EH' abbreviates 'Erzherzog' as in Infantry Regiment *EH Ludwig* No. 8. Austrian regiments that did not have *Inhaber* at the time of the battle (deceased and not yet replaced) are indicated by their number and the former *Inhaber*, for example: Infantry Regiment No. 25 (former *Zedtwitz*).

- The geographic designations of Austrian Grenz Regiments are also given in italics for ease of recognition (e.g., *Gradiska* Grenz Infantry No. 8).

- I refer to Austrian Landwehr battalions by their regional designations in the text, but I have included their commanders' names in the orders of battle as many histories only refer to them in this fashion (e.g. Major Franz Adam Wrtby commanded the 1st Beraun Landwehr).

• The *Inhaber* of German regiments are also shown in italics as in the 7th Bavarian Infantry *Löwenstein*, and German units known only by the names of their *Inhaber* or commanders are presented in italics (Baden Oberst Johann Baptist Lingg commanded Jäger-Bataillon *Lingg*).

• Arabic numerals are used for the French *corps d'armée* (Davout's 3rd Corps) and Roman numerals for the Austrians (Rosenberg's IV Corps). Note that this is simply for clarity and is somewhat anachronistic as there was no standardised rule for corps numbers in either army at the time; both sides most commonly used Arabic numerals, but one occasionally encounters Roman numerals in original Austrian archival materials.

• Battalions or squadrons of a regiment are designated by Roman numerals (II/*Vogelsang* indicates the 2nd Battalion of *Vogelsang* Infantry Regiment No. 47).

• The term 'Rheinbund' refers to the Confederation of the Rhine.

• In most cases, German/Austrian and Polish spellings have been used for geographical names so the reader can locate these on a present-day map or road sign. However, conventional Austrian names have been retained for terrain features and towns in the Czech Republic, Slovakia and Hungary to minimise confusion with other histories of this war. A gazetteer gives the modern names for places such as Znaim (Znojmo).

Comparative Military Ranks

Austrian and German Ranks	French Ranks	Modern British or U.S. Equivalents
Feldmarschall (FM)	(no equivalent)	Field Marshal or General
Feldzeugmeister (FZM) or General der Kavallerie (GdK)	(no equivalent)	Lieutenant General
Feldmarschall-Leutnant (FML) or General-Leutnant (GL)	Général de Division (GD)	Major General
General-Major (GM)	Général de Brigade (GB)	Brigadier General
[staff] Oberst	Adjutant-Commandant	[staff] Colonel
Oberst	Colonel	Colonel
Oberst-Leutnant (OTL)	Major	Lieutenant Colonel
Major	Chef de Bataillon or Chef d'Escadron	Major
Stabs-Hauptmann	Adjoint	[staff] Captain
Hauptmann, Rittmeister, or Kapitän	Capitaine	Captain
Oberleutnant, Premierleutnant or Kapitänleutnant	Lieutenant	Lieutenant, First Lieutenant
Unterleutnant/Leutnant	Sous-Lieutenant	Second Lieutenant

Notes

1. All comparisons are approximate; protocol and functions could vary widely.
2. Contemporary German-language sources frequently use *'Lieutenant'* rather than *'Leutnant'* and *'Obrist'* was often used in place of *'Oberst'* (thus *'Obrist-Lieutenant'*).
3. In the French Army, the title *'Major-Général'* indicated a function rather than a rank and was unique to Berthier. Similarly, the title *'Generalissimus'* was unique to the Archduke Charles. Technically, the French title of 'Marshal' was an appointment rather than a rank.

Conventions

Austrian and German Noble Titles

German (Abbreviation)	English
Erzherzog (EH)	archduke
Freiherr	baron
Fürst	prince
Graf	count
Großherzog	grand duke
Herzog	duke
Kaiser	emperor
Kaiserin	empress
König	king
Kronprinz	crown prince

The prefix 'Erb-' was sometimes used to indicate a hereditary title as in Erbgroßherzog.

Preface

THE BATTLE OF ZNAIM is almost unknown.

Fought on 10 and 11 July 1809, it was one of the major encounters of the Napoleonic epoch with more than 100,000 soldiers engaged at its height, but it is routinely subsumed in the aftermath of the even larger Battle of Wagram (5–6 July). The usual narrative runs thus: Napoleon won a costly victory in the colossal struggle at Wagram; a brief pursuit ensued; and an armistice was concluded after an action near Znaim in Moravia. This hasty treatment is unfortunate as Znaim is interesting in its own right for several reasons. First, from a purely military perspective, it rewards study as an unplanned meeting engagement between two largely veteran armies in the wake of the second-greatest battle of the entire era.[1] The ferocity of the fighting, the sizes of the forces involved and its two-day duration alone suffice to commend it to our attention. Add to these factors the imbalance in numbers (the numerically inferior French attacking the defending Austrians), the drama of a stunning thunderstorm, instant reversals of fortune, military ruses and a sudden ceasefire and it is surprising that the battle has not drawn more detailed examination. Moreover, the period of the pursuit is not without its instructive aspects: gruelling marches, misunderstood orders, sharp rearguard clashes, mass inebriation and, most of all, the challenge of coping with uncertainty about the enemy.

Second, the drums and thunder (quite literally as will be seen) of battle roared in parallel with diplomacy. As the Austrians retreated and the French pursued, Habsburg councils were divided on whether or not to seek an end to hostilities. Advocates of an immediate peace briefly prevailed upon the Kaiser so that, while the two armies were locked in bitter combat, an Austrian emissary was laboriously seeking Napoleon to initiate negotiations. He finally caught up with the French emperor on the battlefield itself. Complex consultations followed along separate military and political tracks ending with a ceasefire and, almost immediately thereafter, a comprehensive armistice. Although a peace treaty would not be signed for another three months, the war of 1809 thus effectively came to an end on the hills around Znaim on the evening of 11 July.

This diplomatic facet of the pursuit and the battle was also intimately entwined with the question of war aims for the two sides. In the aftermath of Wagram, this was an unresolved issue for both belligerents. In the Austrian case, it was the subject of intense, bitter and debilitating debate. The Habsburg leadership would not reconcile itself to its grim fate until the peace treaty in October, but the period between Wagram and Znaim casts a harsh light on this internal dispute and the contending factions of a court in crisis. Furthermore, the decision by the Austrian commander, the Archduke Charles, to agree to the ceasefire and armistice – indeed his efforts to *seek* such outcomes – ultimately left the old empire with capitulation to Napoleon's demands as its only realistic strategic option. As for Napoleon, this brief few days sharpened his sense of what was desirable and achievable, leading him to accept conditions that were punitive but not catastrophic for his foes. Examination of this period also illuminates another overlooked dimension of the 1809 war: the role of Russia. Russia, nominally allied with France, had an army in Poland in the Austrian strategic rear and Tsar Alexander I regarded the fate of Poland and the preservation of the Austrian state as vital security interests. As the French and Austrian forces marched towards Znaim after Wagram, they drew closer to Poland, dramatically increasing the relevance of the tsar's army whether as an ally, an enemy or some admixture of the two. For both military and political reasons, therefore, the Russian Empire was a key factor for both Napoleon and the Habsburgs as they calculated possibilities and evaluated options on the road to Znaim. Whether considering Russia or other aspects of the war, of course, the Battle of Znaim and its antecedents are also examples of contingency in history. That is, the Austrian empire, despite the defeat at Wagram, *could* have continued fighting; the virtual end of the war on a hillside in Moravia on a mid-July evening was not foreordained or inevitable. The fighting and diplomacy surrounding the Znaim episode thus help us understand how and why the history of the war evolved from desperate combat to a sudden ceasefire and an equally sudden armistice, eventually leading to a peace shaped, to no small degree, by the outcome at Znaim.

Finally, this period around the Battle of Znaim is not without its human dimensions. For the Habsburgs, it was the culmination of a vicious contest between Charles as commander-in-chief or 'Generalissimus' and his opponents in the court of his elder brother, Kaiser Franz I. In large part owing to Charles's actions at Znaim, he was unceremoniously cashiered shortly after the battle. One of the Danubian monarchy's most renowned military leaders, he would never again hold a field command. It is also arguably the beginning of the rise of Clemens von Metternich to the prominent role he would play in Austrian and European affairs for the next four decades. On the French side, the battle saw a reflective Napoleon holding a council of war to decide on peace and the surprise elevation of General August Marmont to the marshalate despite the emperor's displeasure with his performance during the pursuit. Though not directly resulting from the actual battle, the events around Znaim and the subsequent peace negotiations also were connected to Napoleon's marriage to the Habsburg Archduchess Marie Louise in 1810. For the local population, of course, the unexpected explosion of war on their doorsteps brought disruption, dislocation, devastation and death.

Whether as a case study in how wars end, as an example of the interrelationship of policy and combat outcomes or as an interesting engagement from a solely military perspective, the Battle of Znaim therefore warrants closer examination. This book is thus an attempt to describe and analyse the combat actions and diplomatic manoeuvrings that ended the 1809 war and forged its results. It is a traditional military history, presented chronologically and focused on marches and battles, but it also highlights how these actions by the armies intersected with political considerations, each informing the other. Although some specifics are lost to us – especially when decisions were based on verbal orders or unrecorded conversations – it endeavours to provide as detailed a picture as possible here two centuries after the events. In addition to 'the usual suspects' within the memoir and secondary literature, this narrative relies heavily on archival accounts from Vienna and Paris; additionally, it draws on material from archives in Munich, Karlsruhe and, to a lesser extent, Darmstadt as troops from Napoleon's Bavarian, Baden and Hessian allies played important roles in the battle. Despite the numerous encroachments by human development over the past two centuries, this study is also informed by visits to the Znaim battlefield and travels along the two principal axes of movement used by the opposing armies. Some of this material has been sketched in abbreviated form in the third volume of *Thunder on the Danube*, but most is new and this book-length treatment affords an opportunity to present considerably more detail and greater nuance than could be included in the earlier overall history of the war.[2] Additionally, of course, this book affords me an opportunity to correct errors in my previous work, filling in gaps and probing more deeply into the actions between 7 and 11 July. The discussion of the background to the war and the conduct of operations prior to Znaim are largely condensed versions of the account presented previously in the three volumes of *Thunder* but, as this book is intended to stand on its own, it begins with a review of the events leading up to the war and the course of hostilities from April through early July 1809.

1. Leipzig, 'the Battle of Nations', 16–19 October 1813, was the largest Napoleonic engagement.
2. The original hardback edition was published by Frontline in London, 2008–10; Frontline issued a revised, paperback edition of all three volumes in 2014. See also the author's '1809: The Most Brilliant and Skillful Maneuvers', in Michael V. Leggiere (ed.), *Napoleon and the Operational Art of War*, Leiden: Brill, 2016, pp. 235–64; and 'From Abensberg to Znaim: The Franco-Austrian War of 1809', in Bruno Colson and Alexander Mikaberidze (eds.), *The Cambridge History of the Napoleonic Wars*, vol. II (forthcoming).

Acknowledgements

Most of the time, the writing and researching of military history is truly fun, exciting, engrossing. At moments, however, the process is better characterised as a struggle, wrestling with lacunae, contradictions and defiant mysteries or engaging in hand-to-hand combat with sentences that simply will not obey as one tries to 'whip order into a yelping pack of probabilities'.[1] Acknowledging the assistance one receives, on the other hand, is always an enjoyable part of the exercise.

Taking a cue from my friend, Dr Sam Mustafa, allow me to reverse the usual order of such things by first thanking my family: Anne Rieman, Grant Gill and Hunter Gill. Anne, who continues to indulge my eccentric hours, who is my best editor, and who sacrificed part of a trip to Vienna so I could scan some of Stadion's memoranda, is beyond all praise. She and our sons have tolerated long hours of absence, endless discussions of early nineteenth century European political-military affairs, diversions to obscure battlefields and incessant reminders of Napoleonic anniversaries. Their patience, understanding and assistance fill one's heart.

Having expressed my gratitude to those closest to home, let me acknowledge, in no order of priority, those in more distant locales who have been instrumental in helping me assemble all the material that has gone into this work and who have proffered a great deal of helpful advice along the way.

---

1. Jack Vance, *The Languages of Pao*, St Albans: Mayflower, 1974, p. 97.

In Austria I have benefited from all manner of assistance, in the first place from two old friends and one new one: Mag Michael Wenzel, Herr Ferdi Wöber and Ms Heidrun Riedl. Michael, who probably knows more about the Battle of Wagram than anyone on the planet, has been enormously helpful with all manner of archival material, good recommendations and even arranged a visit to the famous tower in Markgrafneusiedl on the Wagram battlefield. He and Ferdi were instrumental in making the International Napoleonic Society's annual conference in Vienna in 2018 a huge success. Most especially, Michael had the kindness to review the draft and offer typically cogent recommendations. I have also received generous help on local history from Dr Ernst Bezemek, Dr Rudolf Fürnkranz, Mag Gerhard Hasenhündl, Herr Manuel Köllner and Dr Günter Marian (Niederösterreichische Landesarchiv). Gentlemen: your courtesy, promptitude and kind assistance have greatly enriched this study!

I wish to thank several friends in the Czech Republic for their kindness as well: Dr Jiří Kacetl and Dr Jaromír Kovárník in Znojmo, Mgr Kateřina Rainisová of the National Heritage Institute at the Sychrov Castle and Mgr Jan Kahuda at the National Archives. Dr Kacetl of the South Moravian Museum in Znojmo (he organised an exhibit on 1809 there in the summer of 2019) has been instrumental in helping me find unusual images from the museum's unique collection and in checking my interpretations of 19th century geography; my exchanges with him have been enjoyable and enlightening.

In *la belle France*, I would like to thank Peter Hicks and François Houdecek for their kind and most welcome help, and especially Victor André Masséna, Prince d'Essling, for his courteous assistance. I must also note that the Fondation Napoléon, with which these gentlemen are associated, has been a boon to scholars everywhere, most particularly with the publication of the *Correspondance Général*, an invaluable research tool. M. le Général Eric de Stabenrath, whom I had the pleasure of meeting many years ago at the U.S. Army Command and General Staff College, has also been most courteously helpful as has M. Stanislaus de Stabenrath. The thoughtful and considerate Yves Martin at La Sabretache was a tremendous resource for images; this is the second time that friends at La Sabretache have been unstinting in their offers and courtesy. Claire Khelfaoui and Eymeric Job provided invaluable research. I must also thank M. Antoine Lesveques for French translation assistance.

Friends in Germany have also been helpful. The archives staffs in Munich and Darmstadt in particular, where I must thank Herr Heinz-Jürgen Weber and Dr Klaus-Dieter Rack respectively. Gratitude is also due to old friends, Dr Thomas Hemmann, who has repeatedly helped me locate recondite sources, and Alfred Umhey, who has again come through with illustration assistance. Dr Wolfram Siemann courteously alerted me to materials in the Czech National Archives.

I owe a special debt to Dr Attila Réfi in Hungary for supplying me with invaluable material on Charles and Franz from the archives in Budapest. This work would have been much weaker without his very generous help.

In the UK, Paul Dawson, an expert on matters equine, kindly clarified a number of nagging issues for me. I also owe a great deal to Donald Sommerville for his close reading and thoughtful editing.

Finally, there are those in the USA. I can start with David and Edna Markham of the International Napoleonic Society for many years of friendship and for organising the society's 2018 congress in Vienna. Two friends deserve special mention: Dr Rick Schneid of High Point University who scanned materials in Vincennes on my behalf and always supplies the best advice, and Peter Harrington of the Anne S. K. Brown Collection at Brown University, who has (once again!) come through with a host of useful illustrations. Likewise, Mr. Todd Fisher, another friend of long standing, has courteously permitted us to use images from volumes III and IV of *Napoleonic Uniforms* (Chicago: Emperor's Press, 2000). I would like to note as well the staff at the Pictures Collection in the New York Public Library; although I did not end up using any of the illustrations they uncovered, they could not have been more friendly and helpful. For courteous research support, I must also thank the team at the Napoleon Series Discussion Forum and Mr Stephen Smith.

And thanks yet again to Greenhill. From my first interactions back in 1992 to today, it has been a pleasure to work with Lionel Leventhal, Michael Leventhal and the entire Greenhill team.

Any errors of omission, commission or interpretation, of course, are mine, but I hope that this work will shed some light on this little-known episode in the grand and terrible Napoleonic epoch and spark additional research by other scholars. Most of all, however, I hope that you will find as much enjoyment in reading it as I have had in writing it.

Chapter 1
A Minister, an Archduke and an Emperor
April 1808 – April 1809

THE FRANCO-AUSTRIAN WAR OF 1809, or 'War of the Fifth Coalition', occupies a unique place in the military history of the Napoleonic epoch. Occurring at the midpoint of Napoleon's imperial career, it is one of the most interesting conflicts of the era, replete with insights into the strengths and weaknesses of Napoleon and his system of war as well as the approaches his enemies were adapting to counter him. Although some aspects of this war have been subject to considerable scrutiny, others, equally significant, remain obscure, drawing little scholarly attention despite their inherent importance. One such aspect is the Battle of Znaim, fought on 10 and 11 July, the final major engagement of the war. Though overshadowed by its titanic predecessor, the Battle of Wagram on 5–6 July, it rewards study for at least two reasons. First, for its operational aspects as an encounter battle that illuminates the qualities of the armies and leaderships on both sides. Second, because Znaim is intimately connected with the convoluted process that led to a ceasefire and then to the armistice that effectively ended the war. For both military and political reasons – not to mention the interleaving of these two considerations – Znaim is thus worthy of further analysis. An understanding of Znaim, however, requires an understanding of the antecedent phases of the conflict including strategy disputes within the Habsburg hierarchy, the war aims considered by both sides and the course of combat during the war's preceding campaigns.[1]

Austria in 1808: Anger, Anxiety and Opportunity

Austria launched the war of 1809 motivated by a combination of anger, anxiety and opportunity. Anger arose from the litany of defeats and humiliations the old monarchy had suffered at the hands of Revolutionary and Imperial France since 1792. The treaties of Campo-Formio (17 October 1797) and Lunéville (9 February 1801) resulted in a general retreat of Austrian power from both Germany and Italy, while the Imperial Recess of 25 February 1803 legitimised French possession of all formerly German lands on the west bank of the Rhine and drastically reorganised the Holy Roman Empire of the German Nation (or the *Reich*) more or less in accordance with Napoleon's wishes. It was the beginning of the end for this institution, rule of which had been virtually hereditary within the House of Habsburg since 1438. Most devastating for Vienna was the Treaty of Pressburg, signed on 26 December 1805 in the wake of the disastrous defeat at Austerlitz three weeks earlier. Among other painful stipulations, the treaty forced Austria to cede the Tyrol and the Vorarlberg to Bavaria and granted Venetia, Istria and Dalmatia to Napoleon's newly minted Kingdom of Italy (he had been crowned King of Italy on 5 May 1805), leaving Austria with Trieste and Fiume as its only outlets to the sea.

The next two years brought additional shocks. First, Napoleon established the Confederation of the Rhine, or Rheinbund, on 12 July 1806. This alliance between France and fifteen of the smaller German states solidified Napoleon's hold on Germany between the Elbe and the Rhine and effectively eradicated the Holy Roman Empire. Kaiser Franz of Habsburg had no choice but to surrender his title as Holy Roman Emperor on 6 August 1806; having anticipated this eventuality, however, he had had himself declared 'Emperor of Austria' in 1804 and thus retained his imperial ranking. The second shock was Napoleon's stunning triumph over Prussia at the Battle of Jena–Auerstedt in October 1806. Russian involvement as Prussia's ally meant that what historians came to know as the 'War of the Fourth Coalition' would drag on until June 1807, but Austria, its army still recovering from the debacles of 1805, was unable to intervene. Moreover, the several Treaties of Tilsit that ended the war left Prussia crushed, established a Franco-Russian alliance and installed Napoleon's victorious Grande Armée in garrisons arcing across Poland, Prussia and Germany from the Vistula to the Danube. With the Holy Roman Empire dissolved, French forces in Prussian Silesia on its northern borders, Napoleon's Kingdom of Italy on its southern frontier and its huge eastern neighbour now an ally of France, it is hardly surprising that many in Vienna believed their empire's future was precarious.

These profound territorial and administrative changes not only resulted in a drastic diminution of Habsburg power and influence in Germany and Italy, they also brought a flood of dispossessed princes, nobles, bureaucrats and soldiers to Vienna, all looking to the House of Habsburg to restore their lost fortunes. Among their number were members of the House of Austria-Este (or Habsburg-Este), bitterly anti-Napoleon after having been evicted from their Italian holdings owing to French conquests. The most influential of these was Maria Ludovika, since January 1808 the third wife of Austria's Kaiser Franz; her brothers Ferdinand and Maximilian, both Austrian generals, were also prominent at court, the former earning the nickname 'war trumpet' for his passionate, and often public, advocacy of a renewed confrontation with France.[2] They, along with their mother, other members of the imperial family and many of Franz's most intimate advisors, would become key components of the 'war party' that would push the old empire to confront Napoleon in 1809.

The single most important Austrian proponent of war that year, however, was the foreign minister, Johann Philipp Graf Stadion. The son of an official in the former Prince-Bishopric of Mainz, he had been born and educated in the Holy Roman Empire, began his career as an Austrian diplomat within its comfortable confines and remained a 'conservative *Reichspatriot*' (patriot of the Holy Roman Empire) with a strong attachment to the old, pre-Revolutionary political order combined with an unquenchable enmity towards Napoleon.[3] He was determined, intelligent and energetic, but often allowed his preconceptions to dominate his thinking and had 'a tendency to regard even the most serious matters too lightly and too optimistically'.[4] Moreover, he had little practical knowledge of and little apparent interest in military affairs, a lacuna that repeatedly led him to grasp and cling to unrealistic expectations.

Appointed foreign minister in early 1806 after Austerlitz, Stadion was convinced that Napoleon regarded Austria with hatred and would, sooner or later, seek to destroy the Habsburg state. During the War of the Fourth Coalition in 1806–7, he promoted an aggressive, potentially provocative form of armed neutrality and was inclined towards active military intervention.[5] He could not, however, overcome opposition from the empire's leading military figure, the Archduke Charles, one of Kaiser Franz's younger brothers.[6] Charles, probably Austria's most able senior soldier at the time, was engaged in a long-term project of restoring and reforming the army in the wake of the cataclysms of 1805. To facilitate pursuit of his modernisation goals, he pressed for greater power over all military affairs, to include the Court War Council or Hofkriegsrat. The Kaiser, however, was deeply suspicious of his younger brother, a mistrust that was eagerly nurtured by many of Franz's closest advisors. Nonetheless, he agreed to appoint Charles 'Generalissimus' or overall commander of the armed forces in February 1806, while simultaneously granting him authority over the entire military establishment in peace time.[7] Although this arrangement proved at best a partial success, it meant that Charles 'represented a political power which could not be bypassed'.[8] Charles was absolutely certain that 'a new war with France and its allies would be the death sentence of the Austrian monarchy' as he could envisage no possibility of success against 'the ambition, the will to conquer, the exaggerated sense of vengeance, the enterprise, Napoleon's entire personal character, the superiority of his troops in public opinion, [and] their true worth' when Austria's strength had been 'diminished by humiliations of every sort'.[9]

Fundamental differences of approach between the leading military commander and the dominant minister were evident as early as 1806–7. Although both agreed that drastic reform of the Austrian state's administrative and military apparatus was an urgent necessity, the minister and the archduke differed in significant ways. Stadion, convinced that an apocalyptic confrontation with France was inevitable, was determined to prevent Austria becoming 'one of the tributary states groaning under the French yoke' and actively sought means to contain Napoleon's power while restoring 'the independence of our policies'. His memoranda to the Kaiser and his correspondence through 1806 and 1807 are replete with warnings about what he perceived as the dire, direct and imminent threat Napoleon posed to the Habsburg state's very existence.[10] He was willing to take risks, often ill-informed risks, to promote internal reform and counter these dangers. Charles, on the other hand, was governed by caution – excessive caution from Stadion's point of view – as he laboured to rebuild the army and imbue it with a new spirit. He too watched the war between France and the Russo-Prussian alliance with grave concern ('If Napoleon is victorious, it is doubtful that there will be anything left to call Austria!'[11]), but he wanted to avoid any actions that might give the French emperor an excuse to turn his attention and his army against Austria. His advice prevailed in 1806–7, but the experience left Stadion with the conviction that Charles and his staff were, as he wrote, 'wrong-thinking men' and that the archduke himself was irresolute, perhaps timid, and prone to interminable delay rather than decisive action.[12]

Having kept itself out of the War of the Fourth Coalition, Austria at least hoped to play a major role in its resolution. Indeed, Stadion, the Kaiser and other leading figures were desperate to insert themselves and their interests into the peace negotiations to preclude the conclusion of a separate settlement between Napoleon and his opponents. This was not to be. Events outpaced Vienna's efforts to involve itself and Stadion's fears were realised as Napoleon indeed concluded a set of bilateral treaties with Russian Tsar Alexander I at Tilsit on 7 and 9 July 1807. Austria was left isolated and vulnerable, subject to the whims of the new Franco-Russian condominium. 'Of all the bad outcomes, the worst has come to pass,' Stadion wrote to the Kaiser on 9 July 1807, 'and that under the evilest circumstances.' Two days later he told his imperial master 'We must not fool ourselves, any day now we could find ourselves in the necessity of having to risk everything and the danger will be near that we could lose our existence in one way or another.'[13] Stadion's fears were, in fact, exaggerated, and tensions with France soon subsided, albeit temporarily. Nonetheless, his sentiments were a genuine manifestation of the anxieties that permeated the atmosphere among Vienna's elite circles in 1807. This unquestioned assumption that Napoleon purposed the ruin of the Habsburg monarchy thus added anxiety to the anger many harboured for the setbacks suffered in the wars with France since 1792.

Events on the Iberian Peninsula during the spring of 1808 reignited these Austrian anxieties, building on the extant anger to excite near-panic in the Habsburg hierarchy. Napoleon had declared an embargo of British goods in 1806 after Jena and, since Tilsit, he had been manoeuvring to tighten the grip of what came to be known as the 'Continental System' or 'Continental Blockade' in Spain and Portugal. Spain had been an ally of France since 1796 and had participated in the blockade nominally, but Madrid's enforcement was lax, and Portugal, closely aligned with Britain, was completely outside the system. Furthermore, from the French point of view, Spain's behaviour during the opening phases of the 1806 campaign had been virtually treacherous and concern for his strategic rear had nagged Napoleon throughout the war with Prussia and Russia.

Beginning in late 1807, therefore, he began deploying significant forces to the peninsula: sending Général de Division (GD) Andoche Junot to invade Portugal with a corps of 25,000 and gradually finding reasons to move more than 70,000 additional men across the Pyrenees. Although most of these troops were inexperienced recruits, by early March they controlled key fortresses throughout northern Spain, and Marshal Joachim Murat, Napoleon's brother-in-law, was en route to Madrid to become the emperor's 'Lieutenant General in Spain'.

Reaching the Spanish capital on 24 March 1808, Murat found the court in the throes of a series of complicated intrigues that ended with the vapid King Charles IV abdicating in favour of his son, the inept and obdurate Ferdinand VII, only to regret his decision several days later and plead for French assistance in restoring his throne. Murat, however, refused to recognise either claimant and, with the crown of Spain in dispute, Napoleon lured the entire Bourbon clan to Bayonne to resolve the issue. Disgusted with the weakness, incompetence, and venality of the Spanish court, Napoleon intervened in the family's dynastic politics and cajoled the pathetic Charles IV into a second abdication on 6 May, this time in favour of a Bonaparte. His elder brother, Joseph, whom Napoleon had installed as King of Naples barely two years earlier, seemed a likely candidate and by June the emperor had transferred Joseph from Naples to Madrid. Brother-in-law Murat received the vacant throne in Naples.

All Europe was aghast at Napoleon's high-handed treatment of his putative Spanish ally and its Bourbon dynasty, one of the continent's oldest ruling houses, but nowhere was this rude shock more terrifying than in Vienna. Stadion immediately interpreted the French intervention across the Pyrenees as a vindication of his own convictions, imagining that Napoleon's opportunistic actions in Iberia represented the next step in a long-term strategic plan. In forceful presentations for the Kaiser on 13 and 15 April 1808, he outlined his assessment in dramatic terms: Napoleon, driven by his 'hatred for all old dynasties', especially 'the hate he holds in his heart for the court of Vienna', would quickly eradicate Spanish resistance and turn on the Habsburgs. 'What conceivable cause', he asked rhetorically, 'would restrain Napoleon from falling on Austria as soon as he comes to regard such an enterprise as feasible or indeed easily executed?' Austria had at best five and at worst two months to prepare itself for this supposedly ineluctable confrontation because Napoleon's policy, in Stadion's view, must be aiming to 'subjugate the Austrian imperial house, to break up the monarchy and finally to divide it among his relatives, creatures and generals'.[14]

Charles, likewise alarmed, broadly agreed with the foreign minister. 'Your Majesty can no longer misread Napoleon's plans,' he wrote in a 14 April 1808 memorandum, 'There can be no more doubt as to what he wants – he wants everything.' Both pressed for urgent measures employing all the state's resources to rescue the monarchy from its presumably looming disaster.[15]

The events in Spain and the monarchy's dire future as depicted by Stadion and Charles had a dramatic impact on Kaiser Franz. With uncharacteristic speed, he injected temporary vivacity into Vienna's ponderous governmental machinery with a flurry of decrees. These decisions, promulgated through May and June, provided for an expansion of the monarchy's military establishment through the raising of two reserve battalions for each line infantry regiment and the creation of a national militia, called the Landwehr, in the empire's 'German' lands (including Bohemia, Moravia-Silesia and Carniola as well as modern Austria). Although they served to augment the standing army, these measures were basically defensive in nature. They demonstrated, however, the Habsburgs' pervasive feeling of vulnerability as well as the extent to which Stadion was able to exploit the family's dynastic fears to conjure up a sense of imminent and unavoidable danger.

In addition to enlisting the support of the Kaiser and the court for his war policy, Stadion mobilised public opinion behind his cause with a host of writers, poets, composers and playwrights who served as earnest, often passionate, propagandists. These efforts resulted in 'a unique, if short-lived, popular enthusiasm for war', at least in the monarchy's German-speaking regions, an enthusiasm that gradually grew through the latter half of 1808 to reach a crescendo in early 1809.[16] An atmosphere of anxiety and emergency was thus created not only in court conferences and in elite salons but also in theatres, taverns and popular entertainments. With Stadion portraying a 'looming danger' that Austria must 'either delay, eliminate utterly, or at least resist to the greatest possible extent',[17] a desperate pressure to act gradually built up in the minds of the Habsburg leadership compounding the anger many had nurtured since the late 1790s.

As the weeks passed without Spanish submission, however, an opportunity seemed to emerge from this grim international landscape and Vienna's actions began to assume a decidedly offensive complexion. The defeats inflicted on the French in Iberia during the summer of 1808 were especially encouraging to Napoleon's foes. Indeed, French setbacks followed one another in rapid succession between June and August: repulse at Valencia (26–28 June), defeat at Roliça (17 August), defeat at Vimiero (21 August), the failed first siege of Saragossa, (15 June–17 August) and abortive assaults on Girona (20–21 June and 24 July–16 August). Joseph, installed in Madrid on 20 July, had to flee his capital after less than two weeks as the situation deteriorated.[18] Most infuriating for Napoleon and most heartening for his enemies was GD Pierre Dupont's surrender of more than 20,000 men to a hotchpotch Spanish army at Bailén on 21 July. Napoleon had already sent several regiments from Germany to Spain in June and July,[19] but he now began making arrangements to transfer substantial reinforcements to redeem this 'horrible catastrophe'. Orders were quickly issued for two corps of the Grande Armée (1st and 6th) and two dragoon divisions as well as several unassigned regiments to march for the Pyrenees. Others would soon follow.[20]

For observers such as Stadion, the impact of these events was sensational. Most decision-makers in Vienna still assumed that Napoleon would eventually triumph, but it now seemed that French victory would be neither swift nor easy and that significant French forces would be entangled in Spain well beyond the two- to five-month time frame Stadion had initially envisaged. In their enthusiasm over French military embarrassments, however, Stadion and others were injudicious and superficial in their analyses, overlooking important details as they eagerly transferred supposed lessons from Iberia to central Europe, especially to Germany. They not only ignored the substantial political, social and economic differences between Spain and Germany but also equated the hastily assembled conscript battalions Napoleon had sent across the Pyrenees with the thousands of veterans still billeted between the Rhine and the Vistula. They thus drew facile and erroneous conclusions as Stadion confidently relayed in a 25 August memorandum for the Kaiser: 'The developments in Spain prove that Napoleon's generals are not invincible and even troops that are poorly supplied with cannon and other military necessities may withstand the tactics of the French and overcome them.'[21] The dangerously misleading and ultimately toxic corollary to this sort of glib thinking was that the Austrian army too, *if properly led*, should be able to defeat the overrated French. Stadion, however, repeatedly and pointedly expressed his doubts about the army's leadership. He conveyed his mistrust freely, for example, in a 31 August letter to Clemens von Metternich, the Austrian ambassador in Paris: 'I would characterise [our situation] as good and advantageous if I did not know the indecisiveness and weak commitment of our matadors. They cause me more worry than the entire mass of the Rheinbund states. Even under the most favourable conditions, they would still make me tremble.'[22]

For Stadion, this rapid and unanticipated accumulation of French reverses across the Pyrenees presented an irresistible opportunity to strike a blow against the Napoleonic imperium in Germany, Italy and Poland. An offensive war thus came to seem an increasingly attractive option as the summer progressed. On 8 August, for example, he told Metternich that Vienna 'will do everything to avoid war if it is avoidable, but if it is not, we must begin it and not wait'.[23] Given his conviction that the destruction of the Habsburg Empire was 'the sole goal of Napoleon', however, the inevitability of conflict was hardly in question.[24] As a well-connected diplomat reported from Vienna on 11 October, Stadion was making policy 'in the firm persuasion ... that war is inevitable, and perhaps with the premeditated intention of profiting from the favourable circumstances of the moment by seizing the first pretext to begin it [the war]'.[25] For Stadion, therefore, Austria could only escape its supposedly desperate position by taking advantage of 'these most favourable circumstances, which will perhaps never again offer themselves' to strike Napoleon while he was embroiled in Iberia.[26] The monarchy, however, would have to move soon to 'anticipate the danger and, without waiting for the eruption of Napoleon's plans, to choose the most advantageous moment to bring our tense political relations with France to a quick and permanent decision'.[27]

Stadion's views were bolstered by an increasingly numerous, active and influential war party at court. Inspired by tendentious and highly embellished reports of Spanish triumphs and imbued with Stadion's sense of desperation and opportunity, members of this informal war party fuelled a heady atmosphere in the Habsburg capital where talk of war was commonplace in the late summer of 1808. The crowning of Maria Ludovika as Queen of Hungary at the Hungarian Diet in September that year, for instance, prompted extravagant displays of loyalty to the Habsburg dynasty with the Diet pledging 20,000 additional Hungarian recruits for the regular army, the swift embodiment of the Hungarian militia (known as the 'Insurrectio', 'Nemesi felkelés' or 'Noble Insurrection') at need and yet more sacrifices of blood, treasure and material if required. Although these promises were largely related to fulfilling Hungary's constitutional obligations, many portrayed them as indications of fervent fidelity and reassuring signs of the monarchy's martial strength. Others reacted to the war mood with alarm and scepticism. Septuagenarian Feldmarschall Charles Joseph Prince de Ligne, for example, derided the pageantry and enthusiasm of the coronation as 'a true diet of illusions where one believes much has been accomplished but the results are costly and of little utility'. Observing the surging momentum towards war, the worried de Ligne ridiculed 'this miserable salon diplomacy of *I think* and *I hope* and this miserable politics based on the hypothesis of *perhaps*! Because this is the grand word: *perhaps*, they say, Napoleon will attack us. Why not just let him exhaust himself in the Pyrenees?'[28]

Harbouring similar views to de Ligne and conspicuously absent from the war party was the man who would have to lead the army against Napoleon: the Archduke Charles. Like Stadion, Charles urged rapid and far-reaching reforms in the Austrian system and saw Napoleon as a threat to Europe in general and to the Habsburg monarchy in particular. However, he considered the advocates for war reckless and impatient. He rejected their facile assumptions of French weakness and insisted that they were deluding themselves regarding Austria's military, political and economic capacity vis-à-vis France.[29] 'Our monarchy seems to me comparable to a consumptive man,' he wrote on 20 July, 'He feels a certain restlessness within, wants to be active, to travel, and believes that he is powerful; many regard his red and puffy cheeks as signs of health; but the knowledgeable recognise that these are actually signs of approaching death.'[30] He feared a repetition of Austria's defeat in 1805 and, with Prussia's 1806 catastrophe clearly in mind as well, he viewed the bubbling fervour in Vienna with dread, as manifested in a 16 July 1808 letter to his younger brother Johann.

> The attitude of our cousin Ferdinand, who seems to have taken as his credo that the war is on the point of breaking out, does not sit well with me. Let us not imitate the young officers and mob of Berlin, or things will end for us as they did there. If the war begins before everything is organised, all that will harm rather than serve us. I beg you not to lose sight of these observations and not to believe that the uprisings in Spain have robbed Napoleon of all his power for the indefinite future.[31]

Charles believed he needed more time to rebuild the army and strongly preferred a defensive strategy, as he outlined in a 25 June memorandum, a pessimistic appraisal that contained no mention whatsoever of offensive action by Austria.[32] In late September, with pressure for an aggressive war mounting, he drafted another lengthy assessment that pointedly attacked Stadion's most cherished notions: minimising the immediacy of the threat, disparaging the sense of urgency prevalent in Vienna, and questioning the wisdom of provoking any war with France, let alone one founded on an offensive strategy that would leave Austria as the obvious aggressor. Moreover, he could foresee no favourable long-term outcome, nothing beyond some ephemeral advantage: 'The result of a war could therefore be, in the best case, the liberation of Germany from the French, but it would not be so detrimental for France that it would thereby be weaker than Austria or incapable of hurting it [Austria]; in contrast, the worst case would mean the destruction of the Austrian monarchy.'[33]

Stadion was 'devastated' by the tone of this note and several others he received in a heated correspondence with one of Charles's most trusted staff officers, Feldmarschall-Leutnant (FML) Philipp Graf Grünne, between 27 September and 3 October. While agreeing that war should only be undertaken if unavoidable, he was dismayed that the archduke was displaying 'desperation, indeed the darkest desperation' rather than greeting the possibility of war with 'calmness and hope for success'. He thus saw himself differing completely from Charles 'in the most important question that I have ever handled'.[34] Despite points of agreement, therefore, the attitudes of the two men towards the prospect of war were founded on fundamentally divergent views of the strategic situation. Where Charles saw Austria as weak in comparison to Napoleon's potential power, Stadion, who had at best a limited grasp of military affairs, overestimated Habsburg capabilities and underestimated those of Napoleonic France.

Furthermore, Stadion confidently maintained airy hopes that popular uprisings in Italy and Germany – carefully managed and guided from Vienna – would erupt in the wake of initial Austrian battlefield successes and compensate for any deficiencies in Habsburg arms. Charles (as communicated through Grünne) concurred as far as the importance of exploiting 'the awakening of oppressed peoples' was concerned, but countered that 'their assistance is too dependent on the vagaries of the moment to be made the foundation for military calculation and we can only regard such as a lucky chance and not as a guaranteed result'.[35] For Stadion, these cool, equivocating replies to his passionate convictions only confirmed his negative assessment of Charles and the general staff for their 'dreadful lack of commitment' to a cause that seemed so urgent and obvious to him.[36] Other observers in Vienna bluntly accused Charles of cowardice: 'Above all, it is the pusillanimity of the Archduke Charles which paralyses everything here,' wrote the Prussian ambassador.[37]

As the autumn wore on, however, Charles relented. Under pressure from key members of the court and the imperial family and convinced that war was unavoidable – more owing to Austria's actions than Napoleon's – he gradually abandoned his resistance to Stadion's plans. His motivations are obscure. Writing in the third person several years later, he recalled that 'The archduke had delayed the decision for war for a long time by his opposition. However, rather than hold on at all costs, even at the loss of his position, he eventually gave his assent.'[38] Maria Ludovika's influence probably contributed to the softening of his stance, but he also seems to have simply grown weary of the endless pressure and intriguing (such as attempts by members of the court over the summer to remove the Hofkriegsrat from his authority).[39] Privately, Charles told his adoptive father, Herzog Albert von Sachsen-Teschen, that 'although he had employed all his means to prevent an explosion, he finally came to see that his efforts were useless'.[40] Referring to himself in the third person, he later wrote that, 'The archduke recognised that the ministry [Stadion] had brought things to a state where war was inevitable, and concerned himself from then on with the requisite preparations in order to contribute as much as possible to success.'[41] The monarchy's key military leader thus addressed himself to the prospect of war with a sense of foreboding and weary resignation rather than confidence or enthusiasm.

Charles's elder brother the Kaiser was not eager for war either. He was surrounded, however, by many who were both keen and confident, including his wife, her mother, her brothers and some of his closest personal advisors, not to mention Philipp Stadion, his elder brother Friedrich Lothar von Stadion and their various adherents. Kaiser Franz was neither well-versed in military matters nor the type of leader to impose greater coherence on the state's byzantine policy machinery. Although he desired peace, therefore, he took no serious steps to preserve it.[42] Rather he allowed himself to be slowly persuaded of war's necessity and perhaps did not realise that his ministers and their supporters, anticipating his acquiescence, had pushed Austrian preparations for an offensive war to an almost irrevocable point.[43] His younger brother Johann would later write that the Kaiser 'desired peace but worked for war without wanting it or recognising it'.[44] Though Stadion and the other members of the war party would eventually overcome his reluctance to take a firm decision for war, his initial doubts, compounded by his vacillating nature and his tendency to follow the advice of the last person to speak to him, would inform his thinking throughout the conflict and during the peace negotiations.

The decision over war or peace also had impact on Franz's relations with Charles. Many of those who wanted war saw the archduke as an impediment and fed the Kaiser's pre-existing suspicions by portraying Charles as a Francophile incapable of winning what they believed to be an almost preordained victory of sweeping proportions.[45] Mistrust between the two brothers had grown over the course of the wars with Revolutionary and Imperial France, mistrust nurtured by the sycophants around the Kaiser to include rumours that Charles sought to replace Franz on the throne. Repeatedly slighted or side-lined in the period leading up to Austerlitz and spied upon thereafter, the archduke faced numerous challenges to his personal position and to his attempts to strengthen Austria's military establishment.[46] In the summer of 1808, for instance, as tensions with France were rising, he could only fend off the Kaiser's efforts to remove the Hofkriegsrat from his control by threatening to resign. Writing to his adoptive father in August 1808 about this latest effort to limit his role, he compared the situation to the months preceding Austria's previous disastrous encounter with France: 'The gossip of spring 1805 begins anew . . . if it is not Mack, the army will easily find another fool who will repeat the scenes of 1805 . . . but my decision is made, I will not be accused of contributing to the ruin of the state.'[47] Charles, though unfailingly obedient to his imperial brother, thus sometimes saw a 'higher calling' in his dedication to what he believed were the interests of the Habsburg dynasty; he detested many of the Kaiser's inner circle and resented the various efforts to curtail his authority. Franz, on the other hand, acutely sensitive to any potential threat to his power, harboured doubts about Charles's loyalty and competence. To make matters worse, Wallenstein's ghost hovered over every banquet in Vienna.[48] That is, the fear of an over-powerful military leader who might menace the dynasty corrupted the atmosphere and hampered logical decision-making. Charles, of course, was the principal object of such suspicions. This history of mutual mistrust between the two brothers, exacerbated by the course of combat in 1809, would be another important factor in the events at Znaim.

Winter 1808–1809: Austria Must Seize the Moment

By late October 1808, the question of war, indeed an offensive war, had been tacitly, if not explicitly, decided. Stadion was, as one historian portrays him, 'already a captive of his war policy'. This policy had developed a powerful inertia of its own, creating an 'atmosphere of sustained psychological and administrative pressure' around the Habsburg leadership, including Kaiser Franz.[49] Franz, though fearful of the threat he believed Napoleon posed to his dynasty's future, did not actively seek war, but, like Charles, he eventually succumbed to the pressure which Stadion and the war party had manufactured. The Kaiser would continue to vacillate, but by this stage the momentum towards war was so powerful that only a radical change in Austrian behaviour, including a retreat from the fervid public agitation, could have averted the coming conflict. Such a change or retreat was unthinkable in Vienna's labyrinthine workings without some dramatic external stimulus and, as will be seen, nothing that France or Russia could reasonably offer would suffice to satisfy Stadion's imagined requirements for Austria's security: a complete withdrawal of French troops across the Rhine and eradication of French political influence from Germany.[50] Barring such unlikely developments, he remained firmly set on the road to war, exclaiming to the Russian chargé in late November: 'We have established a system from which we will never depart.'[51] Herzog Albert ruefully recorded that those who 'held to pacific principles' were seen as traitors and 'could not fight against the torrent'.[52]

A meeting between Napoleon and Tsar Alexander that autumn did nothing to deter Austria. Indeed, in some respects it had the opposite effect. Intent on retrieving the situation in Spain, the French emperor arranged a conference with his Russian counterpart in the small city of Erfurt from 27 September to 14 October amidst great pomp and ceremony. Napoleon hoped to enlist Alexander in cajoling and intimidating Austria so as to secure his strategic rear as he turned his attention to Iberia. He was only partially successful. Alexander demurred

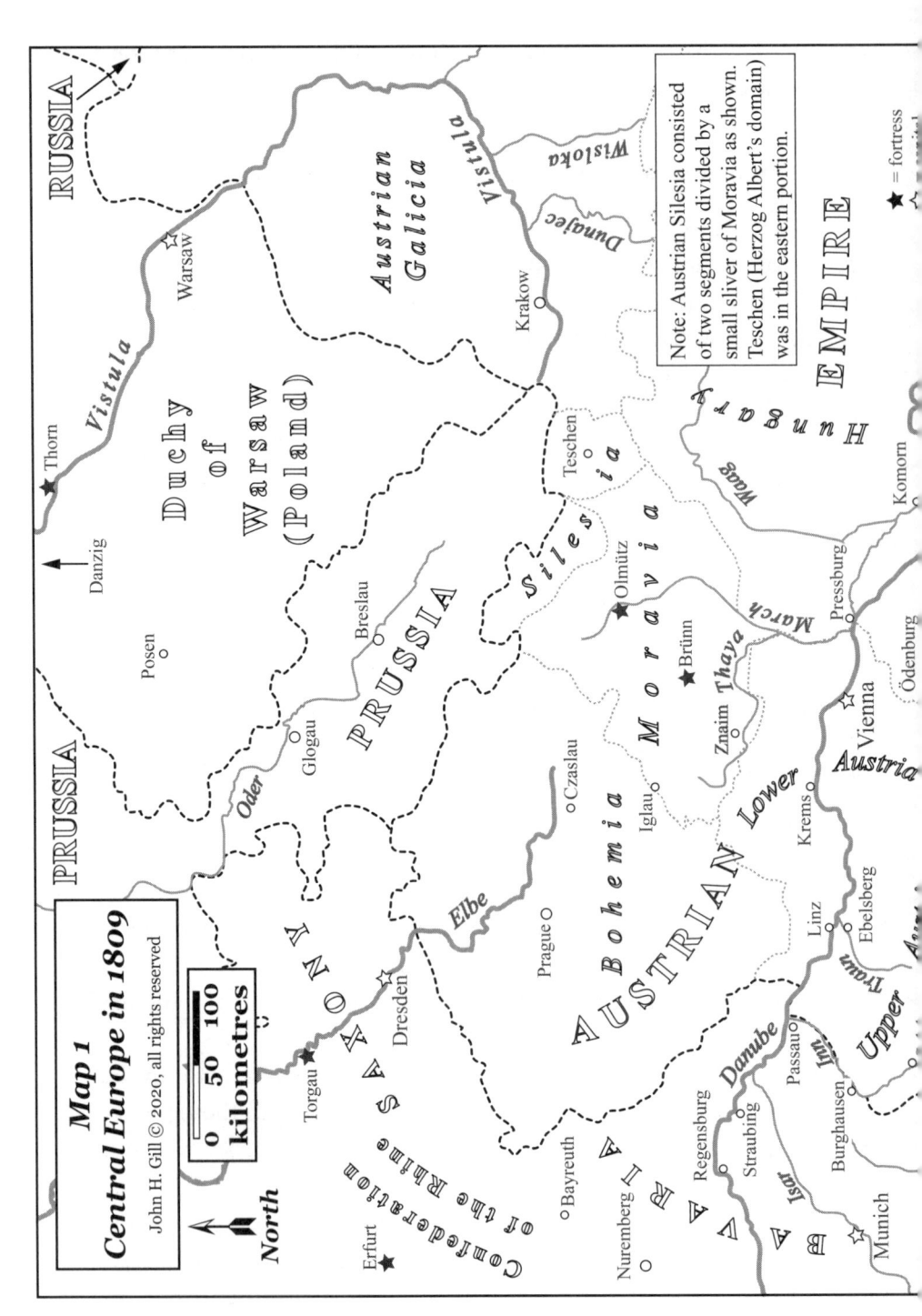

on sending a joint demarche to Vienna demanding a cessation of Austria's re-armament programmes and pugnacious public pronouncements, and the most Napoleon could extract after two weeks of talks and lavish entertainments was a pledge that, 'In case Austria goes to war against France, the Emperor of Russia engages to declare against Austria and to make common cause with France.'[53] This clause, even half-heartedly fulfilled, would have profound ramifications in setting the context for the Battle of Znaim as the 1809 war was coming to a close, but in October 1808 both Napoleon and Stadion misread its significance. Napoleon, for his part, overvalued the Russian commitment and headed for the Pyrenees convinced that Austria had been deterred. Stadion, on the other hand, dismissed the threat of Russian intervention. He had already concluded that Austria could defeat a combined Franco-Russian attack because both of the potential adversaries were distracted elsewhere: France in Spain and Russia by its conflicts with Sweden and the Ottoman Empire. He acknowledged that Russia was acting against Austria's interests but believed that the tsar 'inclined towards us in his heart' and that 'Russia not only completely approves of our present attitude but would itself wish to see it [Austria] stronger and more complete.' Relations with St Petersburg could be improved, he argued in a 22 October memorandum, but, above all, Austria 'must pursue its currently undertaken policy with firmness, persistence and single-mindedness, and unwaveringly continue on the path already trodden'.[54] In other words, it must hold steady on the path to war. The tsar, in an effort to be solicitous of Austria's concerns and specifically 'to calm Mr Stadion's worries',[55] unintentionally contributed to misperception in Vienna by stressing his personal interest in the integrity of the Habsburg empire in his correspondence with Kaiser Franz and by saying nothing about the cessation of Austrian mobilisation in his interview with the Austrian envoy at Erfurt.[56]

The military measures Napoleon took as the Erfurt conclave was concluding could also be seen as encouraging Austria in its aggressive posture. On 12 October, the French emperor issued a decree disbanding the old Grande Armée and dispatching additional reinforcements to join the long lines of veterans who had been on the roads to Iberia since June.[57] By the end of October, therefore, some 108,000 French troops had left Germany for Spain along with tens of thousands of German, Italian and Polish allies. Four other French divisions soon departed Germany for cantonments in France.[58] Left behind was a new entity called the 'Army of the Rhine' under Marshal Louis Nicolas Davout along with a small Franco-Dutch force led by Marshal Jean-Baptiste Bernadotte. The two commands totalled some 90,000 men 'present under arms', potentially to be bolstered by a nearly equal number of German troops from the Rheinbund contingents. The transfers to Spain and back to France thus represented a reduction of the French forces in Germany by more than half, greatly diminishing the threat on Austria's borders. Moreover, Napoleon's instructions shifted almost all of the French forces out of Poland and Prussia to central Germany west of the Elbe and to the Hanseatic cities on the coasts. As a result, the danger of French attack across Austria's northern and north-eastern frontiers was practically nil. Perhaps most significant was Napoleon's decision to take himself out of Germany and assume personal command of his armies across the Pyrenees.

For the war party in Vienna, proceeding from the assumption that war was unavoidable, Napoleon's temporary absence and the removal of so many French troops from Germany created a welcome window of opportunity for Austrian action. The question of timing, however, remained. Now, in the final months of 1808, the foreign minister and other members of the war party, urged the Kaiser to launch an offensive war against France early in 1809.[59] Stadion even recalled Metternich from Paris to increase the pressure on his monarch and, after a series of meetings in December, the decision was made: Austria would invade Germany in the coming March with the aim of expelling all French troops, erasing Napoleon's alliances and re-establishing Habsburg primacy in central Europe. All was premised on attaining dramatic victories in the very opening moments of the coming war, a signal success that Stadion and others had convinced themselves would set Germany ablaze (under Habsburg guidance), attract powerful allies, and preclude an effective response from Napoleon. As Stadion portrayed the concept to the Kaiser in a 4 December memorandum: 'Our troops will simultaneously cross the borders of the monarchy into Germany and Italy in force, using our momentary superiority to make rapid progress and, so far as possible, to cripple all of Napoleon's tributary sovereigns, depriving France of their resources, and exploiting them ourselves.'[60]

Three principal considerations prompted the decision on timing. First, Stadion forcefully and repeatedly reiterated his assessment of Napoleon's hostile intentions, claiming that 'Napoleon's vast superiority cannot co-exist with Austria in its present state,' and that Austria 'must seize the moment which offers us the best advantages against him'.[61] Napoleon unintentionally heightened the state of alarm in Vienna with a 7 December proclamation to the Spanish people that threatened to remove King Joseph to a different throne if Spain did not accept its new monarch. For key leaders in anxious Vienna, this could only mean that Joseph was destined for the Habsburg family's palaces.[62] Second, the military situation seemed likely to favour Austria for the next six months or so. As far as Austria's armed forces were concerned, Charles presented a military analysis stating that the Austrian army could be ready for war by the end of March 1809.[63] As for the enemy, Stadion and Metternich concluded that Napoleon would be unable to generate significant reinforcements for Germany until at least summer and perhaps not before autumn; even then, in their view, nearly half of these would be supposedly unreliable Rheinbund troops and French 'conscripts below proper age for service'. Austria's forces, therefore, 'would be at least equal to those of France initially'.[64] Finally, Finance Minister Graf Joseph O'Donnell informed his colleagues that the pitiful condition of the monarchy's exchequer would not allow Austria to maintain the army in its present state of readiness beyond the following spring.[65] In Vienna's superheated atmosphere, these political, military and fiscal factors seemed to leave no alternative but war, and war at the earliest possible moment in 1809. This brief delay would also allow Stadion time to alleviate the financial strain by negotiating subsidies from Britain, a task he was confident could be accomplished by spring. Indeed, advancing Charles's schedule, he set 1 March 1809 as the deadline for completion of all political, military and financial preparations.[66] Propelled by Stadion's energy, therefore, the Habsburg monarchy picked up momentum in its desperate rush towards conflict with Napoleon as 1808 came to an end.

Austria, early 1809: The Means Not in Proportion with the Ends

Although the general timing of the coming Austrian offensive was thus more or less decided in December 1808, the purpose of the war was problematic. Indeed, owing to the gradual shift from a defensive to an offensive posture, it was only in January 1809 – after the decision for war had been made – that the specifics began to appear in written form. Beyond pre-empting a presumed French attack, what did Stadion and other advocates of conflict hope to achieve? Working in close collaboration with his elder brother, Friedrich Lothar, the Austrian ambassador to Bavaria, the foreign minister did outline some very broad goals at the strategic level. The brothers cast Austria's cause as a noble crusade to 'deliver itself and Europe from the despotic yoke and invasive politics of Napoleon' and leave the Habsburg monarchy with 'an increase in the state's population and income which is commensurate with our military status and the position we should hold in the European political order, [and] a secure, defensible border'.[67] Their breathtakingly ambitious notions, however, envisaged 'the restoration of the old order of things', returning Europe, above all Germany, to the way it had been 'before and after the Peace of Pressburg, up to the introduction of the Rheinbund act'.[68] The Rheinbund, in fact, was a particular target of Austrian policy, characterised as 'that act of the French regime whose destruction is an especial goal of the war'.[69] Not only would Austria regain territories lost in 1805 and supplant France in Germany, but 'every legitimate sovereign' would be 're-established in the possessions which appertained to him prior to the usurpations of Napoleon' (as least as defined by Vienna). This principle was to apply to Spain, Italy, Naples, the Papal States, Sardinia, Germany, Poland, Prussia, Hesse-Kassel, Brunswick and the ruling house of Britain; it would also include the 'liberation' of Belgium and Holland as well as the extension of Austria's frontiers to the Po and Chiesa Rivers in Italy.[70] In other words, the two Stadions saw this 'war of retribution' as a means to overturn two decades of European history.[71] In their imaginations, the post-war continent would resemble the political dispensation that prevailed under the Holy Roman Empire, with the important difference that Vienna would exercise uncontested hegemony in Germany and Italy.[72]

Despite their seeming specificity, the 'war aims' described by the Stadions were open-ended, imprecise and incomplete, a list of unconstrained desires rather than a studied, well-crafted attempt to develop realistically achievable objectives. Grandiose in the extreme, this desired end-state hardly constituted a solid basis for military planning. The foreign minister's concept, for example, called for the invading Austrian forces to simultaneously disperse and concentrate: disperse to lend support to the German uprisings the younger Stadion assumed would ignite as soon as Habsburg troops crossed the border and concentrate to achieve the crucial initial victories upon which the entire vision of an offensive war was predicated. Similarly, the goal of conquering Italy diverted at least one full army corps from the principal theatre of war in Germany. Stadion's wishful thinking and his facile assumptions about military affairs – Napoleon's ability to respond as well as Austria's own offensive potential – thus left Charles in a nearly impossible strategic situation, forcing him to prepare plans for a conflict with uncertain objectives and no clear terminus. As a result, notes eminent Austrian historian Manfried Rauchensteiner, 'The prelude to the military events of 1809 is characterised by unparalleled confusion' because 'The mutual interaction of politics and military strategy was grossly inadequate.'[74] Bitter interpersonal rivalries and power plays within Charles's personal staff were an additional hindrance to coherent planning[75] and the archduke himself did little to bridge the gap between political goals and military action. He handed his chief of staff, General-Major (GM) Anton Mayer von Heldenfeld, some initial guidance on 25 December, but this was so lacking in political context and military substance that Mayer immediately complained he was being asked to draft a plan 'like a blind man speaking of colours'.[76]

The political details Mayer needed, however, proved elusive because of another problem with the expansive war aims Stadion had embraced. The foreign minster's fanciful optimism notwithstanding, it was clear that Austria would need substantial military and financial support from powerful allies to achieve 'the destruction of the Parisian government's influence in Germany and its replacement by that of the Vienna government' envisaged in the various Stadion memoranda,[77] but all attempts to enlist allies in the coming war failed. Vienna's approaches to minor powers such as Naples and Sardinia came far too late to matter and the responses from the major powers, Russia, Prussia and Great Britain, were unsatisfactory.[78]

For Tsar Alexander, Austria's rush to war was foolhardy; he enjoined restraint and repeatedly stated that he would fulfil his obligations to Napoleon if Austria started a war. The best Stadion could elicit from St Petersburg was a promise that Russian forces entering Habsburg territory would endeavour to avoid hostilities with Austrian troops. This message, however, only reached Vienna in early May, almost a month *after* the Austrian invasion of Bavaria; when Austria went to war, therefore, it had no solid information on Russia's stance. As for Prussia, Stadion had placed great hopes in gaining the support of up to 80,000 Prussian troops but, despite some seemingly encouraging military exchanges in Vienna, King Friedrich Wilhelm III followed the tsar's stern advice and declined to engage his battered kingdom in a new war with Napoleon.

Great Britain was another disappointment. Austria counted on substantial British subsidies to fund the war and on a major British amphibious expedition to Germany to arm and inspire local rebels. Stadion's expectations, however, were wildly unrealistic. Foreign Secretary George Canning called the requested subsidy 'beyond all possibility of Compliance' and, mistrusting Austria, would commit nothing until hostilities actually commenced.[79] An agreement for the provision of (significantly reduced) financial assistance was concluded in late April, but, as with Russia, this only came weeks *after* the war had begun. Likewise, the Austrian agent who was to co-ordinate British military support did not return until early May and brought no concrete commitments in any case.

The popular uprisings in which Stadion had invested so many heady hopes also failed to materialise. Rolling rhetoric and nebulous plans notwithstanding, Austrian appeals to Germany's citizens found little echo in 1809. Only in formerly Austrian Tyrol, ceded to Bavaria in 1805, did Habsburg propaganda resonate, but this remained an exception. Outbreaks of anti-French violence were few and ephemeral; there would be no widespread insurrection. As a contemporary observer noted: 'For Austria, the uprising of a few mountain folk was no substitute for its deluded expectations.'[80]

When Charles's battalions crossed the border into Bavaria on 10 April to face 'the very God of War himself', therefore, they were alone.[81] The conflict thus opened with baseless assumptions regarding foreign support and vague hopes that all would change in Austria's favour once those battalions had achieved a few signal victories.

In addition to the lack of allies and strategic confusion, the other problem associated with Stadion's grandiose war aims was the tool charged with achieving them. Embedded in Stadion's formulations was a requirement for aggressive action, rapid movements and dramatic victories early in the war, but the Habsburg army, though markedly improved since 1805, was ill-suited to such tasks. It was still an ungainly instrument and the command, mobility and logistical demands implied in Stadion's vision were beyond its abilities. Charles was painfully aware of 'the great clumsiness' of his army[82] and its manifold deficiencies prompted GM Josef Radetzky to observe in a post-war analysis that 'the means were not in proportion with the ends'.[83] The foreign minister, however, unfamiliar with military matters, was incapable of judging the army's readiness and did not understand what he was asking Charles and the Habsburg soldiery to undertake. Moreover, he did not trust Charles and his generals (nor they him) and feared that the military hierarchy would lose the war through lethargy. The archduke's belief in the war, on the other hand, was tentative, a thin, temporary veneer that threatened to crack at the first setback. He entered into actual operational planning with the conviction that he could only do his best on behalf of a cause that probably could not be won. Given this dissonance between political and military authorities and the gap between goals and resources, it is hardly surprising that Radetzky later concluded 'the campaign of 1809 was lost before it began'.[84]

Austria, February 1809: The Die Is Cast for War

The final decision to launch the army across the empire's borders on 9 April came in a conference with the Kaiser on 8 February 1809. Although it would have been very unlikely that Austria would have altered course at this late date, Stadion apparently overwhelmed all opposition with typically passionate and articulate arguments and Charles emerged deep in one of his pessimistic moods.[85] In a meeting that evening to review operational plans, he told Mayer: 'The die is cast for war, I can do nothing about it, let those who took the decision take the responsibility.'[86]

Dark forebodings notwithstanding, Charles and his staff accelerated their efforts to craft a concept for the Austrian offensive or, more precisely, for the multiple offensives to be launched in early April. The army was organised for the first time along the lines of the French *corps d'armée* system and, in anticipation of active support from Prussia, seven of these (five 'line' or 'standard' corps and two reserve) were to assemble in Bohemia with two others committed to the Danube valley and one each to Italy and Poland (Duchy of Warsaw). The initial target of the Austrian offensive out of Bohemia was to be Davout's Army of the Rhine in central Germany but, blithely assuming Russian neutrality, considerable emphasis was also placed on the invasion of Poland in assumed collaboration with Prussia.

These initial dispositions, however, were soon altered. First, as mentioned above, one corps (VIII) was removed from the Danube valley and placed under Archduke Johann on the Italian border to satisfy his ambitions for a major command and to underwrite a full-scale invasion of both Italy and the Tyrol. Johann's 'Army of Inner Austria' in this secondary theatre would thus consist of VIII and IX Corps as well as a separate detachment allocated to conduct an incursion into Dalmatia. Second, the greater part of the Hauptarmee (Main Army) was shifted from Bohemia to the Danube valley just weeks before hostilities were to open. This last-minute decision was controversial at the time and has remained so ever since. It was apparently motivated by two changes in the external situation in early March. First, intelligence arrived suggesting that the French were concentrating along the Danube in Bavaria, not in central Germany. They could thus pose a danger to an Austrian force debouching from Bohemia and would be in a position to threaten the Austrian heartland by advancing down the Danube valley. Second, Vienna received the discouraging news that the Prussian king would not to risk his army and throne in a new contest with Napoleon. Though Prussia left open the possibility of an alliance at some later point, a key reason for launching the Austrian offensive from Bohemia thereby evaporated. Convinced that the Danube valley was 'the key to the theatre of war and to the Austrian monarchy', Charles, ever cautious, weighed his options and selected the safer course of action, the one that would best protect the heart and capital of the empire.[87] The second half of March 1809 thus saw most of the Habsburg battalions slogging south in wretched weather to cross the Danube and assemble along the Inn River on Bavaria's borders. Only two corps were left in Bohemia: I Corps under General der Kavallerie (GdK) Heinrich Graf Bellegarde and Feldzeugmeister (FZM) Karl Graf Kolowrat-Krakowsky's II Corps. Jointly commanded by Bellegarde, these two formations were charged with advancing north of the Danube while the bulk of the Hauptarmee drove into Bavaria south of the great river.

Here at the very eve of war, Stadion provided a vivid instance of the complete breakdown of Austrian political–military co-ordination. Although he was the chief promoter of the coming conflict and despite the influence his military protégés had exerted to shift the Hauptarmee from Bohemia to the Danube, it seems that Stadion had only the fuzziest notion of the army's plans. On the evening of 6 April, he met with Charles Stuart, an unauthorised but welcome British official. According to Stuart's account of their discussion, Stadion stated that Austria had three of its corps in Bohemia; of these, Bellegarde (I Corps) would strike north towards Dresden and Kolowrat (II Corps) would advance west on Bayreuth, while FML Franz Seraph Fürst Rosenberg-Orsini (IV Corps) marched southwest to defeat a Bavarian division at Straubing before joining Charles 'in the vicinity of Munich'. He even suggested that any French reinforcements withdrawn from Spain would be sent to Italy 'where Bonaparte means to command in person'.

What is one to make of this exposition, so completely at odds with reality? Stadion's description of the military situation included numerous serious errors: there were only two corps in Bohemia, not three; Bellegarde was headed for Bayreuth with Kolowrat, not Dresden by himself; Rosenberg was south of the Danube, not north; Charles was aiming the Hauptarmee at the Regensburg area, not at Munich; and the French emperor would go to Germany, not Italy. These were not arcane bits of military trivia, but important aspects of strategy with direct relevance to key problems in Austria's war diplomacy such as Prussia's stance and the treatment of Napoleon's Rheinbund allies. Napoleon's personal location alone was a matter of crucial importance. As foreign minister, Stadion could reasonably be expected to have mastered such operational information, especially given the life-or-death significance he personally ascribed to this war. Either he had no idea of the army's actual intentions or he was deliberately misleading the presumed agent of a much-sought ally for no apparent reason. In either case, Stuart instantly perceived the weakness of this supposed strategy and offered a prescient assessment: 'I cannot but consider that these corps, like so many rays diverging from the same centre, though at first successful, will progressively grow weaker as they advance towards the enemy's frontier.'[88]

Beyond Germany and Italy, Poland was also an objective for Habsburg forces. Here Archduke Ferdinand d'Este, one of Kaiserin Maria Ludovika's brothers and a vocal proponent of the war, was to invade Napoleon's ally the Duchy of Warsaw at the head of VII Corps (29,800 infantry and cavalry with 94 guns). Austria's leadership hoped that he would quickly knock Poland out of the war and thus remove a potential threat to the monarchy's strategic rear. Ferdinand was then to turn west and join the Main Army in Germany. This extravagant military mission had important political dimensions. In the first place, the arrival of a strong Austrian corps in Poland might force a change in Prussia's stance. Leaders in Vienna thought Ferdinand's presence would compel Friedrich Wilhelm III to ally himself with Austria either by bribing him with Polish territory or by approaching his borders and forcing him to choose sides – a choice which Vienna believed could only result in allegiance to the Austrian cause. Second, the Habsburg hierarchy hoped a swift victory in Poland would reverberate in St Petersburg and provide a powerful incentive for Russia to stay out of the war. Indeed, Austria's military posture on its eastern frontiers was premised on the assumption of Russian neutrality even though Charles had long harboured deep suspicions about Russia's trustworthiness and value as an ally.[89] With Ferdinand focused on defeating the small Polish army (14,200 infantry and cavalry with 41 guns) before marching west through Prussia, the defence of Galicia on Austria's border with Russia was left to a motley collection of fewer than 8,000 border guards and depot troops. Scattered about in those distant districts, they would barely suffice to give notice of a Russian advance should Alexander decide to honour his commitments to Napoleon. Though seemingly remote from the main arena of combat, however, actions in the Polish theatre would become a key piece in the mosaic of politics, strategy and battle as the war approached its end at Znaim.

Napoleon in 1808: I Have Nothing to Fear from Austria

Napoleon had no desire for a war with Austria. Nor is there any evidence to indicate that he intended to turn on Austria as soon as he had solved his Iberian problem. Austria may be excused for harbouring such fears, but its leaders consistently ignored or misunderstood the centrality of the long-term struggle against Great Britain in Napoleon's strategic view and thus overestimated what the tsar termed their 'perhaps imaginary dangers'.[90] Rather than Austria, Napoleon was focused on Spain and the larger contest with Britain, as outlined in a letter French Foreign Minister Jean-Baptiste de Nompère de Champagny wrote to the ambassador in Vienna, GD Antoine Andréossy on 16 August 1808. After relating the impact of the disaster at Bailén, Champagny outlined Napoleon's intentions:

> The emperor will go to war [in Spain], but with the most powerful forces he can employ so that his success will not be in doubt. In such a situation, it is important to him to be sure of the dispositions of Austria. The emperor desires peace, but he prefers war to a perfidious peace that would serve as a trap.[91]

Napoleon seems to have been genuinely baffled that Austria would behave in an actively belligerent fashion, when, from his perspective, its political–military situation was so adverse. He concluded that Austria was arming out of fear and worried that it would make the same mistake Prussia had made in 1806: 'In a feeble government, the party that wants war begins arming under some pretext or another and the ruler, deceived, finds himself engaged in a war he did not want.'[92] Napoleon responded with a combination of threats and blandishments in his efforts to avert a conflict. In August and September 1808, for example, he mobilised the Rheinbund, temporarily halted the withdrawal of the 5th Corps from Germany and called up 160,000 new conscripts at home. He also issued sharp verbal warnings to Austrian envoys. In a famous scene at a diplomatic reception to celebrate the imperial birthday on 15 August, he posed a series of questions and answers to Metternich: 'Do you wish to frighten me? You will not succeed. Do you believe the circumstances favour you? You are fooling yourself ... I will pull 100,000 of my troops from Germany to send them to Spain and I will still be able to match you.'[93] FML Karl Freiherr von Vincent, the Austrian emissary to Erfurt, received a similarly harsh imperial lecture on 1 October: 'Well then, it is war you seek; I have prepared for it, and I will be terrible ... Under these conditions is it propitious for you to attack me?'[94] At the same time, Napoleon repeatedly communicated to the Austrians, to the Russians and to his own subordinates that bilateral relations were good, that he desired peace and that he 'wanted nothing from Austria'.[95]

His letter to Kaiser Franz at the conclusion of the Erfurt conference encapsulated his attitude, mixing a desire for peace with blunt threats:

> There is a faction in Vienna that affects fear in order to push your cabinet into violent measures that will be the cause of miseries far greater than those that have preceded them. I was in a position to dismember Your Majesty's monarchy, or at least to leave it less powerful; I did not wish this. That which it is, it is by my wish: this is the most obvious proof that our accounts are balanced and that I want nothing from you. I will always be prepared to guarantee the integrity of your monarchy. I will never do anything against the principal interests of your estates. But Your Majesty must not bring into question that which has been settled by fifteen years of war ... Let Your Majesty beware of those who speak to you of the dangers to your monarchy ... Those alone are dangerous; those alone call forth the dangers they pretend to fear.[96]

Napoleon also used this missive to remind Franz of the Franco-Russian alliance and his larger confrontation with Britain, but he offered an indication of his desire for reduced tensions and 'the tranquillity of Europe' by apprising Vienna that the Rheinbund troops were being released to return to their home garrisons. In speaking of his desire to 'guarantee the integrity' of the Habsburg monarchy, Napoleon touched directly on a core Austrian concern, one that would arise again at the end of the coming war just as it featured in the antecedent months. The French emperor's hopes of mollifying Austria in this fashion, however, were in vain. For the war party in Vienna, Napoleon's letter with its often-haughty tone was immaterial. 'Napoleon retains his hostile attitudes towards Austria,' summarised Stadion for Franz on 22 October, 'I remain convinced that the day he finds the power to do so will be the day his plans against us are executed.'[97]

As demonstrated by the pomp and ceremony of the Erfurt conference, Napoleon saw the intimate co-operation of his principal ally, Tsar Alexander, as the centrepiece of his Austrian policy in 1808–9. Napoleon thus hoped to use Russia to restrain Austria while simultaneously precluding any inclination on the tsar's part to participate in or even tolerate another coalition aimed against France. From the summer of 1808, as details of Austria's defensive measures reached Paris and tensions rose, Napoleon's communications with Russia consistently touched on the need to deter the Habsburgs. Moderation of Austrian behaviour thus became a key theme at Erfurt. As we have seen, however, Napoleon was only partially successful in securing Alexander's assistance and the tsar's conciliatory communications with Austria threatened to dilute one of the Erfurt conference's concrete achievements: the treaty clause in which Russia promised to support France militarily should Austria attack. Napoleon, however, persuaded himself that he had subdued Austria and renewed his Russian alliance: 'All is well with Russia, I have nothing to fear from Austria,' he told Marshal Davout in late October.[98] Confident that his strategic rear in central Europe was now secure, he accelerated preparations for the campaign in Iberia. Marshal Adolphe Édouard Mortier's 5th Corps therefore resumed its course for Spain and two-thirds of Marshal Jean de Dieu Soult's old 4th Corps headed for either Spain or France. Napoleon himself left Erfurt on 14 October to arrive at Saint Cloud outside Paris on the night of the 18th. He did not tarry long. After ten days of frenetic work, he departed for the Pyrenees. On the evening of 4 November he was in Spain, taking a few moments in the pre-dawn hours the following morning to pen a note to Josephine: 'I hope that all this will soon be finished.'[99]

Napoleon, early 1809:
The Desire of the Emperor is to Conserve Peace

Napoleon may have dissolved the Grande Armée and taken himself across the mountains into Spain, but his vigilance in Germany and Italy did not relax. Likewise, he continued to rebuild the regiments left behind in Germany under Davout's Army of the Rhine; he devoted similar attention to his Army of Italy, commanded by his stepson, Eugène de Beauharnais, the Viceroy of Italy. The rebuilding proceeded at a slow pace as the new Army of Spain had priority, but Napoleon's officers, officials and allies kept a close watch on Austria and supplied him with a steady flow of reliable intelligence from every conceivable source while he campaigned across the Pyrenees. The war in Spain seemed to be proceeding in a satisfactory manner as 1808 came to an end. The Spanish had suffered a series of crushing defeats and Sir John Moore's small British army was conducting a desperate retreat to the coast in hopes of rescue by the Royal Navy. The news from central Europe, however, was disturbing. Not only were reports on Austria growing more alarming, but Napoleon also received letters describing murky plots against him in Paris.[100] Reading a packet of messages by a wintry roadside fire near Astorga on 1 January 1809 as he pursued Moore's ragged army, he decided that these two problems required his immediate return to France. Leaving Marshal Soult to handle the destruction of Moore, he took two hectic weeks to settle his Iberian affairs (or so he hoped) and departed on 17 January to clatter into Paris on the morning of the 23rd.[101]

While dealing with Iberian matters, Napoleon also addressed the Austrian problem with at least twenty-five letters bearing his signature on 14 and 15 January alone. This flood of correspondence illuminates two aspects of the emperor's thinking at this point. First, he was confident that two or three months would elapse before Austria could be ready for war. He therefore had at least the remainder of January, all of February, and probably most of March in which to make his preparations against Austria 'if it wants to stir'.[102] Second, he clearly believed that Austria could still be deterred and, as during the previous summer and autumn, he turned to a combination of diplomatic palliatives and military threats to forestall this war he did not want. Among other military actions, he mobilised the Rheinbund, refurbished fortresses in Bavaria and Italy, alerted reserves inside France and issued secret instructions for the defence of Italy and Dalmatia. He also moved troops closer to the Austrian frontier in Bavaria, sending GD Nicholas Charles Oudinot's corps and a division of cuirassiers to Augsburg with the hope that 'The arrival of this corps, coincident with my return to Paris, will make Austria see that this is no jest.'[103]

On the diplomatic front as well, Napoleon returned to the tactics of 1808, attempting to calm Austrian anxiety by enlisting the tsar's assistance combined with direct communications to Vienna that 'the desire of the emperor is to conserve peace with Austria'.[104] Although the Austrians, as the French chargé in Vienna noted, were now 'too far advanced to turn back',[105] Napoleon maintained his conviction that war could be avoided: 'When Austria sees the French and Russian armies ready to invade its territory, it will accept the guarantee [of its territorial integrity] ... and disarm.'[106] He continued to find Vienna's 'extravagant conduct' puzzling and 'mysterious', asking the Rheinbund princes rhetorically if the waters of the Danube 'had acquired the properties of the Lethe' (the river of forgetfulness in Greek mythology).[107] To the tsar, Napoleon complained that 'Austria's ridiculous armaments' were draining France's exchequer and, above all, paralysing his plans for 'the maritime war' as he called the struggle with Great Britain.[108] He persisted in his belief, however, that Austria would 'return to reasonable thinking'.[109] 'I do not think that they are so foolish as to commence operations having the Russian army on their flanks,' he wrote on 4 March, adding that, 'The Austrians will not be long in recognising that there are more troops in Germany and Italy than they can imagine.'[110]

March 4th also saw Napoleon issue orders to begin assembling these troops. Subsequent instructions designated this gathering mass the 'Armée d'Allemagne' ('Army of Germany') and appointed the faithful Marshal Alexander Berthier as its 'major general' (chief of staff).[111] Thanks to the assiduous efforts of his generals, spies and diplomats, Napoleon knew that the principal Austrian army was concentrated in Bohemia and he positioned his forces to counter an offensive from that direction. The heart of his strategic concept was Davout's Army of the Rhine, now designated as 3rd Corps and collected around Nuremberg,

Bayreuth, Bamberg and Regensburg. To anchor his strategic right flank, he placed Oudinot's temporary command (now named 2nd Corps) and a new 4th Corps under Marshal André Massena between Ulm and Augsburg along the Lech River, while the Bavarian army (designated 7th Corps) screened the frontier with Austria along the Isar. Württemberg's army (later forming the nucleus of 8th Corps) was to be a special reserve, while smaller Rheinbund contingents bolstered 3rd and 4th Corps. The Saxon army, reinforced by a French division, became 9th Corps and was detailed to cover the strategic left at Dresden while the Poles of the Duchy of Warsaw's army, commanded by GD Prince Joseph Poniatowski, were to assemble at Warsaw.[112] Similar preparatory measures were instituted south of the Alps as Napoleon reinforced Viceroy Eugène's Army of Italy with troops from Rome and Naples. GD Auguste Marmont, commanding the small but veteran Army of Dalmatia, was placed under Eugène's orders and directed to concentrate on the Austrian frontier while retaining garrisons in key coastal towns. As usual, Napoleon also paid close attention to rear-area security (his lines of communications and the coasts), allotting these tasks to the Westphalian army (10th Corps), Dutch and Danish allies, along with a host of newly created French second-line units. The organisation, energy and resources required to execute the barrage of imperial orders associated with these measures was extraordinary, but time was short and much remained unfinished when the war began. The Imperial Guard, for example, was still on its way from Spain, as were several key generals; materials and munitions of all sorts were in short supply; thousands of replacements were yet to arrive; and most of the rear-area security formations existed only on paper. The greatest problem for the moment, however, was that the constituent elements of this new army were scattered about southern Germany, not yet concentrated. If Austria could strike quickly, it might have an opportunity to gain the desired early victory before the Army of Germany was assembled under Napoleon's personal command.

Nonetheless, by the middle of March, Napoleon was well on his way to establishing a large army in southern Germany, the principal theatre of war, supplemented by significant forces in Italy as well as small commands in distant Poland and Dalmatia. To minimise provocation, the emperor and his chief of staff would remain inside France unless

Austria attacked. Napoleon thus stayed in Paris while dispatching Berthier to Strasbourg to coordinate the army's movements. As a result of these precautions, Napoleon would be absent from the theatre of war when the conflict opened, leaving Berthier in de facto command of the Army of Germany.

If war could not be prevented, Napoleon intended to start on the defensive. Austria would thus bear the onus of being the aggressor and French forces could launch a counteroffensive on their own terms once the initial Austrian incursion had been contained. Beyond this broad military strategy, the French emperor did not enter into the conflict with any preconceived notions concerning war aims or the military operations that might be necessary to attain them. As he hoped to avoid war in the first place, this is hardly surprising. Unlike the Stadions, therefore, he did not articulate a desired outcome and remained flexible both before the opening of hostilities and as the war unfolded. What was clear in his statements in late 1808 and especially in early 1809, however, was that he harboured no doubts that he would emerge victorious and that his thinking encompassed the possibility of imposing the harshest terms on a defeated Austria, to include the potential removal of Kaiser Franz as emperor and even the dissolution of the monarchy. In a letter to his brother Jérôme, the King of Westphalia, written just before he departed Spain, for instance, he commented that 'The Emperor of Austria, if he makes the slightest hostile movement, will soon cease to reign.'[113] A 6 March 1809 letter to his ambassador in St Petersburg, GD Armand Augustin Caulaincourt, went so far as to propose the possibility of 'separating the three crowns of the Austrian empire', that is, those of Bohemia, Austria and Hungary. These component parts would then become minor independent states under new rulers or perhaps fall under the sceptres of Russia and France in some combination. Though these extreme ideas remained in play until the end of the war, however, they represented little more than a list of options that Russia and France might explore.[114] Nothing was decided.

In considering his future relations with Austria, Napoleon's thinking was informed by his previous experiences with the Habsburgs. He saw the old empire as an enemy he had defeated but preserved from destruction three times (1797, 1800, 1805) and felt especially betrayed after the pledges of peace he had received personally from Kaiser Franz in the days following Austerlitz. Austria 'has articulated no grievances and wants to go back to the shameful campaign of 1805', he told his brother Louis, the King of Holland, 'She is rushing to her ruin.'[115] At the same time, prevention of war remained his central interest. He repeatedly restated that he had no intention of attacking Austria and enjoined his generals to avoid provocative actions along the now tense frontiers.[116] Napoleon, therefore, though open to the destruction of the Habsburg monarchy as a possible outcome, had nothing definitive in mind as far as his war aims were concerned when hostilities finally opened on 10 April.

The weather in early April 1809 was ugly, a nasty mix of rain, freezing rain and snow exacerbated by sharp winds that cut through soldiers' coats and blew the biting precipitation into their faces. For the white-coated battalions of the Austrian Hauptarmee, their miseries were compounded by the long tedious marches required to relocate from Bohemia to the Inn River. Driven by the revanchist beliefs of their leaders in Vienna and momentary popular enthusiasm, they settled down to catch what rest they could before crossing their Rubicon into Bavaria.[117] Stadion's unsound assumptions and vague, visionary war aims, however, dealt the army an almost impossible mission while weak, tardy diplomacy meant it was entering the conflict without allies. The army's leadership contributed little to crafting solutions to its strategic challenges and compounded its problems by diffusing its efforts and squandering an irreplaceable seven to ten days in shifting the army south to the Danube valley. 'Rapid decisions' and 'bold enterprises'[118] might still deliver the crucial early victory over the scattered French and their German allies, but the Austrians had lost valuable time and their window of opportunity was fast closing.

On the opposite side of the Inn and all across southern Germany, thousands of French and Allied soldiers likewise suffered from the execrable weather as they went about the quotidian business of finding food and shelter. Napoleon's vast energy had brought together the beginnings of a great army in a remarkably short period of time and thousands of replacements were collecting in depots or trudging across the muddy miles in march battalions to join their fellows on the

Bavarian frontier. The troops allotted to rear-area security were weeks away from assembling, but the first-line formations and most of these replacements would reach their assigned positions in seven to ten days. This was the period of maximum French vulnerability, made more inviting for the Austrians because Napoleon and several other key senior commanders were not yet present in the theatre of war. The initiative lay with Austria. The question now was whether Archduke Charles and his army could move fast enough and hit hard enough to exploit this French vulnerability, open the campaign with a major victory and redeem the failures of Habsburg diplomacy.

Chapter 2
Armies on the Edge of War

FOR WEEKS, NAPOLEON PERSISTED IN HIS BELIEF that war could be avoided, but intelligence of Austrian preparations continued to mount and, when Habsburg border officials arrested a French courier carrying correspondence from the embassy in Vienna, he told his ambassador in Russia that 'Everything leads me to believe that Austria will attack.'[1] In response, he accelerated his own military measures and dispatched his horses and campaign equipment to the frontier. He remained convinced, however, that Austria would not be able to attack until some time in May[2] and he once again approached the tsar in the hopes that Russian military and diplomatic pressure in the interim would restrain Vienna and avert war. 'I have relied and I rely on Your Majesty,' he wrote to Alexander on 24 March, 'But action must be taken and I trust in you.'[3]

By this point in late March, however, it was already too late to deter Austria. The Habsburg hierarchy was irrecoverably on the path to war, its key leaders issuing bellicose proclamations and its regiments plodding towards the empire's borders. In any event, Napoleon's 24 March missive to Alexander did not reach St Petersburg until 14 April, when the war was already into its fifth day.[4] Even if the tsar had reacted with the greatest alacrity, therefore, the time for prevention had long since passed. As Alexander dined with French Ambassador Caulaincourt on 15 April, the two armies in distant Bavaria were struggling through the mud and sleet towards their first major engagement.

The Habsburg Hauptarmee

The armies that faced each other in Bavaria in April 1809 were unique in several respects.[5] That is, they both represented significant changes from the familiar templates of earlier conflicts. In Austria's case, both the size and the nature of the army were notable. As far as numbers were concerned, the field forces were divided into 46 'German' and 15 Hungarian line infantry regiments, 17 Grenz regiments, 9 new Jäger battalions, and 35 cavalry regiments totalling 283,400 men. Sedentary troops numbering some 314,810 were slated to supplement the regulars: the depots of the line regiments, four garrison battalions, reserves, and the Landwehr. It was hoped that the Hungarian Noble Insurrection would soon provide a further 50,000 infantry and cavalry, raising the total forces available shortly after the start of hostilities to over 640,000 men under arms. Additional 'Insurrection' troops from other border regions were to be added as mobilisation proceeded. These numbers were never attained, however, and the quality of many of the second-line formations fell far short of what their enthusiasts had projected. Nonetheless, the size of the proposed force represented a major exertion for the old empire, indicating the importance Vienna attached to the coming war and the success the war party had achieved in mobilising the monarchy's resources. Given the monarchy's parlous financial situation, however, the army could only be kept on a war footing for a few months.

The product of eight years of sporadic reforms largely led by Charles, the army of 1809 was also notably different in organisation from the forces assembled for the wars of 1792–1805. To a lesser degree, it was also different in composition and tactics. The archduke had long recognised that reforms were imperative if the old monarchy was going to maintain its status as a great power and cope with the severe challenges posed by France since 1792, challenges that multiplied exponentially under the leadership of Napoleon whether as general, first consul or emperor.[6] As Charles observed later: 'Eventually, France's enemies saw themselves, owing to their own setbacks, required to imitate those things that had given the adversary the advantage.'[7] Though this process was retarded by the often eccentric alterations introduced under FML Karl Freiherr Mack von Leiberich in 1805, Charles had laboured for two years to repair Mack's errors and reassert his own ideas to promote fundamental improvements in all aspects of the monarchy's military establishment.

Among Mack's ideas was a complete change in the tactical organisation of the army's infantry to regiments of five battalions (one of these being grenadiers), each with four companies; while the 'Grenz' ('border') regiments each had three battalions, also of four companies. Widely considered unsatisfactory, this was one of the first measures Charles reversed. When he regained authority in 1806, he returned the infantry regiments, both line and Grenz, to their pre-1805 structures. In terms of tactical organisation, therefore, a white-coated line infantry regiment in 1809 consisted of three battalions of six line companies each, for a total of eighteen companies in the field during war time as well as a pair of depot companies (a 'division') in its home station. Not included in the line battalions were the two grenadier companies that belonged to each regiment. Wearing distinctive bearskin caps, these grenadier companies were detached and formed into six-company composite battalions known by the names of their commanders. The *Leiningen* Grenadier Battalion, for example, consisted of two companies each from three 'German' infantry regiments: former *Zedtwitz* No. 25, *Argenteau* No. 35 and *Froon* No. 54. Concentrated in the army's reserve corps, these battalions, *Leiningen* in particular, would play an important role at Znaim. Depending on its recruiting district, each regiment was classified as 'German' or 'Hungarian', the former being drawn from Austria, Bohemia, Moravia, Silesia and Galicia, even though German may not have been the principal language in all those districts. The various regions of the Kingdom of Hungary supplied the remaining line infantry regiments. Hungarian regular infantry wore tight blue trousers as opposed to the white breeches of the German troops and were equipped with tall black shakos instead of the crested helmets still issued to the German regiments. The Hungarian companies were also slightly larger in size (238 rather than 218), but there was no difference in their tactical employment. The Grenz regiments, on the other hand, contained only two battalions each (also of six companies) and were supposed to be the army's principal light troops supplemented by individual Jäger and volunteer battalions. A true innovation was the Landwehr, a form of militia infantry that made its appearance in the Austrian order of battle for the first time in 1809. Organized into battalions on a regional basis in the Habsburg hereditary lands, the Landwehr battalions were initially collected in separate brigades, but most were eventually incorporated into line formations to bolster the size of the regular army and to lend greater steadiness to the inexperienced and poorly trained Landwehr. Most of these battalions would prove fragile and unreliable, but some, notably the six raised in Vienna (the Vienna Volunteers), would gain a reputation for solid performance on a par with the regulars.

The Habsburg regular cavalry consisted of heavy (cuirassiers and dragoons) and light regiments (hussars, chevaulegers and Uhlans). The cuirassier and dragoon regiments, each of six squadrons, were concentrated in the two reserve corps, while most of the light regiments (eight squadrons each) were distributed among the standard corps. The empire's impecunious situation, however, meant that it could not maintain a body of cavalry commensurate with the army's size. The Austrian horse would thus almost always find itself outnumbered by its French opponents. In addition to regular regiments, the reserve corps eventually came to include the only two Hungarian Insurrection units to serve with the Hauptarmee: the Neutra and Primatial Insurrection Hussar Regiments. The bulk of the Insurrection was only embodied after hostilities had opened and only campaigned in Hungary, but these two regiments joined the army in May in time for the Battle of Aspern-Essling and remained with it through Wagram and Znaim. Charles, however, considered them something of a liability 'Because these troops are not practised in fighting on their own and, although they show much courage, they certainly cannot be left alone.'[8]

Beyond returning the infantry to its pre-1805 organisational arrangements, Charles believed that fundamental changes in the army's personnel were needed because the new style of warfare against the French demanded greater independence, initiative and aggressiveness from officers and men alike.[9] At the most basic level, he addressed the conditions of service for common soldiers, reducing terms of enlistment and promulgating new regulations to ameliorate some of the wretchedness and brutality normally suffered by the rank and file. In place of beatings and degradation, for instance, he insisted that soldiers be treated as honourable servants of their emperor, not social misfits or convicts in uniform. Though far from being an army of free citizens, the men were to be motivated by sincere devotion to their monarch, by attachment to their regiments, and by noble ideals of martial virtue. 'Numerous punishments recommend neither the regiment nor its commander,' he adjured his colonels.[10] Physical abuse was not entirely removed from the Austrian army's repertoire, but there was a noticeable improvement in life for the men in the ranks.

Charles was especially concerned with the quality of the army's leadership. Acutely aware of the limitations of the monarchy's generals, he introduced doctrinal publications and a military journal to raise their level of professionalism and overcome the deeply entrenched conservatism of the institutional culture and the 'marked lack of intellectual activity' that characterised the officer corps.[11] Junior to mid-grade leaders were to be edified by detailed tactical examples in the eight-part *Contributions to Practical Instruction in the Field* while Charles's own *Fundamentals of the Higher Art of War for the Generals of the Austrian Army* was to enhance operational competence among the army's senior commanders.[12] He was particularly interested in countering the mobility and energy of the French armies as well as their 'dispersed style of fighting'.[13] These publications, he hoped, would instruct 'the thinking officer' to enhance technical competence and inject a more independent, offensive spirit among his subordinates.[14] To promote the study of military history and generally broaden the outlook of the officer corps, Charles also founded the *Austrian Military Journal* as 'the intellectual centre' of the army, a professional periodical that continues in print to this day.[15] As most of these publications first appeared in 1808, however, there was hardly time to instil the sort of transformative change Charles sought before the new war with France began.

Tactically, too, Charles endeavoured to modernise the army, introducing a new set of drill manuals in 1807 and 1808, the first approved update since 1769. He saw Austrian tactics, both grand and minor, as outmoded, and sought ways to overcome the ingrained norms of linear deployments dating from the era of Maria Theresa in order to cope with the general shift from unitary to articulated armies.[16] The new regulations granted the infantry somewhat greater flexibility and stressed independence, open-order tactics and operations in the field,[17] but the improvement was negligible. In the assessment of the Austrian official history of 1809, the new drill was 'more complicated ... it had incorporated all the refinements of Frederickian drill'.[18] Indeed, the army's ability to co-ordinate attacks above the regimental level may have actually declined.[19] Particularly nettlesome for the Austrian army were light infantry tasks such as skirmishing, screening, advance-guard duties and fighting in rough or wooded terrain, in other words duties that required acting in dispersed or open order rather than in tight, well-drilled formations.[20] Austria had traditionally relied on a mixture of Grenz regiments recruited from its frontiers with the Ottoman Empire and volunteer battalions to handle such functions, but these units had proven increasingly unsatisfactory against the French.[21] Nine new Jäger battalions were raised in 1808 specifically to perform light infantry missions, but these lacked a coherent training regime and were often squandered by commanders who did not know how to use them. Each line infantry battalion was also to allot some soldiers to skirmishing, but this was at best 'a compromise between linear tactics and the new style of fighting'.[22] The overall results were thus marginal. Although much of the fighting at Znaim would take place in skirmish order, the Austrian infantry could not match its French opponents and their more advanced Rheinbund allies in the facility with which they grasped these duties.

As for the other arms, the artillery benefited from being organised into permanent batteries for the first time (rather than being distributed individually in dribs and drabs), from the creation of a unit of battery support personnel (*'Handlanger'* or labourers) and from the militarisation of its train columns. These changes gave commanders the potential for more options in combat and facilitated the formation of larger batteries to suit tactical situations, but there was no artillery reserve at Charles's personal disposal and he remained dissatisfied even after the success at Aspern-Essling.[23] The cavalry, on the other hand, largely languished. Despite the presence of a substantial cavalry reserve in 1809, there was a tendency to dilute the mounted arm's power by distributing it across the battlefield in small packets. Though highly respected across Europe on a man-for-man or regiment-for-regiment basis, therefore, it never developed the ability to operate in large formations on a par with its French adversaries.[24] As a result, the Habsburg horse was regarded more as 'a means to parry enemy attacks rather than a tool to deliver blows'.[25]

Of particular importance for the 1809 war were structural changes at the operational level. As mentioned above, the field army was for the first time arranged in French-style *corps d'armée* in an attempt to enhance its mobility, flexibility and logistical sustainability. The nine standard or line corps were very similar to one another, each consisting of two line divisions, an advance guard division, and supporting elements, for a total of approximately 30,000 men in 25–30 infantry battalions and 16 cavalry squadrons supported by 64–96 guns. While line divisions each consisted of two or three brigades, with two three-battalion line regiments per brigade, each corps' light troops were combined in its advance guard division, usually four to six battalions of supposedly 'light' infantry (Jäger, Grenzer or volunteers) and two light horse regiments (chevaulegers, hussars or Uhlans). In addition to the line or standard corps, the Hauptarmee in Germany began the war with two 'reserve' corps. These were intended to serve as command headquarters for the army's elite grenadier battalions and heavy cavalry regiments. This initial organisation of the army, however, did not last beyond the opening campaign in Bavaria. First, the requirement to protect Bohemia forced Charles to leave most of one corps behind when the army retreated back into Austria. Second, and more directly relevant to the Battle of Znaim, he reconfigured the reserves, placing the component elements of both previous corps under GdK Fürst Johann von Liechtenstein as a single army reserve. In practice, however, this large 'reserve corps' was composed of separate grenadier and cavalry corps that operated as more or less independent formations. Indeed, at Wagram the cavalry reserve was distributed to different parts of the battlefield rather than functioning as a single coherent body.

The corps system provided the Hauptarmee with potentially powerful, self-contained combat formations, each of which could train, march and fight as an integrated entity with resulting benefits for combat effectiveness and unit cohesion. Intended as agile, all-arms manoeuvre elements, they should have eased the command and control burden for the army commander while increasing his range of operational and tactical options; that is, they should have helped Austria move away from the ad hoc 'wings', 'columns' and 'lines' (*'Treffen'* or 'battles') of the linear era when armies had no permanent structure above the regimental level. In the event, only some of these benefits were realised during the war. In the first place, the corps were only designated in February 1809, so the army had no time to train or manoeuvre in this unfamiliar structure before hostilities opened. Frictions and confusions arose as commanders, staff officers and troops did not know one another and were not quite sure what was expected of them as members of these new organisations. Second, the Austrian military establishment 'did not yet understand the true nature of the division' as an organisational echelon, especially the delegation of command and administrative responsibilities to the corps and division level.[26] Many routine functions remained the sole purview of the army headquarters, slowing movement and reaction times. The greatest problem, however, was the weakness of the army's senior leadership. Conservative, hesitant and unaccustomed to thinking for themselves beyond the rigid confines of specific, written orders, the deficiencies of the senior commanders and their staffs obviated many of the advantages of the corps system, especially in fluid operational situations that demanded independence and initiative on the part of subordinate leaders. Commenting on this predicament immediately after the war, an Austrian officer observed:

> I had the opportunity to notice that one of the most conspicuous differences between the French general and one of ours lies in the fact that the Austrian general is completely satisfied and content when he has exactly followed the orders he has received, can demonstrate this by sufficient evidence and can thus see proof that no blame falls on him, regardless of whether or not success was achieved. This is a result of our organisation ... The Frenchman, in contrast, is responsible to his emperor for success. He receives no other order than the military task, the objective; the means to achieve it and all other details are simply left to him.[27]

Charles himself remarked that 'The span of command of most generals seldom exceeded that of a regimental commander.'[28]

The last-minute adoption of the corps system, therefore, did not fulfil Charles's hope of transforming the army into an effective offensive strike force. As he later wrote, the improvement in the army's mobility 'was limited to a few regiments' and the 'larger troop formations had neither

Chart 1: French and Allied Forces on 10 April

Napoleon I, Emperor of the French

In Germany
  Armée d'Allemagne (Army of Germany) Napoleon, commanding in person

In Bavaria
  2nd Corps & 3rd Heavy Cavalry Division GD Oudinot
  3rd Corps & 2nd Heavy Cavalry Division Marshal Davout
  4th Corps Marshal Massena
  7th Corps (Bavarian) Marshal Lefebvre
  8th Corps (Württemberg) GD Vandamme
  1st Heavy Cavalry Division GD Nansouty
  German Division GD Rouyer
  (Cavalry Reserve not yet formed)

En route from France
  Imperial Guard

In Saxony
  9th Corps (forming) Marshal Bernadotte

In Westphalia
  10th Corps (forming) King Jérôme Bonaparte

Along the Rhine
  Reserve formations being established Marshal Kellermann, later GD Junot

In Italy
  Army of Italy Viceroy Eugène de Beauharnais

In Dalmatia
  Army of Dalmatia GD Marmont

In Poland (Duchy of Warsaw)
  Polish army with Saxon detachment GD Poniatowski

Notes: (1) The numbers 1, 5 and 6 were not used to designate army corps in either the Army of Germany or the Army of Italy (multi-division formations in the Army of Italy were called 'wings'). (2) Marshal Augereau was initially slated to command the 8th Corps, but he did not participate in this war and 8th Corps never assumed its planned mixed-nationality configuration. (3) Though nominally part of 9th Corps, the Poles operated as an independent body under Prince Poniatowski.

Chart 2: Austrian Forces on 10 April

Franz I, Emperor of Austria
Johann Philipp Graf Stadion, Foreign Minister
Archduke Charles, Generalissimus

In Germany
    Hauptarmee — Charles, commanding in person
    Friedrich Lothar Stadion, Commissioner to the Army

Invading Bavaria north of the Danube
I Corps	GdK Bellegarde and in overall command of both corps
II Corps	FZM Kolowrat

Invading Bavaria south of the Danube
III Corps	FML Hohenzollern
IV Corps	FML Rosenberg
V Corps	FML Archduke Ludwig
VI Corps	FML Hiller
I Reserve Corps	GdK Liechtenstein
II Reserve Corps	FML Kienmayer

Army of Inner Austria — GdK Archduke Johann

  Invading the Tyrol
Elements of VIII Corps	FML Chasteler

  Invading Italy
Remainder of VIII Corps	FML Albert Gyulai
IX Corps	FML Ignaz Gyulai

  Invading Dalmatia
Separate detachment	GM Stoichevich

Invading Poland
VII Corps	GdK Archduke Ferdinand Habsburg-Este

Notes: (1) II Reserve Corps was abolished in early May, leaving a single formation simply called the Reserve Corps under Liechtenstein. (2) Albert Gyulai reported himself ill in June; Chasteler thus became commander of VIII Corps.

been assembled together nor exercised in combination' prior to the war.²⁹ On the other hand, the new organisation did enhance the army's overall cohesion, making it more resilient and less likely to shatter under pressure.³⁰ At the same time, despite all of the thought and effort, many of Charles's reforms remained half-measures and the army continued to exhibit many of the debilitating defects of the past. Although he inveighed against dispersing forces and condemned cordon-defence strategies in his writings, for instance, Charles and his fellow commanders never lost their passion for detachments. They frequently scattered small batches of troops across the landscape like marbles, weakening the main body and leaving many units absent on the day of battle. Nor did the army overcome its infamous tendency towards torpor. Austrian movements were generally slow and senior Austrian leaders repeatedly expressed surprise at the speed of French operations and the fact that Napoleon did not pause to regroup after every minor action. Charles had stressed the advantages of French mobility in his writings in the 1790s and the army had been fighting the French for almost two decades, but various Habsburg generals and the archduke himself continually expected the French to grant them time to recover from any setback. The Habsburg host of 1809, therefore, suffused with its conservative military culture, remained stolid, cautious and dogged rather than bold, rapid, enterprising or imaginative. It was a formidable foe when on the defensive and when operating in relatively open ground, but it was at best a clumsy offensive instrument and it was at a decided disadvantage if placed in rough terrain or in fast-moving, unexpected situations.

As it prepared to enter Bavaria in April 1809, however, most of these problems were not yet evident. Charles was already haunted by misgivings, but Grünne was not wrong in noting that the army at the start of the war was 'more splendid, proud and numerous than ever before, inspired by a previously unheard of spirit and enthusiasm'.³¹ 'Everything he [Charles] did was intended to raise the spirit of the army,' wrote Radetzky, 'and in this he succeeded.'³² Meanwhile, among the junior officers, Oberleutnant Karl von Grueber of the *Albert* Cuirassiers recalled that: 'Anyone who had seen the enthusiasm of this magnificent army advancing towards Bavaria could hardly have doubted that our brows would be encircled by victory's green laurels.'³³

Napoleon's Armée d'Allemagne

On the French side, the Armée d'Allemagne or Army of Germany was still a work in progress when the war began, neither as veteran nor as cohesive as the Grande Armée that Napoleon had disestablished after Erfurt in October 1808. This new entity evolved as the war progressed, however, rapidly expanding, hardening and cohering to more closely resemble its famous predecessor.

At the tactical level, the Army of Germany differed from the Grande Armée in the structure of its French infantry regiments. There had been considerable disparity in the number of battalions per infantry regiment under the previous French system, but an imperial decree of 8 February 1808 stipulated that each line or light infantry regiment would henceforth consist of at least five battalions: four 'war' or field battalions (numbered one to four) and one depot battalion (the fifth battalion) at the regiment's home station. As part of this reorganisation, the number of companies per battalion was reduced from nine to six (only four companies for each depot battalion) with the excess personnel transferred to become cadres for the new battalions. Each of the reformed line (*ligne*) battalions was thus left with four line or centre companies known as fusiliers and two elite companies, one each of grenadiers and voltigeurs, the latter specially designated for light infantry tasks. The light infantry (*léger*) regiments retained the voltigeur designation for one elite company, but the centre companies were called chasseurs and the counterparts to grenadiers were termed carabiniers.

The vast shifting of personnel and other assets required by this process was barely under way in the summer and autumn of 1808 when Napoleon ordered the massive redeployment of troops from Germany to Spain. The result was an administrative and accounting nightmare that disrupted and delayed this army-wide tactical reorganisation. Many regiments never had a chance to assemble all four field battalions in one location: some were shunted off to fill ad hoc commands in Spain, some remained in Germany and yet others were in the process of forming in depots or training camps. The army's tactical changes and the strategic shift to Spain thus provided the context for the establishment of the Army of Germany.

This new army differed significantly from the past at the higher levels of command as well. Both the Grande Armée and the Armée d'Allemagne were forged around seven numbered corps, a cavalry reserve and the Imperial Guard, but practical differences in composition, training and combat experience belied these superficial similarities. From 1805 through 1807, Napoleon had been able to rely upon a predominantly French army that he had assiduously trained on the Channel coast and then honed in the fire of combat over the course of three successive campaigns. That army, however, no longer existed. The 1st, 5th and 6th Corps had marched away over the Pyrenees in 1808 along with much of the light cavalry and all of the dragoons, while Marshal Soult's old 4th Corps had been broken up and redistributed between Germany and France. Only Davout's 3rd Corps of the Grande Armée, briefly called the Army of the Rhine as noted above, remained more or less as it had been constituted during the previous imperial wars. Other than Davout's command and the heavy cavalry, therefore, all of the corps Napoleon established in April 1809 were almost entirely new creations. Moreover, when the Austrian invasion began, the Guard had not arrived, the components of the cavalry reserve were distributed among other commands, 2nd Corps lacked its largest and most experienced division, several key generals were still en route from Spain (most notably Marshal Jean Lannes, the assigned commander for 2nd Corps) and thousands of fresh conscripts were still on the road to their regiments from depots in France. The actual configuration of the Army of Germany as it faced the Austrian Hauptarmee in April 1809 was thus different not only from the old Grande Armée, but also from Napoleon's desired structure. Napoleon improvised on the spot during the first two weeks of the war to repel the Austrian offensive, dexterously shifting units as needed, but he did not lose sight of his original intention and would return to this basic concept as soon as circumstances permitted.

The quality of the new army was also inferior as compared to its famous forebears. This posed problems of training and acculturation at both the individual and collective levels. At the individual level, there was little time to train the new conscripts in basic skills or to inure them to the hardships of extended marches, living off the land and routine campaign privations. Many of the conscripts joining their regiments in the Army of Germany had only been in uniform for three or four months before enduring forced marches under inclement weather or finding themselves in the most desperate combat. Collective training and unit cohesion were also problems in some cases as there was no time for integrating the new recruits and junior officers into their regiments or for the conduct of battalion, regimental, brigade or higher-echelon manoeuvres. These deficiencies were most acute in the two divisions commanded by GD Oudinot. No longer an elite force of 'combined grenadiers' as in the past, Oudinot's brigades were largely composed of young conscripts in single battalions separated from their parent regiments. They could be as enthusiastic, courageous and impetuous as their compatriots, but their steadiness and their ability to manoeuvre under fire were limited.

If Napoleon's Army of Germany of 1809 was not at the same pinnacle of excellence as the Grande Armée in its prime, however, it is important not to let Oudinot's conscripts represent the entire army. Overall quality had declined somewhat but, in aggregate, the Army of Germany was far superior to the courageous but raw conscript masses who marched into the 1813 campaign in Saxony. They might lack training and experience, but most of the new soldiers in 1809 were young men between the ages of 20 and 24 with greater stamina than the youths who often filled Napoleon's ranks in those final frantic campaigns. In contrast to Oudinot's battalions, most French regiments in the Army of Germany had a solid core of veterans and the Austrians erred badly in concluding that the French army consisted entirely of untried soldiers. Newly assigned to units with high percentages of calm, confident veterans, the new conscripts acclimated quickly and responded well to the leadership provided by their sergeants, their officers and their emperor.

Indeed, leadership at all levels was a major strength of the French army. There were certainly green young subalterns gathered up from military schools or superannuated retirees drafted back into active service who gave their new commanders occasion to complain (Oudinot received a batch of these with large replacement detachments in mid-May), but the officer corps of most front-line units was composed of men who had attained their promotions through courage and competence during many years of service and multiple campaigns. Compared to their Austrian counterparts, they were youthful but experienced, skilled, energetic and bold, often to the point of impetuosity or rashness. They had tremendous confidence in themselves and their leaders, Napoleon above all. 'Everyone viewed these preparations for war with pleasure,' one junior officer wrote in a letter to his brother, 'We were quite disposed to open the ball at any time, too bad for those who could not keep the measure.'[34]

These men understood that they were expected to take the initiative, that no opportunity was to be overlooked, no exertion left untried. For one young French staff officer, the army was possessed of a 'limitless confidence in success' and an enterprising spirit that manifested itself in a 'manner of regarding nothing as impossible'.[35] Writing later in the third person, Charles revealed something of himself as well as his view of the French when he commented that 'Napoleon and his instruments were children of the revolution, who allowed themselves every means to the end and remained in practice through perpetual wars to exploit the same thoroughly, exhaustively and relentlessly... The effectiveness of his opponent, the Archduke Charles, could not be as comprehensive.'[36] The post-war Austrian report cited earlier offered a similar assessment from the enemy's viewpoint:

> He who has the opportunity to observe the eager, restless and anxious striving of everyone without exception, from first to last, from highest to lowest, how each endeavours to do everything that is at all possible, indeed to deduce what is not specifically stated, to exceed that which is expected, he who observes this must share the full conviction that no sovereign in all Europe can be considered better served, more closely obeyed or more wholly satisfied than Napoleon.[37]

Victory, not cautious adherence to meticulously written orders, was the measure of success.

Independent, intrepid and with complete faith in their imperial master, French officers could be entrusted with orders that specified their missions, Napoleon's objectives and the general operational context. Napoleon did tailor his instructions to match his assessment of a commander's capabilities, but in most cases, orders were spare and simple, starting with the phrase 'it is the intention of the emperor' to state Napoleon's general goals. The details of execution were left up to the subordinate. This system was by no means flawless and could lead to misunderstanding and error, especially when the emperor failed to clarify command arrangements among semi-independent subordinates, as would occur during the pursuit after Wagram. In general, however, Napoleon's system worked admirably within the prevailing French military culture, leaving adversaries breathless and confused by the rapid and unremitting pace of French operations. When problems did arise, the competence and experience of the French and their German allies, officers and soldiers alike, granted them room to recover and compensate. In the Austrian structure, the margin for error was much narrower.

In tactics, too, French speed and adaptability contrasted strongly with the Austrian emphasis on stiff formality and the minutiae of the drill book. Flexibility, drive and an uncanny skill at deriving every possible advantage from the terrain were especially prevalent in the French infantry. These qualities gave Napoleon's foot soldiers a significant superiority over most of their continental foes in broken terrain or village fighting, which placed a premium on the agility, open-order tactics and individual initiative that characterised the French infantry. Off the battlefield, the French army enjoyed a well-deserved renown for its marching ability. Combining this mobility, boldness, energy and initiative with a general disregard for march formalities and an almost heedless determination to match the emperor's expectations, the French could conduct rapid, consecutive marches over long distances. Some of their German allies, notably the men of the Bavarian, Baden, Hessian and Württemberg contingents, equalled the French capacity for rapid movement. The 2nd Bavarian Division, for example, covered the more than 200 kilometres from Linz to Wagram in four days. Although Habsburg troops also managed lengthy forced marches on a few occasions,[38] the Austrian army as a whole could not match the speed and mobility that Napoleon's legions demonstrated on a regular basis.

The French mounted arm exhibited the initiative, flexibility and zeal that were so prominent among their infantry compatriots, but most observers considered French horse generally inferior to the Austrians at the regimental level and below. The French compensated for their deficit in individual and small-unit skills by their marked superiority in co-ordinating the actions of multiple regiments to achieve tactical battlefield goals. Where the Austrians tended to employ their squadrons and regiments as isolated entities with little co-ordination above the regimental level, French commanders were adept at combining their formations for large orchestrated attacks of brigade or division size. They could thus overwhelm their opponents and had the potential to have a decisive influence on the outcome of any particular battle. Moreover, the Austrians were keenly aware that the French cavalry was more numerous and Charles had to issue special instructions to counter his army's mounting fear of the French horse after the opening battles in April.

Although the French artillery enjoyed a well-deserved reputation for excellence, the Army of Germany began the war with serious shortfalls in manpower, equipment, and horses for its guns. Like Charles, therefore, Napoleon did not have a central artillery reserve at the start of hostilities, but he speedily repaired these deficiencies during the lull that followed the Battle of Aspern-Essling (21–22 May). Exploiting Vienna's vast arsenals and France's own resources, he re-equipped and expanded the artillery arm. He devoted special attention to the Imperial Guard, increasing the count of guns and howitzers from the eight he had had available at Aspern-Essling in May to sixty pieces by early July. He thereby placed a formidable artillery reserve under his personal control that would earn a place in military history during the Battle of Wagram.

Whether infantry, cavalry or artillery, the French units of the Army of Germany did not confront Austria on their own. One of the most notable features of the army's structure and composition in this war was the heavy reliance on German troops from the Rheinbund. Previously present in relatively small numbers and employed primarily to blockade fortresses or guard lines of communications, Rheinbund contingents emerged as essential elements in the forefront of the 1809 contest with Austria. The 7th Corps was entirely Bavarian, the Württemberg army became the de facto 8th Corps and Marshal Jean-Baptiste Bernadotte's 9th Corps[39] consisted of the Saxon army and a single small French division. A division of troops from the smaller Rheinbund states performed the 'traditional' rear-area roles as did the half-Westphalian, half-Dutch 10th Corps under Westphalia's King Jérôme. By the time the peace treaty was signed in

October, troops from almost every Confederation member would have been involved in the war in one way or another.[40]

Thus stood Napoleon's forces in Bavaria on the eve of war in April 1809. Where almost all of the Austrian Hauptarmee would fight at Znaim, however, only three of the Army of Germany's component parts would arrive in time for the final battle: elements of 4th Corps, one of the Bavarian divisions, and the heavy cavalry. The other major French forces on the field would be the Army of Dalmatia and cavalry of the Imperial Guard. All of these deserve a few words before we proceed with the campaign narrative.

The French 4th Corps of 1809 was in part descended from Marshal Soult's 4th Corps of the old Grande Armée and the regiments of its 1st and 2nd Divisions. That is, those that fought at Znaim had served together in all the imperial campaigns since 1805 before the original 4th Corps was broken up in 1808. After October of that year, some of its component units headed for Spain and others joined Davout's Army of the Rhine, while the regiments that would constitute the new 1st and 2nd Divisions returned to France from Germany. By the time Napoleon sent them back to Germany in early 1809, therefore, these 'divisions' were quite small with only two regiments in the 1st and three in the 2nd as compared to the previous standard of five regiments per division. The 1808 reorganisation of the army's infantry and the urgency of the situation in early 1809 introduced other dislocations: all five of these regiments fought at Znaim with three battalions each, for instance, but the fourth battalions for four of them (e.g. IV/4 Ligne), though present in Austria, were assigned to Oudinot's 2nd Corps and one (IV/46 Ligne) was in Germany on line of communications duties. All five regiments also had parts of their depot battalions allotted to reserve units being formed for rear-area security in Germany or on the Rhine.[41] To make up for losses in the previous conflicts, these regiments had received numerous conscripts in the weeks leading up to the war. This meant that, across the corps, as much as 30 per cent of each regiment's full complement of men seems to have consisted of brand new soldiers in April 1809. Conscripts and changes notwithstanding, Massena's infantry was composed of solid, well-established units with excellent reputations, superb leadership at all levels and valuable unit cohesion based on their earlier service together. Massena reviewed the men in early April, finding them in 'the best appearance' and 'already accustomed to marching'. Although 'the beardless faces of the conscripts contrasted with those of their older comrades', he reported, they were 'vigorous, willing' and, learning from the veterans, 'had already adopted their easy manner, their high spirits and their cheerfulness'.[42] Général de Brigade (GB) François Roch Ledru des Essarts, newly arrived to command one of the brigades of the 1st Division, pronounced his men 'very fine and very numerous'. 'My brigade is superb', he wrote proudly to his sister.[43]

Such impressions were encouraging, but the small size of Massena's 1st and 2nd Divisions led Napoleon to supplement each with a brigade of German troops.[44] Fortunately for Massena, the contingents assigned to his corps would prove to be two of the best among the Rheinbund armies, men who 'rivalled [the French] in zeal and devotion'.[45] The 1st Division received the brigade from the Grand Duchy of Baden: three line infantry regiments, a battalion of Jäger (light infantry), a foot artillery battery and a half-battery of horse artillery. A regiment of light dragoons, assigned to the corps cavalry division, completed the contingent. Baden's cavalry and artillery had good reputations, but the indifferent performance of its infantry in previous campaigns had prompted significant French pressure for thoroughgoing military reforms during 1808. As a result, the contingent's foot soldiers in 1809 were organised such that a line regiment consisted of two 840-man battalions dressed in blue, each mirroring the French pattern of four musketeer or centre companies, a voltigeur company and a grenadier company. On paper, the green-clad light battalion had a similar organisation, but it was short of personnel when the war began and took the field with only four of its six companies. The Badeners retained, however, a high, crested helmet (Raupenhelm) as a distinctive feature of their uniforms. Modelled on the Bavarian Raupenhelm, this unusual piece of headgear would often lead Austrians to misidentify the Baden troops and report themselves in combat with Bavarians.

Owing to the dramatic changes in the grand duchy's small army, especially its rapid expansion, the battalions that joined Massena's corps included large numbers of new recruits. Reviewing them in March, the marshal described the contingent in a letter to Berthier: 'I found them very fine but totally composed of conscripts.'[46] They were, however, 'in the prime of life, of good height, well dressed and perfectly equipped' and 'their commanders assured [Massena] that they were animated by the best spirit'. They would soon demonstrate this good spirit as well as considerable military skill, proving themselves valuable additions to the corps both on the march and in combat.

The 2nd Division was filled out by the contingent from the Grand Duchy of Hesse-Darmstadt. These men brought with them a good martial reputation and Napoleon's favourable opinion. As they were already considered a reliable asset, Napoleon did not interfere with their internal arrangements and the contingent's infantry thus maintained a peculiar organisation. Hesse-Darmstadt fielded two 'brigades', each composed of a two-battalion musketeer (line) infantry regiment and a fusilier (light infantry) battalion; whether musketeer or fusilier, the battalions were all divided into four companies. Although these 'brigades' were the functional equivalent of regiments in other armies, it was not uncommon for the fusilier battalions and the sharpshooters (Schützen) of the line battalions to be detached for special missions as would occur at Znaim. Like the Baden troops, the Hessian infantry wore distinctive headgear, in Hesse's case a bicorne hat that would have been more at home in the previous century. They also resembled Baden in uniforming their musketeers in blue and their fusiliers in dark green. A light cavalry regiment called chevaulegers and a battery of six pieces rounded out the Hessian contingent as a solid professional contribution to 4th Corps.

These men, French and German, veteran and conscript alike, found themselves serving under excellent leaders. The division commanders were all competent, experienced veterans. GD Claude Juste Alexander Legrand, aged forty-seven, a former sergeant of the old royal army who had led the 1st Division since 1805, stood out from the rest as one of the few officers in whom Napoleon descried the 'sacred fire' (*feu sacré*) that distinguished officers of especial dedication, determination and inspirational ability.[47] Pierre Pelleport, colonel of the 18th Ligne in Legrand's division, regarded his commander as skilful on the battlefield and 'one of the most serious generals of our army'. 'It is with veneration that I go to visit his tomb whenever I am in Paris,' Pelleport wrote later, 'No soldier ever received a more deserved honour.'[48] GD Claude Carra

Saint-Cyr, 49, had taken command of 2nd Division in February 1807. He had a reputation for prudence, but was solid and reliable if not especially energetic or imaginative.[49] Battle losses among Massena's brigade commanders would lead to the introduction of new commanders for the French brigades of the 1st and 2nd Divisions by the time 4th Corps marched to Znaim: GB Jean Parfait Friederichs in the 1st and GB Jean Marie Eléonor Léopold de Stabenrath in the 2nd. Although new to their brigades in July 1809, both were accomplished officers with distinguished service records dating back to the early days of the Revolution. Above all, however, 4th Corps benefited from having Massena as its commander. At fifty-one, Massena was an extraordinarily gifted leader, one of the two or three marshals capable of commanding armies on independent operations. His abilities were the result of natural talent rather than study, but he had honed his skills across a lengthy career of victorious service. He had begun as a common soldier in the old royal army and had repeatedly displayed his competence during the wars of the Revolution, most notably during his exemplary campaign in Switzerland in 1799. His passions for women and riches have tarnished the sheen of his reputation, but Napoleon remarked that the marshal was 'eminently noble and brilliant under fire and in the disorder of battle; the sound of cannon clarified his thoughts, gave him spirit, penetrating insight, and cheerfulness'.[50]

Three heavy cavalry divisions from the Army of Germany would also be present at Znaim. While much of the old Grande Armée's infantry, parts of its light cavalry and all of its dragoons had been sent to Spain during 1808, all of the heavy cavalry regiments had remained in Germany, more or less in the same divisions with which they had served in the recent wars. The result was strong bonds of unit cohesion among these elite formations, complemented by experienced leadership. GD Etienne Marie Antoine Champion, Comte de Nansouty, for example, had led the large 1st Heavy Cavalry Division since its creation in 1805 and all six regiments had served continuously in the same brigades for the past four years. Coming from an aristocratic family background, Nansouty exhibited a haughty demeanour and still wore his hair in a powdered queue, but was known as a hard-eyed, competent professional. 'To a rapid *coup d'oeil* he joined a great firmness of character,' wrote a fellow officer, 'and that tone of command, that imposing exterior so precious to a commander.'[51] He was not, however, a general who would seize the initiative instinctively or seek innovative solutions to tactical predicaments and even his admirers found his tendency towards sarcasm and mockery both distasteful and detrimental. In addition to four regiments of cuirassiers, his division included France's two unique regiments of mounted carabiniers. GD Raymond Gaspard de Bonardi, Comte de St Sulpice commanded the 2nd Heavy Cavalry Division. These four cuirassier regiments had served together in the same brigades since the division's formation in the summer of 1805 and St Sulpice had been with them for the entire period, first as a brigade commander and, since 1807, as division commander. The regiments of the 3rd Heavy Cavalry Division had also been together since 1805, but they were under a new general, GD Jean Toussaint Arrighi de Casanova, the Duke of Padua. Arrighi was a veteran of more then twenty years' service, but had only come to the division on 25 May that year to replace the much-regretted GD Jean Louis Brigitte, Comte d'Espagne, who had been killed at Aspern-Essling. The redoubtable cavalry of the Imperial Guard would arrive at Znaim in the company of the cuirassiers: one regiment each of grenadiers-à-cheval, chasseurs-à-cheval, dragoons and Polish chevaulegers along with four batteries of Guard horse artillery with 24 guns.[52] As Nansouty had two mounted batteries and Arrighi one, the entire cavalcade would bring with it a formidable artillery component of 42 pieces.

The talented and ambitious GD Marmont commanded the other major French formation at Znaim: the 'Army of Dalmatia'. Trained as an artilleryman, Marmont had first met the then young General Bonaparte during the siege of Toulon in 1792 and, though only thirty-five in 1809, he had subsequently amassed extensive combat experience, much of it with Bonaparte first in Italy, then in Egypt, and then again in Italy. Despite his close personal connection to the new emperor, he was not among the first tranche of marshals appointed in 1804. Napoleon, however, designated him as commander of the Grande Armée's 2nd Corps in 1805, the only non-marshal to receive such a posting at that time. Charged with occupying and pacifying Dalmatia in 1806, Marmont fought minor engagements, coped with insurgents among the population, initiated numerous civic works projects, and showed himself to be an able administrator as well as a general. The small force he had available for these multifarious tasks became the 'Army of Dalmatia' in June 1806. Most of Marmont's regiments and most of his senior officers had thus been operating together in garrison and pacification duties under his command for up to three years by the time they were called to the war with Austria. The little army's brigade commanders were officers of long service and high quality, especially the talented GB Alexis Joseph Delzons. Two others, GB Louis Auguste Marchand Plauzonne and GB Gilbert Désiré Joseph Bachelu, had been promoted in June 1809 from regimental commands within the Army of Dalmatia (5th and 11th Ligne respectively) to replace brigade commanders wounded in May. All knew the army, its officers, its men and its regiments very well. Only one, the former gunner and experienced staff officer GB Antoine Joseph Bertrand, was new to the command, being recently appointed from his position as Marshal Jean-Baptiste Bessières's chief of staff. GD Bertrand Clauzel, leading 2nd Division, was also familiar with Marmont's army, having been in Dalmatia since January 1808. Held in high regard by Napoleon, he was one of the finest French generals of the period. The 1st Division, on the other hand, had a new commander, GD Michel Marie Claparède. He replaced GD Joseph Hélie Désiré Perruquet de Montrichard whose disappointing performance in the campaign from Dalmatia to Austria led to his being shunted off to command Lobau Island after Wagram. Returning to active duty after being wounded at Aspern-Essling, Claparède was courageous, energetic and tactically skilful but had a reputation for avarice and vanity among some of his compatriots.

The army was composed of solid veteran regiments whose long association had produced a high degree of unit cohesion. Its unusual role as an army of occupation in a ruggedly mountainous region, however, gave it several unique features. First, title notwithstanding, the Army of Dalmatia was small. Numbering only some 12,000 men at the start of the war, it was only the size of a small corps.[53] Second, its role in Dalmatia combined with the broader infantry reorganisation of 1808 meant that its regiments were split between Marmont's Army of Dalmatia and Viceroy Eugène's Army of Italy in 1809. As a result, none of the regiments that appeared at Znaim had all four of its battalions, and only the 11th Ligne had even three battalions. Third, the entire army did not appear at Znaim. Dalmatia could not be left without a garrison, so the 60th Ligne (two battalions) remained behind when Marmont marched north to the Danube and the 18th Léger (two battalions) was detached to escort convoys in Austria. The Army of Dalmatia's infantry at Znaim therefore consisted of only some 8,300 men distributed among thirteen battalions belonging to six different regiments. Finally, when compared with standard French practice, the little army was short of both artillery and cavalry, having only seventeen guns and fewer than 300 horsemen at its disposal. Despite these deficiencies, Marmont reposed tremendous confidence in his cohesive little force. 'I had good soldiers, devoted, brave, trained,' he wrote later, men who became in his opinion 'an elite corps'.[54] Napoleon (overstating their strength) called them '15,000 of the best troops of France'[55] and, by the time they marched up from Dalmatia to join the main army on the banks of the Danube at Vienna, they had fought several significant engagements and covered well over 800 kilometres on foot.

For the pursuit after Wagram and thus for the Battle of Znaim, Napoleon compensated for the Army of Dalmatia's weaknesses by bolstering Marmont with a Rheinbund element, in this case a division of Bavarian troops. The Kingdom of Bavaria supplied the largest German contingent under the Confederation Treaty: 25,000 in 7th Corps under Marshal François Lefebvre and 4,500 on garrison duty in the Tyrol. The Bavarian corps contained three divisions, each with its own brigade of cavalry, as well as an exceptionally powerful artillery complement of 78 guns. Like the Hessians, the Bavarians had acquired a good reputation in their previous service under French eagles and thus experienced little interference in their internal structure or drill practices. Each line infantry regiment consisted of two battalions according to an indigenous Bavarian pattern: four centre companies and a company of grenadiers all dressed in the unique cornflower blue of Bavaria and wearing the distinctive Raupenhelm that had served as the model for Baden. Also under the Raupenhelm but with dark green jackets were the light infantry battalions. Like the line battalions, these were composed of five companies; in combat they were often supplemented by Schützen (specially designated skirmishers) detached from the line units. The cavalry included two regiments of dragoons in white and four of chevaulegers in green, but titles and uniform colours notwithstanding, both types performed the same functions on the battlefield. Having fought and marched alongside the French in the wars of 1805, 1806 and 1807, the Bavarians were experienced, reliable, well-trained and generally well-led. They also understood war against their old foe Austria.[56]

The Bavarian element at Znaim consisted of the 2nd Division supplemented by two artillery batteries borrowed from the 1st Division. This gave the formation two chevaulegers regiments, eight line battalions, a light battalion, and an extraordinarily large artillery component of 36 guns in seven batteries that would compensate for Marmont's weakness in this arm. The division had marched hundreds of kilometres before the post-Wagram pursuit even began. Napoleon had posted the 2nd Division along with the 1st at Linz in late May to protect the army's line of communications along the Danube (the 3rd Division was guarding Bavaria's border with the rebellious Tyrol). As part of the general concentration for the second crossing attempt, he took the risk of thinning his defences along the river and 'invited' the 2nd Division to Lobau Island. He selected this particular division because he valued the energy and skill of its commander, General-Leutnant (GL) Carl Philipp Freiherr von Wrede, an ambitious, experienced and proven officer. Wrede did not disappoint. Leading his division on an epic march of some 200 kilometres, he brought it to the field of Wagram on the morning of 6 July in time to participate in some of the fighting in the battle's concluding stages.

Command and Control

The nature and quality of leadership at the top, of course, would be crucial to the Battle of Znaim and the outcome of the war. In the first instance, this was an issue of the personal characteristics of the two army commanders, Charles and Napoleon. The centrality of the political element in the war's conduct and closure, however, meant that the governmental structures in which these two men functioned were also important, both in imposing strictures and in offering opportunities.

The Habsburg monarchy was fortunate to have Archduke Charles available to lead its army into combat in 1809. Charles, born in September 1771, was not quite thirty-eight years old that summer, an experienced, competent commander and an aspiring military theoretician. He had been engaged in Austria's wars against Revolutionary France starting in 1792 and achieved particular renown for his victories over French forces in Germany during 1796 and 1799. In 1805, he commanded the Habsburg army in Italy against Massena (Vienna had mistakenly calculated that Italy would be the principal theatre of war), but he had never faced Napoleon personally. He was deeply committed to the dynasty's interests, at least as he defined them, and endeavoured to modernise the recalcitrant old empire's military institutions to strengthen the state against the turbulent tides of the era. Enlightened rather than revolutionary,[57] however, he had no interest in undertaking anything that might upset the prevailing political and social order in Austria; he thus maintained a profound scepticism concerning popular militias and notions of 'people's war'.

At the same time, Charles exhibited many of the limitations he decried in his generals. His writings and his campaigns showed him as 'a child of the 18th century, as a man of the old style, the classical positional and manoeuvre warfare, the cautious tactics' rather than the dynamism he had observed in the French in the early 1790s and hoped to emulate.[58] 'He never cut himself loose from the ideas and rules of the *ancien régime*,' commented the nineteenth-century German military historian, Hans Delbrück,[59] and in Clausewitz's judgment he 'lacked enterprise and the thirst for victory'.[60] He was personally courageous, but the killer instinct seemed to be absent, the focus on extracting every advantage from a situation, of exploiting every opportunity to the utmost; in its place was 'caution, the most pronounced caution'.[61] In the field these predilections meant that he would incline towards hoarding reserves to cover his retreat rather than employing them to strike a culminating blow, would be content with tactical, defensive successes, and hesitant to take the risks necessary to achieve more substantive victories.

Compounding his innate caution was a tendency to lapse into extended periods of gloomy pessimism, sometimes even apathy, with concomitant inattention to detail and dissipation of energy. Moreover, he suffered sporadic bouts of epilepsy or nervous exhaustion. There is no evidence that such ailments afflicted him at Znaim, but he was incommunicado during other parts of the war apparently owing to temporary incapacitation resulting from illness. Napoleon respected his talents and had offered him the Habsburg crown in an interview after Austerlitz in 1805 (a meeting that contributed to the Kaiser's fears of disloyalty), but he was clearly daunted by the prospect of facing the terrifying French emperor for the first time.

Charles, of course, was the empire's leading general, not its monarch. He had been endowed with extraordinary powers on his appointment as Generalissimus in February 1806, powers that were restated and expanded in February 1809. He was, however, subject to his brother the Kaiser's wishes. He was the monarch's senior, but by no means his only, military advisor and he had to operate within the confines of the Habsburg state's stultifying bureaucracy. Moreover, he had to respond to and negotiate with Stadion and other major figures at court and had to request rather than order collaboration with Hungary's military institutions owing to the constitutional position of that kingdom within the monarchy. Lingering tensions from the debates leading up to the decision for war tainted the atmosphere in Habsburg leadership circles and Charles was acutely aware of the sceptical if not hostile scrutiny under which he laboured. Intrigue and factionalism within his own staff created additional strains, exacerbated by outsiders attempting to insert their views on military decisions by influencing his immediate subordinates. Sordid scheming thus led to the Hauptarmee having three different chiefs of staff within three months. Mayer von Heldenfeld, who had drafted the original war plan (and was himself no innocent when it came to scheming), was abruptly banished to become commandant of a remote fortress in the Balkans in February and replaced by GM Johann von Prochaska, whom Archduke Johann called 'one of the most mediocre officers of the army'.[62] Prochaska, however, blamed for the defeat in Bavaria, was cashiered in April, his position assumed by newly promoted GM Maximilian Freiherr von Wimpffen who would remain in the job through late August.

The Austrian war effort was thus hobbled by the disaggregation of authority, bureaucratic infighting, pervasive indecision and personal animus that characterised the top levels of the monarchy. These problems and the army's conservative institutional culture aggravated the archduke's considerable personal limitations as a commander, inhibiting the empire's ability to craft cohesive military and political responses to the challenge Napoleon posed in 1809.

Austria was also disadvantaged because it had decided to attack Napoleon and his empire. As soldier–emperor Napoleon embodied unity of command and could issue instructions without cajoling, conniving and endless debate. Moreover, he could (and did) expect that his centralised, bureaucratic state would respond to his demands with reasonable timeliness and efficiency. Austria had expended enormous efforts to prepare itself for war and to sustain its army and basic state functions during the conflict, but its creaky apparatuses could not compete with Napoleon's governmental machinery. Furthermore, the French emperor, in his guise as 'protector' of the Confederation of the Rhine, could draw on the resources of much of Germany for everything from soldiers to shield his lines of communications to billets for his passing troops as well as food, fodder, leather, cloth and supplies of every sort. Austria would eventually receive some financial subsidies from Great Britain, but these funds were too little and too late to alter the course of the war or to give the Habsburg monarchy the means to continue it.

Napoleon was just short of forty years old in the spring of 1809, slightly more than one year older than Charles. Although he was approaching the age at which he claimed he would be too old for campaigning,[63] he showed no lack of vigour during the war (the tale that he slept for thirty-six hours after Aspern-Essling is false). Similarly, his health seems to have been fine with the exception of the period immediately after Wagram, which will intrude on our story later. Indeed, he attended to the immediate operations of the war against Austria, the distant war in Spain and all the other myriad affairs of the empire with all his extraordinary energy throughout this period. His imperial responsibilities, however, did not divert him from his customary minute focus on military detail. 'I always know my position; I am always aware of my strength reports,' he told a councillor just before the war, 'I do not have the memory to retain an Alexandrian verse, but I never forget a syllable of my strength reports.'[64] As just one example of this focus, he personally annotated the Army of Italy's 1 March strength return, calculating the anticipated strengths of sixteen different battalions once they had incorporated conscript detachments varying in size from 80 to 545 men. The total number of recruits involved in this little mathematical exercise was only 5,433 soldiers out of the 94,600 then in Italy.[65] In the meantime, he was running an empire.

Furthermore, the emperor communicated his own drive and will to his officers and men, repeatedly demonstrating his ability to inspire soldiers whether French, German or Italian. 'I double the force of my troops when I am in command,' he remarked in February 1809.[66] As repeatedly demonstrated during the war, this was no idle boast. In describing Napoleon riding along the lines at Wagram, for instance, an admiring staff officer recalled that 'The young army, all the more ardent and susceptible to enthusiasm, responded with cheers and asked for the order to attack: an imposing spectacle that would never be erased from the memory of those who were there.'[67] The confidence he evoked in his own troops derived both from his innate talents as a leader and from the catalogue of military triumphs he had accrued since 1796. He was keenly aware of the value of his aura of victory and was just as keenly determined to maintain it.[68] For Austria, this meant that Wagram must be no less a victory than Austerlitz, that 1809 must equal or exceed 1805 as a success. The confidence this history of victory instilled in his own men was mirrored by the anxiety evinced by his enemies, including Charles. Napoleon could adapt to and anticipate changes on the battlefield 'through the speed of his decisions and their execution', Charles wrote in a subsequent analysis: 'He indeed pushed everything to the limit in the demands he made of his subordinates; but he also knew how to fulfil them. Thus were opponents overpowered who did not aim at such results.'[69]

Skill, energy, charisma and an extraordinary record of battlefield success notwithstanding, some of the French emperor's flaws seem more pronounced in 1809 as compared to earlier wars. In the first place, he regarded his Austrian adversaries with disdain. He was not alone in this judgement; both the Russian tsar and the Prussian king were similarly dismissive of Austria's military capabilities, a key factor for both rulers in choosing not to oppose Napoleon in 1809. Napoleon was not entirely wrong in his assessment of the Habsburg army's torpidity of movement and unsuitability for offensive warfare, but this negative opinion, seemingly confirmed by the opening campaign, led to a serious misappreciation of the Austrians until the Battle of Aspern-Essling in May. Second, he displayed a tendency to underestimate enemy numbers while inflating those of his own forces: always rounding the enemy's strength down, so to speak, while rounding his own up. Third, he occasionally allowed his legendary attention to detail to lapse, most notably on the evening of the first day at Wagram. Additionally, the complete concentration of all authority in his own hands, while often an advantage – especially against a disarticulated state like Austria – could result in confusion in his absence, as would be the case in the opening week of the war before he arrived in Bavaria from Paris. He recognised the potential problems in his personal centrality as a leader, commenting just prior to the war that 'It is perhaps a mistake that I command in person, but it is my essence.'[70] These faults and what may perhaps be described as an incipient dulling of his skills, however, in no way detracted from his consummate mastery of all levels of war in 1809. The problems associated with the concentration of authority solely in his person, for example, which would become serious, indeed debilitating, in later wars were not in evidence when his coach rattled into Donauwörth on 17 April. The vast scope of the war, with its many interrelated campaigns stretching from Germany and Austria to Poland, Italy and Dalmatia, was well within his strategic grasp. Similarly, his operational performance in the April campaign was masterful and Wagram was a remarkable example of improvised grand tactics. Nor should the organisational, administrative and technical efforts involved in assembling the Army of Germany and expanding it on the fly be overlooked. Nascent signs of decline, therefore, however evident in hindsight, were neither as severe as often portrayed nor apparent to most of his enemies in 1809.

If not at the height of his powers, by talent and position Napoleon therefore functioned on a different plane from Charles. He had a phalanx of competent subordinates leading an army that would do its utmost to respond to his demanding expectations and he was backed by the formidable resources of a centralised bureaucratic state. Charles, a general rather than a ruler, lacked the personal abilities and the organisational advantages enjoyed by his imperial foe; and his white-coated army, for all its courage and recent reforms, remained trammelled in the norms of the previous century, durable on the defensive but ill-suited to rapid offensive operations.

Chapter 3

From Regensburg to Wagram
10 April–6 July 1809

THE WAR OF 1809, or 'War of the Fifth Coalition', raged in multiple theatres across the map of central Europe from the Vistula to the Danube, the Elbe, the Scheldt and the Po. The Danube valley from Bavaria to Vienna constituted the principal arena of combat, however, and operations there can be divided into several campaigns. The first, of 10–24 April, consisted of the Austrian invasion of Bavaria and its repulse. This was followed in late April–late May by Napoleon's drive to Vienna culminating in the Battle of Aspern-Essling. While action continued in the subsidiary theatres, June saw a lull along the Danube as both sides recovered from the bloodletting at Aspern and prepared for their next contest. The third campaign in the Danube valley (as broadly defined) occurred in the first two weeks of July, beginning with Napoleon's second crossing of the river and continuing through the Battle of Wagram, the subsequent pursuit and the Battle of Znaim. A few small encounters occurred after the armistice as ceasefire instructions were passed to distant detachments, but the military activities on both sides from July through October were aimed at preparing for a possible renewal of hostilities. For those final three months of the war, the focus shifted from military operations to diplomacy as the two empires trod their slow path to peace.

Regensburg: The First Campaign

Austria initiated hostilities on 10 April when the main body of the Hauptarmee crossed the Inn River to invade Bavaria. The flanking force of I and II Corps debouched from Bohemia on the same day to advance towards Amberg and Regensburg north of the Danube. Though the campaign opened with great optimism, the army seemed afflicted with a peculiar dearth of urgency and the invasion soon ran into trouble. On the military–political side, the Bavarians rebuffed poorly conceived Austrian attempts to get them to defect from their alliance with Napoleon, dashing thereby the inflated Habsburg hopes of weakening the Rheinbund. Operationally, timely communications between the divided wings of the Hauptarmee were already proving almost impossible and the Austrian cavalry was performing poorly in its reconnaissance role, leaving Charles and the corps commanders largely ignorant of French dispositions. The greater problems, however, stemmed from the execrable weather and the army's cumbersome logistical arrangements. Rain, sleet and snow ruined the roads, balky supply columns clogged every defile, and administrative procedures for providing the men with food and shelter broke down. As a result, Charles declared 13 April a rest day for the entire army. Only three days into the invasion, therefore, and having only advanced some 45–50 kilometres from the Inn, the Hauptarmee already had to halt to reorganise and recuperate. This was hardly consistent with the 'rapid decisions' and 'bold enterprises' Charles had urged in his late March orders to Bellegarde.

The rest day did little to improve the army's situation as it trudged ponderously forward on the 14th. The weather remained 'diabolical' in the archduke's words, the roads remained muddy sloughs and logistical support remained inadequate. Nonetheless, the Hauptarmee pushed across the Isar on 16 April after a stiff fight with the well-commanded 3rd Bavarian Division at Landshut. On the far left flank, a division under FML Franz Freiherr Jellacic entered Munich on the 16th to find that the Bavarian court had already evacuated to Ulm. Charles now aimed at Regensburg, hoping to link up there with Bellegarde's flanking force coming from the north. The latter, however, 'true to his previous passivity',[1] was proceeding with extreme caution, advancing hesitantly and halting on receiving false reports of possible French moves against his command. Having expended the 17th in small skirmishes and minor moves, the army finally lurched forward on 18 April. The new advance was determined by solid intelligence that Marshal Davout's corps was

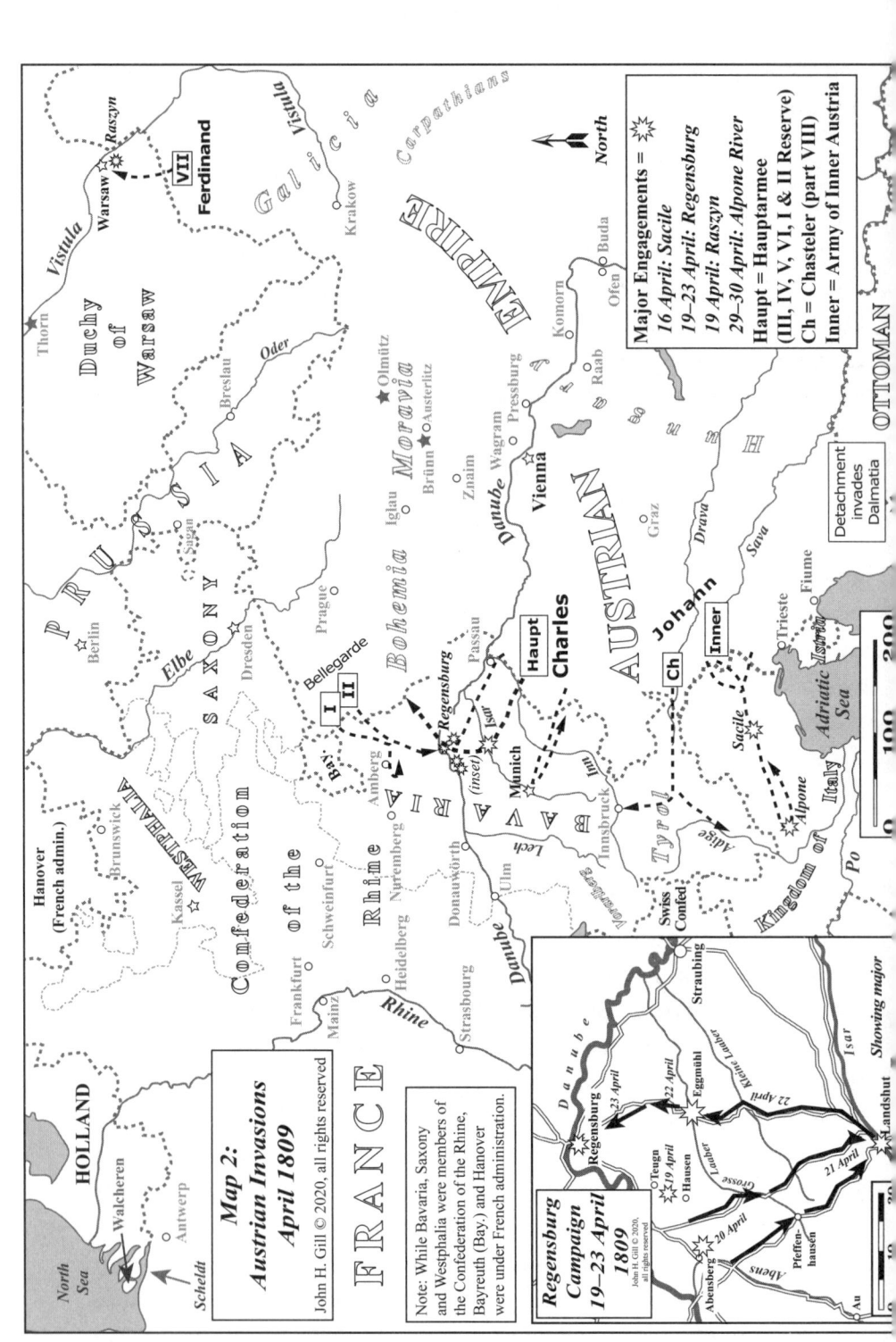

isolated at Regensburg. With Bellegarde to the north of the Danube and the bulk of the Hauptarmee to the south, Charles hoped to trap and destroy this lone French corps before the rest of the enemy army could come to its assistance. Detailing V and VI Corps to protect his left flank along the Abens River, the archduke moved the remainder of his force to the Grosse Laaber with the intention of intercepting and defeating Davout on the following day. Kolowrat, poised just north of Regensburg with his II Corps, was to contribute to the planned battle by doing 'everything possible to eradicate this enemy corps [Davout] completely' on the 19th.[2]

Davout was indeed in danger. Although Napoleon's pre-war instructions to Berthier had included contingency plans in case the Austrians attacked before 15 April, the muddled sequencing of subsequent orders and Berthier's incapacity as de facto army commander left this most powerful French corps and its attendant cavalry (some 52,300 foot and horse) unsupported at Regensburg. The nearest French forces were the 68,700 men of the 2nd, 4th and 8th Corps along the Lech River at least four or five days' march to the southwest. Only the overstretched Bavarian 7th Corps (25,100) connected these two wings and its constituent divisions were poorly placed as well. Moreover, the dreadful weather and the evident confusion in conflicting orders from above had undermined the army's spirits. 'Our anxiety was great, as the enemy's advantage over us increased each day, our position became more and more critical,' noted a brigade commander, 'The simple soldiers themselves were astonished at all of the counter-marches and began to grow uneasy.'[3] Or, as a Bavarian with 7th Corps trenchantly observed, 'After eight days everything closely resembled a retreat.'[4] The Army of Germany was thus disheartened, disarrayed and vulnerable when Napoleon stepped down from his carriage in Donauwörth in the early hours of 17 April.

Thanks to prompt reporting by his military and diplomatic subordinates, Napoleon in Paris learned of the Austrian invasion on the evening of 12 April. Within twelve hours he was seated in his travelling office coach with Josephine, headed east towards war. After two days in the carriage, he parted from the weary Josephine in Strasbourg. In hindsight, this was a poignant moment, as he would return from the Austrian war determined to divorce her and secure his dynasty through marriage with a Habsburg archduchess. As his coach rumbled towards Bavaria on the afternoon of the 15th, however, he was focused on containing the Austrian invasion and turning the tide of war in his favour.

The army's morale soared with Napoleon's arrival, announced via a stirring proclamation to the army. 'Finally!' remembered the brigade commander quoted above, 'an order of the day filled all with confidence; it announced the presence of the emperor.'[5] 'This news produced its customary effect; everyone was animated by a new confidence and certain of victory,' wrote Colonel Pierre Berthezène of the 10th Léger.[6] A soldier of the Bavarian 6th Light Battalion recorded a similar reaction: 'A proclamation issued from Donauwörth on 17 April announced his [Napoleon's] arrival and the coming defeat of the enemy.'[7] 'From then on,' recalled another Bavarian, 'no more retrograde movements took place; everything went forward relentlessly.'[8]

Just as important as the imperial proclamation was the order, purpose and decision that animated the army, reinforcing Napoleon's operational moves and filling his subordinates with his energy and urgency. April 18 was a day of manoeuvre, but the next five days witnessed a succession of five French victories. Often amalgamated as 'the Battle of Abensberg–Eggmühl', this was actually a series of related but separate actions that played out over the rolling and wooded Bavarian landscape south of Regensburg under the grey April skies. On the 19th, Davout's 3rd Corps bested the Austrian III Corps in a savage encounter at Hausen-Teugn that wrecked Charles's plan of defeating Davout and left the Austrians stumbling back in confusion. Thereafter the initiative was firmly in Napoleon's hands. French and German attacks stove in the Austrian left wing in the Battle of Abensberg on the 20th to drive a wedge between it and the remainder of the Hauptarmee. Astonishingly, though he was within 20–25 kilometres of his left wing, Charles did not know of its defeat, did not know therefore that over one-third of his army was retiring on Landshut in growing disorder. This gross lapse and the fact that no one seems to have considered sending patrols to investigate suggests an astonishing degree of disorder and lassitude in the Hauptarmee's headquarters. Fortunately for the Austrians, Regensburg and its ancient stone bridge over the Danube fell into their hands that day. Napoleon, on the other hand, overestimated the success on the 20th, mistakenly thinking he had achieved 'another Jena' at Abensberg.[9] The emperor's misapprehension continued through the 21st as he led most of his army in a pell-mell pursuit of the Austrian left wing to Landshut. Not until 2:00 a.m. on 22 April did Napoleon realise that the principal enemy force was still intact south of Regensburg. Reacting swiftly, he left a small detachment to follow the Austrian left and headed north with the bulk of his army to strike the unsuspecting Charles on the flank at the Battle of Eggmühl on 22 April. The stunned archduke had no option but retreat. Fortunately for Charles, the capture of Regensburg had provided him with a secure bridge. He and his wounded army were thus able to retreat over the Danube on 23 April despite a successful French assault on the city.

The April campaign around Regensburg thus concluded with a clear French victory, but the fact that the Austrians had escaped meant that 'Napoleon's hopes were far from being entirely realised.'[10] He would still have to destroy the Hauptarmee to bring the war to a close. Nonetheless, the Austrians had been severely handled, losing 44,700 men, and 73 guns as well as their entire pontoon train and hundreds of other vehicles. In contrast, French losses totalled approximately 16,300 soldiers. Moreover, Napoleon had entirely overturned the strategic situation: a mere two weeks after the opening of hostilities and one week after his arrival in Bavaria, the Austrian army was in full retreat and his Army of Germany was poised to invade the Habsburg heartland.[11] This was a remarkable achievement and to the end of his days, Napoleon regarded the Regensburg campaign as his greatest manoeuvre.[12]

The psychological repercussions were just as important as the material and strategic results. For Napoleon, the April battles confirmed both his dismissive impressions of Austrian martial prowess and his faith in his own soldiery. In particular, the opening battles validated the superiority of the French and their better German allies when fighting in broken and wooded terrain where open-order tactics and independent leadership were at a premium. Napoleon was not wrong in these judgements, but his negative appraisal of his foes led him to overestimate the damage done to the Hauptarmee and overlook its potential resilience.

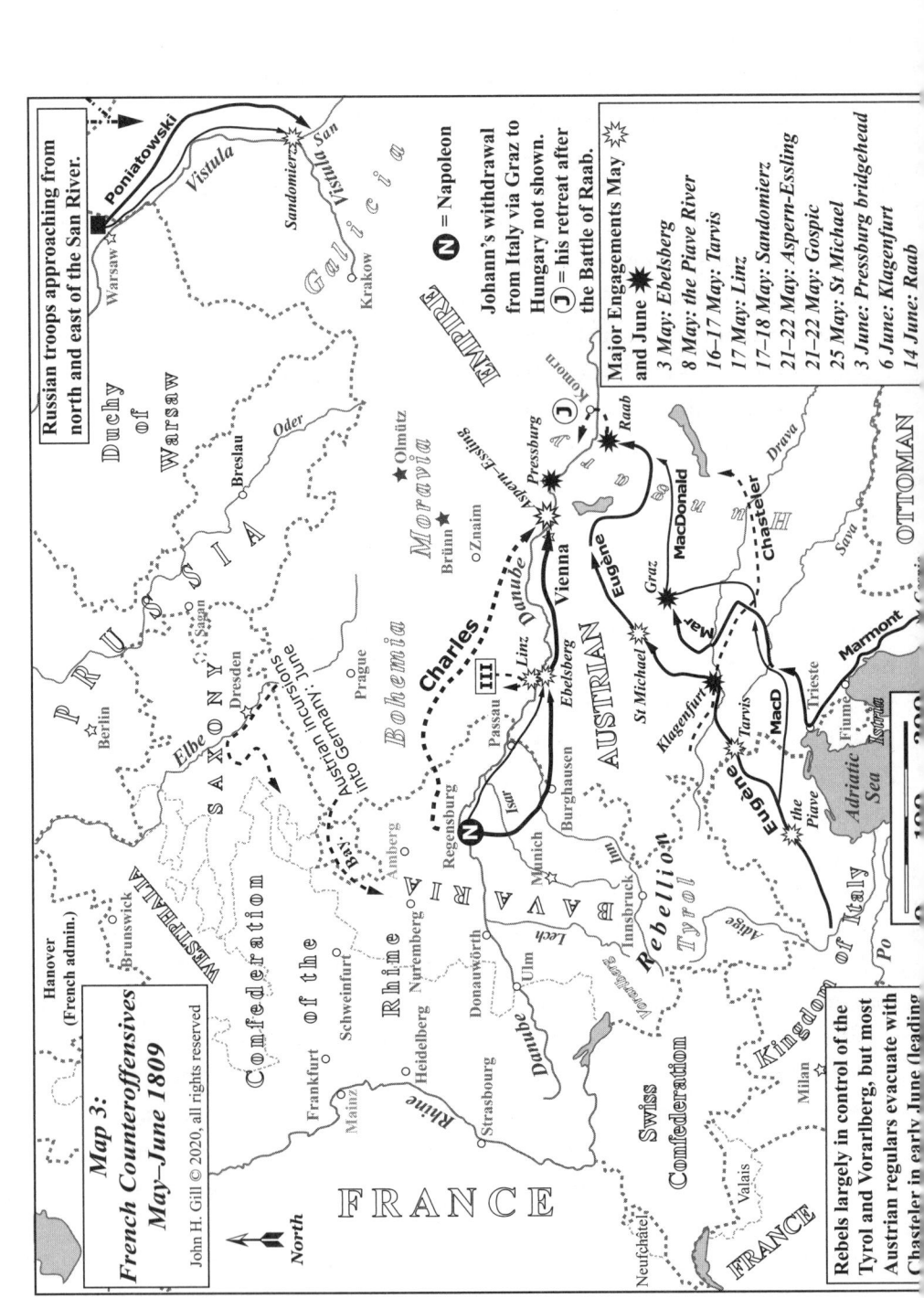

In the war's aftermath, GM Carl von Stutterheim, charged with writing a Habsburg history of the conflict, offered trenchant insights from the other side's point of view. The opening campaign, he wrote in 1811, 'brought the war into the heart of the Austrian monarchy, dashed or changed the moral and political dispositions that could have turned it in its favour, deranged the general plan of that war and decided it, despite the opportunities that later offered themselves to the Austrians'.[13] The defeat in Bavaria was all the more significant as Vienna had pegged its hopes on attaining important early victories and carrying the war into Germany. This thinking was the foundation of Stadion's approach and was reflected in the army's plans as Charles had written in late March: 'Here there can be absolutely no middle way between victory and destruction, and I would regard it as a great misfortune if, right at the beginning, we should be restricted to the defensive within our borders.'[14] This great misfortune had now come to pass and the archduke immediately urged his brother the Kaiser to entertain peace overtures to Napoleon. Only two weeks after having crossed his Rubicon, therefore, Charles had already concluded that the war was lost and that his worst fears for the monarchy's future were on the verge of being realised.

The Drive to Vienna

Meanwhile, Napoleon was marching into Austria. He had considered taking his army over the Danube in the hope of catching the retreating Hauptarmee but elected to drive down the valley to Vienna as he had in 1805. This decision was dictated by his larger strategic concerns. Direct pursuit of the injured Hauptarmee was tempting, but he was confident that a rapid strike at the Habsburg capital would have dramatic strategic effects, forestalling possible Prussian entry into the war, defusing urges towards unrest in Germany, and perhaps dissuading Britain from undertaking amphibious descents along the Channel or North Sea coasts.[15] The Tyrol was already in open rebellion, his Rheinbund allies were anxious, and he knew nothing of developments in either Italy or Poland. These strategic considerations argued for a bold thrust that would capitalise on the recent victories in Bavaria, keep the initiative in his hands, transmit that initiative to the other theatres of war and produce a significant psychological impact on the international stage. It would also serve to outflank and nullify any advances Austria may have made in Italy. Moreover, he hoped Charles would come south of the Danube to defend the Habsburg capital and thereby create an opportunity to crush the Hauptarmee in a grand battle somewhere between Passau and Vienna.[16] Pursuing the Austrians north of the Danube, on the other hand, could result in a protracted and uncertain campaign in Bohemia, prolonging a war that Napoleon wanted to finish as quickly as possible.[17] He thus made Vienna his initial objective, 'a point on his trajectory towards the archduke's army' in the words of a subsequent French commentator.[18] By the 26th, Massena had forced crossings over the Inn. The rest of the army would soon follow. 'All has gone well,' wrote a brigade commander to his wife, 'and we are now in the land of our enemies.'[19]

As for the Austrians, with the opening campaign having ended in failure, the Hauptarmee limped over the mountains into Bohemia and Charles received permission from the Kaiser to make contact with Napoleon. The army's obvious deficiencies in rapid, mobile combat and the repeated blows it had suffered had reawakened all of Charles's misgivings about embarking on an offensive war against the French in the first place. His fears were evident in a letter to the Kaiser from the battlefield on the morning of 23 April, just before the retreat over the Danube. 'Nothing more can be expected from this army, already struggling with a shortage of food, against *this* enemy,' he wrote before stressing that 'Landwehr and Insurrection will certainly not save the state' if the army is 'smashed to bits'. With this preface he hinted at proposing peace while the borders of the hereditary lands were still untouched because 'Once the enemy is in our territory, where he is certainly coming, Your Majesty's lands will be ruined like the Prussians and occupied by the enemy for years.'[20] He reiterated his peace suggestion the following day with greater specificity. The army was in dire condition, he reported and would be 'totally unusable' if it had to endure another major battle. Under such circumstances, he asked, 'Would it not be more advantageous to make an attempt towards negotiations before the enemy crosses our borders and Russia declares against us?'[21] He expressed his worries in a private letter as well, writing to his adoptive father that he might be forced into another battle, but that, 'The outcome of a battle is so uncertain that I wish the pen [diplomacy] would begin to work.'[22] The themes of these missives would remain prominent in the archduke's thinking through Wagram and Znaim: preservation of the army as the guarantor of the state, negotiating before the enemy gained overwhelming advantage and forestalling the Russian threat on the monarchy's vulnerable eastern frontiers. A corporal from the *Argenteau* Infantry Regiment No. 35 summarised the view from the ranks: 'Herewith closed the eighteen-day campaign in Bavaria that had begun with such great hopes and ended with the bleakest prospects.'[23]

The archduke's opponents at court, of course, were incensed by his suggestion of opening negotiations with Napoleon. They held an entirely different appraisal of the monarchy's situation and the causes of the debacle in Bavaria. The monarchy could quickly assemble 120,000 regulars and Landwehr to oppose the French march towards Vienna, they declared; it could stir uprisings in Germany, muster Bohemia's resources and rouse the populace with proclamations and support from the clergy and local notables. Personal attacks on Charles mounted. Stadion, for instance, complained of the archduke's 'baseness and passivity', writing in late April that he was 'full of hope' when he considered Austria's assets, 'but when I examine our instruments I must despair'.[24] 'I fear that his naiveté', he told a colleague, 'will at this opportunity once again ruin us.'[25] Accusing Charles of incompetence and defeatism, Stadion and others attempted to have him removed from command along with his protégé Grünne.[26] The archduke's standing with his brother, already shaky, suffered increased erosion.

As his enemies were mustering their assaults against his position as Generalissimus, Charles received an imperial answer to the dejected note he had sent on 23 April from the field outside Regensburg. Franz's reply, in part, read: 'Your Grace may take upon yourself to attempt a negotiation that takes advantage of the successes my brother Johann has gained in Italy and of the movements of the powers who have decided to tie themselves to those successes.'[27] As an unmistakable signal to Charles, however, the court selected Friedrich Lothar Stadion, to convey this message and additional verbal points.

The elder Stadion reached army headquarters on 28 April and informed Charles that Franz and the imperial court were by no means persuaded of the need for an appeal to Napoleon. Franz had only acceded to the archduke's request to avoid the appearance of rejecting a chance at peace. In the opinion of the court and the Kaiser, Stadion emphasised, the monarchy still had large numbers of regular troops available and would hasten the formation of the Landwehr and Hungarian Insurrection. Stadion's instruction placed special importance on what were seen as dramatic victories in Italy: 'Through Italy we can align ourselves with the policies of the English, Sicilian and Sardinian courts as well as with the success of the Spanish. Italy is Napoleon's most vulnerable point and already offers us a bargaining chip vis-à-vis the French emperor.'[28]

Such reasoning was virtually delusional. Sicily, Sardinia and Spain were practically irrelevant as far as the outcome of the war was concerned and Britain's ability to affect a rapid and decisive influence was doubtful at best. The war party, however, inspired by these hollow hopes, believed that entry into negotiations with Napoleon would throw away these supposed 'advantages' and constitute a dangerous admission of weakness. Charles, however, grasped at the 'hint' that he would not 'be in error' if he sent Napoleon a message that would not compromise the monarchy but might 'open the door to a negotiation'.[29] The result was an abject letter dispatched under the pretext of negotiating a prisoner exchange:

> Your Majesty has announced to me His arrival with cannon shots without leaving me time to offer my compliments. I had hardly been informed of your presence when I could guess it by the losses that you inflicted on me. You have taken many of my men, Sire, and my troops have likewise made many prisoners in the areas where you were not in command. I propose to Your Majesty to exchange them man for man and grade for grade and, if this proposition is agreeable to you, let me know your intentions and the place where this exchange may occur.
>
> I am flattered, Sire, to have crossed swords with the greatest captain of the century. I would be happy if Destiny has chosen me to assure my country the benefits of an unalterable peace. Whatever the hazards of war or the reconciliations of peace, I beg Your Majesty to believe that my ambition always leads me towards you and that I will

always believe myself equally honoured to treat with Your Majesty
with either the sword or the olive branch in my hand.'[30]

Napoleon received this odd note on 1 May in Burghausen on the
Bavarian border with Austria. It only served to confirm his contempt
for his Habsburg foes: 'These people are as vile in adversity as they are
haughty and arrogant at the least glimmer of prosperity,' he told Davout.[31]
'I will respond when I have time,' he continued, but the French reply
would not come until late June when he had Berthier suggest discussion
of a prisoner exchange just prior to Wagram.[32]

In the view of Philipp Stadion's biographer, Charles's letter to
Napoleon was the straw that conclusively broke relations between the
archduke and the Stadion brothers.[33] Whether or not this particular
incident caused the final rupture, both brothers condemned Charles for
the defeat in Bavaria and what they perceived as his lack of zeal for the war
they had promoted. Friedrich Stadion's dismay and disgust were clear
in the 29 April letter he sent describing his meeting with Charles. 'The
inactivity and a certain degree of torpor has increased since the retreat,'
he wrote, 'Everyone is depressed, reproaches himself, fears the worst,
sees only the inadequacy of all means, doubts and despairs of salvation
and has not the courage, rather the indifference of desperation.'[34] Ten
days later, his brother Philipp launched a direct attack on Charles in
a memorandum for the Kaiser, arguing fervently that victory could
be drawn from 'the present oppressive crisis if even a single spark of
strength, will and ability could be found in the top military leadership
... The moment demands a firmness and a determination of will before
which every consideration of kinship, of brotherly affection, every
relationship that does not have a direct reference to the state must give
way.' He urged the Kaiser to listen to the army's generals 'without any
regard for the opinion of the Generalissimus' and 'if the archduke should
refuse to cooperate *fully, frankly, and freely*, then I conjure Your Majesty to
remember that now the state alone must count as *all* for you'.[35]

The same day Kaiserin Maria Ludovika wrote a long letter to Archduke
Johann. 'While two victorious armies advance, one to the Adige the
other as far as Danzig [this was far from accurate],' she lamented, 'the
strongest retreats, exposes the capital and the Fatherland, without giving

any reasonable cause other than this one: we have hands and feet, but neither head nor energy.'[36] Despite the empress' frustration and the anger of the Stadions, Charles was retained in his post and the only personnel casualty from this internecine skirmish was the hapless Prochaska, dismissed as the army's chief of staff and replaced by Wimpffen, now promoted to general-major. However, the rancorous tension between the military and political arms of the Habsburg state had a deleterious effect on the empire's ability to craft coherent strategy during the coming two months of war. This acid atmosphere, stemming from the disaster in Bavaria and the subsequent recriminations, would have an especially significant impact during the climactic week between Wagram and Znaim.

As the pool of sour dissension at court deepened, Charles had to decide on his next operational steps. His situation was hardly enviable. The bulk of the Hauptarmee (I, II, III, IV and I Reserve Corps), battered, disorganised and discouraged, was making its way over miserable roads into Bohemia, fortunately undisturbed by any serious French pursuit. Unfortunately for Austria, approximately one-third of the army (V, VI and II Reserve Corps) was south of the Danube after having been split off on 20 April as a result of the Battle of Abensberg. Placed under the orders of the VI Corps commander, FML Johann Freiherr von Hiller, it was the only obstacle standing between Napoleon and Vienna. Charles therefore regarded union with Hiller as his first priority. Having just experienced his army's awkwardness as an offensive instrument, however, he hoped to bring Hiller north of the Danube and await a French attack in some suitable defensive position. Hiller's obstinacy and the rapid progress of the French advance into Austria scotched this concept. Instead of joining with Charles, Hiller occupied a position at Ebelsberg near Linz only to be evicted by Massena in a vicious battle on 3 May. When he finally retired over the Danube at Krems on the 8th, his actions south of the river had cost the Austrian army some 12,000 men and had contributed nothing to slowing the French advance. Mid-May thus found the Hauptarmee united on the north bank of the Danube northwest of the town of Deutsch-Wagram where Charles would later place his headquarters. The Kaiser and court settled in at the pleasant *Schloss* in Wolkersdorf, some 12 km away.

Napoleon entered Vienna on 13 May, one month to the day after departing Paris, and established himself in the Habsburg summer palace at Schönbrunn for the second time in four years. A young musician in the Baden 3rd Infantry represented the views of many in the army at this stage of the war as he considered the occupation of the Austrian capital in his matter-of-fact if naive manner: 'As steadfast as the Austrians set out to be, everything was useless, nothing they began would bear fruit. The French went to it, as always, without believing that they could lose and won one battle after another so that they soon came to Vienna.'[37] The seizure of the city intact was not an insubstantial accomplishment, but Napoleon did not expect the city's fall to bring Austrian surrender. He knew he would have to eliminate the archduke's army to end the war. As Charles had not obliged by offering battle before Vienna, Napoleon would now have to carry his army over the Danube and force a decisive engagement. This posed a daunting challenge as the Austrians had burned the great span at Floridsdorf that the French had used to great success in 1805 (this bridge is sometimes known as 'am Spitz' for a small community on the north bank that was later incorporated into Floridsdorf). To Napoleon's great consternation, a full week passed before French engineers could complete a series of bridges connecting the southern (right) and northern (left) banks of the river downstream from Vienna. These ad hoc bridges passed over the main channel to a large island called Lobau and thence over a branch of the Danube known as the Stadtler Arm to the Marchfeld, the vast plain stretching along the Danube's northern shore opposite the capital. Unfortunately for the French, the bridges, hastily constructed from local materials, were fragile and subject to breakage by Austrian action and the river's rising waters.

When French troops finally crossed from Lobau onto the Marchfeld on 20 May, they were surprised to find the Hauptarmee present in full force. Napoleon had received only limited intelligence on Austrian movements since late April and thus did not have clear information on Charles's location. Determined to bring the enemy to battle, however, the emperor proceeded with crossing operations despite the unsteady nature of the bridges. The result was the bloody Battle of Aspern-Essling on 21–22 May. On both days, Napoleon was critically hampered by the unreliable chain of bridges. This tenuous link, pounded by rising spring water levels and by flaming rafts pushed into the river upstream by the Austrians, broke repeatedly, leaving the French forces on the northern shore bereft of reinforcements and resupply. When the battle opened on 21 May, for example, the French had only been able to bring across some 32,000 infantry and cavalry before the main bridge snapped for the first time. Faced with 98,000 Austrians, Napoleon was forced onto the defensive, anchoring his flanks in the villages of Aspern and Essling while launching costly cavalry charges to shield his centre. These desperate tactics sufficed to protect his weak bridgehead, but the emperor wanted a decisive victory. He therefore held his ground and, with the bridge repaired, was able to strengthen his force on the Marchfeld to approximately 80,000 men during the night. He launched Marshal Jean Lannes with 2nd Corps in a powerful assault on the Austrian centre shortly after sunrise on 22 May, but was forced to call off the attack when the principal bridge suffered a devastating rupture later in the morning. This irreparable breach left the French constrained to conducting a tenacious defence of the two villages for the remainder of the day, but Charles could not orchestrate a comprehensive offensive and Napoleon was able to withdraw to Lobau more or less undisturbed with a material loss of only three guns. Human casualties, on the other hand, were enormous for both sides: at least 20,000 French (including the promising GD Louis St Hilaire, d'Espagne and the invaluable Lannes) and 23,000 Austrians were counted as dead, wounded or missing over the two days of the battle. The French were battered and temporarily trapped on Lobau Island, but the Austrians, equally exhausted, decided that pursuit was impossible and contented themselves with enjoying their defensive success. Nonetheless, Napoleon's first attempt to cross the Danube had ended in bloody repulse.[38]

The Secondary Theatres: April–July

The awful bloodletting at Aspern-Essling was followed by a six-week lull along the Danube as both sides prepared for the next encounter. Before considering how the battle influenced each belligerent's approach to the remainder of the war, however, it is important to cast an eye on the subsidiary theatres as developments in Italy, Dalmatia, Germany and especially Poland would inform the thinking in both headquarters as the conflict progressed.

From Vienna's perspective, the most important secondary theatre was Italy and the initial operations resulted in considerable progress on this front. Archduke Johann, leading the 'Army of Inner Austria' (VIII and IX Corps) entered Italy on 10 and 11 April while while FML Jean Marquis de Chasteler took a detachment of 13,560 into the Tyrol to support the pre-planned rebellion against Bavaria in that former Habsburg possession. Johann won an early success by dealing Eugène's French Army of Italy a sharp defeat at Sacile on the 16th and forcing the distraught Eugène to retreat almost 150 km to the west. This Austrian advance, shining all the more brightly when contrasted with the dismal outcome in Bavaria, produced the 'advantages' that the Kaiser and Stadion were keen to preserve when they permitted Charles to send his meek letter to Napoleon. By the end of April, however, the Austrian pursuers were exhausted, Eugène had recovered his composure and Napoleon had thrown Charles out of Bavaria. Eugène was thus able to take the offensive and he quickly harried Johann out of Italy and deep into Habsburg territory, inflicting several punishing defeats on the increasingly disorganised Austrians in the process. By 26 May, he had established contact with the Army of Germany's outposts southwest of Vienna. Austrian hopes for the campaign in Italy thus evaporated.

Johann, though battered, remained at large in southern Hungary, concocting unrealistic schemes to cut Napoleon's lines of communication and chafing under orders from his elder brother Charles. In the end, he left most of IX Corps east of Graz and marched the rest of his 'army' (actually only a corps by this point) towards the Danube to unite with the slowly assembling Hungarian Insurrection under yet another Habsburg archduke, Joseph, the Palatine (viceroy) of Hungary. Despite many deficiencies in training, equipment and organisation, this combined army under the two archdukes represented a threat to the French strategic right flank. To neutralise it, Napoleon reinforced Eugène and sent his step-son into Hungary with instructions to shatter the Austro-Hungarian force while remaining close enough to Vienna to be easily recalled. Eugène accomplished these tasks in a brief campaign that ended with a victory over Johann and Joseph at Raab (Györ) on

14 June, the anniversary of Marengo and Friedland. Although the Habsburg force was not destroyed, it was badly damaged and withdrew north of the Danube in disorder.

The other element of what may be termed the Habsburg 'southern strategy' was an offensive into Dalmatia. This too came to naught as the French Army of Dalmatia under Marmont repelled the Austrian invasion force and marched for Vienna in accordance with Napoleon's instructions. Marmont clashed with remnants of the Austrian IX Corps and various newly raised militias along the way and angered Napoleon by moving at what the emperor considered a leisurely pace. Nonetheless, his small but veteran 'army' (actually a small corps) would arrive in time for Wagram.

While these external Habsburg forays ended in defeat or stalemate, the rebellion in the Tyrol was a signal success. Granted to Bavaria by the Treaty of Pressburg in 1805, most of the region's inhabitants detested their new overlords and hoped for a return of Habsburg rule. A small band of prospective rebels had met with Habsburg officers and officials to plot the insurrection before the war. Returning to the mountains, they led a widespread uprising with minimal assistance from Chasteler's mixed detachment of regulars and Landwehr. Bavarian garrisons were evicted or captured, a small French replacement column was destroyed, and raids out of the Tyrol into Bavaria soon posed some threat to Napoleon's lines of communication. With the French focused on the Hauptarmee, the rebels were able to maintain themselves even when Chasteler withdrew most of the Austrian troops in June as part of the general retreat from Italy.

The Tyrol roiled in rebellion, but Habsburg hopes in Rheinbund Germany proved exaggerated. A few instances of unrest and military mutiny that flared in the newly created Kingdom of Westphalia were quickly suppressed and had no wider echo. Likewise, a raid by a renegade Prussian major named Ferdinand von Schill in May spread disruption and panic in Westphalia, but he and his band were trapped and eliminated at Stralsund by Napoleon's Dutch and Danish allies on 31 May.[39] Neither his famous ride nor the other minor disturbances in Germany had any significant impact on the outcome of the war. For Stadion, however, passionately committed to the image of all northern Germany about to explode in anti-French insurrection, these sparks were signs of the inferno to come if only Charles would release significant regular troops to underwrite the presumed rebellions. Though his understanding of military realities was sketchy at best, he believed Austria should 'light fires everywhere at once and save ourselves in the general blaze'.[40] This vague notion of distracting Napoleon with 'fires everywhere' resulted in several small Austrian incursions into Bayreuth and Saxony. These expeditions, numbering 4,400 and 8,500 men respectively under GM Paul von Radivojevich and GM Karl Freiherr Am Ende, had crossed the border from Bohemia into Germany in early June and duly entered Bayreuth (a territory under French administration) and Dresden, the Saxon capital. Small and ineffectually commanded, however, they neither excited rebellion nor distracted Napoleon. He contained these incursions with second-line French and German troops and retained his focus on the Hauptarmee, adjuring one of his rear-area commanders not to dispose 'of a single battalion without my orders if it is not for the defence of Mainz or of my frontiers'.[41]

All of these diffuse subsidiary arenas were considered important in the Habsburg court, but in setting the context for Znaim the most significant secondary front was Poland. This involved not only Polish forces but also the looming menace of Russian intervention. At the head of VII Corps, Archduke Ferdinand crossed the border into the Duchy of Warsaw on 15 April with grandiose expectations of knocking Napoleon's Polish allies out of the war before marching west to the Elbe in collaboration with an allied Prussian army. Although he occupied Warsaw on the 23rd, he soon found himself outmanoeuvred by Poniatowski's inexperienced but enthusiastic Polish army. By early July, as Napoleon was preparing to cross the Danube for the second time, the Poles had evicted the Austrians from almost every corner of the duchy and were advancing towards Krakow and into Austrian Poland (Galicia). These Polish advances were well aligned with Napoleon's interests: tying down enemy troops and menacing the Austrian strategic rear. For the Habsburg court, on the other hand, the Polish theatre gradually transformed from an imagined opportunity to a growing threat. Not only had Napoleon's Polish allies penetrated deep into Galicia and raised a national revolt, but a Russian army had crossed the border and was advancing on Krakow as well.

The Russian move was a consequence of the agreement signed at Erfurt in October 1808. That document bound Tsar Alexander to assist Napoleon militarily if Austria initiated a war with France. The Austrian offensives thus presented Alexander with an exceedingly uncomfortable predicament. On the one hand, he had no interest in breaking his alliance with Napoleon by failing to fulfil the stipulations of the Erfurt convention. At the same time, he did not want to see the Habsburg Empire crushed. He thus attempted to satisfy his own interests while antagonising neither of the two belligerents. Although he dispatched an army over the border, therefore, he instructed his commanders to occupy as much of Galicia as possible while avoiding all hostilities with the Austrians. This policy and the blatant anti-French/anti-Polish sentiments prevalent in the Russian officer corps led to numerous frictions with their putative Polish allies (the Russians and Austrians alike routinely referred to the Poles as 'insurgents'). The torpid Russian advance and the scrupulous avoidance of combat also infuriated Napoleon who had placed excessive faith in the deterrent value of the Russian threat. Nonetheless, the presence of the Russians in Galicia and the uncertainty about their intentions created unease in Austrian leadership circles, unease that grew acute as the Russian corps inexorably advanced. Charles, as we have seen, had been suspicious of the Russians before the war and the archduke had cited the Russian threat as a reason for making peace in his letters to the Kaiser after the defeat in Bavaria.

By late June, the slow but steady progress of the tsar's invading army aroused fears that the supposedly friendly Russians would never leave the Habsburg lands they had occupied and might even take an active part in the war on Napoleon's side. As Kaiser Franz told Ferdinand on 23 June, 'The words of the Russian generals may not be quite open and their friendly declarations may not be entirely genuine.' He worried that they 'could avoid opposition through courteous declarations and place themselves in possession of the greater part of the province without any effort'.[42] In a 20 June memorandum, Wimpffen offered the even more alarming prospect of close strategic collaboration between Russia and France when he described his concern that Austria was being squeezed between 'the two colossi pressing towards their mid-point'. Vastly overestimating the degree of Franco-Russian co-operation, his memorandum even expressed the fear that Napoleon might be prodding the Russians towards the Austrian rear and holding back on crossing the Danube a second time to allow the Russians to penetrate more deeply into Habsburg territory.[43] The safety of Olmütz was a source of particular concern. An important fortress, road hub and supply source, Olmütz lay more than 230 kilometres from Krakow but Napoleon had identified it as a possible pressure point in pre-war correspondence with Russia[44] and it would feature prominently in Austrian calculations during the retreat to Znaim.

Strategic Deliberations

Although Habsburg planners, especially the war party, had attached great expectations to the secondary theatres, by mid-June, all of Austria's subsidiary thrusts had been blunted. In the cases of Italy and Dalmatia, the failed offensives had been accompanied by significant losses for the Habsburg troops involved and, even worse, these defeats had permitted powerful French forces to join Napoleon at Vienna. Remnants of Chasteler's detachment from the Tyrol and IX Corps under FML Ignaz Gyulai, the *Ban* (viceroy) of Croatia, loitered in southern Hungary and Croatia, but these commands were largely composed of militia, Landwehr and new recruits, all short of training and basic equipment. This grim panorama did not daunt Stadion or other members of the war party who continued to propose schemes for operations by Chasteler and Gyulai that were hardly consistent with their actual capabilities. For Charles, on the other hand, the situations in Hungary and Poland only provided more rationale for concluding peace as rapidly as possible while the Hauptarmee was still intact.

Events on the strategic flanks thus set the context as the two sides considered their options in the wake of Aspern-Essling. Though his opinion of Habsburg senior commanders and their 'wretched' Kaiser[45] remained low, Napoleon had gained a better appreciation for the obstinate courage of the Austrian soldiery. His own army recovered rapidly from the setback of the first failed crossing attempt, but he concluded that the inexperience of some of his infantry and the open nature of the terrain on the Marchfeld demanded more guns. On the tactical level, he thus set about increasing the Army of Germany's artillery component. On the strategic plane, he remained committed to ending the war with a decisive battlefield victory. There is no indication that he seriously pursued a peace settlement that would leave Austria unpunished and could be portrayed as a French defeat, but he does not seem to have formulated any definitive war aims. Published statements from imperial headquarters (such as the army's bulletins and orders of the day) frequently depicted Austria's ruling family in demeaning terms or promoted the idea of Hungarian independence from the Habsburg dynasty.[46] Though received with great alarm and indignation in the Kaiser's court, such statements represented public posturing, not a delineation of fixed goals for the conflict.[47]

Napoleon did offer a tenuous peace gesture by sending Graf Johann Anton Pergen, a senior official who had remained behind in Vienna, to the Kaiser under the pretext of arranging food supplies for the capital. For Austrians such as Charles and his brother Archduke Rainer who advocated immediate negotiations, Pergen's appearance and his favourable descriptions of discussions with Berthier suggested that Napoleon did not intend to depose Franz or break up the monarchy. Charles, Rainer and those who believed Austria's best hopes lay in concluding the war quickly thus saw the Pergen mission as an opening to achieve an honourable peace without risking another major engagement. In the absence of peace, Rainer wrote to Franz on 13 June, 'The end of the war may be easily foreseen given Napoleon's great numerical superiority, the means that he employs and the unfavourable attitude of the Russians towards us.'[48] The war party, on the other hand, reacted with anger. Pergen was 'very poorly received' at court and dismissed in disgrace after an audience with the Kaiser. Stadion and his adherents, imagining the raising of new troops by the thousands and perceiving Napoleon 'in a difficult situation', persisted with what one anti-Napoleon diplomat termed their *'plans primitifs'* in pursuing the war.[49] In any case, the Pergen episode was almost certainly a French ploy to gain time rather than an earnest step towards negotiations.[50] Instead of peace, Napoleon devoted all his formidable energies to the next crossing of the Danube, an operation he was absolutely determined to prepare with infinite care and execute with every available musket, sabre and gun.

Napoleon's preparations included completing the organisation of the Army of Germany more or less according to the scheme he had outlined in March. The bulk of the army was lodged on Lobau Island and around Vienna: 2nd, 3rd, 4th and 8th Corps along with the Cavalry Reserve and the Guard. On Lobau itself was Massena's 4th Corps with its four infantry divisions (GD Gabriel Molitor's 3rd and GD Jean Boudet's 4th in addition to Legrand's 1st and Carra St Cyr's 2nd) and a large cavalry component commanded by GD Antoine Charles Lasalle. On the Vienna side of the river, the 2nd Corps, now under GD Oudinot in place of the much-lamented Lannes, consisted of three infantry divisions and GB Pierre David Édouard de Colbert's light cavalry brigade, known as the '*brigade infernale*'. Also in and around Vienna were the fourteen heavy cavalry regiments of the Reserve and the now complete Imperial Guard of twelve elite infantry battalions, sixteen squadrons and 60 guns.

The largest command was Davout's 3rd Corps. This comprised three veteran infantry divisions, a division of recent recruits and a division of light cavalry under GD Louis Pierre Montbrun, one of the empire's finest cavalry commanders. In addition, Napoleon bolstered Davout's corps for the coming battle by attaching the Army of Italy's two dragoon divisions to give the marshal a total of some 6,000 horsemen. As for the Army of Italy, it would arrive in time to play a major role at Wagram with five small infantry divisions, a light cavalry brigade and the Italian Royal Guard. Also slated to join the army on Lobau was the Saxon 9th Corps with its attached French division and Marmont's Army of Dalmatia. Finally, Napoleon called in the 2nd Division of the Bavarian 7th Corps from Linz.

He left Marshal Lefebvre with the 1st Division at Linz to watch the Austrian forces in Upper Austria and Bohemia, buttressing Lefebvre by ordering the 3rd Bavarian Division to march to Linz from its defensive positions north of the Tyrol. With the Bavarians at Linz on the left, Napoleon kept GD Louis Baraguey d'Hilliers with a weak division from the Army of Italy opposite Pressburg, and held Raab with an ad hoc garrison on his right. Stretched thinly along the river between Melk and Vienna was the Württemberg 8th Corps under GD Dominique René Vandamme (some 9,300 men to cover 120 kilometres of river line), engaging in periodic raids and annoyances with the Austrians at Krems. Along with some Württemberg cavalry, a regiment of Nassau infantry garrisoned Vienna, where GD Andréossy, the former ambassador to

Austria, had returned as the occupied city's commandant. Given the city's significance as the army's strategic and administrative hub, however, the number of French and allied troops (including wounded) in and around Vienna in early July could fluctuate from 12,000 to 20,000 men from all branches of service.[51]

On the other side of the Danube, Charles had also reorganised his forces since Regensburg and Aspern. In the first place, he had recalled III Corps from Bohemia, leaving an independent detachment of 7,000 under FML Hannibal Graf Somariva to observe Lefebvre's Bavarians at Linz. Second, he added 25 Landwehr battalions to the army's order of battle, most of these paired with and partially incorporated into line regiments. Third, he retained the Reserve Corps configuration he had instituted prior to Aspern: a single large formation of heavy cavalry and grenadiers under Liechtenstein. He also formed a corps-sized Advance Guard by drawing units from other corps (mostly IV and V), but this would be dissolved on 6 July, its troops absorbed into IV Corps. These major changes and numerous shifts of individual regiments left the Hauptarmee with seven corps-level formations at Wagram in addition to the Advance Guard: I (Bellegarde), II (FML Friedrich Xaver Fürst von Hohenzollern), III (Kolowrat), IV (Rosenberg), V (FZM Heinrich XV Fürst Reuss-Plauen), VI (FML Johann Graf Klenau) and Reserve (GdK Liechtenstein).[52]

As these organisational changes were being implemented and as the soldiers drilled endlessly across the Marchfeld, the Habsburg leadership was embroiled in a heated strategic debate, a debate that grew increasingly bitter as the weeks passed with no offensive action by the Hauptarmee. The contours of the dispute were by now familiar. Charles's opponents scathingly complained about the 'weighty army' that 'rested unmoving on its laurels'[53] and criticised the archduke personally for being 'naturally weak ... too weak to act appropriately, ashamed to have failed'.[54] Many also believed the French to be vulnerable and disparaged Charles for not attacking the presumably feeble foe. Anton Baldacci, one of Kaiser Franz's closest advisors, for instance, blithely remarked that 'The Emperor Napoleon is a wretched person and a completely ordinary, ignorant general, who would certainly have been destroyed long before if Archduke Charles were not an even less competent leader.'[55] Stadion, for his part, was equally dissatisfied with Charles's attitude and tried to goad him into some kind of action through the Kaiser. He repeatedly expressed his faith that German 'hatred' of Napoleon and the support of irrelevant allies would suffice to turn the tide.[56] With his superficial conception of military affairs, he asked rhetorically in a 25 June memorandum if it was not possible to avoid a major battle and achieve the same result though a 'somewhat active and skilful employment and manoeuvre of our various armies' along with diversions in Germany and Italy?

Furthermore, Stadion still hewed to his original war aims, telling the Kaiser as late as 3 July that any peace requiring Austrian territorial concessions would be disastrous. After all, he argued, the war had been launched because Austria's situation after 1805 was unacceptable, so it must end with the empire in a more advantageous position than when it began. That meant significant territorial acquisitions or adjustments in Austria's favour, specifically 'the Tyrol and a contiguous Italian boundary'. His views, he wrote, 'differ entirely from those of His Imperial Highness [Charles]', and he chastised Charles by name for 'the inactivity which has characterised the current campaign' and for Charles's willingness to accept the boundaries of the 1805 Treaty of Pressburg (that is, Austria's boundaries at the start of the 1809 war) or 'even a peace which would involve territorial concessions'. Stadion, in contrast, believed that returning to Austria's pre-war borders (what he called 'the boundaries of the Pressburg Treaty') would 'bring on the early downfall and further territorial cessions the immediate downfall of the monarchy and the end of the Austrian state'. The war must be prosecuted 'with determination, willpower and might' to the very moment a treaty was signed. Otherwise, he warned, he 'could see nothing but the decline and destruction of the state'.[57] With no substantial continental allies (Prussia had again demurred from joining the war on Austria's side), with all Austrian offensive plans foiled, with Napoleon in possession of the Habsburg capital, and much of the monarchy's heartland under French occupation, however, there was more than a 'taint of unreality' in such wishful thinking.[58]

Charles, of course, saw the empire's situation through an entirely different lens. As he told Herzog Albert on 23 June: 'Since the Battle of Regensburg and above all since that of Aspern, I continually preach peace, peace, peace, better to sacrifice a few things than lose everything.'[59] In a letter to the Kaiser that same day, he again outlined his views. 'Our first strike failed and with this our hopes disappeared,' he wrote, and now 'the first lost battle is the death sentence of the monarchy and the current dynasty ... it is physically impossible for Austria to conduct a Russian–Polish and a French–Italian–German war at the same time.'[60] He saw no practicable military options. In a second letter to the Kaiser a few days later, he argued that an Austrian crossing of the Danube would inevitably produce a great battle but one Austria was unlikely to win even if the Hauptarmee was able to pass over the river and sustain itself. If Napoleon were to cross, 'We will probably defeat him but probably with no better success than in the Battle of Aspern.' As before, he founded his analysis on the key assumptions that Aspern had chastened Napoleon and that the French emperor would treat with his Austrian counterpart as long as the latter had a viable army in the field. He thus concluded the second note by once again urging his brother to undertake talks with Napoleon: 'These considerations require me to observe that Your Majesty, at the head of a strong, good army, can negotiate now; later you will not be able to do so.'[61] His underlying conviction thus remained that endangering the army would endanger the continued existence of the state and the dynasty.

At the centre of this strategic debate was Kaiser Franz. Stadion and others pressed for action, but Charles would not attempt an offensive over the Danube without a direct order from his elder brother. 'If he orders it, I will cross,' he wrote to his adoptive father before continuing with barely disguised contempt, 'but I believe I will be beaten, and he and his ministers will pay dearly for their arrogance and impatience.'[62] The hesitant Franz, however, could not bring himself to give such an order. Despite myriad memoranda from all sides and a late June conference with Charles and Stadion in the Kaiser's presence, Habsburg councils remained mired in vacillation, recrimination and, ultimately, indecision. In all of this confusion it is not difficult to detect Napoleon's psychological domination of his adversaries. This was particularly the case with Charles, who remained adamantly convinced that the prospect of crossing a major river against a large French army under Napoleon's personal command was 'a gamble where all probability is against success'.[63] Where Charles was resigned to advocating peace while awaiting Napoleon's next move, others believed the monarchy had to do *something*. The leadership was unable to decide on a move in the primary theatre against their daunting opponent, however, and Austrian strategy devolved into a frantic search for some kind of action on the fringes of the war. The results were half-measures, none of which bore fruit. To the north, diplomatic efforts to cajole Prussia into joining the conflict were quickly dashed and the forays into Bayreuth and Saxony by small detachments (totalling some 15,000 men by the end of June) were contained, albeit clumsily, by the second-line French and Rheinbund troops mentioned earlier. Efforts to exhort Great Britain into active participation in the war were renewed with the dispatch of Graf Ferdinand Ernst von Waldstein to London bearing instructions from both Stadion and Charles urging the prompt landing of 12,000–15,000 British troops in northern Germany on behalf of 'the general European cause'. Waldstein, however, did not depart Wolkersdorf until 22 June and more than a month would pass before he reached his destination.[64]

The Austrians also considered diplomatic and military efforts in the east. On the diplomatic side, GM Joseph Xaver von Stutterheim, a protégé of Stadion's, was dispatched with a letter from Kaiser Franz to Tsar Alexander expressing Franz's 'chagrin and astonishment' at the entry of Russian troops into Galicia. 'I am not accustomed to the idea of seeing in you, my brother, an enemy of my monarchy and my house,' wrote the Kaiser.[65] Stadion hoped that Stutterheim could use the imperial missive as an *entrée* to call on the Russian commander, Prince Sergey Golitsyn, and other generals. He was to persuade them to halt or delay their operations, using 'pecuniary means' (bribes) if necessary.[66] At the same time, Franz sent Archduke Ferdinand orders to demand of the Russians that they 'not advance further into my states' until the tsar had time to answer the letter Stutterheim carried.[67] Charles reinforced these instructions by telling Ferdinand to 'allow the Russians to gain as little terrain as possible without provoking actual hostilities'.[68] He and others in the Habsburg hierarchy continued to worry that ground once lost might never be recovered. They perceived a threat not only to Galicia but to Transylvania and Bukovina in the south as well. 'Russia', wrote Charles, 'is completing what it has declared a hundred times in verbal and written form: it is encompassing the entire eastern arc of our border from the Vistula to Slovenia.'[69]

Stutterheim's mission, however, achieved little. In the first place, by the time he reached Ferdinand's headquarters on 28 June, the Russians had already arrived at the Wisloka River. Second, the Russians politely refused to permit him to meet Golitsyn. The best he could attain was a midnight meeting with Major General Burhardt Maximovic Berg, Golitsyn's chief of staff, at a location far from the Russian headquarters. Berg explained that fear of discovery by a Polish officer in the headquarters dictated the distant venue and odd hour for the meeting, but Stutterheim noted sourly that they 'apparently prefer to see the Austrians at night'.[70] Subsequent discussion brought no improvement. Berg, despite protestations of friendship and sympathy for Austria, asserted that Golitsyn had received definite orders to advance from the Wisloka to the Dunajec River no later than 3 July. Unable to see Golitsyn, Stutterheim was reduced to handing Berg the Kaiser's letter in return for a written receipt. With little to show for his efforts and worried that Napoleon might be orchestrating a combined Franco-Russian operation in Hungary, he reported to Ferdinand on 1 July before departing to render a verbal account to Stadion.[71]

In the meantime, the Austrian court was actively considering the desirability of 'actual hostilities' with the Russians. On 2 July Franz thus instructed Charles to detach 12,000–15,000 men from the Hauptarmee to reinforce Archduke Ferdinand in Galicia 'as rapidly as possible'.[72] The thinking was that if the Main Army was not going to act in the near term, it could 'loan' such a detachment to Ferdinand with the aim of intimidating or, if necessary, attacking the encroaching Russians. As the Main Army 'has stood more than quietly and had no impact on the general military situation of the monarchy', Stadion complained to Wimpffen, it was therefore necessary 'to act all the more briskly at some other point'.[73] Charles was able to forestall this move, but the Franz and Stadion letters highlight both the level of desperation in the Habsburg court and the growing anxiety about Russo-Polish advances. The archduke also ignored suggestions that he send troops to Hungary[74] but he could not evade instructions to reinforce the detachments in Germany. Incredible as it seems, army headquarters prepared a set of orders early

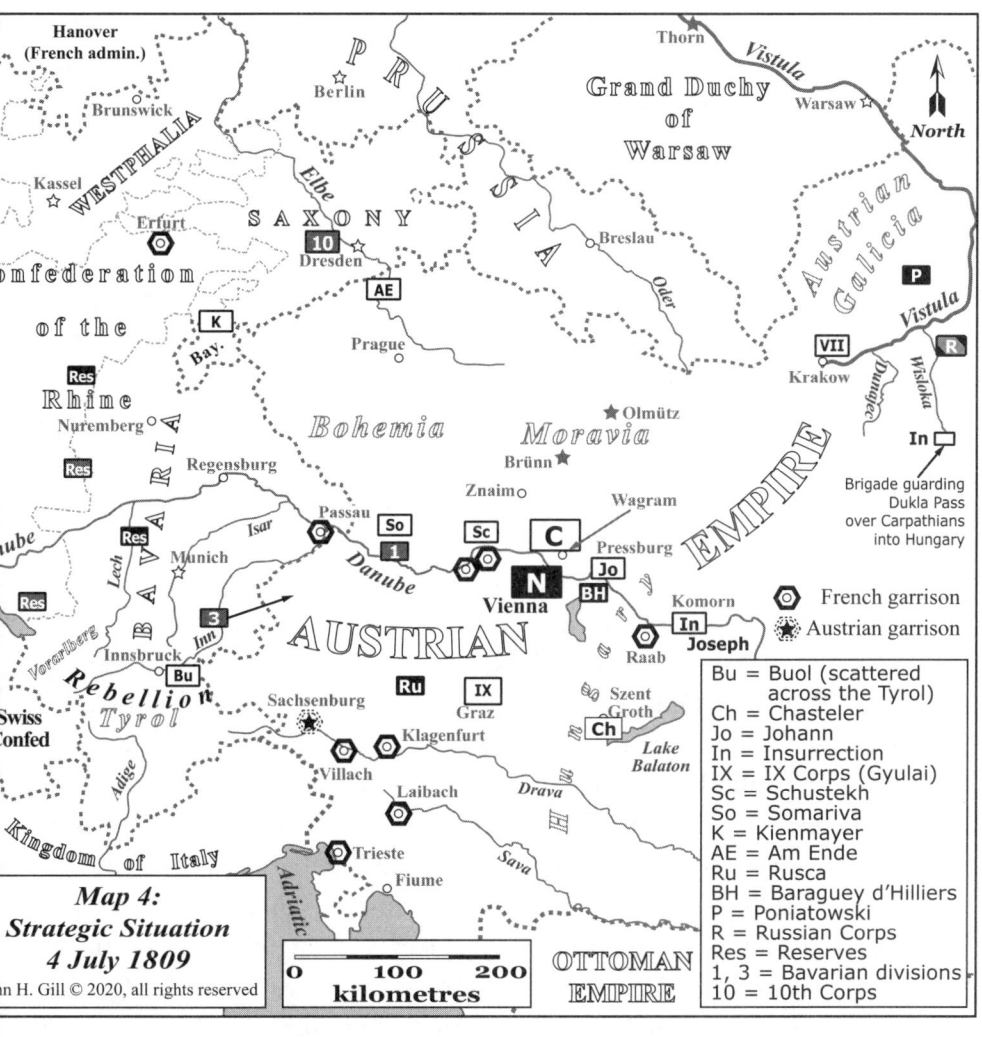

Map 4: Strategic Situation 4 July 1809

on 4 July designating 9,500 men and 'a proportionate number of guns' who were to march for Bohemia on the 6th.[75] A bizarre situation was thus created in which Austrian actions in Germany, far from distracting Napoleon, were on the verge of inducing a substantial weakening of the Hauptarmee on the eve of the war's decisive battle. Nothing better illustrates the strategic–operational confusion and delusion in the Habsburg court and army headquarters. Fortunately for the Habsburgs, there was no time to implement these orders. Indeed, as these were being drafted in Wagram an officer along the riverbank was hastily composing a status report: 'The observation post at the tavern in Essling has just reported that a mass of troops can be seen at Ebersdorf [across the Danube] ... but one cannot determine their strength owing to the dust.'[76] Napoleon was on the move and would unleash his assault across the river that very night.

Wagram

Wagram was one of the largest battles of the nineteenth century and second only to Leipzig in 1813 as far as the Napoleonic era is concerned. Fought on 5 and 6 July, it was a struggle of truly titanic proportions with the two sides deploying more than 300,000 men and nearly 1,000 guns along a 22-km firing line for two long, hot days. The battle was a clear French victory, but a week of pursuit, dispute and combat would pass before the war reached its de facto end at Znaim.

This enormous battle began with one of the greatest offensive river crossings in military history. From May to July, while the Austrians bickered, debated and waited, Napoleon employed all of his energies and all of his empire's resources to prepare for a second crossing of the Danube. First, he transformed Lobau into a huge fortified camp to provide a solid base of operations for the coming attack. Protected by more than 100 heavy guns and mortars, the previously placid island was soon crisscrossed with orderly roads and dotted with powder magazines, bakeries, food stores, workshops and a hospital. At the same time, he addressed the bridging problem. His engineers and artillerymen connected Lobau to the south bank with two sturdy bridges and prepared a series of ingenious prefabricated spans to ensure a rapid crossing from the island, over the Stadtler Arm, and onto the Marchfeld. A flotilla of small gunboats was constructed from scratch to patrol the river and pilings were driven into the riverbed upstream from the bridging site to ward off the fire rafts and floating debris the Austrians had employed against the lone bridge in May. By the beginning of July, therefore, Napoleon could thus justly boast that 'the Danube no longer exists for the French army'.[77] He was also determined to fight the coming battle with overwhelming numbers. To this end, he took risks along his lines of communication, leaving only the thinnest protective screen, but he sequenced the arrival of reinforcements to give the Austrians little time to react to the vast force he planned to assemble. Some of these hard-marching formations would not arrive until 6 July, but this careful planning meant that Napoleon would have a tremendous force of 172,000 infantry and cavalry with 475 guns at his disposal at Wagram, a physical manifestation of his single-minded focus on the strategically decisive action.

The Austrians, in contrast, had neither a coherent strategic concept nor a clear tactical plan on how they would confront Napoleon should he cross onto the Marchfeld. Charles had concentrated the bulk of the monarchy's forces opposite Vienna for a total of some 136,000 infantry and cavalry supported by 388 guns. Significant elements, however, were detached elsewhere. These included, most notably, the remains of Archduke Johann's Army of Inner Austria (about 15,000) downstream at Pressburg and, upstream, a reorganised V Corps of some 16,800, now commanded by the newly promoted FZM Heinrich XV Fürst Reuss-Plauen.[78] Reuss's responsibilities stretched as far as Krems where FML Emanuel Freiherr von Schustekh's division (6,000) watched a brigade of Vandamme's Württemberg corps (1,100) across the river. Further afield, Somariva was north of Linz, while Archduke Joseph's Insurrection troops along with Chasteler and Gyulai covered the many kilometres from the Danube south into Hungary.

The French crossing began on the evening of 4 July under a furious thunderstorm and a heavy covering barrage from the artillery on Lobau. The wild, comingled violence of man and nature led one of the Saxons on the island to call it 'a night out of *Macbeth*'.[79] Despite the storm, the river, and disjointed opposition from the Austrian VI Corps and Advance Guard, Napoleon's meticulous preparations and the skills of his subordinates brought more than 150,000 men, thousands of horses, 400 guns and countless other vehicles across the final arm of the Danube onto the Marchfeld by the late morning of 5 July.

The imposing spectacle of this enormous host unfurling itself across the Marchfeld left an unforgettable image in the minds of observers, but it also contained an oddity: Marshal Massena commanding his corps from a carriage. Injured when his mount stumbled while conducting a reconnaissance with Napoleon on 3 July, Massena could not sit astride a horse for a time and would lead his corps while seated in a light carriage

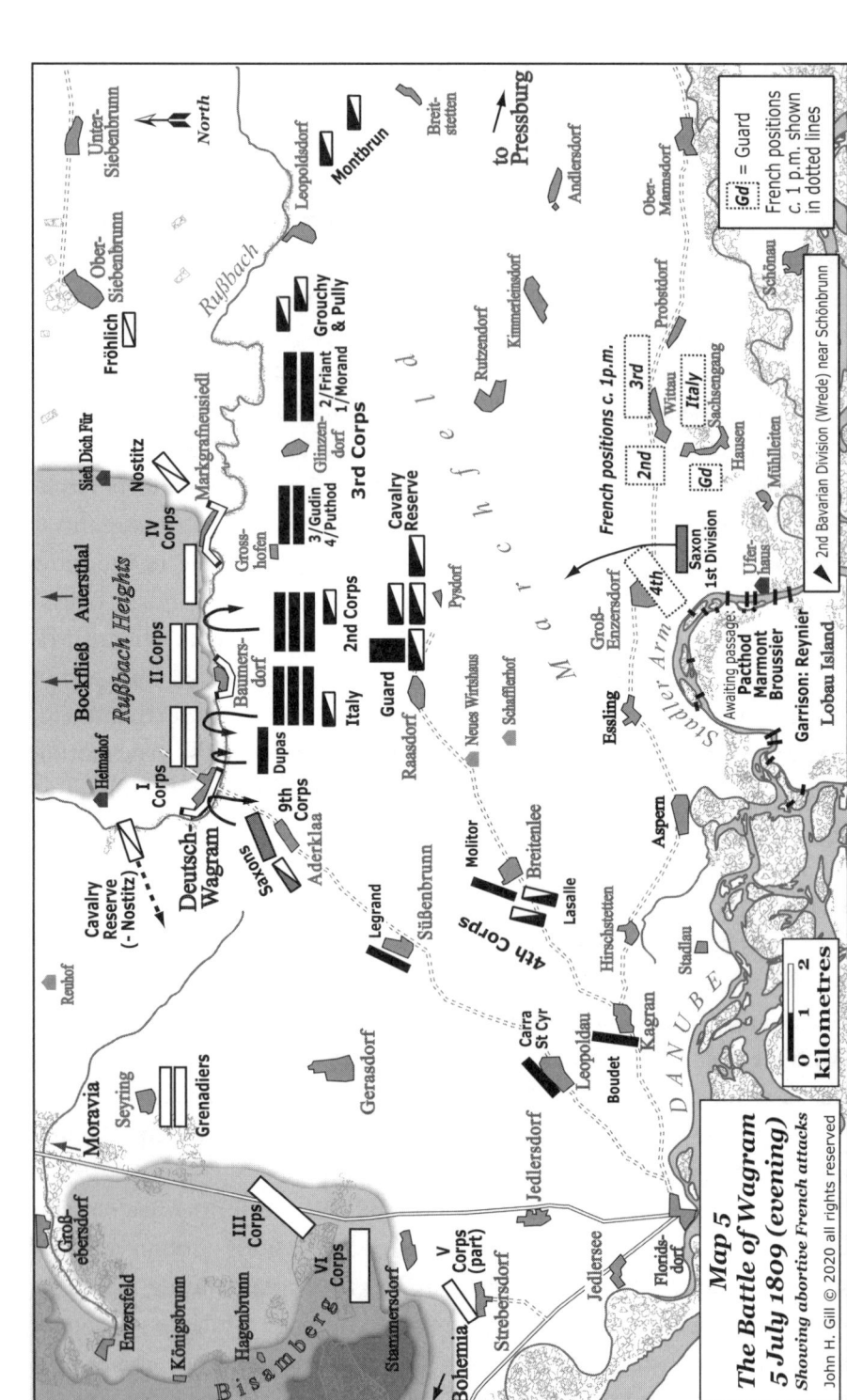

during the coming battle. Despite making a conspicuous target, he emerged unharmed. His contusion was slow to heal, however, and he would remain largely confined to his calash through the pursuit and the Battle of Znaim.

Having won space to deploy, the French and their German allies began to advance across the vast plain. Although cavalry clashed and artillery boomed, there was little major fighting as the Austrians withdrew from the river line. The VI Corps and the Advance Guard suffered badly in their retreat, but they fell back to a formidable defensive position that Charles had chosen arcing from an elevation called the Bisamberg on the Austrian right to the low rise of the Rußbach Heights a few metres above the eponymous stream in the army's centre and left. The Haupatrmee's dispositions were significant for the pursuit to Znaim as the corps locations around Wagram largely determined their routes of retreat. On the far right, VI and III Corps were deployed on the Bisamberg with parts of V Corps some distance to their right and rear; the Grenadiers and Cavalry Reserve filled in the low ground between the Bisamberg and the town of Wagram, while I Corps held Wagram and the heights above; II Corps was placed in the centre of the Rußbach Heights and IV Corps held the far left with cavalry detachments stretched as far as Ober-Siebenbrunn. As the brightly clear and hot day waned, the French drew up opposite, arraying themselves from left to right with Massena's 4th Corps covering the long stretch of open ground to the Danube and the Saxon 9th Corps (Marshal Bernadotte) opposite the town of Wagram at the pivot of the line. Eugène's Army of Italy came next below the heights, followed by Oudinot's 2nd Corps and Davout's 3rd Corps with its strong body of cavalry on the extreme right. The Guard and the Cavalry Reserve were under Napoleon's direct command in the centre. Additional reinforcements were due to arrive on the 6th. So far, all had gone well for the French, but the emperor, evidently wanting to test Austrian determination and make sure his quarry did not escape into the night, launched a poorly managed assault on the Rußbach Heights that evening. French tactical skill almost brought success, but the lack of co-ordination meant that the attacking battalions were repelled, streaming back down the slopes in confusion. As part of this attack, the Saxons had attempted an assault on Wagram itself, only to be repulsed with

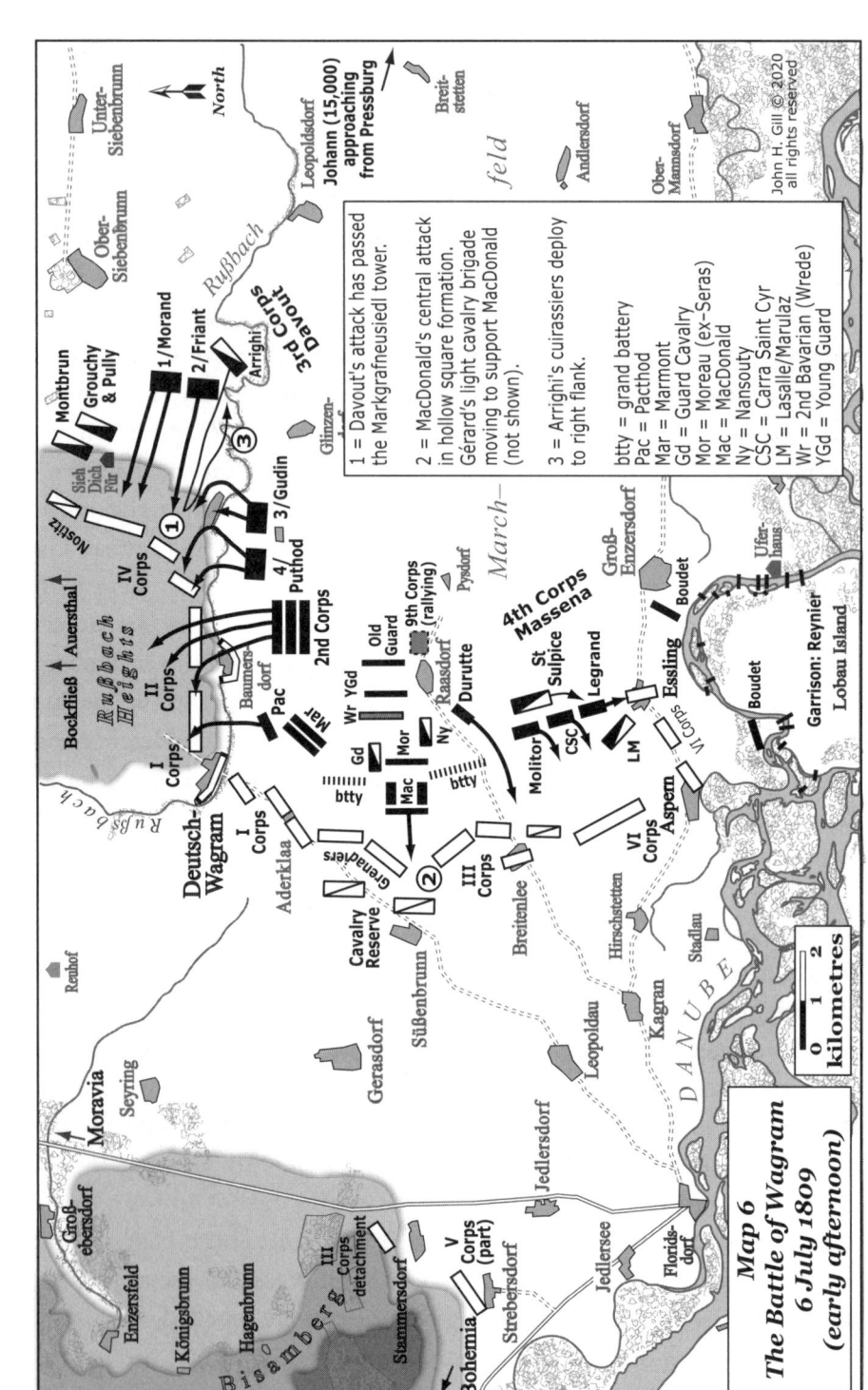

heavy losses, leaving an injured and disordered force at the centre of the French line.

Charles opened the second day of the battle with attacks on both French wings but the effort was poorly orchestrated and the IV Corps attack on the French right was quickly repulsed. On the French centre and left, however, I Corps and the Grenadiers dislodged the shaken Saxons while VI and III Corps advanced stolidly against Massena, eventually gaining enough ground to threaten the French bridges from Lobau Island. Faced with a crisis in his centre and on his left, Napoleon remained calm. Reinforcements had arrived that morning in the form of Marmont's Army of Dalmatia, the 2nd Bavarian Division and two additional divisions belonging to the Army of Italy. He thus had a strong, centrally placed reserve at hand, but he focused his attention on Davout's progress on the right, knowing that success on this flank would unhinge the entire Austrian line. To gain time for Davout's attack to take effect and to prepare for a strike at the Austrian centre, he made a series of rapid decisions. First, he turned Massena's 4th Corps ninety degrees to the left and sent it marching across the front of the Austrian advance to retrieve the situation along the Danube. Second, he shifted three divisions of the Army of Italy under GD Etienne Jacques MacDonald from the centre to the left to launch the main attack. Finally, he massed a battery of more than 100 guns to cover the gap left by Massena and to prepare the way for MacDonald's assault. Meanwhile, Oudinot was to charge the Rußbach Heights and Davout was to redouble his efforts on the right. These moves, conceived and executed on the spot, brought success. Massena retook Aspern and Essling, Davout bent the Austrian left back and Oudinot's men attacked the heights as MacDonald pushed forward in the centre. MacDonald's attack, 'into a volcano' of lead and iron,[80] took heavy losses and slowed to a crawl without achieving the desired breakthrough, but the actions on the flanks were decisive. With Davout and Oudinot threatening to overwhelm his left wing and Massena slowly pushing back his right, Charles could see French infantry massed in the centre 'like a dark storm cloud' but had no reserves of his own to restore the situation.[81] Around 2:30 p.m., therefore, he ordered a retreat.[82]

Napoleon thus had a victory in one of the largest battles of the century, but the success was dearly purchased and incomplete. Casualties on both sides were enormous: 38,870 Austrians and 35,060 French and Germans were dead, wounded, missing or captured during the two long, hot days, but this immense expenditure of blood did not deliver the stunning triumph Napoleon had desired and expected: few prisoners or guns had been taken and the Austrians were retreating in good order. As one of his confidants recalled,

> The emperor was indifferently content with the Battle of Wagram; he wanted a second representation of Marengo, Austerlitz or Jena and he had taken great care to obtain such a result; but far from this, the Austrian army was intact; it was departing to throw itself into some position that would necessitate new planning efforts to bring about an engagement followed by better results.[83]

Watching the battle from French-occupied Vienna was newly promoted FML Nicholas Ungnad Graf Weißenwolff. Like Pergen's delegation, Weißenwolff's presence was another result of the tentative Franco-Austrian interactions during June. Perhaps the most important outcome of these openings was the return of Metternich to the Habsburg fold. Interned by the French since the opening of hostilities in April, he was detained in Vienna for most of June, meeting various of Napoleon's close associates and acquiring the impression that the French were keen to achieve peace. Exchanged for the former French consul in Vienna, Claude Dodun, on 2 July at an outpost in Hungary, he joined the Kaiser's court in Wolkersdorf on the 3rd and began to influence Austrian councils almost as soon as he arrived. In addition to repatriating one another's diplomats, the two sides also had agreed earlier to exchange two captured generals and a small number of other officers. Weißenwolff was ostensibly to discuss further prisoner exchanges, but Charles hoped his mission would open a path to peace. His was to be an exploratory visit, sounding out the French on possible ways to end hostilities, but Kaiser Franz, though aware of this initiative, proffered only the vaguest guidance, airily stating, 'If someone drops a hint, you should pick it up,'[84] and thereby distancing himself from all responsibility should Weißenwolff be rebuffed.

Weißenwolff duly arrived at the French outpost line at 5:00 a.m. on 4 July as arranged. He was met by Captain Nicolas Marie Mauthurin

Galbois, one of Berthier's staff officers, who took him to Berthier. Though blindfolded for his passage to Berthier's tent, he was treated with great courtesy[85] and was escorted from thence almost immediately to see Napoleon 'The interview was quite long,' wrote Galbois, 'and General Weißenwolff had the honour to dine with His Majesty.' The two discussed upcoming military operations as well as prisoners and Weißenwolff was 'delighted with the emperor', but he soon discovered that his embassy was otiose: the French were on the verge of initiating their crossing onto the Marchfeld and any discussion of peace was postponed indefinitely. Indeed, on 2 July, the very day that Berthier and Wimpffen were exchanging letters concerning Weißenwolff's mission, Napoleon issued comprehensive instructions for the passage of the river. Under such circumstances, of course, Weißenwolff could not be allowed to return and, as Galbois recalled, 'Around 11:00 in the morning the emperor gave me the order to conduct the Austrian general to Vienna, to treat him with great consideration but not to leave him for an instant.' Weißenwolff 'complained loudly but there was no way to change the emperor's mind' and Galbois 'left with my unfortunate envoy'. Contrary to Napoleon's instructions, however, Galbois wanted to be on hand for the coming battle and 'did not take these recommendations into account too much'. He thus turned Weißenwolff over to GD Andréossy, the French commandant in Vienna, and rode back to Lobau. Andréossy evidently decided that he had more important tasks than watching an Austrian detainee and handed Weißenwolff off to one of his aides-de-camp.[86] The result of all this was that Weißenwolff, though detained, seems to have been relatively free to move about Vienna from which he apparently watched some aspects of the battle.[87] He would remain a French 'guest' until 9 July when, again escorted by Galbois, he was permitted to return to the Hauptarmee. Despite his annoyance at being interned, his courteous treatment while in French hands would influence the thinking of the Habsburg leadership when he reported to Charles at Znaim on the morning of the 10th.

Chapter 4

Every Night a March, Every Day an Attack

6–9 July 1809

AS NIGHT SPREAD ITS DRAGON WING over the blasted Marchfeld, most of the villages were aflame and burning stands of dry crops consumed those wretched wounded who were too weak to drag themselves out of danger. As a result, the following dawn 'illuminated the frightful spectacle of a battlefield covered with the dead and the dying', wrote a French hussar officer, 'The crops, ready to be harvested, were still burning and smoking, thus the prestige of glory gave place to all the most horrible that war can offer.'[1] 'The wounded sought shelter in the shocks of grain, but there was no safety there, and entire plots of the still standing crops were in flames as was also the case with hundreds of shocks', recalled a Bavarian drummer, 'Men were lying about burned entirely brown.' 'Wherever the eye turned it encountered scenes of suffering humanity and misery,' wrote another Bavarian.[2] Cavalry scouts from Archduke Johann's Army of Inner Austria appeared near Untersiebenbrunn in the late afternoon. Charles had called Johann in from Pressburg to join the main army, but his corps arrived too late to participate in the battle. His patrols, however, induced panic in the French rear among 'the equipment train, spare horses, stragglers, knaves and all the herd of non-combatants that always pullulate in the trail of a victorious army'.[3] Johann's troopers quickly discerned that the battle had moved far to the west and prudently withdrew back towards the March River. Charles would soon blame his brother for the defeat, but in the meantime, the alarm the Habsburg horsemen had occasioned soon subsided and the men of the exhausted armies set about seeking shelter, sustenance and sleep in the short summer's night.

The Night of 6–7 July: Hunger, Thirst and Fatigue

On the French side of the field, the army had pushed the retreating Austrians to the western fringe of the Marchfeld and cleared the Rußbach Heights as far as the Hochleithen ridgeline. In some cases, the action resembled 'following' the enemy more than 'pursuing', but there were numerous sharp combats as well, especially as the French cavalry endeavoured to interrupt the Austrian withdrawal. The legendary GD Antoine Charles Lasalle was killed in one of these engagements leading Massena's light cavalry in the late afternoon. Shortly thereafter, his replacement, GD Jacob François Marulaz, received his nineteenth wound, the one that would end his career as an active field soldier; his brother-in-law, Chef d'Escadron Etienne Maréchal, and Colonel Jean-Baptiste Deban de Laborde, colonel of his old regiment, the 8th Hussars, were killed during the same charge.[4] Marulaz's wounding left the 4th Corps light cavalry under the orders of GB Jean Pierre Joseph Bruyère,[5] but it would not be the last time in this campaign that death or injury would cause a change of command in these divisions. Bruyère and the corps' light cavalry halted between Leopoldau and Stammersdorf for the night with Boudet's small division on their left at Jedlersdorf. Massena's other three infantry divisions and St Sulpice's cuirassiers bivouacked around Leopoldau with the battered Saxon corps just east of the village. To the right of 4th Corps, the Army of Italy was gathered around Gerasdorf with the Bavarian division and 2nd Corps further to the right along the road leading to Groß-Engersdorf. GL von Wrede having been wounded during the afternoon, GM Franz Freiherr von Minucci, the senior brigade commander, was now leading the Bavarian division. Two of Davout's divisions encamped around Wagram, but his other two infantry divisions were 5–10 kilometres further northeast in Bockfließ (where they reported the capture of numerous inebriated Austrians) and Auersthal. The four divisions of Davout's large cavalry component were also on the far right where they had contributed to outflanking Rosenberg's corps during the day. The energetic Montbrun halted his two brigades of light cavalry at Auersthal with a division of dragoons under GD Emmanuel Grouchy in support.[6] Nearby were GD Charles Joseph Pully's division of dragoons and GD Arrighi's 3rd Heavy Cavalry Division, but there was only a thin screen towards the March River where Johann had appeared late in the afternoon. The Guard and Marmont were clustered around the imperial tents on a low rise just north of Raasdorf in the centre of the Marchfeld's vast expanse.

The men were exhausted. Starting on 4 July, they had had a tense and demanding day on Lobau Island, followed by a soaking sleepless night as they waited to cross under the crashing rain and thunder, then two long, hot days in combat with little rest and little to eat or drink. 'We suffered greatly from thirst,' recalled Charles-Henri Lejeune, a trooper of the 11th Chasseurs in Montbrun's division, 'It had been two days since we had seen water or anything else to drink.'[7] A Saxon lieutenant paid three 20-crown pieces for half a flask of water 'and never had a draught refreshed me so much', but a sergeant in Oudinot's corps could not get a sip for any price: 'The batteries tormented us a lot, but thirst and hunger were our greatest afflictions.'[8] Moreover, many elements of the army had just concluded extended forced marches. Marmont from Graz and the Bavarians from Linz had each covered 200 kilometres or more in four days, with little respite, to arrive in time for the grand battle. The emperor was not exempt from the general weariness. 'I am so fatigued that I cannot write any more', he told his arch-chancellor in a letter on 7 July.[9] Exhaustion, disorder, heavy casualties and the gathering darkness all meant that pressure on the Austrians eased as the evening wore on. Marulaz was not wounded until sometime around 8:00 p.m., so fighting in some parts of the field continued until quite late, but this was not the case everywhere and the French lost touch with their opponents during the night. They probably should have pressed harder, fatigue notwithstanding. Among other benefits, pushing a bit farther to occupy Wolkersdorf would have placed French troops at the angle between the two pieces of high ground the Austrians now occupied (Hochleithen and Bisamberg) and might have provided considerable intelligence on future enemy movements as the town had been home to Kaiser Franz's court since May.[10]

In addition to fatigue and the growing darkness, Napoleon likely had other considerations in mind as night fell on 6 July. For one, the Austrians had fought well during the battle, especially on the defensive, and they had retired in fairly good order so he was not facing a defeated enemy that might disintegrate with one more, firm blow. Second, the Hauptarmee's withdrawal had placed it in advantageous defensive positions. The ridges formed by the Bisamberg and the Hochleithen were not high (200–350 metres) but they were rugged and wooded, posing a challenge for the French army should it try to attack uphill out of the Marchfeld plain. Third was the security of his rear areas. Although he was also aware of the potential for trouble south of the Danube from the Austrian forces in Hungary, he does not seem to have harboured great concern for the safety of Vienna. Archduke Johann's command north of the river, on the other hand, was a different matter. Napoleon seems to have credited Johann with some 30,000 men when the actual force Johann was able to bring to Wagram was only half that number.[11] The emperor did not ignore the potential threat from Hungary, but it was Johann's corps that would continue to be a factor in his thinking as he considered his actions immediately after Wagram.

Charles also had Johann in mind as the retreat progressed, seeing his younger brother's tardy arrival as a major contributing factor in the defeat. His immediate concern on the evening of the 6th, however, was to put as much distance as possible between his wounded army and Napoleon's. There is no indication that he gave any thought to renewing the struggle on the 7th from his new positions north and west of the Marchfeld. As Napoleon comes under criticism for not pressing harder late on the afternoon of 6 July, some commentators censure Charles for not accepting a third day of battle. Christian Binder von Kriegelstein in his study, for example, points out that the Hauptarmee suffered significant losses in straggling during its retreat and ended up ensnared in a major battle at Znaim anyway. In his view, that climactic battle could have been fought on the 7th 'in a much stronger position, with greater strength, and under much more favourable conditions'.[12] This was not the sort of risk, however, that the Generalissimus was prepared to run. He confronted a number of serious problems that evening. Perhaps most important was that he knew he was significantly outnumbered. 'I have never seen so many troops,' he told Albert as he described his view from atop the Rußbach Heights on the morning of the 6th, 'Imagine for yourself that they occupied the terrain from the Danube near Raasdorf as far as Siebenbrunn and were formed in many lines in the centre.' He was also deeply angry at his own army's performance, especially the behaviour of the infantry. While some had fought tenaciously (repelling French advances towards the Bisamberg in the late afternoon for instance), he had personally witnessed the overthrow of the left wing. 'The infantry, crushed by cannon fire, did not perform well,' he wrote in a private letter to Albert, 'I rallied it two times' but 'finally it yielded and a rout followed' allowing the French to outflank the Austrian position.[13]

In addition to this private communication, Charles expressed his displeasure with the army's prowess in a harsh circular to his senior generals on the 7th.[14] In this he directly blamed Rosenberg's IV Corps for the defeat but also cited far broader causes for dissatisfaction.

> In yesterday's battle, the troops of the left wing did not perform as I was justified in expecting of them, nor according to what I should have been able to expect given their strength, the advantages of their position and the importance of the day. The loss of the battle is to be attributed to these troops. The confusion there was general, the retreat too hasty and too disorderly. In general I was – discounting a few exceptions – not entirely satisfied with the infantry; many regiments dispersed themselves too rapidly and engaged in skirmishing in clumps in the rear without reason, without purpose, so that our people even fired upon each other.
>
> The officers were mostly in front of these retiring masses and owing to the half-hearted efforts to halt the troops more and more ground was lost. The shouting was so widespread that the voices of the commanders could not be heard. If the colonels had accustomed their troops to more quiet and calm, and were more capable of bringing their troops to follow only the voices of their own commanders, such dissolution would not be possible. I will decimate any regiment that behaves in this manner in the future, distribute its men among other regiments, cashier the commanders and dismiss the officers.
>
> Shouting by the troops shall be forbidden under penalty of death.

He then proceeded to castigate several regiments by name and to dismiss GM Friedrich Freiherr von Riese 'from the service of His Majesty the Kaiser' for poor performance and for being absent from his post.

> The disorder among the troops continues even now and provides proof that the generals and staff officers are not paying attention to anything. To make examples, I will therefore dismiss or, if warranted, cashier those commanders whose troops are not assembled. It is a disgrace to the army that one sees so many stragglers and marauders on all the roads and in all the villages.

This bitter and often unfair critique (none of the Austrian battalion masses was broken, for example) suggests that the archduke and his closest advisors were already seeking to justify their decisions and create excuses for the defeat. Nonetheless, Charles closed with two small bits of praise: awarding the commander's cross of the Maria Theresa Order to Klenau and granting the *Erbach* Infantry Regiment No. 42 the right to beat the 'grenadier march' in recognition of its stalwart performance in the battle.

In addition to these deficiencies as he saw them, Charles knew that the Hauptarmee was weary and disordered. The wounded Oberleutnant von Grueber, for example, noted the confusion while riding in a wagon up the road towards Brünn on the afternoon of the 6th. He recalled 'The retreating infantry of the left wing appeared in disorderly heaps seeking to gain the road and crying that the enemy cavalry was at their heels,' and the 'wild commotion of the retreating army baggage and personal horses' trying to make their way through to the highway.[15] Nor was fatigue an exclusive province of the French. The white-coats had also suffered badly from heat, thirst, hunger and lack of sleep over the previous four days. From standing under the storm on the night of the 4th ('whipped by heavy rain ... burdened with sack and pack, with shouldered musket, sunk up to the ankles in the moist earth' as one wrote[16]) through fighting under the pitiless sun over the following two days 'many soldiers fell down senseless from exhaustion' as they withdrew from the battlefield.[17] Major Antoine François Marcel, Comte de Ségur, commander of the 3rd Brünn Landwehr, for example, left a vivid impression of the army's weariness in his journal: 'Harassed by hunger, thirst and fatigue, and with despair in my soul, a soldier gave me a few drops of water and a morsel of commissary bread, and I slept for a few hours in a ditch bordering the road.'[18] An officer from the 4th Unter-Manhartsberg Landwehr in VI Corps recorded that his 'utterly exhausted troops who had been steadily under fire for two days and consumed nothing but bread and Danube water... were so spent that between Jedlersdorf and the vineyards [Bisamberg] some 100 fell out, many of them dying of thirst'.[19] For Charles on the evening of 6 July, therefore, the enemy's strength, the exhaustion and disorder in his own army as well as the deficiencies he had witnessed over the preceding two days left him no option but retreat to a new 'position' from which he could consider venturing another defensive battle.

The result of these deliberations was an order issued at 8:00 p.m. from the hills above Stammersdorf that directed the bulk of the army to occupy a position along the Kreuzenstein Heights with V Corps on the right athwart the main highway, followed by III Corps, the Grenadier Corps and I Corps stretching to the northeast along the ridge. The Cavalry Corps was to 'remain in the plain behind Korneuburg' and Charles took his headquarters to Oberrohrbach. Much reduced owing to eleven battalions that had retreated with Rosenberg, II Corps withdrew from Enzersfeld to Großrußbach, some twelve kilometres northeast of the position's left flank. The task of rearguard for this portion of the army fell to Klenau's VI Corps, which was to occupy Korneuburg and provide outposts along the army's entire front until at least midnight.[20] Most of the elements of the Cavalry Corps that had been detached to the army's left returned to Liechtenstein by evening, but IV Corps had absorbed the bulk of the now disbanded Advance Guard and Rosenberg also found himself shepherding 'numerous dispersed battalions of the II Army Corps'.[21] This group amounted to eight line battalions – *Zach* No. 15 (2), former I/former *Zedtwitz* No. 25 (1), *Frelich*, No. 28 (3), and *Joseph Colloredo* No. 57 (2) – along with three Landwehr battalions and the meagre remnants of the 8th Jägers.[22] The *Hohenzollern* Cuirassiers No. 8 and one squadron of *EH Johann* Dragoons No. 1 also retreated with IV Corps that evening. They should have rejoined the Cavalry Reserve but would remain with Rosenberg for the next several days.[23] The only instruction for Rosenberg, however, was to 'withdraw to the Hochleithen', more or less where his corps already found itself.[24] In addition to occupying the Hochleithen Heights, Rosenberg was concerned about his route of retreat and thus sent Radetzky with a large detachment to block the defile leading from Groß-Schweinbarth to Gaweinstal[25] 'leading into the rear of the IV Corps and towards the highway to Brünn'.[26]

The Hauptarmee thus began its retreat taking divergent directions: Rosenberg north towards Brünn, the bulk northwest towards Stockerau and ultimately Znaim, with only Hohenzollern more or less between. This dispersal, if not preferred, was the logical consequence of the army's distribution on the battlefield and the nature of the French advance. Moreover, other retreat options all had significant drawbacks in Charles's view. Although Hohenzollern later contended that Charles should have assembled the entire army on the Hochleithen,[27] this would have required shifting most of the corps across the face of the French advance in the middle of a desperate battle and would have left V Corps alone on the road towards Znaim. Withdrawing towards Hungary would have left Bohemia and Moravia open to invasion and might have led to the army being trapped against the March River and its marshy verge. Taking the entire Hauptarmee towards Brünn was also unappealing. Not only would this require a major march to the left for most of the corps, Charles worried he would 'be in danger of being wedged between the French and Russian armies' should he retire towards Brünn or Olmütz.[28] Withdrawing northwest, on the other hand, allowed the various corps to pull back along natural lines and placed him in a position to protect some of the monarchy's key resources.

Kaiser Franz had ridden out to visit the army on the morning of the 6th while his household servants prepared a lunch for him under a makeshift shelter on the Hochleithen Heights. Despite the distance, the members of his suite had a grand view of the battlefield: 'Looking down from these heights, we watched the great tragedy on the plains, that was more a slaughter than a battle,' wrote Johann Baptist Skall, one of the court functionaries, 'Now left, now right, a village went up in flames.' The Kaiser took a meal on the heights in mid-afternoon, ordering his household to 'make sure you get away' as he rode back to the army. As the impromptu lunch pavilion was located next to the main road leading north from Wolkersdorf to Brünn, his servants were witness to the melancholies and absurdities of war.

Around 5:00 p.m. as the k. k. [imperial and royal] butlers were busy with packing up, another crowd of prisoners came up the Hochleithen along with numerous captured enemy cannon and caissons on which the escorting soldiers had wonderfully and curiously stowed their booty. Here was a mattress atop a cannon with half a pig on top of that; there one saw caissons loaded with tubs of flour, chickens, laundry. Captured Portuguese trudged panting up the hill, their rosaries in their hands, k. k. grenadiers offered gold medallions with women's portraits for sale.[29]

Towards evening, the imperial household decamped for Ernstbrunn where Franz arrived around 9:00 p.m. to lodge in the Schloß Sinzendorf just north of the town.

7 July: Reorganisation, Retreat and Reconnaissance

For the French, 7 July was a day of rest, reorganisation, and reconnaissance under 'magnificent weather'.[30] The sights revealed by the rising sun, however, were hardly magnificent. 'What a horrible spectacle now offered itself to my view,' recorded a young conscript of the Guard remembering this his first battle,

> I still shudder with horror when I recall that plain covered with corpses and blood; I still think to hear the crash of the cannon, sounding like thunder, deafening the ears and hardening the hearts, I still think to see all those men lying in a jumble with the horses, dragging themselves along half-crushed and emitting appalling screams, begging for someone to end their sufferings through death.[31]

Others came away with different impressions. Sergeant Marc Desboeufs of the 81st Ligne in Marmont's Army of Dalmatia did not overlook the human cost, but after curiosity led him to wander over for a look at the emperor's tent, he wrote, 'The blood spilt during the day made no impression on me; I was filled with pride to belong to this grand army whose valour overturned empires, and the grandeur of the scene that had just taken place totally absorbed my spirit.'[32] GB Louis Jacques Coëhorn, wounded while commanding his brigade in 2nd Corps, exhibited a

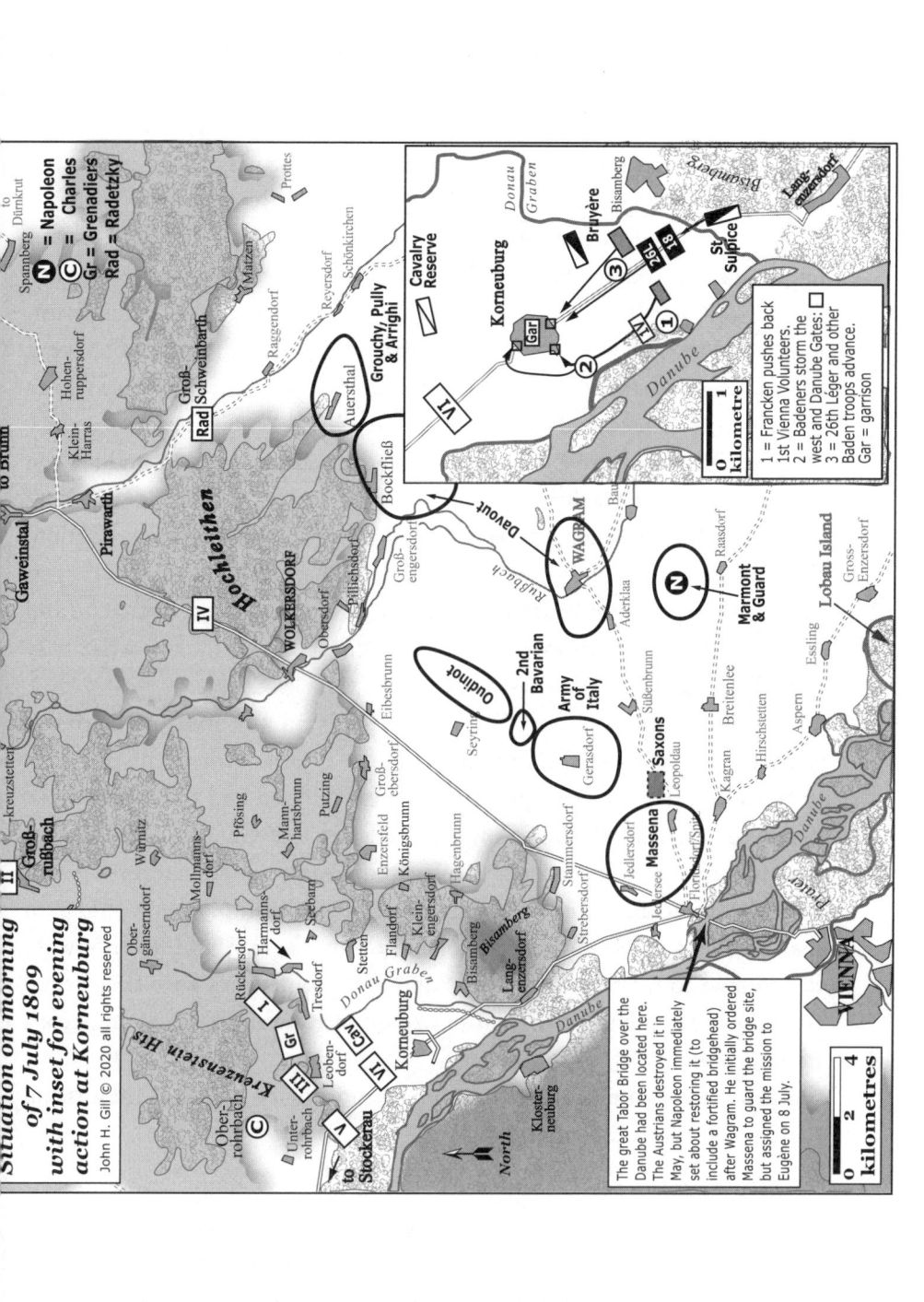

similar attitude. 'I do not believe that, in modern times, a more terrible battle has been given,' he told his wife in a letter on 8 July, but added 'Tell your son that the French are the first soldiers of the world!'[33] 'What a battle, my dear mother!' wrote a lieutenant of the 3rd Léger, 'What genius in the manoeuvres of our great general, whom one may justly call by the title of greatest captain in the world!'[34]

This sort of spirit was pervasive across the army: the battle had been huge, the cost was frightful and the enemy deserved respect for having fought well, but there was no doubt as to who had emerged triumphant. Nor was there any doubt about 'the greatest captain of the world'. Seeing themselves as members of the indisputably victorious army, Napoleon's officers and men would thus continue to display their habitual energy and impetuosity over the coming five days. They would conduct the pursuit with 'an audacity that imposed itself on the archduke',[35] masking French vulnerabilities and reinforcing traditional Habsburg caution. Though the emperor was dissatisfied with the quality of his victory at Wagram, this did not mean that his army was disheartened or that he and his men would lack in fortitude as they chased their foes to what they hoped would be the Hauptarmee's destruction.

As for Napoleon himself, he arose early in the morning, around 4:00 a.m., traversing the dreadful field to inform himself of the state of the army, to ensure proper care of the wounded and to reward those deserving of recognition.[36] Among the latter was General MacDonald, whom Napoleon embraced and elevated to the marshalate in a warm moment of reconciliation and mutual respect. Oudinot, too, would gain his marshal's baton for his performance at Wagram and awards were distributed to many other officers and men, sometimes with the special touch of receiving the cross of the Legion of Honour from the emperor's hand personally.

'It was in such moments that this extraordinary man was interesting to observe,' wrote a civilian official,

> His figure is cool and tranquil during the most lively action; he listens attentively to the reports given to him, he even helps the officers, awed by his presence, to explain themselves and report what they know; but as soon as the affair is over, he seems to forget

his fatigues, his glory, to think only of the care of his army and the reward of the brave who had served him best.[37]

Although some of the details are doubtless embellished or simply amiable legendry, Napoleon clearly devoted some considerable time to visiting the wounded scattered across the plain, offering such succour as he could and issuing instructions for their evacuation and treatment.

What he did not issue were urgent orders to pursue the Hauptarmee. As noted above, the uncertainty of the enemy's situation and his own army's exhaustion militated against an immediate pursuit. Moreover, he needed updated information on the army's status: strengths, losses, exact positions and ammunition stocks after the enormous expenditures of shot and shell on 5 and 6 July.[38] Berthier thus issued instructions that very night requiring reports on these and other items from all commanders.[39] Viceroy Eugène, for example, did not know the locations of all his subordinate formations (Napoleon having shunted them all over the battlefield on the 6th), leave alone their strengths. In the case of 2nd Corps, Napoleon was angered to find the troops dispersed and 'nearly all the men drunk'. Oudinot therefore received a stern rebuke to inspect his corps, make a full report, and issue an order of the day against inebriation.[40] In some respects, 7 July was therefore, as one French historian observes, 'a veritable day of repose' for the army as Napoleon collected information on his own troops as well as those of the enemy to set the stage for the next phase of operations.[41]

If most of the army's movements on the 7th were unhurried shifts to new positions around the Marchfeld, the lack of dramatic marches and combats should not blind us to the high level of activity in command, administration, organisation and reconnaissance. The absence of an immediate, surging, massive pursuit *à la Jena* can create a misleading impression.[42] For one thing, Napoleon did not neglect the strategic situation. Orders issued on the night of the 6th and during the 7th instructed Vandamme at Vienna, GD Jean Reynier, commandant of Lobau Island, and GD Baraguey d'Hilliers, commanding the small division opposite Pressburg, to devote 'the closest attention' to Austrian movements in Hungary, to ensure the safety of the bridges over the Danube and to co-ordinate with one another.[43] The messages written on the 6th specifically ordered their recipients to verify whether Johann had crossed the river to combine with Archduke Joseph. By the 7th these concerns had eased somewhat: 'The victory we have won will probably remove any desire by Archduke Johann to trouble you,' Berthier told Baraguey d'Hilliers. For his part, the latter provided the reassuring news that 'all is perfectly tranquil' along his extensive area of responsibility from Pressburg down to Ödenburg.[44] Though the danger north of the Danube now appeared diminished, it could not be ignored and Eugène was directed to reconnoitre towards Hungary up to the March River.[45] Johann and other Austrian forces in Hungary would remain a factor in Napoleon's thinking, but the precautions he took gave him the freedom to focus on his true strategic targets: Charles and the Hauptarmee.

Locating the archduke and his army proved challenging. 'We are not yet sure of the direction the enemy has taken,' wrote Berthier to Massena late on the morning of the 7th.[46] French and Bavarian reconnaissance elements were active, but much of the intelligence collected during the day was contradictory. The usually reliable Montbrun, for example, reported from the army's far right flank the erroneous information that Austrian cavalry was withdrawing towards Dürnkrut on the March.[47] Numerous indications of enemy activity on the highways north to Brünn in Moravia and northwest to Bohemia did little to clarify the situation. Nonetheless, several points were common among the incoming reports: Charles had been wounded (though the extent of his injury was exaggerated), the French were gathering up large numbers of prisoners and the enemy was retiring in 'the greatest disorder'.[48] Davout went so far as to state 'that the enemy is in disorder and can no longer organise an army'.[49] Like Charles's wound, the degree of disorder would prove exaggerated, but this French impression was not entirely mistaken given the quantity of prisoners collected, the many muskets 'abandoned by the fugitives', and some number of artillery pieces left behind near Wagram.[50] Furthermore, as intelligence from reconnaissance patrols and prisoner interrogations accumulated during the course of the day, it became clear that the Austrian army was split: parts were withdrawing north towards Brünn and parts on the roads to Bohemia via Stockerau. Oudinot reported specifically that the enemy 'was retiring more towards Bohemia than Moravia' and that Charles was personally accompanying the troops retreating to Bohemia.⁵¹ Imperial headquarters, which had moved to Wolkersdorf during the morning, thus focused its attention on those two routes. Which of the two the bulk of the Austrian army had taken remained uncertain, however, despite Oudinot's information.

As was common during this era, intelligence was often gleaned from private letters seized from the local postal system or other sources and the occupation of Wolkersdorf supplied imperial headquarters with a great deal of material when soldiers captured a postal courier. GD Anne-Jean-Marie-René Savary, one of Napoleon's most trusted staff officers, brought the results into a hall in the Wolkersdorf Schloss where other members of the imperial household were dining that evening. 'Gentlemen, amuse yourselves with examining this correspondence,' he told the diners as he deposited two immense baskets stuffed with letters, 'Let us know if you discover anything interesting.' Charles Louis Cadet de Gassicourt, one of the participants in this exercise, recorded that their efforts did not yield much in the way of results except for 'a letter from Archduke Charles and some missives of officers in the enemy army that depicted without deception the extreme distress in which that army found itself'.⁵² This may have been one of the occasions when the French came upon Charles's stern order of the day cited above, although French officers would soon learn of the archduke's order from prisoners as well. Whether or not this particular item was part of this batch of intelligence, the general sense of the Austrian army being 'in extreme distress' became prevalent in French ranks from sources such as these letters.

Among many mundane pieces of correspondence, Gassicourt also came upon a 'very curious' item: a letter from a French émigré in Austrian service who was writing to his commanding general's wife.

> Sweet friend! All conspires against us: not only has fate separated me from Vienna and from you, but once again your husband has not been killed or wounded in the recent battles that we were obliged to sustain. In truth we are most unhappy!

'This wretch deserved to be unmasked,' wrote Gassicourt, but he destroyed the letter 'for the honour of my country'.⁵³

Engagement at Korneuburg: Withdrawing in Perfect Order

If the trove of letters captured near Wolkersdorf provided little specific information on enemy movements, events on the French left late in the day began to shed light on the situation. Massena had pushed patrols 'as far as Korneuburg' in accordance with orders he had received that morning and thus followed the Austrians as they withdrew from the Bisamberg.[54] GB Bruyère, leading the way with the corps' light cavalry, discovered many squadrons and a large body of infantry deployed in and behind the town. The enemy being far beyond his power, Bruyère duly notified Massena and halted to await the arrival of the 4th Corps infantry.[55] With typical light cavalry bravado, however, Bruyère had pressed too far and his regiments now found themselves within range of the Austrian artillery. Though his men suffered considerably, Bruyère was reluctant to withdraw for fear of exposing his command to attack from the nearby Austrian horse. This awkward situation did not escape Massena's notice and the marshal delivered Bruyère a sharp reprimand for leaving his troopers under enemy fire unnecessarily for half an hour or more.[56]

What Bruyère had located, of course, was the main body of the Austrian army. Having marched through the night, the Hauptarmee had reached its planned position north and northwest of Korneuburg around 10:00 a.m. on the 7th undisturbed by the enemy. Klenau, as the army's rearguard, placed a small force in the town, but deployed most of his VI Corps in two lines behind.[57] To his immediate rear was V Corps blocking the highway to Stockerau and, to his left rear, III Corps, the Grenadiers and I Corps arrayed themselves on the Kreuzenstein Heights. The cavalry covered the open ground just north of the town with the *Blankenstein* Hussars No. 6 forward on outpost duty.[58]

Bruyère's patrols first appeared between midday and mid-afternoon, approaching from Langenzersdorf and pushing back the Austrian outpost line as they advanced. Other French and German cavalry soon arrived on Bruyère's flank from across the Bisamberg. To his immediate right was Oberst Friedrich von Lindenau, commander of the 3rd Bavarian Chevaulegers, with two of his squadrons. Napoleon had personally called for the interim Bavarian commander, GM Minucci, that morning and ordered Lindenau to lead a reconnaissance towards Korneuburg and

Stockerau.[59] Making his way forward, the colonel could count at least 'six infantry regiments and a like number of squadrons' deployed behind Korneuburg. The French cavalry, he reported, 'was being received with a lively cannonade'.[60] Further to the right, GB François Joseph Gérard rode up with the Army of Italy's three chasseur regiments followed by Nansouty's 1st Heavy Cavalry Division. Temporarily under Nansouty's command, this mounted force had crossed the Bisamberg ridge from Manhartsbrunn in the late morning and probed towards Harmannsdorf, Tresdorf and Rückersdorf as the afternoon progressed. Nansouty and Gérard were far too weak to attack the estimated 30,000–35,000 Austrians to their front along the Kreuzenstein Heights, but Nansouty dispatched a thorough and largely accurate report on the enemy's dispositions and the 'lively cannonade' he could hear rolling up from the direction of the Danube.[61]

The cannon fire Nansouty heard was occasioned by Massena's attack on the little walled town of Korneuburg. On receiving Bruyère's report of Austrian positions that afternoon, the marshal had informed Napoleon of the enemy situation and immediately headed off with Legrand's 1st Division and some of St Sulpice's cuirassiers, closing his message with 'I hope to capture the town.'[62] As his division moved forward astride the highway, Legrand sent the Baden Jäger Battalion ahead to secure the bridge over a ditch called the Donau-Graben about two kilometres from Korneuburg. Crossing the ditch, he formed his men in line of battle on both sides of the highway and ordered Oberstleutant Karl von Francken, chief of staff of the Baden Brigade, to clear a wooded area on the left along the Danube. At approximately 5:00 p.m., Francken placed himself at the front of the Jäger Battalion and led it towards the wood in what the Austrians later called a 'skirmishing attack'. The defenders were the 1st Vienna Volunteers, who put up a stubborn resistance before withdrawing sometime shortly before 7:00 p.m.[63]

The Baden Jägers had been reinforced by several companies from their brigade's line regiments during the fight for the wood and Francken now used this little ad hoc command to attack the river gate of the walled town (the Donautor) while the French 26th Léger advanced along the highway supported by two guns. At the same time, part of the Jäger Battalion's Voltigeur Company swung around behind Korneuburg despite fire from the VI Corps batteries to the northwest. Here they found that the gate leading to Stockerau had been left open to facilitate the anticipated Austrian retreat. Exploiting this good fortune, the Baden voltigeurs poured into the town through the open entrance as their compatriots clambered over the river gate and dashed through the streets to remove the barricades from the eastern portal, thereby allowing the 26th Léger to enter as well.[64] This tidy feat of arms gained Korneuburg for Massena and netted at least 300 Austrian prisoners for the cost of 20 dead and wounded Badeners and no reported French casualties. Total Austrian losses from the combat and artillery fire in and around Korneuburg, on the other hand, exceeded 400; one company of *Splenyi* Infantry No. 51 was trapped in the village and captured almost in its entirety.[65] As Massena related to Berthier: 'Once we were masters of the wood, the affair was quickly decided.'[66]

The Baden Jägers and the 1st Infantry Regiment hurried through the town to deploy left of the highway on the western side of Korneuburg while the French infantry and heavy cavalry positioned themselves on the right. The light cavalry was brought forward as well in the hopes of pressing the retreating Austrians. Pursuit, however, proved impossible. The Austrian commanders, expecting a cavalry attack,[67] had formed their infantry in battalion masses beyond the town, and the firm countenance of the white-coated infantry, the gross disparity in numbers, and the fall of night precluded any further French advance.[68] Although the French were forced to halt, their artillery left a vivid impression and all of the Austrian after-action reports noted the 'murderous' and 'very heavy' cannon fire. Korneuburg was one victim of the artillery exchange.[69] The town now stood in flames and, with each side blaming the other for the shelling that caused the fires, the Austrians withdrew into the darkness towards Stockerau 'in perfect order'.[70]

Fifteen kilometres away to the north, Hohenzollern's II Corps at Großrußbach was untroubled by the French. Hohenzollern, however, worried that his left flank was vulnerable and decided to retire to Ernstbrunn with his rearguard posted a few kilometres to the south (*Wallach-Illyria* Grenz, 2nd *EH Carl* Legion, 3rd Brünn Landwehr, *Vincent* Chevaulegers No. 4, one cavalry battery). From its starting point at Enzersfeld, the corps had thus covered some 20–25 kilometres

Every Night a March, Every Day an Attack 119

during the day, picking up stray elements of I Corps along the way.[71] At Ernstbrunn Hohenzollern received orders to join the Main Army at Jetzelsdorf by easy marches; in the meantime, he was to establish communications with Rosenberg.

Also trudging through Großrußbach on 7 July was the 4th Unter-Manhartsberg (UMB) Landwehr, whose difficulties were noted earlier. This battalion, badly reduced by casualties and straggling, had reached Königsbrunn around 9:00 p.m. on the night of 6 July. As part of VI Corps, it should have been with Klenau at Korneuburg but it had become lost in the turmoil of the withdrawal during the night. Its commander, Major Ferdinand Graf Colloredo-Mansfeld, had been wounded on the 6th and leadership of the battalion's remnants thus fell to Hauptmann Maximilian Baron von Seckendorff who recorded his travails in an after-action report composed on 12 July. Starting from their halt at Königsbrunn, the frustrated Seckendorff left a dismal account of his command's experience.

> Here too the farms could provide nothing and my men remained without food. All efforts to locate the VI Corps were in vain, even the ammunition train could tell me nothing specific; all I knew for certain was that Mistelbach was the assembly point [this was false for VI Corps]. I departed after 2:00 a.m. on the 7th but, here too, many who could go no further remained behind. I marched through Seebarn to Großrußbach partly to move to the assembly point at Mistelbach, partly to escape the flood of the fleeing artillery parks and stragglers, and partly to secure at least some refreshment for my men. The plundering of our own troops in part and the near presence of the enemy had made my men desperate. In Großrußbach we finally succeeded in grabbing something to eat. Many of my officers, all of whom were on foot, could no longer keep up. At every step on the march from Großrußbach to Siebenhirten near Mistelbach we encountered cellars broken into, wine casks smashed open and plunder and wanton devastation; the discontent and desperation of the troops became so great that they took themselves to the woods in groups and neither pleading nor threats nor punishment could hold them back from hurrying to their homes to limit the destruction of

their own properties. In Siebenhirten my locally born men came to blows with stragglers from the army who had broken into [wine] cellars and plundered them. The darkness of the night contributed to the disorder.[72]

While the units facing the French retained their order and held off pursuit, as the 4th UMB Landwehr's experience demonstrates, there was no lack of chaos in the army's rear areas. Units wandered without orders, trains clogged the roads, Austrian soldiers pillaged their own people, and Landwehr battalions lost their cohesion under the pressures of the retreat. Most of those who lagged behind, of course, eventually fell into French hands.

While Hauptmann von Seckendorff was heading for Mistelbach by mistake, Rosenberg had intentionally and quite understandably chosen that town as his corps' destination. As with Hohenzollern's men, Rosenberg's regiments thus marched between 20 and 25 kilometres in the course of their retreat on 7 July, all the while contending with cumbersome baggage trains that 'jam themselves up in every direction'.[73] Obsessively concerned that his left (eastern) flank would be turned, Rosenberg detailed Radetzky's detachment to cover the route from Groß-Schweinbarth through Pirawarth to Gaweinstal, while withdrawing his main body up the Brünn highway from the heights above Bockfließ.

On the Brünn Highway: The Enemy Is in Full Retreat

The French followed Radetzky closely. It is not clear, however, precisely which French units were involved in the pursuit at this point. The light cavalry brigade of Oudinot's corps (c. 1,400) pressed the enemy up the Brünn highway collecting a considerable number of prisoners, and Montbrun's light cavalry division was certainly active (two brigades, perhaps 3,000 horsemen in all) on the French right. At least some infantry seem to have accompanied Montbrun but the identity of these troops cannot be ascertained.[74] Grouchy's division of dragoons had spent the night nearby and Grouchy had, according to Montbrun, 'as much interest as me in pursuing the enemy', but his dragoons do not seem to have had any role in the pursuit on the 7th.[75] Whatever the exact composition, these forces began exerting pressure on Radetzky's troops at 6:00 a.m. and indeed repeatedly edged around the Austrian left flank, validating

Rosenberg's worries.[76] The intensity of the pursuit increased during the day so that the questing French took Gaweinstal around noon, but the Austrian rearguard conducted itself well and held the pursuit at Schrick as evening came on. 'The enemy is in full retreat,' recorded Captain Maurice Charles Marie de Tascher of the 12th Chasseurs in Montbrun's division, 'but it is being conducted in good order.'[77] The rearguard's skill and the weakness of the pursuit meant that the baggage train was able to escape towards Znaim and Nikolsburg despite the 'monstrous disorder' among the supply wagons. Rosenberg was also pleased to report that most of his artillery had been rescued thanks to 'extraordinary exertions'.[78]

As the baggage wagons rumbled off into the night, the bulk of IV Corps established itself in the hills north of Mistelbach with two squadrons of the *O'Reilly* Chevaulegers No. 3 posted to guard the left flank towards Wilfersdorf and another squadron of the same regiment dispatched much farther north to watch the Brünn road just beyond Drasenhofen.[79] These cavalry deployments seem odd at first glance, but they made sense in light of Rosenberg's conception of his mission and his consequent withdrawal towards Laa: he was simply looking to establish a screen to protect his retreat to the northwest (towards Znaim). He would soon learn that his view of his role in relation to the army was very much mistaken.

Rosenberg's retreat on the 7th was carried out under verbal orders he had received as he was withdrawing from the Wagram battlefield on the evening of 6 July. Delivered by Hauptmann Michael von Schihotzky of the Engineer Corps, these instructions directed Rosenberg to occupy the Hochleithen Heights that night and then to initiate his retreat through Gaweinstal 'such that the army, which is withdrawing to Znaim, will always be covered on its left flank'.[80] This order must have seemed clear and logical to Rosenberg at the time and he reported that evening that he would attempt to maintain himself at Mistelbach 'as long as possible', but would retire towards Laa on the Thaya (Dyje) River 'if pressed by superior force'.[81] The archduke, however, had a different conception of the army's forthcoming movements. Charles, with his penchant for cordon defences and leaving nothing unprotected, regarded the fortresses of Olmütz and Brünn (the latter known as the Spielberg or Spilberk) as critical to the monarchy's security. He thus placed a high premium on retaining control of these positions and the large supply depots they guarded.[82] Neither he nor his staff, however, had apprised Rosenberg of the priority assigned to protecting these places.[83] Where Rosenberg, quite correctly, saw himself obeying orders by directing his future withdrawal northwest towards Laa and thus towards the army's left, Charles assumed IV Corps would retreat directly north along the highway to shield Brünn and Olmütz. This miscommunication between the archduke and the general would soon have grave consequences for the army.

Strategic Intentions: The Fate of a Second Battle?

In addition to the safety of Moravia, Charles addressed the larger strategic situation in his correspondence on the 7th. His attention to Olmütz highlighted the direct connection the Habsburg leadership perceived between events along the Danube and Russo-Polish actions along the Vistula, especially their worries, howsoever misguided, that Napoleon and the Russians were aiming to link up in Moravia.[84] He thus wrote at once to Archduke Ferdinand to inform him of the retreat from Wagram and to describe his orders to Rosenberg enjoining the latter to inform Ferdinand of 'his every step'. He also wrote to Johann, granting his younger brother authority over Chasteler's and Gyulai's forces in Hungary 'as our communications are extremely difficult and may be interrupted'. With these troops and his own, Johann was to see to the security of Hungary in coordination with Archduke Joseph the Palatine. Charles told both fellow archdukes that he intended to occupy the 'position' at Jetzelsdorf on 10 July 'where, circumstances permitting, I am thinking I may dare the fate of a second battle'.[85] He thus seems to have assumed at this stage that the majority of the French army would follow him on the road from Korneuburg through Stockerau towards Znaim.[86] He apparently gave no thought to issuing new instructions for FML Schustekh at Krems, even though Schustekh's division would become dangerously isolated as the Main Army proceeded north from Stockerau.

Charles did not neglect his elder brother in his correspondence as the army retreated. His letter to Kaiser Franz, however, showed him at his most dispirited. Reflecting some of the sentiments he had shared with his corps commanders in the angry circular cited earlier, his missive from his headquarters in Oberrohrbach was grim indeed.

> Yesterday I had a verbal report sent to Your Majesty on the outcome of the battle. Complete exhaustion has followed after two days of such extraordinary exertions and in many regiments actual disintegration. I hope that the enemy does not pursue us too rapidly as I would not be able to offer him much resistance and I cannot conceal from Your Majesty that this army cannot be counted on in its current condition. We have had heavy losses, but our loss will be infinitely heavier owing to the many marauders and stragglers who all fall into the enemy's hands.[87]

This discouraging assessment would set the stage for a change in Austria's approach to the war when the Kaiser met Charles at the latter's headquarters in Göllersdorf on 8 July.

Napoleon would have been gratified to read Charles's gloomy letter, but as midnight approached, the enemy situation was still murky. Berthier could tell Massena that night, however, that 'All intelligence leads to the belief that the enemy is retiring along the route to Nikolsburg and along that to Stockerau.' Rather than lose any more time, therefore, the emperor sent forces in both directions pending greater clarification of Austrian movements. Massena was directed to make himself master of Stockerau, an important magazine and a key junction from which two roads led to Bohemia and another to Krems. Although Napoleon expected that the Austrians would have already abandoned the north bank of the Danube, the marshal was to send strong patrols to the latter town to seize prisoners and establish communications with the Württemberg troops on the south bank of the river. He was also tasked with occupying the area around Floridsdorf, the terminus of the old Danube bridge that the Austrians had burned in May. As a result, he was not at liberty to employ his entire corps during the first two days of the pursuit. Napoleon, however, was also looking beyond the banks of the Danube. He already had his imperial eye on Znaim and informed Massena that 'if the enemy retires to Znaim, the advance guard that will depart from here for Nikolsburg will be in a position to move on the flank of any enemy that marches to Znaim'.[88]

The 'advance guard' mentioned in Massena's instructions was a new command formed around Marmont's Army of Dalmatia. 'The emperor,

'General Marmont, orders that you depart at midnight with your corps to draw as close to Nikolsburg as possible tomorrow, to overthrow the enemy's rearguard and, in sum, to do [the enemy] as much damage as possible,' Berthier wrote, 'H. M. counts on your talents and on your zeal.' Given the small size of Marmont's corps and its lack of both artillery and cavalry, Napoleon placed Minucci's 2nd Bavarian Division and Montbrun's light cavalry division under his orders. In addition to a welcome reinforcement of nine infantry battalions and six light cavalry squadrons (not including the two squadrons detached under Lindenau), the Bavarian division, having been bolstered for Wagram, brought along five artillery batteries with 36 guns to supplement Marmont's meagre 17 pieces, some of which were small mountain guns. Furthermore, the three light horse regiments of the *'brigade infernale'* from 2nd Corps were assigned to Montbrun. Now commanded by Colonel Pierre Edme Gauthrin of the 9th Hussars after Colbert's wounding at Wagram, the addition of this brigade gave Montbrun a total of nine light cavalry regiments for a force of as many as 4,600 troopers.

Berthier also wrote directly to Montbrun both to inform him of the new command arrangements and to instruct him to 'take yourself as far as possible along the route from Vienna to Nikolsburg'. He was to 'push the enemy and reconnoitre the country towards Znaim ... Take prisoners, collect information on the movement and situation of the enemy' and report twice daily to imperial headquarters as well as to Marmont. 'It is probable that you will take a great deal from the enemy at Nikolsburg,' he was told.[89]

As 7 July came to an end, therefore, both armies were still contending with considerable uncertainty. Charles, expecting Napoleon to follow him on the road to Bohemia, had charted out a plan for the next three days to establish the Hauptarmee in a defensive position near Jetzelsdorf and perhaps risk another battle. Rather than call Rosenberg back to participate in this potentially climactic struggle, he envisaged IV Corps protecting the Moravian fortresses of Olmütz and Brünn but had failed to communicate this intention clearly to Rosenberg. Napoleon, unsure of Austrian movements, had launched pursuit forces on both major routes in the hope that the coming day would provide more clarity. The fact that he referred to Marmont's corps as an 'advance guard' suggests that he was inclined, at least for a time, to expect that Charles would retreat up the Brünn highway with the bulk of the Hauptarmee. Indeed, Napoleon may have seen a retreat towards Brünn as the logical choice for Charles as it would have placed the Austrians midway between Bohemia and Hungary, able to protect and draw resources from both regions.[90] Absent more definitive information, however, Napoleon's dispositions remained flexible and he was committed to neither route as yet. He therefore retained the rest of the army in and around the Wagram battlefield: Davout, Oudinot and the Guard near Wolkersdorf; Eugène's Army of Italy and the Saxons encamped on the Marchfeld. From these central locations, he could reinforce either pursuit column or react should Johann make any threatening moves along the banks of the Danube. Both commanders had used Znaim as a reference point during the day, but neither yet expected a confrontation around this ancient Moravian town.

8 July: Uninterrupted Exertions and Continual Alerts

For Austria, 8 July was a day of both military and diplomatic manoeuvring. In what would be the pattern for the next several days, the Hauptarmee (minus II Corps) had marched through the night to occupy new positions as dawn broke on another enervatingly hot day.

On the Znaim Highway: My Troops Are Exhausted

That morning, Charles placed V Corps athwart the highway at Obermallebarn, III Corps at Untergrub and I Corps at Großmugl in what he envisaged as the army's right, centre and left respectively. The Grenadiers bivouacked along the highway behind V Corps in reserve, army headquarters was in Göllersdorf, and the Cavalry Reserve was positioned astride the main road north of Sierndorf in support of VI Corps. Klenau, reinforced by the *Blankenstein* Hussars from Liechtenstein's reserve, retained his mission as rearguard, placing his men on the heights between Sierndorf and Hatzenbach with a strong garrison in Stockerau.[91]

The French were on the move early, however, and Stockerau could not be held. Napoleon had relieved Massena of the requirement to guard the Danube near Floridsdorf, but the only forces the marshal had at hand

that morning were his light cavalry, St Sulpice's cuirassiers and Legrand's 1st Division; the remaining three divisions were echeloned along the road between Langenzersdorf and Jedlersee. Nonetheless, the French and their Baden allies advanced early in the morning. Led by an advance guard composed of the light cavalry and the Baden Jägers, Massena's column appeared east of Stockerau around 8:30 a.m. and attacked at once. They found the outskirts 'barricaded and defended by an entrenched enemy behind a small ravine located in front of that town; but the 2nd Cuirassier Division having arrived with its artillery, they employed it to dislodge all of those troops and enter into the town after chasing them off with loss'.[92]

Klenau, in the midst of drafting a status report to Charles, doubted that the detachment in the town could hold out and, indeed, he had to pen a note in the margins of his report before dispatching it to army headquarters: 'The enemy just took Stockerau at 11:00.'[93] Bavarian Oberst Lindenau, whose detachment had probed as far as Leitzersdorf, watched the advance of Bruyère's light horse and the 2nd Cuirassier Division, reporting that 'The enemy's resistance against these two divisions was not as strong as yesterday.'[94] Indeed, the French light cavalry, followed by the cuirassiers, pushed through Stockerau onto the plateau that carried the highway to Sierndorf and Znaim but were met by an Austrian charge that sent the French troopers tumbling back towards the town. The Baden Jägers, just exiting Stockerau, were surprised but coolly took up positions in buildings and gardens on the edge of town and repelled the Austrian horse. The Jägers pursued the retreating Habsburg troopers for a time until called back by a French staff officer, their place taken by the re-formed French cavalry, light regiments in the first line, cuirassiers in the second.

In the meantime, the capture of Stockerau had allowed Massena to push a task force out towards Krems in accordance with his instructions. He assigned this mission to the competent and energetic Colonel Auguste Jean Joseph Gabriel Ameil, commander of the 24th Chasseurs. With his regiment and the Baden Light Dragoons, Ameil was to 'observe without compromising himself'.[95] Ameil probed as far as Neuaigen, taking a number of prisoners and reporting, as Napoleon and Massena had expected, no contact with formed bodies of Austrian troops.[96]

While Legrand's French and Baden infantry pressed forward on both sides of Stockerau to cover the main roads leading north and northwest, other French forces advanced from Oberrohrbach and Rückersdorf through Leitzersdorf towards Hatzenbach. Among these other units were Gérard's chasseurs who probed as far as Niederfellabrunn, and Lindenau's two Bavarian squadrons who scooped up forty prisoners and deserters in their reconnaissance and skirmishes between Leitzersdorf and Hatzenbach.[97] The activity of the French and German horse as well as their numbers probably explains why Austrian accounts repeatedly refer to the enemy cavalry's numerical superiority. The French may have had more horsemen, but Massena's advance force was, in fact, outnumbered overall and its nearest supports too far away to assist. Aware that at least 100 guns and large numbers of troops had marched up the Znaim highway,[98] the marshal prudently refrained from pressing too hard and the fighting north of Stockerau devolved into a mutual cannonade peppered with heavy skirmishing.[99] Towards evening, Klenau became concerned that the French were preparing an attack and formed his infantry into battalion masses as a precaution, but no attack came and the firing slowly sputtered away.

Losses in dead and wounded on both sides were few (the Badeners had only one killed and three wounded, for example; the *Splenyi* Infantry one dead, four wounded and one missing), but as Charles had feared, the French swept up a considerable number of Austrian laggards. On the whole, therefore, as Colonel Pelleport, commander of Legrand's 18th Ligne, recalled 'Everything that day was limited to a cavalry engagement ... still we took several hundred prisoners, mostly stragglers, and seized what remained of several magazines.' The captured provisions seem to have included a supply of wine 'which delighted the soldiers'.[100] Additionally, Massena could report with some relief that he had been able to mount a horse briefly for the first time in five days. The injury he had sustained when his horse fell on the 3rd still pained him, however, and he travelled almost exclusively in his carriage for the remaining days of the pursuit.

Stockerau represented the end of the war for the small Hessian Chevaulegers Regiment. Not because it had suffered heavily in the fighting that day, but because its losses at Wagram, numerous detach-

Every Night a March, Every Day an Attack 129

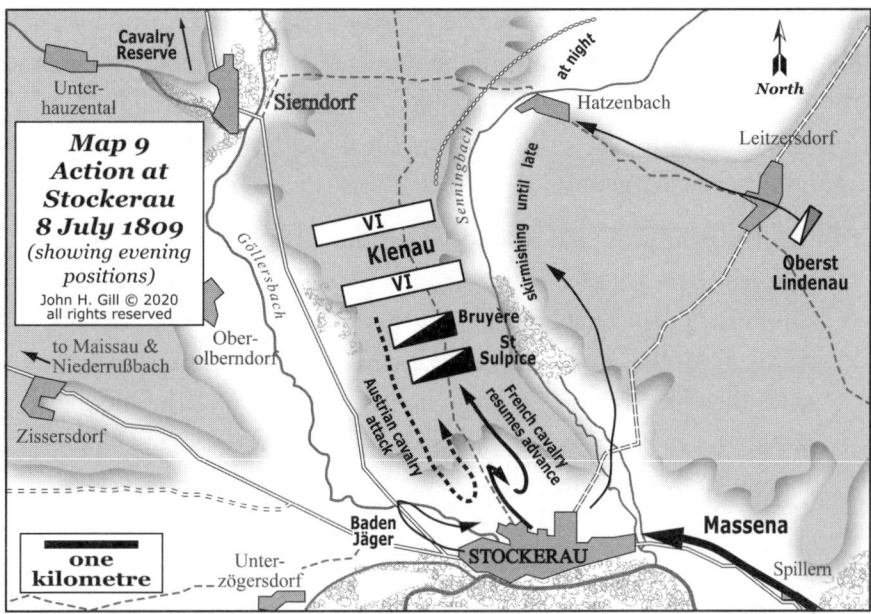

ments and the steady drain of attrition had reduced it to only a few dozen serviceable horses.[101] The small knot of remaining men and their mounts would thus be left behind when Massena marched north again on 9 July. It would not re-join 4th Corps until after the armistice.

Klenau's troops enjoyed no such luxury. Though the combat at Stockerau had not been severe, it was still enervating and the men of VI Corps, having marched through the night of 7/8 July and skirmished all day, now faced another trudge through the darkness. 'Extremely exhausted', they departed just after midnight headed for the next set of rearguard positions to the north.[102]

Klenau's corps, of course, was not the only Austrian formation on the road on the night of 8/9 July: the entire Hauptarmee was again making a march through the darkness, heading for new positions between Hollabrunn and Schöngrabern. The Habsburg host, accustomed to a measured pace of operations, methodical adherence to routine and the regular distribution of rations, was particularly vulnerable to the sort of disruptions it was now experiencing and the negative consequences of these repeated night moves were already becoming evident across the army. 'My troops are exhausted and I will have to use the most extreme means to obtain provisions,' wrote Klenau in an early morning report, 'My losses yesterday were considerable and a great many of my exhausted troops are collapsing by the roadside.' He requested immediate relief from rearguard duties.[103] Liechtenstein's depiction of the state of his cavalry was equally grim:

> The losses in dead and wounded that the Cavalry Reserve Corps suffered on the 5th and 6th are very considerable and its strength is so diminished that some brigades only have 200 files [c. 400 troopers] fit for duty. The uninterrupted exertions and the continual alerts since then have left the men and horses incapable of gathering the so urgently required fodder and food or of realising the recuperation they so badly need after many days of going without. The German breed of horses, as is well known, are badly effected by the lack of fodder and care, awakening in me the immediate worry of the complete exhaustion of all strength and, under such conditions, the danger arises of being thrown back on the army and completely wiped out if the overwhelming enemy attacks.

Like Klenau, Liechtenstein asked that the 'German cavalry' (i.e. the dragoon and cuirassier regiments) be placed 'in reserve behind the army' for a few days of rest out of action while his light regiments supported the rearguard if necessary.[104] How an experienced and courageous senior officer such as Liechtenstein could have imagined that any part of the army could be granted several days to rest and recuperate under the existing circumstances is difficult to comprehend. For Charles, of course, these reports only reaffirmed the deterioration he was witnessing every day with his own eyes.

The archduke had to wrestle with other operational problems as well. Among other things, staff work in army headquarters – never a strong point – seems to have suffered several significant lapses. Not only had the retreat orders for Reuss mistakenly gone to Hohenzollern, but, for a time on 8 July, headquarters did not know where V Corps was. Wimpffen thus sent an appeal to Klenau that morning to report on V Corps' location and to pass on the orders for the withdrawal. At the same time, Liechtenstein was directed to send a platoon of his weary cuirassiers in search of the missing corps.[105] Moreover, information about the enemy was hazy.

Charles specifically enjoined Klenau to collect reliable intelligence 'on the directions in which the enemy is following the army as well as on the strengths of every enemy column and report it to me',[106] but Klenau's subordinates claimed they were hindered by terrain and offered little by way of detail on the composition or strength of the French pursuit forces.[107]

Also slated for a night march was Schustekh's division on the Danube. Stretched along the river for many kilometres from Grafenwörth to Emmersdorf, Schustekh's men were to leave their watch-fires burning and depart that night to reach Maissau on 9 July. In another example of Charles's propensity for cordon-defensive concepts (i.e. defending everything), Schustekh was to post himself on the hills north of the town 'always alert to the movements of the enemy to ensure that the army's right flank cannot be compromised from the Horn highway especially via Sitzendorf'. He was also to cover the road to Bohemia via Horn and maintain liaison with Somariva north of Linz.[108] The Austrian penchant for detachments was also evident in Schustekh's withdrawal as small commands were scattered across the hills north of the river. One of these, under GM Johann Anton Graf von Hardegg, was to march to Sitzendorf to provide a link to the Main Army, while another was to remain at Krems as long as possible before retiring through Gföhl. Yet another detachment was dispatched towards Zwettl where it would join a task force under Oberstleutnant Karl von Scheibler.[109] This small mixed command of cavalry and 4th Jägers had been active along the Danube near Grein since the retreat from Bavaria in May. Scheibler had taken over in mid-June and now, placed under Schustekh's orders, was to screen the area between Zwettl and the Danube while maintaining communications with Somariva.[110] His march undisturbed by the enemy, Schustekh reached Maissau as planned with his main body, but two soldiers from Infantry Regiment No. 40 (former *Joseph Mittrowsky*) died of heat stroke and at least seventy men from the two Landwehr battalions were left behind along the way.[111]

On the eastern flank of the Hauptarmee, Hohenzollern's II Corps had spent the night at Ernstbrunn. His rearguard under GM Johann Ignaz Graf von Hardegg (elder brother of Anton and Heinrich) was in contact with the enemy but under no pressure. 'I find all here completely

> **Chart 3: Misaligned Austrian Units, 7–10 July**
> *(i.e. units unintentionally marching with different corps)*
>
> **With II Corps**
>
> | Unit | Original assigned corps |
> |---|---|
> | *EH Rainer* Infantry, No. 11 (2 companies) | I (returned on 10 July) |
> | *Argenteau* Infantry, No. 35 (II, III) | I (returned on 10 July) |
> | *Vogelsang* Infantry, No. 47 (all) | I (returned on 10 July) |
> | 4th *EH Carl* Legion (3 or 4 companies) | I (returned after armistice) |
>
> **With IV Corps**
>
> | Unit | Original assigned corps |
> |---|---|
> | *Hohenzollern* Cuirassiers, No. 8 | Reserve (to Altstern on 9 July) |
> | *Zach* Infantry, No. 15 (2 battalions) | II (returned on 10 July) |
> | I/former *Zedtwitz* Infantry, No. 25 | II (returned on 10 July) |
> | *Frelich* Infantry, No. 28 (all) | II (returned on 10 July) |
> | *Joseph Colloredo* Infantry, No. 57 (2 btn.) | II (returned on 10 July) |
> | 2nd Znaim Landwehr | II (returned on 10 July) |
> | 1st Brünn Landwehr | II (returned on 10 July) |
> | 3rd Brünn Landwehr | II (returned on 10 July) |
>
> The following had been assigned to other corps, but remained with IV Corps until after the armistice:
>
> | Unit | Original assigned corps |
> |---|---|
> | 'squadron'/*EH Johann* Dragoons, No. 1 | Cavalry Reserve |
> | *Deutschmeister* Infantry, No. 4 (3 btn.) | V Corps |
> | 6th UWW Landwehr | V Corps |
> | *Kerpen* Infantry, No. 49 (3 btn.) | V Corps |
> | 5th UWW Landwehr | V Corps |
> | *Beaulieu* Infantry, No. 4 (I, III) | V Corps |
> | 3rd UMB Landwehr | V Corps |

calm,' Hohenzollern reported.[112] In accordance with instructions from Charles to join the army in the proposed Jetzelsdorf position, he left Hardegg at Ernstbrunn and departed at 2:30 p.m. to make a relatively short, easy march of just over eighteen kilometres to Kammersdorf. Charles also directed Hohenzollern to dispatch a brigade to guard the crossing over the Thaya River at Laa on what would be the army's left flank. Hohenzollern, evidently unaware of the importance of this task, selected his weakest brigade, GM Johann Ritter Allmeyer von Altstern's, for this mission. Altstern's command in fact hardly qualified for the name 'brigade', consisting as it did of the much reduced *Rohan* Infantry No. 21 with only some 800 men and its battery of 6-pounders.[113] Altstern was told that he would find the *Hohenzollern* Cuirassiers, a squadron of *EH Johann* Dragoons and a cavalry battery already in place at Laa, but this was a request to Rosenberg rather than a fact when Altstern's men marched off from Ernstbrunn at 2:30 p.m. Hohenzollern dutifully informed Charles and Rosenberg that the brigade had been sent, while Altstern, as allowed by Hohenzollern's instructions, decided that the twenty-five kilometres to Laa was too much for one day and halted at Eichenbrunn for the night after only marching for four hours or so; he promised to cover the remaining twelve or thirteen kilometres the following day.[114]

As Altstern was heading north towards Laa (albeit slowly), the eight II Corps line battalions and three Landwehr battalions that had retreated with IV Corps were marching west to Seefeld to rejoin Hohenzollern as Charles had ordered.[115] The group was led by the senior regimental colonel, Oberst Carl Johann Baron Mecséry de Tsoor of *Frelich* Infantry No. 28, whose anxiety about his flanks and his vague mission was characteristic of many Austrian commanders during the uncertainties of the retreat after Wagram. Fortunately for Mecséry, he happened upon two weak squadrons of *Blankenstein* Hussars who performed reconnaissance for him and accompanied him to Seefeld where they arrived around 11:00 p.m.[116]

On the Brünn Highway: Your March Is Totally Inappropriate

Hohenzollern's retreat was almost undisturbed and Mecséry easily if nervously made his way to Seefeld, but Rosenberg on the Austrian far right flank was under considerable pressure and without clear, written orders. The French had begun jabbing at his rearguard as early as 5:30 a.m. and when it was eventually forced to withdraw to Mistelbach, Rosenberg sent the majority of his 'extremely fatigued troops' from Mistelbach in two columns back to Asparn an der Zaya and Hörersdorf. Among those men, deeply weary and desperate for sustenance, was Johann Schnierer, a soldier of *Deutschmeister* Infantry No. 4. He vividly recalled the miseries of the retreat as the corps made another march of 20–25 km on the 8th:

> Thirst and heat, which burned our necks and throats on these marches, were so overpowering that – as I can still see for myself now – a frog pond was nothing frightening or disgusting to me, nor to follow the example of others, lying on one's stomach and slurping up the stinking water with or without frog scum.[117]

The pursuit on this flank was now under Marmont's overall command and his troops entered Mistelbach at noon, initiating a fight for the town that went back and forth until French outflanking forces moved through Wilfersdorf and compelled an Austrian withdrawal around 4:00 p.m. With the French edging around his left, Rosenberg found it necessary to order the main body of IV Corps back to Laa on the Thaya River. He posted Radetzky's rearguard just northwest of Mistelbach on the road to Staatz, but the French, manoeuvring unexpectedly across a ridgeline, 'pushed forward so quickly' around 7:00 p.m. that they surprised the Austrians, captured several outposts and shoved Radetzky's line back to Siebenhirten where the fighting petered out as darkness drew on.[118] Radetzky, concerned that his lack of infantry made him vulnerable to another such French surprise, left the *Stipsicz* Hussars Nr. 10 behind in a thin line and withdrew his other three regiments to the slopes of the strikingly prominent hill just outside Staatz.[119]

Rosenberg, who had heard nothing from army headquarters since the brief verbal message delivered by Hauptmann Schihotzky on the evening of the 6th, dutifully reported to Charles. In two messages, he described the weariness of his men, the blockages caused by the baggage train, and 'whole swarms of stragglers from every army corps' that he was attempting to rally. He also asked for orders and, lamenting that he did not know where army headquarters was, asked Hohenzollern to pass on his reports and to reply with information on the overall situation. In outlining the enemy's movements and his own intentions, however, Rosenberg sparked alarm and anger when his notes finally reached Charles. The French, Rosenberg reported, were not only pressing his front in strength, they were also outflanking him on the left with 'a strong column of infantry and cavalry that is marching up the Brünn highway'. Indeed, his rearguard had supplied the specific (if exaggerated) intelligence that two enemy brigades were headed for Feldsberg (Valtice). Rosenberg thus saw himself opposed by enemy forces on his left towards Poysdorf as well as those to his front at Mistelbach. 'Incapable of resisting both corps,' he wrote that afternoon, 'I am forced to withdraw through Staatz towards Laa and, unless I receive orders from Your Imperial Highness late tonight, I will position myself behind the Thaya which I will endeavour to defend to the uttermost.'[120] For Charles, Rosenberg's news was shocking, his plans exactly contrary to the archduke's desires. Where Charles had envisaged IV Corps aligned along a more or less east–west line and facing south, it was now clear that it was actually ninety degrees off his concept, that is, arrayed on a north–south axis and oriented to the east. Rosenberg was already under a cloud for what Charles perceived as a poor showing at Wagram ('the troops of the left wing did not perform as I was justified in expecting of them') and this negative attitude doubtless informed the two stiff messages he sent to IV Corps that afternoon.

Rosenberg was at Laa with the bulk of his corps, thinking he had obeyed his orders to protect the army's left, when he received Charles's two messages of 8 July along with the previously missing orders from the 7th. 'The Feldmarschall-Leutnant will have perceived from my orders of yesterday that it was not my intention that the FML and his corps attach themselves to the left wing of the army,' began Charles, before pointedly specifying that he had wanted Rosenberg to take 'his retreat along the shortest route to Brünn and Olmütz' and provide these places with adequate garrisons. That Rosenberg had retreated towards Laa was 'completely unexpected' and thereby left 'open to the enemy the main access roads to Brünn and Olmütz completely in such as way' that these places could be captured unimpeded by a few advance detachments. Moreover, Rosenberg's actions endangered Archduke Ferdinand 'who is holding himself far forward on the road to Krakow for as long as possible'. This was bad enough, but Charles added a second brief note to restate that, 'I regard your march to Laa as totally inappropriate as I have made the greatest possible protection of the Brünn road and the provision of a garrison for Olmütz your duty.' The archduke's use of the word 'duty' was especially barbed, reiterating a phrase ('your special duty') he had employed in the delayed 7 July orders.[121] This incident with Rosenberg seems to have lodged in Charles's mind and he would refer to his vexation repeatedly in letters to Ferdinand, Johann and even Hohenzollern over the next several days.

Rosenberg must have been horrified to read these curt messages in Laa that night. But he was also indignant and hastened to reply with a justification that he had followed the verbal order delivered by Schihotzky 'exactly' and had only learned of Charles's desires on the evening of the 8th around 7:00 p.m. when he encountered a courier as he was marching to Laa. He promised, of course, to move to the Brünn road with a 'double march' on the following day while co-ordinating with the Moravian Regional Command, dispatching Hohenzollern's troops, providing army headquarters with a corps strength report, and informing Archdukes Ferdinand and Johann of his mission and location. He was troubled, however, that Altstern had not yet arrived in Laa and thus decided to leave *Zach* Infantry No. 15 at the river crossing with the *Hohenzollern* Cuirassiers until Altstern turned up. Additionally, he apprised Hohenzollern of his plans and warned his fellow corps commander to pay close attention to the security of the II Corps' left flank as 'the enemy has already sent a strong column to Feldsberg' and 'is pursuing my rearguard relentlessly'.[122]

Blame for this muddle between Charles and Rosenberg can be distributed in both directions, but the greater culprits would seem to be Charles and the army staff. On Rosenberg's side, although he followed the verbal instructions he had received 'exactly', he does not appear to have forwarded any reports on his corps and its actions on 7 July, a fault that left headquarters in the dark about its left-flank formation. Charles, however, apparently succumbed to wishful thinking in his belief that Rosenberg had intuited his desire to give top priority to the protection of Brünn and Olmütz. With no communication from the corps commander and no confirmation that his orders had been delivered, Charles nonetheless convinced himself that all was proceeding as intended on his left flank. He also displayed his predilection for cordon defences and evinced a curious anxiety about the safety of the supply depots in Brünn and Olmütz, repeatedly reminding Rosenberg of their importance at a time when the safety of the army and indeed the monarchy was at stake. The army staff does not seem to have helped their Generalissimus in this case. It was standard practice in many armies to send multiple copies of important dispatches by different couriers on different routes to ensure delivery. That does not seem to have occurred here. Nor does anyone seem to have thought to send officers or cavalry patrols in search of IV Corps.

Regardless of how one apportions responsibility – and much was simply a matter of the challenges of command and control over long distance in the age of the horse – the upshot was a danger to the archduke's plans and indeed to the army. If all went as Charles ordered, by the evening of 9 July, when Rosenberg marched off to cover the Brünn road and Hohenzollern joined the Main Army at Jetzelsdorf, a gap of some 30–40 km would be created between IV Corps and the left wing of the Hauptarmee in Charles's new 'position'. Other than cavalry patrols and a few odd detachments, the only substantial force in this space would be Altstern's brigade. Yet this small unit of perhaps 800 infantry, 200 cavalry, two artillery batteries and no support in sight was to guard a major road where it crossed a significant river only 12–15 km from the army's left wing. Should the French find this gap and overwhelm Altstern, Charles's chosen defensive line near Jetzelsdorf would be outflanked and his line of retreat to Bohemia in danger. This, of course, is precisely what would transpire in a few short days.

Marmont: Put Myself on the Enemy's Trail

For much of 8 July, however, the French were still uncertain of the Hauptarmee's location. Napoleon knew the Austrians were retreating into Bohemia, but as he wrote to his Minister of War: 'As of now we do not really know what the enemy wants to do.'[123] A number of intelligence and reconnaissance reports suggested that 'only the grand baggage and the artillery' were on the Brünn road and 'the entire army is headed to Iglau (Jihlava) in Bohemia via Znaim', but Massena concluded that he was only facing Klenau supported by some additional cavalry. Even though he correctly identified Charles's headquarters locations on the road to Znaim, he asserted that 'the major portion of the main body has taken the road to Brünn'.[124] Marmont, on the other hand, had a more accurate idea of the enemy's dispositions and intentions. 'The entire Austrian army has quit the road to Nikolsburg,' he wrote from Wilfersdorf at noon, and 'very confused reports' led him to believe that part of the enemy force had left Mistelbach and was retiring towards Laa.[125] Four hours later, he was more confident in the available intelligence and more decisive in his reactions to it:

> I have the honour to report to Your Majesty that the reconnaissance sent to Mistelbach has returned with some prisoners; the reports of the prisoners as well as those of the inhabitants accord in stating that a large portion of the army passed through this town between yesterday and 7:00 this morning and passed on successively; that Prince Rosenberg slept here last night; that all of the troops passed through Siebenhirten and moved towards Ehrendorf [now Ernsdorf]; that the general rumour is that these troops will take themselves to Laa: this uniformity among the reports and the certainty that no one has passed up the grand highway [the Brünn road]; finally the direction taken by the cavalry that we have found has led me to decide to quit the main highway and put myself on the enemy's trail via Mistelbach and Ehrendorf. I count on sleeping in Ehrendorf tonight.[126]

Marmont's troops were also hoping for some rest. 'There was a general dearth of forage and food after these extremely taxing marches,' wrote Unterleutnant Ludwig von Madroux of the Bavarian 2nd Chevaulegers, 'Especially noticeable in the unbroken and unusual heat was the lack of potable water, as all of the villages were abandoned and the wells filled in.' 'The heat and fatigue are very wearing,' noted Captain Tascher of the 12th Chasseurs, 'How precious a little broth is when you've been deprived for a long time!' He also commented on the desolation the armies inflicted on the local populace: 'The damage that we do is incalculable. Everything is sacked, broken, given over to pillage. Either because of carelessness or for other reasons, it often happens that entire villages are reduced to ashes.'[127] 'We took the route to Brünn which was covered with troops hidden in a long cloud of dust,' wrote Sergeant Desboeufs of the 81st Ligne, 'The heat, the thirst and the dust altered our features in such a manner as to render us unrecognisable. The eyes were sunk into the head, the cheeks, forcing their way into the mouth, formed a hollow on either side and the dry tongue could not articulate any sound.'[128] Those who could not sustain the pace of the 'very rapid march' under 'the ardent sun' sometimes suffered from their own officers as well as from the climate. 'The young troops were struggling to keep up,' recalled Cadet de Gassicourt, 'I was mortified to see some officers strike the conscripts who, succumbing to the weight of their arms and the heat, dragged themselves along too slowly... These were the victors, and they were mistreated!' he lamented.[129]

As Marmont was drafting his 4:00 p.m. report and his men were hoping for some respite, Berthier was issuing a stream of orders from imperial headquarters in response to the general's noon message. In the first place, he replied directly to Marmont: 'The emperor gives you a free hand to march towards Znaim if, by this means, you believe you will find yourself closer to the enemy's left.' He also informed Marmont that Davout's corps was on the march to Wilfersdorf and should arrive around 8:00 p.m. Furthermore, that Massena was in Stockerau and, 'if the enemy is on the road to Znaim, he will pursue them and likely be in Hollabrunn this night'.[130] The prediction on Massena's possible progress was hopelessly optimistic, but Napoleon now gave the marshal the liberty to employ his entire corps (part of which had been detained to guard the Danube crossing at Floridsdorf) to pursue the enemy and told him that Marmont was at Wilfersdorf 'turning left to take himself to Znaim'. Indeed, 'It is difficult for me to believe that the enemy is not retreating towards Znaim as the route to Prague through Znaim is much shorter than that which passes through Horn.' As far as Krems was concerned, Massena 'could content himself with sending some patrols to pick up the stragglers, baggage, etc. that have followed the left bank of the Danube'.[131] The flurry of orders bursting out of imperial headquarters that afternoon also directed Davout to march for Wilfersdorf at once and assigned both Grouchy's dragoons and the cuirassiers of Arrighi's division to his command. Additionally, Bernadotte was ordered to reconnoitre towards the March River, Pully's dragoons were returned to the Army of Italy, Viceroy Eugène was instructed to assume responsibility for Floridsdorf from Massena, and Marshal Lefebvre at Linz was informed of Massena's advance to Stockerau.[132]

On the strategic plane, Napoleon was also thinking of Russia. A number of senior Russian officers had been with imperial headquarters for several weeks and had observed the Battle of Wagram first hand. Napoleon now dispatched one of these, Tsar Alexander's trusted aide-de-camp Alexander Ivanovich Chernishev, with a personal letter to his fellow sovereign after a silence of almost three months. Though disappointed and angry at the lethargic and largely non-violent Russian promenade through Poland, it was in Napoleon's interest to maintain the façade of the Russian alliance and to motivate Alexander to pressure Austria. It was also important for him to keep the aura of his military power brightly burnished and to remind the tsar that France was the offended party in this war, inexplicably attacked by a deluded Austria. After providing a few military details of Wagram, his 8 July letter reinforced these points.

> The Battle of Wagram, of which Your Majesty's aide-de-camp, who was present on the battlefield throughout, can render an account, has fully realised my hopes. The Austrian army, cut off from Hungary, is retiring to Bohemia. I am in pursuit; my advanced posts are at Nikolsburg and towards Znaim. During the entire month when we were facing one another, where I was master of Vienna and they a thousand *toises* on the other bank, not only did they show me no insinuation of peace, but I received nothing but evidence of bitterness, and convinced myself of their foolish presumption. This is not to be believed, but it is exact.[133]

In addition to imperial correspondence, Napoleon was careful to treat his Russian guests with meticulous courtesy. With Chernishev's departure, three of the others followed Massena's corps and would be present at Hollabrunn, Schöngrabern and Znaim itself. One of these officers, Vladimir Ivanovich Baron Löwenstern, recorded that 'We received en route every imaginable attention. Napoleon had given very precise orders on this subject. The best houses were placed at our disposal; guards of honour were provided for us, the local commandants furnished us with forage; in sum, nothing was lacking.'[134]

As Chernishev was making for St Petersburg with Napoleon's letter and numerous other instructions were emanating from imperial headquarters, the late afternoon of 8 July did not see any significant orders for Oudinot or for the Guard, however. Oudinot was to round up prisoners and collect intelligence,[135] but otherwise these formations remained encamped in the general vicinity of Wolkersdorf as the army's reserve. Nansouty's large heavy cavalry division and Gérard's light regiments were centrally placed between Rückersdorf and Stetten, but likewise had no new orders. This relative inactivity has occasioned criticism as the two pursuit forces of Marmont and Massena were too far apart to permit mutual support and both were at least two marches distant from the forces at Wolkersdorf (*c.* 50 km in each direction). Indeed, Massena was left in relative isolation, especially as his corps was stretched out over 25 km from Sierndorf to Jedlersee. One French historian of 1809 even disparages the move of Davout to Wilfersdorf as a 'half-measure' because Davout was not committed definitively to the road to Znaim but left to push for Nikolsburg, that is, away from Znaim. Nor was Davout, as the senior general, placed in charge of this ad hoc 'wing', a lapse that has occasioned criticism from some later commentators.[136] He and Marmont were only instructed to communicate and co-operate with one another. Davout duly wrote to apprise Marmont of his arrival and to offer his support, but Marmont blithely told the marshal 'It seems to me that I have all that I need to defeat Rosenberg's corps.' Marmont had a good idea that the force he was chasing numbered no more than 14,000 to 15,000, but he did not know, of course, that he would soon be facing the bulk of the Hauptarmee on his own.[137] Years later, when composing his memoirs, he acknowledged his error:

> I received during that day a letter from Marshal Davout, who had arrived at Wilfersdorf with his corps; he requested the latest information from me and informed me that he was ready to support me if I needed assistance. I told him what had occurred up to that moment and that I was going to Znaim ... I contented myself with informing him of these things without calling him to me or requesting support, and I was wrong. The destruction of the Austrian army, and therefore of the monarchy, may have followed that circumstance. One can conceive of my motives, and they seem excusable. I truly had nothing but inferior forces before me and it is a sort of modesty not to request support when one does not need it; it is also rather ridiculous to do otherwise: I had just rejoined the main army and I did not want to dishonour myself by appearing weak or fearful.

Napoleon suspected that Marmont wanted to operate on his own rather than under some other general, especially the notoriously tough Marshal Davout.[138] Many subsequent commentators have taken this interpretation. Marmont, however, specifically denied this allegation. 'I always had too much conscience, I was always too chary of my soldiers' blood to make such a calculation,' he wrote, 'I thought I would have to wait until the moment when the need seemed evident to me before calling on the assistance that was offered.'[139]

Thus Marmont's thinking and his consequent actions. With the benefit of hindsight, one may also wonder why Napoleon did not shift at least Oudinot and Nansouty to some mid-point between the two pursuit forces. At Ernstbrunn, for example, this reserve would have been placed approximately one *'marche de guerre'* or forced march of some 25 km from both Hollabrunn and Laa, the immediate destinations of Massena and Marmont respectively. From Ernstbrunn, these formations could have followed more or less the route Hohenzollern was taking on his retreat and would have been well positioned to move on Znaim if necessary as the situation evolved. That, again, is hindsight in comfort. In the event, no such orders were issued. The result, however, was that both Massena and Marmont, especially the latter, would be in no little danger on 10 July and Napoleon would be limited in his options on the 11th when he confronted Charles at Znaim.

Charles: A Few Days' Rest

Despite the French advances during the day, as 8 July waned, Charles did not anticipate any threat to his chosen course of action and hoped to grant the army 'a few rest days' in the Jetzelsdorf 'position'.[140] On a series of steep ridges that rise up suddenly behind the Pulkau stream as one approaches the border of Moravia from the south, Jetzelsdorf was one of the commonly known defensive 'positions' throughout the monarchy that was recognised for supposedly affording significant advantages to the defender such as safe routes of retreat and supply, good visibility, ease of movement for reserves and space to array an army appropriate to a formal set-piece battle. As a proper 'position', it simultaneously presented any attacker with formidable difficulties of terrain (attacking uphill, across a water obstacle, and so on). In the words of one of Charles's former staff officers, then Major Ludwig Freiherr von Welden, Jetzelsdorf was 'perfectly suited for the positioning of an army'.[141] These advantages, of course, were all predicated on the attacker approaching from the proper direction. This sort of thinking represented a comfortable old style of warfare for the Austrian leaders, including Charles: slower, more methodical and pedantically focused on geographic objectives. This was not the sort of war waged by Napoleon. Nonetheless, Charles remained confident in the strength of this 'position' as a refuge for the army after its recent setbacks. He seemed equally confident that Napoleon would somehow cease the pursuit and permit the Hauptarmee a few days of rest. This latter assumption was baffling, yet it featured regularly in the calculations of Habsburg commanders throughout 1809 as if the old empire had not been at war with Revolutionary and Imperial France since 1792.

From his headquarters in Göllersdorf, Charles thus told his brother Johann 'I will march to Schöngrabern tonight and arrive at Jetzelsdorf the day after tomorrow with five army corps, the sixth constitutes my rearguard under FML Klenau, and Prince Rosenberg covers the Brünn road.' Even though Rosenberg had reported the 'considerable column' approaching Feldsberg, the archduke does not seem to have had any apprehension that this 'considerable column' might swing to the west against his planned position. Indeed, he may have even begun to think of attacking. At least he wanted to give Johann that impression as he concluded his 8 July letter with 'I will be able to maintain myself at Jetzelsdorf and, according to circumstances, consider making an offensive move.'[142]

While assessing his military options, the archduke was relieved that a first step had been taken towards peace. Franz had discussed the possibility of approaching Napoleon with Stadion and Metternich on the 7th when the imperial entourage was in Ernstbrunn. In the course of long conversations, the Kaiser, against Stadion's urgings, decided to send Liechtenstein to Napoleon to investigate the possibilities for peace: 'If not a negotiation, at least to initiate a sounding that could illuminate Napoleon's intentions; to learn if Napoleon wants peace and what he understands as peace.'[143] In part, this decision seems to have been based on Metternich's experiences during his detention in Vienna in June. In several interactions with French generals and officials, Metternich had gained the strong impression that the French were ready and possibly even eager to enter into negotiations.[144]

The following day, 8 July, the Kaiser and Charles met twice at Charles's headquarters, once in the morning and once after lunch.[145] There is no known written record of their conversations, but Franz clearly indicated his inclination towards opening some sort of negotiation with an aim of achieving an end to the war. He drafted a series of questions for Charles, requesting the archduke's assessment of the army's status, his current and future operational intentions, desirable peace conditions, contingency plans should Napoleon reject Liechtenstein, and ideas on improving Austria's circumstances 'during the necessary duration of negotiations' should any such eventuate. Perhaps he was persuaded of his army's debilities after Wagram. He had Charles's disheartening report of the 7th, and the archduke's answers to the 8 July questions restated his worry about heavy losses from the battle and the large number of stragglers on the retreat. Furthermore, in answering the question on what Austria should do if Napoleon spurned its peace initiative, Charles offered the dramatic but less than encouraging reply: 'Continue the war with the few resources that can be mustered in order to at least succumb with honour'.[146]

Charles doubtless reiterated his anxieties verbally in his conversations with his imperial brother. Additionally, it is hard to believe that Franz did not witness some of the chaos and exhaustion himself as he travelled from Ernstbrunn to Hollabrunn and then to Jetzelsdorf and Znaim that day. Perhaps he expected little from Liechtenstein's mission, but thought it could do no harm and might gain his empire some time. Stadion's biographer, for instance, opined that the Kaiser did not believe Napoleon would accept Liechtenstein and agreed to the mission merely to avoid being accused of not exploring every possible avenue towards peace.[147]

Whatever informed Franz's decision, the upshot of all these discussions and deliberations was a brief note from Franz to Charles sent from his lodgings at the 'Three Princes' inn in Znaim that evening: 'My dear brother Archduke Charles, as I have decided to send Gen. d. Cav. Pr. Liechtenstein to Emperor Napoleon without delay, Your Lordship should at once therefore take the required measures to set an agreement with the enemy outposts and whatever else might be necessary thereto.'[148] Though Charles welcomed the peace mission, his bitterness and frustration over the pointless delay came through in a letter to Herzog Albert. 'Prince Johann has been sent to Napoleon to see if something could not be arranged,' he wrote, 'Did we have to wait until we had lost a battle?'[149]

Stadion's resignation added further drama to the political scene on 8 July. Believing he could not serve as foreign minister under the evolving circumstances, Stadion submitted his resignation to the Kaiser and Franz accepted, designating Metternich to assume Stadion's role at the foreign ministry. Metternich remonstrated with Stadion to no avail and Franz would not reconsider his acceptance, but all eventually agreed that making the change public at such a crucial time would be detrimental to the monarchy's interests. They therefore decided that Metternich would accompany the Kaiser with de facto responsibility for foreign affairs (he would soon be granted the vague title of 'state minister'), while Stadion would remain with Charles and the army both to advise and to monitor the archduke.[150] He would also retain responsibility for relations with Prussia and with the various anti-French factions in Germany. It would seem from this decision that Franz was already determined to remove himself from Bohemia and transfer his court to Hungary. Rather than remaining in proximity to the army when existentially important negotiations were expected to begin, the Habsburg Kaiser would thus take himself days away and be unavailable for personal consultation. It is not clear who convinced Franz to shift to Hungary – even Stadion advised against it[151] – but the adoption of this course of action suggests that 'the vacillating monarch' was once again under the influence of the most fervid advocates of continuing the war.[152] On 8 July there seemed no particular urgency in starting the Kaiser's journey to Hungary, but events would soon accelerate his departure.

9 July: I Am Overwhelmed with Fatigue

As church bells announced the approach of midnight on the night of 8/9 July, the Austrian army was again on the move. The bulk of it wearily trudged off to new positions between Hollabrunn and Schöngrabern with army headquarters further north at Guntersdorf. Klenau's tired corps, reinforced by six squadrons of the *Blankenstein* Hussars, remained the rearguard. Its positions, described in detail in the army 'disposition' issued on the 8th, left it thinly stretched from Oberfellabrunn on the right through Hollabrunn on the highway to Weyerburg and Enzersdorf im Thale on the army's left, a distance of some 17 km. Hohenzollern's II Corps was encamped around Kammersdorf with Mecséry and its missing battalions at Seefeld on what was envisaged as the left flank of the future Jetzelsdorf position. Altstern rested at Eichenbrunn. The main body of Rosenberg's corps was at Laa with Radetzky and most of the rearguard at Staatz and the *Stipsicz* Hussars in a screening position watching the road at Hörersdorf. Only a lone squadron of *O'Reilly* Chevaulegers covered the Brünn highway near Drasenhofen south of Nikolsburg. On the opposite flank, Schustekh was moving to Maissau, with multiple small detachments on the roads leading up from the Danube.

Having thrown a cordon across the entire front from Maissau to Laa and having brusquely ordered Rosenberg to protect the routes to Brünn and Olmütz, Charles looked forward to occupying the Jetzelsdorf position and gaining a few days for the army to rest, recuperate and reorganise. Charles was himself nearing the limits of his physical endurance. Two days earlier, GM Johann von Delmotte, one of the archduke's senior aides-de-camp, had written to Herzog Albert that 'We are without baggage, without servants and are wearing our entire wardrobes on our backs, it has been three days since we have eaten.' Now Charles himself told his uncle, 'I am overwhelmed with fatigue, but at least I can undress tonight and sleep in my bed.'[153] Unfortunately for Charles, his repose would prove short-lived.

Napoleon also needed rest. He was indisposed for much of 9 July, suffering from a 'fever of fatigue' evidently brought on by want of sleep and the extraordinary exertions of the preceding several days.[154] This may explain the relative lack of correspondence from imperial headquarters on the 9th and the paucity of new orders for the army's reserves. Late that night, Nansouty did receive orders to move to Wilfersdorf on the 10th, but Oudinot and the Guard were left in their encampments around Wolkersdorf. Nonetheless, detailed instructions were issued for the security of the army's rear while the pursuit of the Hauptarmee continued. The

Every Night a March, Every Day an Attack

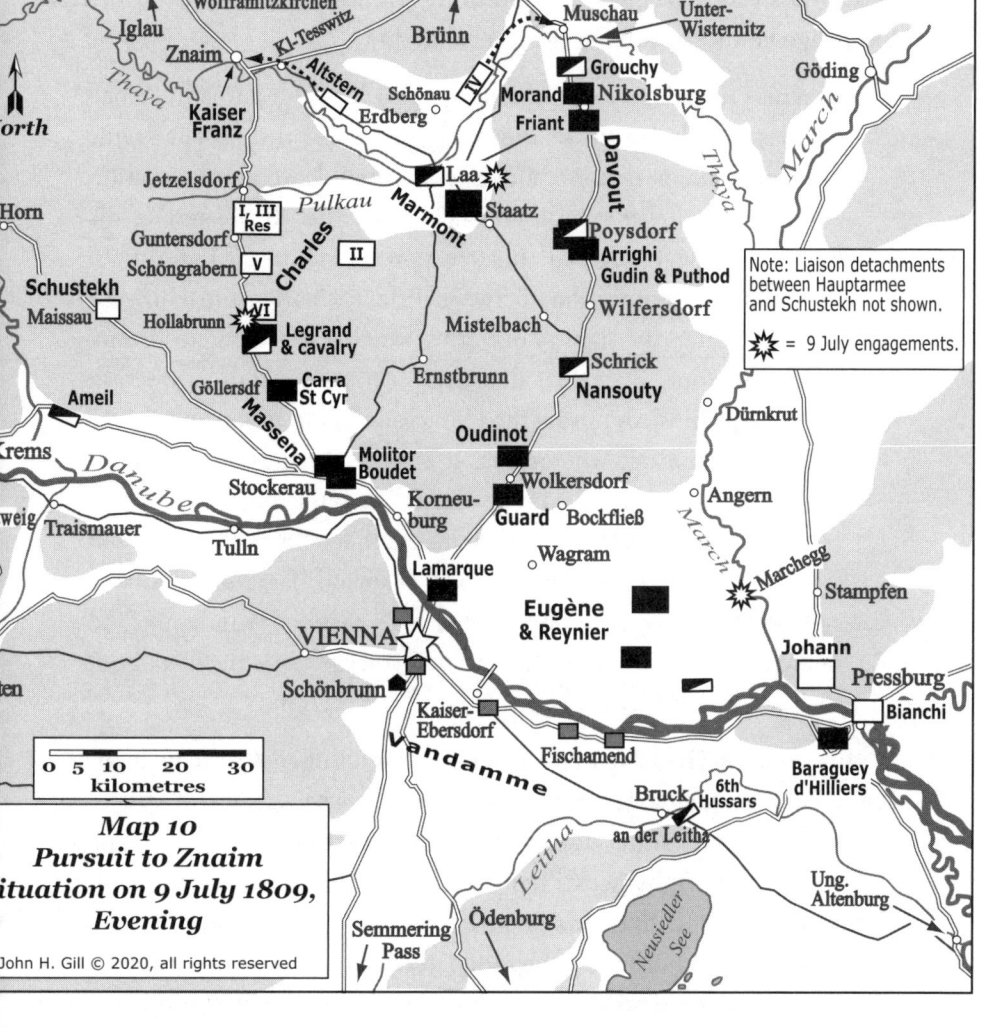

Map 10
Pursuit to Znaim
Situation on 9 July 1809,
Evening

John H. Gill © 2020, all rights reserved

most important of these were orders that placed all troops from the Marchfeld to Carinthia and Styria under Viceroy Eugène. In addition to his own Army of Italy on the Wagram battlefield and Baraguey d'Hilliers at Pressburg, therefore, Eugène would now command Vandamme's Württemberg 8th Corps, the Saxon contingent, GD Jean Rusca who was marching up from Villach to occupy the Semmering Pass southwest of Vienna, and other detachments on the south bank of the Danube.[155] He was also given control over the little flotilla of river gunboats that had been constructed prior to Wagram. Although he was to leave 'a few battalions' to protect the bridge being rebuilt at Floridsdorf, his first order of business was locating and containing Archduke Johann as outlined in a message he received from Berthier that day.[156]

> Where is Archduke Johann? It seems that he wanted to join Prince Charles but the result of the battle prevented this. What seems most probable is that Archduke Johann will leave an observation corps on the lower March and take himself with the rest of his forces and the Hungarian Insurrection to Göding (Hodinin) to maintain communications between Prince Charles and Hungary and to threaten the right of our army which is marching to Brünn. You know, Your Grace, that all of this is conjecture and, as your task has as its purpose opposing the Hungarian Insurrection and Prince Johann, you must go wherever he is. Thus, if it is true that this prince is moving up the March, your headquarters should be placed so as to rejoin the army if Prince Johann rallies to that of Prince Charles. But if he passes the Danube at Pressburg, General Baraguey d'Hilliers can destroy his bridge and, united with General Vandamme, so retard the march of Prince Johann that you can cross the Danube at the Ebersdorf bridge and arrive in time to meet him.

These comprehensive instructions granted Eugène the leeway to cross the March if necessary, but the key object was securing the army's rear. 'The emperor hopes that during the day tomorrow [10 July] you will have swept the entire right [west] bank of the March, that you will be master of the bridges, and that this river will be between you and the enemy'. Vandamme would move his headquarters and most of his troops to the vicinity of Fischamend downstream from Vienna, leaving only enough men behind to garrison Melk, Göttweig and a few other key locales. The flotilla would likewise shift to Fischamend near the confluence of the March with the Danube to support river crossings, intelligence-gathering and combat operations as required.

In hindsight, the French concern for the March River, specifically for Dürnkrut and Göding, seems surprising, but many of the reports arriving in imperial headquarters on the morning of 9 July highlighted the danger to 'the right flank and rear of our army'.[157] Supplied by reliable, experienced officers, this was intelligence Napoleon could not ignore. At the same time, he did not waver in his focus on the Austrian Hauptarmee and, as demonstrated by the weakness of Baraguey d'Hilliers's small division opposite Pressburg (5,200) and the minuscule garrison at Raab (1,100), he was prepared to take considerable risk in his rear areas. Much of the information coming in to Wolkersdorf on the 9th, however, only served to cloud an already murky picture of the enemy situation. Based on reconnaissance and interrogations conducted during the previous day, these reports induced an understandable degree of prudence in the orders issued to the army on 9 July. The veil of uncertainty would not be torn open until the evening hours leading into the 10th.

Beyond the lengthy directive to Eugène, a host of other orders flowed out of Wolkersdorf on 9 July concerning the defence of Vienna and the army's organisation. The Austrian capital was to be placed in a state of readiness and provisioned to sustain a garrison of 6,000 men for six months, the great Tabor highway bridge that the Austrians had burned in May was to be rebuilt, and an independent redoubt was to be constructed near Floridsdorf to protect its north bank terminus.[158] A different order dissolved the 9th Corps.[159] Bernadotte was quietly dismissed and GD Reynier was placed in command of the Saxon contingent as a separate division, initiating an affiliation that would continue through the great trials of 1812 and 1813.[160] In this new configuration the contingent came under Eugène's orders, as noted above, and a scouting detachment engaged in indecisive skirmishing with Johann's men west of Marchegg on 9 July.[161] The two French regiments of the former 9th Corps were assigned to Massena, but these units, having suffered heavy casualties at Wagram, needed time to recover and would not reach their new divisions until after the armistice.[162]

Engagement at Hollabrunn: The Bitterest Fighting

In the meantime, the pursuit continued, leading to sharp engagements on both routes. On the Stockerau–Znaim road, Massena planned to drive north with his substantial cavalry followed by Legrand and Carra St Cyr. He ordered Molitor and Boudet to hold their divisions in Stockerau 'particularly to cover the route to Maissau' because information he had gathered in the town led him to believe that the Austrian V Corps 'would have taken a direction other than Znaim'. He was confident that he could fall back upon these two divisions or call them forward as circumstances required.[163] This misinterpretation doubtless stemmed from the retreat of Schustekh's division, which was after all an element of V Corps, and the fact that Massena had not encountered any V Corps units during the pursuit thus far. In the event, his 4th Corps was so spread out that Molitor and Boudet would not reach Stockerau until late in the day and Carra St Cyr would be well beyond supporting distance when his cavalry and Legrand confronted the Hauptarmee's rearguard at Hollabrunn. By a coincidence of war, Legrand, then leading the 3rd Division of Marshal Soult's 4th Corps, had fought at Hollabrunn in mid-November 1805 with both the 26th Léger and the 18th Ligne under his command.[164]

The ferocious engagement at Hollabrunn opened with a cavalry preliminary as the French horse came upon Klenau's rearguard near Großstelzendorf around 9 a.m. These were *Liechtenstein* Hussars No. 7 under FML Ludwig Georg Thedel Freiherr von Wallmoden-Gimborn and they were quickly pushed back to a low rise some 3.5 km south of Hollabrunn. Klenau had posted two infantry regiments (*Benjovszky* No. 31 and *Spleny* No. 51) on this height to cover the cavalry's withdrawal, but the infantry, too, were soon forced to retire to the town with III/*Benjovszky* making its way through the vineyards east of the highway to protect the left flank.[165] The French cavalry were close behind and Klenau himself was in danger of capture when he and a small escort of hussars ventured too near a French patrol while scouting the terrain.[166]

Hollabrunn, known as Ober-Hollabrunn at the time, sits in a shallow bowl along the Göllersbach with high ground to the north, south, and east. In 1809, it was principally oriented north–south along the highway and the wooded hills to the east combined with the hindrance of the stream made it difficult to approach the town from the south, while a stout walled churchyard in its centre made a good defensive strongpoint. The hills to the northwest afforded artillery good fields of fire on the highway and the low ground west of the town. In all, the position was well suited to the sort of delaying action Klenau was called upon to perform as the army's rearguard.

The VI Corps had reached Hollabrunn at 7:00 a.m. and, leaving his rearguard at Großstelzendorf and on the aforementioned rise south of Hollabrunn, Klenau disposed the bulk of his corps on the hills behind the town. He placed GM Peter Vécsey at Porrau with the *Kienmayer*

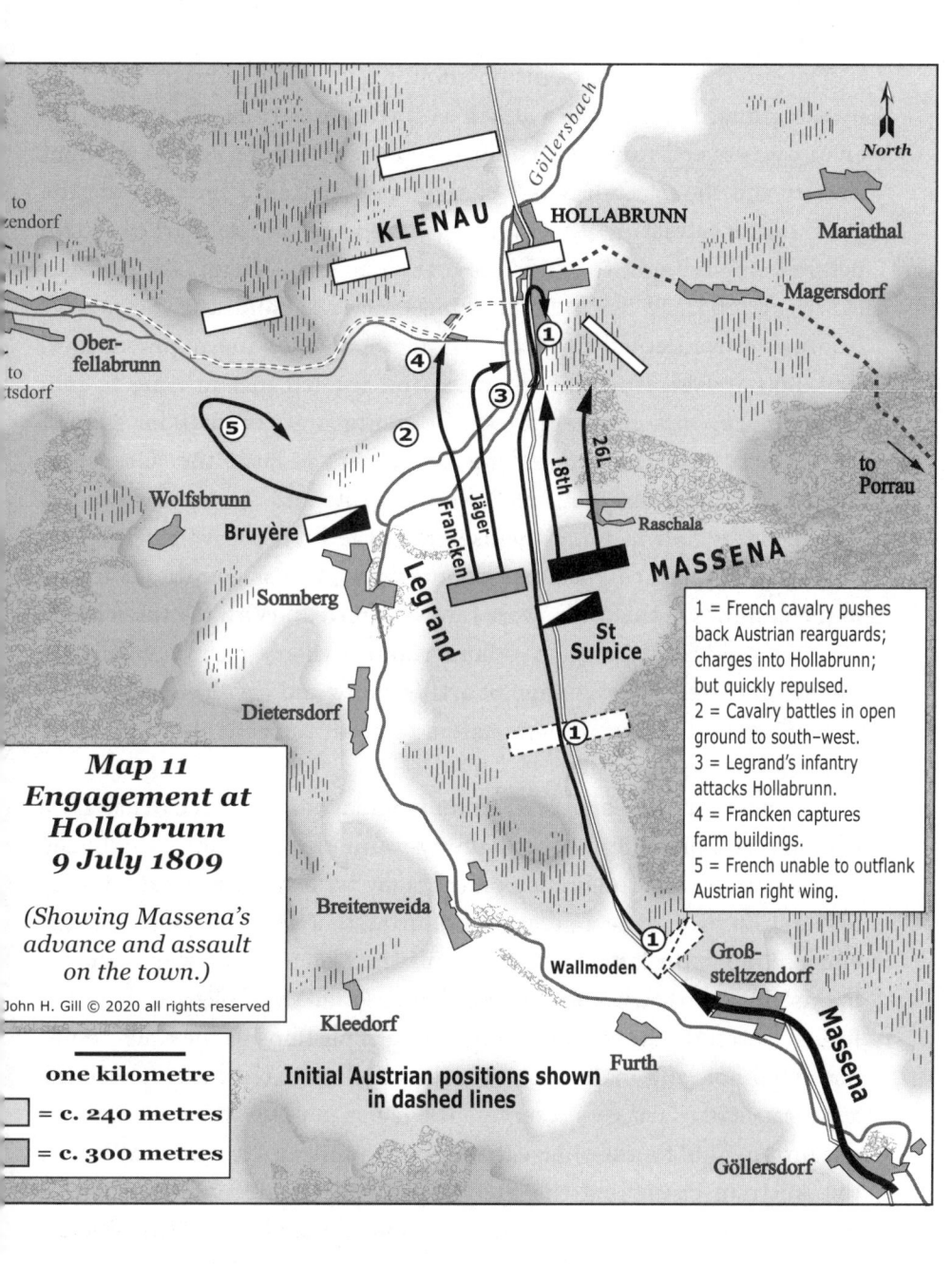

Hussars No. 8 and two battalions of Vienna Volunteers to cover his left and, in the late morning, sent two squadrons of *Blankenstein* Hussars to Gettsdorf to seek contact with Schustekh.[167]

Despite the strength of his position, Klenau faced a crisis when his own rearguard came under attack as it withdrew to Hollabrunn. 'The enemy was overthrown at all points,' reported Bruyère, so that the light cavalry and the 1st Cuirassiers charged pell-mell into the town on the heels of the retreating Austrians, dashing as far as the market square before being brought to a halt.[168] Fortunately for Klenau, GM Andreas Mariássy, charged with Hollabrunn's defence, and the *Benjovszky* Infantry proved equal to this alarming challenge. The regiment's 3rd Battalion arrived from the vineyards on the left just in time to join II/*Benjovszky* in a counterattack. The regimental commander, Oberst Paul Maria Senitzer, ordered his drummers to beat the 'Grenadier March' normally reserved for the army's elite and the two battalions, supported by *Spleny*, flung themselves at the French cavalry. The iron horsemen and their light horse counterparts, at a severe disadvantage in the confines of the town, were forced to retreat. With the town being strongly held and Austrian infantry and artillery clearly visible on the hills beyond, an exchange of artillery fire and cavalry skirmishing ensued as the French troopers halted to await the arrival of Legrand's hurrying infantrymen.

Legrand's division appeared around midday and deployed in battalion columns on both sides of the highway south of Hollabrunn, the Baden Brigade on the left, the French on the right, with swarms of skirmishers to the front provoking a great deal of firing that was 'lively but without effect'. Among the latter were, 'as usual', the Baden Jägers, who managed to push into the town from the meadows around the Göllersbach.[169] The Jägers caused the Austrians in the southern portions of the town to flee but could not long maintain themselves and retreated in turn with the appearance of Mariássy's reserves. The Jägers' repulse was only the start of a furious fight for the village that went on until late that night. Whether the Austrian claim that the French stormed Hollabrunn seven times is accurate or not, it is clear that the contest was vicious. 'The bitterest fighting in the gardens, ditches and vineyards went on until midnight without slackening,' wrote Klenau.[170]

Every Night a March, Every Day an Attack   153

With the southern half of the town in flames owing to French howitzer fire and Baden Jägers who had fired their muskets into straw, entry of formed bodies of troops was nearly impossible. Legrand thus sent ever-growing bands of skirmishers forward while attempting to bypass the Austrian position on both flanks and thereby compel Klenau to withdraw. Neither effort succeeded. On the eastern side, I/26 Léger made little progress among the hillside vineyards, and other vineyards to the west impeded employment of the numerous French cavalry. Nor did Massena and Legrand have sufficient infantry to extend the French line far enough west to encompass the Austrian right flank. In mid-afternoon, three Baden voltigeur companies led by the intrepid Oberstleutnant von Francken managed to seize some farm structures along the road to Oberfellabrunn, but they were too weak to advance further and barely retained their precarious position. Similarly, a French horse battery that was endeavouring to take the Austrian line under enfilade fire from the west was chased off by a detachment from *Duka* Infantry No. 39. French cavalry sparred with the *Liechtenstein* and *Blankenstein* Hussars in the open meadows, skirmishers and gunners kept up heavy fire, and the French and Baden infantry made repeated forays into smoking Hollabrunn to retain their grip on its southern fringe, but the northern half of the town remained in Austrian hands.[171] The Austrian hussars, consistently praised for their efforts on this day, seem to have suffered badly in the fighting with the French reporting the capture of 185–300 of the troopers.[172] Klenau nonetheless accomplished his mission of protecting the Austrian Main Army's withdrawal with his exhausted corps and Massena could only report that each side was left in possession of its portion of the field.[173]

Losses for both sides at Hollabrunn were heavy, apparently more so for Klenau's troops. There are few surviving reports of French losses, but based on the number of officers wounded, the total killed and injured may be estimated at something under 200 with an unknown number captured (the Austrians claimed 'hundreds').[174] Adding Baden losses of 101 dead or wounded and 44 missing yields a total of approximately 320 not including French prisoners of war. The 1st Baden Infantry also had to regret the loss of its band. Left behind in the advance, it was captured entire by a wandering patrol from Oberstleutnant Ludwig

Wilgenheim's squadron of *Erzherzog Carl* Uhlans No. 3.[175] Austrian casualties, on the other hand, came to at least 1,200. It is notable that 595 of the Austrian killed and wounded came from the *Benjovszky* Infantry alone.[176] Moreover, despite the conspicuous courage of that regiment, as well as its compatriots in *Spleny* and the two hussar regiments, Austrian leaders must have worried at the number of prisoners and missing from other units. *Klebek* Infantry No. 14, for instance, reported 114 captured and 77 missing against only 3 dead and 8 wounded; this from a regiment whose only participation in the battle was to send one battalion (III) to support the skirmish line near the end of the day.[177] These figures and the continued anxieties about exhaustion among their troops suggest the precarious condition of VI Corps at this stage of the retreat. In a 1:00 p.m. report, for example, Klenau again begged Charles to send him 'some troops that have been refreshed with food and sleep' as his 'cannot continue'.[178]

The fact that the corps could mount such a determined defence at Hollabrunn thus speaks well for the junior leaders, the common soldiers, and select generals. Klenau, to his credit, was so pleased with Mariássy and Senitzer that he ignored his own weariness and rode to Charles after dark to request the cross of the Maria Theresa Order for both officers. Charles, under his authority as Generalissimus, happily acceded and Klenau was able to reward both men amongst the ashes of Hollabrunn that night.[179] Thanks to the efforts of these officers and the men under their command, the Austrians had delayed Massena's pursuit for a day. Had they not succeeded in this task, Charles would have come under much heavier pressure on the 10th and 11th as he found himself forced back beyond the Thaya to Znaim.[180]

At the same time, Massena, despite being halted at Hollabrunn, could also be satisfied. Like the Austrians, the French and Badeners of his 4th Corps had been marching and fighting with little respite since 4 July, yet they preserved their impetuosity, zeal and tactical skill. In fact, it is worth noting that none of the French reports of the time mention exhaustion or lack of provisions. The marshal may be faulted for not pressing a thorough reconnaissance of the Austrian right to turn Klenau's position, but it is difficult to see how he could have done much more given the paucity of infantry at hand and the hilly, vine-covered terrain.[181]

The fighting left Hollabrunn a smouldering ruin. The journal of Bruyère's division recorded that 'the unfortunate Austrians who had been wounded in the charge at Hollabrunn mostly died as victims of the flames, the fire having progressed too rapidly to permit any rescue. In traversing that town the next day to take ourselves ahead, we found an infinite number of charred cadavers.'[182] These horrors notwithstanding, Massena had orders to 'continue to pursue the enemy towards Znaim'. He intended to do just that, reporting during the night that 'Tomorrow at daybreak I will be on his heels again.'[183]

Meanwhile, on Massena's right, Bavarian Oberst Lindenau and his small detachment had also been active, pushing from up from Leitzersdorf to occupy Großmugl. He advanced as far as Herzogbirbaum, but found it too strongly held and, with 'both flanks completely in the air', he contented himself with observing the Austrian position.[184]

Actions near Laa: A Powerful Shock and Drunken Disorder

While Klenau held Massena's limited pursuit force at Hollabrunn and Lindenau probed past Großmugl in the west, Marmont was grappling with Radetzky and Altstern on the eastern route. Rosenberg and the bulk of his corps, however, would be out of the picture. The IV Corps commander, no doubt smarting after the admonishing orders he had received from Charles late on 8 July, hastened to comply with the demand that he protect the routes to Brünn and Olmütz. At 2:00 a.m. on the 9th, he sent an advance detachment consisting of the *Hessen-Homburg* Hussars No. 4 and a cavalry half-battery from his headquarters in Laa across the Thaya River to protect the crossings at Dürnholz (Drnholec), Muschau (Musov)[185] and Tracht (Strachotín). The corps main body followed three hours later, marching along the north bank of the Thaya. 'I will position myself at Muschau with the army corps to remain master of the two roads to Brünn and Olmütz,' Rosenberg told Charles in a message from Laa before he departed. He sounded rather less confident some hours later when writing to GM Altstern from Dürnholz that he 'hoped to reach Muschau safely'.[186]

Rosenberg left his rearguard under Radetzky south of the Thaya. Relying on Altstern to look after Laa, he wanted Radetzky to protect IV Corps' southern flank as it made its way north and east along the river. The actions on 9 July would thus erupt at Staatz and Neudorf as well as near the bridges around Laa and Ruhhof as Marmont's command advanced.

Marmont was still endeavouring to establish a firm grip on his new corps on the morning of 9 July, but his men were up and moving early.[187] Shortly after dawn, they pushed the *Stipsicz* Hussars out of their advance post near Hörersdorf and drove for Staatz. The French[188] were delayed for a time by a half-battery posted near Staatz, but the appearance of French and Bavarian guns and, more importantly, the arrival of a flanking column from the direction of Poysdorf and Zlabern, made Radetzky's position at Staatz untenable. He withdrew to Neudorf as instructed followed by Bavarian and French light horse (on the left and right flanks respectively). In the press of the pursuit, GM Franz Freiherr von Fröhlich[189] and the *Stipsicz* Hussars became separated from the rest of Radetzky's rearguard and, followed by enemy cavalry skirmishers, retired towards Ruhhof hoping to cross the Thaya there (in vain – *see below*). Radetzky had sent the Primatial Insurrection Hussar squadrons back to Dürnholz during the night, so he was left with only two regiments – *EH Ferdinand* Hussars No. 3 and *O'Reilly* Chevaulegers – some infantry, and his battery to face the oncoming Franco-Bavarian horsemen. The result was 'a powerful shock' around Neudorf in Radetzky's words, but one 'that did not decide much' as the Habsburg horse held the French and Bavarian regiments at bay and Marmont was interested in the road west to Laa, not the routes north.[190] Nonetheless, the fighting was sharp. The remnants of the 8th Jäger Battalion, for instance, were 'wiped out'. As the battalion's after-action report recorded: 'The superiority of the [enemy] cavalry forced ours to retreat, the remainder of the battalion, which consisted of only 140 men, was in the open between Staatz and Neudorf with no support and wanted to throw itself into the village, but was overrun by the enemy cavalry by which occurrence it was finally, the greatest exertions notwithstanding, partly cut down and partly taken prisoner.'[191] In an exchange of charge and counter-charge, the Bavarian cavalry brigade under GM Maximilian von Preysing took Neudorf and a number of prisoners but lost the commander of the 2nd Chevaulegers, Oberst August von Floret, to a pistol shot through the heart. An outstanding officer, who had served with the regiment since 1801, Floret was

Every Night a March, Every Day an Attack

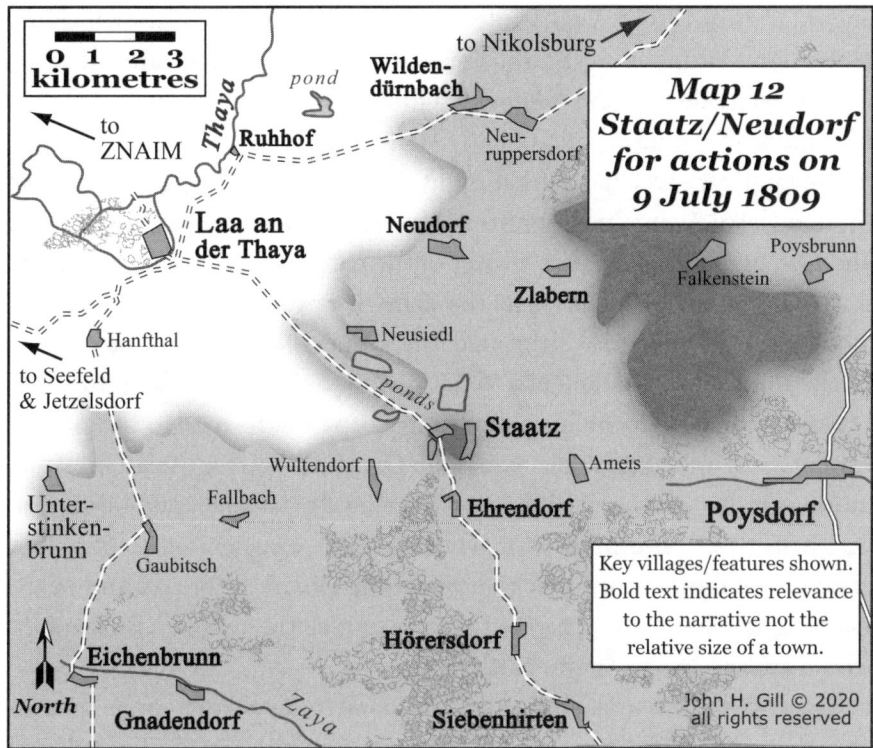

much mourned by his men and was laid to rest near Laa during the night of 9/10 July in a moving ceremony attended by dozens of French officers as well as his entire regiment.[192]

Having lost Neudorf, Radetzky withdrew about four kilometres north to Wildendürnbach but the enemy 'only followed with weak detachments' as 'the bulk' of the enemy's infantry and cavalry 'took the road to Laa'.[193] By late morning, the fighting was over and Radetzky, recalled to IV Corps, crossed the Thaya near Dürnholz where he rejoined Rosenberg and was appointed to command one of the corps' two newly organised divisions. GM Fröhlich and the *Stipsicz* Hussars also rejoined the corps. Fröhlich had attempted to cross at Ruhhof after being separated from the rearguard, but had found French cavalry already skirmishing with Altstern's detachment at the Ruhhof bridges. He had thus headed downstream and crossed south of Dürnholz. With Radetzky now in command of a division, Rosenberg placed Fröhlich in charge of the corps' rearguard. The corps moved off that afternoon, ending the day around 6:00 p.m. with one division (Radetzky's) posted between Weistätten (Pasohlávky) and Mariahilf (Nová Ves) while the other (under FML Ludwig Fürst Hohenlohe-Waldenburg-Bartenstein) occupied Muschau and vicinity. The lone squadron of *EH Johann* Dragoons still with IV Corps was left at Dürnholz to maintain contact with Altstern at Laa and Ruhhof.

In a message to Charles that night, Rosenberg was satisfied to report that he was now in a position to cover 'the shortest line' to both Brünn and Olmütz, but noted that 'owing to the extraordinary heat' the march from Laa was 'so difficult that the army corps left some 30 men dead along the way'. He also informed the Generalissimus that, according to the unanimous statements of the prisoners taken that day, 'Marshal Davout is following with his entire army corps' on the road to Laa.[194] This erroneous if understandable assessment would colour Austrian interpretations for the remainder of the war and would even appear in many post-war histories.[195] Specifically, it would lead to exaggerated impressions of both the number of French approaching Znaim from Laa and of the likely time when these French troops – under the renowned Davout – would appear on the Znaim battlefield.

Rosenberg was not the only commander labouring under a misapprehension that afternoon. Marmont did not detect Rosenberg's turn towards the north after crossing the Thaya. 'Within one hour I will march to Laa by which Rosenberg's entire corps is retiring to Znaim,' he reported to Berthier at 10:00 a.m., 'I will pass Laa and go as far as possible.' He evinced the same conviction in a message to Davout, noting that he had taken 300 or so prisoners from a 'feeble rearguard', that 'the totality of Rosenberg's corps' had retired from Staatz 'to take itself to Znaim', and that he planned to move on Znaim at a very early hour the following day. Otherwise, he had little to report and required no assistance from 3rd Corps.[196]

As for Davout's actual whereabouts, 3rd Corps was indeed on the march, but not in the direction Rosenberg – and later Charles – assumed. Marmont having expressed no need for support, the 'Iron Marshal' continued his advance north up the Brünn highway towards Nikolsburg. It was clear from all incoming reports that the road from Wilfersdorf to Nikolsburg was 'entirely open' and he set half of his corps in motion towards the latter town that afternoon.[197] Grouchy led the advance with his dragoons, supported by two battalions of the 13th Léger. Arriving at Nikolsburg after dark, his men took some scattered fire but he boldly ordered the elite company of the 7th Dragoons to 'traverse the village at the gallop' with the rest of the regiment in support. As the defenders consisted of a lone squadron of *O'Reilly* Chevaulegers that Rosenberg had posted there on the 7th, the daring and numerically superior French were soon masters of the town. Grouchy pushed on in the darkness hoping to seize a crossing over the Thaya, but with Rosenberg's corps already in Muschau, the French found the bridge firmly held and Grouchy called a halt to his adventurous advance. Grouchy's success at Nikolsburg allowed Davout to emplace his 1st Division around the town that night with the 2nd Division just south at Drasenhofen. Intelligence from Grouchy and other sources validated his earlier assessment that no major Austrian formations had passed up the Brünn road.[198] The marshal, already concerned about Marmont's situation, therefore prudently decided to leave his 3rd and 4th Divisions as well as Arrighi's cuirassiers encamped around Poysdorf, only one good march from Laa.

GM von Altstern now re-enters the picture. Having marched the thirteen or so kilometres up from Eichenbrunn, Altstern found that Rosenberg had left behind the *Hohenzollern* Cuirassiers and their cavalry battery as promised. To his dismay, however, he also discovered Marmont's mounted skirmishers already engaged with the *Hohenzollern* troopers near the bridge over the Thaya at Ruhhof (the fighting that caused the retreating GM Fröhlich to head north away from Ruhhof). He quickly took command of the *Hohenzollern* Cuirassiers as intended and led one squadron of the weakened regiment forward to hold off the probing French and win time for his infantry and artillery to cross at Ruhhof. Once his infantry and guns were safely on the northern bank, he dismantled several of the numerous little bridges[199] that crossed the marshy river banks, left some cuirassiers behind as a screen, and marched off for Znaim. Although his orders specifically stated that he was to 'cover the passage over the Thaya near Laa', he apparently decided that he had done enough in observing the enemy and removing the bridges. Whether he feared being overwhelmed or simply misunderstood Hohenzollern's instructions is unclear; his artless report, sent from Znaim that night, merely recounted his actions during the day with no explanation. The instructions Hohenzollern and Rosenberg had supplied should have left no doubt about the importance of his mission and his role as a linchpin between the different elements of the army, but he ignored the implications of his actions, left three squadrons of cuirassiers at Tasswitz (not to be confused with Klein-Tesswitz near Znaim), and took his weak infantry regiment towards Znaim 'to defend the city as long as possible'.[200] Having balked at marching 25 km from Ernstbrunn to Laa the day before, he now undertook to push his troops more than 40 km from Eichenbrunn through Ruhhof to Znaim in the heat of the day. His inexplicable decision to withdraw without even attempting a fight thus compounded the errors Charles and Hohenzollern had made in sending such a weak brigade (800 infantry and 150 cavalry with two batteries) under such an unimaginative officer to perform such a significant mission. We shall return to the alarm Altstern caused with his report later, but for the moment it suffices to note that the French quickly repaired the bridges and that French cavalry patrols were probing up to road towards Znaim that very afternoon. Altstern's retreat had left the door to the Austrian line of communications wide open.

Marmont, despite his mistaken conclusions concerning Rosenberg's destination, had thus far done well on 9 July, brushing aside Radetzky's rearguard, restoring the Thaya crossing and pushing reconnaissance up the road towards Znaim. Among other bits of intelligence, these patrols detained and interrogated a postilion who provided detailed information on the colourful cavalcade ('forming a column of more than 200 coaches, barouches and other vehicles') that had accompanied Kaiser Franz to Ernstbrunn and then on to Znaim, including the Kaiser's times of arrival and departure and the name of the inn where he was lodged in the latter town. The cavalry that had collected this remarkable information were part of Montbrun's command.[201] With Montbrun having joined him on the banks of the Thaya, therefore, Marmont's entire corps was now concentrated for the anticipated thrust towards Znaim. He faced, however, an unanticipated problem that rendered much of his command useless for the remainder of the day: mass inebriation.

The region through which the armies were passing was rich in vineyards and the abundance of wine combined with the extreme heat and lack of water created an irresistible temptation for many thirsty men on both sides. 'The heat was stifling,' recalled Sergeant Desboeufs, and soldiers, on discovering the wine caves dug into the hillsides 'ran into them in crowds and the press increased so much that some suffocated'. He claimed that he and his comrades discovered large numbers of Austrian stragglers in the caves as well, many of whom also succumbed to the urgent onrush of thirsty men.[202] Davout had reported an estimated two million litres in the Wilfersdorf area alone and detailed a *chef de bataillon* with four companies to maintain order. Friedrich Mändler, recently conscripted into the Bavarian 6th Light Infantry, recounted that he and his countrymen 'often suffered a lack of water in our bivouacs during this march; but this never happened with wine. I remember quite well that our soldiers cooked their meat in wine owing to the lack of water and our cavalry watered their horses with wine.'[203] For Marmont on 9 July, these circumstances resulted in an embarrassing setback. 'Nothing can express the heat that the troops suffered during that day,' he wrote later, 'Many soldiers remained behind and the harm was augmented by drunkenness and disorder.' The wine caves of Staatz were forced open 'and drunkenness, added to the heat and the fatigue, annihilated, so to speak, in a moment, all the infantry of my army corps'. Unable to advance in strength, he secured the far side of the Thaya 'and the multitude of bridges', chastised his officers 'for the lack of supervision', visited company bivouacs to exhort his men to better behaviour, published a severe order of the day, and, 'to impose a salutary fear, I had two men tried and executed for insubordination'. The disgraceful comportment of his corps cost at least half a day and he 'awaited the dawn with impatience to march for Znaim where all the columns of the enemy army were heading and where I feared to find nothing more than a rearguard'.[204]

Peace with the Emperor of the French?

Amidst all the manoeuvring and combat, diplomacy continued, albeit haltingly. On Franz's decision to send Liechtenstein to Napoleon, instructions were prepared to guide the prince in his interactions with the French emperor. Although the Kaiser apparently supplied some broad verbal advice, Liechtenstein's written directions were simple, vague and potentially dangerous as it would be easy for Liechtenstein to overstep his remit or to make a commitment the Kaiser would find unacceptable: 'My dear prince, We authorise you to sign a peace with the Emperor of the French in the case that H. I. M. [His Imperial Majesty] offers me one, under the condition of the perfect integrity of the monarchy.'[205] The next problem was arranging Liechtenstein's safe passage through the lines of two armies that were engaged in active combat. In the knowledge that Napoleon was still in Wolkersdorf, Liechtenstein was to proceed from the Reserve Corps headquarters near Schöngrabern through Klenau's corps to Massena on the Vienna–Znaim highway. Altered battlefield circumstances would delay Liechtenstein until the afternoon of 10 July, but preparations began at once. The exact sequence of actions is unclear, but at some time during the morning of 9 July Klenau sent a note to 'the general commanding the French advance guard' requesting unhindered passage for Liechtenstein. The French initially took this as a *ruse de guerre*, but Bruyère, not believing himself authorised for such interactions, passed the messenger on to Massena. This exchange produced a temporary lull in the French advance, as both Klenau and Bruyère reported, but the delay was brief.[206] As Trooper Wilhelmus Kenis of the 3rd Chasseurs observed, once the envoy had passed 'The firing began again on all sides and we fought on until the evening.'[207]

That same morning, Oberst Emanuel St Quentin of the 1st Vienna Volunteers reported that one of Massena's aides-de-camp had relayed a message from Napoleon to the effect that the French emperor 'would await with pleasure' the arrival of Liechtenstein.[208] Additionally, Berthier informed Massena that Napoleon had authorised FML Weißenwolff's return and instructed the marshal to issue the necessary orders for his safe passage through the outpost lines. Massena also encountered Weißenwolff at Schloß Schönborn near Göllersdorf later that day, escorted, as before, by Captain Galbois of Berthier's staff.[209] Indicating the importance Napoleon attached to Weißenwolff's potential utility, Galbois had been the victim of momentary imperial annoyance when Napoleon, supposing the captain was monitoring the Austrian general in Vienna, saw Galbois at headquarters on the battlefield at Wagram on the 6th. 'What are you doing here?' the emperor demanded. 'What have you done with General Weißenwolff? Go find him at once!' Returning with Weißenwolff on 7 July, Galbois recalled later that, 'The emperor received Count Weißenwolff very well and expressed his regrets, in a manner most flattering, concerning the rigour with which he had been obliged to treat him, and charged me with conducting him back to the Austrian army.'[210] Weißenwolff would thus bear a favourable report of his courteous treatment in French captivity and his impression that Napoleon was decidedly interested in concluding peace in the near term. Although Massena reported that night that the Austrian general could not pass through because 'the fire was too lively to risk a trumpeter', he would be blindfolded and permitted to cross the outpost line the following morning (10 July).[211] Despite suspicions, heavy fighting, misunderstandings and the frailties of nineteenth-century communications, therefore, both sides seemed to be fumbling towards the beginnings of peace overtures as 9 July came to an end.[212]

By evening, Charles could be pleased with these developments on the diplomatic front and, unaware of Altstern's overhasty retreat, he could also be relatively satisfied with the combat actions during the day. He knew that Klenau had held at Hollabrunn and that Rosenberg was en route to the Brünn highway as directed and he had every reason to believe that Altstern was guarding the Thaya at Laa. He could thus anticipate occupying the Jetzelsdorf position on 10 July as planned and could contemplate his future actions from what he expected to be a degree of safety.

Charles: There's Not a Moment to Lose

Messages arriving that night, however, put an end to all Charles's hopes. Two came from his brother the Kaiser in Znaim. The first of these, dispatched at 3:00 p.m., stated that a hussar officer had ridden in from the east to report excitedly that enemy cavalry were present in Erdberg (Hrádek) on the road from Laa and that from that point to Znaim no formed Austrian troops were to be seen. This enemy cavalry could thus 'come here with no hindrance and cause all manner of disorder', warned Franz. The second message, sent an hour later, expressed concern for the safety of Olmütz, citing a report that Rosenberg was retreating in a disorderly manner while the enemy was approaching Nikolsburg 'with a strong column'.

Charles seems to have treated these messages with some scepticism. The first appeared especially dubious. As Laa 'was held by a brigade from Hohenzollern's corps', it seemed to him highly improbable that 'an enemy detachment could come through unnoticed'. Nonetheless, 'to avoid the consequences of a false alarm', at 8:00 p.m. he instructed Kolowrat to send GM Andreas von Schneller with the *Schwarzenberg* Uhlans No. 2 to investigate the story that the road to Znaim was open. His concern for the security of Znaim seems to have grown quickly, however, as he issued a new disposition for the Jetzelsdorf position at 9:00 p.m. before hearing anything from Schneller. This new disposition represented a half-measure, clinging to the Jetzelsdorf concept while addressing the possible danger to Znaim. The remains of the Jetzelsdorf plan were evident in Klenau, finally relieved of rearguard duties, moving to a ridge between Guntersdorf and Jetzelsdorf, Kolowrat shifting to Haugsdorf, and Bellegarde to Hadres. Reuss and V Corps would replace VI Corps as rearguard at Hollabrunn with the *Blankenstein* Hussars coming under his command.

Worries about Znaim, on the other hand, were clear in the directions given to the Reserve Cavalry and Grenadiers to march for that town 'on receipt of these orders', shoving all baggage and other hindrances aside if necessary 'to speed the march as much as possible'. An hour later (10:00 p.m.), Charles instructed Hohenzollern to 'march for Laa with his entire corps immediately upon receipt of this, and endeavour to dislodge the enemy if you do not find him too strong, and master the passages over the Thaya'. If, however, Hohenzollern thought that 'the enemy at Laa was so strong that you cannot promise yourself any good success in this enterprise', he was to cross the river upstream towards Znaim and 'secure the road from Laa and Nikolsburg to Znaim' until the army arrived.[213] As will be seen, the Reserve Cavalry and Grenadiers marched with commendable haste to appear just in time, but Hohenzollern proved unequal to his task.

Yet another disposition, issued on 3:30 a.m. on 10 July, abandoned any notion of holding the Jetzelsdorf position. Altstern's report from Znaim and a message from Hohenzollern stating that he would have to withdraw because the French were at Laa in strength apparently spurred this decision.[214] 'There was not a moment to lose in securing the defile over the Thaya at Znaim before the arrival of the enemy,' wrote Charles afterwards in a letter to the Minister of War, 'otherwise, the army would have found itself between two fires and would have been compelled, at the cost of its artillery and supply trains, to force a crossing of the Thaya or to throw itself into the mountains towards Retz and leave open the road to Prague'.[215] This new order thus directed I, III and VI Corps to march for the Thaya without stopping, to cross by bridges or fords depending on what was available and to follow the instructions of general staff officers who would guide them to their respective positions on the northern bank of the river. Kolowrat, however, was directed to leave a brigade (Infantry Regiments *Schröder* No. 7 and *Wenzel Colloredo* No. 56) and four guns on the heights north of Haugsdorf to cover the left flank of V Corps as the new rearguard. In his rearguard role, Reuss was to withdraw slowly, defending '*the advantageous heights*' north of Jetzelsdorf 'to the uttermost, which I make the particular duty of FZM Fürst Reuss'. He was further enjoined to 'spare no sacrifice' to win time for the army, 'especially for the large artillery train', to cross the Thaya.[216] These phrases – 'particular duty' and 'spare no sacrifice' – in the section of the disposition directed at the V Corps commander provide a good gauge of Charles's anxiety. All of these orders and dispositions issued from the night of 9 July through the pre-dawn hours of the 10th meant that the Hauptarmee was once again destined for a night march, this time straight into battle.

Franz: I Must Take Myself to Hungary

By the time these orders were on the way to their destinations, Kaiser Franz was long gone from Znaim. The hussar officer who had ridden into town and disturbed the imperial lunch at 'The Three Princes' had excited, as one may imagine, considerable alarm. The rumour that made its way within the imperial household was that two French cavalry regiments had been ordered to capture Franz and his entire suite. Agitation increased exponentially when an officer attached to the imperial household who rode out towards Laa to verify this assertion quickly returned to affirm that he had encountered enemy mounted patrols within a few kilometres of the town. Part of the Kaiser's baggage had already been sent off to Prague and the remainder was now hastily packed up so that Franz and his attendant staff, servants, family members, table silver, cashbox and other paraphernalia were all on their way north by 5:30 p.m. By 8:00 p.m., Franz had reached Mährisch-Budwitz (Moravské Budějovice) where he parted from Stadion before leaving for Czaslau (Čáslav) that very night, taking Metternich as a companion in his coach for the first portion of this extraordinarily rapid journey.[217]

In addition to his two afternoon notes providing intelligence reports from the war front, Franz dispatched two other messages to Charles on 9 July. Although they did not reach the archduke until the 10th and 11th as the combat at Znaim was raging, they are worth mentioning now because they illustrate the shift in the Kaiser's attitude and the prevailing mood in the Habsburg court only one day after the decision to send Liechtenstein to Napoleon. First, before leaving Znaim, Franz sent a third note to Charles, this one demonstrating that the war party at court was once again in the ascendency. 'Overpowering reasons will have it that I must take myself to Hungary,' he wrote. Without deigning to elaborate on what those 'reasons' might be, he proceeded to remark that each army would now have to operate on its own as communications might be 'completely cut off' as a result of his transfer. Charles was therefore to prepare an operations plan 'as quickly as possible' to cover all possibilities and 'rapidly' forward it to Franz for his approval 'as my departure could come about very quickly'.[218]

The Kaiser's letter also introduced a memorandum from Stadion that outlined three possible outcomes for Liechtenstein's mission: the French could reject him outright, the peace conditions could be unbearable, or Napoleon could offer an acceptable peace; the first two cases were, Stadion observed, 'inseparable from a continuation of the war'. The minister then highlighted the likely breakdown in communications once Franz shifted 'the true central point of the monarchy' to Hungary from its prior location with the Hauptarmee.[219] Given Stadion's background, this formulation implied that continuation of the war was both the more likely result of Liechtenstein's mission and the preferable course of action for the Habsburg monarchy under current conditions. Furthermore, although not stated directly, Stadion was clearly laying the foundation for an imperial decision to deprive Charles of his post of overall commander as Generalissimus, relegating him to a lesser position as simply the leader of one among several armies. In any event, considering the Kaiser's imminent departure from the vicinity of the Main Army, the demand for immediate preparation of an 'operations plan' suited to all situations was out-dated almost as soon as the ink was dry.

Second, on reaching Czaslau that night, Franz sent Charles a brief personal letter. Decidedly cool and imperially haughty in tone, this note informed the archduke of the Kaiser's move to Hungary 'where my presence is necessary' and delivered a stern, demeaning admonishment ordering Charles 'to exercise all your care to maintain the courage and good spirit of the army entrusted to your command, implement order and discipline within the same, and do the enemy as much damage as possible'. Franz would endeavour to mobilise the strength of the monarchy, but his efforts could only succeed 'if Your Grace cooperates properly from your side'. The Kaiser then announced that Charles's sphere of responsibility would now be restricted 'only to the army under your command' and to the pertinent resources 'from the provinces in your rear that are as yet unoccupied by the enemy'. In other words, Charles was no longer to be Generalissimus. Finally, this second letter instructed Charles to relieve Rosenberg of command and, in a personal attack, Franz demanded that Charles dismiss FML Grünne from his staff.[220] Grünne, though widely unpopular, was one of the archduke's closest associates and it was well understood at court that demanding his removal was a way of derogating and diminishing Charles himself.

The letter made no mention whatsoever of Liechtenstein's mission or of negotiations with Napoleon. Nor did it explain how the Kaiser's presence in Hungary could possibly be more important to the monarchy's future than the forthcoming meeting with the French emperor. Perhaps Franz was tired and overwrought, perhaps he was influenced by spending all day driving through the wretched human, animal and material detritus choking the roads in the army's rear. These circumstances and the sudden appearance of the French outside Znaim (supposedly to capture his imperial person!) may have made him more susceptible to the whispers and insinuations of the anti-Charles factions in his entourage. The sudden decision to remove the court to Hungary certainly suggests that key advisors wanted to separate the Kaiser from the army to retard negotiations with Napoleon and perhaps render them impossible. We may speculate that they may have also wanted to distance Franz physically from an army that might be on the verge of another defeat. Whatever the case, these letters did not fail to have an impact on Franz's younger brother. Indeed, the second was practically insulting. Charles, who, as noted above, received them on the battlefield on 10 and 11 July, certainly read them as assaults on his authority and dignity. Moreover, as unmistakable signs that the fervently bellicose personalities at court were again dominating Franz's thinking, they reignited his fears that the war would be continued to the ultimate ruin of the monarchy and ruling house. These imperial letters and the Stadion memorandum would thus influence his own decisions as events evolved over the coming three days.

With the events of 9 July, the post-Wagram phase of the war begins its transition from pursuit and retreat to battle, thus offering us a moment to consider the preceding three days before continuing with the narrative. Several observations are pertinent at this stage.

First, the Austrians had thus far conducted a skilful and successful retreat. Charles had held his army together, fended off incessant French probes, shielded his large and unwieldy baggage train, and was attempting to execute a coherent operational concept (occupation of the Jetzelsdorf position). This was only possible, of course, because the soldiers of the Hauptarmee had fought with courage and stamina despite their trying circumstances. The light cavalry rearguards were especially crucial in parrying the more numerous French horse and the infantry at Hollabrunn displayed tremendous tenacity. At the same time, the archduke's actions were almost entirely defensive and he could not detach himself from his urge to protect everything with his cordon-defence thinking. Although he mentioned possibly making an 'offensive move' in several letters to his fellow archdukes, there is little evidence that he had any thought of doing so before occupying the 'position' behind the Pulkau at Jetzelsdorf and perhaps resting his army for a few days (how he could imagine that a French army under Napoleon's leadership would grant him even a day's respite remains incomprehensible). Given that his overriding aim was the preservation of the monarchy's principal army, his defensive outlook is understandable, but it meant that he missed his opportunity to deal Massena a severe, perhaps crushing blow. The same situation would prevail when he faced Marmont on 10 July.

Furthermore, his concern with throwing a cordon across the entire theatre of operations to protect everything meant that he deprived himself of significant formations just at the point when he was likely to face another major battle with Napoleon. Schustekh's division is the lesser example. Comprised mostly of Landwehr and volunteer units, it would not have been a deciding factor in a large engagement, but it could have been called towards the Stockerau–Znaim road to threaten Massena's flank or bolster Klenau's enervated rearguard. Instead, Schustekh's 6,000 men were scattered across the hills far off on the army's right flank and several hussar squadrons had to be detached to retain liaison with them. They faced the two depleted light horse regiments of Ameil's detachment (perhaps 300 to 400 troopers with no artillery) and the possibility that several hundred Württembergers might have crossed the Danube from Melk to scout north. The contrast with Napoleon's focused concentration against the Hauptarmee is stark. The greater lapse was sending the chastised Rosenberg off to protect Brünn and Olmütz. Although Charles could not know that the French were not marching on these two cities, he might have deployed a screen across the Brünn highway and deterred such a thrust by posting a strong force around Staatz and Laa to threaten the flank of any French troops advancing in that direction.

The most serious danger arising from ordering Rosenberg to Muschau, of course, was that his absence left the door to Znaim ajar. With powerful French forces known to be at Mistelbach and pushing towards Nikolsburg, it is difficult to comprehend how Charles and Hohenzollern thought Altstern's weak brigade would suffice to protect an obvious route from the Brünn highway into the rear of the prospective Jetzelsdorf position. Leaving aside Altstern's timid behaviour, Laa seemed the logical place for all or most of Rosenberg's corps to halt. There he could have tied in closely with Hohenzollern and protected the eastern approaches to the Hauptarmee's main position while adding 8,000 to 12,000 men (depending on size of the screen detached to Brünn) to the army's overall strength.[221] Rosenberg, whatever other criticisms one may level at his performance in corps command, clearly recognised this danger. Charles, in his anxiety about the Moravian fortresses, thus provided the French an opportunity which Marmont, albeit adventitiously, would exploit.

Second, its bravery and fortitude notwithstanding, the Hauptarmee, under relentless French pressure, was clearly fraying at the edges. The repeated night movements, the constant skirmishing and the continual alerts in the immediate wake of one of the greatest battles of the era eroded the white-coated battalions at an alarming rate. 'Every night a march and every day an attack,' wrote Charles. As he had feared, the army shed thousands of stragglers on the pitiless retreat as it suffered the combined effects of heat, thirst, dust and lack of regular provisions. Some units, unable to recover from losses at Wagram, ceased to exist. After suffering heavily in the great battle, for example, the remains of the 8th Jäger Battalion, had been 'completely wiped out' at Neudorf on 9 July as we have seen, and many Landwehr battalions, like the 4th UMB of the unfortunate Hauptmann von Seckendorff, simply disintegrated. It was not uncommon for line infantry regiments to have only a battalion's worth of men fit for duty (such as the *Rohan* Infantry with Altstern) and many mounted regiments were worn down to half strength or less.[222] The army's circumstances fed Charles's pessimism and, compounding his innate caution and the sense of intimidation he felt opposing Napoleon, contributed to his worry that his army had reached the limits of its endurance. If pushed much farther, it would likely collapse and with it, he feared, would go the monarchy.

A third observation relates to Napoleon's actions after Wagram. Although the emperor is sometimes criticised for 'inactivity' or 'indecision' immediately following the great battle, there is reason to reconsider this assumption.[223] He had accepted considerable short-term risk in his rear areas to gather the largest possible army for Wagram, but this level of risk could not be sustained indefinitely. The massive exertion involved in staging that battle having delivered only partial results, he had to assure himself of the security of Vienna and his lines of communication while simultaneously seeking the retreating Hauptarmee. Archduke Johann, whose strength the French generally overestimated, was the greatest variable in this equation. In addition to granting his weary army some time to recuperate and reorganise, therefore, Napoleon faced two operational problems in the days immediately following Wagram: locating Charles – his true target – and deterring forays against his rear while he undertook this second effort to encompass the Hauptarmee's destruction. With only contradictory information at hand for the first several days, holding the bulk of the army on and around the Marchfeld while corps-size pursuit forces were sent to follow the two most likely enemy retreat routes was thus his most logical course of action. As noted earlier, he might have moved at least part of his reserve to the area around Ernstbrunn, but by 8 July he had reinforced the pursuit forces on both routes (releasing Massena's entire corps and sending Davout towards Nikolsburg) and he pushed Eugène's newly constructed command toward the March River the following day to keep Johann in check. He therefore lost an opportunity to catch the exhausted Hauptarmee as it crossed the Thaya because his central reserve (Oudinot and the Guard) as well as Davout were simply too far away on 10 and 11 July. Other than the Ernstbrunn option, however, it is difficult to see how Napoleon could have justified moving any earlier than he did given the circumstances at the time and the available intelligence.

It is also important to note that Napoleon accepted the risk of sending his two pursuit forces off on widely separated routes out of mutually supporting distance. Though he never specifically so stated, it is reasonable to speculate that this decision resulted from his confidence in the corps system, in his commanders and in his troops.[224] If either corps ran into an overwhelmingly superior enemy force, it could delay and withdraw for a day or so while awaiting reinforcement. The French also benefited from their recent success at Wagram and from the energy of the pursuit, as well as assumptions of the Austrian archduke's caution and defensive outlook. As noted in Massena's memoirs, 'The ascendancy given by victory defeats the most skilful enemy, and the prince [Charles] allowed himself to be dominated in this circumstance by the audacious manoeuvres of his opponent.' Marmont made similar remarks in his immediate after-action report.[225] Although the French army was also under great strain, dropping stragglers as it spent long, dusty hours on the road with little food or water, it carried with it a significant psychological advantage that was continually reinforced by its boldness, its seeming tirelessness and its superior numbers of cavalry. The tactical benefit derived from these factors was evident in the French persistently pressing their adversaries, even though they did not enjoy any overall numerical edge in terms of forces engaged. Figures can only be estimated, but at Hollabrunn, for example, Klenau probably deployed slightly more in total forces, likely 9,000 in VI Corps compared to Massena's 8,000 or so (light cavalry, St Sulpice's cuirassiers and Legrand's infantry). Nonetheless, the battle was hard-fought and the Austrians suffered greater casualties.

Likewise, though Marmont had a numerical superiority over Rosenberg by 9 July, most of his corps was not engaged and the various French pursuit forces on the previous two days had consisted primarily of active light cavalry supported by small numbers of infantry. Bold and aggressive action, however, especially threatening the sensitive Austrian flanks, repeatedly resulted in Rosenberg's troops being compelled to retreat.

Finally, the close interplay of combat, diplomacy and Habsburg court politics is notable. Napoleon's war aims at this point are unknown – he probably had not made a final determination himself – but the costly and partly disappointing results of Wagram, the dogged resistance Massena had faced at Hollabrunn and his desire to end the war quickly likely meant that he was willing to consider an outcome that would be less than catastrophic for Franz and his monarchy. He, of course, was the sole arbiter of this question on the French side and he had the ability to alter his terms at will and on the spot.

On the Austrian side, where different factions vied for the Kaiser's ear, the situation was more complex. Here, too, the shape of the desired end-state was undecided: Charles hoped for an immediate peace that would preserve the dynasty from destruction, while the advocates of war continued to entertain illusions of external assistance and domestic military regeneration, the latter largely predicated on demoting or removing Charles. It is more than a little ironic – for Charles bitterly so – that the war party at court suddenly returned to ascendancy just as the tentative Austria peace mission was about to be launched. He did not know it as he rode through the darkness to Znaim from Guntersdorf, but his brother's letter from Czaslau would make painfully clear that his hopes for a quickly concluded negotiation were threatened and his options for action drastically narrowed during the night of 9/10 July.

Intermezzo
The Other Theatres of War
6–9 July 1809

BEFORE PROCEEDING, IT IS USEFUL to cast our eyes across the broad canvas of this war to note actions occurring in other theatres that would have a bearing on the thinking of both parties as they approached the encounter at Znaim.[1]

Germany

Accompanied by the tiny 'armies' of two deposed German princes, two small Austrian detachments had marched into Germany, locus of so many of Stadion's hopes, in early June as a putative alternative to taking action along the Danube after Aspern-Essling: one to Saxony, the other to Bayreuth. A series of complex manoeuvres and skirmishes with French and Rheinbund second-line troops ensued, including raids to Leipzig, Bamberg and Nuremberg during June and a fairly significant clash at Gefrees northeast of Bayreuth on 8 July. Although Charles had dispatched the energetic and able FML Michael Freiherr von Kienmayer in late June to inject some coherence and drive into these incursions, they did not incite the sort of widespread rebellion Stadion had envisaged and the Franco-Rheinbund reserve forces, though often bumbling, sufficed to contain them. Napoleon's arrangements for the security of his strategic rear thus functioned as intended and these expeditions did nothing to diminish French strength on the Danube.

Another Habsburg hope for Germany was that a major British amphibious landing at the mouth of the Elbe or the Weser would spark a German uprising. Several days after Znaim, news arrived that the

British had indeed landed near Cuxhaven on 8 July with, reportedly, as many as 30,000 men. The excitement thus generated, however, was dispelled when it emerged that the landing force was a raiding party of some 320 sailors and marines under Commander William Goate of HMS *Mosquito*. A major British assault was being prepared – the ill-fated Walcheren expedition – but it would land in Holland, not Germany. Graf Waldstein, sent from Wolkersdorf to the Court of St James to urge British intervention in Germany, had boarded a Royal Navy cutter on the German coast on 5 July but encountered extended delays en route. He did not arrive in Harwich until the night of 25/26 July – two weeks after the armistice – and then only to learn 'the unfortunate news' that the British expedition 'had a destination completely foreign to my object'.[2]

Hungary and Styria

The broad expanse of Habsburg territory south of the Danube, more or less from Pressburg to Graz, was another repository of Austrian military hopes after Wagram. The largest force in this area was Gyulai's IX Corps (at most 25,000), a hotch-potch of Landwehr, militia, reserves, recruits and a few regulars. Gyulai occupied Graz on 3 July and sent detachments towards Bruck an der Mur and the Semmering Pass. French GD Rusca (*c.* 2,200), marching for those same destinations from Villach and Klagenfurt, shattered one of Gyulai's detachments at Loeben on 6 July, but being grossly outnumbered, he retreated west to Salzburg. Chasteler, often cited as a key reinforcement for Archduke Johann, was around Szent Gróth (Zalaszentgrót, north of the western end of Lake Balaton), but he counted fewer than 5,000 in his ranks. Pushing ahead to Steinamanger (Szombathely), he learned to his dismay of the defeat at Wagram. Finding himself 'all alone in this flat region all about with such a small corps, without sufficient cavalry, and hanging in the air with no support',[3] he decided to march north to join Archduke Joseph's Hungarian Insurrection army, perhaps 20,000 to 30,000, most of which was collected around Komorn (Komárom). All of these forces, while impressive in numbers, were gravely deficient in experience, training, equipment and leadership. Charles, as we have seen, had placed them all under Johann's command, but their manifold debilities meant they would not serve to redeem the empire's fortunes.

Johann himself and his Army of Inner Austria (actually a corps-sized formation), left a modest detachment at Pressburg under GM Friedrich Baron Bianchi, and withdrew to Komorn to contemplate his future options. GD Baraguey d'Hilliers, encouraged by the victory at Wagram, made an attack on the Austrian bridgehead on the south side of the Danube across from Pressburg on 8 July, but this was unsuccessful and the two sides returned to wary observation of one another.

Poland/Galicia

Other than Johann on the Danube, the most important subsidiary force from a Habsburg perspective was Archduke's Ferdinand's VII Corps in Poland. Ferdinand's projects, however, had not prospered. Manoeuvred out of the Duchy of Warsaw and most of Galicia, he had been forced into a small corner of the province and had deployed his corps north of the Vistula to protect Krakow. The Russian corps, south of the Vistula, continued to encroach on Habsburg territory, repeated protestations of friendship and sympathy for the Austrian cause notwithstanding. The Poles, after a brief pause, renewed their advances in early July north of the Vistula, clashing with Ferdinand's defences about 60 km northeast of Krakow on the 9th. Although the Poles and Russians distrusted and detested one another, pressure from their two prongs would increase in the coming days, creating an impossible situation for Ferdinand. Moreover, the Russians in particular featured prominently in Habsburg strategic worries as the leadership feared a tsarist corps from the east and a Napoleonic army from the south would converge on Olmütz to collaborate against the monarchy. Writing to Ferdinand on 8 July, Charles highlighted this presumed danger, instructed his cousin to provide a garrison for Olmütz, and cautioned him not to 'hold too long too far forward' for fear of being driven into the Carpathians where his VII Corps might be 'wiped out' owing to lack of supplies. Ferdinand, receiving Charles's letter on 11 July, thought there was no chance he could reach Olmütz before the French, but he dutifully placed a battalion of *Baillet* Infantry No. 63 in wagons and sent it trundling off to Moravia.[4]

Beyond the more prominent anxieties about Krakow and Olmütz, the Austrian hierarchy also worried about Russian moves even further to the east opposite Bukovina. Though these fears proved imaginary, the consistent reports from generals, civilian officials and imperial family members in this remote corner of the monarchy contributed to the broad sense of suspicion and mistrust vis-à-vis Russia.

Rebellions in the Tyrol and Vorarlberg

Farther afield, the Tyrolian rebels and their confederates in the Vorarlberg continued to govern the lands they had captured after evicting the largely Bavarian garrisons in April and May. Although raids from these regions into southern Germany and northern Italy were bothersome, Napoleon, focused on the Hauptarmee, was content to contain these insurrections with second-line forces for the time being.

Dalmatia

In distant Dalmatia, an Austrian attempt to seize Trieste in conjunction with the Royal Navy on 5–8 July failed, but Habsburg authorities persisted in hoping that they could regain lost territory in the absence of Marmont's army. Planning for an offensive effort thus continued, but it would take further weeks to organise and would do nothing to distract Napoleon on the Danube.

Chapter 5

I Found Myself in the Rear of the Austrian Army

10 July 1809

ALTHOUGH NEITHER YET KNEW IT, the morning of 10 July found the two armies on the verge of a major engagement. The flurry of orders from Austrian headquarters during the night sent first GM Schneller with the *Schwarzenberg* Uhlans and then almost the entire Habsburg host on the march for Znaim. Altstern's small brigade, as we have seen, was already established near the town in the vineyards west of Klein-Tesswitz. Hohenzollern, however, rather than making direct for Znaim, was to 'dislodge' the French from around Laa if possible, or cross the Thaya upstream and block the road with his II Corps until the remainder of the army could arrive. Left behind as rearguard on the Stockerau–Znaim highway was FZM Reuss, with his own outposts on the hills north of Hollabrunn. To the east, Rosenberg had finally fulfilled his orders to cover the road to Brünn and Olmütz. With his dragoon squadron at Dürnholz, the main body of his IV Corps arced along a line from Weistätten to Tracht with the *Hessen-Homburg* Hussars posted to cover the bridges at Muschau and Unter-Wisternitz (Dolni Vestonice). A lone squadron of *O'Reilly* Chevaulegers remained south of the Thaya on the Brünn road.

On the Hauptarmee's western flank, Schustekh's small liaison detachment under GM Anton Hardegg departed Sitzendorf for Retz on the night of 9/10 July even though the Main Army's rearguard was still around Schöngrabern. The increasingly anxious Schustekh, on learning of Hardegg's move, decided that his flanks and rear were in dire peril and would thus shift his division further west on the 10th. Somariva remained in place north of Linz, periodically skirmishing and exchanging raids with Lefebvre's Bavarians. He received a message from Schustekh on 9 July informing him with wonderful euphemism that the Hauptarmee, after a mighty battle, 'had taken up a position to the rear', but with no orders himself, he remained in place for the remainder of the war.[1]

While most of the Austrian Hauptarmee was again making a night march, the French bivouacked where they had been at nightfall, awaiting the dawn before continuing the pursuit. Massena's 4th Corps was on the Stockerau–Znaim road with its cavalry component and Legrand's division just south of Hollabrunn, Carra St Cyr at Großstelzendorf and the other two infantry divisions around Stockerau (Boudet) and between Göllersdorf and Schönborn (Molitor).[2] Colonel Ameil's small cavalry detachment was active along the Danube from its base at Krems. To Massena's right was Oberst Lindenau with his two Bavarian light horse squadrons at Großmugl, but Lindenau does not seem to have been in touch with Massena and there was no significant body of French troops between his detachment and Marmont at Laa, a distance of some 25 km. Although French cavalry patrolled in this gap, the nearest formed French troops on Lindenau's right seem to have been Nansouty's heavy division around Rückersdorf and Stetten, that is 16 km southeast of Lindenau's position. Gérard's light cavalry having returned to the Army of Italy on the 9th, Nansouty was left with his six regiments of cuirassiers and carabiniers, fine battle cavalry, but ill-suited for reconnaissance missions. Moreover, Nansouty was under orders to move to Wilfersdorf on the 10th.

As for Marmont at Laa, many of his infantrymen were doubtless recovering from their excesses of the previous day, but the crossing over the Thaya was secure and some of his light cavalry, having pushed as far as Erdberg and Schönau (Šanov) on 9 July, would be out scouting towards Znaim at first light. Two of Davout's infantry divisions and Grouchy's dragoons had spent the night between Nikolsburg and Drasenhofen, while the rest of his infantry and Arrighi's cuirassier division were gathered around Poysdorf. The Guard and Oudinot were encamped near Wolkersdorf, the latter complaining about the lack of water in the area, while Viceroy Eugène prepared to move most of his new command towards the March River north of the Danube.

South of the great river, the French held Raab and Baraguey d'Hilliers watched Bianchi's Austrians in the bridgehead opposite Pressburg while patrolling as far as Ödenburg. Vandamme, in accordance with Napoleon's instructions, was in the process of shifting his headquarters and most of the Württemberg 8th Corps downstream towards Fischamend to bolster the defences against any possible Habsburg probe towards Vienna from Hungary. Although Schustekh continued to worry about Württemberg forays across the Danube from Melk and Göttweig, Vandamme had at most 2,500 troops to garrison both those miniature fortresses while simultaneously covering 40–50 km of riverfront. The low density of troops and the paucity of boats to transport them meant that the Württembergers could put only put 300 or so men across the river at any one time, hardly a decisive threat to Schustekh's command. Marshal Lefebvre and the Bavarian 1st Division held Linz and also guarded a significant stretch of the Danube. Lefebvre was to be reinforced by the 3rd Bavarian Division, ordered to Linz by Napoleon on 3 July. This division had already departed its defensive positions north of the Tyrol but would not reach its destination until after the armistice.

Two Roads to Znaim

The first troops Charles had dispatched to Znaim from the Hauptarmee arrived sometime around 6:00 on the morning of 10 July. These were the troopers of the *Schwarzenberg* Uhlans under the command of GM von Schneller. The men and their mounts were exhausted. The regiment had been in the saddle from noon to 10:00 p.m. the previous day before departing Schöngrabern at midnight after a mere two hours' rest to ride the 30 km or so to Znaim. Schneller consulted with Altstern and Oberstleutnant Robert Martyn, commander of the *Hohenzollern* Cuirassiers, and learned that all seemed calm: the enemy cavalry that had probed to Erdberg on the 9th had retired during the night and cuirassier outposts watched the road towards Laa. Schneller thus concluded that he could give his men a break and allow the horses to be fed and watered, but this process had hardly begun 'when a man from the *Hohenzollern* outposts galloped up with the news that the enemy was advancing from Erdberg towards Znaim and was only a half an hour away from the town'. Schneller did not tarry in responding to this alarming report. Leaving behind the one squadron that had already begun to tend its horses, he had the rest of the regiment remount at once and hastened off towards Klein-Tesswitz (Dobšice).[3] He found Altstern's infantry was on the vine-covered slopes west of the village and the *Hohenzollern* Cuirassiers were on the heights above skirmishing with French horsemen, so Schneller sent two or three platoons of Uhlans to support them, while dispatching two squadrons to the left to cover the gap between the Rother Hof and the Burgholz; he kept the rest of the regiment in the low ground southwest of Klein-Tesswitz. Though the Austrian cavalry had little difficulty in pushing back the brash and active French light horse, the situation was precarious as there was as yet no sign of the Main Army and the highway through Znaim was jammed with every conceivable kind of vehicle. Fortunately for Schneller and Altstern, major elements of the Hauptarmee and Charles himself would soon arrive.

The Battlefield: Vineyards, Rolling Hills and Deep Ravines

The landscape Schneller's men observed as they trotted east towards the rising sun was a pleasant rural mix of rolling hills, small villages, fields of grain, orchards and innumerable vineyards cut up by deep, steep-sided ravines that the region's watercourses had carved out over the years.[4] Most of the fighting in the coming battle would take place in a relatively confined space bounded on the north by a large wood called the Burgholz (Purkrábka) and on the southwest by the town of Znaim, a distance of only five or six kilometres. The site of an old Moravian fortress since at least the eleventh century, Znaim in 1809 was a district (*Kreis*) centre with a population of some 5,200 souls. Well situated for defence, it sat atop a high cliff above the Thaya River and was still surrounded by its medieval walls so that access was only possible through three principal gates: Upper (northwest), Kaiser Franz's or New (northeast), and Lower (southeast). A fourth gate opened on a narrow incline leading down to the Thaya on the town's southern side and north–south traffic heading towards Iglau could use a ring road of sorts that curved around just outside the town walls to the east. West of town a rill called the

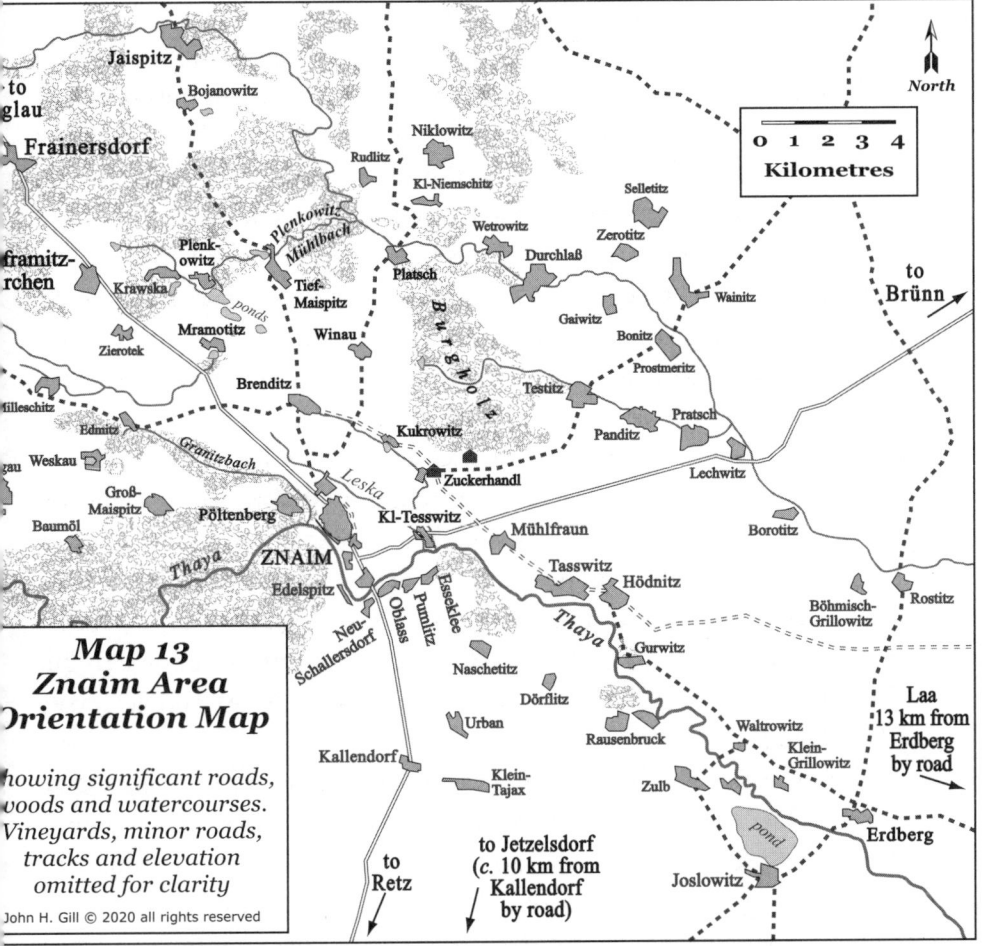

**Map 13
Znaim Area
Orientation Map**

showing significant roads, woods and watercourses. Vineyards, minor roads, tracks and elevation omitted for clarity

John H. Gill © 2020 all rights reserved

Granitzbach (Gránický potok) wound through a constricted gorge separating Znaim from Pöltenberg (Hradiště), a virtually inaccessible settlement and cloister perched on the wooded bluffs above the Thaya. Almost as difficult for any formed military unit was the approach to the town from the Kühberg (Kraví Hora) southwest across the Thaya. To the south, however, the land sloped away gently from Znaim to a pair of bridges that carried the Vienna highway across the Thaya and its island from Oblass (Oblekovice) and Neuschallersdorf (Nový Šaldorf) on the southern bank past Altschallersdorf (Starý Šaldorf) to the town's Lower Gate. West of the highway was the imposing compound of Klosterbruck (Louka), a former abbey that had been converted into a tobacco factory. Several small earthworks had been dug in the open ground near

Altschallersdorf where the brand-new Brünn highway joined that from Vienna. These afforded some shelter to Austrian guns on both days, but were otherwise of limited military value and did not figure prominently in either side's battle reports.[5] The slopes to the east towards Klein-Tesswitz and Zuckerhandl (Suchohrdly), on the other hand, were covered with vineyards and thus represented an obstacle to formed bodies of troops.

This segment of the Thaya, from Neuschallersdorf to Klein-Tesswitz, afforded the only practicable crossing points over the river as the sturdy bridges were supplemented by several fords in summer when the water level was usually low. The Austrians, for example, would rely on the ford near the pheasantry at Pumlitz (Bohumilice). The river's narrow gorge upstream from Edelspitz (Sedlošovice) and the rugged bluffs downstream between Klein-Tesswitz and Mühlfraun (Milfron, now Dyje), on the other hand, essentially precluded the crossing of significant military formations, especially if opposed. Fords at almost every village allowed passage over the river as it proceeded southeast towards Laa, especially downstream from Tasswitz (Tasovice) and Hödnitz (Hodonice), but the only fixed bridges were at Waltrowitz (Valtrovice) and Joslowitz (Jaroslavice).

South of the Thaya, the ground rose steadily from the riverbank to a low ridge approximately two kilometres south along the highway. This would be Massena's route of approach on the 11th and the marshal, topping the ridge, would have been greeted with a spectacular panorama with generally open farmland laid out before him, Naschetitz (Načeratice) in the low ground to his right front, the hilly Pelzwald (Palice) and Sexenberg (Načeratický kopec) just beyond, the Thaya glinting in the sun, and the unique towers of Znaim surmounting the hills in the distance a mere five kilometres to the north.

East of Znaim the terrain was more challenging, so much so that Charles, wedded as he was to eighteenth-century concepts, did not consider it a proper 'position'. That is, unlike Jetzelsdorf with its convenient stream as a natural moat, its protected routes of retreat, and its high ridge for troop deployment and observation, Znaim was not one of the places in the empire that provided the defender with potentially decisive advantages.[6] Instead, the Austrian line of communications to the northwest would be almost parallel to the line of battle here and

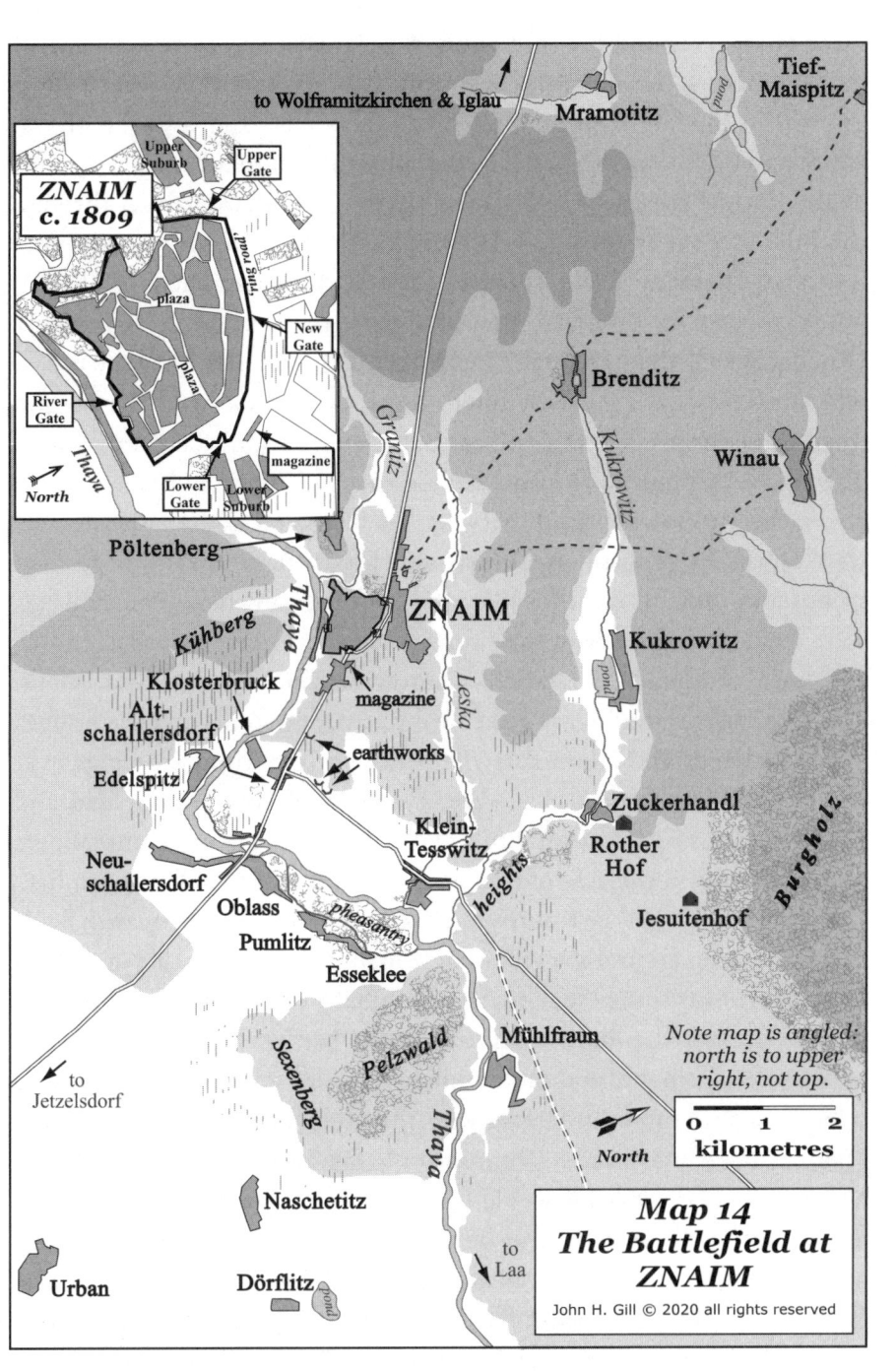

the ground was broken up by obstructions that hindered the movement of reserves and the formation of a classical defensive array. Most notable among the obstacles were the two streams that etched deep grooves in the landscape as they made their ways south to the Thaya. Closest to town was the Leska or Leskabach, a rill that began just south of Brenditz (Přímětice) and cut its narrow, wooded channel through the hills to pass about one kilometre east of Znaim before emptying into the Thaya at Klein-Tesswitz. The Kukrowitzerbach (Dobšický potok) began at Brenditz, flowed into a large pond at Kukrowitz (Kuchařovice), then through Zuckerhandl to find the Thaya just east of Klein-Tesswitz. Although small, these two brooks and the ravines they formed represented significant challenges to military movement. The Leska through most of its course east of Znaim and steep slopes above the Kukrowitzerbach between Zuckerhandl and Klein-Tesswitz were especially problematic: impassable for artillery, cavalry or formed troops and difficult even for loose groups of skirmishers. Four villages were located in the low ground formed by the Kukrowitzerbach north and east of Znaim: Brenditz, Kukrowitz, Zuckerhandl and Klein-Tesswitz. These could serve either army as strongpoints and the bridges at Zuckerhandl and Klein-Tesswitz provided important crossings over the little stream. As such, they were keys to control of the battlefield, and would be the targets of intense interest to the opposing commanders and, especially in the case of Klein-Tesswitz, the scene of fierce combat.

North and east of the Kukrowitzerbach, the land opened up with fields of crops rolling around the village of Winau (Únanov) nestled in its own little dale, towards the Plenkowitzer Mühlbach (Plenkovický potok) that formed the northernmost boundary of the battlefield. The narrow gap between Zuckerhandl and the Burgholz provided access to this relatively open area and, more importantly, to the highway leading to Iglau, the Hauptarmee's line of retreat running only five kilometres west of Winau and Brenditz. These fields would thus be the site of considerable cavalry action during the battle. The Burgholz itself was an extensive forest, approximately four kilometres deep and six kilometres on its long axis from northwest to southeast. Its location made it perfect for a concealed approach to the vulnerable Austrian left flank. Two large, walled farmsteads sat in the gap south of the Burgholz, the Jesuitenhof (or Hof

Burgholz) and the Rother Hof (or Zuckerhandlerhof). The former would be quickly occupied by the French and played no role in the fighting but the latter would be the venue for the some of the discussions that brought the battle and the war to a conclusion.

Across the battle area, the villages were small, generally numbering 250–600 inhabitants, and connected to one another and to Znaim by a network of secondary roads and dirt farm tracks. As noted above, the two major paved highways in the region intersected between Znaim and the Thaya. The Brünn highway, coming from the east, connected Znaim with the Moravian capital some 65 km away to the northeast and was still being completed in July 1809. The Iglau highway made its way from Jedlersdorf to Stockerau along the Danube (20–25 km) and thence north to Znaim, a distance of approximately another 61 km. Massena would therefore follow the bulk of the Hauptarmee as it retreated along this major thoroughfare. Marmont's route from Laa, on the other hand, took him on secondary roads along the broad plateau east and above the Thaya. The principal of these roads (sometimes called the Nikolsburg road) went first through Erdberg and then past Hödnitz and Mühlfraun to join the Brünn highway on the heights east of Klein-Tesswitz. Although the land was generally open, the nature of the terrain was such that he would not have a view of Znaim and the Vienna–Iglau road until he mounted the heights above Klein-Tesswitz where the Brünn highway coming from the east plunged into the little valley of the Kukrowitzerbach.

Nothing Here but a Rearguard

Charles reached Znaim not long after GM von Schneller, that is, some time between 8:00 and 9:00 a.m.[7] Given the terrain and the situation, he faced several uncomfortable problems. First, the terrain was not to his liking. As noted above, it did not constitute a proper 'position' with defensive advantages, ease of movement for reserves and protected routes of retreat. Major von Welden, the staff officer cited earlier regarding Jetzelsdorf, regarded the area around Znaim as 'one grand defile', that is, a narrow space that could only be traversed slowly and with difficulty during which time the army would be vulnerable to attack, defeat and destruction. Listing all of the disadvantages associated with Znaim, he concluded that 'The Austrians would certainly never have designated this as the point from which to fight an enemy coming from one direction, let alone from two directions.'[8] Indeed, as one Austrian military historian later remarked, the area around Znaim was 'not at all suited to the combat methods of the Austrian army'.[9] In his own later writings, Charles repeatedly stressed secure flanks as a defining characteristic of a good 'position' and commented that the relative lack of an anchoring feature on his left at Znaim required him to deploy the left flank of the army in echelon.[10] Second, Charles had not had time to plan his movement to Znaim and issue a detailed 'disposition' as was the norm in Habsburg practice. Instead, he would have to place his formations as they arrived and fight an encounter battle rather than the methodical, set-piece action he preferred. This was the sort of engagement at which the impetuous French excelled, but Charles was painfully aware that his army had repeatedly shown itself awkward and slow in such circumstances, especially when attempting to take the offensive. Finally, the enormous baggage train, clumsily making its way northwest towards Iglau in fits and starts, not only impeded the movement of his combat units but left him no choice but to accept battle under conditions that were, for him, far from ideal.

On his arrival, however, Charles does not seem to have regarded the danger as acute. Although displeased with the overall situation and aware that significant French forces were reported to be approaching, the only enemy troops in evidence at that hour were small groups of probing cavalry. His first report to the Kaiser thus sounded quite confident: 'Shortly after my arrival, some enemy cavalry showed itself on both banks of the Thaya about an hour from here. These began to skirmish with our Uhlans during which some cannon fire occurred. Up to now it does not seem likely to develop into a serious engagement and I will have the corps, as they arrive, assume positions in front of the town towards the Brünn highway.' Beyond what seemed a relatively benign enemy situation, Charles was buoyed by what he believed to be the imminent prospect of peace.

> From the Emperor Napoleon the reply has come that he awaits the arrival of Prince Liechtenstein with pleasure. The emperor was in Wolkersdorf yesterday, currently finds himself on the Brünn

highway, and Prince Liechtenstein has already departed in that direction via Hollabrunn. FML Weißenwolff has returned this morning with high praise for the good reception he had from the Emperor Napoleon both before and after the battle. The latter opined that only his great [numerical] superiority gave him the possibility to outflank our left wing and turn the battle in his favour, that his left was entirely defeated. In these circumstances and as a response from Emperor Napoleon is most certainly to be expected very soon, according to which Prince Liechtenstein will request more definitive orders from Your Majesty, I must urgently ask that Your Majesty not to distance Himself too far from Mährisch-Budwitz so that the proceedings of the initiated negotiations, upon which the existence of the state now depends, are not interrupted by delays.[11]

Unfortunately for the archduke, his brother was already far beyond Mährisch-Budwitz and the battle situation was about to change dramatically.

As Charles had directed in his orders during the night, the Cavalry Reserve Corps and the Grenadier Corps had led the Hauptarmee's march to Znaim on the morning of 10 July, arriving around the same time as the Generalissimus (i.e. between 8:00 and 9:00 a.m.). Following the cavalry, the four grenadier brigades were able to deploy with relative ease, more troubled by their own army's baggage train than by the still distant French. The three leading brigades made their way to the north bank of the Thaya and were initially posted west of Klein-Tesswitz. Before long, however, GM Karl Ritter Steyrer von Edelberg's brigade of five battalions, reinforced by a trio of 3-pounders, was sent to hold the heights above the village in conjunction with the cavalry that was already engaged in desultory skirmishing with the French horse. Here he came under Schneller's temporary command. GM Albrecht Joseph Graf Murray de Melgum's brigade occupied the vineyard-covered slopes between Tesswitz and Znaim while GM Anton von Hammer placed his men astride the highway on Murray's right. Altstern's little command was now withdrawn: the *Hohenzollern* Cuirassiers rejoined the Reserve Cavalry Corps and Altstern, once again reduced to a lone infantry regiment and an artillery battery, was placed in reserve northwest of Znaim.

As for the Cavalry Reserve Corps, Liechtenstein had arrived just before the grenadiers. He initially placed three of the heavy regiments between Znaim and Klein-Tesswitz, but these were redistributed as the rest of the corps arrived and Steyrer's brigade headed for the heights: GM Leopold Freiherr von Rothkirch und Panthen's brigade (*EH Johann* Dragoons No. 1 and *Riesch* Dragoons No. 6) northeast of Kukrowitz, and the six cuirassier regiments (including *Hohenzollern*) north of Znaim just west of the highway and opposite Brenditz. Around the same time, Schneller reinforced the two squadrons between the Burgholz and the Rother Hof with the rest of the *Schwarzenberg* Uhlans, retaining only three platoons near Klein-Tesswitz as part of his temporary little command.

Army headquarters was established in Brenditz but the arriving caravan of officers, soldiers, and servants found it largely vacant. Most of the inhabitants had fled and 'almost the entire village was empty' wrote the local priest. With a large number of officers lodged in the vicinity, therefore, this individual found himself nearly overwhelmed trying to support them on his own. 'Fürst von Schwarzenberg and Fürst Moritz von Liechtenstein as well as a host of staff and senior officers stayed in my priory,' he recorded, 'Every day for the entire two days from 4:00 in the morning until 10:00 at night, more than 300 officers were fed in the two lower rooms and more than 80 senior ranks in the upper rooms, lunch as well as the evening meal, more than 60 *Eimers* of wine were supplied from my cellar unrecompensed both in my house and in the field.'[12]

The remaining elements of the army reserve deployed south of the Thaya. Wimpffen, watching the army's movement from the hill above Naschetitz, gave direct orders to the fourth of the grenadier brigades, that commanded by Oberstleutnant Heinrich Franz von Scovaud de la Bastide (the former commander, GM Franz Freiherr Mauroy de Merville, had been wounded at Wagram). Wimpffen was alarmed to observe French troops approaching Naschetitz from the southeast and enemy skirmishers appearing to the east across the Thaya between Mühlfraun and Tasswitz. Taking advantage of the fact that Scovaud's brigade had been displaced in the march column by a mass of artillery vehicles and had not yet crossed the river, he ordered one battalion

(*Scharlach*) and two guns to cover Oblass and the bridge, placed another at Pumlitz (*Brzezinski*), and directed Scovaud to march the remaining two battalions to the hill upon which he stood. FML Johann Nostitz-Reineck and four cavalry regiments (*Knesevich* Dragoons No. 3, *Rosenberg* Chevaulegers No. 6, and the two Insurrection regiments) were detached to support the grenadiers.[13]

The extent of combat activity here on the right, or south, bank of the Thaya during the day is difficult to discern. Austrian accounts provide detailed depictions of the Hauptarmee's deployments and repeatedly mention enemy 'columns' advancing from Joslowitz to threaten Naschetitz. The after-action report that FML Prochaska[14] submitted for the Grenadier Corps, for example, describes Scovaud's men advancing to occupy Naschetitz and capturing some prisoners as the French withdrew rather than contest possession of the village.[15] French and Bavarian reports, on the other hand, say almost nothing about actions on the right bank. Marmont detached two cavalry squadrons to screen the Thaya southeast of Mühlfraun,[16] but it seems probable that he sent nothing more than a few scouting detachments across the river. These may have engaged in some minor firefights with the Habsburg forces around Naschetitz. Bavarian skirmishers did fire on the Austrians from across the river between Mühlfraun and Tasswitz early in the action (that is, late morning) and some French from Claparède's division seem to have crossed the shallow Thaya near these two villages to harass the enemy on the far shore later. None of this represented a serious threat to the Hauptarmee or a major part of Marmont's planning – he was focused on developments north of the little river. The most likely explanation for this discrepancy would seem to be that the Austrians exaggerated the enemy presence on the right bank, while the French and their Bavarian allies regarded these small reconnaissance patrols as too routine and too insignificant to warrant subsequent mention.

Indeed, the day's fighting took place north, not south, of the Thaya. Montbrun's division had departed Laa at 3:00 a.m., followed by Preysing's Bavarian brigade. He left the 7th Chasseurs behind at Laa to guard the bridges and serve as a link to Davout's corps. Similarly, Grouchy detached 100 dragoons to make the connection from his end. Coordination between these two forces was seriously deficient, however, because the chasseurs left to rejoin their brigade sometime during the day but the dragoons never seem to have assumed responsibility for the town and the vital bridges. It is not clear which unit was to blame for this gross lapse (Napoleon quite understandably faulted Marmont – *see below*), but there were no French troops at Laa when the emperor arrived that afternoon. This error aroused Napoleon's ire, not only because any Austrian patrol could have destroyed the bridges and thus cut Marmont's line of retreat, but also because the absence of friendly cavalry posts meant there was no secure line of communications for reports and orders between Marmont and imperial headquarters. Fortunately for the French, few Austrian commanders were enterprising enough to capitalise on such a mistake. Marmont's line of retreat remained untroubled by enemy action and the worst outcome was the severe scolding he suffered from his imperial master.

As Montbrun's troopers were riding towards Znaim that morning, however, Napoleon's anger lay in the future. Trotting along the road on the left bank of the Thaya, Montbrun's reconnaissance parties appeared opposite the Tesswitz heights around mid-morning to engage in skirmishing with the *Hohenzollern* Cuirassiers and Schneller's *Schwarzenberg* Uhlans. His main body arrived shortly thereafter as the cuirassiers were retiring and Steyrer's grenadiers were climbing up the steep slope from Klein-Tesswitz to post themselves on the heights above. Steyrer's men would not be dislodged without infantry, but the French and Bavarian foot soldiers and their artillery batteries were still making their way up the road from Laa. For the moment, therefore, Montbrun was limited to observing and occupying the enemy while he awaited the rest of the corps. Moreover, with the Austrians holding the heights, he and Marmont, who rode up between 10:00 and 11:00 a.m., had no visibility into the basin around Tesswitz nor could they see beyond to the Iglau highway crammed with the struggling Habsburg baggage train. Marmont thus continued to believe that 'the enemy army had passed Znaim and there was nothing here but a rearguard'.[17]

While awaiting the infantry, Montbrun's inquisitive and acquisitive light horsemen explored the local area, including the Burgholz. There among the trees they came upon a great mass of vehicles trapped in the mud of a poor forest trail. 'Three large wagons filled with silverware fell prey to our hussars who shared it among themselves with an incredible rapidity,' recalled Captain Hippolyte d'Espinchal of the 5th Hussars, 'Four heavy vehicles, massive and of antique design, very rich, containing ten ladies, including six who were young and very pretty, fell into our hands as well as two caleches containing three aged person in court dress with plaques and grand ribbons, ten equipment wagons, and sixty horses of the Austrian emperor's imperial stable.'[18] French generals intervened before the hussars could make off with all of this amazing booty and in any case the regiments would soon be called to battle as the sweating French and Bavarian foot soldiers, toiling up from Laa, were beginning to arrive on the field.

Marmont's infantry had been delayed by the need to restore the many small bridges over the marshes north of Laa and had then endured a strenuous march under oppressive heat that morning, so that the head of the column only began to appear near Mühlfraun some time after 11:00 a.m. Marmont, eager to exploit his presumed opportunity, allowed little time to rest and deployed his divisions as soon as they were on hand. The lead infantry division, Clauzel's 2nd, crossed the Brünn highway and took up a position on the right near the Jesuitenhof while Claparède's 1st Division peeled off to the left nearer Mühlfraun. The Bavarian infantry took a route via the Thaya valley and, as noted earlier, Schützen from the 3rd and 13th Regiments skirmished with the Austrians across the river between Mühlfraun and Tasswitz during their approach to the battlefield. As the main body of the Bavarians came up, Marmont slotted them in on his left astride the Brünn highway between the two French divisions. Parallel to and facing the Tesswitz heights, Minucci arrayed his troops in nine battalion columns with proper intervals, echeloned slightly to the left, and with skirmishers to the front.

The French could not help but notice that they were opposed by grenadiers in their distinctive bearskin caps; this was a troop type usually held as an elite reserve and unlikely to be committed to rearguard tasks. Prisoners, however, stated that they had indeed been assigned to shield the army's retreat.[19] This was true as far as it went, but the common soldiers being questioned could not know that the entire Hauptarmee was en route for Znaim. Their comments thus unintentionally bolstered Marmont's preconception that he only faced a weak rearguard. Proceeding from this erroneous assumption, he initially imagined that he might drive off the enemy force on the north bank of the Thaya, seize the bridge at Oblass, and 'deliver those on the other bank of the river to Marshal Massena'.[20] He would soon learn how mistaken his assessment was.

Opposite Marmont's line, Schneller and Steyrer had deployed the five grenadier battalions in a single line of squares, with the *Hromada* Grenadiers on the left (north), *Hahn* on the right, and the remaining three battalions echeloned in towards the centre. To their left, the weary *Schwarzenberg* Uhlans covered the open ground between Zuckerhandl and the Burgholz, but lack of infantry meant that Zuckerhandl was not occupied in strength.[21] Steyrer's skirmishers were scattered among the vineyards and began exchanging fire with the French and Bavarians as their respective divisions, clearly visible from the heights, moved into place. The Habsburg position was perilous. Steyrer's left flank was vulnerable, he was badly outnumbered, his artillery consisted of three puny 3-pounders, and his nearest supports were west of Klein-Tesswitz some 3 km to his rear. Perhaps because Schneller was technically in command on the heights, the Grenadier Corps commander, FML Prochaska, seemed content to occupy the hills closer to Znaim and leave Schneller and Steyrer to fend more or less for themselves.

Fortunately for Steyrer, the French approach march and deployment had consumed some considerable time and it was not until early afternoon that Marmont was prepared to attack. Assisted by his powerful artillery, his advance began with swarms of skirmishers creeping through 'the bushes and gullies' to pepper the grenadiers with a galling fire.[22] GB Delzons and the 8th Léger led the way on the right with the 23rd Ligne in support. Minucci's Bavarians advanced on the left with the 6th Light Battalion bolstered by the division's combined Schützen. The Austrians resisted stubbornly, but the allied artillery almost immediately dismounted two of Steyrer's three little 3-pounders and musketry from the skirmishers caused numerous casualties among the defending grenadiers. The Austrians also began to run out of cartridges, but Schneller's and Steyrer's requests for more ammunition and replacement artillery went unanswered. Still, the grenadiers held and both the French and the Bavarians had to commit additional formed troops to press their advance. Before long, however, GB Delzons, directing his brigade 'with his usual skill', forced Steyrer's battalions back on the French right.[23] The Bavarians on the left had an equally hard fight but, with support from two artillery batteries firing canister and several additional infantry companies, they were equally successful in driving their opponents back. The danger to the grenadiers' position was compounded as French infantry pressed into Zuckerhandl and Montbrun's horse chased off the Uhlans beyond, leaving the Austrian left in the air. Outflanked on both sides, Schneller had no choice but to evacuate the heights. After holding off a numerically superior enemy for several hours, he and Steyrer conducted the withdrawal in an orderly manner, but they were fortunate that the rearguard, the *Hromada* Grenadiers, repulsed a charge by the Bavarian cavalry that might have turned the retreat into a rout. Schneller, his mission on the heights over, relinquished command of Steyrer's brigade, collected his three platoons of Uhlans, and rode off to join the rest of the regiment on the army's left flank.

The Austrian retreat allowed Marmont to reach the crest above Tesswitz sometime between 2:00 and 3:00 p.m. Here he found that the force opposing him was something rather more than a mere rearguard. 'I discovered Znaim in front of me and, on the other side of the Thaya on the road to Hollabrunn, an immense quantity of troops, artillery and baggage,' he wrote later, 'I thus found myself in the rear of the Austrian army.' 'Znaim was occupied,' he continued, and 'One could perceive, behind Znaim on the route to Bohemia, many troops and much artillery as well as the columns passing the Thaya bridge to follow the general movement of assembly that was taking place around that town.'[24] He estimated 10,000–12,000 men in the basin north of the Thaya and another 15,000 south of the river. This daunting prospect notwithstanding, he discerned at a great distance to the south what he believed were artillery flashes indicating Massena's near approach and wanted to do something to disturb and possibly block the enemy's passage. Before committing himself, however, he needed a picture of the Austrians on his right. 'If the enemy was not in force behind Znaim, I could, despite being alone, attempt the movement which the presence of Davout would have made infallible.'[25] He thus sent Montbrun to advance into the open ground beyond Zuckerhandl and press towards the highway beyond.[26]

Montbrun moved with alacrity, his light horsemen overwhelming the *Schwarzenberg* Uhlans that Schneller had posted near Zuckerhandl and driving them to the northwest in disarray. Rothkirch, waiting in support between Winau and Kukrowitz about 2 km behind the Uhlans, attempted to retrieve the situation by advancing with his two dragoon regiments only to be defeated in turn. Thrown into 'the greatest disorder and complete dissolution',[27] his men fled for Mramotitz (Mramotice) and Tief Maispitz (Hluboké Mašůvky) while Montbrun turned west towards the Iglau highway.

This was a moment of considerable danger for the Hauptarmee. With his regiments arrayed between Brenditz and Winau, Montbrun was only some three kilometres away from the highway and its confused collection of lumbering baggage, artillery, wounded, stragglers and every other variety of rear-area personnel and vehicles trundling towards Iglau in a double column 'wagon after wagon very slowly'.[28] Although Montbrun was himself somewhat out on a limb, beyond supporting distance of the rest of Marmont's corps, his horsemen would have induced destructive panic among this congested mass had they been able to cover those final few kilometres. Even if the French had not been able to sustain themselves long across the Austrian line of communications, the chaos that would have attended even a temporary interruption might have been devastating for Charles and his army. As it was, however, the threat proved transitory. The six cuirassier regiments that had been posted near the highway trotted forward to position themselves on the ridge southeast of Brenditz where they threatened Montbrun's open left flank across the shallow valley of the Kukrowitzerbach. The *Schwarzenberg* Uhlans, re-formed northwest of Brenditz, also helped constrain the French advance.[29] Furthermore, some Habsburg officer had the presence of mind to order a 12-pounder position battery out of the column of vehicles on the highway and its shot and shell were soon bounding and bursting among the French ranks.[30]

Montbrun thus prudently withdrew to the open ground in front of the Burgholz and the moment of danger for the Hauptarmee passed. This incident, though fleeting, was not without impact as it instilled in minds of the Austrian generals, their Generalissimus above all, that their adversary's active, energetic, and very numerous cavalry might exploit the

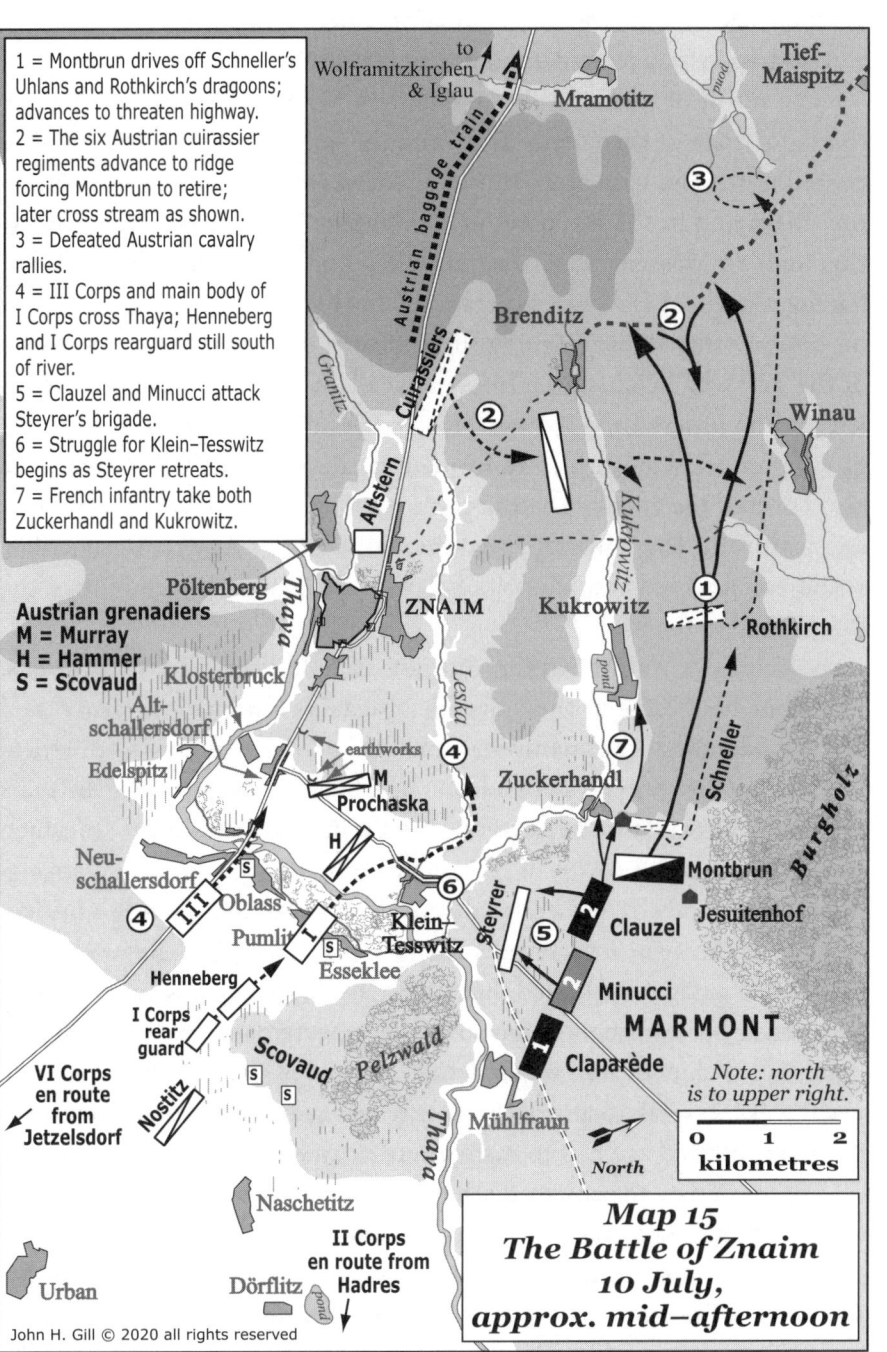

vulnerability of their left flank to cut their line of retreat and trap the entire Hauptarmee in and around Znaim. This brief moment of peril therefore elevated, even exaggerated, their extant fears for the safety of the army.

As a result of these cavalry encounters Marmont learned that 'close to 40,000 men of the enemy army and the entire park of artillery' were posted north and east of Znaim in addition to those on the far bank of the Thaya and in the basin below the heights. His hopes of 'delivering' this force to Massena were thus dispelled and he 'keenly regretted' not having requested Davout's assistance.[31] In this perilous situation he saw no option other than resigning himself to 'a defensive role'. Possession of the Tesswitz heights gave him an excellent defensive position for his left and he ordered the Rother Hof and Jesuitenhof fortified as points of support for Montbrun's re-formed cavalry to anchor his right. He also covered the edge of the Burgholz with light infantry to control this key feature of the landscape. Additionally, as the Austrian grenadiers withdrew, he lined the Tesswitz heights with artillery to dominate the low ground to the west.

A 'defensive role', however, did not exclude local offensive thrusts. Marmont had faith in 'the spirit that sustains a victorious army' and was confident that the enemy was unaware of his command's numerical inferiority. With Steyrer's brigade in retreat and the Bavarian skirmishers in pursuit, he therefore decided to seize Klein-Tesswitz, capture of which would threaten the Austrian retreat over the Thaya, gain him a strongpoint that would strengthen his defensive posture, and provide a bridgehead over the two little brooks for future operations.[32] Beyond these tactical advantages, he hoped that such a display of aggressiveness would help mask his command's weakness for the remaining hours of daylight. As his chief of staff would write in his after-action report, the little corps was too weak to attack the enemy on the right as would have been desirable, instead 'we had to manoeuvre in an entirely different manner, seek to intimidate the enemy on the right and attack vigorously on the left to cause him the greatest disquiet . . . to make him believe that the entire army was in support, that it would soon debouch on our right.' In this fashion, the French hoped to lock the Austrian commander 'in a state of uncertainty that would prevent him from taking any decisive resolution before the next day'.[33]

Klein-Tesswitz: A Sanguinary Combat

The task of assaulting Klein-Tesswitz fell to the Bavarian division, initiating what would be the bloodiest day of the war for that kingdom's contingent. Indeed, as expressed in the Army of Dalmatia's after-action report, it would be a 'sanguinary combat' for all concerned.[34]

As Steyrer's grenadiers fell back into the low ground near the two streams, the Bavarians lost no time in employing their powerful artillery. In short order, the three dozen Bavarian guns rumbled up to the edge of the heights, unlimbered, and opened a lively fire on the Austrians in the basin below, driving the white-coats back from the village. Some Bavarian infantry elements entered Klein-Tesswitz at this point in a more or less unsupervised fashion, exploiting the Austrian retreat to gain a momentary hold on the village. They were soon evicted, and Marmont directed Minucci to take Klein-Tesswitz and the hill to its immediate north. Though he ordered the attack, Marmont seems to have been chastened by the news from Montbrun as his orders indicate he was not yet committed to an all-out fight for Klein-Tesswitz. Most tellingly, he instructed Minucci to retreat and set the village afire if it could not be held. Additionally, he was determined to maintain his position on the heights and thus retained the Bavarian 1st Brigade to occupy the centre of his line to the right of the highway; he also held back the six Bavarian cavalry squadrons (who would have been of little use in capturing the village in any case). This left GM Karl von Beckers and his 2nd Brigade to attack Klein-Tesswitz. The brigade's 7th Infantry having already been allotted to protect the artillery, however, Beckers was reduced to conducting his assault with the 6th Infantry Regiment alone. Despite this formidable prospect, II/6 successfully stormed Klein-Tesswitz and I/6, flanked on its right by skirmishers from the 13th Infantry, captured the vine-covered slope just to the north as directed. Pushing beyond, however, proved impossible in the face of the three enemy grenadier brigades and fire from two Austrian guns on the south bank of the river.

Thus began a protracted and bloody struggle for Klein-Tesswitz that saw the greater part of the village change hands multiple times (anything from three to six times depending on the account). After being pushed out the first time, Beckers rallied his men on the eastern edge of the village and quickly returned to the attack only to be again repulsed. Reinforced by I/7 Infantry, two companies of the 13th Infantry, and a French voltigeur company from the 81st Ligne, he stormed the town once more, but came under heavy fire as he attempted to push into the open ground on the western side and retired back among the houses.

At this stage of the battle, Bellegarde's I Corps entered the scene. As we have seen, the urgent 'disposition' Charles had issued at 3:30 that morning had directed Bellegarde not to halt in the Jetzelsdorf position, but to march on via Dörflitz (Derflice) and Naschetitz to cross the Thaya by a bridge or ford and occupy an unspecified position north of the river. When the corps was about an hour south of the river, however, Bellegarde could see the combat on the Tesswitz heights and sent an officer to ask for new orders from Charles. Fortuitously, Bellegarde's chief of staff, GM Franz Xaver Richter von Binnenthal, was already at Znaim, reconnoitring the terrain on his own initiative. He had joined the headquarters staff when Charles arrived that morning and was thus present when Bellegarde's courier rode up with the request for orders.[35]

Receiving new instructions from the archduke, Binnenthal hastened back to report that I Corps should cross the Thaya using the ford at Pumlitz and then proceed to take up a position between Znaim and Brenditz. It was approximately early afternoon, a time when the heights and Klein-Tesswitz were still in Austrian hands. The lead elements of the corps (five squadrons of *Klenau* Chevaulegers, three batteries and the *Anton Mittrowsky*, *Erbach*, and *Reuss-Plauen* Infantry Regiments[36]) thus crossed the river safely, and passed up the Leska ravine to occupy their designated position.

The next I Corps elements to cross were the *Kolowrat* and *EH Rainer* Infantry Regiments under the command of GM Joseph Freiherr von Henneberg, but the situation had changed by the time these men reached the river. The Bavarians now held Klein-Tesswitz, parts of which were burning, and the ford was under continuous artillery and small-arms fire.[37] Henneberg, undeterred, inspired his men with a 'suitable speech' and led them across the river by platoons. Once on the northern bank, Henneberg re-formed his regiments behind a skirmish line before launching them into an attack that drove the Bavarians out of Klein-Tesswitz once more. With the village in Henneberg's possession, the

I Corps rearguard (two companies of III/*Reuss-Plauen* and the remaining three squadrons of *Klenau*) could traverse the ford undisturbed to join the bulk of the corps near Brenditz. Henneberg likewise withdrew. Conceiving that his mission had been accomplished, he left Klein-Tesswitz and retired to the slopes to the northwest near Znaim where he remained until the arrival of V Corps during the night.[38] The grenadiers once again took responsibility for the fight at Klein-Tesswitz.

As the seesaw contest for the village raged, the two sides also struggled to control the low ridge just north of Klein-Tesswitz. On the Bavarian side, the 6th Light Battalion fought a prolonged battle with the grenadiers under the afternoon sun as Mändler recalled:

> The fighting for possession of this hill was long and fierce until we finally, despite the enemy's obstinate resistance, gained the upper hand and drove them down the slope through the vineyards and into the low ground, whereupon we took our position in an extended line. We punished the enemy severely with our heavy fire by files, but suffered likewise from the equally heavy fire of our opponents, which became ever more painful and disadvantageous for us as we began to run out of ammunition. Taking ammunition from the dead and wounded to distribute among the troops did not help much. It was not long before all of these cartridges had also been fired off and we had to allow the enemy to take aim at us without responding. To make the misfortune complete, the sergeants and soldiers we sent out for ammunition returned with the news that infantry ammunition was nowhere to be found. Finally, towards evening, we were relieved by a battalion of the 13th Line Regiment and retired to the back side of the hill.

The 6th Light received an odd reinforcement during this struggle: what the men called a 'donkey battery' of two mountain guns that Marmont's corps had brought from Dalmatia. These small cannon appeared packed on four donkeys accompanied by 'several French or Italian artillerymen'. Finding an acceptable firing point on the battalion's flank, the crews unpacked and assembled their weapons with a speed and dexterity that astonished the curious Bavarians. They only fired five or six rounds, however, before Austrian counterbattery fire caused them to repack and trot off with equal rapidity. The light infantrymen were happy to see their odd supports depart owing to the decidedly unwelcome attention they had attracted from the Habsburg gunners.

The desperation of combat notwithstanding, Mändler and other Bavarians also remembered the irresistible lure that the region's many cherry trees exerted on the troops. The enticing fruit proved a considerable distraction as 'the day was hot and humid and our thirst was therefore great'. 'Only with effort could we drag our soldiers away from these refreshing trees', he wrote afterwards, noting that 'some soldiers, especially the drummers, even climbed up into the trees' only to pay a heavy price with serious wounds or even death for their adventures.[39]

The battle for the village, meanwhile, had taken a new turn. The sequence of actions is not entirely clear, but sometime after Henneberg's intervention, Marmont noticed that Beckers was struggling to re-form the Bavarian infantry in the eastern parts of Klein-Tesswitz. Fearing that the village might be lost, he personally rode to Preysing, whose brigade was waiting in a cherry orchard on the Tesswitz heights.

> You see, general, the desperate situation of your infantry and how much it needs support; in this terrain and under the prevailing conditions, I cannot order you to provide this assistance with your cavalry. However, if you wish to undertake this and if you think you can do so, you will do me and the entire cause a great service; but I say again, I cannot order this!

Preysing, of course, could not resist such an appeal. He placed himself at the head of the 2nd Chevaulegers *König*, and, with the two squadrons of *Leiningen* following in reserve, set off down the steep slopes towards Klein-Tesswitz some time around 5:00 p.m. Riding through the village, the troopers crossed the little bridge over the Leska, quickly formed on the other side despite a terrible fire, galloped forward, 'and broke into the ranks of the astonished grenadiers who certainly never expected a cavalry attack'.[40] The grenadier commanders hastened to form their men into battalion masses to resist the onrushing Bavarians, but the *Kirchenbetter* Grenadiers and two attached companies from *Leiningen* Grenadiers were slow to react.[41] Placed to cover the Brünn highway west of Klein-Tesswitz, they were hurrying to the rear 'shaken and in considerable disorder' when FML Prochaska rode up in dismay. He was able to rally them and lead them against the cavalry, however.[42] Indeed, the Bavarian horse were in considerable peril. Extremely vulnerable in the open ground west of the village, nearly surrounded by enemy infantry, and under fire from artillery in the partially completed earthworks, they were in danger of being crushed. Preysing wisely sounded the retreat, fortunate that there was no Habsburg horse at hand to exploit his predicament. The charge did prompt the Austrians to send two squadrons of Neutra Insurrection Hussars north of the river from Nostitz's command on the south bank, but these were posted behind the battalion masses of the grenadiers and were not engaged.

If the *Kirchenbetter* Grenadiers fell into disarray, others defended themselves with great tenacity. Unterleutnant von Madroux of the *König* Chevaulegers related a story of 20–25 grenadiers led by a tall sergeant who gathered around a fruit tree when they were cut off from their battalion. Forming an impromptu knot as they had been trained to do when caught by cavalry, they refused to surrender and held off repeated efforts by the Bavarian chevaulegers until the latter were forced to withdraw.[43] Madroux, admiring the grenadier sergeant's courage, regretted that he could not identify their stalwart opponent.

The drama of the cavalry charge notwithstanding, the battle for Klein-Tesswitz was far from over. Marmont, while tightening his line between the Burgholz, Kukrowitz and Zuckerhandl, decided that the village must be defended 'with vigour and every exertion'. During the course of the afternoon and evening, therefore, 'bit by bit', almost all of the Bavarian infantry was committed to the bitter struggle in one way or another.[44] Only a few companies of the 1st Brigade remained on the heights to cover the artillery. Two pieces were even employed in close action as the Bavarian artillery commander, Major Karl Julian Freiherr von Zoller, boldly brought a 6-pounder and a howitzer into the valley north of the village to provide much-needed support. The fight also expanded as Austrian II Corps intervened. Around the time of Preysing's cavalry attack, one of Hohenzollern's batteries unlimbered on the south bank of the Thaya and took the Bavarians under fire from their left flank. White-coated skirmishers of the *Zach* Infantry also emerged from the trees on the far side of the river to harass the Bavarians contesting possession of the village. Turning some of their pieces to face south, Bavarian gunners on the heights put an end to the Austrian bombardment and II/7 Infantry was deployed along the river to chase off the skirmishers, but the fight in the village roared on. Sometimes hand-to-hand with bayonets and musket butts, the combat surged back and forth, with the Bavarians capturing and losing all or part of Klein-Tesswitz at least twice more before the firing petered out around 9:00 p.m. The day concluded, however, with the Bavarians and French in control of all or most of the village. Prochaska's grenadiers retired, some covering the open low ground west of the village with the two squadrons of Insurrection hussars, others joining Henneberg on the slopes below Znaim.[45] For the Bavarians, this was a victory all the more welcome because it brought with it the capture of a large magazine of bread and flour sufficient to feed the division.[46]

Nor was it solely a Bavarian battle with the Habsburg grenadiers. Small French detachments had been engaged in and around Klein-Tesswitz at various points, and, by the end of the day, Marmont had thrown both battalions of the 81st Ligne from Clarparède's division into the fray. Exactly when the French regiment entered the battle is not clear, but the 7th Bavarian Infantry credited their French comrades in arms with saving I/7 from potential disaster as the battalion had exhausted its ammunition.[47] Its precise role in the fighting also went unrecorded, but it was sufficiently significant for Marmont to praise its colonel, Michel Louis Joseph Bonté, for his regiment's fine performance. In any case, the 81st assumed responsibility for the village that night while the 79th Ligne occupied the hill to the north, allowing Minucci's men to retire to the Tesswitz heights to enjoy their captured provisions.[48]

The intensity of the fighting both on the Tesswitz heights and especially in and around the little village is reflected in the casualties both sides suffered during the day. As noted earlier, this proved to be the most costly day of the entire war for the Bavarian contingent. Despite being heavily engaged in the April battles in their homeland, the 901 casualties (including 84 killed) lost in the struggle for Klein-Tesswitz surpassed any other single day's loss. It is hardly surprising that the 6th Infantry accounted for one-third of these (310), but the 7th and 13th Regiments also took significant losses and the 2nd Chevaulegers paid for their charge with 40 casualties. On the Austrian side, the bulk of the losses came from Steyrer's brigade: 559 out of a total of approximately 1,100. French losses are unknown, but it may be assumed that the 81st Ligne took some casualties and possibly, though less likely, the 79th as well. Adding perhaps several dozen or more French dead, wounded, and missing to the Bavarian total would yield an overall figure only slightly below that of the Austrian side.[49]

Notable among the Austrian losses were those of the 1st Ober-Manhartsberg Landwehr Battalion attached to GM Hammer's brigade that had entered the battle with 188 officers and men. With 93 men listed as 'missing' and only one wounded, half of the battalion disappeared during the course of the day, not because of enemy action but because of soldiers taking advantage of night marches and combat confusion to leave the ranks.[50] The 1st OMB thus serves as another example of the problems the monarchy experienced with this new institution during the course of the war.

Both sides regarded the fight for the heights and village of Klein-Tesswitz as a success. For the Austrians, the grenadiers and Henneberg had held off a dire threat to the Thaya crossings and had allowed the Hauptarmee to pass safely over the river. The official Habsburg account offered extravagant praise for Steyrer and Henneberg (Schneller was not mentioned) while lauding Prochaska 'and his brave grenadiers' for having 'thwarted the enemy's intentions on the 10th and opening the passage over the Thaya for the army'.[51] If the threat was not as great as portrayed, the courage and steadiness of the grenadiers and I Corps infantry was well recompensed in this official recognition. Commanders on the other side also commended their troops and subordinate officers. Marmont expressed his appreciation to Minucci several times and rode especially to Beckers the following day to convey 'his particular satisfaction' with the general's actions. He further told Beckers that he had reported 'the brave conduct of the troops' to Napoleon and his 14 July after-action report indeed praised Beckers for attacking Klein-Tesswitz with 'great vigour' and defending it 'stubbornly'. His 12 July order of the day likewise complimented the division for 'the courageous attacks which it made on the village of [Klein-]Tesswitz and the obstinacy with which it defended the same'. He also lavished accolades on Preysing for the Bavarian cavalry charge and, as noted earlier, lauded Colonel Bonté and the men of the 81st for their efforts in the battle.[52]

The actions on the heights and in the village also illustrated the nature of combat on this portion of the field. An officer of the Bavarian 13th Infantry, writing some years later, observed that 'During the two days in a cut-up terrain of hills and vineyards fighting was almost entirely conducted in skirmish order without the battlefield changing more than fifteen minutes; on both sides, one thrust first forward – then back again.'[53] These are useful insights as far as tactics are concerned, but the relative lack of movement was also a function of the weakness of Marmont's corps; had he had more infantry at hand, he might have endeavoured to press harder and farther. The presence of Davout's corps, of course, would have changed the entire complexion of the battle. From the information available, it seems that deployment in skirmish order was somewhat less prevalent on the Austrian side as Schneller and Steyrer initially arrayed the latter's brigade in squares on the heights and Prochaska repeatedly employed battalion masses in the open ground west of Klein-Tesswitz. Even the grenadiers, however, deployed some men in skirmish order.[54] Likewise, this Bavarian officer's observations are less relevant to the northern part of the battlefield, where the rolling hills afforded more scope for cavalry operations and where infantry would adopt close-order formations.

Another tactic common to the Bavarians and the French was exploiting the region's bounty. Captain Jules Antoine Paulin, one of the staff officers on the heights with Napoleon on 11 July, observed scenes that echoed the Bavarian experiences of the previous day, the 'amusing aspect', as he framed it, 'of even the most serious things'. He was watching French infantrymen 'who gave and received death, right next to the furious cavalry charges', but saw 'bands of soldiers leave the ranks and climb the fruit-laden cherry trees that covered the plain. When they had staunched their thirst, they returned to their places to resume firing while others replaced them in the trees to quench their thirst in turn ... I had my share of these refreshing cherries,' he concluded.[55] Had we more personal accounts from the Austrian side, it seems likely we would find similar stories of Habsburg soldiers sneaking off to raid the numerous orchards for which the region was justly renowned.

Zuckerhandl and Kukrowitz

As the bitter struggle for Klein-Tesswitz rolled back and forth, the situation on the other half of the battlefield was also evolving. Minus GM Henneberg's ad hoc command, Austrian I Corps had slipped past the fighting at Tesswitz and made its way though the narrow Leska valley to take position on a hill southeast of Brenditz. Though harassed by the brisk fire of French batteries near Zuckerhandl, Bellegarde placed a battalion of *Anton Mittrowsky* No. 10 in Brenditz and arrayed his corps (five and two-thirds battalions) on the hill in a single line facing south and east with three squadrons of *Klenau* and a cavalry battery in reserve. The other two *Klenau* squadrons were posted just outside Brenditz on his left and two companies of *Reuss-Plauen* were detached to a hill about a kilometre south of his right flank to establish a link with the grenadiers. With the latter engaged at Klein-Tesswitz and on the slopes immediately north thereof, however, for a considerable time during the late afternoon there was a gap of approximately two kilometres in the Austrian line between Bellegarde's right and the left grenadier brigade (Steyrer's) in the vineyards to the south. The choppy nature of the terrain disguised this weakness and Marmont lacked sufficient forces to have exploited it in any case, but it was indicative of the challenge the Hauptarmee faced in entering into an unplanned encounter battle or meeting engagement.

Kolowrat's III Corps arrived as Bellegarde's men were arranging themselves on their ridge. The corps had departed its bivouac at Schöngrabern around midnight, reached Haugsdorf at 8:00 a.m. and deposited six battalions and four guns north of Haugsdorf to support the rearguard before making its way towards the Thaya at 9:00. It crossed the river via the Oblass bridges at approximately the same time that I Corps was wading its way through the Pumlitz ford and 'hurried around the city of Znaim at double time' just outside the walls to take up a position as 'the outermost left wing' of the army on the heights beyond Brenditz. Here Kolowrat had the infantry form squares, doubtless owing to the open terrain and the presence of Montbrun's formidable cavalry force. The corps had been on the road for fifteen or sixteen hours by this time and had covered more than 35 km, but its operations journal recorded that it advanced 'in fine form'[56] with its artillery to the fore to support the Cavalry Reserve to its front. This move brought it to a position on

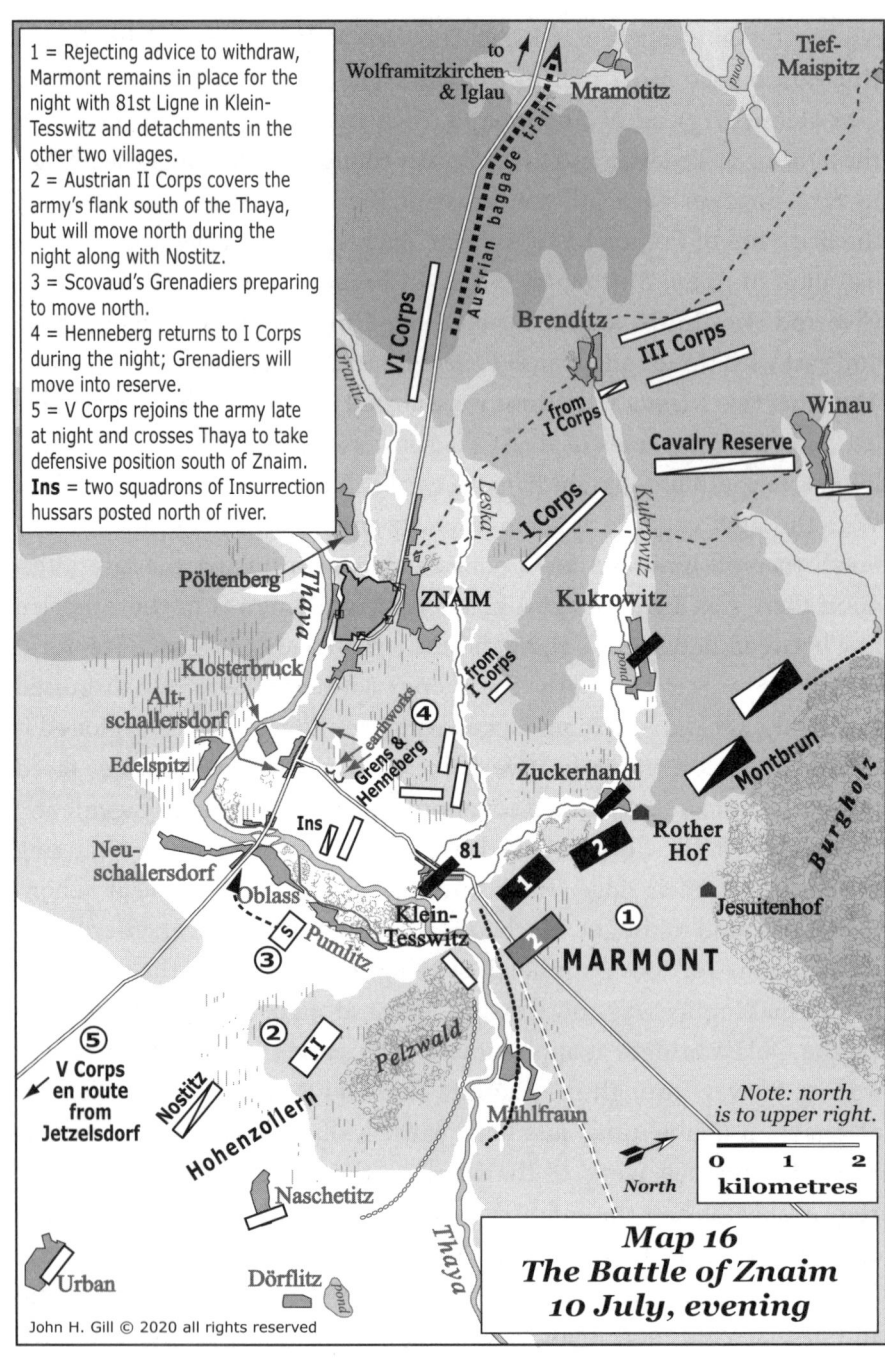

Map 16
The Battle of Znaim
10 July, evening

the hills just south and west of Winau where it halted until nightfall.[57] The Cavalry Reserve regiments on this flank also advanced slowly and ended up forward of III Corps west of Winau, deploying two batteries to maintain a harassing fire against Montbrun's ranks along the edge of the Burgholz.

Among those enduring this artillery fire was Captain d'Espinchal of the 5th Hussars:

> Thus commenced the fire of the batteries that lasted for two hours and did us much damage as we were obliged to protect the movements of our infantry and the play of our own batteries.
>
> In a few moments we had many hussars and horses killed; an officer had his head carried off by a ball; Adjutant-Major Othenin, my friend, was covered with rocks from a howitzer shell that exploded near him; his head was in a frightful state, but, fortunately, without mortal danger.
>
> The 11th Chasseurs, placed behind us, suffered even more than us owing to the ricochet of balls that passed over our heads.
>
> This position, though very bad, was essential, and we had to hold it until a battalion dislodged the enemy from a small village that almost touched the town.[58]

Trooper Lejeune of the 11th Chasseurs was one of those holding firm behind Espinchal under this harrowing fire. 'We had to hold the positions we took, which was very dangerous,' he recalled. 'We stood a cannonade from twelve pieces for a good hour ... We lost many in that affair. From one ball we had eight men out of action.' The Austrians, advancing several guns to canister range, forced the horsemen to fall back 'behind a small rise that masked us' from the enemy fire before nightfall brought an end to the shelling.[59] Despite the travails they experienced in this phase of the battle, the steadiness displayed by Espinchal, Lejeune and their compatriots allowed Montbrun to retain the ground he had gained and dissuaded their Habsburg opponents from attempting further advances.

This general forward movement of the Hauptarmee's left did not prevent the loss of both Zuckerhandl and Kukrowitz. By 5:00 or 6:00 p.m., that is around the time the Bavarian 2nd Chevaulegers were executing their bold charge at Klein-Tesswitz, the French had occupied both villages. The army's operations journal states that Charles did not believe he could risk 'an offensive movement' with troops who were exhausted from the retreat and the forced marches. 'The day's engagement thus acquired an entirely defensive character' in which each party sought only to prepare for the next day's action.[60] Nonetheless, having had a chance to survey the field, the archduke evidently hoped to gain some ground on his left. He therefore ordered Bellegarde to seize Zuckerhandl and personally rode over to I Corps to supervise the attack. The corps' five battalions had already initiated an advance and their skirmishers were exchanging fire with the French when this order was abruptly countermanded. Charles, from his position near I Corps, could see motion among Montbrun's cavalry that suggested it was preparing to support the infantry in the village. He decided that the attack could not be undertaken with any hope of success without first 'dislodging' the French horse from its position beyond Zuckerhandl and that the imminent fall of night would not allow enough time for this preliminary operation. He thus cancelled the advance and the I Corps troops returned to their previous defensive positions, bringing action on this portion of the field to a close for the day.

The late afternoon also saw the arrival of VI Corps in the Austrian position. Relieved of its rearguard mission by FZM Reuss's V Corps, it departed Hollabrunn shortly after midnight and was assigned a position west of and aligned with the Iglau highway about two kilometres beyond Znaim. Arrayed facing the highway and Brenditz, it was to be the army's reserve.[61]

The passage of VI Corps over the Oblass bridge meant that the bulk of the Hauptarmee was now north of the Thaya: I, III and VI Corps along with most of the Grenadiers and the Cavalry Reserve. V Corps, as the new rearguard, was near Hollabrunn, but II Corps and some elements of the reserve were still immediately south of the river as night fell. This was not where Charles had hoped Hohenzollern and his corps would be. As we have seen, the orders sent to Hohenzollern during the night of 9/10 July instructed him to make himself master of the crossing at Laa or, if the enemy proved too strong there, to cross upstream towards Znaim and block the road from Laa to gain time for the army to arrive.[62] Hohenzollern, however, decided that these courses of action were too risky. He was beset by worries and troubles. Cannon fire was audible from across the Thaya, he had heard nothing from Altstern, the officers he had sent to find that general had not returned, he was low on ammunition of all sorts, and he had only 200 cavalry. His operations journal recorded that 'all incoming reports' indicated the enemy was firmly established at Laa. It is not clear what these 'reports' were, but he concluded that the French must have already advanced half-way to Znaim on the east bank of the river. Rather than attempt a serious armed probe towards Laa or make a cavalry reconnaissance across the Thaya further upstream, Hohenzollern assumed that Altstern must have retreated to Znaim and decided to make that his destination as well. He thus reported his decision to Charles and proceeded to march via Mailberg (16 km from Laa), Hadres and Klein-Tajax (Dyjákovičky) to Naschetitz. He kept the main body of his corps well west of the river as he marched and made no effort either to threaten the French on the eastern bank or even to gain more detailed information about their strength and composition. He had picked up Mecséry and his missing battalions at Mailberg and still had the errant *Argenteau* and *Vogelsang* Infantry Regiments (Nos. 35 and 47) from I Corps giving him a strength of 20,000 infantry by his own reckoning.[63] Though he had only three artillery batteries (the others had retreated with Rosenberg) and was numerically inferior to Marmont's command (decidedly so in cavalry), even a demonstration by a force of this size along the western bank of the river would have forced the French general to halt and would have thereby granted Charles time to array his army in relative leisure while the Austrian baggage train cleared Znaim.

As II Corps reached Dörflitz, the officer who had carried Hohenzollern's report to Charles returned with new orders: the corps was now to cross the Thaya at Pumlitz as I Corps had done. The column had just set out towards the ford when revised instructions arrived according to which the corps would remain on the south bank of the river, relieving the grenadier brigade and holding the vine-covered hills between Oblass and Naschetitz. Hohenzollern therefore occupied the high ground with part of his corps facing east and posted troops in Naschetitz, Urban (Vrbovec), and Klein-Tajax facing southeast. He also detached a battalion and a battery to the hills on the south bank of the Thaya to participate in the fight for Klein-Tesswitz and deployed two companies of

Zach Infantry as skirmishers in the Pelzwald. These were the troops that engaged the Bavarians and caused some diversion of Minucci's division before being silenced or driven off. Twenty-seven of them were killed or wounded in the course of this skirmishing.[64]

As the day came to a close, therefore, Habsburg forces immediately south of the Thaya included Hohenzollern's II Corps, the four light cavalry regiments under Nostitz (minus the two squadrons of Insurrection hussars that had shifted to the north bank), and Scovaud's brigade of grenadiers who were preparing to march north. This made at least 20,000 infantry and cavalry supported by a reasonable number of guns. As far as can be discovered, they faced only French scouting parties and occasional forays across the Thaya by French and Bavarian skirmishers in the vicinity of Mühlfraun. Given that V Corps was still at least 30 km south of Znaim on the Vienna highway, it was important for the Hauptarmee to hold the area around Naschetitz to protect Reuss's withdrawal. Moreover, the enemy situation was very uncertain. The Austrians thought they were facing Davout's large corps and a major French force could have appeared on the right bank of the Thaya. However, it is inexplicable and perhaps inexcusable that Hohenzollern remained inert throughout the afternoon and evening, making no serious effort to threaten the enemy's left flank and giving Marmont no reason to worry about his communications back to Laa.[65] More thorough Austrian reconnaissance might have revealed that Marmont was weak and isolated, but there is no indication such patrolling was proposed. The army was probably too exhausted and the evening was probably too far advanced to consider a bolder move, such as a co-ordinated attack on Marmont's flanks by I and III Corps north of the Thaya combined with II Corps from the south. Still, there is no indication that any such notion was ever entertained in Charles's headquarters for 10 or 11 July. The focus remained defensive: shielding the lumbering baggage train, gaining time to recuperate, and hoping that the peace initiative would bear fruit.

In regards to negotiations with Napoleon, Charles may have felt a degree of hope and urgency as 10 July came to an end. Urgency because he had received during the day the first of the two demeaning and discouraging letters from his brother the Kaiser, this the one with its accompanying memorandum from Stadion. These would have left him in little doubt about the negative mood at court as far as peace was concerned. Moreover, the missive and the memorandum foreshadowed the imminent curtailment of his authority as Generalissimus. He may have harboured some hope, however, because Liechtenstein had turned over command of the Cavalry Reserve to FML Carl Furst zu Schwarzenberg and departed around 2:00 p.m. on the road towards Hollabrunn to seek the French emperor.[66]

Action at Schöngrabern: Gaining Time for the Army's Retreat

Although Marmont later wrote that Massena's 'cannon responded to ours' as the battle for Klein-Tesswitz was coming to a close, there was no direct communication between the two French commanders and the bulk of Massena's 4th Corps was still at least 20–25 km from the battlefield as night fell on 10 July.[67] Massena began the day south of Hollabrunn with approximately 14,000 infantry and cavalry, but his command now faced a new opponent: the 11,400 infantry and cavalry of FZM Reuss's Austrian V Corps. Reuss's men had conducted a smooth 'passage of lines' with VI Corps during the predawn hours of the 10th. That is, most of Klenau's weary men slowly withdrew during the night, leaving a screen in position until V Corps troops arrived to assume their rearguard tasks. Just before daybreak, the final VI Corps outposts pulled out of Hollabrunn and passed through the forward line of V Corps vedettes to head north for Haugsdorf and Znaim.

These vedettes were provided by two squadrons of *Blankenstein* Hussars commanded by Rittmeister Franz Graf St Quentin. The regiment had been reassigned from VI to V Corps and now belonged to GM Johann Nepomuk Joseph Graf von Klebelsberg's brigade of light troops: a regiment of Grenzer, the 3rd Jäger Battalion, and seven squadrons of *Erzherzog Carl* Uhlans as well as the *Blankenstein* Hussars. With Klebelsberg forward as the corps' covering force, Reuss held his other two brigades on a low ridge near Grund in a position fronted by a brook whose steep sides and marshy borders would hinder the passage of cavalry. On his far right flank in Gettsdorf 12 km to the southwest, he had inherited the two squadrons of *Blankenstein* who were to connect him with Schustekh's division now moving to Maissau. His left was tied

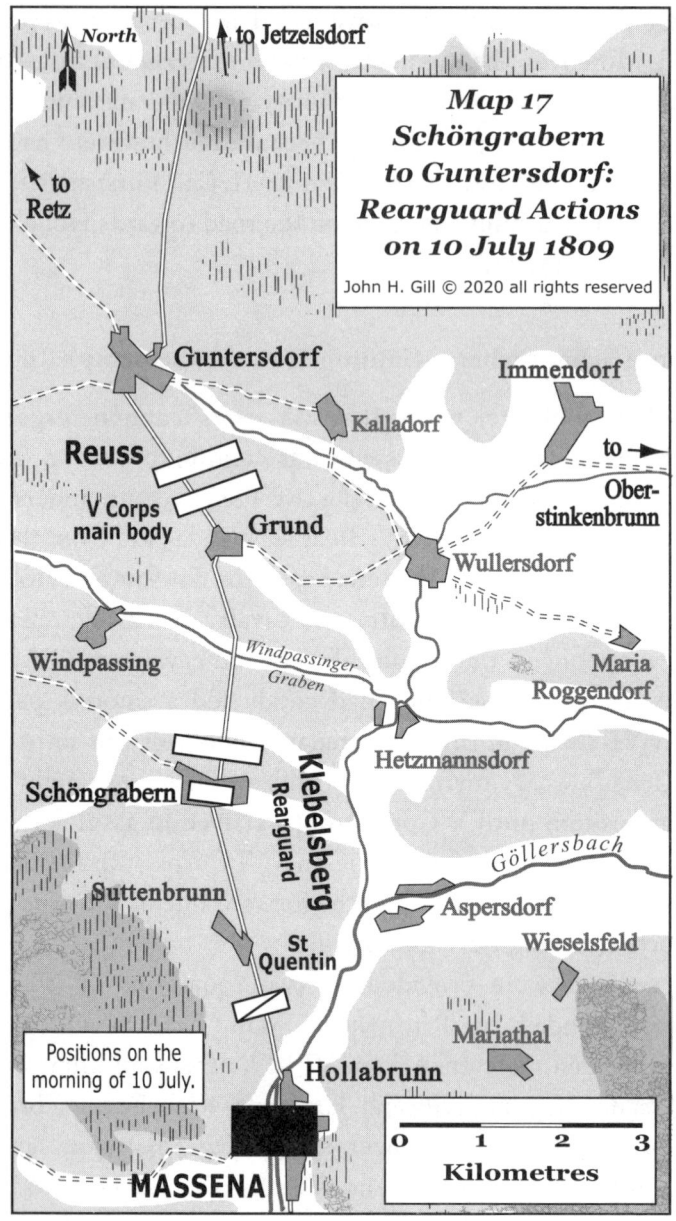

to II Corps by Oberstleutnant Wilgenheim 8–10 km to the northeast at Oberstinkenbrunn and beyond. Wilgenheim's detachment, of which we shall hear more later, consisted of the 4th Jäger Battalion (five companies) and his squadron of *EH Carl* Uhlans (the ones who had captured the Baden 1st Infantry's musicians). Klebelsberg, as the corps' rearguard, had some 3,800 infantry and cavalry under his command. He placed the 3rd Jägers in the village of Schöngrabern, set the remainder of his brigade on the high ground north of the village, and screened his position with the two hussar squadrons forward along the ridge between Hollabrunn and Suttenbrunn.

Massena's light cavalry thus first encountered St Quentin's hussars as they pushed north along the highway from Hollabrunn at approximately 8:00 a.m. Through astute use of his two squadrons, St Quentin managed to outflank and repel the initial French probe, but he was soon forced to fall back and retire through Schöngrabern. Resting in a shallow valley between rolling hills, Schöngrabern is a small village that stretches along a stream perpendicular to the highway. It was 9:00 a.m. by the time the French horsemen appeared on the slopes south of the village, hard on the heels of St Quentin's troopers. Thus began a long, hot day of small-scale combat, continuous and intense, the first instalment of which would engulf tiny Schöngrabern.

As the Austrian hussars made their way up the hill north of the village, the French cavalry attempted to charge in, only to be repulsed by well-directed fire from the defending 3rd Jäger Battalion. Legrand's division now arrived on the scene, led, as usual, by the Baden Jägers. The division had started from Hollabrunn several hours after dawn as Massena was waiting for Carra St Cyr's division to come within supporting distance. With its appearance near Hollabrunn he finally had, after three days of pursuit, two of his four infantry divisions at hand and he lost no time in sending Legrand forward. Marching through 'burned out Hollabrunn' with its 'hideous spectacle of scorched men', Legrand's column passed through the ashen wreck of Suttenbrunn (which they believed had been purposely fired by the retreating Austrians) and soon came up behind the light cavalry.[68] The Baden Jägers, with support from their brigade's foot battery, split in two directions: part persuaded Austrian Uhlans to leave the wood on the western side of the field and part moved to attack Schöngrabern as the rest of Legrand's division deployed in column west of the highway and St Cyr's, likewise in column, unfolded to the east. A Hessian officer described the scene as the 2nd Division arrived: 'We found the 1st Division on this side of the place formed and prepared to deploy, and we at once set ourselves in the same posture to the right.

The cavalry was deployed; the artillery was already working in a lively fashion; Schöngrabern stood in flames.'[69]

Austrian accounts claimed the fires were caused by French howitzer shells, while French and Baden participants accused the Austrians of setting the blaze to cover their imminent retreat. Whatever the case (and perhaps both were true), Schöngrabern, which had barely recovered from destruction suffered during the 1805 war, was once again subjected to ruin and misery. The fires also had a tactical impact as they made the place too hot for the Austrian Jägers to hold and prevented the French infantry from traversing the village for a time. Instead, in what would become the pattern for the day, Massena pushed his light cavalry west of the town threatening to outflank Klebelsberg's position. The Austrian commander thus abandoned Schöngrabern and withdrew to the heights above. Leading the French light horse regiments, Bruyère was severely wounded, taking a ball in the left shoulder and another in the right thigh that put him out of action for the remainder of the war.[70] GB Hippolyte Comte de Piré took Bruyère's place, making this the third occasion since 6 July when death or wounding forced a change of command in Massena's light cavalry.[71] Klebelsberg, with the French cavalry outflanking his right and the French infantry deploying in overwhelming numbers to his front, wisely decided to withdraw. Oberst Johann Heinrich von Hardegg-Glatz of the *Carl* Uhlans, the third of this family of Habsburg officers we have met, led charges by his own regiment and the *Blankenstein* Hussars to hold off the French and allow the rest of Klebelsberg's brigade to retire. Massena pursued: 'We followed them in line beyond Schöngrabern and then stacked arms for the night's rest.'[72]

While the fight for Schöngrabern was in progress, Reuss received the order to retreat. He immediately set the bulk of V Corps on the road to Znaim, but concerns about a perceived threat to his left led him to send the 5th Vienna Volunteers to Immendorf to guard this flank. The main body of the corps reached the Thaya at 11:00 p.m. without incident and crossed to the northern bank. Only the *Lindenau* Infantry Regiment No. 29 and its brigade battery remained behind to support Klebelsberg.

Reuss's withdrawal meant that Klebelsberg was more or less isolated as he continued his rearguard mission. From Schöngrabern, his next possible position was the ridge between that village and the Windpassing stream, but he considered this area a dangerous defile and did not feel confident in stopping there. Instead, behind the protection of Hardegg's horsemen (Hardegg was serving as ad hoc commander of both mounted regiments) and the Jäger battalion, he halted for a short time north of this brook before retiring to the ridge north of the hamlet of Grund. Here too, his stay was brief. He stationed three companies of *Gradiska* Grenz Infantry No. 8 in the town and posted Jägers in a small copse to the east, but was battered by French artillery and soon feared that he would again be outflanked on his right. He therefore waited only until he knew that Reuss had cleared Guntersdorf before making his own rapid retreat to that village. The French thus recorded that this part of the advance was made 'without finding much resistance'.[73]

Like Schöngrabern and Grund, Guntersdorf sits in the valley of a small stream, dominated by heights both north and south. Klebelsberg knew he had to cross the Pulkau in the course of his withdrawal and worried that his little brigade might be overwhelmed in the open terrain between Guntersdorf and the stream. He was also concerned about his position at Guntersdorf, especially his relatively open right flank. In what was by now his routine, he again turned to the three companies of Grenzer to hold the village and placed most of his command on the ridge above.

At this point in the waning afternoon, he received the doubtless welcome order to withdraw and hurried up the highway to establish his brigade in a position north of the Pulkau beyond Jetzelsdorf. Oberst Heinrich Hardegg would cover the brigade's withdrawal with the Grenzers, the two cavalry regiments, and the cavalry battery. Klebelsberg reinforced him with the brigade battery left behind with the *Lindenau* Infantry to give Hardegg a substantial fourteen guns for his little sub-command. Nonetheless, the French had more and Massena was again deploying Legrand to the left and St Cyr to the right of the highway with his light cavalry swinging wide to the west to outflank the Austrian position. Hardegg thus soon found himself hard-pressed and ordered the Grenzers out of Guntersdorf to initiate his own retreat. These three companies, already under heavy fire from enemy guns, were set upon by French cavalry as they tried to exit the village. Hastily forming two impromptu masses, they fended off two attacks as they made their escape. Fortunately for their survival, two guns firing canister were able to dissuade the French from attempting a third charge. Rejoining their regiment, they were assembled into two proper battalion masses and retreated up the highway with the rest of Hardegg's command as, so to speak, the rearguard's rearguard. The day was now closing and French pursuit slackened appreciably. Far to the rear of the retreating Austrians, however, the French could hear 'the distant cannons of Marmont which augmented our regret at not being able to advance more rapidly'.[74]

Hardegg, skilfully employing all three arms in combination, made his way safely across the open plateau beyond Guntersdorf 'followed only by a few weak patrols'.[75] He gained the protection of the hills south of the Pulkau and eventually, as night fell, passed over that stream to establish himself north of Jetzelsdorf. Here his command rested for a time before marching north to cross the Thaya at 2:00 a.m. on 11 July and bivouac near Znaim.

The 5th Vienna Volunteers, meanwhile, had experienced a more stressful withdrawal. Commanded by Major Rudolph Graf Salis-Zizers, the battalion had been posted at Immendorf to protect Reuss's left and was supposed to keep pace with the corps as it withdrew to Jetzelsdorf. When these instructions were issued, the plan was for V Corps to halt for the night behind the Pulkau and the battalion duly withdrew as ordered during the afternoon and evening, halting north of the stream around nightfall. Sometime after the 5th Vienna had marched off to Immendorf, however, Reuss had received Charles's new orders directing V Corps to retire to Znaim without stopping at the Pulkau. Somehow, no one informed the 5th Vienna of this change in plans. Unaware of Reuss's departure and having heard nothing from his higher headquarters, Salis assumed that his previous orders were still valid. His men thus spent a watchful and largely sleepless night north of the Pulkau and marched off towards Znaim at 4:00 a.m. on 11 July as they assumed the rest of the corps was doing.

They were disabused of this comfortable notion when they approached the highway somewhere between the Pulkau and the Thaya. Here they saw French cavalry columns trotting along with no concern for tactical security. Realising at once that they had been cut off during the night, Salis and his officers led the men away from the highway and proceeded north with great caution, using the terrain to screen their march from view where possible and moving in mass when enemy horsemen came into sight. French cavalry patrols spotted the battalion several times, but neither attacked nor brought in reinforcements to encircle the Viennese. The battalion now faced the obstacle of the river. Friendly locals informed them that the Thaya bridge had been barricaded but suggested that the river was fordable in many spots. With this hopeful thought, the battalion wended its way to the Thaya, located a sufficiently shallow point, and waded across, the stronger men helping the weaker. Rather to their own surprise, therefore, the men of the 5th Vienna Volunteers evaded capture to return to V Corps somewhere between 9:00 and 10:00 a.m. on the 11th, just as the battle was beginning. In view of its exhaustion and the fact that its ammunition and muskets had been rendered useless by splashing through the Thaya, Reuss sent the battalion to the town square of Znaim to rest and re-arm. Some eighty men fell out of the ranks during this enervating and stressful escapade, but the battalion retained its cohesion and would play an important role later in the day.[76]

The Vienna Volunteers at least reported to V Corps by the morning of the 11th. From Wilgenheim at Oberstinkenbrunn, on the other hand, Reuss had no word. Even several days later, when writing his after-action report, he could only refer to what French officers had told him and hope that Wilgenheim's little detachment (approximately 730 men of 4th Jägers and 90–100 Uhlans) had somehow found its way through the French army to safety in Hungary or some other friendly region.

The French and their German allies in Massena's corps were not lost, but they were bone weary. They camped where they were around Guntersdorf: Legrand to the west, St Cyr to the east and the cuirassiers in the centre. On the northern side of the village, the light cavalry patrolled beyond the Pulkau, but these regiments were now so worn that some cuirassiers had to be committed to outpost duty during the night, a task for which they were wholly unsuited. As had become the norm in 4th Corps, the Baden Jägers joined their French mounted comrades on the outpost line.[77] The rest of the corps remained far behind: Molitor at Göllersdorf and Boudet still at Stockerau. Notably, however, some of Piré's exploring patrols rode as far as the Thaya and made contact, albeit tentative, with Marmont's outposts.[78]

Despite the long day's combat, casualties on both sides seem to have been fairly light. For Massena's corps, most losses would have been taken by the light cavalry (perhaps 40–50 men) as the French and Baden infantry were hardly engaged (the Badeners only reported two wounded Jägers).[79] The Hessian contingent with St Cyr's division appeared in combat for the first time since Wagram, but suffered no losses other than a dismounted cannon. Austrian combat losses were likely more evenly distributed between the cavalry and infantry, but were probably not heavy. The history of the *EH Carl* Uhlans, for example, cites that regiment's casualties as only 1 dead, 20 wounded, and 13 missing for a total of 34. The Grenzer claimed only 20 casualties and the 3rd Jägers reported losing 101: 7 killed, only 3 wounded, and 91 missing or captured (29 of whom soon rejoined the battalion). Total Austrian losses were thus likely less than 200.

At the same time, the history of the *Lindenau* Infantry records that the regiment lost 70 men on 10 July when Klebelsberg's and Reuss's after-action reports make no mention of the regiment being involved in combat at all.[80] Given the likely low battle losses on both sides and the fact that the French reported sweeping up a substantial number of deserters and stragglers, it is probable that these were men who were leaving the ranks to desert or falling out from fatigue.[81] It was probably from these deserters that Massena and his staff learned of the order of the day Charles had issued on 7 July excoriating the army for poor performance at Wagram and threatening to decimate regiments who failed to meet his expectations. Although they admired the conduct of their enemy's withdrawal, the numerous deserters and news of Charles's harsh 7 July order of the day led French officers to conclude that the Austrian army was disintegrating. 'We pursued the enemy until 8 o'clock at night,' reported Massena, 'They seem very fatigued ... The reports of the prisoners and deserters that are beginning to appear in great numbers, tell that the entire army is in the greatest disorder.'[82]

This image of the state of the Hauptarmee did nothing to tarnish the impression the French gained of Klebelsberg as a result of the day's actions. He had demonstrated great competence in selecting good positions, withdrawing at the right moments in an orderly fashion, making the best use of all three arms and, above all, holding his command

I Found Myself in the Rear of the Austrian Army

together despite the enemy's evident superiority. All of this was clearly visible to his French pursuers. Indeed, the skill he and Heinrich Hardegg displayed earned the admiration of their foes and friends alike. In his history of the war, for example, Jean-Jacques Pelet, then a chef de bataillon on Massena's staff, wrote that Klebelsberg conducted this withdrawal 'in the finest order' and 'thereby gained a great deal of time for the retreat of the army'.[83] Reuss, of course, was grateful as well as impressed and recommended Klebelsberg and Hardegg to Charles for their exemplary conduct during this difficult day. The archduke was only too pleased to oblige and used his authority as Generalissimus to recognize both with award of the Maria Theresa Order shortly after the armistice, an honour he also bestowed on Reuss.

In addition to the combat along this axis of advance on 10 July, Austrian emissaries passed between the lines, one going in each direction. The first of these was FML Weißenwolff, released from French captivity after ostentatiously courteous treatment and carrying with him what seemed to be Napoleon's wishes to engage in negotiations. He rode north early in the morning[84] and seems to have crossed to the Austrian side around the time that Klebelsberg was withdrawing towards Grund. Though nowhere stated in contemporary after-action reports or histories, it seems likely that his safe passage may have occasioned some lull in the combat and perhaps a delay in the French advance. The second individual was Liechtenstein. Having departed the Znaim battlefield in the mid-afternoon, he went south and reached Massena's lines sometime after dark.

Although Charles had written to his brother early in the day that Napoleon had been in Wolkersdorf and was moving towards the Brünn highway, Liechtenstein seems to have been operating under the assumption that the French emperor was in Stockerau or elsewhere on the Vienna–Znaim highway. Whatever the cause of this confusion, he passed through Massena's corps that night and rode south into the darkness in search of Napoleon.

The Civilian Population: Fear, Misfortune and Misery

Beyond the narrative of combat and diplomacy, the fighting along the Vienna highway corridor is a poignant illustration of the miseries inflicted upon the local civilian population as the armies swept over their lands and through their villages. Anton Fidelis Namiesky, the local parish priest in Göllersdorf, for example, reflected the anxiety of the town's inhabitants as the war approached their doorsteps.

> Now commenced our fear, misfortune and misery. Our army retired en masse along the routes of Brünn and Prague, it camped in the best fields of wheat, already ripe for harvest, and trampled everything. During this retreat, the Generalissimus, His Grace, the Archduke Charles, brother of His Majesty Kaiser Franz, took his quarters in the priory. More than fifty grenadiers camped in the courtyard as bodyguard, these had had nothing to eat for three days and were not seen to until later, but nothing, not even the barnyard fowl, was touched ... Now the French had already pushed forward as far as Stockerau and villages were burning as far as one could see. One may imagine the fear in which we passed the night. Most people fled into the woods or to nearby hamlets. Hardly ten heads of household remained here. The next day, towards 7 o'clock in the morning of 9 July, the first French galloped into the square ...

French and Badeners (he thought they were Bavarians) robbed Namiesky of everything he had: food, wine, cloth and clothing. He was also required to provide meals for numerous French officers, including Massena, of whom he formed no favourable opinion: 'This man is defiance and brutality itself.' His church was looted, papers scattered, clerical garments robbed of their decorative braid, 'and rubbish of all sorts lay strewn all about'. Still he could console himself somewhat in saving some chickens and two cows. He also felt that he had to 'honestly acknowledge' that nothing in his priory was wantonly destroyed: 'Not even a window was broken and we were also preserved from fire.'[85]

Other villages were not so fortunate as far as fire was concerned, especially those that witnessed heavy combat. Schöngrabern was one of the hardest hit. The village had largely burned to the ground as a result of the fighting in 1805 only to fall prey to fire again four years later. 'The inhabitants had hardly rebuilt their homes and had not even recovered from their previous losses', recorded the church chronicle,

> when, in the year 1809 after the Battle of Wagram, the French drove through Oberhollabrunn [Hollabrunn] and the Austrians opposed them here to prevent their advance through Schöngrabern.
>
> But the enemy bombarded the market square, church, priory, [and] school, the entire place was soon aflame. The Austrians could not hold off the impetuously advancing enemy any longer. The inhabitants had mostly fled and found on their return nothing but horribly ruined homes. The older registers and other documents in the priory were destroyed.[86]

Similar destruction was visited upon Hollabrunn but with an even grislier aspect owing to the intense combat that had taken place in its streets, courtyards and gardens. 'The place had suffered tremendously from yesterday's fire,' wrote Baden surgeon Wilhelm Meier when he entered the village on the morning of 10 July, 'The half-burned corpses in the collapsed and still partly burning houses offered an especially jarring sight.'[87] Even in Sierndorf, which had not been a battleground, many homes were destroyed by fire as the Austrians withdrew and the French arrived. Though probably the result of an accident in Sierndorf's case, the impact on the villagers was just as devastating.

Locals could also suffer death or injury as a direct result of the passage of the armies, whether from the simple misfortune of being caught in the crossfire or from being executed as suspected spies, as was the case for three hapless farmers from Großstelzendorf who had furtively returned to town to check on their properties. The French and their German allies were especially vengeful in cases where they were fired on by local people. A particularly infamous case occurred in Pulkau on 13 July, when townspeople who were unaware of the armistice attacked a Bavarian artillery quartering party and killed two men. The remainder of the Bavarian party fled but soon returned with reinforcements who threatened dire retribution. On the desperate pleas of the town's leaders, General Minucci agreed to spare people's lives, but the town had to submit to being sacked for an hour by the angry troops. One man died as a result of mistreatment and Pulkau was thoroughly pillaged.[88]

Plunder, thievery and abuse, of course, were not limited to Massena's avenue of advance. Laa, for example, barely escaped devastation after a curious incident. The French entered the town around 10:00 a.m. on 9 July and the mayor was handing the city keys to the senior French officers, when a lone Austrian dragoon who had been caught in town by the French advance suddenly dashed out of an alleyway, fired his carbine at the astonished French, and galloped out of town through the Staatz Gate. The French officers, believing they had been deceived and fearing there might be more Austrian soldiers hiding in town, threatened to burn Laa to the ground. Urgent entreaties persuaded the French to spare the town but the citizens had to deliver a sort of 'fire insurance fee' consisting of a substantial amount of cash and 600 loaves of bread to avoid destruction. That was not the last of Laa's contributions. With a number of French soldiers remaining in town, 'All the livestock and fodder was taken for their use, many cows and calves were slaughtered, [and] the oats and hay removed,' along with, of course, 'many casks of wine'. Matthias Fischer of Laa recorded in his diary that the French 'immediately began to plunder and rob' as soon as they arrived. After cataloguing all that was taken from his family, Fischer bitterly wrote that these losses were an injury 'we and our children's children will remember'. Jakob Frint, the town priest, had to flee disguised as a layman because the French found letters to the Habsburg imperial household among his papers and suspected him of espionage.[89]

Inhabitants north of the Thaya had similar experiences. In Hödnitz, the village teacher recounted that Heinrich and Rosalia Tulipan, owners of the local mill, were set upon first by Bavarian cavalry (whom they mistakenly thought were Württembergers), then by French and Bavarian infantry who stole money, wine, bread and clothing. These troops were followed by five marauders, including a female sutler, who proceeded to beat Frau Tulipan when their demands for money could not be met. Fortunately for the Tulipans, who will reappear later, a French officer intervened to apprehend their abusers. He could not restore their lost property but could at least promise that they would not be further disturbed. Such scenes of passing theft and occasional violence were all too common, and villagers were faced with the painful dilemma of whether to remain with their homes in the hopes of protecting their property or to flee and hope there would be something left when they returned. Many escaped to local forests as soon as they heard that the enemy was approaching, taking whatever belongings they could carry and frequently herding their animals along as well. Whether they stayed or fled, most tried to hide their possessions, but the pillaging soldiers, with endlessly cunning diligence, usually found the concealed cash boxes, clothing, larders and wine cellars. Even the forests were not always secure as the locals near Mühlfraun learned when the cattle they had attempted to hide in the Burgholz were discovered by the Bavarian division.[90]

Some of the damage was simply callous depravity. If Pastor Namiesky in Hollabrunn could take some comfort in the relative absence of truly wanton destruction in his priory, this was by no measure the experience elsewhere. The abundance of wine seems to have brought out the worst in men who were not only hot, weary and thirsty but also likely overwhelmed by the luxury of consuming as much as they wished of an expensive item that would normally have been beyond their financial reach. A common practice was to knock the taps off barrels or shoot holes in them, drink what could be drunk on the spot, carry off whatever could be caught in a bucket or similar container, and simply leave the rest to gush out onto the floor. A Bavarian artillery drummer remembered that the bottoms of his white pantaloons were dyed red with wine after wading into a cellar with a pail ('This looked very odd,' he wrote) and such incidents of appalling waste and wantonness occurred repeatedly.[91] Marmont's summary executions seem to have curtailed such undisciplined behaviour in his command to a significant degree and soldiers in Massena's corps were also executed or otherwise punished,[92] but abuses persisted along both avenues of advance as long as the war was on.

Citizens were sometimes protected by unit officers or compassionate soldiers, and senior commanders were not oblivious to the detrimental impact of indiscipline on unit effectiveness or on the local population. Massena, for instance, employed his Baden aide-de-camp, the young Markgraf Wilhelm, to limit the damage 'as the soldiers plundered everywhere'.[93] Punishments were imposed that could include, as Marmont demonstrated, execution. Still depredations were common.

Furthermore the protection of helpful officers might be only transitory; once a regiment moved on, the next occupants might be less lenient, eventually leaving hopeful villagers destitute even though they had been temporarily shielded by some troops. Nor were the French and their German allies the only offenders. As noted earlier, Austrian soldiers could also loot their fellow citizens, especially where wine was involved. Retreating Habsburg troops broke into the cellars in Breitenweida south of Hollabrunn on 8 July taking all they could grab in their haste, while others invaded the priory and carried off silver vessels, the church treasury and all the livestock.[94] Several white-coated marauders pillaged a church in Znaim during the battle (one was caught and executed on the spot) and local civilians – 'plunder-hungry riffraff from the villages and city' in the words of a local history – sometimes took advantage of the chaos to scoop up wine by the bucket or grab other valuables.[95] It is clear, however, that the principal perpetrators were French and German soldiers of Napoleon's army. A later chronicler called them 'a horde of Gallic barbarians'.[96] Indeed, if locals were usually paid for official requisitions, the depredations of 1809 seemed even worse than 1805 for most inhabitants.[97]

Beyond the immediate suffering of robbery, abuse and destruction, there were also longer-term impacts to consider from the point of view of local people and local administrations. Stolen or ruined farm implements and wagons that were damaged or impressed for use by the armies meant that what remained of the harvest was difficult to reap, while burned barns left farmers no place to store what they had gathered. 'The people have been robbed of all grapes, grain and fodder, the manor has been plundered and the village of Schöngrabern turned into a ruin,' lamented local officials, 'The harvest cannot be brought in because the French have confiscated all the vehicles.' The resultant shortages of everything from common foodstuffs to utilitarian household items and luxury goods brought staggering price rises that led to additional hardship.[98] School schedules and church services were disrupted as the relevant buildings were burned and looted. Describing his experiences after the French had departed, for instance, the schoolmaster in Schöngrabern plaintively observed that owing to the dislocations occasioned by war, marches and occupation, he 'did not find that attentiveness among the pupils that is so necessary for the instruction to have its desired effect'.[99] Village registers were often arbitrarily destroyed as soldiers searched for money or other valuables in churches and town halls. The concomitant loss of birth and death records, land titles and all manner of other administrative data threw local governance into disarray for months or years. Less affected communities did provide assistance once the fighting stopped and the government in Vienna made solemn pledges when its authority was restored, but help from neighbours could not replace all that had been lost and financial assistance from the central government was often slow in arriving and inadequate in amount. Coming less than four years after the travails of 1805, it is hardly surprising that the local populace remembered 1809 as a year of hardship, fire and fear.[100]

Nightfall at Znaim: The Enemy's March Has Been Much Delayed

The night of 10/11 July meant more marching and little rest for much of the Hauptarmee. Although Charles would have preferred to withdraw to Iglau or a similar position to the north under the cover of darkness, the massive baggage train still blocked the road making a retreat into the night impossible. 'The news of the complete congestion and confusion of the vehicles in the defiles between Frainersdorf [Vranovská Ves] and Scheletau [Želetava] led the archduke to the risky decision to desist from a continuation of the retreat on the following day and to await the enemy in the current position,' he wrote later, adding 'but simultaneously to send the VI Army Corps off to Wolframitzkirchen [Olbramkostel] for the protection of the artillery park.'[101] He and his men would thus have to spend another day around Znaim to grant time for the army's encumbrances to escape.

The Hauptarmee, however, could not remain as it was: dispersed and straddling the Thaya. The units on the right bank in particular were too vulnerable to being destroyed if driven into the river by the presumably superior French forces approaching from Laa and Jetzelsdorf. At 10:00 p.m., Charles thus issued a new 'disposition' to concentrate the entire army north of the Thaya.[102] Scovaud's grenadier brigade had moved at some time in the evening and it was followed late that night by II Corps and the four cavalry regiments under Nostitz. Both of these formations were destined for the army's left wing. Nostitz and his mounted regiments returned to the Cavalry Reserve Corps now under Schwarzenberg's command and deployed north of Winau in multiple overlapping echelons. Hohenzollern's men established themselves halfway between Brenditz and Tief-Maispitz about a kilometre behind the cavalry and oriented generally to the east. Third Corps remained in its position between Winau and Brenditz, but 'to oppose any night attack', Kolowrat deployed it in squares with cavalry in the intervals.[103] The infantry brigade and battery temporarily left behind in Haugsdorf (*Schröder* and *Wenzel Colloredo*) rejoined the corps sometime after dark. The grenadiers, once more united, shifted to a reserve position on the slopes just northwest of Brenditz. These movements illustrate the Austrian concern for security of the army's left flank as the dawn found three of the six regular corps and both of the reserve formations poised to counter any French advance towards the area around Brenditz.

The tasks assigned to VI Corps also reflected this anxiety about attack from the left. Klenau remained the army's reserve but marched at midnight to take up a new position some 14 km northwest of Znaim between Wolframitzkirchen and Frainersdorf. In addition to protecting what Charles assumed would be his line of retreat, Klenau was specifically instructed to send a detachment to Jaispitz (Jevišovice) in the army's left rear 'to observe the route there'. Two squadrons of *Liechtenstein* Hussars under Oberstleutnant Joseph Struppy were duly dispatched and patrolled far and wide only to find almost nothing to report.[104] Struppy's was not the only force patrolling the Austrian left. GM Ignaz Hardegg of II Corps was sent off to the east with a mixed detachment of cavalry and a Landwehr battalion to establish contact with Rosenberg and to secure the army's left flank. He too ended up in Jaispitz, but found neither IV Corps nor notable enemy forces to report.[105]

The new orders left Bellegarde in generally the same position he had held during the day, his left on the opposite side of the Kukrowitzerbach vale from III Corps, and his right resting on the hills above the Leska across from Zuckerhandl. He thus continued to form the army's centre. On his right, Reuss was instructed to cross the Thaya bridge after II Corps, destroy the bridge, leave a 'light chain of outposts' along the north bank of the river, occupy Klein-Tesswitz and defend 'all the approaches to Znaim'. It was soon apparent, however, that the bridge could not be demolished, so Reuss had it barricaded instead, as Salis's Vienna Volunteers discovered when they appeared after daylight. Likewise, Klein-Tesswitz was in the possession of Claparède's men and Reuss had no orders to re-open that struggle. He therefore placed several battalions along the Thaya while arraying the rest of his infantry in the vineyards above Klein-Tesswitz on his left and on the slopes south of Znaim on his right. He posted his Jägers in the nearly unassailable Pöltenberg with one gun and dispatched two squadrons of *Blankenstein* Hussars to screen the upper reaches of the Thaya. The rest of his cavalry was placed behind Znaim in reserve and, on arrival, the exhausted 5th Vienna, as we have seen, were told to clean their muskets and collect dry ammunition while recuperating in the town square.[106]

The new location of army headquarters also indicated the archduke's intention to retreat at the earliest opportunity. It was to move from Brenditz to Wolframitzkirchen at 4:00 a.m. on 11 July where it was to be protected by VI Corps. For himself, Charles seems to have remained at Znaim where he had been lodged the previous night.[107]

While rearranging his army, Charles turned to subterfuge to gain time and afford his troops some much-needed rest. At some point between 8:00 and 9:00 p.m. on the 10th, therefore, FML Johann Carl Hennequin Graf von Fresnel appeared at Montbrun's outpost line under a flag of truce. Fresnel, one of the division commanders in I Corps, bore a message proposing an immediate ceasefire. Though purportedly from Bellegarde and accompanied by Bellegarde's word of honour, this was actually the archduke's idea and the substance was that the two sides should avoid further bloodshed for the moment and agree to a ceasefire, considering that Liechtenstein was on his way to Napoleon's headquarters to discuss peace. Instead of serving Charles's purposes, however, this initiative provided an opportunity for Marmont to disguise his own weakness. His reply was thus full of aggressive bluster and self-assurance, as he reported to Berthier that evening: 'I told him that I had the order to attack all out and that I would not agree to an armistice of even a quarter of an hour; moreover, that his story was badly conceived because His Majesty has been announced to me and will arrive momentarily with a large number of troops and that I hope to capture a good part of his army tomorrow morning.'[108] Charles was doubtless disappointed but probably not surprised by this brassy response. Marmont, however, evidently made some mention of Austria receiving a reply the following day after Napoleon had arrived – at least all of the Austrian accounts refer to the promise of an answer on the morrow.

This brief episode on the evening of 10 July generated several implications for the near future. First, it meant that most of the Hauptarmee would remain under arms during the night and thus enjoy little rest or recovery. Second, it confirmed in Austrian minds their assessment that they were, or soon would be, opposed by numerically superior French forces under Napoleon's personal leadership. Though erroneous as far as French numbers were concerned, this conviction would inform Austrian decision-making over the coming twenty-four hours.[109] Third, it provided a precedent, a hook upon which Napoleon could hang his own ceasefire offer the following day, portraying his proposal as a reply to that made by Charles on 10 July. Finally, it is not amiss to note once again the psychological dominance enjoyed by Napoleon and his generals over their Austrian counterparts, especially as Marmont's brashness reinforced preconceived notions already entertained in the headquarters of the Hauptarmee. This psychological dimension would also form part of the context for the coming day's developments.

Like Charles, Marmont had decided to remain in place overnight. A number of his generals advised him to withdraw, but for him 'If we retired, it was admitting we had lost when we were the victors.'[110] Moreover, he believed that the enemy would retreat during the night if he did not stay close and he hoped, albeit unrealistically, that Davout would soon arrive in support. His corps would thus stay in place, retaining the positions it had won: Montbrun's cavalry on the right in front of the Burgholz, Clauzel in the centre on the heights with detachments holding Kukrowitz and Zuckerhandl, Claparède's division on the left side of the heights with the 81st Ligne in Klein-Tesswitz, and the Bavarians in reserve to the rear. As his weary men sought food and shelter in a night that was turning rainy, Marmont could take some satisfaction in the day's outcome. Despite the risk he had run with his impetuous pursuit of the supposed Austrian rearguard, he had succeeding in delaying the

Hauptarmee's escape. He was therefore justified to report that night with some pride: 'Independent of the very great loss suffered by the enemy because his masses were exposed to [our] cannon for a long time and the fusillade was lively, I think the affair today has at least had as a result that the enemy's march has been much delayed.'[111]

At the same time, Marmont was acutely aware of his peril. Although he tried to minimise the danger facing his isolated corps in his report to Berthier that night, he had already sent a letter to Davout at 5:00 p.m. requesting help, albeit in oblique terms. 'It appears that the entire enemy army is united here,' he wrote, noting that the Austrians numbered at least 40,000 and might vanish during the night before concluding with: 'It would be extremely useful if you could come promptly.'[112]

Napoleon: Marching to the Sound of the Guns

Davout was already on the march by the time Marmont drafted his request. Indeed, barring Viceroy Eugène's expanded command, the entire French army would be hurrying towards Znaim by the end of the day, but little of it would be able to arrive as 'promptly' as Marmont hoped. The reports that flowed into imperial headquarters in Wolkersdorf during the night of 9/10 July confirmed Napoleon's suspicion that Charles and the Hauptarmee were retreating via Znaim. He was soon on the road to Wilfersdorf himself. At 8:30 a.m., just before departing, he outlined his view of the strategic situation and his intentions in a message from Berthier to Davout.

> Marshal, the Duke of Rivoli [Massena] had an engagement at Holla-brunn yesterday at three in the afternoon. The entire enemy army is retiring on Znaim; it is thus necessary to march to General Marmont in all haste. That general halted at Laa yesterday, and marches on Znaim today; he must be engaged with the enemy during the day. It is therefore important that you march to his assistance within the hour. The emperor is marching at the head of the cavalry of his Guard and his artillery to direct himself towards General Marmont and will go where he hears the sound of the guns. General Oudinot and the Foot Guards will follow in the same direction this evening when they are rested ... Everything leads to the conclusion that if

there is not a serious engagement today, there will be a very serious one on the morrow.[113]

Napoleon's urgency and the priority attached to the 3rd Corps' march to Znaim could not have been clearer. Although Davout was directed to leave 'some troops' to watch the Brünn highway, if he thought these needed additional support 'the emperor would send one of Oudinot's divisions there'. Orders issued to Oudinot, Nansouty and the Guard later in the morning instructed all of them to take their commands to Znaim by way of Laa.[114] Berthier apprised Marmont of all these moves in a 9:30 a.m. letter from Wilfersdorf, providing the doubtless welcome news that the emperor would be departing in an hour with his Guard for Znaim so that there would be 'important forces' in place the following day 'to battle the enemy if he remains in position', even though it seemed more likely that the Austrians would decamp and retire into Bohemia. The same missive chastised Marmont for failing to provide frequent situation reports and noted pointedly the Napoleon expected such a report 'at any moment'.[115]

As for Massena, he was to 'form the pivot of a grand turning movement that Napoleon was executing by the right'.[116] In a conceptual sense, this meant that 4th Corps on the army's left south of Znaim, would be the hinge upon which the rest of the army would turn to strike Charles. The message Massena received, however, supplied an update on the overall situation but contained no reference to this grand concept and no specific orders. 'I write to inform you, my duke, that General Marmont attacked the enemy rearguard near Laa yesterday and continues his march to Znaim today,' wrote Berthier from Wilfersdorf, 'The Duke of Auerstedt [Davout] is between here and Nikolsburg and marches today on Znaim. The emperor has arrived here and HM will also depart for Znaim in an hour.'[117] The marshal, already annoyed and baffled at having heard nothing from headquarters since the afternoon of 8 July, was unsure where he should halt and was especially keen to be granted permission to call up Molitor's and Boudet's divisions from their positions at Göllersdorf and Stockerau respectively.[118] Fortunately, for Napoleon, Massena could infer from this note – especially as Napoleon himself was headed for Znaim – that he was to press the pursuit. On the other hand, it could

Napoleon (1769–1821): Frau Anna Maria Gebauer, a citizen of Laa, prepared this silhouette of the French emperor when he passed through the town in 1809.

Napoleon at Eggmühl, 22 April 1809: the defeat suffered in Bavaria in April overturned all Habsburg hopes for an early offensive success and cast a pall over the rest of the war, convincing Charles that the empire's salvation lay in rapidly concluding peace while confirming for his enemies at court that the archduke had to be removed.

Marshal Massena at Wagram: injured when his horse stumbled during a reconnaissance with Napo[leon] on 3 July, Massena was confined to a light carriage at Wagram and throughout the pursuit to Znai[m].

GD Michel Marie Claparède (1770–1840) was wounded twice in 1809, first at Aspern-Essling and, after his recovery, at Znaim.

Oberstleutnant August Graf zu Leininger[-]Westerburg (1770–1849) commanded a bo[ld] attack on the Thaya bridges on 11 July.

Austrian grenadiers from 'German' companies were dressed in white breeches and wore distinctive grenadier bearskin caps.

Austrian line infantry from a 'German' regiment in white breeches and the helmet these regiments still wore in 1809.

Austrian Grenz regiments were adopting own jackets with tight blue trousers similar to the Hungarian infantry.

Troopers of the Austrian *Schwarzenberg* and *Carl* Uhlans wore this green uniform with Polish-style *czapka* headgear.

Baden Jäger: clad in typical Jäger green with Baden's tall Raupenhelm and black leather equipment, this small battalion was heavily engaged in all of Legrand's actions from 7 through 11 July.

Baden line infantry: Baden's line regiments also wore the Raupenhelm but had blue coats and white breeches or trousers. Despite many new recruits in the ranks, these regiments performed well.

Hessian light infantry: the battalions of Hesse-Darms light infantry wore green w their musketeer comrad were dressed in blue; all h bicorne hats that by 180 seemed outmoded compa to the shakos most armies adopting.

French grenadier: each line infantry battalion included one company of picked grenadiers with tall bearskin hats and red epaulettes to show their elite status.

French chasseur-à-cheval: wearing green uniforms that were relatively plain compared to the gaudy hussars, these regiments constituted the bulk of the French light horse.

French light infantry: the of the 26th and 24th Lég Regiments in 4th Corps a the 8th Léger under Marm would have had uniform similar to this soldier's.

ch cuirassier: these French avy cavalrymen were an posing sight in their steel nets and breastplates; four ments supported Massena nd eight more (plus two carabiniers) arrived with Napoleon on 11 July.

Bavarian line infantry: the kingdom's line troops wore coats of a unique cornflower blue with their distinctive tall Raupenhelms and white breeches or trousers.

Bavarian chevauleger: the two regiments of Preysing's Bavarian light cavalry brigade at Znaim and Lindenau's two detached squadrons all wore this green jacket with red facings.

ve: Bavarian artillery: dressed in dark blue, the Bavarian and gunners played a key role on Marmont's side of the field aim. Train personnel (left rear) wore grey.

t: Bavarian light infantry: men of the 6th Light, like young cript Mändler quoted in the text, wore this hunter's green rm with the ubiquitous Raupenhelm.

Engagement at Hollabrunn, 9 July 1809: Hollabrunn is in the distance with Legrand's infantry in the foreground and light cavalry beyond the road. French and Baden guns are exchanging fire with Austrian artillery while St Sulpice's cuirassiers wait on the left.

The *Schloß* at Wolkersdorf: this tidy manor was Kaiser Franz's residence from 16 May until the afternoon of 6 July; Napoleon occupied it during 7–10 July.

Attack on Zuckerhandl: this riflery [target] from 1826 shows French [troops] attacking the Rother Hof [at] Zuckerhandl on 10 July.

[South] Vienna at the Znaim [Gate]: another target from 1826 [displays] an idealised image of [South] Vienna Volunteers in [perfect] alignment and impeccable [uniforms] chasing French [cuirassiers] from the town's [main] gate.

The Battle of Znaim: the view from Massena's side of the field with troops approaching on the high in the foreground and blocks of reinforcements deploying south of the Thaya; the firing line of Legrand's division is visible north of the river and Znaim's skyline emerges in the distance.

The Battle of Znaim: this painting by Bavarian artist Johann Lorenz Rugendas shows Napoleon surveying the scene from the heights above Klein-Tesswitz. The roofs of Zuckerhandl and the Roth Hof are on his right along with French horse artillery; on his left are cuirassiers and Bavarian artille

...duke Charles (1771–1847): though endowed
... considerable military talent and an earnest
...ern for the future of the dynasty, he could fall
... periods of pessimism and only entered the
... with resignation, seeking to end it as soon as
...ible after the opening defeats in Bavaria.
...im, the war party's desperate enthusiasm
...09 was a repeat of the follies of 1805.

...ngraving published in 1809 in praise of the
...evements of Archduke Charles. The central
...ge is of Charles leading his troops at Aspern-
...ing with the smaller images surrounding it
...cting battlefield successes against the French
...er in his career from 1793 through 1805.

Kaiser Franz I (1768–1835): emperor and head of the Habsburg family, the vacillating Franz tended to become absorbed in minutiae and allowed himself to be swayed by urgent entreaties from the war party, traits that helped bring on the war and delay the peace.

Johann Philipp Graf Stadion (1763–1824): Stadion was the driving engine of the war party, but his limited understanding of military affairs hampered realistic planning.

Clemens von Metternich (1773–1859): Austri ambassador in Paris before the war, he adopt a policy of accommodation with Napoleon wh he became foreign minister.

FML Franz Seraph Fürst von Rosenberg-Orsini (1761–1832): while his corps conducted largely effective rearguard actions, confusion in the orders he received initially led him to march to Laa rather than Brünn as Charles desired.

FML Friedrich Franz Xaver Fürst von Hohenzollern-Hechingen (1757–1844): his decision to send a very weak brigade to Laa on 9 July and his timid behaviour on the 10th opened the way for Marmont to march to Znaim.

FZM Johann Nepomuk Karl Joseph Graf Kolowrat-Krakowsky (1748–1816): III Corps was the least engaged element of Hauptarmee during the retreat and at Znaim.

GdK Heinrich Graf Bellegarde (1760–1845): the most senior of the corps commanders, Charles recommended him as his replacement in late July, but the Kaiser selected Liechtenstein instead.

FML Johann Joseph Cajetan Graf Klenau (1755–1819) commanded VI Corps at Wagram and as the army's rearguard during 7–9 July.

GdK Johann Joseph Fürst von und zu Liechtenstein (1760–1836) replaced Charles commander of the Hauptarmee in late July a finally signed the peace treaty on 14 Octobe

GM Maximilian Alexander Freiherr von Wimpffen (1770–1854) was the Hauptarmee's chief of staff from May until after Znaim; he apparently wrote or co-wrote some of the essays published later in support of Archduke Charles.

FZM Heinrich XV Fürst zu Reuss-Plauen (1751–1825): Charles, overly worried about French forays across the Danube, did not ca Reuss to Wagram, but his V Corps played a crucial role on 10 and 11 July.

Austrian troops and allies near Nuremberg, June 1809: a mixed collection of Austrian regulars and Landwehr rest outside Nuremberg with volunteers from the Duke of Brunswick's legion. Despite grand Austrian hopes, these incursions did not distract Napoleon or ignite serious rebellion in Germany.

Bavarian light infantry storm a bridge in the Tyrol, 27 July 1809: as with the Austrian forays into Germany, Napoleon did not allow the active rebellion in the Tyrol to divert his attention from the Habsburg Hauptarmee. He withdrew almost all regular Bavarian troops from the region in preparation for Wagram and only sent them back after Znaim (as shown here).

Marshal André Massena, Duke of Rivoli (1758–1817): though his 4th Corps had suffered considerable losses at Wagram, Massena led a relentlessly aggressive pursuit of the Hauptarmee from Korneuburg to Znaim.

GD Gabriel Jean Joseph Molitor (1770–184 by dint of prodigious marching, his 3rd Divis arrived south of the Thaya late on 11 July ar would have been available had combat bee renewed on the 12th.

GD Claude Carra St Cyr (1760–1834): his 2nd Division was present for the pursuit engagements on 10 July; his French brigade and parts of the Hessian brigade also fought at Znaim.

GD Claude Juste Alexandre Legrand (1762– the energetic Legrand's 1st Division, along w the light and heavy cavalry, formed the bulk Massena's pursuit force from 7 through 9 Ju

ssena and GD François Nicolas Fririon (1766–
.o): painted in October 1809, Massena is seen
:h his chief of staff (*right*) and, on horseback,
son, Jacques Prosper (1793–1821), who served
as an aide-de-camp in 1809.

GD Louis Pierre Montbrun (1770–1812):
one of the most competent cavalry commanders
in the Army of Germany, Montbrun was a
hard-bitten warrior known for his tactical
acumen and thorough reconnaissance.

Auguste Frédéric Louis Viesse de Marmont,
uke of Ragusa (1772–1852): made a marshal
on 12 July 1809, he later gained infamy by
urrendering his forces to the Allies in 1814.

GD Bertrand Clauzel (1772–1842): Napoleon
considered the talented Clauzel one of his most
promising subordinates; he had served with the
Army of Dalmatia since 1808.

Charles at Aspern: Charles hoped his defensive success at Aspern would create an opportunity to negotiate with a chastened Napoleon, but the war party at court saw things differently.

Napoleon and the mortally wounded Marshal Lannes at Aspern. Lannes was a close friend and one Napoleon's most capable commanders; his death and the loss of several other senior generals seem have weighed on the emperor's mind when considering the armistice on the afternoon of 11 July

Above: French bridges over the main arm of the Danube before Wagram: the bridging of the Danube was a major achievement of military engineering; the scale of the preparatory measures undertaken before Wagram heightened Napoleon's frustration that the battle did not conclude with the crushing triumph he had worked so hard to obtain.

Left: Napoleon at Wagram, July 1809: the French emperor calmly issued orders from the centre of his extended battle line despite the crisis early in the second day's fighting. His firmly confident demeanour left a vivid impression on officers and men.

Charles at Wagram, 5 July 1809: Charles received a slight wound while rallying troops of I Corps on the evening of the battle's first day; French patrols learned of this on 7 July but their initial reports exaggerated the extent of his injury.

Napoleon and Austrian prisoners, a drawing by Hippolyte Bellangé: French light cavalrymen escort captured Austrian grenadiers past Napoleon after Wagram.

Oberstleutnant Karl von Francken (1774–1828): as the Baden brigade's chief of staff, the able and energetic Francken frequently led attacks during the pursuit.

Major Rudolph Graf Salis-Zizers (1779–1840): his 5th Vienna Volunteers halted the French cuirassiers who were driving towards Znaim on the afternoon of 11 July.

GB Jean Marie Eléonor Léopold de Stabenrath (1770–1853): this capable officer took command of Gratien/St Cyr's French brigade on 3 July and led it until Znaim where he was severely wounded.

GB Jean Pierre Joseph Bruyère (1772–1813): badly wounded at Schöngrabern on 10 July, he was promoted to general of division after the armistice.

Parlementaire at Hollabrunn, 9 July 1809: an Austrian officer delivers a message (likely the request to allow Liechtenstein to pass) to the French at Hollabrunn during a pause in the fighting.

Znaim from the west: this perspective clearly shows the very steep bluffs above the Thaya upstream from Znaim and the narrow valley of the Granitzbach; the Pöltenberg abbey (not visible) crowns the promontory on the far left.

General Franz von Minucci (1767–1812) at Znaim. As senior brigade commander, the competent and respected GM von Minucci led the 2nd Bavarian Division in place of the wounded GL von Wrede during the pursuit and at Znaim; he died of illness after the hardships in Russia 1812.

Znaim from the east: this image exaggerates the steepness of the slopes immediately east of Znaim, but the town's spires and walls can be seen across the intervening fields and vineyards.

French troops charge across the bridge over the Thaya: this well-known image gives a good sense of
French troops and the advantageous positioning of the French guns on the south bank on 11 July, b
the bridge is too wide and the lines likely too orderly.

Napoleon interviews Austria
this scene by Benjamin Zix ('
Day After the Battle of Wagra
shows the emperor talking to
Austrian officers and provide
sense of what Napoleon's tent
would have looked like above
Klein-Tesswitz.

Above: Marshal Louis Alexander Berthier, Prince of Neufchâtel (1753–1815): Napoleon's faithful and hardworking chief of staff, Berthier negotiated the ceasefire and armistice with Wimpffen and was named Prince of Wagram after the war for his contributions to the victory.

Below: The Hödnitz Mill: Frau Tulipan hosted Napoleon and his staff in this mill on the night of 12/13 July.

An imperial review at Schönbrunn Palace: Napoleon frequently reviewed troops in the expansi Schönbrunn courtyard before and after Wagram and Znaim; it was during one such parade that would-be assassin Friedrich Staps attempted to stab the emperor.

Napoleon meets Marie Louise at Compiègne, 27 March 1810: a major outcome of the 1809 wa was Franco-Austrian accommodation, dramatically embodied in personal union when Napole married Kaiser Franz's daughter Marie Louise in 1810. Their son was born the following year, seeming to secure Napoleon's dynasty.

only have been vexing that this 'laconic' message neither provided definitive instructions nor addressed his request for release of his other two divisions (this permission had been sent at 4:00 p.m. on 8 July, but the letter seems to have been delayed).[119]

In addition to laconic messages, French operations were hampered by the lack of direct communications between Massena and Marmont. Each knew the general whereabouts of the other and each could hear the other's guns in the distance, but they were unable to co-ordinate their movements in any meaningful way. Other than the remote sound of cannon fire, Massena had to rely on information from the local citizens to gain news about his fellow corps commander. Two patrol reports that Piré brought in around midnight provided some clarity. In one, villagers claimed that the Imperial Guard and three marshals had arrived at Klein-Tesswitz and that the French had had the worst of a great combat. In the second, a carter who had returned from Brenditz stated that Charles and the Austrian army were passing through Znaim, that the French had cavalry and guns on the heights above Klein-Tesswitz and 'The entire population was alarmed.' As vague as this intelligence was, it confirmed for Massena that Marmont was opposite Znaim (he doubtless discounted the claim about the Imperial Guard). He already knew from Berthier's brief missive that the emperor himself, the Guard and several corps were en route to Znaim. His mission for the next day, therefore, could only be to march north as early and as rapidly as possible to participate in what was likely to be a major engagement.[120]

Massena may have felt rather left in the dark, but by sunset the tremendous activity on the other avenue to Znaim had resulted in a large concentration of French forces between Mistelbach and Laa. In and around Laa were the Guard cavalry, Davout's 3rd Corps with Arrighi's 3rd Heavy Cavalry Division, and Nansouty's 1st Heavy Cavalry Division, in all at least 32,000 infantry and cavalry. As noted, Nansouty had received orders during the night of 9/10 July to march at dawn for Wilfersdorf.[121] He was thus already on the road when the new instructions on the 10th directed him to turn northwest from the Brünn highway at Schrick and make for Laa via Mistelbach. Davout acknowledged receipt of the new orders at 10:30 a.m. and set about turning his corps to the west from its previous northerly orientation on Muschau.[122] Arrighi's cuirassiers simply rode west from Poysdorf through Neudorf, while Davout's 3rd and 4th Divisions marched from Nikolsburg by way of Wildendürnbach (23 km). The marshal's other two divisions were approaching Muschau when they received the recall order. They had a long march of some 30 km along the south bank of the Thaya through Prerau (Nový Přerov). Evening thus found 3rd Corps east of the river between Laa and Wildendürnbach. Left behind along the Thaya near Muschau and Unter-Wisternitz was Grouchy with his dragoon division, two battalions of the 13th Léger, and one battalion of the 30th Ligne at Eisgrub.

We shall return to Grouchy's exploits presently, but it is worth noting at this point that Davout seems to have been frustrated at having to abandon his pursuit of Rosenberg.[123] While his information indicated that the Austrians would not stand at Znaim, Grouchy's reports of success against Rosenberg's rearguard led him to believe he had a chance to inflict serious injury on the Habsburg IV Corps, perhaps destroying two regiments. Berthier responded in the evening that Davout was authorised to march towards Znaim via Irritz (Jiřice u Miroslavi) and thereby move closer to Znaim while possibly accomplishing the destruction of Rosenberg's corps, a prospect that also seems to have enticed Napoleon. By the time this note was dispatched (6:30 p.m.), Davout's divisions were closing on Laa and the opportunity, if such it was, no longer existed.[124] This little incident is interesting not only because it shows how the lure of crushing a significant enemy formation could appeal to Napoleon and Davout, but more importantly because it illuminates the prevailing attitude among the French commanders on 10 July: few, if any, expected to find the Habsburg Hauptarmee at Znaim the following morning. Marching to Znaim was essential to prevent Charles from turning on Marmont and punishing him for his brash advance; Napoleon's swift action on the 10th had set all in motion, albeit belatedly, to achieve this goal. As it seemed highly unlikely that Charles would await Napoleon's arrival, however, the notion of diverting Davout to defeat Rosenberg was not illogical. In the end, it was probably fortunate for the French that Berthier's reply came too late to alter Davout's march. While possible, it is improbable that Rosenberg would have allowed Davout to march across his front to Irritz unmolested. Instead, it is easy to imagine Davout becoming entangled with Rosenberg for a day or more and thus being partially or entirely unavailable for a clash at Znaim even if the fighting had been prolonged to 12 July. Though events did not evolve in this fashion, this brief speculative exercise illustrates how outcomes are contingent upon a concatenation of incidents and how relatively small shifts in circumstances can introduce a significant degree of unpredictability.

While the men of 3rd Corps were trudging towards Laa and Berthier was exchanging notes with Davout, Oudinot and the Foot Guards (more than 50,000 infantry) were hastening up the Brünn highway towards the same destination. They took the same route as Nansouty through Mistelbach, but with between 30 and 40 km to cover, the column's weary lead elements only reached Staatz before bivouacking for the night.

Also in Laa that night was the emperor. Greeted by the town's dignitaries, he had his headquarters set up in a house in the town square while his household established his lodgings in the priory. He knew that it would take at least one day, probably two, to gather the army at Znaim, but he could take satisfaction that all of its components were on the march in response to his urgent orders. Marmont, however, excited his concern. 'We have no news from the Duke of Ragusa [Marmont], who departed this morning for Znaim,' wrote Berthier to Davout in his 6:30 letter that evening.[125] Chef de Bataillon Charles Jean Pernet was thus dispatched with 140 'well-mounted' troopers of the Guard's Polish Chevaulegers Regiment to find Marmont and report on his situation.[126] Pernet's report has not survived (it was probably verbal), but Captain Adam Dezydery Chlapowski, one of Napoleon's junior aides-de-camp, returned to Laa to find Napoleon soaking in a hot bath to ease the discomfort of a lingering head cold. Ordered to sketch Marmont's position, Chlapowski took out pencil and paper and began to draw, but the impatient emperor exclaimed that he was familiar with the terrain and grabbed the paper and pencil himself. This action, of course, splashed water all about and ruined the paper, so Napoleon called short the interview and sent Chlapowski to Berthier with instructions to have the Guard cavalry move at once. Chlapowski was then to return to Marmont to inform him that reinforcements were on the way.[127]

After nothing had been heard from Marmont all day, an officer bearing his report of the fighting near Znaim arrived at imperial headquarters at midnight. The quality of Marmont's report, however, was far from satisfactory in Napoleon's eyes and the officer, either too ignorant or too intimidated by having to face the demanding emperor, could not elaborate on the report's contents. The result was a stern reprimand for Marmont:

> The Italian engineer you dispatched arrived at midnight; it took him six hours to conduct this mission. Since then no one has arrived. This officer could have got lost. The rules of war dictate that you should send three with a half hour's separation between them. I found no commandant, no garrison at Laa, not even a guard at your bridges; therefore, if the hussars who lurk about on the plains had burned them, your retreat would have been compromised. You did not acquire such insouciance in my service. Why did you not leave cavalry posts to mark the route and ensure that your reports arrived promptly?

This opening paragraph did not exhaust Napoleon's ire. He informed Marmont that Davout and Oudinot were under orders to march for Znaim, but further rebuked him for the lack of urgency in his letter to Davout that day and insinuated that Marmont had allowed his desire for independence to take priority over the demands of service. 'I am mounting up with all the cavalry, but it is already two o'clock in the morning,' he continued, 'Take care not to engage seriously until I am close to you.' He concluded with additional demands.

> Send me someone who knows your position and that of the enemy well. What is the village that was taken and retaken? Make me a sketch and send it to me en route.[128]

In his reply, Marmont acknowledged that he had delayed in requesting Davout's support but offered as explanation that he 'did not want to influence Your Majesty's combinations by a premature alarm'. He also outlined his rationale for aggressively pursuing what he believed to be 'a simple rearguard' and described with some pride his army's performance, the virtues of his position, and his decision to retain it rather than retreat. His excuse for leaving Laa unguarded, however, was weak (he lamely claimed that Grouchy's dragoons had taken over watching the Thaya) and he glossed over the failure to keep Napoleon and Davout

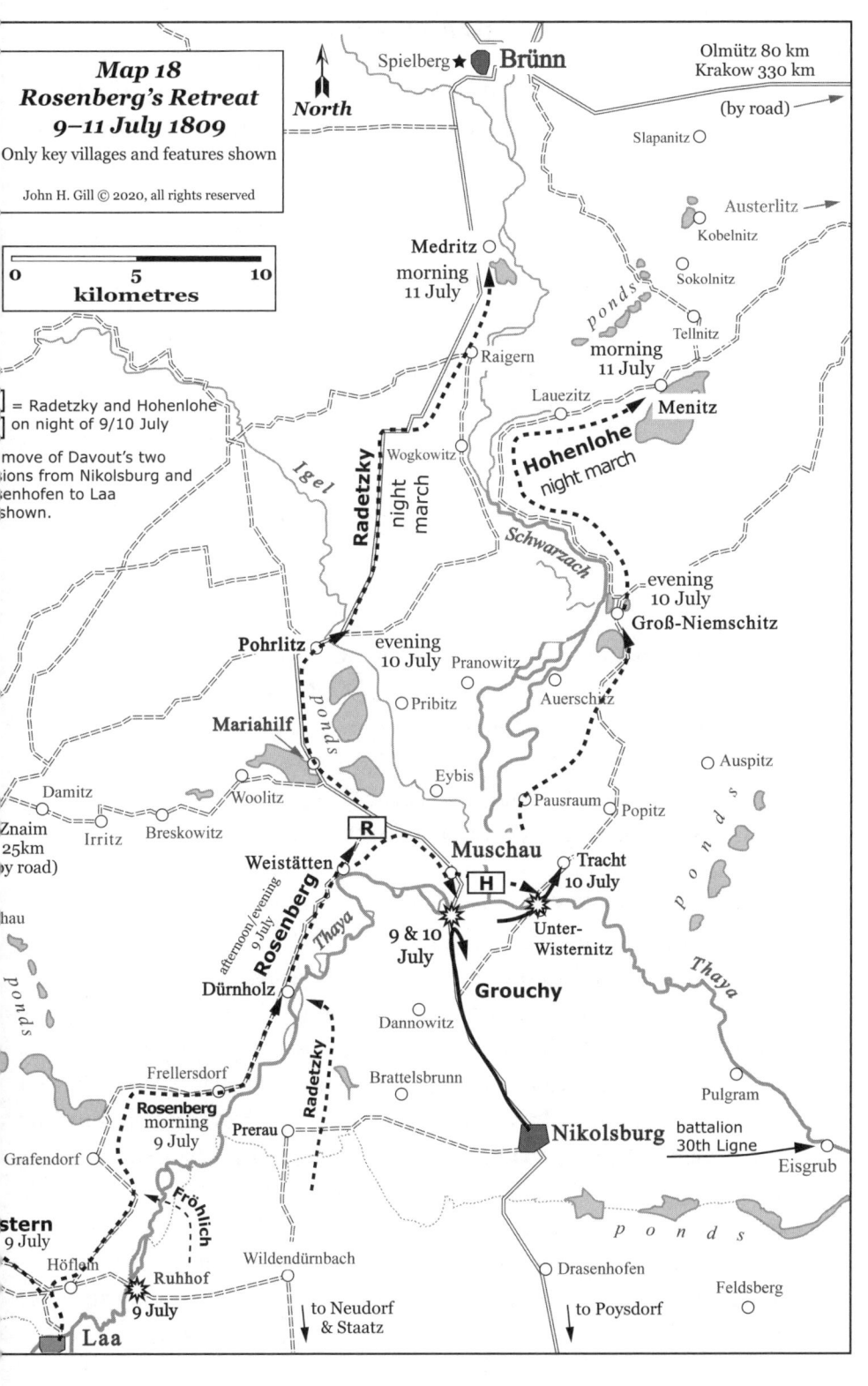

apprised of his situation.[129] As noted earlier, the measures he had taken to protect his line of communications were dangerously inadequate and he had utterly neglected his responsibility to supply imperial headquarters with frequent and detailed reports on his status.

Across the Thaya and Back to Brünn

General Grouchy had remained opposite Muschau with his small command to observe Rosenberg when Davout marched off to Laa on the afternoon of the 10th. He and his dragoons had seized Nikolsburg in a daring night charge the preceding evening but Austrian defenders had stymied his efforts to exploit this success by capturing the Muschau bridge intact. Early on the morning of 10 July, however, before Berthier's new instructions had arrived, he received orders from Davout to continue his advance up the Brünn highway, throw the Austrians across the Thaya and seize the bridge over the river. Grouchy thus pushed forward with the 7th Dragoons and a battalion of the 13th Léger as dawn was breaking. The French overthrew the squadron of *O'Reilly* Chevaulegers south of the river, but encountered 'very superior forces'[130] as they approached Muschau and recoiled, pursued by the two squadrons of *Hessen-Homburg* Hussars Rosenberg had stationed at the bridge.

Grouchy found the enemy's strength and the degree of resistance surprising as he had seen no evidence of major Austrian units retreating up the highway over the past two days and did not know that Rosenberg's men had passed the Thaya at Laa to make their way north along the left bank of the river. He asked for reinforcements, but did not wait before making a second attempt at the bridge. Bringing up the 30th Dragoons and his other battalion of the 13th Léger, he advanced again, but the Austrians on the south bank withdrew so swiftly that the French, to Grouchy's frustration, could not prevent them burning the bridge. Although the fighting degenerated into what the IV Corps operations journal called 'an insignificant cannonade', this little engagement at Muschau cost the *Hiller* Infantry No. 2 thirty casualties along with an unknown number from *Stain* Infantry, the 4th Unter-Wienerwald Landwehr and the hussars.[131] French losses are likewise not recorded.

Not to be denied, Grouchy slipped to his right (east) and marched on Unter-Wisternitz, driving before him the two other squadrons of *Hessen-Homburg* Hussars posted on the southern bank. Reaching Unter-Wisternitz 'hard on the heels' of the hussars,[132] the impetuous French thwarted attempts to burn the three little bridges that carried the road over two small islands and across the Thaya. The best the Austrians could do was to toss some of the planking into the river. The defenders here belonged to Fröhlich's rearguard brigade of Hohenlohe's division in the newly reorganised IV Corps. Behind the two hastily retreating hussar squadrons was I/*EH Carl*; this battalion was responsible for the protection of the bridges, backed up by the rest of *EH Carl* Infantry, its attached 4th OMB Landwehr Battalion and the 1st *EH Carl* Legion (Major Watterich). The dragoons alone therefore could not force a passage, but they dismounted and engaged in a firefight with the Austrians to hinder their continued efforts to dismantle the three little spans. The 1st Battalion of the 13th Léger soon arrived, however, and Grouchy launched an immediate attack. As part of the battalion stormed straight across the bridges, one company commandeered a rather shaky barge and paddled across to surprise the defenders on the far bank. The 7th Dragoons followed the light infantrymen, some trotting over parts of the bridges, some swimming across the river on both sides. Led by the dragoon regiment's elite company, the French pursued the retreating white-coats to capture the village of Tracht, a little more than a kilometre beyond the bridges, apparently knocking I/*EH Carl* apart in the process. Covered by II/*EH Carl*, the Austrians fell back in some disorder to collect themselves on the hills above the village. Grouchy, receiving instructions not to press too far in light of the 3rd Corps' revised mission, reigned in his troopers and retired to the river to repair and retain the bridges for future use. His opponents withdrew to Groß-Niemschitz (Velké Němčice) during the night.

Casualties during this engagement at Unter-Wisternitz are unclear. Grouchy claimed capturing some 500 men and picking up 458 abandoned muskets after the fighting. The *EH Carl* after-action report admitted to 53 officers and men killed or wounded and 89 captured, but losses for the other Austrian units are unknown and Grouchy did not give a French casualty count in his after-action report.[133] Whatever the casualties, GM

Fröhlich was dismayed and baffled by the outcome of the French attack and the performance of his infantry. The enemy 'cuirassiers', he reported, 'had so shattered a battalion of *EH Carl*' that the battalion commander could only assemble sixty men. 'How the cuirassiers [*sic*] could shatter the infantry in those water meadows is still a puzzle to me,' he remarked with no little disgust.[134] Grouchy thus accomplished his mission of securing a passage over the Thaya. Although Rosenberg was planning to retire anyway, this was still no mean achievement given his limited forces and the advantageous Austrian position.

As Grouchy settled in to guard the passage he had won and patrol the Thaya as far as Laa, Rosenberg withdrew further to the north. Perhaps in part as a result of Grouchy's aggressive advances, Rosenberg remained concerned about his flanks and sent patrols left and right both to provide advance warning of any French threat and to establish contact with Archdukes Charles and Johann. One of these liaison detachments, a lieutenant and six men of the *Hessen-Homburg* Hussars, was captured when it blundered into French patrols near Znaim as it tried to make its way to the Hauptarmee.[135] The bulk of IV Corps withdrew to the north to cover the roads leading towards Brünn and Olmütz: Radetzky to Pohrlitz (Pohořelice) on the right and Hohenlohe to Groß-Niemschitz on the left. This retreat of 8–10 km, however, still left Rosenberg feeling vulnerable. He therefore ordered another withdrawal at 8:00 p.m. so that the main bodies of Radetzky's and Hohenlohe's divisions dragged themselves through the night to reach Medritz (Modřice) and Menitz (Měnín) just south of Brünn as dawn was breaking on 11 July. For Hohenlohe, this was a march of an additional 10–12 km, but Radetzky's weary men had to cover nearly 20 km to assuage their corps commander's anxieties. The chastened Rosenberg thus positioned himself to protect Brünn as directed, but in the process he exhausted his 14,000 soldiers, retreated before the numerically inferior Grouchy (*c*. 3,000), and essentially lost touch with the enemy to his front.

As 10 July ended, it was clear that distance would be the key element in determining the next day's actions, both combat and diplomatic. On the French side, the question was whether support could reach the outnumbered Marmont – facing Charles at Znaim more or less on his own – in time to forestall catastrophe. Bivouac fires for his possible reinforcements were burning along both approaches to the town, but they were scattered and Napoleon's regiments would have many wearing kilometres to cover if they were to join the fight. Massena, encamped around Guntersdorf in the west with his cavalry and two of his infantry divisions, was closest, but more than 20 km south of the Thaya.[136] His other two divisions were further to the rear: Molitor could conceivably reach Znaim late on the 11th, but Boudet at Stockerau was far too distant. Distance was also a problem for the formidable force Napoleon had gathered in and around Laa. The Guard cavalry and the two cuirassier divisions would have to march some 25 km or so and Davout's infantry 35 km or more before they would be in a position to support Marmont. Even worse, from the French perspective, was the situation of Oudinot's corps and the Guard infantry: stretched east along the road to Staatz, they would have to march a minimum of 40 kilometres to reach the prospective battlefield. Moreover, many of these formations were slated to pass through Laa raising the prospect of congestion and substantial delays.

Charles, on the other hand, could expect no reinforcements. Rosenberg's right flank division was some 60 km to the east and barely in contact with the Hauptarmee. Given the distance and the persistent worries Franz and Charles expressed for the safety of Brünn and Olmütz, Rosenberg would not be recalled. Off to the west, Schustekh was even further away. Submitting to his anxieties, he had left a rearguard at Horn and withdrawn his main body beyond Göpfitz on the 10th, thereby placing himself 62 km west of Znaim. In any case, he received verbal instructions that day to screen the approaches to Prague. GM Anton Hardegg's small liaison detachment also moved on 10 July, departing Retz for Frain (Vranov ad Dyjí) 20 km west of the army's right flank.[137] Although Hardegg was in touch with the Hauptarmee, therefore, Schustekh's division would not be a factor either. The archduke enjoyed a dramatic numerical advantage over Marmont and, contrary to French expectations, had decided to remain in place for the night, but it was not clear that he would or could exploit his advantage before additional French forces arrived.

Meanwhile, Kaiser Franz was intentionally distancing himself from the scene and Liechtenstein, having inexplicably taken the long road, was riding through the night in search of Napoleon. Many extra hours would therefore elapse before the envoy located the French emperor and the reigning Habsburg monarch would be too far away to exert any direct influence on the developments of 11 July.

Chapter 6

Can't You Hear the Cannon?

11 July 1809

NAPOLEON AND THE MASS OF CAVALRY he had collected around Laa were up and moving well before the sun crept over the eastern horizon on the morning of 11 July. This made a seemingly endless column of more than 7,000 horsemen and another 500–600 artillerymen and artillery train personnel, jingling, jangling, swaying and swearing as they made their way north towards Znaim with their horses, guns, forges and caissons. They had had a few hours to rest, scrounge up some food and care for their mounts during the previous evening, but they were doubtless weary after several days of hard riding and they had many kilometres to cover to reach the battlefield.

The urgency of the march did not prevent the men of one lucky unit from exploiting what must have seemed an incredible stroke of good fortune, creating thereby what Cadet de Gassicourt called 'a singular spectacle'.

> A Moravian shepherd, leading a herd of more than a hundred sheep, came recklessly into our column. A cry arises: in an instant the herd is dispersed across the fields; four or five hundred soldiers, sabres in hand, chase after the sheep, seize them, strip them, skin them. In ten minutes, the herd had disappeared, and the soldiers had rejoined their ranks, one having a leg, another a rack of mutton on the tip of his bayonet. I have never seen a stupefaction to parallel that of the poor shepherd, who instead of a hundred and some sheep, now had only his two dogs, almost as astonished as him at the loss of their companions.[1]

The troopers, gunners and foot soldiers of the Guard shared the road, of course, with the vehicles of the imperial headquarters, a circumstance that produced some frictions as the march proceeded. Coming upon a rushing rivulet formed by the night's rain, one of the imperial household's wagons overturned when trying to cross and the column halted as servants, officials and staff officers tried to decide how to right the vehicle and resume their movement. Guns could be heard off to the northwest as an artillery company with its pieces came upon this scene.

> The captain in command was indignant to find the passage obstructed. 'What!' he exclaimed, 'Can't you hear the cannon? It is the Prince of Essling [Massena] attacking the Austrian rearguard. I must join them at all costs; they have need of us. Forward, gunners, smash everything and pass!' The prefect of the palace, the colonel of the gendarmerie, wanted to hold him back; he paid no attention. Pistol in hand, cursing like one possessed, he opened a passage, knocked over two or three vehicles, and crossed the ravine with his six artillery pieces more quickly than a schoolboy would have jumped a stream.[2]

Napoleon would doubtless have approved of the captain's impetuosity and impertinence, but he could not act as heedlessly as the duty-conscious battery commander. By the time he left Laa at 2:00 a.m. or so, he had some information about the situation from the staff officers who had been sent to find Marmont. It is also likely that on the way he read a message Marmont sent to Berthier at 6:00 o'clock that morning. Apparently confused by all the Austrian repositioning that had transpired during the night as they moved north of the Thaya, Marmont reported that the enemy was 'in full retreat', provided some incomplete information on Austrian strength, and hoped Davout would soon be on hand so he could initiate a pursuit.[3] On its own, this unsatisfactory report did little to clarify the situation, but Napoleon may have received additional information verbally from the courier, who was one of Berthier's staff officers. It is possible that this individual would have been able to elaborate on Marmont's imprecise text and perhaps even supply the sketch map Napoleon had requested. In the end, however, this sort of encounter battle presented a situation in which he would have to conduct a personal reconnaissance before deciding on a course of action. As was his normal practice, therefore, he approached Znaim on the morning of the 11th with a desired outcome in mind, but no specific tactical plan on how he was going to achieve it. That is, he wanted to lock Charles in place, forestalling an Austrian retreat until he could bring his superior forces to bear and threaten the Habsburg Hauptarmee with destruction so as to conclude this unwanted war as rapidly as possible. The major variables for Napoleon would be the speed with which his own reinforcements could arrive and what Charles might do in the interim. Weighing those two variables, he would formulate a plan once he reached the battlefield.

Charles did have a plan and, from a strictly military point of view, it was simple. His overriding aim was the preservation of the monarchy's army. He therefore intended to hold the Znaim position – awkward as it was from his perspective – only as long as necessary to let the army's baggage clear the highway to the north. He would then withdraw to a true, old-school-style 'position' such as Iglau where he could defend himself with greater confidence. These considerations placed a premium on the security of his left flank, where the French could most dangerously threaten his vulnerable line of retreat. His exaggerated estimate of French strength and his fear of the French cavalry made concern for this flank all the more acute. He thus weighted his left with two-thirds of his army: two of the infantry corps (II, III) and the entire Cavalry Reserve, with the Grenadier Corps in close reserve and VI Corps to the rear guarding the road north. He would therefore fight a strictly defensive battle with the intention of retreating during the night. At the same time, Charles also had to consider the strategic and political angles of his situation. He knew that his position as Generalissimus was in danger and that the war party was ascendant at court. He too wanted a quick end to the war, and he hoped that delaying a battlefield defeat would grant Liechtenstein time to find Napoleon and enter into negotiations while he still retained significant authority and while the Hauptarmee was still intact.

Indeed, Charles was deeply worried about the state of his army. In this respect, Marmont's 6:00 a.m. report was not far off the mark. Although mistaken about the Hauptarmee being 'in full retreat', the French general had written to Berthier that 'The enemy troops must be extremely tired.'

They arrived here yesterday at the same time as us after having marched all night. They remained under arms [i.e. they remained awake and in their ranks ready for action all night], manoeuvred or fought all day, and commenced marching at midnight according to the reports of deserters.[4]

Charles's assessment was similar. His troops were 'nearly exhausted' from 'hunger, thirst and weariness' and the army had suffered 'painful' losses 'owing to stragglers left behind from exhaustion on the march from Stammersdorf to Znaim and a part of the Landwehr that had disintegrated'. Not only did he believe he was already facing Davout, but 'the enemy had been considerably reinforced overnight' and 'prisoners said that the Emperor Napoleon and the bulk of his army were approaching from Laa'. 'It was thus in my interest for the army to gain an undisturbed lead' ahead of the French. He would have one more battle to fight, however, before he could attempt 'to gain an undisturbed lead'.[5] Neither he nor Napoleon, of course, knew at the time that this would be the last action of the war.

Massena and Reuss: More Resolution then Prudence

Despite the prospect of renewed fighting, the rising sun doubtless brought no little relief to the soldiers of both sides as its light spread across the soggy fields on the morning of 11 July. Overnight rain had softened the soil, hampering the movement of artillery pieces and compounding the discomfort of the weary men, whether Austrian, Bavarian, Hessian or French. 'Exhausted from hunger, worn with fatigue, it was not until 10:00 at night that we could dismount,' wrote Captain Tascher of the 12th Chasseurs, 'The mud did not permit us to lie down, so it was necessary to remain upright.'

As Marmont assumed, the Austrians, standing in formation through the night, were likely in even worse condition. In the artillery and cavalry units, equine care further impinged on the hours available for rest and food, especially as water sources were often far from a squadron's or battery's place in the line of battle. Tascher and his compatriots, for example, had to walk some distance to water their mounts. 'We were barely back when the day began to break and the call "to horse" was

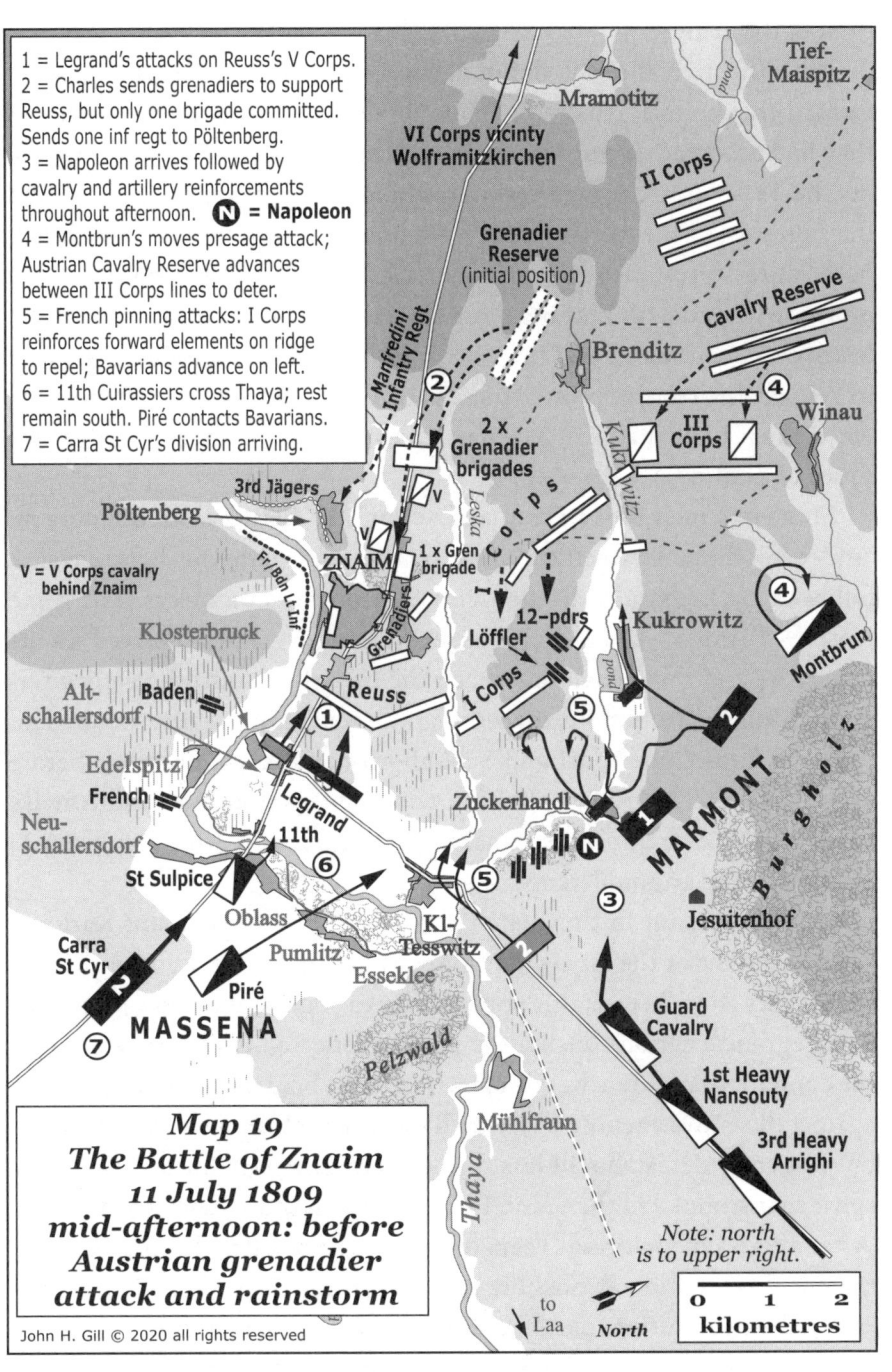

sounded,' he wrote, 'We resumed our positions of the previous day on the right of the army.'[6]

With the arrival of the damp dawn, French and Bavarian troops reformed their ranks, Austrians made final adjustments to the positions they had occupied during the night, and the hundreds of vehicles making up the Habsburg baggage train continued their laborious trundle up the highway to the north. There was, however, little gunfire. Although both sides were braced for a major clash, the first few hours of the morning passed with nothing more than desultory skirmishing between Marmont's command and the opposing Austrians from Klein-Tesswitz to Winau. The relative calm of these early hours changed in mid-morning when the lead elements of Massena's corps began to appear on the hills south of Znaim.

Massena's men broke camp and set off for Znaim around 4:00 a.m. 'under abominable weather',[7] Piré in the lead with the light cavalry, followed by Legrand's division and St Sulpice's cuirassiers. For some reason, Carra St Cyr's division seems to have been delayed in its departure and thus would not reach the battlefield until the early afternoon. Molitor also put his division on the road, but the distance he had to cover from Göllersdorf and Schönborn made his appearance before evening unlikely. Boudet's division remained at Stockerau and Ameil's small cavalry detachment was making its way back to 4th Corps from its mission in and around Krems.[8]

One participant in this march was young Premierleutnant Karl von Zech, adjutant of the 1st Baden Infantry. Writing his history of the war some years later, he took this opportunity to comment on how Massena's and Legrand's actions during the pursuit reflected his interpretation of the contemporary French style of warfare. 'The bold thrust of this division against the entire enemy army, which was certainly shaken and retreating but not truly defeated still less disintegrating, was characteristic of the spirit that stimulated the grand French army in those days,' wrote Zech. 'After a series of victorious years of war and unparalleled successes, they regarded everything as possible and everything as permitted and often scorned basic caution, partly from complacency, partly from contempt for the enemy.' Setbacks might instil greater circumspection for a time, but only until 'the next sunny ray of fortune aroused the peculiar high spirits of the French character'⁹. Zech overstates the degree to which boldness transformed into recklessness in this case, but his observations offer useful insights not only into how the French were perceived by military professionals at the time, but how they actually behaved on campaign. His remarks thus help explain the audacity displayed by, indeed expected of, officers such as Massena, Marmont and Legrand. In circumstances such as the pursuit to Znaim, 'scorning basic caution' was an understandable, perhaps necessary, risk. Relentlessly exploiting the momentum generated by Wagram, they intimidated their conservative and methodical foe, used speed and daring to conceal vulnerabilities, and ultimately imposed their will on Charles and the Hauptarmee to achieve a satisfactory outcome to the war.

This characteristic alacrity and audacity now brought Legrand's 1st Division to the banks of the Thaya, well ahead of Carra St Cyr's men. French mounted patrols may have reached the Thaya shortly after dawn, but the main combat elements of Massena's corps did not arrive on the slopes overlooking the river until around 10:00 o'clock that morning. By this time, all of Reuss's V Corps had crossed over to the north bank. Even Oberst Heinrich Hardegg's rearguard and the tardy 5th Vienna Volunteers had returned safely to the fold. Enjoined to defend the heights at Znaim to the last,[10] Reuss posted GM Johann Gottlieb Freiherr von Neustädter on the left to cover the slopes above Klein-Tesswitz with his brigade's two regular regiments and their associated Moravian Landwehr battalions. The Leska stream divided Neustädter's position from the right flank of I Corps. Reuss entrusted the V Corps right flank to Oberst Philipp Freiherr Pflüger von Lindenfels with his own *Lindenau* Infantry Regiment and the two battalions of *Gradiska* Grenzers. Pflüger would thus have responsibility for the sector that would see the heaviest fighting: Klosterbruck, Altschallersdorf, the bridges over the Thaya and the highway leading into Znaim. The 3rd Battalion of *Lindenau* had initially been tasked with the destruction of the bridges, but this proved impossible. The Austrians had to settle for barricading them in the hopes of slowing the anticipated French assault and III/*Lindenau* withdrew early in the morning as French scouts and skirmishers began to appear on the south bank. This withdrawal left protection of the river in the hands of the *Gradiska* Grenzers, their 2nd Battalion covering

Klosterbruck and Altschallersdorf on the right, the 1st Battalion to the left towards Klein-Tesswitz with a chain of skirmishers lining the north bank of river. Pflüger put his two regular battalions on the high ground behind the Grenzers: II/*Lindenau* athwart the highway and III/*Lindenau* slightly to the left rear near the Znaim magazine. A few guns were rolled up into the small earthworks to cover the bridge and support the *Gradiskaners*. Beyond his main position, Reuss placed the 3rd Jägers and a cannon atop the Pöltenberg promontory and sent two squadrons of *Blankenstein* (c. 200) upstream to screen the Thaya and prevent surprises on his right. The rest of his cavalry (c. 1,170) was held in reserve north of town as the terrain to the south seemed to provide few opportunities for mounted action. Finally, as we have seen, Major Salis and the 5th Vienna Volunteers were in Znaim itself, recuperating from their escapade during the night.[11]

Curiously, Charles pulled away I/*Lindenau* with a 'specific written order'.[12] It is not clear what Charles had in mind in ordering this move and the battalion's actions during the day are unknown (it may have been sent off to guard the road leading northwest from Pöltenberg), but it played no role in the fighting and its detachment deprived Reuss's small corps of 700–800 regular infantry. Whatever the archduke had in mind, this odd decision certainly baffled and irritated both Pflüger and Reuss. Without lending too much weight to the employment of one battalion, this small occurrence suggests two things about Charles. First, it is consistent with the archduke's cordon-defence mind-set and his predilection for detaching units for tertiary tasks even when a major engagement was in the offing. Second, it represents another example of the exaggerated Austrian anxiety about their flanks, even when there seemed little reason for concern. That same morning, *Manfredini* Infantry No. 12 would be dispatched from III Corps to supplement the 3rd Jägers and hussars in their positions from the Pöltenberg Abbey upstream along the steep bluffs above the Thaya. This meant that there would eventually be some 2,500 Austrians to watch the fifty or so Baden light infantrymen and perhaps some French skirmishers on the far bank.[13]

Although he only had some 9,000 infantry (after subtracting I/*Lindenau*), Reuss's position was a strong one. The Jägers were almost invulnerable perched above the Thaya around the Pöltenberg Abbey and the two brigades south of the city were well situated on high ground with a number of manmade structures they could potentially use as strongpoints. The irregularities of the terrain presented some difficulties and the south bank was in some places higher than the north, but the Thaya formed a veritable moat for the position and at least a few of the Habsburg guns could benefit from some minimal cover by occupying the small earthworks. One serious disadvantage was that the bend in the river near Edelspitz allowed cannon placed there or on the Kühberg above the village to enfilade the Austrians between Znaim and the bridges. On the other hand, the nature of the terrain afforded very little scope for the French to employ the cavalry that caused such worry to Austrian commanders. This meant that the battle – despite some dramatic and surprising mounted action – would basically be an infantry fight. Here Reuss enjoyed another advantage. He did not know it, but his infantry significantly outnumbered the foot soldiers Massena would be able to bring to bear in the early stages of the coming struggle.

It was now mid-morning and those French and Baden regiments were becoming visible in the fields of ochre grain that cloaked the gentle ridge south of the Thaya.[14] The marshal, though still commanding from his carriage, rapidly deployed his men as they came on the scene under the lowering skies. While Piré's light horsemen trotted off to the right towards Klein-Tesswitz, Legrand's infantry unfolded from their march columns and shook out skirmish lines as horse batteries unlimbered on the hillside. Cannon on both sides soon opened up, the deeper booming of the guns joined by the increasing crackle of musketry as the light infantry spread out along the riverbank. French foot artillery added to the growing din as perspiring gunners manhandled their pieces into position across the muddy ground. Meanwhile, the Baden Jägers were advancing straight towards the southernmost bridge in the centre of Legrand's line with the four Baden light companies on their left and the French brigade's voltigeurs to their right around Oblass. Once in position and formed into four large closed columns, the rest of the French and Baden infantry began to roll forward towards the river, accompanied by most of the artillery. Although two 12-pounders remained on the ridge to engage in a counterbattery duel with the Habsburg guns, most of the pieces moved closer to the Thaya to place a heavy fire on the Grenzer immediately on the other side of the river. Three pieces established near Edelspitz to the left of the skirmishers were especially effective, punishing the Austrians along the bank with enfilading canister fire and quickly forcing those working to barricade the bridges and their supports to retire. To complete the devastating ensemble of French artillery, several guns on the French right delivered flanking fire against the left of I/*Gradiska* in the low ground towards Klein-Tesswitz. Austrian efforts to retake the bridges failed because the troops 'had no protection against the effect of the enemy guns whose placement was favoured by the advantageous heights on the right bank' of the river.[15]

With support from their artillery and the dense columns of formed infantry behind, the French and Baden light troops began to advance. The Carabinier Company of the Baden Jäger Battalion grappled with the task of removing the barricade on the southern bridge, but most of the men splashed into the Thaya and waded across, driving the Austrian skirmishers from the far bank and gradually pushing them back on Reuss's main position. The light cavalry likewise made its way through the chilly waters to establish itself on the northern shore near Klein-Tesswitz and complete the connection to Marmont's men on the French right wing. Massena also sent the 11th Cuirassier Regiment across the river, apparently using a ford. Coming out of the water on the northern bank, they arranged themselves in a small open area near the end of the northern bridge and just to the right (east) of the road. Lacking space to deploy, the other three cuirassier regiments were held near the bridge but south of the river. The French and Baden artillery likewise remained on the southern bank of the Thaya, providing effective fire support, albeit from something of a distance. The lone cuirassier regiment, however, even though more or less immobilised by the muddy ground, excited great concern among the Grenzer officers. Worried that this 'substantial cavalry unit' looked like it might 'fall on the 1st Battalion in the flat ground or outflank the 2nd Battalion at the bridge', Oberst Pflüger pulled I/*Gradiska* back north of the Brünn highway, withdrew the cannon from the earthworks and directed II/*Gradiska* to retire to Klosterbruck, abandoning both the bridges and Altschallersdorf.[16] The French seem to have been unaware of the impact of the 11th Cuirassiers. Their attention was focused on the Baden Jägers clearing the obstructions on the bridges and on the French and Baden light infantry who were splashing ahead through the river at the same time that the horsemen were making their way across the ford. In any event, with the bridges open, the rest of Legrand's infantry soon surged over the Thaya, the French fanning out to the right, the Badeners to the left to form in closed masses while cannon balls from both sides' guns flew overhead.

The hour was probably approaching noon. Legrand's men were preparing to advance and the battle was rapidly intensifying. The manner in which the fighting now evolved, however, was peculiar in several respects.

In the first place, Legrand, though outnumbered, was attacking. The French general probably had some 5,000 infantry under his command on 11 July with only a lone cuirassier regiment on the northern bank of the river for support (perhaps 400 troopers). The light cavalry would have little opportunity for employment given the terrain and the need to maintain contact with Marmont. Massena's artillery on the southern shore would be helpful, but the gunners would be unlikely to use canister owing to range and fear of hitting their own men. In contrast, Reuss could deploy up to 9,000 infantry on the hills in front of Znaim and his gunners would have no compunction about employing canister for close-range work.

Second, the choppy terrain with its vineyards and buildings dictated that, by and by, most of the infantry would end up deployed in open order as the combat progressed. Though open, these French and Baden formations would be more dense than was common in standard skirmishing tactics. In a later commentary, one of Massena's staff officers would term this *en grande bande*: that is, a loose formation of 'a battalion, a regiment, even an entire brigade' that could negotiate difficult terrain to overcome a position while a formed body of troops menaced the enemy's front.[17] The physical space the French brigade had to cover on the right also made skirmish order more appropriate than tightly closed formations. Fortunately for Massena and Legrand, this was a tactical form at which the French and their German allies excelled. As will be seen, however, there were risks in not having sufficient formed units at hand when the skirmishers encountered trouble. It is also notable that many of the Austrian units dispersed in skirmish order for much of the battle.

Third, although timing cannot be determined with any great precision, it seems that Legrand's assault began before any French reserves were available. Reuss could call upon the entire Grenadier Corps behind Znaim (9,500), but the nearest French reinforcements – the French and Hessians of Carra St Cyr's division (at most 5,000 infantry) – had not yet appeared on the field when Legrand advanced. These remarkable circumstances notwithstanding, Massena and Legrand did not hesitate to attack and their French and Baden troops were soon straining the Habsburg defences.

On the left of Legrand's line, the ubiquitous Oberstleutnant von Francken assembled the eight companies of the 1st Baden Infantry beyond the Klosterbruck complex and to the west of the highway to support the advancing light troops; these in turn were reinforced by II/2 Baden. Of the brigade's infantry, only I/2 Baden remained formed in reserve near the highway. The 1st and 2nd Battalions of the 18th Ligne pressed forward along and just to the right of the highway in skirmish order, while III/18 remained behind in column. Similarly, I/26 Léger led the attack on the division's right flank dispersed in open order, while the other two battalions kept back and tried to extend the regiment's line towards Klein-Tesswitz.[18] Reuss, pressured in front, suffering heavily from Massena's artillery fire, and apprehensive about Bavarian skirmishers emerging from Klein-Tesswitz to threaten his left flank, pulled his line back closer to Znaim. The French eagerly pursued. They overran the small earthworks and pushed about half the distance from the bridges to the town, but they advanced 'with more resolution than prudence' and were brought to a halt as they tried to exploit their momentum.[19]

Here in the first hours of the afternoon, the battle swayed back and forth for a time as first one side, then the other, seemed to have the advantage.[20] The intensity of the fighting soon forced both Reuss and Legrand to commit almost all of their reserves. The 2nd and 3rd Battalions of the 26th, for example, gradually found themselves drawn into the firing line. Though the effort cost the life of Louis Raymond, one of the battalion commanders, these battalions restored the situation when the Austrians threatened to outflank Legrand on his right. Reuss, lamenting the absence of I/*Lindenau* as 'the engagement roared on without a break', worried that 'all the little reserve was already in combat', while from his perspective at least, 'The enemy constantly supported his [line] with fresh troops.'[21] As the hour neared 2 o'clock, therefore, all Reuss had left was the exhausted 5th Vienna Volunteers in Znaim and Legrand's only untouched infantry was part of the 18th Ligne and perhaps one Baden battalion. None of these concerns diminished the ferocity of the struggle, but Reuss was about to receive welcome reinforcements and nature was on the verge of intervening in a most dramatic fashion.

The Emperor Arrives

Massena's appearance south of Znaim coincided with Napoleon's arrival on the heights south of Zuckerhandl. Watching from the opposite side of the field was Major Georg Freiherr von Valentini, a Prussian officer who had taken Habsburg service. He could see 'a senior general with a large staff reconnoitring, probably Napoleon himself'.

> The suspicion became near certainty as one saw a great tent being erected on the heights just like the bivouac of the imperial commander-in-chief. An orderly deployment of the enemy occurred opposite the Austrian front, and lines of skirmishers advancing on all sides in the usual manner indicated without any doubt the beginning of a great battle.[22]

As usual, the emperor's appearance had a dramatic effect on his army. 'He rode along in front of the loudly cheering troops,' wrote Leutnant Madroux of the 2nd Bavarian Chevaulegers, 'No one doubted victory any more'. 'The Emperor Napoleon was there and with him his Guard; our highly dangerous situation had changed,' remembered another Bavarian, 'Arriving and grasping the battle with a mighty hand was the work of a moment.' 'We received him with the most lively acclamations as he rode along in front of our posts despite the incessant fire of the enemy artillery, which did not prevent him from coolly studying the position,' recalled Captain Espinchal. As was his custom, Napoleon dedicated some of his time to interactions with junior officers and common soldiers, personally praising the Bavarian gunners and stopping by a French battery that was hotly engaged with the Austrians opposite. 'It was there that one saw Napoleon, impassive amidst the most terrible fire, himself aim a cannon whose shot fell in the middle of the Austrian batteries,' observed Lieutenant Victor Dupuy, 'He was awaiting impatiently the arrival of Marshal Davout and his corps.'[23]

The heights afforded a spectacular view and Napoleon quickly took in the scene laid out before him like some panoramic battle painting beneath the grim, grey skies: on his left, Massena's men, under cover of their guns, were skirmishing along the river bank with the defenders; sweeping his eye from his left front to his right, he could see Marmont's command stretched from Klein-Tesswitz to Zuckerhandl and Kukrowitz; and to his right rear, Montbrun's horsemen were arrayed in front of the Burgholz. He could also see the defects in Charles's position, notably the proximity of the Austrian left flank to the Hauptarmee's line of retreat, still crammed with ungainly baggage of all sorts. He did not have the necessary force to exploit this vulnerability, but as Espinchal noted, 'He made dispositions to attack that left no doubt of his intention to fight a decisive battle the following day.' For the moment, however, 'He forbade the troops to commit too much.'[24]

As the emperor was examining the battlefield, the reinforcements he had led were arraying themselves in dark mounted masses behind him: the Guard cavalry, Nansouty's 1st Heavy Division, and Arrighi's 3rd for a total of more than 7,000 horsemen and 42 guns. This was an impressive force by any measure, 'a numberless host of French soldiers, especially the vast line of cavalry that established itself in a fairly concentrated position' in the words of a Bavarian lieutenant.[25] What Napoleon needed, however, was infantry, but the hard-marching battalions of Davout, Oudinot and the Guard were still many kilometres away. In their absence, he would use Marmont's small corps both to assist Massena and to lock Charles in place. He had to hope that either the rest of his foot soldiers would arrive before nightfall or that the two armies would become so entangled that the Austrians would be unable to escape.

Charles had no intention of remaining through the night. Indeed, as Massena and Marmont were moving against V Corps and I Corps respectively, the Austrian army staff back in Wolframitzkirchen were preparing new orders to retire to Mährisch-Budwitz during the coming night. Issued at 11:00 a.m., this 'disposition' called for VI Corps to move first, withdrawing from its position around Wolframitzkirchen at 6:00 p.m. and followed in sequence by the Grenadiers, III, II and I Corps between 8:00 and 11:00 p.m. Reuss, protected by the Cavalry Reserve, was to pull out at midnight before assuming the rearguard role while the cavalry withdrew north to Mährisch-Budwitz.[26] The fact that V Corps was again selected for the demanding rearguard mission suggests that Charles and his senior staff officers did not expect much fighting south of Znaim on 11 July. Either III Corps or II Corps would have seemed more logical choices as neither had seen much action at all since 6 July and each had enjoyed at least one day of rest. The choice of V Corps may have represented an acknowledgement of Reuss's fine performance as rearguard on the 10th, but the archduke and his officers feared for their left flank and may have assumed that V Corps on the right would not be seriously engaged during the day. Drafting and copying out their disposition in distant Wolframitzkirchen that morning, they did not know that Massena was about to unleash a terrible storm south of Znaim, one that would absorb Reuss and his men in fierce fighting through the remaining daylight hours and into the evening.

As the army staff officers were composing this disposition, they and their Generalissimus were labouring under the erroneous belief that the Hauptarmee was already outnumbered or soon would be. Not only was it evident that Napoleon himself had arrived, but some of the incoming reports sounded truly alarming. As noted earlier, army headquarters was convinced that they were already facing all or part of Davout's 3rd Corps. How the Austrians could believe this when they had been engaged with Marmont for more than a day is unclear, but now they heard from prisoners that the French Army of Italy was also headed for Znaim![27] Many officers, anxious about the security of the army's left wing, seem to have regarded the Burgholz with special concern, fearing that all manner of French forces might be lurking among the trees. 'The enemy had been reinforced during the night,' recorded the main operations journal, 'In particular, one saw more infantry and, on the heights along the edge of the woods towards [Klein-]Tesswitz, more and more columns forming up.'[28] All of this fed a pre-existing bias towards anxiety and inferiority as far as numbers were concerned. The worry was reversed when regarded from the French perspective. In the early morning hours before Napoleon's arrival with the heavy cavalry, Montbrun had all of his division's servants, *cantinières* and spare horses placed behind his regiments to simulate a second line of troopers.[29] The appearance of the Horse Guards and the two heavy cavalry divisions eased this concern, but the French remained at a substantial numerical disadvantage. Although it is difficult to determine each side's exact strength following the losses occasioned by Wagram, multiple rearguard engagements, and march attrition, the Austrians outnumbered the French by roughly two to one even after the arrival of Massena's two divisions and the heavy cavalry (*see* Chart 4 and Appendix 5E).

The Austrian array had changed somewhat compared to the previous evening as units shifted and absent regiments returned to their assigned corps. III Corps continued to hold the far left flank. Kolowrat placed a battalion in Winau but deployed the bulk of his infantry in two lines, the first (twelve battalions) south of Winau and the second (nine battalions) about a kilometre behind, between that village and Brenditz. The *Schwarzenberg* Uhlans were distributed in a light chain across the front of the corps. As he had during the night, he kept his men under arms in squares throughout the day, but at some point on the 11th, he was directed to detach an infantry regiment (he selected *Manfredini* Infantry) to strengthen the 3rd Jägers around the Pöltenberg monastery complex. The twelve regiments of the Cavalry Reserve Corps were deployed to Kolowrat's left rear behind Winau facing southeast. Further to the rear was Hohenzollern's II Corps in five lines about two kilometres north of Brenditz, more or less west of and aligned with the road to Tief-Maispitz.[30] The Grenadier Corps stood in two equal lines between Brenditz and the Iglau highway, while VI Corps, as we have seen, had retired during the night to a position between Wolframitzkirchen and Frainersdorf, approximately ten kilometres (straight-line) distance northwest of Brenditz.

I Corps covered the peninsula of broken terrain between the Leska and Kukrowitz streams that constituted the centre of the Hauptarmee's position. The main body of the corps stood across the Kukrowitzerbach from III Corps in two lines angled to the right to face southeast: the eleven battalions in the first line coming under Henneberg, and GM Joseph Graf Clary und Aldringen commanding the five squadrons and

> **Chart 4: Rough Comparative Strengths on 10 and 11 July**
> *(Infantry and cavalry figures only)*
>
> **10 July/midday**
>
> French: 17,500
> Marmont (incl. Montbrun, Minucci)
>
> Austrian: 63,500
> I, II, III, VI, Gren, Cav
> (V Corps opposing Massena)
>
> **11 July/midday**
>
> French: 37,800
> Marmont (incl. Montbrun, Minucci)
> *Added:* Massena: 1st, 2nd Divs, Piré, St Sulpice
> *Added:* Guard Cavalry, 1st and 3rd Heavy Cavalry
>
> Austrian: 74,900
> I, II, III, V, VI, Gren, Cav
> (65,200 if deduct VI)
>
> **Potential 12 July/morning**
>
> French: 91,200
> Marmont (incl. Montbrun, Minucci)
> Massena: 1st, 2nd Divs, Piré, St Sulpice
> Guard Cavalry, 1st and 3rd Heavy Cavalry
> *Added:* Davout, Oudinot, Molitor, Foot Guards
>
> Austrian: 47,300*
> I, III, V, part Gren, Cav
> (deducting II, VI and part Gren)
>
> * The Hauptarmee could have had as many as 74,900 (or even 65,200 if VI Corps is excluded) on the morning of the 12th had Charles not ordered II Corps, VI Corps and two grenadier brigades to withdraw on the night of 11/12 July.
>
> Note: All figures are estimated, casualties on 10 and 11 July not deducted. See Appendix 5E for details.

five battalions of the second line. Additionally, four companies of I/*Anton Mittrowsky* were detailed to guard the approaches to Brenditz.[31] The remaining three battalions and three squadrons were spread between the two streams 1½–2 km to the southeast as a sort of forward element: a battalion of *Reuss-Plauen* stood above the Leska on the right, the 2nd Jägers and the remnants of two companies from the 4th *EH Carl* Legion held the centre, and II/*Anton Mittrowsky* covered a 12-pounder battery atop a prominent hill on the left. The placement of this battery allowed it to fire into the valley near Zuckerhandl and onto the plateau beyond. The three squadrons of *Klenau* were to use patrols to connect this advanced line with Neustädter's brigade of V Corps across the Leska on the right. This advance element comprised only some 2,000 of Bellegarde's 12,000 men, yet they were the ones who would be the targets of Marmont's most serious probing attacks in the late morning and afternoon of 11 July.

While waiting for his imperial master during the morning, Marmont had wisely disposed his troops to facilitate a rapid transition to the attack. The Bavarians assumed responsibility for Klein-Tesswitz on the left, Clauzel shifted to the area east of the valley that connects Zuckerhandl and Kukrowitz in the centre, Montbrun remained in front of the Burgholz on the right, and Claparède's division arranged itself behind Clauzel in reserve. Marmont's command was thus well positioned when the emperor appeared to assume personal control of the battle.[32]

It did not take Napoleon long to assess the situation and organise a series of pinning attacks with the forces he had at hand. The skirmishing that had nattered along between Marmont and Bellegarde throughout the early hours thus began to assume more earnest proportions shortly after his arrival on the field. Though he only intended pinning or holding attacks against the Habsburg centre and left, these had to be sufficiently menacing so as to occupy Austrian attention, assist Massena and embroil the Hauptarmee in a fight from which it could not easily disengage. He therefore activated Marmont's entire command and Austrian observers soon noticed increased pressure from skirmishers around Klein-Tesswitz and the formation of what they perceived as 'three assault columns' on the plateau around Zuckerhandl. 'We were under arms when we heard cannon on our left; this led us to believe it was Marshal Massena who was attacking the enemy on that side,' recalled Colonel Roch Godart of the 79th Ligne, 'The Duke of Ragusa [Marmont] ordered the attack at once and we were soon engaged.' Napoleon, however, sought little more than a vigorous and convincing demonstration. 'We limited ourselves to maintaining the positions we had on the previous day,' wrote Godart, 'I was charged with defending a village with my regiment.'[33] On the other side of the field, the Austrians drew dire conclusions from the French movements. They assumed Napoleon's objective was 'to master the heights we held and to open a way to Znaim across the vineyards and ravines' west of Zuckerhandl and Kukrowitz.[34]

It was probably about noon when the French attack columns moved forward. Of the three the Austrians defined, one halted on the plateau north of the Kukrowitz stream before reaching the village and the second remained in the valley just north of Zuckerhandl. It is not clear that these were stopped by Austrian action; it is equally possible that they were held back by French orders to avoid being committed to what would likely have been a futile and costly attack.[35] The third column, as outlined in Austrian accounts, emerged from Zuckerhandl and climbed up the slopes towards the west to threaten the 12-pounder battery. The Austrians countered this French advance with II/*Mittrowsky* posted to cover the 12-pounder battery and the 'effective fire' of the guns themselves, but Bellegarde was sufficiently concerned to order up III/*Kolowrat* and two 6-pounders from his main body's first line in the rear. These reinforcements, especially the well-handled pair of guns under Oberleutnant Franz Löffler, sufficed to repel this initial French attack. Austrian accounts also mention help from the *Klenau* squadrons that repulsed small French cavalry forays.

This first French probing attack revealed the weaknesses of the I Corps position, especially what is termed here the advance element. Strangely, neither Bellegarde, nor his staff, nor Charles seems to have noticed the vulnerability of the 'now important heights by Zuckerhandl' earlier. Hastening to repair this oversight, Bellegarde quickly brought four more battalions from the main body to strengthen his defences: one each of *Reuss-Plauen*, *Erbach*, *EH Rainer* and *Kolowrat* (so two battalions from this regiment were now engaged). Command of the reinforced advance element was entrusted to FML Fresnel.[36] He would face a second French attack in short order.[37]

As these initial attacks were under way, Montbrun attempted to threaten the Austrian left. In view of his limited resources and the reinforcements Charles had placed around Winau, however, this effort did not prosper. When French movements seemed to portend an imminent attack, Schwarzenberg advanced four of his brigades into the space between the two lines of III Corps infantry between Brenditz and Winau.

Deployed in columns, the Austrian horse maintained this post until nightfall while their infantry compatriots remained formed in masses. Schwarzenberg's defensive response sufficed to forestall any serious adventures on Montbrun's part and, as the Austrians had no intention of taking the offensive, no appreciable action occurred on this part of the field for the rest of the day.[38] The diary of the Baden Light Dragoons thus recorded with some regret that the cavalry here 'was not given much to do'.[39]

In contrast to the relative quiet on Marmont's right, the fighting on his left was lively, if limited. 'With the first rays of the sun on the 11th, the firing of the skirmishers began again' and the numerous Bavarian batteries once more unlimbered on the crest of the Tesswitz heights despite the difficulties presented by the muddy ground. This deployment brought the Bavarian gunners into close proximity to Napoleon as he was using the same area for his observation post. 'The emperor in the midst of his glittering staff was very easy to recognise,' wrote an artillery officer who had seen him in April, 'He was as simply clad as at Abensberg.' Napoleon had dismounted and was surveying the battle from a campstool when several Austrian cannon balls struck the soft earth only ten paces away from his seat. Whether or not the Austrians were intentionally aiming for him and the obvious staff suite surrounding him as the Bavarians believed, he was unperturbed. He calmly remounted, rode some thirty paces to one side, dismounted, resumed his seat on the stool, 'and the entire incident sank into oblivion'. For their part, the Bavarian pieces and a French battery that joined them took Bellegarde's 12-pounder battery for their particular target, albeit with little evident success. Their fire, however, garnered Napoleon's praise and provided valuable support to the attacks Marmont was conducting against the high ground beyond the Kukrowitz stream.[40]

As the Bavarian gunners were busily engaged, their infantry countrymen were moving into the valley below. 'On the morning of the 11th, in the same moment that the Duke of Rivoli [Massena] appeared on the far side of the Thaya,' the 2nd Division received orders to advance. After halting for a time on the heights, the division descended into the low ground and deployed, pushing its 1st Brigade forward towards Znaim on the division's right. However, as General Minucci reported,

'The infantry did not come to a major attack on this day, and only the Schützen of the 1st Brigade along with some sections of the 6th [Light] Battalion that were pushed forward as skirmishers participated in the infantry battle.' The division's exact location at this point is not clear from the records. Most likely it was just north of Klein-Tesswitz with its skirmishers probing forwards among the vineyards on the tongue of land between the Kukrowitz and Leska streams.[41] Two Bavarian batteries that were supposed to move into the vale via Zuckerhandl, however, came under heavy fire when their vehicles mired in the soft ground near the Kukrowitzerbach. As the gunners and train personnel of the first battery were struggling to extricate their equipment, a lucky Austrian shot hit one of the ammunition caissons causing an explosion that killed two horses, wounded two men and excited untold confusion. The Austrians exacerbated the battery's travails by opening up on it with canister fire. Slowly and painfully, the men extracted their guns and unlimbered in a small flat space south of Zuckerhandl. The second battery, seeing these problems, turned around and, after enormous effort, resumed its position on the heights.[42]

These actions may not have constituted a 'major attack' in Minucci's view, but they cost the division an additional forty casualties and, in the words of the 6th Light's Mändler, 'Both sides fought with the greatest exertion and, especially from the enemy side, with the greatest bitterness.' The division's performance also burnished its reputation among its French allies with Pelet praising it for giving 'proofs of zeal and courage'.[43] Moreover, the Bavarian skirmishers unsettled Reuss. He perceived them as a threat to his left flank, and their advance, portrayed as lively and aggressive by the Austrians, was an additional motivation for him to pull his line back towards Znaim. Indeed, we must now return to Reuss and Massena to address the next developments across this complex field.

Massena and Reuss: A Heavy and Violent Storm

While Marmont's first attack was being repulsed and as his second was being prepared, Legrand's outnumbered division was making slow but steady progress towards Znaim. Reuss had used up nearly all of his reserves and the French were pushing close to the city's suburbs. Charles responded to this threat by shifting the Grenadier Corps towards Znaim from its initial position west of Brenditz. Rather than punishing the bold French and perhaps wrecking Legrand's division by driving it into the Thaya, however, the archduke was content simply to bolster the V Corps' defence. In addition to his strictly defensive approach to the battle, Charles's reluctance to commit any more of the grenadiers was likely motivated by his exaggerated notions of French strength on the field and his overriding worry that Napoleon would use this power to strike for the Hauptarmee's vulnerable line of retreat. As a result, two of the four grenadier brigades (Steyrer and Hammer) were left astride the Iglau highway about two kilometres northwest of Znaim, one was moved closer to the town 'ready to be sent forward' (Scovaud), and only one brigade (Murray) was actually sent to Reuss's immediate assistance. Of the seventeen grenadier battalions, therefore, only four (some 2,200 men) were to be employed to address the impending danger to V Corps directly. Two of these were stationed in the southeastern suburbs to strengthen Reuss's left flank and one remained in reserve, leaving one battalion to be posted at the southern gate to Znaim. Commanding this battalion was Oberstleutnant August Graf zu Leiningen-Westerburg, a German from the old Bavarian Rhineland territories who had served the Habsburgs for seventeen years and had earned the Knight's Cross of the Maria Theresa Order in 1805. Hurrying around the ring road just outside the city's walls, Leiningen's grenadiers and the other three battalions were in place by about 2:00 o'clock or so on that cloudy afternoon.

One of the most dramatic moments in a war that seemed overcrowded with dramatic moments now ensued. 'The enemy had succeeded in driving almost to the Vienna Gate,' Reuss recorded, 'but the Murray Grenadier Brigade rushed up [and] the *Leiningen* Battalion was immediately ordered to attack.' Reuss's counterattack plan was simple: the grenadiers would thrust straight down the highway toward the bridges with several companies of *Lindenau* accompanying them on their flanks; one battalion of *Lindenau* would remain in reserve in front of the city gate. Reuss does not seem to have expected anything beyond a temporary reprieve from the mounting French pressure, but nature now decided to intervene. 'In the very moment of a violent cloudburst,' continued Reuss, 'the attack was begun.' Rolling in from the south, heavy storm clouds loosed a sudden pelting deluge of terrifying ferocity on the combatants. In seconds all was chaos and confusion.

Muskets refused to fire, visibility dropped to a few dozen paces, the obscurity halted artillery fire and commands were drowned out by the noise. 'Water spouted out of the musket barrels, the cartridges were soaked through, firing ceased along the entire line, and the battle was involuntarily suspended,' wrote Leutnant von Zech. Startled French and Baden troops scattered in all directions seeking shelter as the rain poured down in sheets. The slow but steady advance collapsed. Another Baden officer, Unterleutnant Philipp le Beau of the 2nd Infantry, had pushed too far ahead in his enthusiasm when he saw Leiningen's men preparing to attack. 'I shouted to my grenadiers to turn around and hurry so that we would not be caught,' he noted in his diary, 'And then it was a headlong rush up the hill and then down the other side to reach the regiment. At just that moment, it began to rain so hard, such a cloudburst, as if every drop was a bucket full of water ... thus I ended up with my grenadiers at the bridge thirty paces ahead of the Austrians.' This desperate scrambling seems to have been most prevalent among those French and Baden units (such as le Beau's) that were already spread out in loose, independent skirmish order. Le Beau, for instance, had temporarily found himself more or less on his own with his section of grenadiers and had rushed forward hoping to capture some Austrians he saw milling about in a swale towards Znaim.[44] Formed units, on the other hand, in tight ranks under the immediate control of their officers and sergeants, seem to have retained their cohesion in most instances.

Compounding the disorder in Legrand's division was an unfortunate incident of 'friendly fire'. Held in reserve, I/2 Baden Infantry was one of the few units that had not been fighting in open order. Called forward to support the wavering skirmish line on the division's right just before Leiningen's attack, the battalion came under fire from Massena's 12-pounders on the southern bank of the river. Solid shot killed the battalion commander and several soldiers in the first volley, and the battalion, thrown into disorder, began to recoil just as the storm broke. Errant balls from the 12-pounders also fell among the other formed Baden units and among the troops in the skirmish line.[45] Infuriating and disheartening under any situation, these mistaken cannon shots exacerbated the disorder attendant upon the downpour and contributed to stymieing officers' efforts to rally their men.

All these circumstances gave the Austrians a momentary advantage. They disposed of greater numbers overall, had more units in formation, and were already preparing a counterattack. Now the enemy was in disarray and the guns across the river had stopped firing. Furthermore, they benefited from a determined leader in Oberstleutnant zu Leiningen. Despite the confusion occasioned by the downpour, Leiningen kept his head and launched his men down the highway towards the centre of Legrand's line and the bridges beyond. 'The advance began at a walking pace, then at double-time, then changed into an all-out run,' recorded Reuss. Resistance disintegrated under the combined impact of the deluge, the friendly fire and Leiningen's charge as French and Baden troops fled towards the bridges or sought refuge in Klosterbruck and Altschallersdorf. Contributing to the confusion was the sudden appearance – 'as if called forth from the earth by magic' – of 'a not inconsiderable number of Austrian infantrymen who had hidden themselves in the barns and cellars of Klosterbruck and in the houses along the highway' during Legrand's rapid advance.[46]

The Austrians cut off many of the skirmishers and captured several hundred men outright, including Massena's corps engineer, GB Joseph Félix Lazowksi. Another prisoner was the commander of Carra St Cyr's French brigade, GB de Stabenrath. Carra St Cyr's 2nd Division was now approaching the field and apparently received an order from GB François Nicolas Fririon, Massena's chief of staff, to send reinforcements across the river at once. De Stabenrath's brigade of three French regiments led the march and Carra St Cyr directed him to cross the bridges without delay and hasten to the assistance of Legrand. De Stabenrath protested that the congestion at the bridges made this order both unreasonable and dangerous, but Carra St Cyr insisted on instant obedience.

Angry and disgusted at what he perceived as pusillanimous acceptance of unsuitable orders, de Stabenrath forged a path through the 'veritable torrent' of soldiers on the bridges with great difficulty. Only some 400 men of the 46th Ligne were able to follow him, however, and these quickly fell victim to the prevailing disorder on the French side and the pressure of the onrushing Austrians. De Stabenrath, who had just taken command of the brigade on 3 July after recovering from a wound suffered on 22 May at Aspern-Essling, took five sabre cuts, including three to the head and a very serious one on his left arm.[47] Though he would remain a soldier for the rest of his life, the severity of his wounds was such that he would never again hold field command.

Another of those caught in the chaos was Colonel Pelleport, commander of the 18th Ligne.

> [As the division was advancing on Znaim] there followed a rain so violent and so heavy that everything was inundated in an instant; weapons would not fire and the combat was suspended. The enemy profited from this circumstance to send a column of grenadiers against us. The determined march of this elite unit intimidated our skirmishers; they retired and carried with them the troops charged with supporting them and even the reserves. I made vain efforts to remedy this shameful setback: I was carried along as well and thrown into the Thaya.[48]

Fririon, Massena's chief of staff, likewise ended up in the now flooding river. Fririon was on the northern bank when he saw 'a strong column of Hungarian grenadiers ... advancing in mass towards the Thaya and pushing back our skirmishers'.[49] He became worried that Massena, who had returned to his carriage that day owing to the inclement weather, might be captured, and assembled all the soldiers of the 18th Ligne that he could find: 'I formed them into two platoons and placed myself at their head to march against the enemy and stop them if possible or at least to slow them down.' He also sent word to Massena about the danger. His courageous effort, however, quickly crumpled. 'I was thrown from my horse and driven back to the bridge,' he wrote later, 'The Hungarians were so drunk that they forgot they had bayonets ... they struck us, my brave soldiers and me, with their musket butts.' 'The Hungarians had already taken my horse from me and were about to strip me of all my possessions,' he continued, 'when, maintaining my composure, I saw our cuirassiers advancing to the bridge to free us!' Seizing the opportunity, Fririon elected to free himself. 'Engaged as I was on the bridge, at the point of being killed or taken prisoner by the enemy; on the other hand, exposed to being crushed by our cavalrymen, I took the course of desperation and jumped into the river.'[50]

The marshal may have been in some danger of being taken as Fririon feared. Massena was being driven towards the bridges when the Austrian counterattack opened. As he was approaching the bridges, however, an Austrian cannon ball struck the seat of his carriage and knocked over the servant who was sitting on it (miraculously without serious injury) just as Leiningen was beginning his charge. This near miss and the deteriorating situation to his front notwithstanding, Massena remained calm. He swiftly had his carriage turned about, remounted despite the pain of his pre-Wagram injury, and started issuing orders.[51] Whether or not Fririon 'saved' Massena from imminent capture is an open question, but his prompt and valorous action certainly granted the marshal precious time to react to the potentially disastrous situation facing his corps.[52]

One of Massena's decisions was to exploit the bend in the river by placing a battery atop the Kühberg above Edelspitz on the French left. From there, the guns would be able to enfilade much of the Austrian line and place effective fire on the Habsburg troops in front of Znaim. Whether he gave this order just prior to Leiningen's attack or just as the grenadiers began their charge is unclear, but the task fell to the Baden foot battery. Dragging the guns up the slippery soft soil of this seemingly minor hill proved a major challenge and local chroniclers claimed the men had to double-team their pieces and caissons.[53] Once in position, however, the battery was nearly invulnerable to Austrian guns trying to fire up at it from lower elevations. Unfortunately, the Baden gunners discovered to their frustration that many of the French cannon balls they had been issued were of slightly larger calibre than their pieces and the balls stuck when loaded. Nonetheless, the battery would play a helpful role once the rain cleared enough for the gunners to avoid hitting their own men. Also providing flank support to the late afternoon attacks would be some fifty Baden Schützen who dispersed themselves along the south bank below the Kühberg to pester the opposing Austrians with long-range fire.[54]

Meanwhile, on the Austrian side of the muddy field, much of Reuss's line had joined in Leiningen's drive towards the bridges. 'The brave behaviour of this grenadier battalion and the rapid success of the attack, inspired all the troops and it was not possible to hold back the established reserves,' lamented Reuss, 'All ran forward, but not in formation, and with them went two 6-pounder cannons without orders. All wanted to participate, it was not possible to bring order to the troops or to recall them.' The scene at the northern end of the bridge was now a wild, disorganised melee of Austrians, French and Badeners all tangled together under the driving rain. As the storm had rendered firearms useless, it was also a bitter, personal fight of bayonets and musket butts as de Stabenrath and Fririon experienced personally. The Habsburg grenadiers, however, had lost their momentum and become vulnerable. Although the disordered crowd of other Austrian troops was endeavouring to press forward in its enthusiasm, Leiningen's men were largely on their own as Massena launched his counterstroke.

With Legrand's division in disarray and Carra St Cyr's blocked on the far side of the river by the chaos on the bridges,[55] Massena turned to his heavy cavalry to restore the situation. The 11th Cuirassiers on the northern bank of the river would have been ideally placed to strike the Austrian flank, but the downpour had made the already sodden ground even worse and a proper charge was impossible. The marshal thus sent the young Markgraf Wilhelm of Baden to the regiments poised south of the bridges with orders to charge at once. The 10th Cuirassiers, led by GB Adrien François Marie Guiton and the regimental commander, Colonel Samuel François Lhéritier, surged across the bridges and slammed into the unsuspecting grenadiers.[56] The onslaught was so sudden that 'The foremost ranks hardly had time to bring their bayonets down.'[57] In moments, Leiningen's battalion disintegrated, losing 323 men as it fled back towards Znaim. The iron horsemen of the 10th, joined by their fellow regiments, coursed ahead, sweeping up hundreds of prisoners and freeing almost all of their countrymen, including the two captured generals. 'In this critical moment, two French cuirassier regiments appeared, charged in column at full gallop across the bridge, freed all of our people and made prisoner an entire battalion of Austrian grenadiers,' noted Francken in the Baden war diary.[58] 'In fifteen minutes the matter was closed,' observed a Hessian watching from the southern side of the Thaya, 'and a battalion of hacked-up Hungarian grenadiers was brought to this bank.'[59] The 'grenadier battalion was largely cut to pieces, part taken prisoner,' recorded the Hauparmee's operations journal, 'Our rapidly retreating troops [were] pursued to the city gate for the second time.'[60] One unfortunate grenadier, attempting to hide himself in a pile of hay at the Klosterbruck tobacco factory, was stabbed when the pursuing French probed for fugitives with their bayonets.[61] Reuss blamed the *Lindenau* Infantry for the debacle, claiming that the regiment had failed to support the 'brave grenadiers', but he also noted ruefully that 'The fact that the violent rain meant no musket would fire now became very useful to the enemy.'[62]

The momentum of the French charge, however, was not yet expended. Groups of re-formed French and Baden infantry followed in the wake of the cuirassiers. Owing to the confusion 'every individual officer was more or less left to rely on his own courage and good sense, and many of the bravest followed the cuirassiers and rushed towards Znaim with whatever men they could grab together in a hurry.'[63] Among them was General Fririon. Thoroughly soaked, he pulled himself out of the river, borrowed a horse from a light cavalryman, and rode up to join the attack. Charging alongside the cuirassiers, Markgraf Wilhelm was splattered with the brains of the rider to his left when the unfortunate man's head was taken off by a cannon ball. Such horrors aside, losses among the cuirassiers were few and the iron tide rolled on towards Znaim. Back at the river, the bridge 'was covered with the dead and the wounded, almost all Hungarian grenadiers', wrote the Russian Löwenstern, 'We had trouble getting across it.'[64]

The situation on Reuss's front was now critical. The only troops near the gate seem to have been Hauptmann Peter von Petit's company of the *Scovaud* Grenadier Battalion and the 5th Pioneer Division of Reuss's corps. Fortunately for the Austrians, Major Salis and the 5th Vienna Volunteers were still in reserve in the town square. Apparently alerted by Oberst Menrad von Geppert, the V Corps chief of staff, Salis and his men hurriedly assembled and hastened to the southern gate. Here they found that Oberleutnant Franz Dobesch of the 5th Pioneers had had the good sense to lower the striped barrier pole (*Schlagbaum*) that controlled access to the city in normal times.[65] Now this pole served to stall the French horsemen for a few vital minutes. Salis's battalion thus encountered the cuirassiers as soon as it reached the gate. Not far behind the horsemen, the men could see that enemy skirmishers were already approaching as well. Salis understood that,

> In order to turn the engagement in a favourable direction, it was not simply a matter of defending the city, but also of pushing far enough forward along the highway again to come into line with our troops who were still holding their positions to the right and left. Recognising this, the battalion formed itself into a half-company mass, the barrier pole was raised, and the battalion charged towards the enemy cavalry with lowered bayonets.[66]

Faced with this determined attack, the cuirassiers recoiled and the French infantry skirmishers hesitated in their advance. A strange scene now ensued. The cuirassiers moved to attack the Viennese, but they came on slowly. Their mounts were doubtless blown after battling nearly 2½ km from the bridges, they had little room to manoeuvre, and they were hampered by the soggy ground. As result, the best they could manage was to canter up to the bayonets of the first rank. The Austrians, of course, could not fire owing to the rain, so 'the bayonet was the only protective weapon for the mass'.

'Numerous men in the first rank were wounded by the cavalry's sabre blows, and some were killed, but nothing could shake the courage and composure of the battalion,' reported Salis with understandable pride, 'and the enemy cavalry finally found itself forced to go back as it was not possible to penetrate into the mass.' The French retired 'all the more hurriedly', he continued, 'as some muskets in the rear ranks were already beginning to be capable of firing, from which every shot would hit at least one man of the cavalry standing so close by'. Unable to dislodge the stalwart battalion, the cuirassiers retreated and Salis moved his men forward to align with the Habsburg troops on either side of the highway.

The firm stand of the 5th Vienna Volunteers had averted the immediate crisis for Reuss, but the battle was not over. Massena now had Carra St Cyr's 2nd Division at hand as well as Legrand's disordered men and his substantial cavalry force. The hasty Austrian retreat from the bridges allowed the 2nd Division to cross the river in proper order (unlike de Stabenrath's courageous foray) and also granted Legrand time and space to rally his men. Carra St Cyr's three French regiments hurried over the river to deploy east of the highway and thus in the centre of Massena's new line of battle. For the moment, the Hessian brigade remained on the south shore in reserve, a position that offered a splendid view of the evolving battle despite the menacing clouds and occasional drizzling rain. 'Both armies stood in battle order,' recorded the Hessian brigade, 'and it seemed the day of the Battle of Wagram was to begin for a second time.' 'But off to the right up on the heights the cannonade was sharp,' wrote a Hessian officer, 'One could perceive that the emperor himself had arrived there with the main army.'[67]

Marmont, Bellegarde and Napoleon: Imposing on the Enemy

The stunning cloudburst, of course, was not limited to the portion of the battlefield Massena and Reuss were contesting. 'A heavy storm arose on the horizon', wrote Leutnant Madroux with the Bavarian cavalry brigade above Klein-Tesswitz, 'that now turned into such a frightful rain that neither of the two opposing parties could see the other any more and the battle of the elements for a moment imposed a halt on the battle of men.'[68] While its timing initially facilitated an Austrian charge on Reuss's front, on the other side of the field it struck just before Marmont launched what his adversaries viewed as the second French attack.

Fresnel, commanding the I Corps troops opposite Zuckerhandl, noted that the downpour had neutralised his soldiers' muskets,[69] but the storm did not lead to dramatic charges and counter-charges as it did immediately south of Znaim. Instead, 'The enemy formed for the second attack on the heights around the Zuckerhandlerhof.' An infantry column soon advanced to attack the vineyards on the Austrian right while 'a strong column of cavalry debouched in the low ground' and attempted to form itself under canister fire from Löffler's two 6-pounders supported by the 12-pounder battery. This Austrian artillery fire disrupted the French horsemen and they quickly withdrew, seen off by the three squadrons of *Klenau* Chevaulegers No. 5. A French cavalry attack thus never materialised. The infantry attack was also brief. The advance hit II/*Mittrowsky*, driving in the battalion's skirmishers and pushing it back on its supports, the two battalions of *Kolowrat* Infantry. The three battalions, however, now turned the tables on the French. Counterattacking 'with the bayonet' from the front while the battalion of *Reuss-Plauen* struck the enemy's left flank, the Austrians shoved the French off the slopes and back into the ravine near Zuckerhandl.[70] This minor success ended the 'second French attack'.

If these advances were contained, French skirmishers remained very active and the Austrian guns had to be employed to discourage them as the French repeatedly crept forward to annoy the white-coats on the western side of the Kukrowitz stream. Covered by this skirmisher action, the French brought more infantry into Zuckerhandl, formed their attack columns in the village and 'debouched from there in the greatest order' with what the Austrians estimated to be 'three complete battalions'. At the same time, a cavalry regiment deployed in column hard by Zuckerhandl, and a second infantry column assembled itself on the heights above near the farmstead. 'The enemy, who had gathered a large number of troops by the aforementioned Zuckerhandlerhof, repeated a fresh attack with cavalry and infantry supported by well-directed canister fire and by fresh troops being pushed forwards.'[71] Observing these preparations, the Austrians pulled the battered II/*Mittrowsky* out of the line and substituted it with the *Erbach* battalion that had been brought up earlier. Additionally, a battalion of *Argenteau* was called forward from the main body's second line, and a 6-pounder brigade battery replaced the 12-pounder battery and Löffler's two 6-pounders; the battery and Löffler's section, having been engaged since midday, had by this time exhausted their ammunition and suffered heavily from French and Bavarian counter-battery fire.

From the Austrian viewpoint, these measures were eminently successful. The French infantry near Zuckerhandl was hit with such effective artillery fire that it took serious losses before wavering and retreating into the village. The other column advanced but was repelled 'despite exerting all efforts to break through' and Binnenthal recorded that the I Corps troops 'maintained the position held at the beginning of the affair'.[72] Fresnel thus exuded satisfaction when composing his own after-action report: 'With great courage and endurance, I Corps succeeded in maintaining this important position, loss of which would have unfailingly resulted in the loss of Znaim and a difficult, fatiguing retreat for the troops that were defending it.'[73] These Austrian perspectives are not without merit, but they overlook a crucial point: Napoleon had neither intention nor expectation of breaking through I Corps on 11 July. French accounts of the second day at Znaim make almost no mention of the fighting on Marmont's front. Although this could be explained by a desire to hide the failure of the attacks on I Corps, the far more likely reason is that these were simply pinning attacks to distract and engage the Hauptarmee. Napoleon was completely cognisant of his available strength and knew that there was no realistic prospect of driving the Austrians back on their line of retreat to disorder and possible destruction that day. From the French side of the field, his officers and men understood this. As Bavarian Leutnant Christian Schaller observed, 'It seemed that one did not want to undertake anything decisive and simply await the coming day for a major battle.'[74] The Austrians 'were trapped in a funnel with only one exit', wrote Lieutenant Esprit Victor Castellane, 'We awaited a grand battle.'[75] At the same time, the emperor knew that Liechtenstein was en route to initiate negotiations and he clearly understood that 'In an arrangement where imposing on the enemy was a necessity, the conditions [to be negotiated] would depend on the situations of the two armies.'[76] Napoleon thus sent multiple couriers to urge Davout and Oudinot to hasten their marches and tried to ensure that the prince and the other Habsburg observers would indeed be treated to an imposing scene as they travelled past the ranks of the gathering French army.

Napoleon and his officers would have been gratified to learn that their adversaries already believed themselves outnumbered and in danger of destruction. In the wake of the storm, recalled Major Valentini:

> One could once again overlook the wide battlefield. But as objects became more clearly discernable, no favourable outcome could be foreseen for Austria. Locked in a most extensive, elevated position and with the enemy having his right wing on heights that favoured every movement to get around our left flank; the enemy's numerous cavalry lying in wait to exploit any rearward movement or disorder; and a terrain in the rear that easily permitted this [enemy cavalry attack]; for whom would the situation of the army not appear highly dangerous?[77]

Though adventitious (that is, not planned by Napoleon), Liechtenstein's route would take him through the countless bivouacs of Oudinot's and Davout's corps as he rode north from Laa that night, creating a vivid impression of power that reinforced these Austrian preconceptions.

Massena and Reuss: A Fusillade of Prolonged Severity

French reinforcements were also approaching on Massena's side of the field as Molitor's 3rd Division hastened up the muddy miles from Göllersdorf and Schönborn. For the moment, however, the marshal remained limited to Legrand and Carra St Cyr along with his two cavalry divisions. Nonetheless, 'pushing the attack hard', his men were once again pressing into the suburbs on the southern edge of Znaim.[78] The Baden brigade on the left flank advanced with the Jägers and I/2 Infantry in the lead, while the 1st Infantry and II/2 reorganised themselves in Klosterbruck to be sent forward in small detachments as the advance progressed.[79] The cuirassier division seems to have remained assembled on the highway, posing a threat but not actually engaging in further combat. To the right of the highway, however, 'fired by the new successes and assisted by the new reinforcements', Legrand's regiments reassembled and returned to the fight in remarkably short order. Contributing to this swift recovery was the fact that 'The largest number of our skirmishers [were] spread among the vineyards to the right of the great road, unaware of what was happening there.' They thus 'conserved their positions and continued their fire as much as possible in the rain that was still falling in sheets'.[80] As the rain slackened, these men were able to resume the battle despite the near catastrophe that had befallen the units on and to the left of the highway. 'Legrand's division rallied itself, the 26th and the 18th carried themselves forward and reoccupied the line they had abandoned,' wrote Colonel Pelleport, 'Soon they entered the first houses outside the town.'[81]

Reuss's men held on in the face of 'the most vigorous, repeated attacks of the enemy and a murderous fire'.[82] The 5th Vienna and the *Lindenau* Infantry defended the city gate with support from two guns and two companies of grenadiers, the latter switching out with two fresh companies every hour or so. Like the French and Badeners, many of the Austrians were deployed as skirmishers in the vineyards, now advancing, now retreating as enemy pressure allowed.[83] Although Leiningen's battalion had been destroyed, seven other battalions from Murray's and Scovaud's grenadier brigades were available to support V Corps. Based on the casualties they reported, four saw considerable action: *Frisch* lost 101 men or approximately a quarter of its strength, and *Scharlach* somehow managed to have 42 men captured for only 12 otherwise wounded. The other three battalions remained largely in reserve and suffered few casualties. The *Scovaud* Grenadiers (minus Hauptmann Petit's company), for instance, were posted to guard the little gate at the top of the incline that wound up from the Thaya on the southwestern side of the city walls.[84] The presence of these men meant that Reuss could call on an additional 3,000 or so infantry even after subtracting the *Leiningen* Grenadiers. As a result, he maintained his numerical superiority over Massena even as Carra St Cyr's 2nd Division was entering the battle.

Carra St Cyr's French troops, initially deployed behind Legrand's men, soon found themselves heavily engaged. These regiments had taken severe losses at Wagram, especially the 4th Ligne and the 24th Léger, both of which had lost their colonels and their eagles in the brutal fighting around Aderklaa on 6 July. Retaining their cohesion, the two regiments actually regained some of their strength during the pursuit as men who had been captured escaped to rejoin the ranks. On 10 July, for example, three officers and an unknown number of men caught up with the 4th Ligne after having freed themselves from Austrian captivity. The regiment, however, was the size of a battalion when it arrived on the slopes below Znaim that afternoon: only some 500 men under command of Captain Jean Lanes, the senior remaining officer. The 24th Léger, slightly better off, likely had between 900 and 1,000 men under arms at Znaim. Despite their losses, these regiments and their compatriots in the 46th Ligne first deployed in support of Legrand, then sent skirmishers forward up the vineyard-covered slopes on the right, and finally moved into the line of battle. The case of the 4th Ligne is illustrative:

> It [the regiment] was ordered to take the heights to the right of Znaim. It was not long before it met the enemy. The captain commanding sent the skirmishers forward and remained in readiness with the rest of the regiment, which, as already mentioned, did not form

more than a battalion. The skirmishers, having encountered superior forces, were obliged to withdraw to the main body. Captain Lanes ordered a charge. The regiment repulsed the enemy and seized a position that it held for about two hours. It was pushed back some 200 paces and maintained itself in this position until eight o'clock at night.[85]

As Carra St Cyr's men fought, around 5:00 p.m. Massena decided to call up part of the Hessian brigade from the far bank of the Thaya. Their vantage point on the hills to the south afforded the Hessians a view of the French brigades advancing 'from terrace to terrace in the most ferocious musket fire'. 'I have never heard a fusillade of the same prolonged severity,' wrote one officer. Ordered forward, the two Hessian fusilier battalions and I/Leib-Garde made their way over the Thaya on the right towards Klein-Tesswitz, partly by wading, partly by scrambling across impromptu bridges of ladders and boards. Passing through Klein-Tesswitz almost unseen by the Austrians (where they happily availed themselves of bread from the enormous magazine the Bavarians had discovered), these three battalions sent their Schützen up into the vineyards with 'determination and skill', while a formed company remained below in support.[86] There were only some 160 of these light infantrymen, but they rapidly gained ground, driving the Austrian skirmishers back and exciting the admiration of the French and Hessian officers watching from the southern side of the river.[87] 'The infantry fire from both battle lines became heavier and the thunder of the artillery presaged the beginning of a new battle,' recorded the Hessian brigade's diary, 'The battle was already general, the orders for the decisive attack were already given, when suddenly the armistice that had come about in the meantime put an end to the bloody work and silenced the fire of both armies.'[88]

Cease Fire! Cease Fire!

'All at once, as if by magic, the fire stopped all along the line,' wrote Captain Espinchal from his position near the Burgholz, and 'Each returned to his respective position.'[89]

It was now between 7:00 and 7:30 p.m. and the grey light was slowly ebbing from the leaden skies overhead as officers from both sides rode out to deliver 'the completely unexpected order' to cease firing.[90] Jean Baptiste Fournier of Arrighi's staff remembered 'The aides-de-camp or officers of the emperor's staff were seen riding rapidly, with a white handkerchief tied to the arm, and the emperor himself, with a smile on his lips, galloped past our lines with a map unfolded in his hand, assuring that peace would be achieved.'[91] This proved a relatively simple matter on the far eastern side of the field where Espinchal was and where there had not been much combat in the first place. Despite the bitterness of the fighting, the action in the centre was likewise soon quelled, perhaps because of the proximity of the respective army headquarters. 'Our corps had been skirmishing continually since morning,' noted Colonel Godart, when, towards evening, 'an officer of the emperor's staff came to order us to stop firing as a ceasefire had been signed.' 'The word "peace" then circulated through all the ranks,' recalled Lieutenant Dupuy of the 11th Chasseurs, 'The joy was general!'[92]

The story was very different in the area south of Znaim. The long hours of uninterrupted combat here had been especially vicious and neither side seemed interested in relenting. The two officers charged with informing the men in the battle line suffered as a result. On the Austrian side this was the young Hauptmann Constantin d'Aspre von Hoobreuck of the General Staff Corps, just twenty years old, whose father had been mortally wounded at Wagram only five days earlier. He rode out from the V Corps lines and down the highway but 'without using the necessary precautions'. Trotting towards a French column on the road with a small delegation, he was greeted with a salvo and fell from his horse with a wound in the shoulder. D'Aspre fell into enemy hands, but his comrades 'sought their safety in flight', pursued by several hundred French. According to the V Corps operations journal, the French would have followed the fleeing Austrian riders into the city but for the quick action of Hauptmann Petit's grenadier company from Scovaud's battalion. The grenadiers dashed to the city gate and prevented any further advance until the French could be convinced that an armistice had actually been concluded.[93]

The French emissary, Captain Marbot of Massena's staff, had a similarly trying experience but his account differs from the Austrian operations journal. As other officers rode to different parts of the line, Massena assigned Marbot to inform the brigade closest to the city gate.

Coming up in the rear of these regiments, I vainly tried to speak; my voice was drowned out by cries of *'Vive l'Empereur!'* which always preceded combat, and the bayonets were already crossing. A moment later and one of those terrible infantry melees would take place, which once started, cannot be checked. I hesitated no longer and, passing through the files, I got between the lines, which were on the point of meeting. As I was shouting 'Peace! Peace!' and with my left hand giving the sign for a halt, suddenly a bullet from the town suburbs struck me on the wrist. Some of our officers, understanding at length that I brought the order to suspend hostilities, halted their companies; others, seeing [that] the Austrian battalions were coming towards them and were only a hundred paces away, were doubtful. At the same moment, an aide-de-camp from Prince Charles also came between the two lines, with a view of preventing the attack, and got a bullet in the shoulder from the same quarter. I hastened towards him, and to make both sides see for what purpose we had been sent, we testified to it by embracing each other. At the sight of this, the officers of both sides had no more hesitation about ordering a halt.[94]

Whichever of these accounts is more accurate, there is no question that both of these officers were involved outside the lower gate of Znaim and that both were wounded in the process, d'Aspre quite severely and Marbot lightly but very painfully with what Markgraf Wilhelm wryly called 'the last bullet of this campaign'.[95] All accounts also agree on how difficult it was to stop the fighting, especially on this front. Gradually, however, 'The cries of peace and amity replaced the cries of carnage.'[96] Reuss and Legrand met at the city gate to discuss arrangements and a strange calm fell over the field as night came on.

On Marmont's front the scene was almost surreal, as described by Colonel Louis-François Lejeune with his artist's eye from the hills above Zuckerhandl where Napoleon's tents had been pitched:

The last rays of the setting sun lit up a scene of unrivalled beauty. At the base of the wooded hills flowed the pretty river, and beyond stretched a smiling landscape dotted with gardens, just now rendered animated by the numerous soldiers, some of whom were eagerly climbing the cherry trees and devouring the fruit, which I believe they would have been just as ready to pick if the firing had still been going on, though this pause in the hostilities in such a delightful neighbourhood was a regular fête for them.[97]

The Battle of Znaim thus came to a sudden, unexpected conclusion and Markgraf Wilhelm's witticism proved to be correct: the ball that wounded Marbot was the last – or one of the last – rounds fired in the war of 1809, at least between the two principal armies. For most of the officers and men on the field that night, however, it was by no means clear that the battle, never mind the war, was over. 'We anticipated a general engagement' for the next day, recalled Sous-Lieutenant Charles Denis Parquin of the 20th Chasseurs, and Colonel Claude Etienne Guyot of the Guard Chasseurs-à-Cheval noted in his journal: 'Tonight our entire army is going into line in a fine position; tomorrow there will probably be a battle.' 'Finally night comes', wrote the weary Captain Tascher, 'Tomorrow morning we will know if we should embrace or cut one another's throats.'[98]

The uncertainty among the majority of the men is hardly surprising. As the rainy day turned into a damp night, all that had been agreed was a temporary battlefield ceasefire. Negotiations for a longer armistice were still under way as quiet and darkness descended on the field and men sought to light fires and prepare hot meals, for thousands the first warm food in many days. We shall take up the ceasefire and the subsequent armistice in the next chapter, but before doing so it is important to highlight several points about the battle on 10 and 11 July.

First, although not on the scale of grand battles such as Wagram, the cost of Znaim was substantial for both armies. However, just as the Austrians outnumbered the French on both days, Habsburg casualties were considerably higher than those suffered by their French and German opponents. The scarcity of French data and the fact that both sides tended to treat losses from Wagram, the various rearguard actions and Znaim as one aggregate figure leaves us heavily reliant on estimation, but a reasonable approximation gives total casualty figures (dead, wounded, missing, captured) of between 5,000 and 6,000 for the Austrians as against some 3,000 for the French and Germans.[99]

The Austrians had no general officer casualties, but Generals Bertrand, Claparède, Delzons and de Stabenrath were among the wounded on the French side, the last three each struck for the second time during this brief war. On the Austrian side, the casualties were distributed fairly evenly among the principal formations involved: I and V Corps with approximately 1,700 each, plus 1,400 for the Grenadiers. As far as individual units were concerned, beyond the destruction of the *Leiningen* Grenadiers, the *Kolowrat* Infantry, with only two battalions engaged, reported 887 casualties, substantially higher than any other regiment in any other corps.[100] The Bavarian division, as noted above, paid the highest price on the other side with its loss of 901 men in the struggle for Klein-Tesswitz. No other single French or German formation came close to this figure. Massena's two divisions lost approximately 1,200 (over 500 each) on 11 July, including 184 Badeners. The Hessians, on the other hand, with their limited involvement late in the afternoon of the second day, only reported eight men wounded.[101]

Curiously, the Austrians seem to have abused many of the prisoners they took during *Leiningen*'s charge. 'At the Battle of Znaim, this otherwise upright army dishonoured itself', wrote a Hessian officer, 'in that it treated Generals Lazowksi and de Stabenrath to blows with fists and musket butts and drove the other officers and men with stabs of the bayonet.' Wilhelm Meier, a Baden surgeon who treated a number of these men, recalled that 'The Austrians took many prisoners: many were quite battered with musket butt strikes and bayonet stabs.'[102]

The sequence of charge and counter-charge between Massena and Reuss was the only incident in the battle where large numbers of prisoners were taken. Most of the French, as noted above, were soon freed, but the French accurately stated that their counterattack and the subsequent fighting netted some 800 Austrians. As far as the other standard indicators of battlefield success were concerned, there was little for either side to claim. The only guns known to have been taken were the two Austrian cannon captured in the French countercharge south of Znaim on the second day. Nor is there any indication that either side lost any regimental or battalion standards.

Second, both sides heavily favoured open-order, skirmishing tactics during the battle. Such tactics, of course, were dictated by the broken terrain in the western and central portions of the battlefield (that is, immediately south and east of Znaim) with its vineyards, deep ravines and small villages. Although such loose formations had become standard for the French and their German allies (as Valentini observed watching Marmont's regiments prepare their attacks on 11 July), Austrian regiments also resorted to deploying relatively large numbers of skirmishers (*tirailleurs*, *Plänkler*) throughout the battle. The use of skirmishers was not limited to 'traditional' Austrian light troops such as Grenzer, but was a feature of action by regular line regiments and even grenadiers. The French and Germans seem to have easily retained their superiority in such tactics, but it is notable how frequently the Habsburg troops deployed skirmishers as well. Unsurprisingly, the Austrians employed the newly adopted battalion masses or traditional squares ('*Quarres*') on the open eastern flank owing to their worries about French cavalry attack.[103]

Third, at what we may term the grand tactical level, the Battle of Znaim was a meeting engagement.[104] That is, an unplanned battle where the two sides encounter each other on the march and engage wherever they happen to meet rather than in carefully selected positions. For Napoleon, his subordinates and his army, such engagements were simply part of their combat repertoire; the flexibility of the army's organisations and the independence and initiative expected of leaders at all levels meant the French and their allies easily adapted to this form of warfare. Charles and the Habsburg host, on the other hand, were clearly uncomfortable being forced to conduct such a battle. The repeated, relentless hammer blows the Hauptarmee had suffered in April during the series of meeting engagements in Bavaria had left a deep impression on the archduke. He assessed his army as totally unsuited for offensive operations in congested terrain and far preferred fighting from well-ordered defensive positions or, if forced to attack, to do so in open ground where all action could be orchestrated through a written 'disposition' and visually observed by him as overall commander. These considerations help explain his strong desire to occupy a recognised defensive 'position' such as Jetzelsdorf or Iglau and his unease at being forced to fight at Znaim. In an unplanned engagement, with an army that was extremely awkward in the attack, and convinced that he was both outnumbered and outgeneralled, his only concern was to escape with his army intact. He and his subordinate commanders discovered anxieties in all directions: the fear of the numerous French cavalry, excessive worries about being outflanked, exaggerated estimates of enemy strength. He thus fought a strictly defensive battle at Znaim, forgoing opportunities perhaps to slow or halt the chase by inflicting a stunning and unexpected offensive blow against his brash French pursuers.

Finally, it is worth noting that Znaim presents a further instance in this war of outnumbered French forces overcoming, or nearly overcoming, Austrian troops in strong defensive positions. The storming of the bridge at Ebelsberg is one example and the French evening attack on the Rußbach Heights at Wagram on 5 July provides another, even though that poorly organised assault was eventually repelled. Here at Znaim, a combination of energy and audacity undergirded by excellent tactics (such as artillery employment and the threat of cavalry attack) allowed Legrand's outnumbered division to force a passage of the Thaya against a force approximately twice its size and drive the enemy back on the city. The Hauptarmee's defensive orientation was certainly a major factor as well, but successes such as this are worth recalling when considering the strengths and weaknesses of the French army in 1809.

Chapter 7

An Armistice Saved Us

12 July–14 October 1809

'THE EMPEROR ESTABLISHED HIS HEADQUARTERS on the plateau captured in the morning, surrounded by his guard and the artillery, all ready to act at the first moment; in all, more than 100,000 combatants were present on a terrain of eight kilometres; a thought, a word, a gesture would suffice to set them at each other and let spill a flood of blood,' wrote Captain Espinchal. But that word never came. Instead, 'Day arrives and "to horse" is not sounded. The two armies hold their respective lines and negotiate,' noted Tascher in his journal, 'We hurry to build fires and we can finally eat soup for the first time in eight days.' Castellane and Chlapowski had gone to sleep the previous evening near the Burgholz 'to the sound of the fusillade'. They had expected a grand battle in the morning and 'were most astonished when we woke up to see that our watches showed seven o'clock in the morning, and even more surprised at the calm that prevailed'. 'Despite our warlike ardour, this news filled us with joy; we were exhausted from all the efforts expended over such a short period of time,' recalled Fournier, 'Everyone, more or less, had some repairs to make and for twelve days we had not taken off our clothes or removed our boots.'[1] On Massena's side of the field, Philippe René Girault, a musician with the 93rd Ligne of Boudet's division, 'had heard the guns rumble in the morning, and when we met a regiment turning its back on the enemy, we at first thought we were retreating. But the trumpet-major, who I approached, announced to me that an armistice had just been signed . . . The division was halted and all the canteens were emptied to celebrate this good news.'[2]

An Agreement Before Dawn

Though many details are murky, the general chronology of how the two armies arrived at the ceasefire and armistice Girault and his comrades were celebrating is fairly straightforward. Sometime in the late afternoon of 11 July, General Montbrun approached the Austrian Reserve Cavalry as a *parlementaire* with the message that, 'In accordance with the proposal made by the Austrian side [on 10 July], a general was awaited in the French headquarters for the conclusion of a ceasefire.'[3] Charles quickly acceded to this request and designated Wimpffen to conduct the negotiations with Berthier on his behalf. He would not yet permit Wimpffen to go to the French side of the field, so this initial interaction between the two chiefs of staff seems to have taken place along the outpost line. Wimpffen returned an hour later with a grim report. Berthier had told him that 'His emperor had arrived with his entire army and that his advantage permitted him to engage us in a new decisive battle on the following day for which all dispositions had already been made and for which the army, as we could ourselves observe, was already prepared.' However, Berthier also said that Napoleon was open to concluding 'a general armistice if we could reach an agreement on the conditions before the break of day'.[4] Charles agreed, Wimpffen returned to negotiate with Berthier and orders issued by both sides sent d'Aspre, Marbot and numerous other staff officers riding off to announce the temporary battlefield ceasefire.

At the same time, Charles altered the withdrawal order he had issued earlier in the day: II Corps, VI Corps and two of the grenadier brigades would march north during the night as previously planned, but I Corps, III Corps, the Cavalry Reserve and V Corps with two of the grenadier brigades were to remain in their present positions around Znaim.[5] These instructions removed some 27,000 infantry and cavalry from the field,[6] thereby reducing the available Austrian forces by more than one-third and leaving the bulk of the army more or less at Napoleon's mercy should the French emperor elect to continue the battle on 12 July. Rather than retreating into the night, therefore, much of the Hauptarmee remained in place as the firing died away and the two chiefs of staff sat down in the Rother Hof above Zuckerhandl to hammer out the details of an agreement that would halt the fighting in all theatres of war. The grave risks attendant upon this decision would have been unambiguous to a commander of Charles's experience and competence.

The two parties completed a draft during the night of 11/12 July, apparently before midnight. Napoleon reviewed it, evidently added the occupation of Pressburg and the Sachsenburg fortress to his demands, and Wimpffen rode back to the Austrian lines to seek his commander's approval. He encountered Charles as the archduke was riding to Brenditz early on the morning of the 12th. Presented with the terms of the armistice, Charles had little choice but to acquiesce in what was, in effect, a French ultimatum. With minimal delay, therefore, Wimpffen signed for Austria, Berthier affixed his signature for France and the general armistice went into effect immediately.

What of Liechtenstein and his mission to Napoleon? The prince finally reached the French emperor's tents above Klein-Tesswitz sometime between midnight and 1:00 a.m. on 12 July after a long and doubtless exhausting ride via Hollabrunn and Wolkersdorf. They were well acquainted with one another as Liechtenstein had served in a similar diplomatic capacity after Austerlitz in 1805 and Napoleon 'held him in particularly high regard'.[7] This time, Napoleon seems to have received him with a combination of grace and brusque irritation.[8] It is not clear whether Wimpffen and Berthier were still in conference when Liechtenstein arrived. It is likely they had just finished an hour or two earlier, but no one seems to have informed him that the two chiefs of staff were meeting or had just met only some 500 metres away. Charles claimed that Wimpffen did not even know Liechtenstein was close by.[9] Aware or not, Liechtenstein was certainly not included in the negotiations and the discussions were not suspended to await his arrival. Instead, Napoleon personally engaged him in a lengthy disquisition regarding his future plans, to include blunt reference to the possible abdication of Kaiser Franz and the division of the Habsburg monarchy into three or more independent states. The emperor may have even presented these drastic moves as preconditions for conclusion of a final peace, at least that was the impression Liechtenstein received. The prince quite reasonably responded that such questions were far beyond his remit and the audience closed after some hours with no resolution. Liechtenstein then rode off to find Charles. In the meantime, Berthier and Wimpffen had finished their work and Charles had seen and approved the terms. All this seems to have transpired before Liechtenstein located Charles; that is, it is unlikely that Liechtenstein had a chance to review the draft before it was concluded. In either case, he had no impact on its provisions. His experience of riding through the numerous French encampments to find Napoleon, however, served to confirm the archduke's conviction that the entire French army was assembled, numerically superior and poised for battle on the other side of the field. His mission having achieved nothing for the Habsburg cause, Liechtenstein remained with Charles for several more days before riding off via Vienna to Komorn in Hungary where he would report to Kaiser Franz.

Also missing from the armistice deliberations was Stadion. As we have seen, the former minister had remained behind in Mährisch-Budwitz when Franz fled to Hungary with Metternich. Among other tasks, he was supposed to serve as a foreign policy advisor to Charles. He therefore wrote to Charles on the 10th to apprise him of the Kaiser's departure and establish contact, but with the archduke absorbed in managing the battle, Stadion received no reply. The following day, he attempted to ride to Znaim only to claim that the traffic jamming the Iglau highway thwarted his efforts. Returning to Mährisch-Budwitz, he waited through the night and all the next day until Charles ('expected any moment') and Liechtenstein finally arrived around 6:00 p.m. on 12 July. Unsurprisingly, there is no evidence that Charles sought to call for Stadion's advice as he contemplated his ceasefire proposal on the 10th or when he sent Wimpffen to Berthier on the 11th.

Meeting with Charles, Liechtenstein and Wimpffen that night and the next day, Stadion could only be dismayed by what he learned of the armistice and the state of the army. He quickly composed two lengthy, rambling epistles to Franz conveying his impressions and advice. Despite the bravery of the troops, Charles and Liechtenstein told him, the army would have been in danger of 'total destruction' had the armistice not been signed. Wimpffen grimly related that 'the superiority in numbers (not to mention the decisive superiority in leadership) would always favour Napoleon', even if Austria were able to unite its dispersed forces. 'Renewal of the war', opined the general, 'would mean the renewal of the misfortunes of our arms'. Such declarations, combined with his own observations and preconceptions, led Stadion to report to the Kaiser that 'The army here, such as it is ... cannot be counted on at all and that even after the expired period of the armistice, nothing more may be expected of it but the speedy continuation of the current retreat up to the borders of the monarchy.' Writing to Metternich several days later, he expressed his dismay at the 'distressing impression' of 'the lack of will and means' he had found during his visit to army headquarters. 'The generals shrug their shoulders, they do not say anything untoward about the archduke, but they are all the less sparing about his entourage, above all Wimpffen, who indeed in this current crisis is showing himself very poorly.'[10] With his cavalier understanding of military affairs, he persisted in placing faith in the forces of the other archdukes in collaboration with Generals Chasteler and Gyulai. The degree of mistrust he felt towards the army was evident in a comment to Metternich twelve days later. Noting that he had received a letter from Metternich through army headquarters, he thought it necessary to tell Metternich that he had examined the seal on the letter well and 'according to all indications it remained intact'; in other words, he feared that officers in army headquarters might be intercepting and reading his mail.[11]

As far as the armistice was concerned, Stadion found the provisions 'very hard', indeed, *'more than hard'* considering the clauses that dictated Austrian evacuation of Fiume and the Tyrol. He feared Napoleon would demand nothing less than 'a capitulation' that would 'strike deep wounds in both the honour and the existence of the monarchy'. He thus urged the Kaiser to undertake negotiations swiftly and directly with the French emperor as the best means of ameliorating these onerous conditions and forestalling perhaps worse to come. He even recommended that Franz consider alignment or alliance with Napoleon, as Tsar Alexander had done after Tilsit in 1807. He concluded his second report by advising his imperial master that it was now 'perhaps more important than ever' to be near the army in Bohemia; an understandable notion, but odd in that he knew Franz was already on the road to Hungary.[12]

Stadion also used these missives to renew his resignation. It is not clear why he felt this was necessary, but he seems to have sunk into a mire of indignant despair in the wake of Wagram and the armistice. Lamenting the monarchy's situation, he wrote to a colleague to explain his decision to leave his post. 'I have experienced, to my misfortune, and unfortunately also that of the state, that there is a degree of nullity and baseness that transcends the imagination of a decent man. I could only remain in my place by abandoning all my principles, and even if I were capable of such a sacrifice, I would still have to leave the ministry because in the future I would be unable to represent my master's interests properly.'[13] In this state of despondency, the former minister retired to his family in Prague. He would continue to bombard the Kaiser and Metternich with memoranda from a distance and would join the court in Hungary for a brief time later, but from now on Metternich would be the dominant voice on foreign affairs.

Although Stadion regarded the armistice as *'more than hard'*, it was not as punitive as it might have been had the Hauptarmee been crushed in a third day of battle on 12 July. With one major exception, each side would essentially retain the territory it currently occupied. This meant that French troops would remain in possession of Upper and Lower Austria, Styria, Carniola, Istria and the Adriatic coast to include Fiume, Austria's sole outlet to the sea and thus its sole secure means of receiving payments from Great Britain. The major exception was Moravia, where Austria was required to turn over the districts (*Kreise*) of Znaim and Brünn. In all, the provinces and districts under French occupation would thus amount to approximately one-third of the monarchy's land area. Moreover, the evacuation of all these territories was to include the fortresses of Brünn in Moravia, Graz in Styria and Sachsenburg in Carinthia, as well as the city of Pressburg on the Danube. Austria was also to remove its few remaining troops from the Tyrol and the Vorarlberg, a most agonising stipulation for Kaiser Franz as he had just renewed his pledge to make their liberation from foreign rule a central goal of the war.[14] At the particular insistence of the Austrians, the armies in Poland would hold the positions they occupied at the time of the signing and the Russian commander would be informed of the agreement's details.[15] The term of the initial armistice was set at one month with both sides naming commissioners to oversee implementation and both having the option to recommence hostilities upon giving the other party fifteen days' advance notice.

On 12 July, therefore, the Hauptarmee marched away from Znaim, heading north towards Mährisch-Budwitz and beyond. The French swiftly moved in to occupy the districts allotted to them under the armistice. Massena shifted his headquarters to Znaim itself where Napoleon viewed a parade of parts of 4th Corps during the day before departing for Hödnitz on the road to Laa. Davout headed to Brünn and the other corps dispersed to assembly areas closer to the Danube. Despite occasional disagreements occasioned by the rapid transition from war to peace, the two sides generally conducted themselves with professional courtesy as they moved to their respective cantonments. 'We join the grand highway which is fine and well-shaded', noted Tascher, 'We meet along the way some Austrian regiments: yesterday we would have gone after one another, sabres held high; today we salute politely.' He also observed, however, 'the damage we caused in the fields around Znaim':

> The land was covered with magnificent crops; in manoeuvring, our horses' legs were often hampered by the thickness of the wheat and when they were taken to the trot, we could see the bouncing heads of the wheat already at a stage to be cut. The rain that fell in torrents rendered the damage more considerable. Often the same field, covered with a rich harvest whose fecundity the eye admired, offered nothing after an hour but a vast terrain covered with mud and cluttered with debris! What a spectacle for the poor labourer![16]

Arrighi's aide-de-camp, on the other hand, rejoiced in 'the first shave, the first bath when, on returning to Vienna, we were installed in our lodgings'.[17]

For most on both sides, the armistice was indeed a most welcome reprieve from the rigours and privations of the previous two weeks. Some, however, were left dissatisfied. Some of Napoleon's generals called for destroying the Austrian army and many of the junior officers and soldiers were dismayed by the apparent clemency towards a foe they considered an 'irreconcilable enemy', perpetually the junction point for anti-French coalitions. The Guard Horse Grenadiers reportedly broke their sabres over their knees on hearing the news, and Colonel Berthezène recorded that 'This resolution by the emperor was poorly received by the troops,' who believed the Austrian army had 'reached a moment to be vanquished one final time and perhaps erased entirely'. Whatever their opinions on the virtues of the ceasefire and armistice, for the French and their German allies, there was no question that they and their emperor had once again triumphed over the Habsburg Empire. 'This was the last battle fought against the Austrians in 1809,' wrote Captain Louis Bro of the 7th Hussars, 'They humbly asked for peace.'[18]

Some on the Austrian side were equally distraught at the outcome of the battle. Having convinced themselves that their exhausted army was facing an overwhelmingly superior enemy from a disadvantageous defensive position, they were congratulating themselves for their great success in offering staunch resistance on the 10th and 11th. The withdrawal of the Hauptarmee over the Thaya on 10 July during the combat with Marmont was trumpeted as an especially notable accomplishment. In fact, as we have seen, the French were numerically inferior on both days by wide margins, but the vivacity of their actions, their brazen bluffs and Austrian preconceptions had led many white-coats to believe they had fended off powerful assaults by a French army under Napoleon's personal command. If they were winning, or at least avoiding defeat, why was such a harsh armistice necessary? Soldiers may have retained their affection for Charles, but many officers had long been dissatisfied with him, holding him personally responsible for the army's misfortunes during the war and for the terms of the armistice specifically.[19] Furthermore, many no doubt sensed that the Generalissimus had fallen into disfavour with the court and felt freer in expressing their criticisms.[20]

Beyond disaffection with Charles among some officers, the army's morale was eroding. Despite the dogged endurance demonstrated at Znaim, even the stalwart Radetzky noted that 'the spirit of the army' had degenerated appreciably 'after the lost battles'.[21] Hohenzollern was so disturbed by 'the listlessness, the despondency, the decline in military spirit' that he observed during his corps' withdrawal to its armistice positions that he issued a stern order of the day admonishing his officers and men. 'The battalion commanders will have persuaded themselves how little attentiveness and obedience is evident among the troops, that all falls into disorder at the least movement in front of the enemy and no one is able to form the troops; it will be their task and that of the brigade commanders to introduce fear and obedience, the only means of restoring order.'[22] Wimpffen reflected his worries in a blunt 17 August memorandum to the Kaiser. He reported that the army was 'psychologically shaken' and, though not 'despondent', required leaders to ignite 'an electrical spark' to restore morale. There was no unity of command or administration, he warned, highlighting that 'an extraordinary lack of enterprise' prevailed on the Austrian side 'that stands in stark contrast to the activity of our adversary'. He was especially troubled at the absence of discipline among the general officers and predicted that this would worsen in the absence of an imperial family member as overall commander with the power to dispense rewards and punishments on his own authority.[23] As Wimpffen indicated, all of this did not mean that the army was on the verge of collapse, but the situation did not bode well for rapid recovery and resumption of war, especially as these problems would be exacerbated by the confusion and loss of confidence that ensued when Charles stepped down from command at the end of the month.

Enough Blood Has Flowed

The circumstances surrounding the signature of the armistice illuminate the thinking of both commanders and, for the Austrian side, of the contending attitudes within the Habsburg state. On the French side, Napoleon's aim in revisiting the Austrian ceasefire offer was simple and practical. Despite Berthier's bluff on the 11th when he spoke to Wimpffen of 'the entire army', he had at most 38,000 men on hand that afternoon and he knew he was significantly outnumbered. A decisive battle would have to await the arrival of the 55,000 infantry making their way towards Znaim by forced marches. Davout's lead division only reached the battlefield sometime after nightfall having marched via Laa. Oudinot, on the other hand, had come through Joslowitz to avoid the congestion at Laa, but then found his further progress blocked by one of Davout's divisions at Erdberg anyway. By 7:00 p.m., therefore, he only had one division across the Thaya and it would be 9:00 or 10:00 p.m. before his corps was assembled around Erdberg (approximately 17 km from Zuckerhandl). By dint of extraordinary marching, Molitor's division was also on hand. Having reached Kallendorf (Chvalovice) late that night, it was only five or so kilometres south of the Thaya.[24] This concentration of forces would give Napoleon an overwhelming numerical advantage on

12 July and the prospects for a crushing victory would then be high. It is noteworthy that Napoleon directed all of the arriving reinforcements (the Guard, 3rd Corps, 2nd Corps) to deploy north of the Thaya; none were sent to Massena south of the river (via Naschetitz, for instance). This certainly indicates that he intended to exploit – as Charles feared – the vulnerability of the Austrian left had combat been resumed. 'The position of the Austrian army was extremely bad, very confined, and the Archduke Charles could not remain in it any longer without running the risk of losing a battle more decisive battle than that of Wagram,' commented GB Mathieu Dumas of Berthier's staff, and the historian of Davout's 3rd Corps wrote that 'The ruin of the Austrian army seemed inevitable.'[25]

Assuming, that is, that the Austrians did not depart under cover of darkness. Many in the French camp, however, were convinced that their enemy was 'already in retreat' and the emperor feared that the Austrians would escape entirely during the night, depriving him of an immediate triumph and dragging his weary army yet further north into Bohemia. Not only was Bohemia 'a land studded with natural obstacles and sown with fortified places where the enemy would find new resources',[26] but shifting the theatre of war there would carry the French army an uncomfortable distance from Vienna with no guarantee of a decisive, war-ending battle in the near term. Napoleon, of course, did not know that Charles had already issued orders for a withdrawal, but he was clearly concerned that failure to hold the Hauptarmee around Znaim would mean 'he was going to have to enter into a system of complicated manoeuvres to force it into a new battle, that is, recommence a calculation of the probabilities, the chances for and against, and indeed put everything back into question'. For Napoleon, who above all wanted to end the war quickly, any such prolongation was highly undesirable. Acceptance of the local ceasefire, on the other hand, would cost him nothing and might nail Charles in place for the night. Then, on the 12th, he would be in a position to eliminate the Austrian army if the archduke rejected his armistice terms. He thus 'seized on the pretext of the answer to be given' to the Austrian ceasefire proposal of 10 July.[27]

As part of his decision process, Napoleon convened an impromptu council of war at his tent. The timing of this extraordinary session is uncertain, but it seems likely it occurred some time in the afternoon before Napoleon dispatched Montbrun to communicate his acceptance of the ceasefire proposal. According to Pelet, the participants included Berthier, Davout, Hughes Bernard Maret, GD Géraud Christophe Michel Duroc, GD Jean Ambroise Baston, Comte de Lariboisière, 'and several others'.[28] Asked for their opinions, this informal group quickly divided into two factions.

On the one side were those such as Berthier and Davout who advocated completing the destruction of the Austrian army 'to finish with this Austria, the irreconcilable enemy of the new France' that continually 'violated the most solemn treaties'. 'It would only take two hours to unite 30,000 men on the archduke's left and across his line of retreat,' argued Davout. In addition to other grievances against Austria, they urged 'the necessity of preventing these ceaselessly returning coalitions by dividing Austria that was their perpetual point of unification'. This was a sentiment that resonated with Napoleon who held the Kaiser and his court in contempt and who felt personally betrayed by what he viewed as their repeated and senseless attacks on France.

The other faction promoted preservation of the Habsburg monarchy in a reduced but more or less intact form. They were concerned about the impact in Europe more broadly and hoped for the establishment of a continental equilibrium that would favour France but also sustain an extended peace. They saw both dangers and opportunities in the situation that afternoon. Among the dangers, their chief fear was that the Austrian army would escape into the night. If it could avoid defeat, the Habsburg host might inspire uprisings across Germany and could induce Prussia to alter its stance and perhaps enter the war on Austria's side. An armistice and 'a stable peace', on the other hand, would create an opportunity to build a new relationship with a subdued Austria, one founded on the common interests of the two states. This could be especially important as none of Napoleon's advisors trusted Russia, given its tepid support during the war thus far. Napoleon certainly shared this deep, and for him personal, disappointment with the behaviour of his putative Russian ally and may have worried that the tsar would change sides in the event of an extended war or a significant French setback.[29] Finally, those recommending acceptance of the armistice set their concerns against the backdrop of the unresolved war in Spain and the possibility of British intervention elsewhere on the continent.

War aims, that is, the shape of the final peace, also entered into Napoleon's calculations as he listened to his various advisors. What terms did he want to impose on Austria? If he intended to dissolve the monarchy, he would need to destroy the Austrian army utterly. If, however, he could be satisfied with a weakened but intact Habsburg realm, then an immediate cessation of hostilities was acceptable, even preferable. In the circumstances as they existed that afternoon and evening on the field at Znaim he seems to have reached several conclusions. First that the probability of the Austrians slipping away overnight was high and that the uncertainties attendant upon a new campaign with his victorious but fatigued and weakened army were too great to take the chance of hoping for a decisive battle on 12 July. Second, that his military superiority over the Austrian forces was such that he would be able to destroy their main army at a later date if the Habsburg leadership balked at his peace terms and opted to reopen the war. Third, that he could defer a final decision on peace conditions to a later date, specifically as far as the dissolution of the monarchy and the fate of Kaiser Franz were concerned.

Personal matters may have been a factor as well. He too was physically weary, he was likely still suffering from his recent indisposition, and he was dissatisfied with the results of Wagram after huge expense in blood and effort to bring about what he had expected would be another stunning triumph as this unwanted war's culminating battle. Furthermore, he was not insensible to the costs this war had inflicted, particularly among his senior officers. Although Bruyère was not among the brightest stars in the galaxy of imperial generals, he was something of a favourite, and Napoleon seems to have been unusually effected by the news of his severe wounding after the loss of such extraordinary talents as St Hilaire, d'Espagne, Lasalle and the irreplaceable Lannes.[30] 'As you can see, death hangs over my generals,' he reportedly told Davout, 'Who knows if, in two hours, I would not learn that you yourself had been hit.'[31] Whatever weights we assign to these various considerations, Napoleon ended the discussion in his tent that night by stating 'enough blood has flowed'.[32] This memorable phrase resulted in Berthier arranging the armistice with Wimpffen and the termination of the active phase of the war.

Although he had not yet decided what peace terms he would accept, Napoleon was adamant about two aspects of the armistice as a stepping-stone towards a final peace. First, it must be the equivalent of the peace terms incorporated in the 1805 Treaty of Pressburg. That is, for the purposes of both the Habsburg court and the wider European audience, Wagram was to be portrayed as no less a victory than Austerlitz: Austria must be seen as having been conclusively defeated by France.[33] Second, he was careful to ensure that the provisions of the agreement granted his forces every possible advantage should hostilities recommence.[34] He stipulated, for example, that his troops must remain in occupation of provinces they had *traversed* over the past three months, not simply those where they were present in significant numbers on 12 July. Styria, Carinthia and parts of Hungary were included in the French zone because they ensured communications to Italy and Dalmatia even though the only substantial forces there when the armistice was signed were Gyulai's Austrians. Similarly, the allocation of the districts of Znaim and Brünn to the French zone was also strategic as it conveniently placed his forces in a position to block communication and collaboration between Austrian armies in Bohemia and Hungary. The occupation of key fortresses and cities such as Brünn, Pressburg and Graz solidified his hold on these regions, while possession of Fiume hampered Austrian efforts to collect subsidies from Britain.[35] The armistice thus left Napoleon in the heart of the Habsburg empire and able to manoeuvre in any direction with Vienna as a secure base of operations. Moreover, his army was to a large degree living at Austrian expense while encamped in Habsburg lands, drawing food, wine, firewood, clothing, animals and other essentials as well as large monetary 'contributions' from the Kaiser's subjects.[36]

Outside of Austrian territory, Napoleon subsequently insisted that the armistice be applied to the Austrian detachments in south-central Germany as well.[37] The withdrawal of these small commands not only removed a menace to his line of communications and to the security of his German allies but also allowed him to present his forces in Germany as a threat to the Austrian rear in Bohemia (no matter that the threat was largely hollow given the size and composition of the second-line troops he had deployed between Bayreuth and Dresden).

Finally, the duration of the armistice, even if not extended, would suffice for him to accomplish considerable reinforcement, reorganisation, re-equipping and redistribution of his forces. Thousands of replacements were already en route to the Army of Germany and many more would be sent over the coming weeks. Although it is beyond the scope of this study, it is useful to note that the period of the armistice saw intense industry on the French side of the demarcation line. The level of effort mirrored the activity just prior to the war in every sphere from training the infantry to remounting the cavalry and expanding the artillery. Napoleon, in an unconscious echo of Stadion, saw the armistice as a capitulation by a defeated foe.[38] He had no interest in renewing the war, but he would be as prepared as possible should Austria reject his terms for peace.

To Save the Army

Unlike Napoleon, of course, Charles was not a sovereign ruler. Consequently, the ceasefire and armistice decisions were both complex and fraught with personal risk for him. Like Napoleon, he also wanted to end the war at the earliest possible moment, but where the French emperor was annoyed at being distracted from his larger strategic interests, the archduke feared for the very existence of the Austrian empire and the House of Habsburg. On the evening of 11 July, therefore, he deliberately endeavoured to create a situation where ceasefire and armistice were the only viable choices for Austria, hoping thereby to lay a foundation for a conclusive peace. His acts of commission and omission both point in this direction. In the first place, he accepted Napoleon's offer immediately. He was certainly under time pressure as the French emperor had intended by making his proposition contingent upon overnight agreement, but there is no evidence that Charles made any attempt to temporise or extend the deadline. He did not defer to his brother the Kaiser or request a delay to allow for Liechtenstein's arrival as he might have done. He certainly did not send for Stadion. Instead, he dispatched Wimpffen at once to conclude an armistice according to the compressed French timetable. Second, he did not retreat under the cover of darkness. His previous decision to hold his positions through the night of 10/11 July was logical, indeed unavoidable, to allow time for

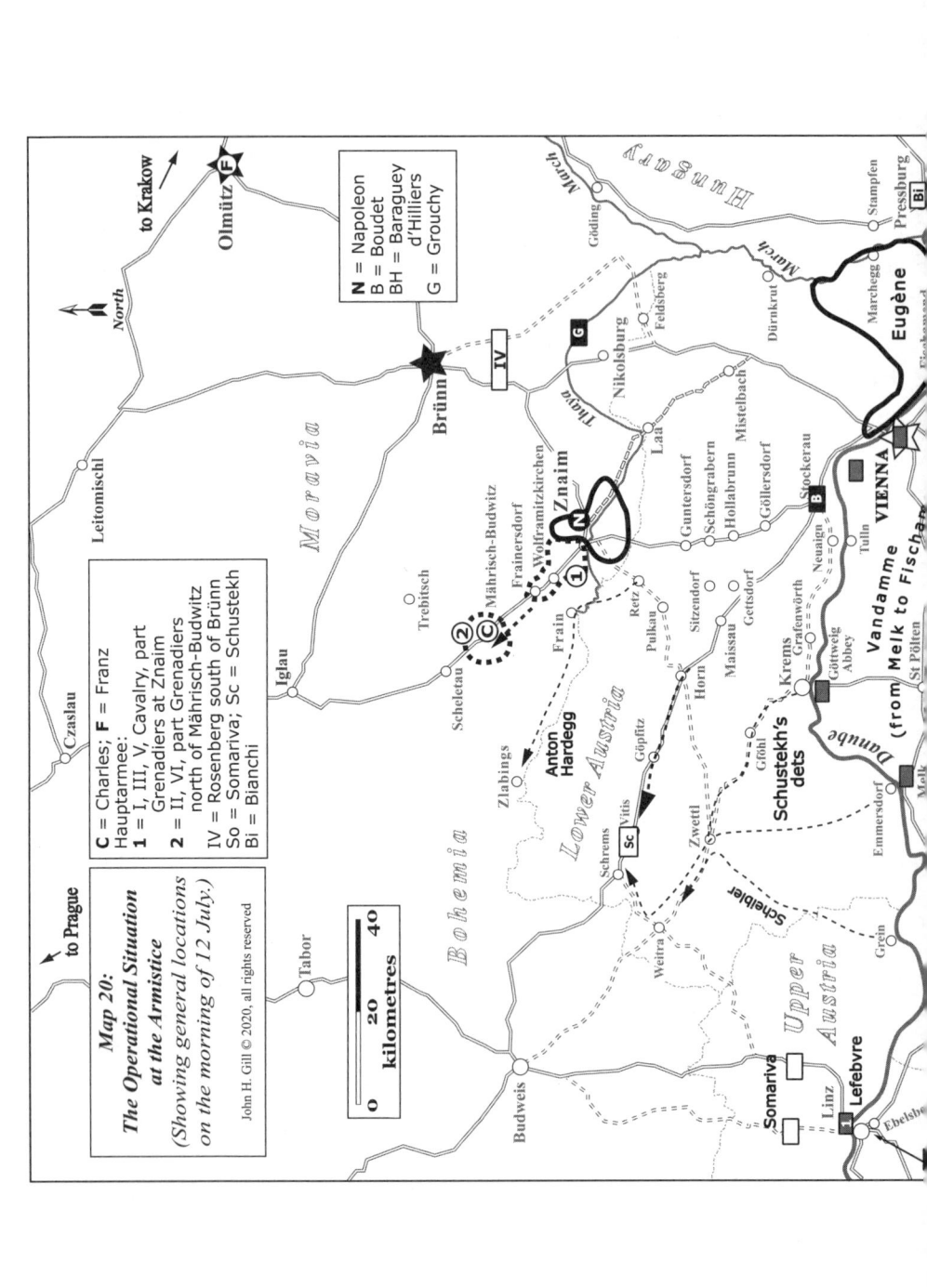

the jammed baggage trains to clear the Iglau highway. By mid-morning of the 11th, these conditions no longer applied: the army's cumbersome trains had largely moved on and the way was clear for his retreat on the night of 11/12 July as he had ordered in his 11:00 a.m. disposition. Instead of withdrawing and extending the war, he countermanded his orders and left most of the army in place, vulnerable to the truly overwhelming power that Napoleon had by then assembled on the opposite side of the field.[39] Furthermore, he compounded his army's vulnerability by sending off II Corps and two of the grenadier brigades and by instructing VI Corps to continue its movement north in such a way that it would be completely out of supporting distance should combat resume on 12 July. He was likely exaggerating for effect when he told Stadion that night that his army was outnumbered two to one, but in fact, he would have had only some 47,000 infantry and cavalry to face approximately 91,000 French and Germans had the armistice not been signed.

Several factors account for the archduke's decisions that evening. First, was his fundamental scepticism concerning the necessity of this war. As we have seen, he had harboured deep misgivings about challenging Napoleon in an offensive war when the idea was first raised in the second half of 1808 and he had only consented with resignation and the greatest reluctance when the course to conflict seemed ineluctable. He had urged negotiations in the immediate aftermath of the defeats in Bavaria and, as noted earlier, had 'preached peace, peace, peace' since Aspern-Essling in May. His scepticism, reluctance and desire for near-term peace were all driven, of course, by his conviction that Napoleon, with his superior military power and his personal prowess in the field, might decide to end the war by dismantling the Habsburg monarchy.

For Charles, the weary white-coats under his command were the surety of that monarchy and the second major factor was his assessment of his forces. Not only was the Hauptarmee facing a numerically superior enemy under the personal command of the dreaded 'emperor of battles', but his men were exhausted by unremitting marches, they had not cooked a warm meal in days and his regiments had left thousands of stragglers by the roadside during the retreat from Wagram. His interest in peace may have led him to overstate the army's deficiencies in his talks with Stadion and his reports to the Kaiser, but he had received repeated pleas for rest and reinforcement from his subordinates and had personally witnessed the army's struggles over the preceding week. He was daunted by the prospect of 'continuing a retreat when one could not determine the stopping point' and was convinced that a new battle, even a defensive one, would likely result in defeat.[40] An offensive was out of the question. This war had supplied him with plentiful evidence of his army's clumsiness as an offensive instrument. Even with the Hauptarmee, the best of the monarchy's troops, an offensive now would be 'an act of desperation' and he scoffed at the notion that the largely second-line forces under Johann, Joseph, Chasteler and Gyulai could pose a serious threat to Napoleon. The Kaiser, he wrote 'forgot that I also know what troops and what kind of troops are available in Hungary'. All the adventurous schemes proposed by Johann and other enthusiasts were 'much ado, little substance' (*'multum clamoris parum lanae'*).[41]

Third, the Russians were never far from his thoughts, a looming threat to the east. Like most in the Habsburg leadership, he worried that the tsar's battalions, advancing inexorably despite repeated expressions of friendship, would combine with Napoleon's men to squeeze the Austrian forces from two sides.

The physical and mental strain on his frail constitution since the beginning of the month may have been a fourth factor. 'Extremely fatigued' and possibly suffering from several enervating maladies, Charles claimed to be so tired that he could barely mount his horse.[42] His usual professionalism and dedication notwithstanding, these physical impingements may have influenced his judgement and reinforced his innate pessimism.

The single most important consideration for Charles, however, was the attitude of the court and his brother the Kaiser. The revived dominance of the war party was painfully apparent in the letters he had received from Franz on the battlefield over the previous two days, particularly the demeaning note he had opened around noon on 11 July. This sudden shift in the imperial court must have been especially shocking and disheartening to him as it came immediately after the hopes he had entertained when Franz had agreed to send Liechtenstein to Napoleon. Now Liechtenstein's mission went unmentioned and his own authority as Generalissimus was clearly in danger of revocation; with this would go his ability to influence events. Indeed, from his perspective, his ability to save the empire from ruin was on the verge of being fatally compromised. Napoleon's unexpected acceptance of the 10 July ceasefire offer thus provided him an opportunity to act on his own convictions, halt the progress of the French pursuit, save the army from what he was certain would be 'total destruction' and present the war party at court with a *fait accompli* in 'an armistice that is the first step towards peace'. Driven by the need to act before his powers were curtailed, he seized the moment without hesitation and agreed to Napoleon's severe terms. 'Napoleon arrived with his entire army,' he told his adoptive father the next day, 'but an armistice concluded that night saved us.'[43]

Charles grasped the opportunity for an armistice out of what he perceived to be his patriotic duty and dynastic loyalty, but he knew full well that he was acting against the prevailing mood at court and he braced himself for disapprobation. He feared 'the ministers and the emigrés' of the old Reich and made plans to send Liechtenstein to the Kaiser 'provided he does not disavow this armistice and that he follows the path of peace, without which we are lost'. At the same time, his weariness, exasperation and distrust were evident in a scornful remark about Franz that he made in a private letter to Albert: 'If the Kaiser does not ratify the armistice and does not make peace quickly, he can go begging for alms.'[44]

Having taken his parlous decision, Charles now had to explain himself to the Kaiser, the court, the army and the public at large. To Franz he sent a brief personal letter and an extensive formal report, both to be delivered by Liechtenstein. In the personal letter, he rather testily defended his impugned honour (from the insinuations in the Kaiser's 10 July messages), opining that he had displayed sufficient 'courage and determination' by maintaining the 'bad position' at Znaim despite the enemy's numerical superiority. He affirmed that Rosenberg would be relieved of command at once but strenuously asserted the personal importance he attached to Grünne regardless of what some 'popinjays' might say of him. 'I feel too keenly the significance of the burden that rests on my shoulders to believe that I can carry it alone, that I can do everything alone,' he wrote.[45]

In his lengthy formal report, Charles outlined in detail his rationale for agreeing to the armistice, endeavouring in the process to pre-empt all possible objections. He began by reviewing all of the army's sufferings and deficiencies, a theme he reinforced throughout this letter: 51,626 men and 7,482 horses lost since Wagram, pervasive exhaustion, lack of proper provisions, thousands of stragglers left behind every day, the dissolution of much of the Landwehr, the demoralisation of his own troops and the power of the enemy. It was under these circumstances, he explained, that he had received the armistice provisions from the French that Berthier had presented as 'an unalterable ultimatum':

> Between acceptance of this ultimatum and the battle, for which we clearly could see that the French had made all preparations against my far inferior army, there was no choice. In order to save the army, I had to make use of the authority that Your Majesty had granted me to conclude an armistice in order not to leave Your Majesty and the monarchy at the mercy of the conqueror.

He then discussed the various stipulations of the agreement to demonstrate how 'The continuance of Your Majesty's reign has been preserved with the least possible sacrifice.' Not only was it 'better to enter into an armistice than lose a second battle' but in his assessment even a relatively safe retreat could hardly have ended before Prague, leaving all of Moravia and most of Bohemia in French hands and opening the way for Napoleon to establish direct liaison with the Russians. Instead, 'We have given up through the armistice almost nothing that the French did not already occupy.' Much of Galicia had been saved (including its valuable salt works), the Russians and Poles would have to halt where they were on 12 July, and the army, with a welcome chance to recuperate, would now be in a position to operate in conjunction with the empire's forces in Hungary. He dismissed Gyulai's corps as too weak to maintain itself in Styria or Carinthia (most of which the French controlled anyway) or to pose a serious threat to the French in Vienna. As for the fortresses lost, he characterised these as being of little military value and pointed out that Austria still retained other important citadels. Aware of the Kaiser's sensitivity regarding the Tyrol, Charles depicted the situation there as bleak given that the tiny force of 5,000 or so men was 'totally cut off from the monarchy and would be lost sooner or later'. At the same time, he attempted to hold out the hope that evacuation of the Tyrol might be drawn out under one pretext or another.

He summarised by acknowledging that the armistice at first glance seemed unfavourable, but averred that it achieved two great advantages that far outweighed its negative aspects: first, that Napoleon was no longer considering the abolition of the dynasty; and second, that the army had been preserved. With the time and resources now available, he wrote hopefully, the army could be made ready to take the field for another trial of combat should the enemy's demands at the peace table be unacceptable. His own opinion, however, was completely clear and he ended his exposition by reiterating the importance of a quick end to the war: 'I am totally convinced that the conclusion of peace is the only way to preserve the greater part of the monarchy between the pressure of France and Russia.'[46]

The archduke was equally direct in reports to Franz on 16, 22 and 23 July and in his official report to the war ministry on the 21st. In addition to repeating his call for an early peace, he used these letters to his brother to announce his plan to move the army to Hungary as the local authorities in Bohemia claimed they could not supply his men for more than six days. The armistice was essential for this transfer, he argued, otherwise the army might be trapped between the French and Russian armies on one side and the Carpathian Mountains on the other where it would be unable to defend or sustain itself. His report to the ministry on 21 July was similar in content. After reviewing the reasons he had outlined to Franz for acceding to the armistice, he concluded with his assessment that the armistice,

> was the only way in which it would be possible to preserve for His Majesty a proven, excellent army; to safeguard the resources of all Bohemia and the best parts of Moravia; to contain the advances of the Russians and the insurgents [Poles] in Galicia; to protect Krakow and the salt works from enemy capture; to rescue the entire right bank of the Danube, with the exception of Raab, from enemy raids and pillage; and, finally, to pave the way for a rapprochement which must eventually come if the monarchy is not to be entirely destroyed.[47]

Charles made the same points in an unusual circular to the corps commanders issued on 26 July to address the discontent within the army, stressing that the Hauptarmee had retreated in good order and was resolutely holding off the superior French when *Napoleon* took the initiative to request the ceasefire.[48] For some, of course, this begged a question: if Napoleon's situation was so dire that he had to ask for a pause, why did Austria agree to such stern terms?[49] The same basic rationale also appeared in several pamphlets published after the war by Charles's adherents to justify his actions in the eyes of 'soldiers and statesmen'.[50] Some of what Charles and his protégés wrote was tendentious, overdrawn or painted in excessively grim colours owing to his own pessimism and his ardent desire to convince the Kaiser to make peace. Most of his observations, however, were accurate, but neither his analysis nor his actions were welcome at court.

Curiously, despite the gravity of the armistice decision and the urgency of implementing its provisions, no one in Charles's headquarters seemed to think it necessary to expedite a messenger to the Kaiser with this unexpected news. As Franz later complained, it seems almost certain that the French would have allowed, perhaps encouraged, the sending of a courier through their lines by the most direct route to Hungary. No one requested such permission. Instead, Liechtenstein, who was to carry the archduke's personal letter and formal report, went off to one of his Moravian estates for a day or two before traveling to Vienna in hopes of meeting Napoleon. A week would pass before he reached Komorn and the imperial court. As far as can be determined, no other courier was sent to hurry this crucial information to Franz.

As Liechtenstein was resting at his nearby estate and Charles was leading the army north towards Leitomischl (Litomyšl) in Bohemia, Napoleon was returning to the Schönbrunn Palace outside Vienna. After reviewing Massena's men in Znaim, he and his immediate staff arrived in Hödnitz around midnight. Knocking on the door of the mill, they awakened the astonished and alarmed Frau Tulipan whose first thought seems to have been that she could not meet such exalted personages in the meagre clothes previous marauders had left her. One of the senior officers loaned her his blue mantle and led her to the sitting room where she was introduced to Napoleon and Berthier. She and Napoleon sat together on a sofa and, with one of his suite interpreting, the emperor asked her a few questions and reassured her that she and her property would not be harmed. Meanwhile staff officers laid out maps on a nearby table to which Napoleon periodically addressed himself, standing up to point to various spots as Frau Tulipan looked on. She answered in the affirmative when asked if she owned a calf; the creature was soon slaughtered and prepared for a meal that occurred around 2:00 a.m. The emperor, officers, staff and servants then took their rest in the miller's home and outbuildings. Napoleon departed the following morning, but not before paying Frau Tulipan 300 golden ducats and, at her request, placing her home under protection with several guards posted to ensure she was not further mistreated. Furthermore, when she complained that her cow had been stolen, Berthier ordered that she be given one from the French herd in the village, a boon from which the rest of Hödnitz also benefited as more than forty head were distributed to other inhabitants. Unfortunately for Frau Tulipan, an imperial paymaster later returned claiming he 'had forgotten his cap'. In retrieving his cap, however, he also swept up all the coins that she had not stowed away and departed with the money pursued by her outraged protests.[51]

Also surprised on 12 July was Marmont, but in the most gratifying fashion. Reporting to Napoleon, he found the emperor 'radiant'. Walking back and forth together in front of the imperial tents, they discussed the just-concluded battle and Marmont's march up from Dalmatia in great detail with Napoleon asking innumerable, and often critical questions, and the general justifying his decisions at various points during his campaign. After an extended time, Napoleon departed to work with Berthier, and Marmont, 'overcome with fatigue and dissatisfied', returned to his 'miserable cabin'. He was reviewing the 'singular and fatiguing conversation' with his chief of staff, Adjutant-Commandant Marie Joseph Raymond Delort, when Colonel Alexander Louis Robert Girardin d'Ermenonville arrived to announce that the emperor had elevated Marmont to the marshalate. Given his recent conversation, Marmont claimed to be 'a thousand miles' from thinking of any such outcome, especially considering his disappointment at not having been named in the first batch of marshals in 1804. He was 'content' rather than overjoyed but noticed after a few days 'the immense step' his life had taken and the difference in how other generals now related to him.[52]

As for Napoleon, he departed Hödnitz on the morning of the 13th, inspected the new bridge at Floridsdorf en route to Schönbrunn and resumed his customary management of all the manifold affairs of the empire. Liechtenstein arrived on 15 July but was denied an audience after waiting four fruitless hours. On the following day, however, Napoleon received him with great courtesy and spoke in a comparatively mild manner about the terms he would demand for peace. In particular, there was no more talk of dividing the monarchy or dethroning Franz. Liechtenstein, much relieved, departed for Komorn to report to the Kaiser.[53]

The Emperor Wants to Be Rid of Me

Liechtenstein would have been better advised to ride directly to the Kaiser from the battlefield. Franz and his court had arrived in Komorn on the evening of 14 July after their hasty flight from Znaim. He first learned of the armistice from French officers who had handed a copy to Bianchi's pickets along the outpost line west of Pressburg, a circumstance that aroused no little imperial annoyance. Worse than the manner in which he heard of the armistice were the contents of the draft the French had provided. He was astonished to read that it 'included conditions which an army could only enter into if the only choice was between certain defeat and capitulation, conditions the fulfilment of which is not in our power and the evacuation of areas that are presently occupied by my troops and which comprise a large part of my monarchy'. 'I could never think to enter into an armistice that costs me more than the enemy,' he told Charles that day. The Kaiser and his advisors immediately suspected a French ruse. Mindful of the deception practiced by some French commanders in 1805 to capture the great bridge over the Danube intact, and perhaps that the Russians successfully fooled the French several days later, he ordered Johann, Bianchi, Rosenberg and Palatine Joseph to ignore the supposed armistice until they received personal notification from him. Reading between the lines of this 15 July letter to the archduke, it is not difficult to imagine that Franz was already worried that his brother the Generalissimus had approved what he regarded as scandalously disgraceful and unnecessary stipulations.[54]

Furthermore, the defeat at Wagram and the subsequent retreat had not improved the image of the Hauptarmee's leadership in the eyes of the court. Graf Karl Zichy, the Army Minister, sketched an alarming picture in a 15 July report to the Kaiser.

> I must candidly state, partly from my own experience and partly from the information gathered at headquarters, that I found the Generalissimus so completely dejected over the current situation, that one can hardly count on a favourable outcome in the case of renewed war. They are so persuaded of Napoleon's superiority in men, cavalry and guns that they consider all resistance with enduring effect to be nearly impossible.[55]

Stadion's letters, when they arrived, would only reinforce these pre-existing impressions.

Given this background, it is hardly surprising that the Kaiser and his court reacted with outrage and indignant vociferations when Liechtenstein presented himself for an imperial audience on 18 July.[56] While Liechtenstein escaped censure and indeed enjoyed praise for 'conducting his mission very well', Metternich reflected the mood at court in writing to a colleague that day: 'Everything about that headquarters is rotten but it will cease to exist' and Austria, with its rich resources, could always fight another battle.[57] The result was a series of letters to Charles over the next several days that severely admonished him and – as he had anticipated – strictly limited his authority. Charles's 13 July report had confirmed his fears, wrote the Kaiser. He could understand the need for a ceasefire given the weakened state of the army, but he could not comprehend accepting 'such hard conditions', conditions that 'took out of our hands in one blow all the advantages that we had' and forced Austria to accommodate all the arbitrary requirements of the enemy or face renewed hostilities at a disadvantage. He claimed to be especially surprised and dismayed to receive news of the armistice just when he was about to gather 60,000 men at Ödenburg and lead them to Vienna. This was an odd objection given that he had dismissed Johann's actions along these lines as militarily useless in his 15 July letter, but it was the comment that later led Charles to deprecate these troops in his private communication to Herzog Albert.

Franz also expressed his distress at the failure to involve Liechtenstein in the armistice negotiations. He not only believed the conditions would have been less odious had Liechtenstein been consulted, but feared that the conduct of simultaneous but separate talks with different Austrian representatives would lead Napoleon to conclude that everyone in the Habsburg hierarchy was acting according to his own agenda. Moreover, he chastised Charles for the long delay in apprising him of the armistice. The archduke 'should have and could have' sent a courier through the French army to deliver a report by the shortest possible route. Instead, he only learned the details when Liechtenstein reported on 18 July, six days after the event. In addition to his anger at the slow notification, he seems to have been deeply annoyed at having to rescind his earlier orders to ignore all references to a ceasefire or armistice. 'Most painful of all' for Franz, however, was 'the compromising of my honour' vis-à-vis 'the brave Tyrolians and Vorarlbergers' after he had promised that these regions *'would never more be separated from the body of the Austrian imperial state'* and that he *'would sign no peace* other than *that which would tie this land inseparably to my monarchy'*.[58]

The price Charles had to pay for his bold decision on the armistice was loss of his special status as Generalissimus. 'The experience of the present campaign has adequately demonstrated', wrote Franz on 18 July, that commanding one great army, overseeing all others and managing parts of the War Ministry's affairs was too much for Charles, his zeal notwithstanding. This and the fact that the 'continued existence of the monarchy' would be at stake should hostilities resume, led him, he continued, to 'retain for myself alone' the supreme command of all armies from this point forwards. Charles would be concerned 'only with command of the troops I have entrusted solely and exclusively to you'.

There followed a set of detailed instructions – including a demand for situation reports every 24 hours – of the sort that a superior officer would issue to a dilatory, fractious or inexperienced subordinate. Similar requirements were imposed in additional imperial letters over the coming five days. Having commanded hundreds of thousands of men in multiple complex campaigns over nearly two decades and held the field against Napoleon, Charles would have seen such instructions for exactly what they were: a tactic crafted by dilettante members of the

Kaiser's household and designed to belittle him personally in the hope that he would resign.[59] The entire correspondence also clearly illustrated that Franz, always jealous of his powers, perceived Charles's actions as transgressions upon his own imperial prerogatives. Influenced by the coterie of strongly anti-Charles advisors at court, he thus decided to treat the errant archduke as a very junior subordinate. These demeaning directions culminated in a 23 July instruction addressed to Charles as one of 'my commanders-in-chief' with a lengthy and detailed list of all the items each 'commander-in-chief' was to report on a routine basis. The same day that this further diminution of Charles was being signed, however, the archduke was putting his own pen to a letter requesting relief from command.

'From the three letters of 15th, 18th and 19th, I have, with the deepest sorrow, noted Your Majesty's dissatisfaction. A commander who has attracted such a degree of Your Majesty's dissatisfaction can no longer enjoy your trust and thus can no longer be of use to the state as commander of the army. These considerations have moved me to lay the command of the army at Your Majesty's feet.' Thus wrote Charles on 23 July 1809. 'I believe that the emperor or rather the behind the scenes manipulators, because the emperor counts for nothing, want to be rid of me and lead me to leave, and I see myself as an impediment to the good of the service and the state as no one has confidence in me,' he told Albert in a long letter several days later. 'You know that I have always devoted myself and sacrificed myself, but when you see that this leads to nothing and that the sovereign does not want to listen to you, your urge [to devote yourself to the state] wanes, and you become selfish in spite of yourself.' In later years, he wrote that he had the option of either resigning his position or hurrying to Hungary to resolve the disagreements with his elder brother. Physically and mentally exhausted from the struggles against both Napoleon and against his enemies at court, he chose to resign. The curt imperial reply to Charles's letter came with unseemly haste. In his tiny, tidy script on the bottom of his brother's missive, Franz penned two sentences. The first read: 'I regard the resignation of command of the army as a sacrifice for the state by Your Grace and only regret that the state thereby loses a courageous field commander, nonetheless I find myself moved, in the current circumstances, to accept.' The second granted permission for Grünne to remain with Charles until the new commander was in place as this would smooth the transfer and ensure that the Kaiser's instructions were carried out to the fullest extent.[60] That was all. With these words, Charles turned command of the Hauptarmee over to Liechtenstein (not to Bellegarde whom he had recommended by virtue of seniority), issued an order of the day thanking the soldiers and retired to Teschen with Herzog Albert. Although he would indulge in writing histories of his campaigns and treatises on military theory, he would never again hold field command.

Mustard after the Meal

By the time this sordid drama between Charles and the court had played itself out, the principal armies had moved to their armistice camps and the two sides had begun to focus on both the initiation of a peace process and on preparations for war should peace not eventuate. Some time would elapse, however, before word of the armistice reached all the corners of this wide war. Fighting at various levels of intensity thus continued for several days after Berthier and Wimpffen put their signatures to the formal agreement. In a few cases, combat connected with the war persisted for weeks or months as Great Britain was not a party to the armistice and some belligerents simply decided to ignore its stipulations.

Most closely related to the Battle of Znaim were Austrian Oberstleutnant Wilgenheim's detachment and Bavarian Oberst von Lindenau's two squadrons of light horse. Both of these small commands were operating in the broad space south of the Pulkau and between the two main roads to Znaim during the time of the battle. Where Lindenau was scouting and screening this area in accordance with orders he had received from Napoleon immediately after Wagram, Wilgenheim was present by accident, having been cut off from V Corps during Reuss's retreat on 10 July.

One of Wilgenheim's patrols, as we have seen, had scooped up the band of the 1st Baden Infantry on the 10th, but his detachment of Jägers and Uhlans found the way back to V Corps blocked when it reached Hadres that day as ordered. Wilgenheim thus turned to the southeast and

Chart 5: Major Forces in Other Theatres of War
(Infantry and cavalry figures only, as of mid-July)

In Linz and vicinity north of the Danube

Austria	FML Sommariva	7,200
French & allied	Marshal Lefebvre, 7th Corps	
	Bavarian 1st Division	6,870
	Bavarian 3rd Division en route	6,220

In and Opposite Hungary and Croatia

Austria	Archduke Johann	
	Johann (Army of Inner Austria)	16,920
	Chasteler	4,520
	Gyulai (IX Corps)	29,110
	Joseph: Hungarian Insurrection	c. 30,000

(Only about a third of the Austrian troops could be considered regulars.)

French & allied	Viceroy Eugene	
	Army of Italy (includes Baraguey and Raab)	26,820
	Saxon Contingent (GD Reynier)	10,320
	Württemberg 8th Corps (GD Vandamme)	9,860
	Vienna garrison (GD Andréossy)	1,970
	Other (6th Hussars, 18th Léger)	1,500

(Small garrisons held Klagenfurt and Villach; GD Rusca en route with small detachment.)

sought refuge in the large Ernstbrunner Wald on the 11th. His men picked up some prisoners and collected Austrian stragglers as they retreated but they were fortunate that there were few French or German troops in the area. Here they stayed for the next four days, hiding in the forest, attempting to gather information and sustained by victuals provided by helpful locals. Lindenau, meanwhile, marched from Großmugl to

Ernstbrunn on 10 July. His scouts found the Austrians, but Wilgenheim refused a surrender demand and Lindenau's troopers continued north to Gnadendorf on the 12th. Both commanders reported occasional skirmishes, sometimes with one another, at other times with different scouting parties, but casualties were few. Both also picked up a number of allies along the way: stragglers, men who had evaded capture or those who were simply lost. The Bavarian detachment, for example, thus ended up with a tiny ad hoc platoon of French and Bavarian infantrymen. With these men and his troopers, Lindenau reached Laa on the 13th, pleased with the performance of his two squadrons in gathering intelligence and capturing 401 prisoners when they 'stood completely isolated between the Brünn and Znaim highways and could expect neither liaison nor support for three hours distance to left, right or rear'. Wilgenheim was likewise satisfied with his men. Learning of the ceasefire, they headed out of the forest on the night of 15/16 July, crossed the Thaya at Joslowitz past sleepy French troops and reached Erdberg at 3:00 a.m., where they left their 78 French prisoners in exchange for free passage north. Hungry and exhausted, the weary band arrived in Trebitsch (Třebíč) on 17 July and was soon reunited with V Corps.[61]

Along the Danube, the Württemberg light infantry in Melk noticed the departure of the Austrians on the opposite bank and launched a successful reconnaissance on 10 July. Skirmishing and cross-river raids also continued between the Bavarians around Linz and Somariva's command, the last of these occurring on 12 July before the two sides learned of the armistice. Schustekh and his multifarious detachments from the Danube had by this time withdrawn to Schrems, while Anton Hardegg's small flanking force shifted to Zlabings to maintain contact with the Hauptarmee. The Bavarian 3rd Division arrived in Linz on 13 and 14 July, but the armistice made its presence superfluous and it departed again on the 17th to resume its duties on the borders of the Tyrol. Minucci marched the 2nd Division back to Linz after Znaim as Marmont's command, now designated as 11th Corps, established cantonments around Krems. With Wrede back in command, the 2nd Division relieved the 1st, which departed for Salzburg on 23 July. Wrede and his men would also be called to the Tyrol come early October.

Germany and Holland

Much to the indignation of the war party at court, the Austrian invading forces in Saxony and Bayreuth withdrew to Bohemia in accordance with the modified terms of the armistice that Charles had accepted. Neither they nor the tiny British raid near Cuxhaven generated the sort of widespread German uprising Stadion and others had imagined. The deposed Duke Friedrich Wilhelm of Brunswick, on the other hand, refused to acknowledge the armistice. He and a small band of some 2,000 adherents called the 'Black Corps' or 'Army of Vengeance' had marched with the Austrians during the incursion into southern Germany. On 24 July, however, he turned north instead of returning to Bohemia. His appearance in his former homeland, now part of Jérôme Bonaparte's Kingdom of Westphalia, did not spark the desired rebellion, but he defeated a Westphalian garrison at Halberstadt on 29 July, fought other Westphalian troops to a draw at Oelper on 1 August and reached the Weser estuary on 7 August. From here he and his men sailed to Britain, eventually serving with the British army in the Peninsular War and the Waterloo campaign.

Britain did launch a major amphibious assault on the continent, but this, in pursuit of British interests, was aimed at the French naval facilities in Antwerp not the incitement of insurrection in Germany. Landing at Walcheren in Holland on 30 July, this 'Grand Expedition' as it was called, enjoyed some initial success, but soon bogged down in the coastal marshes. Napoleon contained the invasion with second-line forces, content to let the region's notorious fevers deplete the attackers. By the time the last troops departed on 23 December, some 4,000 had died and 12,000 or so were incapacitated for an indefinite time, mostly from 'Walcheren fever' and other ailments. The attack did nothing for the Habsburg cause. None of Napoleon's troops were diverted and no rebellion ensued. Moreover, the British ships did not even appear off the coast of Holland until 28 July, more than two weeks after the armistice. 'It is the mustard after the meal,' wrote Charles of these British enterprises.[62]

Hungary, Styria and Dalmatia

The long frontier from Hungary down to Dalmatia saw little action during the period around the Battle of Znaim and the signing of the

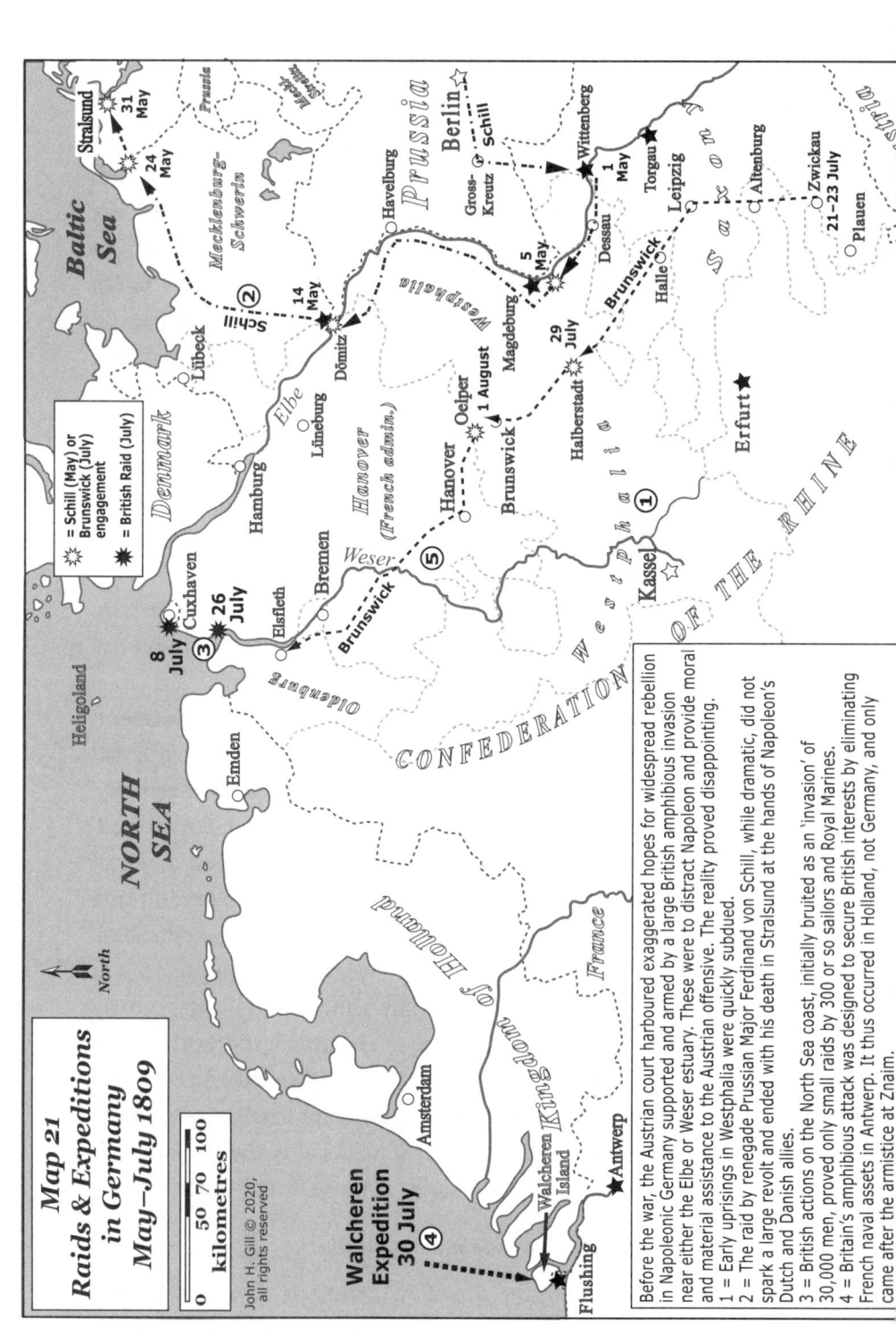

armistice. Archduke Johann moved most of his corps from the March River to Komorn where he arrived on 13 July. He then shifted south of the Danube and busily indulged himself in concocting various schemes for attacking Vienna from the south and east. He left GM Bianchi to hold Pressburg and ordered him to abandon the bridgehead on the southern bank of the Danube, a task Bianchi accomplished despite a French attempt to interrupt the evacuation. A more serious skirmish occurred on 13 July at Stampfen as the Saxon division crossed the March River and approached Pressburg from the north. Bianchi's men, disbelieving the ceasefire claims, attacked the Saxons only to be handed a humiliating defeat that cost them 400 casualties in dead, wounded and prisoners. This action occasioned a pointed exchange between Berthier and Wimpffen, but the Saxons occupied Pressburg the following day as instructed.

Elsewhere, despite some frictions generated by Austrian stalling tactics, Gyulai withdrew as required by the armistice terms and the French eventually took possession of Sachsenburg and the Graz citadel. News of the armistice did not reach Dalmatia until late July. Small-scale fighting had flared here as the Austrians took advantage of Marmont's absence to occupy much of the region before the end of the month.

The Tyrol and Vorarlberg

The insurrection in the Vorarlberg had also sputtered away by early August. In the Tyrol, on the other hand, the rebellion burned on brightly. Franco-Bavarian forces suffered severe setbacks in August and the flames were only quenched in the later months of the year after the peace treaty was signed. Napoleon could then concentrate the necessary forces under Viceroy Eugène to flood the region with troops from all directions. Though the insurgency ceased to function in any co-ordinated fashion after a time, hard fighting continued through much of the winter and peace was not restored until January 1810, six months after the formal end of the war.[63]

Poland/Galicia

The Poles, having initiated an advance on 9 July, were approaching Krakow as the Battle of Znaim was raging. Archduke Ferdinand, unable to defend the city with his VII Corps, had to decide who should gain control of the city as the Habsburg troops withdrew. His choice, unsurprisingly, fell on the Russians as the lesser of the two available evils. Additionally, he hoped that the Russians would form a 'barrier wall' blocking Polish access to other Habsburg territories. He therefore notified the Russian commanders of his intentions and ordered his own subordinates to hold the city long enough for the tsar's men to arrive. A tiny force of Cossacks and Russian dragoons thus managed to clatter into Krakow late on 14 July and additional troops arrived the following day as the Austrians withdrew. The Poles also reached the city on the morning of 15 July and the two supposed allies almost came to blows before the Poles, protecting themselves by proclaiming that they were acting in Napoleon's name, were able to take possession of their ancient capital. Russo-Polish tensions remained high even after a courier arrived with news of the armistice. Ferdinand was pleased with the subterfuge that had created another 'opportunity for misunderstanding' between the Russians and Poles. The standard Austrian interpretation became that 'It was not military developments [the advance of the Polish troops] but only the arrival of the Russian army – about which we could do nothing – that forced us to depart this land.'[64] At the same time, there was a common recognition in Habsburg leadership circles that the entire foray into Poland had ended to Austria's disadvantage and the presence of substantial Russian forces along the monarchy's eastern frontiers would continue to be a significant factor in decision-making as the question of peace or renewed war was debated.

The Phantom of a Glorious End

As the guns fell silent in one area after another, there ensued a lengthy and convoluted peace process. The meandering negotiations followed two paths, one formal between representatives of the two governments and one more personal and direct between the two sovereigns.

The formal track took place in Ungarisch-Altenburg, a small town approximately halfway between Napoleon's residence in Schönbrunn and the Kaiser's court in Hungary. Beginning on 17 August after an extension of the armistice, these talks were conducted by Foreign Minister Champagny on the French side and Metternich, the foreign

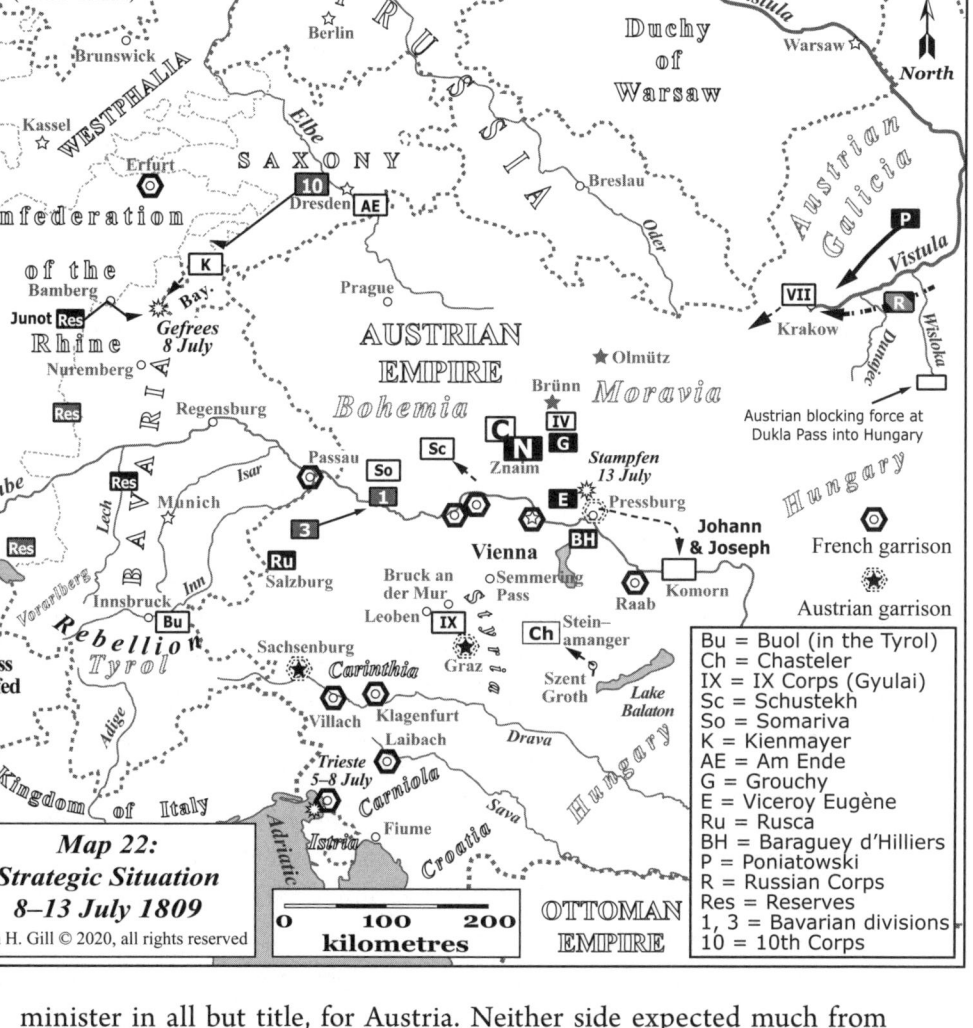

Map 22: Strategic Situation 8–13 July 1809

minister in all but title, for Austria. Neither side expected much from these exchanges. Metternich had been instructed to prolong the talks until at least the end of August so that the army could recover and reorganise in preparation for a renewal of hostilities. He was to probe Napoleon's intentions through these interactions, that is, 'whether he wants an acceptable peace or makes demands which would bring about the destruction of the monarchy or new wars'.[65] He was also to learn what he could about Russia, where Austria continued to harbour a mix of hopes and fears. Champagny was likewise to delay and discover. Moreover, like Austria, Napoleon had serious concerns about his putative Russian ally.

Before making a serious proposal to the Austrians, Napoleon wanted to learn the tsar's views on the disposition of territory captured in Austrian Galicia and on the sensitive Polish issue. He knew that the resurrection of anything resembling the old Polish kingdom was anathema to Alexander. As the tsar's foreign minister had told Napoleon's ambassador in St Petersburg back in May, Russia would renounce its alliance with France and 'sacrifice to the last man before suffering an augmentation of the Polish domain, as that would threaten our existence'.[66] With both parties playing a waiting game, it is hardly surprising that the Altenburg conference became 'a combat of finesse and deception' between the two diplomats that yielded little of substance.[67] As Champagny recalled, 'Neither side had truly decided on peace.'[68]

The channel that would ultimately produce results was that between the two imperial rulers. Although French staff officers delivered messages to the Austrian court, the principal interlocutors were Liechtenstein and FML Ferdinand Graf Bubna von Littitz[69] as personal emissaries from the Kaiser to the emperor. Indeed, Bubna made his first journey to Vienna in late July in order to convince Napoleon that Austria was serious about pursuing negotiations so that the Altenburg talks could be arranged. In the following weeks, the two officers would make numerous trips between Schönbrunn and Totis (Tata), the latter a small castle not quite 20 km southeast of Komorn where the Kaiser's court moved on 22 August. Before long, these personal interactions completely overshadowed the tedious exchanges of notes in Altenburg. The first of these missions occurred after Champagny had finally presented a complete list of French demands to Metternich on 5 September. Having received satisfactory assurance of non-interference from Tsar Alexander, Napoleon proposed, among other conditions, that Austria cede territory containing some nine million people (about one-third of the monarchy's total population) and pay a substantial indemnity. These demands ignited immediate outrage in Totis and Franz sent Bubna back to Vienna on 8 September with an indignant note protesting the delays at Altenburg generally and the ultimatum specifically. Similar fruitless exchanges continued until a stormy council session in Totis on 25 September. This meeting, which apparently included angry outbursts by several participants in the Kaiser's presence, concluded with a decision to send Liechtenstein to Schönbrunn accompanied by Bubna and equipped with plenipotentiary powers to negotiate an acceptable end to the war. Against the fervent protestations and last-minute manoeuvrings of the war party, the advocates of peace had finally persuaded the Kaiser to change course. This new tack naturally spelt the end of the Altenburg talks and Metternich, much vexed at being superseded by someone he considered unqualified, departed for Totis on 26 September.

Liechtenstein remained in Vienna for two weeks of seemingly ceaseless discussions with both Maret and Champagny, whom Napoleon had recalled from Altenburg after Metternich's departure. He attempted to procure milder peace terms but found himself completely outflanked by Napoleon and the French diplomats. In the end, he was reduced to accepting trivial territorial concessions and a 15 per cent reduction in the indemnity. Overwhelmed by his task and French pressure, he signed a treaty at Napoleon's residence in the Schönbrunn Palace on 14 October. To his horror, the French announced the peace that morning with a celebratory cannon salute, even though it had not yet been sanctioned by the Kaiser.

The conclusion of the treaty may have been hastened by a young German named Friedrich Staps who attempted to assassinate Napoleon with a knife at one of the military reviews that were a regular feature of life at Schönbrunn palace. GD Jean Rapp intercepted Staps before he could strike and Napoleon interviewed him at length later in the day, but emerged baffled from the bizarre interrogation with this calm but single-minded young man. Staps was executed, but his attempt and demeanour made a 'profound impression' on the emperor. Napoleon was already eager to leave and impatient with the sluggish pace of negotiations towards what he saw as an ineluctable outcome. The Staps incident thus seems to have heightened his annoyance and impelled him to reduce the indemnity demand to achieve a faster conclusion to the war. According to Champagny, Napoleon approached him immediately after the attempted assassination and said 'Peace will be made ... do everything possible to have the peace signed within twenty-four hours.'[70]

Whatever the impact of Staps's act, while Napoleon's household prepared for an imminent return to France, the unfortunate Liechtenstein rode south to report to his master. He knew that he, like Charles at

Znaim, had overstepped his remit and he correctly anticipated that his decision would generate new outrage at court. Alighting from his carriage upon his return, he told Metternich: 'I bring peace but also my head; the Kaiser will dispose of the one as well as the other as he wishes.'[71] Franz was indeed shocked by the terms of the treaty: among other indignities, Austria's population was reduced by more than 3.5 million subjects, it lost its access to the sea, its army was limited to 150,000 men, and it was burdened with an indemnity of 85 million gulden. 'The conditions it imposes on us', Metternich wrote shortly afterwards, 'are such as to leave in Austria a long and dolorous memory of the struggle that has just ended.'[72] Nonetheless, Franz had little choice but to ratify the treaty with minimal delay.

Throughout the period of the armistice, Bubna's efforts, and later Liechtenstein's, were hobbled by the 'uncertainty, helplessness and anarchy' that characterised the consideration of strategy in Totis.[73] As in the months prior to the conflict, so now at its ending, the war faction at court fulminated against France and demanded military action, but the military instrument of policy was incapable of meeting the demands placed upon it. There was no national strategy, no operations plan and, with Charles out of the picture, no true army commander, certainly none qualified to take the field against Napoleon. Though men like Stadion were relieved to be rid of 'the archduke who made great mistakes in the recent war', there was no one to take his place.[74]

Liechtenstein, supposedly the senior general, seems to have believed that his responsibilities would only begin if hostilities resumed.[75] Even Bubna, a close friend of Liechtenstein's, opined that 'it would be an absurdity' to believe that Liechtenstein 'was capable of commanding an army, above all against a general such as Bonaparte'.[76] Moreover, he soon became the central figure in the peace negotiations at the enemy's headquarters, hardly the place for the designated commander of a major field army.

Nominally, Franz had taken command into his own hands in mid-July, but he soon decided that he could not address all the details of supreme command because he was 'over-taxed with many other affairs of state'.[77] Command, such as it was, thus devolved upon a committee with indecisive meetings and debates, all confounded by endless interruptions and intrigues as other would-be advisers, qualified or not, endeavoured to have their grand operations plan placed into the Kaiser's hands or attempted to issue instructions in his name. Radetzky, brought in (very much against his will) to replace Wimpffen as army chief of staff, was in near despair. 'A command of this nature was an impossibility,' he wrote later, 'and I was convinced with all these gentlemen that a continuation of the war in December was infeasible.'[78] Retired, superannuated and disgraced generals were temporarily rehabilitated or offered advice on their own initiatives and even Stadion was recalled from Prague.[79] 'No centre, no unity, how can this work?' asked a frustrated Archduke Joseph on 22 August: 'Instead of acting, the Kaiser goes almost daily to watch the exercises of the Insurrection infantry.' He remained disconsolate a month later as he lamented 'our dreadful military position, our weakened army, [and] even though the Kaiser has been inclined towards war up till now, no preparations, dispositions, march plans drafted, nothing settled for the situation [of war], rather all is just talk'.[80]

Even had a plan been developed and issued, the army was in a poor state of readiness. Logistical shortfalls hampered efforts to re-equip or even feed battered regiments, morale was questionable, sickness was rampant in poorly managed encampments (more than 50,000 out of 180,000 men were ill from 'Hungarian fever' in early September), and the majority of senior officers wanted a rapid end to hostilities.[81] Indeed, the desire for peace was widespread and growing. Asked for his opinion, for example, Bellegarde in late August told Metternich (after an excursion through a garden of flowery circumlocutions) that 'In the extreme crisis in which the monarchy finds itself, I regard a mediocre peace as a benefit.' He wanted to maintain the 'honour and existence of the state', but battle 'depends too much on chance' and he was 'intimately persuaded' that 'peace is desirable'.[82]

The army, though fundamental as Charles had consistently argued, was not Austria's only challenge as it weighed its options in the waning days of summer. Among the monarchy's pre-eminent problems were its fragile financial situation and its international isolation. All the feeble and disjointed attempts at rebellion in Germany had failed and there were no foreign allies to call upon for succour. Russia held itself aloof, Britain's Walcheren expedition had stagnated and its forces were in retreat in

Spain following the Battle of Talavera (28 July). For a time, Prussia represented a potential bright spot on this otherwise bleak horizon. Oberst Karl Friedrich von dem Knesebeck, a personal representative from King Friedrich Wilhelm III, arrived in Totis with plenipotentiary powers to pledge active Prussian military support if Austria truly seemed committed to war and if he judged the Austrian army fit to oppose the French under Napoleon. Knesebeck and the Prussian ambassador gradually concluded that neither of these conditions applied. The Habsburg hierarchy was in chaos over the issue of war or peace and was, in any case, incapable of using its large and courageous army to advantage. Prussia would not join the war. Austria remained alone.

The uncertainty about allies contributed to the absence of comprehensive war plans. Radetzky did eventually draft two, but did not seem especially confident in either. Lack of clear war aims at this stage was another gap. Having begun the war with unrealistic intentions that were as vague as they were grandiose, Austria once again found itself in a strategic wilderness. Some advocates of war still imagined recovering the pre-1805 borders, others hoped to at least return to what the monarchy had controlled at the start of the conflict, still others called for renewing hostilities with no greater notion than 'perishing with arms in hand' or, as Friedrich von Gentz, one most incisive observers in Totis, termed it: 'the phantom of a glorious end'.[83] Those promoting peace, on the other hand, perceived only ruin should the war resume. Their aim in the conflict was to end it.

At the top of the policy pyramid was Franz, but the Kaiser himself was an impediment to sober assessment, consequential decision-making and determined implementation. Continually vacillating, Franz was prone to adopting the opinions of the last person he saw ('You cannot count on that man for a quarter of an hour,' exclaimed Stadion privately[84]) and shifted unpredictably from bold bellicosity to dull resignation.[85] He issued a defiant war manifesto on 16 August just before the Altenburg exchange was to open and made clear that he did not want to give over an inch of territory or pay a florin in compensation to the reviled Napoleon.[86] Giving his ear to a small body of pro-war confidants who continued to 'shout for war', he grasped at illusions: 'The Kaiser, who still relies on landings, uprisings, etc. despite his experiences, secretly wants war,' wrote Joseph.[87] All this in circumstances where the enemy occupied a third of his state, where he had no allies and where his army was only slowly recovering from the manifold trials and losses it had endured since April. Incapable of providing the leadership his complex empire required in this difficult hour, this was the missing 'centre' that caused Joseph and others to despair. As the days of summer slipped away into autumn and the long list of painful realities became unavoidable, the advocates of peace began to gain the upper hand in Totis, but it still took Liechtenstein's dramatic act in Schönbrunn to present Franz with a *fait accompli* and bring about a finalised treaty.

The situation in Schönbrunn was completely different. As Napoleon combined military and diplomatic functions in one person, he closely managed the negotiations while simultaneously rebuilding his army. On the military side, he was in a comfortable central position from a strategic perspective and was busily applying his customary energy to strengthening and training his forces. More than 43,000 replacements and reinforcements were already en route as the armies moved to their armistice locations and by 1 September he had more than 227,000 present under arms in Austria with another 75,000 in Germany and around the Tyrol.[88] As he told Bubna on 20 September:

> Kaiser Franz should ask his marshals and generals if it is possible to dislodge me from here. People who push the pen do not understand this; not in four campaigns would Austria be able to remove me from his lands. You will lose another fourteen days and still have to agree to my conditions; you cannot ignore the danger.[89]

On the political front, he used his knowledge of the confusion and indecision in Franz's court and his sense of Austrian military capabilities to calibrate his peace demands as he refined them during the course of the armistice period. For practical political and strategic reasons, it was essential that he maintain his aura of military predominance on the continent, so the terms imposed on Austria in 1809 must be at least equal to those of 1805. If he could gain something more, so much the better. He also harboured a personal desire to punish Austria for what he considered the Kaiser's repeated attacks on his and France's interests. At the same time, there were dangers to be avoided and opportunities to exploit if he limited his demands. A key concern was Russia's reaction. He was keenly aware of the tsar's views on Austria and that pushing it too far could lead to an utterly unwanted war with Russia. 'The destruction of that monarchy would be a calamity for Europe ... as well as a misfortune for our alliance,' Alexander had told Napoleon's ambassador in April. Austria 'deserved a vigorous lesson ... but it must not be destroyed'.[90] The situation, however, also presented opportunities. As Maret had highlighted in the tent on the battlefield at Znaim, some French and Austrian interests were compatible and a reduced but still intact Habsburg monarchy could be beneficial in the future. The threats of breaking up the empire or of replacing Franz with a more amenable Habsburg such as Großherzog Ferdinand of Würzburg were just that: threats. Although he may have flirted with such notions at the beginning of the war, by the time he reached Znaim and during the weeks of the armistice, mention of such drastic outcomes was simply a useful tool to speed Austrian acceptance of his other and, in comparison, lesser terms.[91] In his mind, the Treaty of Schönbrunn 'was the most advantageous peace they could hope to achieve'.[92] He thereby preserved Austria, albeit diminished, as a potential future ally and opened the way for an alliance of a different sort with the House of Habsburg through marriage to Kaiser Franz's daughter Marie Louise.

The Battle of Znaim and the ensuing armistice began the process that led to the end of the war and the culminating Treaty of Schönbrunn of 14 October. That document cost Austria 110,000 square kilometres of territory containing some 3.5 million inhabitants and imposed a heavy financial indemnity (albeit insufficient to cover Napoleon's expenses in the war). The old empire not only lost its access to the sea, but also agreed to join Napoleon's continental blockade against Great Britain and to grant formal recognition to Joachim Murat as King of Naples and Joseph Bonaparte as King of Spain. As guerdon for its hesitant but consequential involvement in the conflict, Russia received part of Austrian Galicia with a population of 400,000 (which the tsar deemed insufficient recompense). By early January, French troops had evacuated occupied Habsburg territory and, consistent with Metternich's new policy of alignment with France, Napoleon and Marie Louise were married by proxy in Vienna on

11 March that year, with Archduke Charles serving as Napoleon's stand-in during the ceremony. Additional rituals ensued when the new bride arrived in Paris and Napoleon II was born the following year, seeming to secure Napoleon's imperial dynasty. The Franco-Austrian affiliation culminated in a formal alliance signed on 14 March 1812 by Maret, Napoleon's new foreign minister, and Schwarzenberg, now the Austrian ambassador to France.[93] This treaty resulted in Austria contributing an auxiliary corps to the invasion of Russia three months later. Commanded by Schwarzenberg, it would thus participate in a war in part caused by Franco-Russian frictions over the fate of Poland in 1809.

Epilogue

THE PURSUIT AFTER WAGRAM and the Battle of Znaim left strong impressions on those who fought there. On the French side, one of those accompanying the army through Wagram, the pursuit and Znaim, was GB Louis Bertrand Pierre Brun de Villeret who was delivering dispatches from Marshal Soult in Spain. From his unique vantage point, Brun observed that,

> The Archduke Charles was able to make an honourable retreat ... but his troops were demoralised, his rearguards did not hold and every day after the battle [of Wagram] he suffered great losses. He thus arrived at Znaim where the activity of our marches forced him to deploy for battle. We attacked with vigour and the *coup de grâce* probably would have been given to his army if his emperor had not asked for peace and if an armistice had not been signed when the armies were most engaged.

The view from the other side was rather different. For Hohenzollern, 'The retreat without the loss of a single cannon, with exhausted troops, in the presence of an enemy who pursued relentlessly, over many days, [and] in the best order, will shine just as brightly in the annals of Austria as the battles on the 10th and 11th at Znaim that turned out to our advantage and moved Napoleon to the armistice.' Hohenzollern saw the Hauptarmee passing over a river and through a difficult defile under fire, fighting its way into its positions, and holding on for two days 'against superior numbers and Napoleon'. He thus proudly asserted that 'only firm determination to conquer or die, loyalty to the commander, the fatherland and the monarchy' could evoke 'such deeds of heroism'. The Bavarians and Badeners were equally proud of their actions in this part of the war, but they also remembered more prosaic aspects: 'What made this bloody and extremely arduous day even more difficult', recorded the Baden brigade in its war diary for 11 July, 'was a dreadful rainstorm ... that crashed down from the sky in streams, soaked the previously overheated men to the skin and rendered their muskets useless.' Bavarian Leutnant Schaller, welcoming the end of the fighting, passed through Klein-Tesswitz and over the Thaya bridge by Altschallersdorf with the rest of the 2nd Division on 13 July: 'For the last time here we had to recall the horrors of the previous days. The vineyards, the roads, the bridge were covered with dead from whose frightful appearance one's eye recoiled. I will leave undrawn the curtain that covered this scene, as the sight behind it would offend humanity and fill the heart with revulsion and dread'.[1]

Looking back with the perspective of 210 years from July 2019, we can examine the pursuit and the battle through a number of analytic lenses. From the strictly military standpoint, several aspects of the days after Wagram are notable. The Austrian retreat, for instance, is broadly and correctly acknowledged – not least by the French pursuers as we have seen – as having been conducted in good order under the protection of rearguards that were both tenacious and skilful in almost all cases. At the same time, Charles deprived himself of troops and options through his excessive concern for defending everything rather than concentrating for what was likely to be another major battle. Not keeping Schustekh closer to at least cause the French concerns about their western flank was a minor issue, but detaching Rosenberg with his entire corps to the protection of Brünn and Olmütz was significant. The danger was compounded by sending only Altstern's tiny 'brigade' to protect the Thaya crossings at Laa. These two decisions sent some 14,000 to 15,000 men of IV Corps off on a secondary mission and created a vulnerability on the Hauptarmee's left flank. His planned occupation of the 'position' at Jetzelsdorf was thus undone before it could be attempted and the way was open for Marmont to threaten the Austrian line of retreat. Although some contemporary Austrian commentators would claim that the retreat was too slow,[2] the principal problem with the Austrian withdrawal of

7–9 July was Charles's single-minded focus on placing his army in the Jetzelsdorf position. Intent on his plan, he does not seem to have even considered counterattacking to exploit the relative isolation of the two French pursuit forces. Massena was particularly vulnerable, but French audacity and Austrian caution meant that he and Marmont could exploit what a later commentator called 'the temerity of victory' to maintain constant pressure on the retreating white-coats.[3] Charles reacted with the speed and decision the situation demanded on the night of 9/10 July in sending the Reserve Corps to block Marmont's approach to Znaim, but the general sense of caution and anxiety remained intact. Hohenzollern's timorous behaviour on the 10th has been discussed above and there is no indication of anyone in the Hauptarmee's headquarters contemplating a serious attack to turn the tables on the brash Marmont that day.

A theme throughout these four days of the retreat is the Austrian overestimation of the enemy. There is no indication that Charles and his commanders considered that their pursuers might be just as tired, just as hungry, just as oppressed by the heat as their own troops were. Although they were operating in their own country, they seem to have had only vague notions of French strength and dispositions. The persistent belief that Davout rather than Marmont was advancing from Laa on 10 July is only the most prominent of several examples of misreading the enemy. Overwhelmed with their own woes and overawed by the vigorous activity of the impetuous French and Germans, Charles and his officers remained locked in their preconceptions of French numerical superiority, especially in cavalry. Unlike Marmont, who eagerly reported that the enemy's night marches and losses on the 10th would make his adversaries vulnerable to attack on the 11th, the Austrians were so absorbed in their own seemingly insurmountable challenges that they overlooked their opportunities.

The most serious error on the French side during the pursuit was losing touch with their foe on the afternoon of Wagram and into the night of 6/7 July. This resulted in the uncertainty about the direction or directions of the Austrian retreat that delayed the initiation of an earnest pursuit for one or two critical days. This delay, of course, meant that Davout, Oudinot, Molitor and the Guard could not arrive in time to participate in a potentially decisive battle on 11 July, but it is hard to see how Napoleon could have acted otherwise once the initial loss of contact had occurred.

Several aspects of his situation are worth considering. First, is the context. Napoleon had staked everything on Wagram being another Austerlitz or Jena, he had thus stripped his rear areas and concentrated every possible soldier at the vital point. When the shattering triumph he had expected did not eventuate, the exertions preceding and during the great battle left his army almost as disorganised and exhausted in victory as the Hauptarmee was in defeat.[4] The 'freshest' troops he had at hand were the 2nd Bavarian Division and Marmont's small Army of Dalmatia, each of which had marched more than 200 km over the previous several days to arrive on 6 July. Some time was needed to rest, reorder and resupply. Moreover, the enemy was not broken as the Prussians had been after Jena–Auerstedt, so a wild, hurtling cavalry pursuit was not possible that night or the next day. Nor could Napoleon leave his rear unprotected as he went in search of Charles. Although he was certainly misled by his overestimation of Johann's force, he would have had to protect his rear areas, especially Vienna, under any circumstances. Second, the information he had on the enemy did not permit him to commit to one route of pursuit at first. Early reports suggested that Charles might be retreating towards the March River (i.e. Hungary), towards Brünn, towards Znaim or in several of these directions. It was soon apparent that the Austrians were not heading for Hungary, but he could not order the bulk of his army to one avenue until he had more definitive information on the enemy. This situation only clarified on the night of 9/10 July. In the meantime, he trusted that 'the temerity of victory' and the qualitative advantages his forces enjoyed would allow them to confront the cautious and methodical Austrians even though his subordinates were operating beyond immediate supporting distance of his reserve at Wolkersdorf. Third, the absence of major force movements on 7 July does not mean that the Armée d'Allemagne was inactive. The patrolling and pursuit initiated that day, albeit limited, set in motion the process by which the enemy was located and the true pursuit could be launched.

This concatenation of considerations helps explain why Napoleon acted as he did between 7 and 9 July. The key point, however, is that the 12–24 hours lost in this period, whether avoidable or unavoidable, were lost irretrievably. The consequence of those lost hours was his inability to deliver a crushing blow at Znaim on 11 July and therefore the need to contemplate an armistice instead of continued war.

The ensuing battle on 10 and 11 July is an illustrative example of the two armies in a meeting engagement. For the Austrians this was a decidedly uncomfortable situation. The Habsburg commanders preferred battles where they could prepare in advance, issue detailed dispositions and carefully place their troops on the ground in advantageous positions before the enemy attacked. The Hauptarmee had fared poorly in the unplanned encounters south of Regensburg in April and no one had any desire to repeat those very fresh and humiliating experiences. Likewise, the broken terrain with its ravines and vineyards did not favour the Austrians when compared with the 'superior agility' of the French and their German allies.[5] The only advantage at Znaim was that the compressed battlefield and relative lack of forestation allowed Charles and his subordinates visibility over the fighting, something that had been largely absent in the earlier battles in Bavaria. The one area where their vision was blocked, however, was the Burgholz and the possibility of the French massing large forces in that wood on their left coincided with Austrian anxieties about the vulnerability of their line of retreat to Iglau.

The nature of the field and the unexpectedness of the encounter, combined with Charles's innate caution and his mistrust of his army as an offensive instrument, led him to conduct the battle in a strictly defensive manner. He thus missed a chance to hand Marmont a sharp rebuff on 10 July and gave no thought to ruining Legrand's isolated and outnumbered division the following day. In contrast, none of the French commanders was nonplussed by dealing with an unplanned engagement. Marmont on the first day and Napoleon on the second treated the battle as a means to hold the Austrians in place. They limited themselves to pinning attacks and manoeuvres that would 'impose on' or intimidate their opponents, conveying an impression of being stronger on the field than they actually were. Only Massena launched an all-out attack, and one that was surprisingly effective.

Almost all contemporary Austrian interpretations of the battle, however, were founded on the erroneous assumption that the Hauptarmee was overwhelmingly outnumbered. Many subsequent Austrian analyses presented the same skewed picture. Without in any way denigrating the stoic endurance of the Habsburg soldiery or the skill of some junior leaders, the threat posed by Marmont on 10 July was hardly sufficient to prevent the Hauptarmee's crossing of the Thaya even if some units had to shove their way through the jam of their own vehicles on the bridges or ford the river under fire from the Bavarian guns on the heights above Klein-Tesswitz. Likewise, Marmont's attacks on 11 July were not intended to break through to Znaim, but to preclude further Austrian withdrawal so French reinforcements could arrive. A breakthrough of some sort would have been most welcome, but there is no indication that anyone on the French side expected such a happy outcome. If we return to the comments from Hohenzollern and Brun at the opening of this section, then we may conclude that Hohenzollern, while justly proud of the steadfastness his men displayed, was fundamentally mistaken in his view of the severity of the test to which they were subjected. Brun, on the other hand, was correct: 'The *coup de grâce* probably would have been given to his army ... if an armistice had not been signed.'

Doubtless contributing to these later Austrian assessments was the remarkable success Massena had south of Znaim, where his numerically inferior command levered Reuss out of a strong defensive position and almost forced its way into the town. Legrand's lone division made such an impression that Charles had to send two grenadier brigades to support Reuss. The *Leiningen* Grenadiers certainly conducted a bold and effective counterattack in the rainstorm, but with support from Carra St Cyr, Legrand's regiments recovered with surprising speed and returned to the attack. Even the arrival of Carra St Cyr's division did not give Massena a numerical advantage, yet Reuss found himself hard-pressed until the moment of the ceasefire.

This combat south of Znaim and similar situations throughout the 1809 war suggest the need for nuance in evaluating the qualities of the French army that year. That is, while the men in the ranks may not have been 'the soldiers of Austerlitz', they were not all raw recruits incapable of manoeuvre or tactical flexibility. Colonel Gueheneuc of the 26th Léger, for instance, was deeply concerned that the new soldiers that year did not measure up to their predecessors, yet he offered a trenchant observation on the fighting at Znaim. 'The enemy, despite his superior numbers and the advantages of his fine position, was pushed back at all points until the white flag was raised,' he wrote, 'This was the last feat of arms in this short and brilliant campaign.'[6]

Moving beyond the tactical battlefield to the strategic plane, one of the most overlooked dimensions of the 1809 war is the military significance of Russia's involvement. Russia's political importance is broadly acknowledged, but the Russian military role is treated as an afterthought in most accounts. Yet the presence of a Russian army in Galicia was a central element in how both sides assessed the strategic situation, especially after Wagram as the campaign shifted east of the Danube and a genuine threat to Olmütz developed. Howsoever disappointing to Napoleon, the tsar's regiments and, to a lesser degree what the Austrians termed the Polish 'insurgents', represented an abiding anxiety for the Habsburg leadership from Franz to Stadion and the array of archdukes. The military and diplomatic correspondence of the time and the subsequent commentaries are replete with references to the fear that Russian and French forces might unite and collaborate to trap the Hauptarmee or to seize Olmütz and thereby split the monarchy in two. A subordinate, though no less real, worry was that the Russians might enter Hungary, diverting Insurrection troops and endangering the empire's integrity.

Napoleon would have been bitterly amused by these Habsburg fears. As we have noted, he was deeply frustrated by what he perceived as the tsar's failure to abide by the terms of the Erfurt accord and angered by the undisguised pro-Austrian sentiments of the Russian officer corps. Despite his irritation, he skilfully used the Russian threat in the armistice period to help force Austrian concessions and he may have held out some hope that the Russian army would become actively engaged on his side should hostilities resume. In the main, however, the half-hearted Russian performance in the war instilled in him a sense of having been duped or betrayed. This assessment would inform his interactions with Tsar Alexander during the armistice, influencing his views on the amount of Galician territory Russia and the Duchy of Warsaw (in effect Poland) would each receive in the peace settlement and thus contributing to the decline in Franco-Russian relations beyond 1809.

The capture of Krakow by the Russians and Poles was also a factor in Charles's calculations regarding the ceasefire and armistice, reinforcing his conviction that the war was irredeemably lost and that his army, the sole support of the state, was in danger of annihilation. Where some members of the Habsburg leadership were willing to engage in histrionics about 'perishing with arms in hand' as Stadion and others pronounced, Charles was not. He feared that acting upon such sentiments would drag the empire and the dynasty to destruction. This had been his objection as far back as 1808. The war party had launched the monarchy into a war with an unprovoked offensive but with weak military–political co-ordination and aims that can only be described as grandiose, vague and open-ended. They thereby encountered, albeit unknowingly, what Christopher Duffy calls 'the central problem' in Austrian planning: 'how to implement an offensive grand strategy without hazarding the army'.[7] Charles had resignedly acquiesced to the offensive concept in February 1809, but his own view of the monarchy's war aims had diverged from the notions entertained at his brother's court after the first defeats in Bavaria. With the army having recovered and having secured a defensive success at Aspern-Essling, he had promoted a peace policy through May and June. This failed in the face of adamantine opposition from Stadion and others around the Kaiser. In the process, Charles only further sullied his reputation in the eyes of many of his brother's closest advisors.

At Znaim, with the army facing what he believed to be certain destruction (whether then and there or later was irrelevant), and with his special authority as Generalissimus on the verge of vanishing, he acted on what he fervently believed to be the state's and the family's best interests. He never itemised any specific goals for the war before embarking upon it, but he had certainly modified them, whatever they were, after April. The aim of the war in his mind was now the preservation of the state, threatened as it was by a powerful enemy who seemed capable of anything, even the imminent dissolution of the monarchy. In avoiding another Austerlitz and achieving the armistice, its harsh terms notwithstanding, Charles had therefore saved the army and thereby saved the state. In effect, he accomplished his own revised version of the monarchy's war aims.

The archduke's enemies at court, of course, saw him as weak, incompetent and excessively pessimistic. They too recognised the importance of the army, but they could not formulate a set of war aims or a political–military strategy commensurate with the army's strengths and weaknesses. Radetzky's rueful remarks about the failure to align means and ends at the beginning of the war thus applied at the end as well. As Bubna's friend Gentz wrote to him on 8 October, 'the monarchy exists in the army'. Renewed hostilities would not be a case of Austria having a chance for a once-and-for-all victory, rather the best that could be hoped for was 'a victory that decides nothing'. In other words, he was convinced that Austria would be risking 'everything for a precarious and secondary gain'.[8] Nonetheless, some of the most influential voices at Komorn and later Totis were willing to put the entire state in jeopardy by hazarding the army in a renewed contest with Napoleon. Fortunately for Franz, a second act of desperate defiance of his wishes, that by Liechtenstein in Vienna, brought peace and an end to these potentially fatal delusions. Thus none of the lofty, ill-defined goals imagined by the war party when they set the monarchy on the path to confrontation with Napoleon were achieved. The most that could be claimed was that the Habsburg state had survived. With Metternich now at the helm and a policy of accommodation with France in place, a much-reduced Austria would persevere in the hopes that Napoleon's domination would collapse of its own weight and afford in that moment an opportunity for the House of Habsburg to redress the reverses of the past twenty years.

Unlike his opponents, Napoleon, as the victim of aggression in this case, did not have 'war aims' per se when the Austrians attacked. As he told his confidants later: 'This war had no purpose, it was the Austrians who declared war on me.'[9] Indeed, his chief aim before April was to avert hostilities entirely. He found it incredible that Vienna would actually launch a war in 1809 given its frailties and the larger political–military environment in central Europe that spring. Nonetheless, he certainly considered the idea of what might eventuate should this unlikely conflict occur. Some of his words were clearly efforts to deter Austria by outlining dire consequences should it take the road to war. References to the House of Habsburg 'ceasing to reign' in correspondence with his brothers and with Rheinbund sovereigns, on the other hand, indicate he was at least considering such radical action in the event of war, but none of this is to suggest that Napoleon marched into Austria that April with a fixed set of goals in mind. Rather, from its beginning in April to its end in July,

Napoleon's main aim in this unwanted war was its rapid ending. That ending, however, had to include punishments no less severe than those codified after Austerlitz in the 1805 Treaty of Pressburg. Regardless of the future of the House of Habsburg, his primary goals thus remained two: a swift ending to the war and the imposition of terms equivalent to Pressburg. By the time he reached Znaim on 11 July, he determined that he could achieve both of these. The moment was thus propitious for an armistice. He could accept the continued existence of an undeniably defeated Austrian empire with Kaiser Franz on its throne to avoid the military risk of dragging his fatigued troops on an endless chase into Bohemia and to minimise problems with the tsar on the political front. The terms Berthier and Wimpffen signed that night on the battlefield provided this satisfactory outcome, an end to hostilities and the public confirmation that Wagram was no less a victory than Austerlitz. What he saw as clemency to the Habsburgs was a small sacrifice for these larger goals.

For Napoleon, the period of the armistice was simply a time of hoping to avoid further fighting (but preparing for its possible outbreak), while using every tool available to compel concessions from his adversary. Among other measures, he threatened to replace Austria's currency with his own and to 'revolutionise' the social system in the French-occupied regions by abolishing old feudal structures. He also continued to raise the possibility of dividing the monarchy or installing Großherzog Ferdinand on the Habsburg throne.[10] How serious was he at this point? Although he likely would have accepted an abdication by Franz in favour of Ferdinand had it been sincerely proposed and pursued by the Austrian side, this course of action was so improbable as to be imaginary and he was certainly not going to renew the war to achieve such an outcome. As noted earlier, these threats during the months of the armistice primarily served as powerful means to pressure the Habsburg court. In exile on St Helena, he several times expressed regret at not imposing harsher terms: 'I committed a great fault after the Battle of Wagram in not reducing the power of Austria still more.'[11] In 1809, however, his principal purpose in suggesting these drastic options was to speed the negotiations and make his other demands seem mild and tolerable by comparison.

Though he grew impatient with the long delay at Altenburg and with the extended discussions between Champagny and Liechtenstein in

Vienna, in the end Napoleon's persistence was rewarded with the Treaty of Schönbrunn. Reporting to his emperor on the morning of 14 October, Champagny recalled that Napoleon approached 'with an air of concern':

> 'Well, monsieur', asked Napoleon 'what have you done this night?'
> 'The peace, sire.'
> 'What, the peace! And the treaty is signed?'
> 'Yes, sire, here it is.'
> His face brightened; he frankly expressed his satisfaction.[12]

Well might he have been satisfied. Whatever the deficiencies of his Armée d'Allemagne, whatever the incipient corrosion of his own skills, only three months had been required for his mastery of the operational art, his skilful diplomacy and the hard fighting and marching of his troops to inflict another defeat on the Habsburgs and place him on the heights opposite Znaim in a position to eradicate the principal Austrian army.[13] He elected not to do so. While Austria entered a period of biding its time in murmuring discontent, Wagram and Znaim had granted Napoleon new opportunities and soon a new family.[14] What remained to be seen was how he would use the time thus afforded.

Endnotes

Chapter 1: A Minister, an Archduke and an Emperor

1. The term '1809 war' is used here rather than '1809 campaign' to comport with modern U.S. and NATO terminology. The *war* in 1809 thus consisted of multiple, sometimes overlapping, *campaigns*.
2. Criste, *Erzherzog Karl und die Armee*, Vienna: Stern, 1906, p. 30.
3. Thomas Nipperdey, *Deutsche Geschichte 1800–1866*, Munich: Beck 1983, p. 23. Stadion's repugnance for Napoleon's hegemony in Germany in general and the Rheinbund in particular was doubtless further inflamed when newly crowned King Friedrich of Württemberg appropriated the income from the Stadion estate in Württemberg in 1806 (Hellmuth Rössler, *Graf Johann Philipp Stadion: Napoleons deutscher Gegenspieler*, Vienna: Herold, 1966, vol. I, pp. 281–2; August von Schloßberger, 'Aus der Zeit des französisch-österreichischen Krieges im Jahre 1809', *Besondere Beilage des Staats-Anzeigers für Württemberg*, 13 July 1887).
4. Walter Consuelo Langsam, 'Count Stadion and Archduke Charles', *Journal of Central European Affairs*, vol. VI, no. 2, July 1946, p. 147; also Franz Krones, *Geschichte der Neuzeit Oesterreichs*, Berlin: Hofmann, 1879, p. 513.
5. Adolf Beer, *Zehn Jahre österreichischer Politik*, Leipzig: Brockhaus, 1877, pp. 277–8.
6. Charles, *Ausgewählte Schriften weiland seiner kaiserlichen Hoheit Erzherzog Carl von Oesterreich*, Archdukes Albert and Wilhelm, eds., Vienna: Braumüller, 1894, vol. VI, pp. 328–9.
7. Gunther E. Rothenberg, *Napoleon's Great Adversaries: The Archduke Charles and the Austrian Army 1792–1814*, Bloomington: Indiana University Press, 1982, pp. 104–5.
8. Manfried Rauchensteiner, *Kaiser Franz und Erzherzog Carl: Dynastie und Heerwesen in Österreich 1796–1809*, Vienna: Verlag für Geschichte und Politik, 1972, p. 83.
9. Charles, *Ausgewählte Schriften*, 'Meinungsäusserung des Erzherzogs Carl über die gegenüber Frankreich und Russland einzunehmende Haltung', 29 April 1806, vol. VI, p. 202.
10. In a 27 March 1807 memorandum, for example, he wrote 'We will be able, so to speak, to calculate the actual day of our destruction' should the fortunes of war further expand French power vis-à-vis Austria; similarly, on 24 October 1807 he described Austria as

'the most exposed power' in Europe having to 'exert all of its strength ... just to secure its existence' (in Beer, *Zehn Jahre*, p. 279 and p. 300).
11. 'Siegt Napoleon, so wird es zweifelhaft, was noch künftig Österreich heisse!' from 'Gutachten über Stadion's Mémoire vom 27. März 1807', 29 March 1807, in Charles, *Ausgewählte Schriften*, vol. VI, p. 242.
12. Stadion memorandum cited in Rössler, *Stadion*, vol. I, p. 275. In effort to influence the archduke's thinking, Stadion attempted to have one of his protégés, Oberstleutnant Joseph von Stutterheim, appointed as Charles's adjutant as early as 1806 (ibid., p. 266).
13. Beer, *Zehn Jahre*, pp. 292–3. Kaiser Franz likewise viewed a peace without Austria's involvement as 'the most unhappy outcome for us' (response to a 3 July 1807 Stadion memorandum); Charles also feared a separate agreement among the warring parties, see Eduard Wertheimer, *Geschichte Österreichs und Ungarns im ersten Jahrzehnt des 19. Jahrhunderts*, Leipzig: Brockhaus, 1890, vol. II, pp. 177–9.
14. Stadion memoranda of 13 & 15 April 1808 in Rössler, *Österreichs Kampf*, vol. I, pp. 304–5.
15. Oskar Criste, *Erzherzog Carl von Oesterreich: Ein Lebensbild*, vol. II, p. 436.
16. Rothenberg, *Great Adversaries*, p. 121.
17. Stadion memorandum of 13 April 1808 in Rössler, *Österreichs Kampf*, vol. I, p. 304.
18. The litany of early French reverses in Iberia could be expanded with events such as the capture of the French naval squadron at Cadiz (14 June) and the repulse at Roses (or Rosas, 11 July); the French victory at Medina de Rióseco on 14 July could not counterbalance these blows. Good starting points for the complex war in Spain and Portugal are Nick Lipscombe, *The Peninsular War Atlas*, revised edition, Oxford: Osprey, 2014; and Charles Esdaile, *The Peninsular War*, London: Allen Lane, 2002.
19. Paul Balagny, *Campagne de l'Empereur Napoléon en Espagne*, Paris: Berger-Levrault, 1902, vol. I, p. 11.
20. Napoleon to Clarke, 5 August 1808 and 16 August 1808, Napoleon I, *Correspondance Générale* [hereafter CG], Paris: Fayard, 2011, nos. 18,689 and 18,702, vol. VIII, pp. 949, 955.
21. Stadion memorandum of 25 August 1808 in Rössler, *Österreichs Kampf*, vol. I, p. 315.
22. Stadion to Metternich, 31 August 1808, in ibid., vol. I, p. 376.
23. Stadion to Metternich, 8 August 1808, in ibid., vol. I, p. 373.
24. Former Hanoverian minister Ernst Christian Georg August von Hardenberg in Vienna relating a conversation with Stadion to Ernst Friedrich Herbert zu Münster in London, 8 October 1808, in Paul Hassel, *Geschichte der Preussischen Politik 1807 bis 1815*, Leipzig: Hirzel, 1881, pp. 537–8.
25. Hardenberg to Münster, 11 October 1808, in ibid., pp. 538–9.
26. Stadion to Feldmarschall-Leutnant Philipp Grünne (Charles's adjutant-general), 27 September 1808, in Rössler, *Österreichs Kampf*, vol. I, p. 373.
27. Stadion memorandum of 12 October 1808, in ibid, vol. I, p. 393.
28. Charles Joseph Prince de Ligne, *Fragments de l'Histoire de ma Vie*, Paris: Plon, 1928, vol. II, pp. 185, 170; emphasis in the original.
29. Beer, *Zehn Jahre*, p. 327. 'Reckless' used here for '*leichten Sinn*' or '*leichtsinnig*'.

30. Helmut Hertenberger and Franz Wilschek, *Erzherzog Karl*, Graz: Verlag Styria, 1983, pp. 205–6.
31. Charles to Johann, 16 July 1808, in *Krieg 1809*, Vienna: Seidel & Sohn, 1907, vol. I, pp. 55–6. In the period just before Prussia's 1806 defeat, young Prussian Guard officers had ostentatiously sharpened their sabres on the steps of the French embassy in Berlin.
32. 'Erwägungen für einen neuerlichen Krieg gegen Frankreich', 25 June 1808, in Charles, *Ausgewählte Schriften*, vol. VI, pp. 295–9. Comparisons between Austria and pre-Jena Prussia abounded during 1808–9, including in reports from the French embassy in Vienna, such as Andréossy, no. 54, 3 December 1808, and Dodun, no. 4, 11 March 1809, Archives du Ministère des Affaires Étrangères, Correspondence politique: Autriche [hereafter AE], vol. 382.
33. 'Vortrag an den Kaiser, ob ein Krieg gegen Frankreich im gegenwärtigen Momente zweckmässig wäre', undated, in Charles, *Ausgewählte Schriften*, vol. VI, pp. 300–3. The editors of Charles's writings thought this document was written sometime in January 1809, but, as Rössler cogently argues, it clearly comes from late September or, at the latest, mid-October 1808 (see Rössler, *Österreichs Kampf*, vol. II, p. 305, n. 178).
34. Stadion to Grünne, 29 September 1809, in Rössler, *Österreichs Kampf*, vol. II, p. 383.
35. Grünne to Stadion, 2 October 1809, in ibid., vol. II, p. 384.
36. '... vor diesem furchtbaren halben Willen', Stadion to Metternich, 8 and 31 August 1808, in ibid., vol. I, pp. 373, 376.
37. Karl Reichsgraf Finck von Finckenstein to King Friedrich Wilhelm III, 17 September 1808, in Hassel, *Preussischen Politik*, p. 524.
38. Charles, 'Ein Beitrag zur Geschichte des Krieges zwischen Österreich und Frankreich im Jahre 1809', *Ausgewählte Schriften*, vol. VI, p. 357.
39. Criste, *Carl*, vol. II, p. 470; Hertenberger/Wiltschek, *Karl*, p. 207.
40. Herzog Albert von Sachsen-Teschen, 'Mémoire sur la Guerre éclatée en 1809 entre l'Autriche et la France et sur les Evénements qui l'ont précédé et amené', Hungarian National Archives (Magyar Nemzeti Levéltár, hereafter MNL) P300/1/100. Charles's old military mentor, Carl Friedrich von Lindenau, concluded that 'The decision for war was seen as already made, so his objections had become utterly superfluous,' 'Ausweis über den Stand, die Eintheilung und Stellung der beiderseitigen Armeen im Jahr 1809', MNL, P300/1/98.
41. Charles, 'Denkschrift über die militärisch-politischen Verhältnisse Oesterreichs von 1801–1809', *Ausgewählte Schriften*, vol. VI, p. 329.
42. Johann, *Erzherzog Johanns 'Feldzugserzählung' 1809*, ed. Alois Veltzé, *Supplement zu den Mitteilungen des K. und K. Kriegsarchivs*, Vienna: Seidel & Sohn, 1909, p. 13.
43. Rössler's comment in *Österreichs Kampf*, vol. I, p. 306, n. 212.
44. Johann, 'Feldzugserzählung', p. 14.
45. Rothenberg, *Great Adversaries*, pp. 104–6.
46. See Rauchensteiner's *Kaiser Franz und Erzherzog Carl* and Rothenberg, *Great Adversaries*, pp. 55, 77, 104–6.

47. Carl to Albert, in Criste, *Carl*, vol. II, pp. 445–9. FML Karl Freiherr Mack von Leiberich became the principal military advisor to the Kaiser in 1804 and instituted a set of controversial army reforms (overturning those of Charles); as de facto commander of the Austrian invading forces in Bavaria in 1805, he was largely responsible for the debacle at Ulm that year.
48. Albert Eusebius von Wallenstein (1583–1634) had left a legacy of a powerful military leader of independent means, who was beyond the control of the reigning emperor and thus posed a challenge to the dynasty. See Johann Christoph Allmayer-Beck and Erich Lessing, *Das Heer unter dem Doppeladler: Habsburgs Armeen 1718–1848*, Munich: Bertelsmann, 1981, p. 184; Gunter E. Rothenberg, *The Army of Francis Joseph*, West Lafayette: Purdue University Press, 1976, p. 6; and Gordon A. Craig, 'Command and Staff Problems in the Austrian Army, 1740–1866', in his *War, Politics, and Diplomacy*, New York: Praeger, 1966.
49. Manfred Botzenhart, *Metternichs Pariser Botschafterzeit*, Münster: Aschendorff, 1967, pp. 262, 270–1.
50. Rössler, *Österreichs Kampf*, vol. I, p. 376 (paraphrasing a 27 September 1808 memorandum from Stadion).
51. Chargé Ivan O. Anstett to Count Alexander Saltykoff, 23 November 1808, in Fedor Martens, *Recueil des Traités et Conventions conclus par la Russie avec les Puissances Étrangères*, St Petersburg, 1876–1908, vol. III, p. 32.
52. 'Mémoire sur la Guerre éclatée en 1809', MNL, P300/1/100.
53. Article 10 of the 'Convention d'alliance' signed at Erfurt on 12 October 1808, in M. de Clercq, *Recueil des Traités de la France*, Paris: Amyot, 1864, vol. II, pp. 284–6.
54. Stadion, 22 October 1808 memorandum, quoted in Ernst D. Petritsch, 'Österreich und der Fürstenkongreß', in Rudolf Benl, ed., *Der Erfurter Fürstenkongreß 1808*, Erfurt: Stadtarchiv Erfurt, 2008, p. 230.
55. Alexander to Kurakin, 16 October 1808, *Vneshniaia Politika Rossii*, Moscow, 1965, vol. IV, pp. 364–5.
56. Alexander would soon worry that his courtesy was being misinterpreted as acquiescence but by then it was too late to change the impression he had created. See Gill, *Thunder*, vol. I, pp. 79–80.
57. 'Décret portant organization de l'armée du rhin', 12 October 1808, Napoleon I, *Correspondance de Napoléon Ier publiée par ordre de l'Empereur Napoléon III* [hereafter *CdN*], Paris: Imprimerie Impériale, 1858–70, no. 14,376, vol. XVII, pp. 549–54.
58. See Balagny, *Napoléon en Espagne*, vol. I, pp. 10–20.
59. Stadion had already proposed spring 1809 for the initiation of hostilities in his 27 September 1808 memorandum for the Kaiser.
60. Stadion, memorandum of 4 December 1808, Haus-, Hof- und Staatsarchiv [hereafter HHStA], Vorträge 1808/XII, 180.
61. Ibid.
62. 'Proclamation aux Espagnols', *CdN*, no. 14,537, vol. XVIII, pp. 103–4. For Austria's reaction, see Caulaincourt to Napoleon, 15 January 1809, in Grand Duke Nicholas Mikhaïlowitch

(ed.), *Les Relations Diplomatiques de la Russie et de la France d'aprés les Rapports des Ambassadeurs d'Alexandre et de Napoléon*, St Petersburg, 1905, vol. III, p. 25. The Prussian ambassador, Finckenstein, believed this proclamation finally pushed Charles into the war faction (Finckenstein's reports of 4 and 21 January 1809, cited in Udo Gaede, *Preussens Stellung zur Kriegsfrage im Jahre 1809*, Hanover: Hahn, 1897, pp. 25–6).
63. Charles to Stadion, 26 November 1808, in Rössler, *Österreichs Kampf*, vol. I, pp. 385, 397; and Stadion's 4 December memorandum, HHStA.
64. Metternich, 'Armée française. Guerre d'Espagne,' 4 December 1808, in Beer, *Zehn Jahre*, pp. 529–35. Granting excessive credence to malcontents in Paris, Metternich also contended that Napoleon was insecure at home, alienated from the French people and facing a cohesive political opposition that did not in fact exist in any meaningful form (Metternich, 'Mémoire', 4 December 1808, in ibid., pp. 516–25).
65. Botzenhart, *Metternichs Pariser Botschafterzeit*, pp. 250–1; Stadion's 4 December memorandum, HHStA.
66. Stadion, memorandum of 10 December 1808, in Beer, *Zehn Jahre*, p. 338.
67. Quotes from Stadion, 'Instructions données au Lieutenant Wagner lors de sa mission à Londres', 28 January 1809, in Wladyslaw de Fedorowicz, *1809: Campagne de Pologne*, Paris: Plon, 1911, vol. I, pp. 67–71; and Stadion, memorandum of 22 January 1809, in Rössler, *Oesterreichs Kampf*, vol. I, p. 533.
68. Undated and unsigned memorandum attributed to Philipp Stadion: 'Bemerkungen über den Marsch der Kays. Königl. Armeen nach Deutschland', quoted in Rössler, *Oesterreichs Kampf*, vol. I, pp. 503, 505.
69. 'Allgemeine Gesichtspunkt über die bevorstehenden Krieg in Beziehung auf Deutschland', attributed to Friedrich Stadion, in August Fournier, 'Oesterreichs Kriegsziele im Jahre 1809', *Beiträge zur neueren Geschichte Oesterreichs*, vol. IV, December 1908, p. 223.
70. Stadion, 'Instructions données au Lieutenant Wagner', Fedorowicz, *1809*, vol. I, pp. 69–70; Stadion's 4 December 1808 memorandum, HHStA; and Wagner's 12 March 1809 note to the British government (PRO/FO 7/90).
71. 'War of retribution', from a letter unofficial British envoy Charles Stuart sent to George Canning, 12 April 1809, no. 1 (PRO/FO 342/2).
72. As Enno E. Kraehe noted, the conclusion seems 'inescapable' that the Stadions were aiming to start 'a war to restore the Reich', see his *Metternich's German Policy*, Princeton: Princeton University Press, 1963, vol. I, p. 80.
73. See discussion in *Thunder on the Danube*, vol. I, pp. 44–9.
74. Rothenberg, *Great Adversaries*, p. 94.
75. Ibid. pp. 88–98.
76. Ibid., p. 95.
77. Stadion, memorandum of 22 January 1809, in Rössler, *Oesterreichs Kampf*, vol. I, p. 535.
78. For details on Stadion's attempts to engage allies, see *Thunder on the Danube*, vol. I. pp. 16–33.
79. Canning to Adair, 2 December 1808, PRO/FO 78/60.

80. Heinrich Zschokke, *Der Krieg Oesterreichs gegen Frankreich und den rheinischen Bund im Jahre 1809*, Aarau: Remigius, 1810, p. 29. Other contemporaries made similar observations; for example: Johann Gottfried von Pahl, a Württemberger writing under the pseudonym Alethinos, *Der Krieg in Deutschland im Jahre 1809 und dessen Resultate politisch und militärisch betrachtet*, Munich: Lentner, 1810, p. 131.
81. Carl von Clausewitz, *On War*, ed. and trans. Michael Howard and Peter Paret, Princeton: Princeton University Press, 1984, pp. 583–4.
82. Charles, 'Denkschrift', *Ausgewählte Schriften*, vol. VI, p. 326.
83. Radetzky to Liechtenstein, 1 December 1809, published as 'Ein Memoire Radetzky's, das Heerwesen Oesterreichs beleuchtend, aus dem Jahre 1809', *Mittheilungen des k. k. Kriegsarchivs*, vol. VIII (1884), p. 362ff.
84. Josef von Radetzky, 'Erinnerungen aus dem Leben des FM. Grafen Radetzky', *Mittheilungen des k. k. Kriegsarchivs*, new series I (1887), p. 64.
85. *Krieg 1809*, vol. I, pp. 178–9.
86. Mayer, 'Journal für das Jahr 809', Österreichisches Kriegsarchiv [KA], Militärische Nachlässe 857 (B).
87. Quote from a late March note to Johann, in 'Feldzugserzählungen', p. 36.
88. Stuart to Canning, 12 April 1809, no. 1 (PRO/FO 342/2). The observant but indiscreet Stuart (later Baron Stuart de Rothesay) arrived in Vienna on 6 April but, having journeyed to Austria 'without the authority or knowledge' of his government, Canning ordered him to return at once (Canning to Stuart, 13 May 1809, PRO/FO 342/2).
89. See his sarcastic comments in a lengthy memorandum prepared for the Kaiser on 3 March 1804 in Moritz Edlen von Angeli, *Erzherzog Carl von Oesterreich als Feldherr und Heeresorganisator*, Vienna: Braumüller, 1897, vol. III, pp. 213–16. In 1806, he had confidently predicted 'we can defeat the Russians' if the two came to blows (memorandum of 29 April 1806 in Criste, *Carl*, vol. II, p. 418).
90. Alexander to Rumiantsev, 14 February 1809, in *Vneshniaia Politika Rossii*, vol. IV, p. 493.
91. Champagny to Andréossy, 16 August 1808, AE 381.
92. Napoleon to Jérôme, 25 July 1808, *CdN*, no. 14,320, vol. XVII, pp. 417–18.
93. Champagny to Andréossy, 16 August 1808, AE 381.
94. Champagny to Andréossy, 1 October 1808, AE 381.
95. For example: Andréossy to Champagny, no. 34, 18 July 1808, AE 381.
96. Napoleon to Franz, 14 October 1808, *CdN*, no. 14,380, vol. XVII, pp. 557–8.
97. Stadion, memorandum of 22 October 1808, in Rössler, *Oesterreichs Kampf*, vol. I, p. 395.
98. Napoleon to Davout, 25 October 1808, *CdN*, no. 14,410, vol. XVIII, pp. 18–19.
99. Napoleon to Josephine, 5 November 1808, *CdN*, no. 14,441, vol. XVIII, pp. 37.
100. For a good summary, see Thierry Lentz, *Napoléon et la Conquête de l'Europe*, Paris: Fayard, 2001, pp. 424–34.
101. Napoleon spent this period in Astorga, Benevente and Vallodolid.
102. Napoleon to Clarke, 1 January 1809, *CdN*, no. 14,634, vol. XVIII, pp. 165–6.
103. Napoleon to Otto, 15 January 1809, *CdN*, no. 14,710, vol. XVIII, pp. 219–20. Oudinot's men had been at Hanau; the cuirassiers at Erlangen.

104. Champagny to Andréossy, 17 and 25 January 1809, AE, vol. 382; see also Napoleon to Champagny, 7 January 1809, CG, no. 19,707, vol. VIII, p. 1418.
105. Dodun to Champagny, no. 2, 6 March 1809, AE, vol. 382.
106. Napoleon to King Friedrich of Württemberg, 21 February 1809, *CdN*, no. 14,800, vol. XVIII, pp. 280–1.
107. Napoleon's letters to the Rheinbund rulers, 15 January 1809, *CdN*, nos. 14,710 and 14,718 through 14725, vol. XVIII, pp. 219–33.
108. Napoleon to Caulaincourt, 6 and 21 February 1809, *CG*, nos. 19,976 and 20,105, vol. IX, pp. 27–8, 97–8.
109. Napoleon to Dalberg, 15 January 1809, *CdN*, no. 14,725, vol. XVIII, p. 233.
110. Napoleon to Otto, 4 March 1809, *CdN*, no. 14,849, vol. XVIII, pp. 309–10.
111. Napoleon to Berthier ('Instructions pour le major general'), 30 March 1809, and Napoleon to Berthier, 8 April 1809, *CG*, nos. 20,619 and 20,749, vol. IX, pp. 378–90, 448–50.
112. The Poles were nominally under Marshal Bernadotte in his guise as commander of the Saxon troops, but this was a physical impossibility and Poniatowski exercised de facto command.
113. Napoleon to Jérôme, 16 January 1809, *CdN*, no.14731, vol. XVIII, p. 237.
114. Napoleon to Caulaincourt, 6 March 1809, *CG*, no. 20,238, vol. IX, pp. 165–8.
115. Napoleon to Louis, 21 March 1809, *CG*, no. 20,484, vol. IX, p. 307.
116. Napoleon to Champagny and Napoleon to Caulaincourt, 21 March 1809, *CG*, nos. 20,472 and 20,473, vol. IX, pp. 299–301.
117. Charles used the Rubicon metaphor in an 8 April 1809 letter to Herzog Albert, in Criste, *Carl*, vol. III, p. 475.
118. Charles used these phrases in a 27 March 1809 instruction to Bellegarde, KAFA, 1451.

Chapter 2: Armies on the Edge of War

1. Napoleon to Caulaincourt, 24 March 1809, *CG*, no. 20,525, vol. IX, pp. 328–30. Among other indications, Napoleon was especially disturbed by militant declarations Charles issued to several volunteer units in early March (see, for example, the *Wiener Zeitung* of 11 March 1809; French translations were published in the 22 March issue of the *Gazette Nationale ou Moniteur Universel* and in the 23 and 24 March issues of the *Journal de l'Empire*).
2. Napoleon to Eugène, 27 March 1809, *CG*, no. 20,570, vol. IX, p. 353.
3. Napoleon to Alexander, 24 March 1809, *CG*, no. 20,521, vol. IX, p. 327.
4. Caulaincourt to Napoleon, 16 April 1809, in Mikhaïlowitch (ed.), *Les Relations Diplomatiques de la Russie et de la France*, vol. III, p. 208.
5. In addition to *Thunder on the Danube*, vol. I and the other sources noted below, this section draws on John H. Gill, 'Responding to Military Defeat: The Habsburg Case', unpublished paper presented to the Consortium in the Revolutionary Era, Feb. 2016.

6. Charles, 'Über den Krieg mit den Neufranken' (1795), *Ausgewählte Schriften*, vol. V, pp. 5–15; Charles, 'Observationspunkte für die Generäle bei der Armee in Deutschland im Jahre 1796', in 'Beiträge zur Geschichte des österreichischen Heerwesens', *Österreichische Militärische Zeitschrift*, vol. IX, no. 4, 1868, pp. 180–4.
7. Charles, 'Das Kriegswesen in Folge der französischen Revolutionskriege' (1838), *Ausgewählte Schriften*, vol. V, p. 344.
8. Charles to Liechtenstein, 19 May 1809, *Krieg 1809*, vol. IV, p. 365. The Primatial Insurrection Hussars had been raised from volunteers by Archduke Karl Ambrosius at his own expense; one of the Este brothers, he was the Catholic Primate of Hungary. The Neutra (Nyitra) Hussars were part of the conventional Insurrection, but volunteered to serve outside Hungary.
9. Charles, 'Kriegswesen', *Ausgewählte Schriften*, vol. V, pp. 346–7.
10. *Dienst-Reglement für die kaiserliche königliche Infanterie*, Vienna: kaiserlich-königlichen Hof- und Staats-Druckerey, 1807, vol. I, p. 83; see also vol. II, p. 11.
11. Rothenberg, *Great Adversaries*, pp. 22, 49, 71; Allmayer-Beck/Lessing, *Heer unter dem Doppeladler*, p. 185; Kurt Peball, 'Zum Kriegsbild der österreichischen Armee und seiner geschichtlichen Bedeutung in den Kriegen gegen die französische Revolution und Napoleon I. in den Jahren von 1792 bis 1815', in W. von Groote and K. J. Müller (eds.), *Napoleon I. und das Militärwesen seiner Zeit*, Freiburg, 1968, p. 138.
12. Charles, *Beiträge zum praktischen Unterrichte im Felde für die Officiere der Österreichischen Armee* and *Grundsätze der höheren Kriegskunst für die Generäle der Österreichischen Armee*, in *Ausgewählte Schriften*, vol. I, pp. 1–85 and 89–219. Walter Wagner, *Von Austerlitz bis Königgrätz: Österreichische Kampftaktik im Spiegel der Reglements 1805–1864*, Osnabrück: Biblio-Verlag, 1978, p. 6.
13. *Grundsätze der höheren Kriegskunst und Beyspeile ihrer zweckmässigen Anwendung für die Generale der Österreichischen Armee*, Vienna: Kaiserl. Königl. Hof- und Staatsdruckerey, 1808, p. 40.
14. *Beiträge zum praktischen Unterricht im Felde* and *Grundsätze der Strategie erläutert durch die Darstellung des Feldzuges von 1796 in Deutschland*, in *Ausgewählte Schriften*, vol. I, pp. 89, 231–3.
15. The journal is the *Österreichische Militärische Zeitschrift*, see Karl Zitterhofer, *Streffleurs Militärische Zeitschrift 1808–1908*, Vienna, 1908. On the importance Charles attached to military history, see *Grundsätze der Strategie*, in *Ausgewählte Schriften*, vol. I, p. 232.
16. This is one way to describe the shift from 'linear warfare' with 'unitary' armies that approached battle and fought largely as single entities on a single axis of advance without permanent formations above the regimental level (i.e. no permanent divisions or corps) to the sort of army organisations that arose in the course of the French Revolution with the creation of standing command echelons such as brigades, divisions and corps between the regiment and the overall commander; this sort of new organisation facilitated approaches to battle on multiple lines by formations that could be moved around the theatre of operations or the battlefield with great flexibility. An alternative term is Brent Nosworthy's 'impulse tactics' (see his *Battle Tactics of Napoleon and His Enemies*, London:

Constable, 1995). For the pre-Revolutionary Austrian army, see Christopher Duffy, *The Army of Maria Theresa*, Doncaster: Terence Wise, 1990; and his *Instrument of War*, Chicago: Emperor's Press, 2000; as well as the extended discussion in *Krieg gegen die Französische Revolution 1792–1797*, Vienna: Seidel & Sohn, 1905, vol. I, pp. 321–541.
17. Wagner, *Von Austerlitz bis Königgrätz*, pp. 8–18.
18. *Krieg 1809*, vol. I, p. 102.
19. Rothenberg, *Great Adversaries*, 111; *Krieg 1809*, vol. I, pp. 110–11.
20. The word 'skirmisher' is used here for contemporary terms such as '*Plänkler*' and '*tirailleur*' (interestingly, contemporary German-language military writings frequently employed the French term '*tirailleur*' as both a noun and a verb).
21. This was another case of Austria attempting to fight Napoleon with unadapted tools from Maria Theresa's age. On the Grenzer, see especially Gunther E. Rothenberg, *The Military Border in Croatia 1740–1881*, Chicago: University of Chicago Press, 1966.
22. [FML Josef Freiherr von Gallina], 'Reglements und Instructionen für die Ausbildung der Truppe und ihrer Führer', *Österreichische militärische Zeitschrift*, Jahrgang 24, 1881, p. 186.
23. Circular of 7 June 1809, in *Beiträge zur Geschichte des österreichischen Heerwesens*, vol. I, p. 225.
24. Charles, 'Denkschrift', *Ausgewählte Schriften*, vol. VI, pp. 333–4.
25. *Krieg 1809*, vol. I, p. 114.
26. [Gallina], 'Reglements und Instructionen', pp. 160–1.
27. An anonymous 1810 memorandum entitled 'Bemerkungen über die französische Armee und unsere Lage', cited in 'Die Armee Napoleon I. im Jahre 1809, mit vergleichenden Rückblicken auf das österriechische Heer; dargestellt nach dem Urtheile von Zeitgenossen', *Mittheilungen des k. k. Kriegs-Archivs*, Vienna, 1881, p. 389.
28. Charles, 'Denkschrift', *Ausgewählte Schriften*, vol. VI, p. 330.
29. Ibid. Gallina, noting that Austrian manoeuvres in 1828 still reflected the old linear order, bemoaned 'the power of habit' and 'the law of inertia': 'Twelve campaigns in which the Austrian army participated and which stretched over a period of twenty-four years were not sufficient to bring the advantages of the Napoleonic system of army organisation into clear awareness', in [Gallina], 'Reglements und Instructionen', pp. 176–7.
30. Robert M. Epstein, *Napoleon's Last Victory and the Emergence of Modern War*, Lawrence: University of Kansas Press, 1994, p. 6.
31. Grünne to de Ligne, 23 September 1809, in Josef Freiherr Hormayr, *Das Heer von Innerösterreich unter den Befehlen des Erzherzogs Johann im Kriege von 1809 in Italien, Tyrol und Ungarn*, Leipzig and Altenburg: Brockhaus, 1817, p. 393.
32. Radetzky, 'Erinnerungen', p. 63.
33. Karl Johann Ritter von Grueber, *Lebenserinnerungen eines Reiteroffiziers vor Hundert Jahren*, Vienna: Seidel & Sohn, 1906, p. 62.
34. Letter of 26 March 1809, in Alexander Coudreux, *Lettres du Commandant Coudreux à Son Frère 1804–1815*, ed. Gustave Schlumberger, Paris: Plon, 1908, p. 147.

35. Raymond-Aimery-Philippe-Joseph de Montesquiou-Fezensac, *Souvenirs Militaires de 1804 à 1814*, Paris: Dumaine, 1870, p. 129.
36. Charles, 'Beitrag', *Ausgewählte Schriften*, vol. VI, p. 356.
37. 'Bemerkungen über die französische Armee', *Mittheilungen des k. k. Kriegs-Archivs*, Vienna, 1881, p. 393.
38. The II Reserve Corps marched 48 km in 23 hours on 10–11 May and some of the troops invading the Tyrol covered an extraordinary 65 km on 11 April. See *Thunder on the Danube*, vol. II, pp. 91, 210.
39. Bernadotte was nominally responsible for the Polish forces as well.
40. For an overview of the Rheinbund contingent histories, see John H. Gill, 'Armies of the Confederation of the Rhine', in *Armies of the Napoleonic Wars*, Gregory Fremont-Barnes (ed.), Barnsley: Pen & Sword, 2011.
41. Service Historique de la Défense, Archives de la Guerre et de l'Armée de Terre [hereafter SHD], C11/180, 'Ordre Numérique', 15 June–1 July 1809.
42. Jean Baptiste Koch, *Mémoires d'André Massena*, Paris: Bonnot, 1967, vol. VI, p. 55–6.
43. Letters of 7 and 17 April 1809, in Jean-Louis Bonnéry, *Ledru des Essarts: Un Grand Patriote Sarthois Méconnu*, Le Mans: Imprimerie Maine Libre, 1988, pp. 61, 66.
44. For background on these two German contingents see Gill, *Eagles*, Chapters 4 and 5.
45. Koch, *Massena*, vol. VI, p. 51.
46. Massena to Berthier, 19 March 1809, in Charles Saski, *Campagne de 1809 en Allemagne et en Autriche*, Paris: Berger-Levrault, 1899–1902, vol. I, p. 301.
47. Ernest Picard, *Préceptes et Jugements de Napoléon*, Paris: Berger-Levrault, 1913, p. 465; Legrand's personnel file, SHD, GR 7Y D316.
48. Pierre Pelleport, *Souvenirs Militaires et Intimes*, Paris: Didier, 1857, vol. I, p. 254.
49. Alain Pigeard, *Les Étoiles de Napoléon*, Paris: Quatuor, 1996, p. 263.
50. Ibid., p. 482.
51. Charles Pierre Lubin Griois, *Mémoires du Général Griois*, Paris: Plon-Nourrit, 1909, vol. II, p. 283. See also Pigeard, *Étoiles*, pp. 502–3.
52. Note that the Poles were not yet armed with the lance, although the experience at Wagram would contribute to their transition to this weapon later in the year.
53. Though historians often refer to the Army of Dalmatia as the '11th Corps', it did not acquire this designation until 17 July 1809 during the armistice. This work will thus use the original title: Army of Dalmatia.
54. Marmont, *Mémoires du Maréchal Duc de Raguse*, Paris: Perrotin, 1857, vol. III, pp. 132, 154.
55. Napoleon to Eugène, 14 January 1809, *CG*, no. 19,833, vol. VIII, pp. 1485–6. Note that Napoleon, though exaggerating the numbers, was counting the regiments not present at Znaim as well as artillery, cavalry and other troops.
56. For background on the Bavarians in 1809, see Gill, *Eagles*, Chapter 2.
57. Rothenberg, *Great Adversaries*, p. 41; see also Lee W. Eysturlid, *The Formative Influences, Theories and Campaigns of Archduke Carl of Austria*, Westport: Greenwood, 2000.
58. Allmayer-Beck/Lessing, *Heer unter dem Doppeladler*, p. 182.
59. Hans Delbrück, *Erinnerungen, Aufsätze und Reden*, Berlin: Stilke, 1905, p. 603.

60. Carl von Clausewitz, *Die Feldzüge von 1799 in Italien und der Schweiz*, Berlin: Dümmler, 1833, vol. I, p. 153.
61. Rudolf von Caemmerer, *Die Entwicklung der strategischen Wissenschaft im 19. Jahrhundert*, Berlin: Baensch, 1904, p. 47. Also: Arnaud Blin, *Wagram*, Paris: Tallandier, 2010, p. 196.
62. Johann, 'Feldzugserzählung', p. 28.
63. At Austerlitz he had said that 'a man has but one time for war; I shall be good for six years yet, but after that I shall have to stop'; in Louis Constant Wairy, *Memoirs of Constant*, New York: Scribner's Sons, 1985, vol. III, p. 261.
64. Pierre Louis Roederer, *Oeuvres du Comte P. L. Roederer*, Paris: Firmin Didot Frères, 1854, vol. III, p. 537.
65. See *Thunder on the Danube*, vol. I, p. 92.
66. To Roederer, 11 February 1809, in *Oeuvres*, vol. III, p. 537.
67. Jean-Jacques Pelet, *Mémoires sur la guerre de 1809 en Allemagne*, Paris: Roret, 1824–6, vol. IV, p. 208.
68. Dupont's surrender at Bailén in 1808 was thus an unpardonable offence only mitigated by the fact that Napoleon himself was not in Spain at the time.
79. Charles, 'Beitrag', *Ausgewählte Schriften*, vol. VI, pp. 364–5.
70. Roederer, *Oeuvres*, vol. III, p. 537.

Chapter 3: From Regensburg to Wagram

1. Charles to Albert, 12 April 1809, in Wertheimer, *Geschichte Österreichs und Ungarns*, vol. II, pp. 302; *Krieg 1809*, vol. I, pp. 323–5.
2. Ibid., vol. I, p. 361.
3. Guillaume de Latrille, comte de Lorencez, 'État Raisonné de mes Services', *Le Carnet Historique & Litteraire*, vol. X (1901), pp. 415.
4. Albrecht Adam, *Aus dem Leben eines Schlachtenmalers*, Stuttgart: Cotta, 1886, pp. 55–6.
5. Lorencez, 'État Raisonné', p. 415
6. Pierre Berthezène, *Souvenirs Militaires de la République et de l'Empire*, Paris: Dumaine, 1855, p. 189.
7. Friedrich Mändler, *Erinnerungen aus meinen Feldzügen*, Nürnberg: Lotzbeck, 1854, p. 3.
8. Adam, *Aus dem Leben*, p. 59.
9. Napoleon to Davout, 21 April 1809, 0500, in Saski, *Campagne de 1809*, vol. II, p. 304.
10. Philippe-Paul Ségur, *Histoire et Mémoires*, Paris: Didot, 1873, p. 324.
11. Helmut von Moltke, 'Der Feldzug 1809, in Bayern', *Moltkes Militärische Werke*, Berlin, 1899, vol. III, p. 46.
12. See 'Notes sur le manuscrit venu de Sainte-Hélène', *CdN*, vol. XXXI, p. 235; 'Notes sur l'ouvrage intitulé Considerations sur l'Art de la Guerre', *CdN*, vol. XXXI, p. 359; Henri Gatien Bertrand, *Cahiers de Sainte-Hélène*, Paris: Flammarion, 1949, vol. II, pp. 93–4; Gaspard Gourgaud, *Talks of Napoleon at St. Helena*, Chicago: McClurg, 1904, p. 143.
13. [Carl von Stutterheim], *La Guerre de l'An 1809 entre l'Autriche et la France*, Vienna: Strauss, 1811, p. 283.

14. Charles to Bellegarde, 27 March 1809, KAFA, 1451.
15. Napoleon to St Marsan, 29 April 1809, *CG*, no. 20,938, vol. IX, p. 546.
16. Napoleon to Davout, 26 April 1809, 1500, and Napoleon to Davout, 27 April 1809, 0900, in Saski, *Campagne de 1809*, vol. III, pp. 33–4 and 44–5.
17. Some commentators portray the advance on Vienna as a strategic error, see Henry Bonnal, *La Manoeuvre de Landshut*, Paris: Chapelot, 1905, pp. 260, 345–51; Edmond Buat, *1809 De Ratisbonne à Znaim*, Paris: Chapelot, 1909, vol. I, pp. 16–22; and F. Lorraine Petre, *Napoleon and the Archduke Charles*, London: John Lane, 1909, pp. 201–6.
18. Hubert Camon, *La Manoeuvre de Wagram*, Paris: Berger-Levrault, 1926, pp. 5, 75.
19. GB Coëhorn to Sophie, 28 April 1809, in Joseph Ernest Baron de Méneval, *Le Général Baron de Coëhorn: Un Bayard Alsacien*, Paris: Fischbacher, 1912, p. 176.
20. Charles to Franz, 23 April 1809, in *Krieg 1809*, vol. I, p. 581. Emphasis in the original.
21. Charles to Franz, 24 April 1809, in *Krieg 1809*, vol. IV, p. 731.
22. Charles to Albert, 28 April 1809, in Wertheimer, *Geschichte Österreichs und Ungarns*, vol. II, pp. 309–10.
23. F. A. Brandner, *Aus dem Tagebuch eines österreichischen Soldaten im Jahre 1809*, Lobau: Breyer, n.d., p. 51.
24. Stadion comments on diplomatic correspondence, in late April and early May, Rössler, *Oesterreichs Kampf*, vol. II, p. 14.
25. Rössler, *Stadion*, vol. II, p. 47.
26. Rössler, *Oesterreichs Kampf*, vol. II, p. 11–15; Rauchensteiner, *Kaiser Franz und Erzherzog Carl*, pp. 99–101.
27. Franz to Charles, 24 April 1809, in *Criste*, vol. III, p. 78.
28. 'Punktation' (Instructions) for Friedrich Stadion, in 'Operations-Journal der Haupt-Armee vom Anfange der Feindseligkeiten bis 24. Mai', Op. J. 1, Kriegsarchiv, Alte Feldakten, Karton 1381, 1809 (1) Operationsjournale der Hauptarmee und Korps (1809) [all items from the Alte Feldakten hereafter simply indicated by 'KAFA']; extract in Wertheimer, *Geschichte Österreichs und Ungarns*, vol. II, p. 310.
29. Charles to Franz, 28 April 1809, in *Criste*, vol. III, p. 79.
30. *Krieg 1809*, vol. IV, pp. 47–8.
31. Napoleon to Davout, 1 May 1809, in Saski, *Campagne de 1809*, vol. III, p. 96.
32. For example, Berthier to Wimpffen, 3 July 1809 (KAFA, 1461), with a list of officers from the 65th Ligne captured at Regensburg in April to be exchanged for Austrians taken at Raab in June.
33. Rössler, *Stadion*, vol. II, p. 47.
34. Friedrich to Philipp Stadion, 3 May 1809, Rössler, *Oesterreichs Kampf*, vol. II, p. 11.
35. Stadion, memorandum to the Kaiser, 9 May 1809, Rössler, *Oesterreichs Kampf*, vol. II, p. 15; a full version in English is printed in Langsam, 'Count Stadion', pp. 147–8.
36. Maria Ludovika to Johann, 9 May 1809, in Hans von Zwiedineck-Südenhorst, *Erzherzog Johann von Oesterreich im Feldzuge von 1809*, Graz: Styria, 1892, pp. 20–4.
37. Balthasar Eccardt, *Als badischer Militärmusiker in Napoleons Kriegen*, Mirielle Geering (ed.), Stuttgart: Kohlhammer, 2013, p. 65

38. For observations on the controversies surrounding this initial crossing attempt, see Gill, '1809', in Leggiere (ed.), *Napoleon and the Operational Art*, pp. 251–2.
39. On Schill, see Sam Mustafa, *The Long Ride of Major von Schill*, Lanham: Rowman & Littlefield, 2008.
40. Stadion, 1 May 1809, cited in Rössler, *Stadion*, vol. II, p. 48.
41. Berthier to Kellermann, 17 May 1809, Saski, *Campagne de 1809*, vol. III, pp. 312–13.
42. Franz to Ferdinand, 23 June 1809, Bronislaw Pawlowski, *Historja Wojny Polsko-Austrajackiej 1809 Roku*, Warsaw, 1935, pp. 444–5.
43. Wimpffen, 'Beweggrunde zum Uebergang über die Donau', 20 June 1809, in Pawlowski, *Historja Wojny*, pp. 440–1; Charles to Albert, 27 June 1809, Criste, *Carl*, vol. III, p. 490.
44. Napoleon to Caulaincourt, 24 March 1809, *CG*, no. 20,523, vol. IX, pp. 328–9.
45. Napoleon to Clarke, 8 July 1809, *CG*, no. 21,473, vol. IX, p. 836. Herta Steiner provides many other examples of Napoleon's low regard for Franz in her 'Das Urteil Napoleons I. über Oesterreich', dissertation, University of Vienna, 1946, pp. 103–8.
46. The appeals to Hungary were ineffectual, see Domokos G. Király, 'The French Revolutionary and Napoleonic Wars and Hungarian Society', in Béla K. Király (ed.), *East Central European Society and War in the Era of Revolutions, 1775–1856*, New York: Brooklyn College Press, 1984, pp. 11–18.
47. The Habsburgs were indignant and anxious when Napoleon referred to the dynasty as 'the House of Lorraine' in a 13 May order of the day and in several of the army's periodic bulletins (16 May, 28 May, 28 June). By referring to Austria's rulers in this manner, Napoleon intended to denigrate the dynasty's standing and hint at its removal: see Appendix 2. Napoleon issued a proclamation to the Hungarians on 15 May and referred to the alleged Hungarian desire for independence in several of the army's bulletins (e.g. the 19th Bulletin of 16 June 1809). For the 1809 bulletins, see vol. V of Adrien Pascal, *Les Bulletins de la Grande Armée*, Paris: Prieur, 1844.
48. Rainer to Franz, 13 June 1809, in Friedrich Reschounig, 'Das Jahr 1809 im Urtheile der Zeitgenossen', dissertation, University of Vienna, 1939, pp. 119–20.
49. Hardenberg to Adair, 7 July 1809, HHStA, Diplomatie und Außenpolitik vor 1848/Kriegsakten/423.
50. Criste, *Carl*, vol. III, pp. 178–9; Rössler, *Oesterreichs Kampf*, vol. II, p. 37; Wertheimer, *Geschichte Österreichs und Ungarns*, vol. II, pp. 355–7; Friedrich von Gentz, *Tagebücher* (ed.), K. A. Varnhagen von Ense, Leipzig: Brockhaus, 1861, pp. 86–7.
51. Situations for the Vienna garrison for 7 and 8 July 1809 from SHD, C13/67 (of slightly more than 20,000 men recorded on 8 July, approximately 11,000 were wounded).
52. Charles had switched Kolowrat (from II to III) and Hohenzollern (from III to II) after Regensburg. Missing from the Austrian command pantheon at Wagram was Hiller, the former VI Corps commander. Peeved by what he perceived as unjust treatment by Charles, he departed the army on 4 July claiming ill health.
53. Joseph to Johann, 8 June 1809, in Sandor Domanovszky (ed.), *Palatin Josephs Schriften*, Budapest, 1991, vol. IV, p. 66.

54. Maria Ludovika to Johann, 6 and 28 June 1809, in Zwiedineck-Südenhorst, *Erzherzog Johann*, pp. 114–17.
55. Cited in Carl Friedrich Freiherr Kübeck von Kübau, *Tagebücher*, Vienna: Gerold, 1909, p. 270. The quotation is from early May but provides a sense of the prevailing atmosphere at court.
56. Stadion, 'Bemerkungen auf eine mir von Seiner Majestät allergnädigst mitgetheilte Note vom 23ten Junius 1809', in 'Rössler, *Oesterreichs Kampf*, vol. II, p. 37.
57. Stadion memorandum for Kaiser Franz, 3 July 1809, in Langsam, 'Count Stadion', pp. 149–51.
58. The quote is from a work of fiction: Jack Vance, *The Green Pearl*, New York: Berkley, 1986, p. 248.
59. Charles to Albert, 23 June 1809, in Criste, *Carl*, vol. III, p. 489.
60. Charles to Franz, 23 June 1809, in Criste, *Carl*, vol. III, pp. 176–7; Reschounig, 'Das Jahr 1809', p. 122.
61. In Criste, *Carl*, vol. III, p. 184.
62. Charles to Albert, 23 June 1809, in Criste, *Carl*, vol. III, p. 489.
63. Charles to Franz, 23 June 1809, in Criste, *Carl*, vol. III, p. 177.
64. Charles to Waldstein, 16 June 1809 and Stadion to Waldstein, 21 June 1809 (quote from this letter), in Joseph von Hormayr, *Lebensbilder aus dem Befreiungskriege*, Jena: Frommann, 1844, vol. I, pt. 2, pp. 36–8; see also correspondence relating to Waldstein, in Andreas Joseph von Thürheim, *Ludwig Fürst Starhemberg: eine Lebens-Skizze*, Graz: Styria, 1889, pp. 211–25.
65. Franz to Alexander, 24 June 1809, HHStA, Kriegsakten, 424.
66. Stadion, instructions for Stutterheim, 23 June 1809, HHStA, Russland III, 50 Varia (Stutterheim).
67. Franz to Ferdinand, 23 June 1809, HHStA, Russland III, 50 Varia (Stutterheim).
68. Charles to Ferdinand, 23 June 1809, KAFA, 1429.
69. Charles, memorandum of 23 June 1809, in Criste, *Carl*, vol. III, p. 176.
70. Stutterheim to Stadion, 29 June 1809, HHStA, Kriegsakten, 424.
71. Stutterheim to Stadion, 30 June 1809, HHStA, Russland III, 50 Varia (Stutterheim).
72. Franz to Charles, 2 July 1809, KAFA, 1461.
73. Stadion to Wimpffen, 2 July 1809, in Christian Freiherr Binder von Kriegelstein, *Der Krieg Napoleons gegen Oesterreich 1809*, Maximilian Ritter von Hoen (ed.), Berlin: Voss, 1906, vol., II, p. 294.
74. Franz to Charles, 3 July 1809, KAFA, 1461.
75. Unsigned orders, 4 July 1809, KAFA, 1461.
76. Kottulinsky to Charles, 1500, 4 July 1809, KAFA, 1422.
77. 'Vingt-Quatrième Bulletin de la Armée d'Allemagne', 3 July 1809, *CdN*, vol. XIX, pp. 212–14.
78. All figures include infantry and cavalry only. An additional 4,300 men were assigned to garrison Pressburg and Marchegg.

79. Johann Jacob Otto August Rühle von Lilienstern, *Reise mit der Armee im Jahre 1809*, Rudolstadt: Hof- Buch- und Kunsthandlung, 1810, p. 277.
80. *Journal historique de la Division Broussier, pendant la campagne de 1809*, SHD, C4/10.
81. The quote is from an eyewitness, Major Georg Freiherr von Valentini, a Prussian staff officer who had signed on to serve the Habsburgs, in his *Versuch einer Geschichte des Feldzugs von 1809 an der Donau*, 2nd edn., Berlin: Nikolai, 1818, p. 198. Hohenzollern described the French as 'deployed in countless lines like one mass', 'Bermerkungen ueber die Schlachten von Wagram und Znaym', June 1810, II Corps, Op. J. 15, KAFA, 1382.
82. Disposition, Breitenlee, 1430, 6 July 1809, KAFA, 1422.
83. Anne-Jean-Marie-René Savary, *Mémoires du Duc de Rovigo*, Paris, Bossange, 1828, vol. IV, pp. 182–3.
84. My rendition of '*Wenn man ein Hölzel fallen läßt, so heben Sie es auf*', in Wertheimer, *Geschichte Österreichs und Ungarns*, vol. II, pp. 360–1. In addition to Wertheimer, see the following on Weißenwolff's mission and the exchange of officers: Gustav Just, *Der Friede von Schönbrunn*, Vienna: Stern, 1909, p. 10; Maximilian Ritter von Hoen, *Wagram*, Vienna: Stern, 1909, pp. 23–4; Rössler, *Oesterreichs Kampf*, vol. II, p. 40; Wimpffen to Berthier, 2 July 1809, SHD, C2/93; Berthier to Wimpffen, 2 July 1809, no. 15,486, *CdN*, vol. XIX, pp. 211–12.
85. Report of the Württemberg representative at imperial headquarters, Oberst Josef Ignaz von Beroldingen, no. 41, 4 July 1809, Württemberg Hauptstaatsarchiv, Stuttgart (WHStA), E 270 a Bü 94 (Meldungen des Obersten v. Beroldingen).
86. All quotes from Galbois's notes published in Paul Robiquet, 'Le Général de Galbois 1778–1850', *Revue Historique*, vol. CXX, 1915, p. 8.
87. It is possible that Weißenwolff was the officer who watched the battle 'from a tower in Vienna' as related in an anonymous piece that appeared the following year: 'Darstellung der Schlachten auf dem Marchfelde', *Europäischen Annalen*, vol. X, 1810, p. 207.

Chapter 4: Every Night a March, Every Day an Attack

1. Hippolyte d'Espinchal, *Souvenirs Militaires*, Paris: Ollendorff, 1901, vol. I, p. 272.
2. Nicholas Reichold, *Soldaten-Sohn und das Kriegsleben von 1805 bis 1815*, Munich, 1851, p. 115; Christian Schaller, *Fragmente aus dem Feldzuge gegen Oestreich im Jahr 1809*, Augsburg: Burglen, 1810, p. 81.
3. Jules Antoine Paulin, *Les Souvenirs du Général Baron Paulin*, Paris: Plon, 1895, p. 209.
4. Jean Noubel and Olivier Lapray, 'Le Général Marulaz et le 8e Hussards à Wagram', *Traditions*, no. 22, October 2018.
5. His name is sometimes spelt 'Bruyères'. I have used the spelling from his Legion of Honour records: http://www2.culture.gouv.fr/public/mistral/leonore_fr?action=chercher&field_1=nom&value_1=bruyer.

6. Friant's after-action report, 'Historique des différents affaires ou la 2e Division du 3e Corps de l'Armée d'Allemagne commandé par Gal Friant s'est trouvée', SHD, manuscript MR 668; Grouchy's after-action report, 6 July 1809, SHD, 2C/93.
7. 'Souvenirs du cavalier Charles-Henri Lejeune', *Carnet de la Sabretache*, no. 213, September 1910, p. 524.
8. [Ferdinand von Larisch], 'Meine zweite Campagne (Aus dem Tagebuche eines Verstorbenen)', *Bautzener Nachrichten*, vols. 21–5, 1883; and Louis Frèche, *Mémoire de mes Campagnes (1803–1809)*, Levallois: Centre d'Etudes Napoléoniennes, 1994, p. 119.
9. Napoleon to Cambacérès, 7 July 1809, *CG*, no. 21,464, vol. IX, p. 832, and Napoleon to Josephine, 7 July 1809, *CG*, nos. 21,467 and 21,468, vol. IX, pp. 833–4. Napoleon also mentioned being 'burned by the sun' in one of these letters to Josephine; doubtless many others, French and Austrian alike, also suffered from sunburn as well as heat exhaustion and heat stroke.
10. Buat, *1809*, vol. II, p. 277. Stéphane Béraud terms the lack of pursuit 'undeniable negligence' on Napoleon's part: *La Révolution Militaire Napoléonienne*, vol. II, *Les Batailles*, Paris: Giovangeli, 2013, p. 233.
11. Binder von Kriegelstein, *Der Krieg Napoleons*, vol. II, p. 356.
12. Binder, *Der Krieg Napoleons*, vol. II, pp. 357–8. Liechtenstein may have proposed shifting the entire army, including V Corps, to the Hochleithen Heights along the Brünn highway to fight for a third day (Alexandre de Laborde, *Précis Historique de la Guerre entre la France et l'Autriche en 1809*, Paris: Anselin et Pochard, 1823, p. 309).
13. Charles to Albert, 9 July 1809, Criste, *Carl*, vol. III, p. 493. See also Charles to Colloredo, 21 July 1809, in *Ausgewählte Schriften*, vol. VI, pp. 306: 'the entire enemy army in a strength that has hardly every been united at one point since ancient times'.
14. 'An den Herrn Corps Commandanten', 7 July 1809, KAFA, 1461.
15. Grueber, *Lebenserinnerungen*, p. 83.
16. Johann Schnierer, *Aus der Franzosenzeit, Innviertler Volksbücher*, nos. 4 and 5, Braunau: Stampfl, 1914, p. 19.
17. 'Relation der feindlichen Vorfälle bei dem 6. Armee Corps vom 30. Juni, bis inklusiv 9. July 809', KAFA, 1461.
18. Auguste François Marcel, Comte de Ségur-Cabanac, *Journal*, Vienna: Stern, 1910, p. 110, courtesy of Herr Ferdi Wöber.
19. Hauptmann Baron Seckendorff, after-action report, 4th Unter-Manhartsberg (UMB) Landwehr, 12 July 1809, KAFA, 1461.
20. 'Disposition am 6ten July 809 zum Ruckzug', 6 July 1809, 2000, KAFA, 1422.
21. 'Beitrag zur Geschichte des Feldzugs vom J. 1809, das IV Armee-Corps unter F.M.L. Fürst Rosenberg betreffend', Op. J. 22, KAFA, 1383.
22. II Corps, Op. J. 10, KAFA, 1382. The Landwehr battalions were 2nd Znaim, 1st Brünn and 3rd Brünn. Note name of the *Frelich* Infantry's Inhaber is sometimes spelt 'Fröhlich' or 'Frehlich'; 'Frelich' is used here as it appears in the *Schematismus der Kais. Königl. Armée auf das Jahr 1808*, the *Schematismus der Oesterreichisch-Kaiserlichen Armée für das Jahr 1810*

(Vienna: Graeffer, 1808 and 1810), and in Alphons Freiherr von Wrede, *Geschichte der K. und K. Wehrmacht*, Vienna: Seidel & Sohn, 1898, vol. I.

23. The *Hohenzollern* Cuirassiers had been sent to support II Corps on the 6th, but Hohenzollern dispatched them to assist Rosenberg; as they did not belong to the division sent to the left wing under FML Johann Nostitz-Reineck, they evidently received no new orders and remained with IV Corps. The dragoon squadron probably just became lost or it may have been a composite 'squadron' assembled from parts of the regiment that became separated from the main body during the confusion of combat and retreat.
24. 'Disposition am 6ten July 809 zum Ruckzug', 2000, 6 July 1809, KAFA, 1422. Known today as 'Hochleithen', this area was called the 'hohe Leithen' or 'Hoheleithen' in 1809.
25. Gaweinstal was known as Gaunersdorf in 1809.
26. IV Corps, Op. J. 22, KAFA, 1383; and 'Beschluß des Feldzugs 1809: Die Division des Herrn General F.M.Ls. Grafen Radetzky vom 4ten Armee-Corps betreffend', KAFA, 1461.
27. 'Bermerkungen', II Corps, Op. J. 15, KAFA, 1382.
28. The quotation is from a post-war exculpatory essay likely written by one of the archduke's adherents, but the concern about being jammed between the Russians and the French was certainly prevalent in the army's thinking before and after Wagram: *Berichtigung über die letzten Ereignisse des Krieges zwischen Österreich und Frankreich im Jahr 1809*, Frankfurt: n.p., 1810, pp. 74–5.
29. Johann Baptist Skall, 'Feldzugsreise des Kaisers Franz I. von Österreich im Jahre 1809', *Mitteilungen des K. und K. Kriegsarchivs*, vol. V, 1907, pp. 243–5. Oudinot's corps included a small Portuguese brigade.
30. J.-P. Vergnes, 'Le Lendemain de la Bataille de Wagram', *Revue de l'Empire*, vol. IV, 1845, pp. 54–7.
31. Jean-Baptiste Godin, 'Abrégé de mes Voyages Faits Pendant les Annés 1808–1809–1810–1811–1812 et 1813', *La Giberne*, IX/1, July 1907, edited by Chantal Prévaost and re-released by the Fondation Napoléon at http://bibliotheque-martial-lapeyre.napoleon.org/Default/doc/syracuseE/71733/abrege-de-mes-voyages-faits-pendant-les-annees-1808-1809-1810-1811-1812-et-1813-de-jean-baptiste-god (accessed 29 May 2019) with thanks to M. François Houdecek.
32. Marc Desboeufs, *Souvenirs du Capitaine Desboeufs*, Paris: Picard et fils, 1901, p. 111.
33. Méneval, *Le Général Baron de Coëhorn*, pp. 194–5.
34. 'Deux Lettres de 1809 du Lieutenant de Marbotin à sa Mère', *Carnet de la Sabretache*, 1909, pp. 519–20.
35. Pelet, *Guerre de 1809*, vol. IV, p. 266.
36. Savary, vol. IV, pp. 185–8; Louis François Lejeune, *Memoirs of Baron Lejeune*, Felling: Worley reprint, 1987, vol. II, pp. 325–6; Claude François de Méneval, *Mémoires pour server à l'Histoire de Napoléon Ier*, Paris: Dentu, 1894, vol. II, pp. 254–5.
37. Laborde, *Précis Historique*, p. 311.

38. Napoleon to Berthier, 7 July 1809, *CG*, no. 21,463, vol. IX, pp. 831–2. Some commanders complained of shortages of ammunition (Grouchy to Napoleon, 6 July 1809, SHD, C2/93), but others retained substantial quantities, certainly enough for another major engagement (Davout to Berthier, 0515, 7 July 1809, SHD C2/93). Naulet observes that the army replenished its ammunition supplies with surprising speed owing to the thorough preparations in advance (Frédéric Naulet, *Wagram: Le Canon Tonne sur les Bords du Danube*, Paris: Economica, 2009, p. 249).
39. Davout's morning message to Berthier (0515, 7 July 1809, SHD C2/93) refers to instructions Berthier sent at 2300 on the 6th requesting a status report, so Berthier clearly sent similar instructions to all formations that night, but these have not been preserved; Berthier also issued an order of the day to this effect on the 7th (SHD, C2/93).
40. Berthier to Oudinot, 2300, 7 July 1809, SHD, C2/93. According to the 1837 edition of the memoirs of Lieutenant Elzéar Blaze (108th Ligne), 'The entire French army was drunk on the night after the Battle of Wagram' (*La Vie Militaire sous l'Empire*, Paris: Bureau de l'Album des Théatres, 1837, vol. I, p. 365); this passage is absent from the edition published under the same title in 1901 by Garnier Frères of Paris, an English version of which was translated and edited by John R. Elting and published as *Military Life under Napoleon*, Chicago: The Emperor's Press, 1995. See also Thomas Joseph Aubry, *Souvenirs du 12e Chasseurs*, Paris: Librairie des Deux Empires, 2002, p. 135.
41. Buat, *1809*, vol. II, p. 320. See also Naulet, *Wagram*, p. 255.
42. Indeed, in many respects, the post-Jena pursuit, though dramatic, took place in relatively unique circumstances and may not be the most useful metric for other situations.
43. Berthier to Vandamme and to Reynier, both 2200, 6 July 1809, SHD, C2/93.
44. Minute of Berthier to Baraguey d'Hilliers, 7 July 1809; Baraguey d'Hilliers to Berthier, 1000 and 2100, 7 July 1809, SHD, C2/93.
45. Napoleon to Eugène, midnight, 7 July 1809, *CG*, no. 21,465, vol. IX, pp. 832–3.
46. Berthier to Massena, 7 July 1809, Koch, *Massena*, 'Pièce Justificative XXVII', vol. VI, p. 436.
47. Montbrun report and Girardin to Napoleon, both sent on the morning of 7 July 1809, SHD, C2/93.
48. Quote from Lieutenant Jean Hippolyte Irénée Gabriel Lazillière of the Guard Dragoons to Walther, 7 July 1809, SHD, C2/93.
49. Davout to Napoleon, 0715, 7 July 1809, SHD, C2/93.
50. Davout to Napoleon, 0715, 7 July 1809; and 2nd Corps report, 7 July 1809, SHD, C2/93.
51. Oudinot to Napoleon, 7 July 1809, SHD, C2/93. Like Massena, Oudinot often neglected to mention the time of day in his reports.
52. Charles Louis Cadet de Gassicourt, *Voyage en Autriche, en Moravie et en Bavière fait a la Suite de l'Armée Française pendant la Campagne de 1809*, Paris: L'Huillier, 1818, pp. 238–9.
53. Ibid.
54. Berthier to Massena, 7 July 1809, Koch, *Massena*, 'Pièce Justificative XXVII', vol. VI, p. 436.

55. Massena to Napoleon, [7 July 1809], SHD, C2/93. Note that this missive is mistakenly dated '8 July'.
56. This anecdote is from one of Massena's staff officers, Jean-Baptiste Antoine Marcellin Marbot, in *The Memoirs of Baron de Marbot*, New York: Longmans, Green, 1905, vol. II, p. 394. Another renowned French cavalry commander called Bruyère 'a very mediocre officer' (Auguste Jean Joseph Gabriel Ameil, *Notes et Documents provenant des Archives du Général Baron Ameil*, Paris: Teissedre, 1997, p. 215).
57. Klenau to Charles, 1015, 7 July 1809, KAFA, 1422.
58. 'Freimüthige Beiträge zu der Kriegsgeschichte der Campagne 1809 das Reserve Corps der k. k. Armee betreffend', Op. J. 77, KAFA, 1388.
59. Minucci's after-action report, 26 July 1809, BayHStA, B445.
60. Lindenau report, 1400, 7 July 1809 (misdated as 6 July), SHD, C2/93; Oscar von Sichlern, *Geschichte des königlich bayerischen 5. Chevaulegers-Regiments*, Munich: regimental, 1876, p. 82.
61. Nansouty report, evening, 7 July 1809, SHD, C2/93.
62. Massena to Napoleon, [7 July 1809], SHD, C2/93. Note that this missive is mistakenly dated '8 July'; Pelet, *Guerre de 1809*, vol. IV, p. 253.
63. The VI Corps after-action report heaped praise on the 1st Vienna Volunteers (KAFA, 1461). The 1st Vienna claimed that they had not withdrawn until outflanked on their left: 'Relation über die seit dem 5. dieses von dem obbenannten Bataillon beigewohnten Affairen', KAFA, 1461.
64. Although Jean-Jacques Pelet's generally excellent history of the 1809 war credits the 26th Léger with the capture of Korneuburg (*Guerre de 1809*, vol. IV, p. 524), the history of the 26th Léger, written by its new colonel immediately after the war, gives the regiment only a minor role (Charles Louis Joseph Olivier Gueheneuc, 'Historique du 26e Léger pendant la Campagne de 1809', August 1810, SHD, manuscript MR1843); the Baden accounts are very detailed and persuasive. The other French regiment of Legrand's division, the 18th Ligne, was present but not involved in the fighting on 7 July.
65. This counts only those listed as casualties in the regimental histories of the five line infantry regiments of VI Corps; there may have been more. Maximilian Maendl, *Geschichte des K. und K. Infanterie-Regiments Nr. 51*, Klausenburg: regimental, 1899, p. 92. Édouard Gachot gives the count of Austrian prisoners alone as 575 in *1809: Napoléon en Allemagne*, Paris: Plon, 1913, p. 292.
66. Massena to Berthier, [7 July 1809], SHD, C2/93. This is also mistakenly dated '8 July'; many of Massena's reports do not include times.
67. Spleny to Klenau, 1800, 7 July 1809, KAFA, 1422.
68. Sources for the capture of Korneuburg: 'Journal der Operationen der Haupt-Armee vom 6ten July bis zum 10t July 809', Op. J. 1f, KAFA, 1381; 'Relation der Campagne 1809' (Klenau's personal journal), Op. J. 32, KAFA, 1384; '6tes Armée Corps: Tage-Buch der Begebenheiten im Feldzug 1809 unter F.Z.M. Bron Hiller', Op. J. 35, KAFA, 1384; 'Journal vom Großherzoglich Badischen Contingents Corps in der Campagne gegen Oestreich a[nn]o 1809', General Landesarchiv Karlsruhe [hereafter GLA], 48/4286;

Gueheneuc, 'Historique du 26e Léger'; Pelet, *Guerre de 1809*, vol. IV, pp. 251–4; Koch, *Massena*, vol. VI, pp. 336–7; Karl von Zech and Friedrich von Porbeck, *Geschichte der Badischen Truppen 1809*, Heidelberg: Winter, 1909, pp. 169–72; Austrian, Baden and French regimental histories.

69. For example, those of VI Corps and Hohenfeld's division, KAFA, 1461.
70. Pelleport, *Souvenirs Militaries*, vol. I, p. 286.
71. The *Vogelsang* Infantry Regiment and two battalions of *Argenteau* (II, III) as well as two companies of *EH Rainer* ('2tes Armee Corps: Operations Journal unter F.M.L. Fürst Hohenzollern vom 7t Juni 1809 bis 19t December', Op. J. 10, KAFA, 1382; *Argenteau* after-action report, KAFA, 1461).
72. Seckendorff, after-action report, KAFA, 1461.
73. Rosenberg to Charles, 7 July 1809, in Hauptarmee, Op. J. 1f, KAFA, 1381.
74. Girardin's 7 July 1809 report refers to voltigeurs, SHD, C2/93.
75. Montbrun to Davout, morning, 7 July 1809, SHD, C2/93. Pully's dragoons and Arrighi's cuirassiers were also in the area, but took no part in the pursuit.
76. Girardin noted the Austrian sensitivity to flank threats in his report to Napoleon from Hohenruppersdorf on the morning of 7 July 1809, SHD, C2/93.
77. Maurice Charles Marie de Tascher, *Journal de Campagne d'un Cousin de l'Impératrice*, Paris: Plon, 1933, p. 236.
78. Hauptarmee, Op. J. 1f, KAFA, 1381.
79. Another squadron of *O'Reilly* escorted the baggage train towards Znaim.
80. IV Corps, Op. J. 22, KAFA, 1383. This phrase is not recorded in the other version of the corps operations journal: 'IVtes Armee Corps: F.M.L. Fürst Rosenberg Operations Journal vom 26t März bis 1t Decbr. 1809', Op. J. 24, KAFA, 1383.
81. Rosenberg to Charles, (evening), 7 July 1809, in Hauptarmee, Op. J. 1f, KAFA, 1381.
82. As in Charles to Ferdinand, 7 July 1809, KAFA, 1461; the archduke's correspondence on the 8th would be even more specific.
83. Binder, *Der Krieg Napoleons*, vol. II, p. 381.
84. Even Charles's critics agreed on the Russian danger: 'Darstellung der Schlachten', p. 11.
85. Both letters are in Hauptarmee, Op. J. 1f, KAFA, 1381.
86. Binder, *Der Krieg Napoleons*, vol. II, p. 382.
87. Ibid.
88. Berthier to Massena, 2300, 7 July 1809, SHD, 2C/93; Berthier to Massena, 7 July 1809, Koch, *Massena*, 'Pièce Justificative XXVIII', vol. VI, p. 437.
89. Berthier orders to Marmont and Montbrun, both 2300, 7 July 1809, SHD, C2/93.
90. Adolphe Thiers, *Histoire du Consulat et de l'Empire*, Paris: Paulin, 1868, vol. X, p. 479. As noted above, Charles perceived numerous reasons *not* to retreat towards Brünn and Olmütz.
91. 'Disposition zu dem Marsch in das Lager bey Göllersdorf', 7 July 1809, KAFA, 1422; Hauptarmee, Op. J. 1f, KAFA, 1381.

92. Bruyère, 'Notices Historiques et Topographiques sur les Marches et Combats des Troupes aux Ordres de Général Bruyère en 1809', *Carnet de la Sabretache*, no. 198, June 1909, p. 368.
93. Vincent to Klenau, 0830, 8 July 1809, and Klenau to Charles, 1000, 8 July 1809, KAFA, 1422 (Klenau had already placed a time on his report before learning that Stockerau had been lost).
94. Lindenau report, 8 July 1809, SHD, 2C/93.
95. Bruyère, 'Notices Historiques et Topographiques', p. 369.
96. Zech/Porbeck, *Badischen Truppen 1809*, pp. 172–7; Baden Brigade journal, GLA 48/4286; Maendl, *Infanterie-Regiments Nr. 51*, vol. II, p. 93; Ameil reports, 8 July (no time) and 0700, 9 July 1809, SHD, C2/93.
97. Martin Vignolle, 'Armée d'Italie: Journal Historique de la Campagne de 1809', SHD, MR734; Lindenau report, 8 July 1809, SHD, 2C/93.
98. Pelet, *Guerre de 1809*, vol. IV, p. 254–5.
99. VI Corps, Op. J. 35, KAFA, 1384.
100. Pelleport, *Souvenirs Militaries*, vol. I, p. 286; Marbot, *Memoirs*, vol. II, p. 395. Gachot gives the number of prisoners as 417 (*1809*, p. 295).
101. The number fit for duty was between 26 and 40, Karl von Zimmermann, *Geschichte des 1. Großherzoglich Hessischen Dragoner-Regiments*, Darmstadt: Bergsträßer, 1878, vol. I, p. 148.
102. Klenau to Charles, 1000, 8 July 1809, KAFA, 1422. The III Corps, which was under no pressure, provides an example: it departed the Kreuzenstein Heights position at 10:00 p.m. on the 7th; arrived near Göllersdorf at 9:00 the following morning where the men had time to prepare a meal before marching again at 9:00 p.m. to reach their new bivouac near Schöngrabern at 7:00 a.m. on the 9th (Op. J. 13, KAFA, 1382).
103. Klenau to Charles, 0500, 8 July 1809, in Hauptarmee, Op. J. 1f, KAFA, 1381; VI Corps, Op. J. 32, KAFA, 1384.
104. Liechtenstein to Charles, 8 July 1809, KAFA, 1461.
105. Wimpffen to Klenau, 0600, 8 July 1809, KAFA, 1422; and Ites Corps de Reserve, 'Operations-Journal vom 27t Febr bis 31 Deber 1809', Op. J. 75, KAFA, 1388.
106. 'Disposition für den Marsch in das Lager bei Schöngrabern', 8 July 1809, KAFA, 1422.
107. For example, Spleny to Klenau, 0645, 8 July 1809, KAFA, 1422.
108. Charles to Schustekh, 8 July 1809; Schustekh, 'Disposition auf den 8t July 809', both KAFA, 1416.
109. 'Task force' is used here for the German '*Streifcommando*'.
110. Charles to Scheibler, 8 July 1809, KAFA, 1416.
111. Oskar Posselt, *Geschichte des k. und k. Infanterieregiments Ritter v. Pino Nr. 40*, Rzeszow: regimental, 1913, pp. 338–9; and Schustekh to Reuss, 10 July 1809, KAFA, 1416.
112. Hohenzollern to Charles, 8 July 1809, KAFA, 1409.
113. The strength of Altstern's infantry is uncertain. In his 9 July report, he claimed only 800 men in *Rohan*, but a summary of Morning Reports of 7–10 July gives the regiment 1,721 men (KAFA, 1461). The discrepancy could arise from several factors: the return

of stragglers and lost detachments by 10 July or Altstern underplaying his strength to excuse his hasty retreat on 9 July.

114. Correspondence between Charles and Hohenzollern and between Hohenzollern and Altstern, 8 July 1809, KAFA, 1409.
115. The 8th Jägers were supposed to be part of this group, but the battalion had been destroyed near Neudorf, as we have seen.
116. Mecséry's reports to Hohenzollern, 8 and 9 July 1809, KAFA, 1409. It is not clear how this division of *Blankenstein* Hussars appeared here on the army's left flank; it may have remained with IV Corps during the retreat on 6 July or retreated on its own between II and IV Corps. The bulk of the regiment was on the Znaim road, but a Rittmeister Blankenstein (there were two with this name and rank in the regiment at the time) had 100–120 troopers under his command in the area between II and IV Corps (from Hohenzollern's and Mecséry's correspondence).
117. Schnierer, *Aus der Franzosenzeit*, p. 25.
118. IV Corps, Op. J. 22, KAFA, 1383.
119. Parts of *EH Ferdinand* Hussars No. 3 and *O'Reilly* Chevaulegers No. 3 along with two squadrons of Primatial Insurrection Hussars and a cavalry battery (Radetzky's after-action report, KAFA, 1461).
120. Rosenberg to Charles, morning and afternoon, 8 July 1809, Hauptarmee, Op. J. 1f, KAFA, 1381; and Rosenberg to Hohenzollern, 1100, 8 July 1809, KAFA, 1409.
121. Charles to Rosenberg, 7 July and 8 July (two letters) 1809, KAFA, 1413.
122. Rosenberg to Charles, and Rosenberg to Moravian Regional Command, both 8 July 1809, KA, Nachlass Rosenberg, B/1504, 1809/1; Rosenberg to Hohenzollern, 8 July 1809, KAFA, 1409; and IV Corps correspondence log, KAFA, 1414.
123. Napoleon to Clarke, 8 July 1809, *CG*, no. 21,473, vol. IX, p. 836.
124. Three reports from Massena to Berthier (no times noted), 8 July 1809, SHD, C2/93. In one of these messages, the marshal noted that he was beginning to walk about a bit with a cane and hoped to be able to ride soon.
125. Marmont to Napoleon, noon, 8 July 1809, SHD, C2/93.
126. Marmont to Napoleon, 1600, 8 July 1809, SHD, C2/93; note that Buat (vol. II, p. 327, n. 6) mistakenly cites this missive as being sent at noon.
127. Ludwig von Madroux, 'August von Floret', *Archiv für Offiziere aller Waffen*, III/2, 1846, p. 192; Tascher, *Journal de Campagne*, entries for 9 and 8 July respectively, p. 237.
128. Desboeufs, *Souvenirs*, p. 113.
129. Cadet de Gassicourt, *Voyage en Autriche*, p. 244.
130. Berthier to Marmont, 1500, 8 July 1809, SHD, C2/93.
131. Napoleon to Berthier, 8 July 1809, *CG*, no. 21,470, vol. IX, p. 835; Berthier to Massena, 1600, 8 July 1809, SHD, C2/93.
132. Orders from Berthier to the respective commanders, 1600, 8 July 1809, SHD, C2/93.
133. Napoleon to Alexander, 8 July 1809, *CG*, no. 21,474, vol. IX, p. 837. The '1,000 *toise*' distance would be approximately 2,000 metres.

134. Vladimir Ivanovich Baron Löwenstern, *Mémoires du Général-Major Russe Baron de Löwenstern*, M. H. Weil (ed.), Paris: Fontemoing, 1903, vol. I, p. 136.
135. Berthier to Oudinot, 1600, 8 July 1809, SHD, C2/93.
136. Buat, *1809*, vol. II, pp. 328, 358–9; Naulet, *Wagram*, p. 258; Béraud, *La Révolution Militaire*, p. 238.
137. Marmont to Davout, 8 July 1809, SHD, C2/93.
138. Napoleon to Marmont, 0200, 11 July 1809, *CG*, vol. IX, no. 21,480, p. 839. For a caustic contemporary critique, see Laurent de l'Ardeche, *Réfutation des Mémoires du Maréchal Marmont*, Paris: Plon, 1857, pp. 207–12, 269–81.
139. Marmont, *Mémoires*, vol. III, pp. 246–7; see also his *De l'Esprit des Institutions Militaires*, Paris: Librairie Militaire, 1845, pp. 193–4.
140. Charles to Franz, 13 July 1809, KAFA, 1461.
141. Ludwig Freiherr von Welden, *Der Krieg von 1809 zwischen Oesterreich und Frankreich*, Vienna: Gerold, 1872, p. 196.
142. Charles to Johann, 8 July 1809, Hauptarmee, Op. J. 1f, KAFA, 1381. On the assumption that Napoleon would somehow allow time for the Hauptarmee to recuperate, see the sections on Charles in April, Hiller in May and Johann from May through June in the three volumes of *Thunder on the Danube*.
143. Franz quoted in Just, *Friede von Schönbrunn*, p. 13.
144. 'Précis de la marche des négociations qui ont amené le traité de Vienne', in Clemens von Klinkowström, *Aus der alten Registratur der Staatskanzlei*, Vienna: Braumüller, 1870, p. 156; Gentz, diary entry for 17 August 1809, relating his conversations with an Austrian diplomat who had accompanied Franz throughout Wagram and the retreat, Gentz, *Tagebücher*, p. 121; Kraehe, *Metternich's German Policy*, p. 89. Metternich's typically tendentious and dramatised account of his stay in Vienna is in Metternich, *Aus Metternichs Nachgelassenen Papieren*, Vienna: Braumüller, 1880, vol. I, pp. 77–80. Liechtenstein's biographer, Oscar Criste, states that Napoleon replied in the affirmative when asked if he would accept Liechtenstein's embassy (*Feldmarschall Johannes Fürst von Liechtenstein*, Vienna: Seidel & Sohn, 1905, p. 133); while not impossible, it is difficult to imagine how the question could have been communicated to Napoleon and an answer received in the short space of time (7–8 July) and amidst the uncertainties and confusions associated with the retreat and pursuit; there is no reference to such a communication in available French sources.
145. Skall, 'Feldzugsreise', p. 245.
146. Charles to Franz, 1700, 8 July 1809, as well as the Kaiser's questions, in Criste, *Carl*, vol. III, pp. 250–1.
147. Rössler, *Österreichs Kampf*, vol. II, p. 43.
148. Franz to Charles, 8 July 1809, KAFA, 1461.
149. Charles to Albert, 9 July 1809, in Criste, *Carl*, vol. III, p. 494.
150. Fedor von Demelitsch, *Metternichs auswärtige Politik*, Stuttgart: Cotta, 1898, pp. 27–8; Rössler, *Österreichs Kampf*, vol. II, p. 43. On Metternich's life and career, see the new

biography using previously underutilised sources by Wolfram Siemann, *Metternich: Strategist and Visionary*, Cambridge, Massachusetts: Harvard University Press, 2019.
151. Stadion to Franz, 12 July 1809, No. 1, HHStA, Vorträge 1809 (V–X), 182.
152. Beer, *Zehn Jahre*, p. 422. We may speculate that this physical distance was also a way to remove Franz from direct responsibility for the negotiations.
153. Delmotte to Albert, 7 July 1809, in Wertheimer, *Geschichte Österreichs und Ungarns*, vol. II, p. 375; Charles to Albert, 9 July 1809, in Criste, *Carl*, vol. III, p. 492.
154. Savary, *Mémoires*, vol. IV, pp. 188, 195.
155. These other detachments were the 6th Hussars from the Army of Italy at Bruck an der Leitha and the 18th Léger of Marmont's corps on the road to Vienna from Bruck an der Mur.
156. Berthier to Eugène, 9 July 1809, *CdN*, no. 15,506 vol. XIX, pp. 232–4; and Berthier to Eugène, 1700, 9 July 1809, SHD, C2/93.
157. Grouchy to Davout, 0200, 9 July 1809; also reports by Montbrun (8 July, forwarded by Davout at 0130, 9 July) and Oudinot (9 July); all SHD, C2/93.
158. Ordre, 9 July 1809, in Pelet, *Guerre de 1809*, vol. IV, pp. 408–9.
159. Ordre, 9 July 1809, *CdN*, no. 15,507, vol. XIX, p. 234.
160. Contrary to Marbot's colourful story (*Memoirs*, vol. II, pp. 385–7), Bernadotte was not cashiered on the battlefield at Wagram. Though it is certainly possible that he and the emperor exchanged angry words on 6 July leaving Bernadotte in some disgrace, correspondence between the marshal and imperial headquarters was completely normal through the afternoon of 9 July, when a courteous letter from Berthier informed Bernadotte that he would be receiving a new assignment (1700, 9 July, SHD, C2/93).
161. See Gill, *Eagles*, pp. 306–7.
162. Comprising GD Pierre Louis Dupas's division of 9th Corps: the 5th Léger and Dupas's artillery were allotted to Boudet's division while the 19th Ligne was to join Legrand; Dupas was designated to replace the wounded GD Bernard Georges François Frère in 2nd Corps, but declined the assignment.
163. Massena to Berthier, morning, 9 July 1809, SHD, C2/93; Massena to Boudet, 9 July 1809, in Gachot, *1809*, p. 296/N2. The marshal sent the Baden Jägers with some light cavalry up the northwest highway towards Maissau, but this detachment had hardly reached Niederrußbach (then Unter-Rußbach) when it was recalled; it rejoined the corps at Großstelzendorf.
164. Rainer Egger, *Das Gefecht bei Hollabrunn und Schöngrabern 1805*, Vienna: Heeresgeschichtliches Museum, 1982.
165. *Benjovszky* Infantry had only two battalions at this time (II and III) as I/*Benjovszky* had been distributed among the other two after the heavy losses at Aspern-Essling in May.
166. Amon Ritter von Treuenfest, *Geschichte des k. k. Huszaren-Regimentes Alexander Freiherr v. Koller Nr. 8*, Vienna: Mayer, 1880, p. 469. This anecdote indicates that at least some of the *Kienmayer* Hussars, even if only an escort detachment, had remained with the main body of VI Corps along with the *Blankenstein* and *Liechtenstein* Regiments.

167. Technically, there were three battalions of Vienna Volunteers (2nd, 3rd and 4th); but the 3rd and 4th had been combined owing to their losses. For the hussars: Teschenberg to Klenau, (evening), 9 July 1809, KAFA, 1422.
168. Bruyère, 'Notices Historiques et Topographiques', p. 369. The report from Bruyère's division only mentions light cavalry, but it is clear that cuirassiers were involved, most likely the 1st Regiment as this unit received special notice from Massena. See also Gachot, *1809*, p. 297.
169. Both quotations from the Baden brigade journal, GLA, 48/4286.
170. Klenau, VI Corps, Op. J. 35, KAFA, 1384.
171. Troops involved in the struggle for the town on the Austrian side included *Benjovszky*, *Spleny* and two companies of *Gyulai*; the 1st Vienna Volunteers were engaged in the meadows west of town and III/*Klebek* moved up to support late in the day; the rest of the corps seems to have been in position on the hills northwest of town (minus Vécsey and the two squadrons of *Blankenstein* detached). The entire Baden brigade minus II/2 Infantry (in reserve) was heavily engaged as was I/26 Léger (the other two battalions in reserve) and most of the cavalry; based on the number of officers wounded (seven), it would seem that the 18th Ligne did most of the fighting in the town on the French side. Massena offered special praise for the 1st Cuirassiers, so it is likely that this regiment joined the light cavalry charge into Hollabrunn in the opening phase of the battle; it is unclear which other regiment(s) were involved.
172. Bruyère, 'Notices Historiques et Topographiques', p. 369; Gachot, *1809*, p. 297.
173. Massena to Berthier, 2200, 9 July 1809, SHD, C2/93.
174. Multiplying the number of officer losses from Aristide Martinien (*Tableaux par corps et par batailles des Officiers Tués et Blessés pendant les Guerres de l'Empire*, Paris: Éditions Militaires Européenes, 1984 reprint) by twelve for the 18th Ligne (the approximate ratio of officers to men reported for the 26th Léger in Gueheneuc and for the Badeners) and an estimate of one officer to ten men for the cavalry regiments. Gachot gives a total of 315 dead and wounded for Massena's troops (*1809*, p. 297).
175. Neuenstein to Großherzog Carl Friedrich, 15 July 1809, GLA, 48/4266.
176. Karl von Blazekovic and Julius Pössl, *Chronik des k. u. k. Infanterieregiments Nr. 31*, Regimental Verlag: 1909, vol. I, pp. 292–6; Maendl, *Infanterie-Regiments Nr. 51*, p. 96.
177. *Klebek* Infantry after-action report for 30 June to 9 July, 13 July 1809, KAFA, 1461. Massena's chief of staff told Molitor 'we took 400 or 500 prisoners yesterday', Fririon to Molitor, 10 July 1809, SHD, C2/93. Gachot gives the total number of prisoners taken as 715 (*1809*, p. 297).
178. Klenau to Charles, 1300, 9 July 1809, KAFA, 1422.
179. 'Der k. k. Feldmarschall-Lieutenant Graf Klenau im Gefechte bei Hollabrunn, 1809', *Österreichische militärische Zeitschrift*, vol. VII/1, 1866, pp. 12–4.
180. Welden, *Der Krieg von 1809*, p. 198.
181. Sources for the engagement at Hollabrunn: Hauptarmee, Op. J. 1f, KAFA, 1381; VI Corps, Op. J. 35, KAFA, 1384; after-action reports of the 1st, 3rd and 4th Vienna Volunteer Battalions, KAFA, 1422; after-action reports of GM Mariássy, *Klebek* Infantry,

Benjovszky Infantry, Splenyi Infantry and Gyulai Infantry, all in KAFA, 1461; Baden brigade journal, GLA, 48/4286; Bruyère, 'Notices Historiques et Topographiques', pp. 369–70; Gueheneuc, 'Historique du 26e Léger'; Pelet, *Guerre de 1809*, vol. IV, pp. 258–9; Koch, *Massena*, vol. VI, pp. 339–41; Zech/Porbeck, *Badischen Truppen 1809*, pp. 175–82; Austrian, Baden and French regimental histories.

182. 'Notices Historiques et Topographiques', p. 370.
183. Berthier to Massena, 0530, 9 July 1809, Archives Nationales, fonds Masséna, 304 Mi 48–49 [311 AP 48-49]; Massena to Berthier, 2100, 9 July 1809, SHD, C2/93.
184. Lindenau's after-action report, 19 July 1809, Bayerisches Hauptstaatsarchiv, B Feldzüge 445 [hereafter BayHStA, B445].
185. Note that the community of Musov (Muschau) was dissolved in 1980 as the area had been transformed into a lake.
186. Rosenberg to Charles, 9 July 1809 (from Laa) and Rosenberg to Altstern, 9 July 1809 (from Dürnholz), both KA, Nachlass Rosenberg, B/1504, 1809/1.
187. On the night of the 8th, he complained to Berthier from Mistelbach that Colbert was up the road to Nikolsburg and that Montbrun had not yet arrived (Marmont to Berthier, 2200, 8 July 1809, SHD, C2/93).
188. Marmont reported that he had conducted the attacks at Staatz and Neudorf with Colbert's brigade and the Bavarians. The term 'French' is used here for convenience, but the lack of unit after-action reports from the French side makes it impossible to know precisely which elements were indeed French and which were Bavarian – the Austrians did not distinguish between the two enemies in their reporting. The artillery deployed at Staatz, for instance, was a Bavarian light battery.
189. Fröhlich's name is sometimes spelt 'Frehlich' or 'Frelich'; 'Fröhlich' is used here as in the Army's *Schematismus* of 1810. Note that the same official publication uses 'Frelich' for Infantry Regiment No. 28.
190. Radetzky's after-action report, KAFA, 1461. Radetzky's force at Staatz/Neudorf on 9 July (with number of squadrons): *EH Ferdinand* Hussars (8) *Stipsicz* Hussars (4½), *O'Reilly* Chevaulegers (4), a cavalry battery and several hundred infantry. Radetzky does not mention any infantry in his report, but the tiny band of 8th Jägers was clearly present as well as likely the 1st *EH Carl* Legion under Major Philip Watterich (or Wadrich) and possibly the remnants of the 1st and 7th Jägers.
191. Major Hieronymus Mumb, 8th Jäger Battalion after-action report, 16 July 1809, KAFA, 1409.
192. Preysing to Minucci, 9 July 1809; the 2nd Chevaulegers after-action report (both BayHStA, B445); and Ludwig von Madroux, in 'August von Floret', pp. 192–205. Madroux, the regimental adjutant in 1809, provides a detailed account of this cavalry action and his much-admired colonel's talents.
193. Radetzky's after-action report, KAFA, 1461.
194. Rosenberg to Charles, evening, 9 July 1809 (from Muschau), KA, Nachlass Rosenberg, B/1504, 1809/1.

195. As in the Austrian official account: *Relation über die Schlacht bei Deutsch-Wagram auf dem Marchfelde am 5ten und 6ten July 1809, und die Gefechte, welche derselben bis zum Abschlusse des Waffenstillstandes am 12ten des nämlichen Monats folgten*, Pest, 1809, p. 28; or Welden, *Der Krieg von 1809*, pp. 196–7.
196. Marmont to Berthier and to Davout, 9 July 1809, SHD, C2/93.
197. Davout to Napoleon, 0130, 9 July 1809, SHD, C2/93.
198. Grouchy, after-action report, 11 July 1809, in Emmanuel Grouchy, *Mémoires du Maréchal de Grouchy*, Paris: Dentu, 1873, vol. III, pp. 39–41; and Grouchy to Davout, 2200, 9 July 1809, SHD, C2/93.
199. It is not clear how many bridges there were at the time (Austrian sources mention seven bridges, the Army of Dalmatia wrote of nine), but there were clearly several and they posed a significant obstacle.
200. Altstern's 9 July 1809 report, in Hauptarmee, Op. J. 1f, KAFA, 1381; Hohenzollern to Altstern, 8 July 1809, KAFA, 1409; also II Corps, Op. J. 10 and Op. J. 15, KAFA, 1382.
201. Montbrun to Berthier, 9 July 1809 from Laa, SHD, C2.93.
202. Desboeufs, *Souvenirs*, p. 113.
203. Davout to Napoleon, 1600, 9 July 1809, SHD, C2/93; Mändler, *Erinnerungen*, p. 37.
204. Marmont, *Mémoires*, vol. III, pp. 245–6.
205. Undated draft, HHStA, Vorträge 1809 (V–X), 182; Charles to Franz, 13 July 1809, MNL, P300, Carton 18.
206. Bruyère, 'Notices Historiques et Topographiques', p. 369. Both Massena's memoirs (Koch, vol. VI, p. 339) and Pelet (vol. IV, p. 258) record dismissively that the Austrian messenger was chased off with a few cannon shots.
207. Wilhelmus Kenis, *Soldaten van Napoleon*, K. C. Peeters, ed., Antwerp: de Vlijt, 1955, p. 90.
208. Klenau note, 9 July 1809, SHD, C2/93; Klenau to Charles, 1300, 9 July 1809, KAFA, 1422; St Quentin report, 1000, 9 July 1809, KAFA, 1422. There is a lacuna here as Napoleon's reply (awaiting Liechtenstein with pleasure) could not have resulted from Klenau's 9 July note; Wolkersdorf is some 50 km from Hollabrunn and it is hardly conceivable that a rider could have carried Klenau's note via Massena to Napoleon, received the emperor's response, and returned by 10:00 the same morning. This suggests that the Austrian court had in some fashion communicated with Napoleon on 7 or 8 July. If so, as seems the case, this would likely have been an initiative of Metternich's. A letter in the French Foreign Ministry archives to an unspecified recipient dated 7 July from Znaim *refers to* Metternich; although this innocuous letter of transmittal (the attachments are missing) does not address the question of peace or mention an Austrian envoy, its existence suggests that some channel of communication could have been open to allow Napoleon to learn of the Habsburg interest in initiating negotiations (unsigned, unaddressed letter, dated Znaim, 7 July 1809, AE, vol. 383). Adding further complication is Just's unelaborated statement that Charles's emissary reached the outpost line at 2:00 p.m. on the 9th to deliver his message, and that Massena responded that night (*Friede von Schönbrunn*, pp. 14–15).

209. Two 9 July 1809 letters from Berthier to Massena (one at 0530, the other with no time indicated), Archives Nationales, fonds Masséna, 304 Mi 48–49 [311 AP 48–49] (with thanks to the Prince d'Essling and friends at the Fondation Napoléon); Wilhelm von Baden, *Denkwürdigkeiten des Markgrafen Wilhelm von Baden*, Karl Obser (ed.), Heidelberg: Winter, 1906, vol. I, p. 95.
210. Robiquet, 'Le Général de Galbois', p. 8.
211. Massena to Berthier, 2200, 9 July 1809, SHD, C2/93. Massena does not name the '*général parlementaire*' whose delay he describes, but it seems logical that this must have been Weißenwolff.
212. The French were not alone in trying to influence the other side through solicitous treatment of captured generals. GD Antoine Jean Auguste Henri, Comte Durosnel, one of Napoleon's personal aides-de-camp, had been wounded and taken prisoner on 22 May at Aspern-Essling. His fate had been the subject of considerable interest to both sides prior to Wagram and Metternich seems to have regarded him as a channel to influence the French emperor. Despite the hectic confusion of 6 July, Metternich sent a personal note to the captive Durosnel from Ernstbrunn (i.e. during the retreat after Wagram) forwarding several letters for the French general that Metternich had been given while being detained in Vienna; he also offered to defray Durosnel's expenses in captivity 'if perhaps you find yourself momentarily denuded of pecuniary resources' (Metternich to 'M. le Gl. Durosnel, prisonnier de guerre', 6 July 1809, Národni Archiv, Metternich Family Archive, AC 8/34 [hereafter NA]). Charles, in consultation with Stadion, then ordered Durosnel's release on 12 July in hopes of advantageously working on Napoleon's good opinion (Charles to Franz, 23 July 1809, KAFA, 1462). Durosnel expressed his appreciation for Metternich's courtesy before departing for the French lines (Durosnel to Metternich, 12 July 1809 from Brünn, NA, AC 10/232), but there is no evidence that his return had any substantial effect on the emperor's actions. The Austrians had seen Durosnel as a bargaining chip in the controversy surrounding Napoleon's branding of Chasteler as a war criminal for allegedly ordering the murder of French and Bavarian prisoners in the Tyrol.
213. Charles to Hohenzollern, 2200, 9 July 1809, KAFA, 1409.
214. Angeli, *Carl*, vol. IV, p. 533.
215. Charles, 'Über den Verlauf der Schlacht bei Wagram' (Charles to Colloredo, 21 July 1809), *Ausgewählte Schriften*, vol. VI, p. 308.
216. 'Disposition zur Fortsetzung des Marches des 1t, 3, 5, und 6t Corps in die Aufstellung beÿ Znaÿm', 0330, 10 July 1809, KAFA, 1416; emphasis in the original.
217. Skall, 'Feldzugsreise', pp. 246–7.
218. The letter does not have a time of writing or dispatch, but Criste (*Carl*, vol. III, p. 262) states that it reached Charles early on 10 July, leading to the conclusion that it was written shortly before Franz left Znaim or perhaps from Mährisch-Budwitz.
219. Franz to Charles, 9 July 1809 from Znaim with Stadion memorandum, KAFA, 1461.
220. Franz to Charles, 9 July 1809 from Czaslau, MNL, P300, Carton 44; parts in Criste, *Carl*, vol. III, p. 266; and Hertenberger/Wiltschek, *Carl*, p. 287. Binder von Kriegelstein

relates that an unnamed Prussian met Franz in Czaslau that night and reported to Berlin that the Kaiser intended to continue the war, that negotiations were not being considered, and that Charles would likely soon be replaced (*Der Krieg Napoleons*, vol. II, p. 399).

221. Rosenberg had an estimated 12,700 infantry and 1,360 cavalry on/about 10 July (Heller gives him 12,237 infantry and 1,117 cavalry, in *Feldzug des Jahres 1809*, vol. II, p. 244). Karl Bornemann also addresses this point in his study, but makes the unsubstantiated assumption that Charles initially intended for Rosenberg to march to Laa (*Napoleon bei Znaim*, Geislingen/Steige: Verlag der Südmährischen Landschaftsrates, 1975, pp. 18–21). While entirely reasonable, there is nothing in the record to suggest that this thought entered the archduke's mind.
222. Liechtenstein was not the only corps commander to complain about the drastic reduction in mounted strength; Hohenzollern lamented that his *Vincent* Chevaulegers No. 4 only had 300 troopers available owing to losses, exhaustion and numerous detachments (Hohenzollern to Charles, 8 July 1809, KAFA, 1409).
223. Such as Buat, *1809*, Vol. II, pp. 330–41.
224. Napoleon would later admonish Marmont, but not for pursuing the enemy closely, rather for lacking circumspection in that Marmont's attack might have entangled him with a superior enemy and made it impossible to disengage.
225. Koch, *Massena*, vol. VI, p. 341; Marmont to Berthier, 14 July 1809, SHD, C2/93.

Intermezzo: The Other Theatres of War

1. For summaries of these operations, see *Thunder on the Danube*, vol. III, Chapters 1, 3, 4 and 7.
2. Waldstein, 'Rapport confidential & détaillé sur les circonstances & négociations relatives au Project d'Insurrection dans le Nord de l'Allemagne', London, 20 September 1809, NA, AC 8/34. See also his report of 16 October 1809, in Hormayr *Lebensbilder*, vol. I, pt. 2, pp. 39–47. Of course, given the timing of his departure from Wolkersdorf and the difficulties of traveling surreptitiously to Britain, Waldstein's mission was far too late to influence the armistice decision Charles made on 11/12 July.
3. VIII Corps, Op. J. 46, KAFA, 1386.
4. Charles to Ferdinand, 8 July 1809, KAFA, 1461; Ferdinand to Charles, 12 July 1809, KAFA, 1462.

Chapter 5: I Found Myself in the Rear of the Austrian Army

1. Schustekh's and Somariva's operations journals (Op. J. 28, 68, and 69, KAFA, 1383 and 1387); Schustekh to Reuss, 10 July 1809, KAFA, 1416.
2. Fririon to Molitor, 10 July 1809, SHD, C2/93.
3. Schneller's after-action report, 15 July 1809, KAFA, 1462.
4. In addition to visits to the battlefield, the following draws on Karl Georg Rumi, *Geographisch-statistisches Wörterbuch des österreichischen Kaierstaates*, Vienna: Doll, 1809;

Joseph Marx Freyherrn von Liechtenstern, *Handbuch der neuesten Geographie des Österreichischen Kaiserstaates,* Vienna: Bauer, 1817; Friedrich Anton Heller von Hellwald, *Der Feldzug des Jahres 1809, in Süddeutschland,* Vienna: Carl Gerold's Sohn, 1864, vol. II, pp. 253–6; as well as courteous personal communications from Dr Jiří Kacetl of the South Moravian Museum in Znojmo.

5. On these earthworks (*Schanzen*) see Appendix 7.
6. While noting that the archduke was 'astonishingly' familiar with all of the 'positions' within the monarchy, Binder von Kriegelstein (*Der Krieg Napoleons,* vol. II, p. 403) uses this as another opportunity to criticise Charles for his persistent adherence to 'the lessons of the old school'.
7. This is the time given in Criste, *Carl,* vol. III, p. 257; Hoen, *Wagram,* p. 117, also gives 9:00 a.m. The main operations journal, on the other hand states that Charles arrived at 6:00 a.m., which seems rather too early.
8. Welden, *Krieg von 1809,* p. 199. See also Valentini, *Versuch einer Geschichte,* pp. 226. Znaim could have been considered a 'position' of sorts as long the enemy approached *only* from the south via the Vienna highway and did not threaten the eastern/left flank as would be the case on 10/11 July.
9. Hoen, *Wagram,* pp. 118–19.
10. Charles, 'Geist des Kriegswesens Überhaupt', *Ausgewählte Schriften,* vol. V, pp. 53–4; Heinrich Ommen, *Die Kriegsführung des Erzherzogs Carl,* Berlin, 1900, p. 95.
11. Charles to Franz, 10 July 1809, in Criste, *Carl,* vol. III, pp. 257–8. Massena had indeed sent an aide-de-camp to inform the Austrians that Liechtenstein could come to imperial headquarters but, as of the morning of 10 July, Liechtenstein had not appeared (Massena to Berthier, 10 July 1809, SHD, C2/93).
12. The unnamed priest's chronicle, translated from Latin and published in Anton Hübner, *Denkwürdigkeiten der königl. Stadt Znaim,* Znaim: Lenk, 1869, p. 896. An '*Eimer*' was a liquid measure that was approximately equivalent to 16 gallons or 60 litres (according to Thomas Mortimer and William Dickinson, *A General Commerical Dictionary,* London, 1823); the law that introduced the metric system into Austria defined the *Eimer* as 56.589 litres; meaning the anonymous cleric was claiming to have delivered considerably more than 3,000 litres of wine over the two days!
13. Grenadier Corps after-action report, 17 July 1809, KAFA, 1462; Reserve Corps, Op. J. 76, KAFA, 1388.
14. This was the same Prochaska who had served briefly as army chief of staff early in the war. He was now one of two division commanders (two brigades each) in the Grenadier Corps, but had become acting commander of all four brigades when his counterpart, FML Constantin Freiherr d'Aspre, was mortally wounded at Wagram.
15. Grenadier Corps after-action report, 17 July 1809, KAFA, 1462.
16. Marmont to Napoleon, 11 July 1809, SHD, C2/93.
17. Marmont's after-action report to Berthier, 14 July 1809, SHD, C2/93.
18. Espinchal, *Souvenirs,* p. 274.

19. Marmont to Napoleon, 11 July 1809, SHD, C2/93, also in Marmont, *Mémoires*, vol. III, pp. 517–19.
20. Marmont's after-action report to Berthier, 14 July 1809, SHD, C2/93.
21. The identity and strength of the Austrian troops in Zuckerhandl is unclear.
22. Grenadier Corps after-action report, KAFA, 1462.
23. Marmont's after-action report to Berthier, 14 July 1809, SHD, C2/93.
24. Marmont, *Mémoires*, vol. VI, p. 249.
25. Ibid., p. 250.
26. This section draws on a composite of Marmont's 10 July report to Berthier, his 14 July 1809 after-action report and his memoirs. As the memoirs closely follow the after-action report, it would seem that he had a copy at hand when he composed his subsequent account.
27. Reserve Corps, Op. J. 77, KAFA, 1388.
28. Ibid.
29. *Schwarzenberg* Uhlans after-action report, KAFA, 1412.
30. Although authors such as Heller von Hellwald credit Charles with personally ordering the cuirassiers forward and Welden credits Schwarzenberg, none of the Austrian operations journals give any indication as to who issued the orders.
31. In words that unconsciously echoed a letter Charles wrote to Franz on 13 July, Marmont asserted that the Austian army would have been 'gravely compromised' had Davout been present. With no route of retreat, it would have been forced to march upstream along the Thaya on poor roads in difficult terrain and 'would have lost all its materiel and become completely disorganised' (Marmont, *Mémoires*, vol. VI, pp. 249–50). See below for discussion of Charles's letter.
32. Marmont's 14 July 1809 after-action report (SHD, C2/93) and his memoirs (vol. VI, pp. 250–1). The statement about Bavarian skirmishers following Steyrer, however, is my conclusion as (1) this would have been a natural consequence of the attack on the heights and (2) it seems from the Bavarian after-action reports that some Bavarian troops had entered Klein-Tesswitz before the more or less 'formal' assault by the 2nd Brigade.
33. Army of Dalmatia after-action report, 17 July 1809, SHD, C2/94 (written by Adjutant-Commandant Delort).
34. Ibid.
35. Binnenthal, 'Selbstbiografie', KAFA, Nachlässe, 698 (B); with thanks to Herr Michael Wenzel.
36. *Anton Mittrowsky* and *Erbach* each consisted of two battalions; *Reuss-Plauen* forded the river with two battalions and four companies; the remaining two companies were part of the corps rearguard and crossed later.
37. Austrian accounts also mention the threat of enemy light cavalry. It is entirely possible that some few Bavarian horsemen were in the valley at this point, but there is no mention of such in the detailed Bavarian reports.

38. Binnenthal's after-action report, I Corps, Op. J. 5, KAFA, 1382; 'Relation über die Gefechte beÿ Znaim am 10ten und 11ten July 809', (also written by Binnenthal), KAFA, 1462.
39. Mändler, *Erinnerungen*, pp. 38–9; also Madroux, 'August von Floret', p. 206; and Reichold, *Soldaten-Sohn*, p. 123.
40. Madroux, 'August von Floret', p. 208; Madroux had this story from Preysing himself.
41. These were the two grenadier companies of Infantry Regt No. 25 (former *Zedtwitz*).
42. Grenadier Corps after-action report, 17 July 1809, KAFA, 1462.
43. Madroux, 'August von Floret', pp. 208–9.
44. Bavarian 2nd Division after-action report, 26 July 1809, BayHStA, B445.
45. Some Austrian reports also claim to have held Klein-Tesswitz at the end of the fighting, but this seems unlikely.
46. A contemporary Austrian commentator claimed that this magazine contained 40,000 loaves of bread ('Der letzte Akt des französich–österreichischen Feldzugs im Jahre 1809', *Europäische Annalen*, vol. V, 1811, p. 158).
47. Bavarian 7th Infantry after-action report, 12 July 1809, BayHStA, B445; French Sergeant Desboeufs of the 81st Ligne describes considerable fighting in his vivid memoirs (*Souvenirs*, pp. 113–16).
48. After-action reports from the participating units and commanders represent the principal sources for the fighting at Klein-Tesswitz. Austria: Schneller, Cavalry Reserve Corps, Grenadier Corps, I Corps (KAFA, 1462), Binnenthal's operations journal (Op. J. 5), and the Hauptarmee's operations journal (Op. J. 1f). Bavaria: 2nd Division (two reports: 12 and 26 July), 2nd Brigade, 6th Infantry, 7th Infantry, 2nd Chevaulegers (BayHStA, B445). France: Marmont's 14 July 1809 report (SHD, C2/93). These were supplemented by regimental histories (especially on the Bavarian side), Marmont's memoirs, Bavarian memoirs and the Austrian official 'Relation'.
49. Bavarian figures are based on specific day-by-day losses listed in a 'Verzeichniss' prepared on 12 July 1809 (BayHStA, B445). French regimental histories give no figures and Martinien lists no officer casualties for 10 July specifically; all of the killed and wounded in Martinien are listed under 11 July, but it is entirely possible that this was merely a matter of convenience or accounting and that some were indeed lost on the 10th. Austrian casualties are from the Grenadier Corps after-action report and from the regimental histories of *EH Rainer* and *Kolowrat*. However, in Austria's case, casualties for 10 and 11 July are combined, so some estimation is required. For the grenadiers, the estimate here is based on the assumption that most or all of the losses taken by Steyrer's and Hammer's brigades occurred on the 10th as they were not engaged on the 11th; for Murray's brigade, I did not count the heavy losses of the *Leiningen* Grenadiers (as most of these fell on 11 July), but did count all the casualties of the other three battalions (which were engaged but peripheral on 11 July) on the assumption that these would balance out (those suffered by *Leiningen* on the 10th balancing those suffered by the other three on the 11th); I did not count any from the Merville/Scovaud brigade as it was south of the Thaya on the 10th. *Rainer* had 126 casualties for the two days, but

was barely involved on the 11th, so we may assume most of those were lost in the fight for Klein-Tesswitz; *Kolowrat*, on the other hand, lost 887 men on 10–11 July and was heavily engaged on both days. Although it probably underestimates *Kolowrat's* losses at Klein-Tesswitz, I have applied the figure of 120 from *Rainer* to arrive at what seems a reasonable figure for the Austrian side.

50. Casualty table in the Grenadier Corps after-action report, 17 July 1809, KAFA, 1462.
51. *Relation über die Schlacht bei Deutsch-Wagram*, pp. 29–38.
52. Marmont's after-action report to Berthier, 14 July 1809, SHD, C2/93; and extract from the 12 July 1809 order of the day in Eduard Freiherr von Völderndorff und Waradein, *Kriegsgeschichte von Bayern unter König Maximilian Joseph I.*, Munich, 1826, vol. II, pp. 258–9. In his memoirs (vol. III, pp. 251–2), Marmont disparaged the Bavarian performance at Znaim, but this petty disdain, the opposite of his remarks at the time, was perhaps an effort to appeal to his French readership in the 1850s.
53. 'Skizzen einer Geschichte des 11ten k. baierischen Linien-Infanterie-Regiments', *Kriegs-Schriften, herausgegeben von baierischen Offizieren*, vol. I, Munich, 1820, p. 119. In measuring distances, soldiers of the era often used time as their metric with one hour equating to approximately 4 km of march; so this officer's reference to 'fifteen minutes' meant that the opposing lines only shifted 1 km or so despite fighting for two days. Note that the 13th Infantry became the 11th in 1811 as part of a renumbering of Bavarian regiments, thus the seeming anomaly of the regimental numbers.
54. Gottfried Uhlig, *Militärische Erinnerungen vom Jahre 1701 bis 1838 mit besonderer Berücksichtigung des aus den Divisionen des 35., 36. und 42. Linien-Infanterie-Regiments bestehenden Grenadier-Bataillons John*, Prague: Thabor, 1839, p. 53.
55. Jules Antoine Paulin, *Les Souvenirs du Général Baron Paulin*, Paris: Plon, 1895, p. 216.
56. My rendering of the German idiom '*mit klingendem Spiel*'.
57. All of the corps' operations journals specifically state that the infantry formed '*Quarrés*' not masses (Operations Journals 12, 13, 15 and 18, KAFA, 1382). All quotes from III Corps, Op. J. 12.
58. Espinchal, *Souvenirs*, vol. I, pp. 275–6.
59. Lejeune, 'Souvenirs', p. 525.
60. Hauptarmee, Op. J. 1f, KAFA, 1381.
61. Principal sources for actions on this part of the field are the operations journals of the Hauptarmee (Op. J. 1f) and the respective corps: Op. J. 5, 12, 13, 15, 18, 30, 35, 77 (KAFA, 1381, 1382, 1383, 1384, 1388).
62. Charles to Hohenzollern, 2200, 9 July 1809, KAFA, 1409.
63. Drawn from the II Corps operations journal (Op. J. 10) and Hohenzollern's personal journal (Op. J. 15), KAFA, 1382. In his personal journal (composed in the spring of 1810), Hohenzollern credited Altstern's 'intelligent actions' with preventing the Kaiser's capture.
64. Actions of II Corps are taken from its operations journal: II Corps, Op. J. 10, KAFA, 1382.

65. Binder von Kriegelstein (*Der Krieg Napoleons*, vol. II, p. 391) excoriates Hohenzollern for 'The characteristic reluctance to undertake independent operations ... the spirit of the direct and strict defensive was so ingrained in the Austrian leaders that they could not grasp the concept that the best means of defence consisted in the application of offensive force over the shortest distance.'
66. This is the time given in Liechtenstein's personal record (Reserve Corps, Op. J. 76, KAFA, 1388); the main operations journal places his departure from Znaim in the morning. Massena, writing in the morning from Göllersdorf, states that Liechtenstein had not yet appeared (to Berthier, 10 July 1809, SHD, C2/93).
67. Bornemann maintained that what Marmont heard were Austrian guns firing south of the Thaya around Naschetitz (*Napoleon bei Znaim*, p. 33).
68. Baden brigade journal, GLA 48/4286. The Hessians likewise thought the Austrians burned many villages intentionally: 'Feldzug der 2ten Division 4ten Armeecorps der Armee von Teutschland im Jahre 1809', *Pallas*, vol. II, no. 6, 1810, p. 638. Many common French soldiers also made this assumption, for example: François-Joseph Jacquin of the 37th Ligne in Molitor's division: *Carnet de Route d'un Grognard de la Révolution et de l'Empire*, Paris: Clavreuil, 1960, p. 72.
69. 'Feldzug der 2ten Division', p. 635.
70. Bruyère, 'Notices Historiques et Topographiques', p. 370. Six (vol. I, p. 171) mistakenly dates Bruyère's wounding to Wagram. Gachot (*1809*, p. 299) claims that the loss of Bruyère introduced disorder into the French cavalry and that the French squadrons were handed an unpleasant rebuff by their Habsburg foes; unfortunately, his timing for this entire affair is confused, so it is difficult to treat his depiction as reliable.
71. Piré had recently recovered from a wound to the head received at Aspern-Essling, Piré's personnel file, SHD, GR 7Y D601.
72. 'Feldzug der 2ten Division', p. 635.
73. 'Notes sur les operations du 4eme Corps de la grande armée pendant la champagne de 1809, en Autriche', 12 July 1809, SHD, MR 661. These seem to have been Pelet's notes made just after the battle.
74. Pelet, *Guerre de 1809*, vol. IV, p. 264.
75. Klebelsberg, after-action report, KAFA, 1462.
76. 'Historische Darstellung des Antheils, welchen das 5te Wiener Frey-Bataillon an dem Feldzuge des Jahres 1809 genommen hat', *Neue militärische Zeitschrift*, vol. III, 1811, pp. 81–4. Though published anonymously, this account was almost certainly written by Salis himself as an after-action report.
77. Zech/Porbeck, *Badischen Truppen 1809*, p. 186.
78. Naulet, *Wagram*, p. 263.
79. Martinien lists only three or four officers wounded. If the ratio of approximately 10–12 soldier casualties for each officer is applied, this yields perhaps 40–50 French cavalrymen lost on 10 July. Gachot, on the other hand (*1809*, p. 299), gives French losses as 413 but does not cite a source for this figure.

80. Erich Freiherr Riedl von Riedenau, *Geschichte des k. und k. Uhlanen-Regiments Erzherzog Karl Nr. 3*, Vienna: Hof- und Staatsdruckerei, 1901, p. 72; Karl Kandelsdorfer, *Geschichte des k. und k. Feld-Jäger-Bataillons Nr. 3*, Vienna: Vergani, 1899, vol. I, p. 75; Rudolf von Hödl, *Geschichte des k. und k. Infanterieregiments Nr. 29*, Temesvár: regimental, 1906, p. 259.
81. Sadly, the casualty list that accompanied Klebelsberg's after-action report is lost. The *Gradiska* Grenz report only lists nine captured and eleven missing, but it hardly seems credible that the regiment had no dead or wounded after the day's fighting. In addition to regimental histories, sources for the actions from Schöngrabern to Guntersdorf include: after-action reports for Reuss, Klebelsberg and the *Gradiska* Grenzer, KAFA, 1462; Heller, *Feldzug des Jahres 1809*, vol. II, pp. 261–3; 'Notes sur les operations du 4eme Corps', 12 July 1809, SHD, MR 661; Koch, *Massena*, vol. VI, pp. 345–6; Pelet, *Guerre de 1809*, vol. IV, pp. 260–4; Baden Brigade journal, GLA 48/4286; Zech/Porbeck, *Badischen Truppen 1809*, pp. 182–6.
82. Massena to Berthier, 2100, 10 July 1809, SHD, C2/93.
83. Pelet, *Guerre de 1809*, vol. IV, p. 263.
84. Massena to Berthier, 10 July 1809, SHD, C2/93. In a different note from Göllersdorf that morning, Massena reported that Liechtenstein had not yet appeared.
85. From the excellent collection of local chronicles available at: http://www3.htl-hl.ac.at/homepage/bok/dt/fr1805-9/bericht1.htm [accessed April 2019]; many of these and some additional ones are collected (in French translation) in Robert Ouvrard, *1809: Les Français à Vienne*, Paris: Nouveau Monde, 2009, pp. 239–72.
86. Local chronicles at: http://www3.htl-hl.ac.at/homepage/bok/dt/fr1805-9/bericht1.htm [accessed April 2019].
87. Wilhelm Meier, *Erinnerungen aus den Feldzügen 1806 bis 1815*, Karlsruhe: Müller, 1854, p. 63.
88. *Heimatbuch des Bezirkes Hollabrunn*, Hollabrunn, n.p., 1951, vol. II, pp. 230–4. Austrian accounts routinely blame the French for this incident, but the detailed history of the Bavarian artillery is very clear on attributing the retaliation to Bavarian troops (Rudolf Ritter von Xylander, *Geschichte des 1. Feld-Artillerie-Regiments Prinz-Regent Luitpold*, Berlin: Mittler und Sohn, 1909, vol. II, p. 188); also Minucci to Wrede and Gravenreuth to Minucci, both 13 July 1809, SHD, C2/93.
89. With thanks to Dr Rudolf Fürnkranz for excerpts from his book *Laa an der Thaya 1800–2000*, Gösling: Edition Weinviertel, 2009. See also Friedrich Kohlhauser and Karl Müller, *Heimatmuseum der Stadt Laa a. d. Thaya und Umgebung*, Laa an der Thaya: Heimatmuseum, 1930, p. 50.
90. Hübner, *Denkwürdigkeiten*, p. 835; Karl Fitzka, *Geschichte der Stadt Mistelbach*, Mistelbach: Stadtgemeinde, 1901, pp. 197–8.
91. Reichold, *Soldaten-Sohn*, p. 131; Hübner, *Denkwürdigkeiten*, p. 864.
92. *Heimatbuch des Bezirkes Hollabrunn*, Hollabrunn, 1951, vol. II, p. 234.
93. Wilhelm, *Denkwürdigkeiten*, vol. I, p. 95; see also Gassicourt, pp. 248–9; Zech and Porbeck list many of the measures taken in Massena's corps to enforce discipline, see *Badische Truppen 1809*, pp. 202–11.

94. Heimatbuch des Bezirkes Hollabrunn, vol. II, p. 227.
95. Hübner, Denkwürdigkeiten, p. 865.
96. Ibid., p. 890.
97. Willibald Rosner, 'Der Bezirk Hollabrunn von 1648 bis 1848', in Ernst Bezemerk and Willibald Rosner, eds., Vergangenheit und Gegenwart: Der Bezirk Hollabrunn und seine Gemeinden, Hollabrunn, 1993, p. 154.
98. Anton Eggendorfer, ed., Guntersdorf und Großnondorf: Die Geschichte der Marktgemeinde Guntersdorf, Wien: Berger, 2008, p. 136; Heimatbuch des Bezirkes Hollabrunn, vol. II, p. 229; Ernst von Kwiatowski, 'Die Kämpfe bei Schöngrabern und Ober-Hollabrunn 1805, 1809', Mittheilungen des K. K. Archivs für Nieder-Österreich, I/4, 1908, pp. 34–5.
99. Karl Pleyer, 'Zwei Berichte über Schöngrabern im Jahr 1809', Unsere Heimat, vol. XXX, 8/10, 1959, p. 171. With thanks to Herr Gerhard Hasenhündl.
100. Overview and quote from Franz Wolf, Schöngrabern im Wandel der Zeiten, Schöngrabern: self-published, 1995, p. 73. With thanks to Herr Manuel Köllner.
101. Charles to Colloredo, 21 July 1809, in Ausgewählte Schriften, vol. VI, p. 383.
102. 'Disposition', 2200, 10 July 1809, KAFA, 1422.
103. III Corps, Op. J. 12, KAFA, 1382.
104. 'Disposition', 2200, 10 July 1809, KAFA, 1422; and Struppy to Klenau, 0900, 11 July 1809, KAFA, 1422.
105. Hardegg had 2nd Znaim Landwehr from II Corps and four cavalry squadrons: one division each from *Rosenberg* Chevaulegers and *Schwarzenberg* Uhlans (Hauptarmee, Op. J. 1; Reserve Corps, Op. J. 75; Charles to Kolowrat, 11 July 1809, KAFA, 1381, 1388, 1412).
106. 'Disposition', 2200, 10 July 1809, KAFA, 1412; and V Corps, Op. J. 26, KAFA, 1383.
107. Although army headquarters was in Brenditz, the archduke (and doubtless other senior officers) spent the night in Znaim itself.
108. Marmont to Berthier, 10 July 1809 (evening), SHD, C2/93.
109. Weißenwolff may have contributed to the Austrian misconception about being outnumbered. One French secondary source claims he told Charles that Massena was approaching with 40,000 men and 120 guns (Gachot, *1809*, p. 305).
110. Marmont, Mémoires, vol. VI, p. 252.
111. Marmont to Berthier, 10 July 1809 (evening), SHD, C2/93.
112. Marmont to Berthier, 10 July 1809 (evening); Marmont to Davout, 1700, 10 July 1809, SHD, C2/93.
113. Berthier to Davout, 0830, 10 July 1809, CdN, no. 15,510, vol. XIX, pp. 235–6. Buat (vol. II, p. 342) criticises Berthier for sending a message lacking in specificity, but it was to be delivered by Captain Jules-Henri-Charles-Frédéric, comte de Pourtalès, one of Berthier's aides-de-camp who almost certainly could have explained any vague points.
114. Napoleon to Berthier, 10 July 1809, CdN, nos. 15,511 and 15,512, vol. XIX, pp. 236; Berthier to Oudinot, noon, 10 July 1809, SHD, C2/93.
115. Berthier to Marmont, 0930, 10 July 1809, SHD, C2/93.
116. Pelet, Guerre de 1809, vol. IV, p. 266; also Koch, Massena, vol. VI, p. 341.
117. Berthier to Massena, 0930, 10 July 1809, SHD, C2/93.

118. Massena to Berthier, morning, 10 July 1809, SHD, C2/93.
119. Buat, *1809*, vol. II, p. 343.
120. Gachot, *1809*, pp. 308–9.
121. Berthier to Nansouty, 2000, 9 July 1809, SHD, C2/93.
122. Davout to Napoleon, 1500, 10 July 1809, SHD, C2/93.
123. See Buat, *1809*, vol. II, pp. 344–6.
124. Davout to Berthier, 10 July 1809, in Charles de Mazade, ed., *Correspondance du Maréchal Davout*, Paris: Plon, 1885, vol. III, pp. 87–9; and Berthier to Davout, 1830, 10 July, SHD, C2/93. As Davout received Berthier's orders at 10:30 a.m. (report to Napoleon, 1500, 10 July 1809, SHD, C2/93), Buat reasonably assumes that this reply to Berthier was dispatched at approximately 11:00 a.m.
125. Berthier to Davout, 1830, 10 July 1809, SHD, C2/93.
126. Berthier to Pernet, 10 July 1809, SHD, C2/93.
127. Adam Dezydery Chlapowski, *Memoirs of a Polish Lancer*, Chicago: Emperor's Press, 1992, p. 90. It is not clear if Chlapowski rode with Pernet or was sent separately. Chlapowski refers to Napoleon's indisposition as 'croup'.
128. Napoleon to Marmont, 0200, 11 July 1809, *CG*, no. 21,480, vol. IX, p. 839.
129. Marmont to Napoleon, 11 July 1809, SHD, C2/93.
130. Grouchy to Davout, 0415, 10 July 1809, SHD, C2/93.
131. IV Corps, Op. J. 22; Friedrich von Hermannsthal, *Geschichte des Tyroler Feld- und Land-, später 46. Linien-Infanterie-Regiments*, Krakau: Czas., 1859, p. 253; Ludwig Kirchthaler, *Geschichte des k. k. Infanterie-Regimentes Nr. 2*, Vienna: n.p., 1895, p. 324.
132. 'So schnell auf den Fersen' from the IV Corps Op. J. 24. KAFA, 1383.
133. Sources for the action at Unter-Wisternitz: Grouchy's 10 July 1809 reports to Davout (0415, 0700, 1000, 1700, and one with no time indicated), SHD, C2/93; Grouchy's after-action report, 11 July 1809, in Grouchy, *Mémoires*, vol. II, pp. 39–43; IV Corps Operations Journals, 22 and 24; EH Carl after-action report, 27 July 1809, KAFA, 1409; Julius Stanka, *Geschichte des K. und K. Infanterie-Regimentes Erzherzog Carl No. 3*, Vienna: regimental, 1894, vol. I, pp. 454–5.
134. Fröhlich to Rosenberg, 1900, 10 July 1809, KA, Nachlass Rosenberg, B/1504, 1809/1. 'Water meadows' is used here for the German term *'Aue'* which indicates open, perhaps partly wooded, lowlands near water where the damp, spongy soil would be disadvantageous for cavalry.
135. Amon Ritter von Treuenfest, *Geschichte des k. u. k. Husaren-Regiments Nr. 4*, Vienna: regimental, 1903, p. 370.
136. This distance and all of the others below are estimates of how far units would have to travel by road (i.e., not straight-line distances).
137. Schustekh's Operations Journal, Op. J. 28, KAFA, 1383; Schustekh to Reuss, 10 July 1809, KAFA, 1416.

Chapter 6: Can't You Hear the Cannon?

1. Gassicourt, *Voyage*, pp. 246–7.
2. Ibid., pp. 247–8.
3. Marmont to Berthier, 0600, 11 July 1809, SHD, C2/93.
4. Ibid.
5. Quotes from two of Charles's reports: 13 July to Franz (KAFA, 1462) and 21 July to Minister of War Colloredo (*Ausgewählte Schriften*, vol. VI, pp. 308–10). The conviction that Davout was at Znaim appears again and again. At least two explanations are possible, alone or in combination: the Austrian command may have been simply adhering to what Rosenberg had reported on 9 July (see above), and the Austrians, understandably associating Montbrun with Davout, may have concluded that Montbrun's presence meant Davout's entire corps was on hand.
6. Tascher, *Journal de Campagne*, p. 239.
7. Wilhelm, *Denkwürdigkeiten*, vol. I, p. 96.
8. 'Tagebuch des Großherzoglich badischen Dragoner Regiments vom 1sten Juni bis 20ten Juli 1809', GLA, 48/4271.
9. Zech/Porbeck, *Badischen Truppen 1809*, p. 187. Although parts of this book were compiled by two different officers over many years, this section clearly stems from the pen of 1809 veteran Zech.
10. Charles to Reuss, 11 July 1809 (two notes), KAFA, 1416.
11. Dispositions taken from V Corps after-action report (KAFA, 1462); operations journal (Op. J. 26, KAFA, 1383); and the after-action reports of the two regiments. These arrangements seem to have left the talented Klebelsberg with nothing to do; he may have been relegated to commanding the cavalry in reserve or posted on the Pöltenberg with the 3rd Jägers.
12. Pflüger's after-action report, in Hödl, *Infanterieregiments Nr. 29*, pp. 259–61.
13. Charles to Kolowrat, 0945, 11 July 1809, KAFA, 1412.
14. French and Baden sources are unanimous in placing Massena's arrival around 10:00 a.m. or between 9:00 and 10:00. In contrast, the Austrian V Corps after-action report (echoed by the main operations journal which follows V Corps very closely) claims the attack began at 6:00 a.m.; but this is hardly credible given the distance 4th Corps had to march from Guntersdorf. The most likely explanation is that light cavalry outriders appeared early in the morning and engaged in some exchange of fire thus leading the Austrians to see an earlier start to the fighting.
15. V Corps after-action report for 11 July 1809, and *Gradiska* Grenz after-action report, 13 July 1809, both KAFA, 1462. These state that the Austrians regained the bridge twice but could not maintain themselves there; French and Baden reports say nothing of this.
16. *Gradiska* Grenz after-action report, 13 July 1809, KAFA, 1462.
17. Marcellin Marbot, *Remarques Critiques sur l'Ouvrage de M. le Lieutenant-Général Rogniat, intitulé Considérations sur l'Art de la Guerre*, Paris: Anselin et Pochard, 1820, pp. 60–2.

18. Gueheneuc, 'Historique du 26e Léger'; Jean Henri Éliacin Labouche, *Historique du 18me Régiment d'Infanterie*, Pau: Garet, 1891, p. 218.
19. Pelet, *Guerre de 1809*, vol. IV, p. 268.
20. According to local historians, the combat did not prevent some French soldiers from sporting and stealing in the church, including playing the organ while the cannon thundered outside (Hübner, *Denkwürdigkeiten*, p. 861).
21. V Corps after-action report for 11 July 1809, KAFA, 1462.
22. Valentini, *Versuch einer Geschichte*, p. 228.
23. Victor Dupuy, *Souvenirs Militaires*, Paris: Lévy, 1892, p. 133.
24. Espinchal, *Souvenirs*, p. 276–7; Madroux, 'August von Floret', p. 212; Reichold, *Soldaten-Sohn*, p. 127.
25. Schaller, *Fragmente*, p. 89.
26. 'Disposition zum Marsch der Armee in das Lager bey Budwitz', 1100, 11 July 1809, KAFA, 1422.
27. Valentini, *Versuch einer Geschichte*, p. 228; Heller, *Feldzug des Jahres 1809*, vol. II, p. 270.
28. Hauptarmee, Op. J. 1f, KAFA, 1381.
29. Tascher, *Journal de Campagne*, p. 239.
30. Arrayed left to right as follows: *Zach, Joseph Colloredo, Wallach-Illyria* Grenz (first line); former *Zedtwitz* and *Froon* (second line); *Frelich* alone (third line); *d'Aspre* and *Rohan* (fourth line); the three Landwehr battalions (fifth line). The 2nd *EH Carl* Legion and *Vincent* Chevaulegers were to the rear near corps headquarters (II Corps *Marschzettel*, 11 July 1809, KAFA, 1409).
31. The regimental history states that the other two companies were 'with the rearguard', so perhaps they were guarding the corps wagon train (*Geschichte des K. K. Infanterie-Regimentes Oskar II. Friedrich König von Schweden und König von Norwegen No. 10*, Vienna: regimental, 1888, p. 259).
32. Buat, *1809*, vol. II, p. 356.
33. Roch Godart, *Mémoires*, Paris: Flammarion, 1895, p. 133.
34. Hauptarmee, Op. J. 1f, KAFA, 1381; I Corps after-action report, 26 July 1809, KAFA, 1462.
35. These two may have been comprised of Clauzel's troops as depicted on Buat's maps; in the absence of more detailed French accounts, it is impossible to know.
36. I Corps after-action report and Op. J. 5, KAFA, 1462 and 1382.
37. It is analytically convenient to employ this framework of 'three French attacks' as adopted from Austrian accounts. There are no detailed French reports of this fighting extant, so readers should not assume that Napoleon or Marmont viewed things in this manner.
38. Schwarzenberg's after-action report, KAFA, 1462; III Corps operations journals Op. J. 12, 16 and 18, KAFA, 1382.
39. A detachment of fifty Baden light dragoons under Leutnant Franz Georg von Stern reached the field during the 11th after having been released from previous duty along the Danube; they ended up with Marmont even though their proper assignment was with Massena (where the rest of their regiment would arrive by evening): 'Tagebuch

des Großherzoglich badischen Dragoner Regiments vom 1sten Juni bis 20ten Juli 1809', GLA, 48/4271.
40. Schaller, *Fragmente*, pp. 91–2; Xylander, *Geschichte des 1. Feld-Artillerie-Regiments*, vol. II, pp. 186–7. Xylander's excellent history drew on the battle reports of the Bavarian battery commanders involved.
41. Minucci's after-action report, 26 July 1809; Minucci to Wrede, 12 July 1809. The timing of the Bavarian advance (that is, before or after the downpour) and its exact location are difficult to ascertain. Pelet says Napoleon ordered this move on seeing the Austrian grenadier counterattack (Pelet, vol. IV, p. 272), but Minucci's report indicates a much earlier hour.
42. Xylander, *Geschichte des 1. Feld-Artillerie-Regiments*, vol. II, pp. 187–8. The timing of the artillery's attempt to relocate is not clear – it may have been *after* the great downpour.
43. Mändler, *Erinnerungen*, p. 40; Pelet, *Guerre de 1809*, vol. IV, p. 272.
44. Unterleutnant Philipp le Beau, 2nd Baden Infantry, diary extract courteously provided by Reinhard Franz Kaufmann and published in his 'Die Schlacht bei Znaim veränderte die Landkarte Europas', Zusammenfassung der Beiträge zum Napoleon Symposium 'Feldzug 1809', Vienna: Delta Druckproduktionen, 2009, pp. 74–5.
45. Zech/Porbeck, *Badischen Truppen 1809*, p. 193.
46. Ibid., p. 194.
47. This account is taken from de Stabenrath's obituary. None of the other French accounts mention anything about de Stabenrath beyond his wounding, capture and release (there is no word of Fririon's order to Carra St Cyr or the presence of 400 men from the 46th Ligne). However, the obituary was composed by an engineer officer who was related to the de Stabenrath family by marriage and the level of detail is such that the account seems to have come from de Stabenrath himself; it is not a standard 'he served with distinction' obituary, but reads like a personal narrative or the results of an interview. If the obituary is accurate, de Stabenrath had little use for either Carra St Cyr or Fririon. See Alexandre Genet, *Notice Nécrologique sur le Général de Stabenrath*, Paris: Christophe, 1858, pp. 29–36. The general sometimes signed his name 'Destabenrath' or simply 'Stabenrath' during this period, but the proper written form is 'de Stabenrath'.
48. Pelleport, *Souvenirs Militaires*, vol. I, p. 287.
49. French accounts routinely and indiscriminately speak of 'Hungarian grenadiers' as if these were a more ferocious species of foe (just as many Austrian units only seemed to be opposed by French Imperial Guards). In fact, all of *Leiningen*'s grenadier companies came from 'German' regiments, not Hungarian.
50. Fririon's partial 'Souvenirs' published in Jean Moisette, 'Le Général François-Nicolas Fririon', *Le Pays Lorrain*, vol. XXX, January 1938, p. 228.
51. Wilhelm, *Denkwürdigkeiten*, vol. I, p. 96. Koch, *Massena*, vol. VI, p. 350. Wilhelm writes that Massena had his carriage turned around, while Massena's memoirs state that he once again mounted a horse; it seems reasonable to speculate that both are correct: that the carriage turned around, after which Massena mounted up.

52. The question of who 'saved' Massena (Fririon by his actions or Lhéritier's cuirassiers) led to a petty, pointless and unseemly debate between Pelet and Fririon's son, Jules Joseph (also an army officer). The feud began with a reference to Znaim in Fririon's *Journal Historique de la Campagne de Portugal* (Paris: Lenevu, 1841, p. 5) and played out in one of France's premier military journals: see *Spectateur Militaire*, letters to the editor, 5 May, 8 June and 28 June 1841, in the May, June and July issues of that year.
53. Hübner, *Denkwürdigkeiten*, p. 835.
54. Alexander Ferber, *Geschichte des 1. Badischen Feld-Artillerie-Regiments Nr. 14*, Karlsruhe: Müller, p. 77; Zech/Porbeck, *Badischen Truppen 1809*, pp. 195–6.
55. Efforts by French sappers to establish another bridge had not succeeded owing to lack of boats (Gachot, *1809*, p. 312).
56. The identity of the regiment(s) involved and the details of the orders they received are the subject of controversy, see discussion in Appendix 6.
57. Marbot, *Memoirs*, vol. II, p. 399.
58. Baden Brigade journal, GLA 48/4287.
59. *Theilnahme der Grossherz. Hess. Truppen an dem Kriege zwischen Oestreich und Frankreich im Jahre 1809*, Darmstadt: Auw, 1850 (written in October 1809).
60. Hauptarmee, Op. J. 1f, KAFA, 1381.
61. From local cleric P. Gräf who was himself hiding in the tobacco factory, cited in Hübner, *Denkwürdigkeiten*, p. 864.
62. V Corps after-action report, KAFA, 1462.
63. Zech/Porbeck, *Badischen Truppen 1809*, pp. 197–8.
64. Löwenstern, *Mémoires*, vol. I, p. 136.
65. Wilhelm Brinner, *Geschichte des k. k. Pionier-Regimentes*, Vienna: Seidel & Sohn, 1878, vol. I/2, p. 92. Petit commanded the 1st Grenadier Company of the *Kerpen* Infantry Regiment No. 49. His company seems to have been tasked with guarding the lower gate, and may have been involved in lowering the pole too: 'Geschichte des k. k. 49. Linien-Infanterie-Regiments Baron Kerpen in den Feldzügen von 1809, 1813, 1814 und 1815', *Oestreichische militärische Zeitschrift*, 1821, no. 10, p. 32.
66. [Salis], 'Historische Darstellung', pp. 85–6.
67. 'Tagebuch des Hess. Truppencontingent betr. von 18. April bis 4. November 1809', Hessisches Staatsarchiv Darmstadt, G61, 17/2; and 'Feldzug der 2ten Division', p. 635.
68. Madroux, 'August von Floret,' p. 211.
69. Fresnel's after-action report, 15 July 1809, KAFA, 1462.
70. I Corps after-action report, 26 July 1809, KAFA, 1462.
71. Fresnel's after-action report, 15 July 1809, KAFA, 1462.
72. I Corps after-action report, 26 July 1809, KAFA, 1462.
73. Fresnel's after-action report, 15 July 1809, KAFA, 1462.
74. Schaller, *Fragmente*, p. 89.
75. Esprit Victor Elisabeth Boniface de Castellane, *Journal du Maréchal de Castellane*, Paris: Plon, 1895, vol. I, p. 64.
76. Pelet, *Guerre de 1809*, vol. IV, pp. 272–3.

77. Valentini, *Versuch einer Geschichte*, pp. 232–3.
78. Ibid., p. 273.
79. Zech/ Porbeck, *Badischen Truppen 1809*, pp. 198–9.
80. Gueheneuc, 'Historique du 26e Léger'.
81. Pelleport, *Souvenirs Militaries*, p. 287.
82. *Gradiska* Grenz Regiment after-action report, KAFA, 1462.
83. Pflüger's after-action report, in Hödl, *Infanterieregiments Nr. 29*, pp. 259–61; [Salis], 'Historische Darstellung', p. 87.
84. Casualty list attached to the Grenadier Corps after-action report, KAFA, 1462. The other battalions and their losses were: *Jambline* (35), *Scovaud* (5), *Brzezinski* (6), *Georgy* (33), and *Portner* (16). One company from *Scovaud* was serving as headquarters guard (2nd Grenadier Company of *Kerpen* Infantry).
85. Louis Léger Boyeldieu, 'Itinéraire et Notes Historiques du 4e Régiment de Ligne', in Léon Charles Emile Auguste Loÿ, 'Le Général de Division Baron Boyeldieu', *Carnet de la Sabretache*, August 1914–May 1919, p. 499. The 4th Ligne's strength also taken from this source. The strength of the 24th Léger estimated from *Historique du 99e Régiment d'Infanterie de Ligne*, SHD, manuscript, 1889 (the 99th carried on the traditions of the 24th Léger). There are no precise figures for the 46th Ligne, but it had 1,330 officers and men on 15 July, so its strength at Znaim was likely 1,200–1,500.
86. 'Der letzte Akt', p. 158.
87. 'Feldzug der 2ten Division', pp. 635–7; Carl Christian Freiherr von Röder von Diersburg, *Geschichte des 1. Grossherzoglich Hessischen Infanterie- (Leibgarde-) Regiments Nr. 115*, (ed.) Fritz Beck, Berlin: Mittler & Sohn, 1899, pp. 162–3.
88. 'Tagebuch des Hess. Truppencontingent', Hessisches Staatsarchiv Darmstadt, G61, 17/2.
89. Espinchal, *Souvenirs*, p. 277.
90. Baden Brigade journal, GLA 48/4287.
91. Jean Baptiste Fournier, *Souvenirs*, Maurepas: La Vouivre, 2009, p. 32.
92. Godart, *Mémoires*, p. 133; Dupuy, *Souvenirs*, p. 135.
93. V Corps, Op. J. 26, KAFA, 1383. Implied in the after-action report, the 1821 *Kerpen* regimental account cited earlier specifically credits Petit with this action.
94. Marbot, *Memoirs*, vol. II, p. 400 (with slight emendations based on the French edition of 1891).
95. Wilhelm, *Denkwürdigkeiten*, vol. I, p. 97.
96. Gueheneuc, 'Historique du 26e Léger'.
97. Lejeune, *Memoirs*, vol. II, pp. 328.
98. Charles Denis Parquin, *Souvenirs et Campagnes d'un Vieux Soldat de l'Empire*, A. Aubier (ed.), Paris: Berger-Levrault, 1903, p. 205; Claude Etienne Guyot, *Carnets de Campagnes*, Jean Hugues de Font-Réaulx (ed.), Paris: Teissèdre, 1999, p. 104; Tascher, *Journal de Campagne*, p. 240.
99. Calculated independently, these figures are similar to Binder's (vol II, p. 414). Charles stated that he had lost 6,000 at Znaim (letter to Albert, 13 July 1809, Criste, *Carl*,

vol. III, p. 494) and a later Austrian historian gave a figure of 6,500 Austrian casualties: Eberhard Mayerhoffer von Vedropolje, *Oesterreichs Krieg mit Napoleon I. 1809*, Vienna: Seidel & Sohn, 1904, p. 165.

100. Figures do not include the V Corps losses on 10 July. Estimates derived from the afteraction reports of I Corps, V Corps, the Grenadier Corps and regimental histories checked against 'Summarischer Ausweis des in den verschiedenen Affairen vom 29ten Juny bis incls. 11ten July 809 erlittenen Verlustes' (KAFA, 1460) and additional archival material courtesy of Michael Wenzel.

101. This number does not include Massena's losses on 10 July in the rearguard engagements. French casualty figures require more estimation than the Austrian as few of the French regimental histories supply details. This figure was developed by taking the data from the few units that provide loss statistics and applying those to other regiments in the same area as adjusted for the officer losses presented in Martinien's massive work (see Orders of Battle, Appendix 5).

102. 'Feldzug der 2ten Division', pp. 639–40; Meier, *Erinnerungen*, p. 64. Of course, there were also incidents during the war when captured Austrians were mistreated by the French and Germans.

103. As noted above, III Corps repeatedly referred to its infantry being formed in 'squares' owing to the cavalry threat, even though the army's preferred formation in 1809 was the 'battalion mass'.

104. The U.S. military and NATO define a 'meeting engagement' as 'A combat action that occurs when a moving force, incompletely deployed for battle, engages an enemy at an unexpected time and place,' U.S. Department of Defense, *Dictionary of Military and Associated Terms* (JP 1-02), Washington DC: U.S. Government, 2001 as amended through 2006, p. 337.

Chapter 7: An Armistice Saved Us

1. Espinchal, *Souvenirs Militaires*, vol. I, p. 272; Tascher, *Journal de Campagne*, p. 240; Castellane, *Journal*, vol. I, p. 64; Fournier, *Souvenirs*, p. 32.
2. Philippe René Girault, *Mes Campagnes sous la Révolution et l'Empire*, Paris: Le Sycomore, 1983, p. 187. One may speculate that the regiment's canteens contained a liquid other than water.
3. Hauptarmee, Op. J. 1f, KAFA, 1381.
4. Charles to Colloredo, 21 July 1809, in *Ausgewählte Schriften*, vol VI, p. 310.
5. Hauptarmee, Op. J. 1f, KAFA, 1381
6. This figure includes VI Corps.
7. Savary, *Mémoires*, vol. IV, p. 209.
8. Sources such as Criste (*Liechtenstein*, p. 133) and 'Précis de la marche des négociations' (Klinkowström, *Aus der alten Registratur*, p. 157) portray Napoleon as gracious. Observing Liechtenstein's arrival, Chef de Bataillon Joseph Szymanowski, one of Davout's staff officers, described him being received 'with full military honours' (*Mémoires*, Paris:

Lavauzelle, 1900, p. 50). On the other side, Charles wrote that Napoleon displayed 'choler and bitterness' (to Albert, 13 July 1809, in Criste, *Carl*, vol. III, pp. 494–5), while other Austrians sources describe Napoleon as being angry or ill-humoured.

9. Among the uncertain details of the armistice negotiations is the timing of the Berthier–Wimpffen meeting. Charles told Franz that the armistice had been completed before Liechtenstein arrived, but he was responding to the Kaiser's anger by that point and may have been less than precise with the sequence of events. This data point comes from Charles to Franz, 23 July 1809 (excerpt in Angeli, *Erzherzog Carl*, vol. IV, p. 554); note that this is *different* from the letter Charles sent on 23 July requesting relief from command. See also Jean Tulard and Louis Garros, *Itinéraire de Napoléon au Jour le Jour*, Paris: Tallandier, 1992, p 321; the *Itinéraire*, without specifying a source, has the Berthier–Wimpffen meeting occurring between approximately 9:00 and 11:00 p.m. on the 11th.

10. Stadion to Franz, 12 and 13 July 1809, HHStA, Vorträge 1809 (V–X), 182; and Stadion to Metternich, 18 July 1809, NA, AC 2/62 C 10/6. Note that the parenthetical comment about leadership was Stadion's recounting of Wimpffen's words.

11. Stadion to Metternich, 24 July 1809, NA, AC 2/62 C 10/6.

12. Stadion to Franz, 12 and 13 July 1809, HHStA, Vorträge 1809 (V–X), 182. Emphasis in the original.

13. Stadion to Hudelist, 24 July 1809, in Rössler, *Österreichs Kampf*, vol. II, p. 43.

14. See Josef Hirn, 'Das kaiserliche Handbillet aus Wolkersdorf (29. Mai 1809) für Tirol', *Beiträge zur neueren Geschichte Österreichs*, September 1906, pp. 104–15.

15. Pelet, *Guerre de 1809*, vol. IV, p. 279.

16. Tascher, *Journal de Campagne*, pp. 240–1.

17. Fournier, *Souvenirs*, p. 32.

18. Pelet, *Guerre de 1809*, vol. IV, pp. 277–8; Berthezène, *Souvenirs*, pp. 259–60. Observation regarding the Horse Grenadiers is from an excised portion of Larrey's memoirs, in Paul Triare, *Dominique Larrey*, Tours: Mame, 1902, p. 64; Louis Bro, *Mémoires*, Paris: Plon, 1914, p. 78.

19. Rauchensteiner, *Kaiser Franz und Erzherzog Carl*, pp. 109–10. See also *Darstellung des Feldzugs* pp. 177–8.

20. With thanks to Michael Wenzel for this insight.

21. Radetzky, 'Erinnerungen', p. 69.

22. II Corps Order of the Day, 22 July 1809, KAFA, 1410.

23. Wimpffen to Franz, 17 August 1809, in Criste, *Carl*, vol. III, pp. 503–9.

24. Friant's after-action report, SHD, MR668; Oudinot to Berthier, 1900, 11 July 1809, SHD, C2/93; 'Rapport historique des operations de la Division du Général Molitor', 12 November 1809, SHD, MR662. As for the Guard infantry, Davout's 2nd Division report states it bivouacked that night with a large forest on the right (the Burgholz) and the light infantry of the Guard on its left, indicating that the Guard infantry had indeed arrived by the night of 11 July.

25. Mathieu Dumas, *Memoirs of His Own Time*, Philadelphia: Lea & Blanchard, 1839, vol. II, p. 208; 'Opérations du 3e Corps dans la campagne d'Allemagne en 1809', SHD,

MR667. Dumas was appointed as the French commissioner for implementation of the armistice; his Austrian counterpart was Rothkirch.
26. Koch, *Masséna*, vol. VI, p. 352.
27. Savary, *Mémoires*, vol. IV, pp. 196–7.
28. Maret, as secretary of state, fulfilled a civilian role analogous to Berthier's role in military affairs; Lariboisière was the army's artillery chief; and Duroc, one of Napoleon's closest associates, held the title Grand Master of the Palace.
29. Savary, *Mémoires*, vol. IV, p. 196.
30. César Nicolas, *Une Famille de Sommiérois*, Nîmes: Revue du Midi, 1904, pp. 106–8.
31. 'Opérations du 3e Corps dans la campagne d'Allemagne en 1809', SHD, MR667; Philippe-Paul Ségur, *Histoire et Mémoires*, Paris: Didot, 1873, vol. III, pp. 385–6.
32. Sourcing for this crucial meeting is essentially limited to Pelet, who related what he had learned 'from one of the interlocutors' who was present (*Guerre de 1809*, vol. IV, pp. 275–8). To this may be added a few comments Davout made to Ségur (*Histoire et Mémoires*, vol. III, pp. 386). GD François Roguet's statement that Napoleon was counselled to break up the Austrian Empire and distribute most of it to German princes (*Mémoires Militaires*, vol. IV, p. 88) suggests that advisors and generals continued to make this recommendation to the emperor after his return to Schönbrunn.
33. In some cases, he would publicly portray Wagram as *more* complete than Austerlitz, as in the 28 September 1809 issue of the *Journal de l'Empire*.
34. Thiers, *Histoire du Consulat*, vol. X, pp. 496–7.
35. Fiume was a point on which Napoleon would not relent: Berthier to Wimpffen, 13 July 1809, SHD, C2/94.
36. Karl Venturini, *Geschichte unserer Zeit*, Leipzig: Steinacker, 1811, vol. I, p. 212.
37. Napoleon to Berthier, 14 July 1809, *CG*, no. 21,492, vol. XIX, p. 844; Berthier to Wimpffen, 14 July 1809 and Wimpffen's acceptance of this condition in Charles's name, 15 July 1809, SHD, C2/94. The recall order is Charles to Riesch, 17 July 1809, KAFA, 1462; printed in 'Journal über der Operation des kais. österreichischen Truppen-Corps unter dem Generalmajor von Am-Ende von 12ten bis 22ten July 1809, in Sachsen', *Europäische Annalen*, vol. VI, 1810, pp. 259–75.
38. Napoleon to Champagny, 19 August 1809, *CG*, no. 21,847, vol. IX, pp. 1037–9.
39. Binder von Kriegelstein, *Der Krieg Napoleons*, vol. II, pp. 415–17. See also: Hoen, *Wagram*, p. 122; Just, *Schönbrunn*, p. 21.
40. Herzog Albert, 'Mémoire sur la Guerre éclatée en 1809', MNL, P300/1/100. It is interesting to note that both Charles and Napoleon found the notion of carrying the war deeper into Bohemia unpalatable.
41. Charles to Albert, 23 and 27 July 1809, Criste, *Carl*, vol. III, pp. 497–501. 'Adventurous' is from 'Anmerkungen über die im 8ten und 10ten Stück der europäische Annalen Jahrgang 1810 enthaltene Darstellung der Schlachten auf dem Marchfelde', *Europäische Annalen*, vol. VIII, 1811, p. 144.

42. Charles to Albert, 13 and 18/19 July 1809 (in the latter he stated that he had been ailing from 'colic and dysentery' for several days), Criste, *Carl*, vol. III, pp. 494–7; Charles, 'Beitrag', *Ausgewählte Schriften*, vol. VI, p. 384.
43. Charles to Albert, 13 and 18/19 July 1809, Criste, *Carl*, vol. III, pp. 494–7.
44. Charles to Albert, 19 July 1809, in ibid.
45. Charles to Franz, 12 July 1809, MNL, P300 Carton 18; also in Criste, *Carl*, vol. III, p. 273.
46. Charles to Franz, 13 July 1809, MNL, P300 Carton 18; also in Criste, *Carl*, vol. III, pp. 268–74. Napoleon indirectly affirmed the importance Charles attached to the Austrian army: in mid-August he told a Russian emissary 'I negotiate with Austria because she still has an army in the field' (Alexander to Rumiantsev, 16 August 1809, *Vneshniaia Politika Rossii*, vol. V, pp. 130–1.
47. Charles to Franz, 16, 22 and 23 July 1809, KAFA, 1462; Charles to Colloredo, 21 July 1809, in *Ausgewählte Schriften*, vol. VI, pp. 304–13. The quote is from the 16 July report. Note that the 23 July report cited here is not the same as the personal letter of the same date in which Charles offered his resignation.
48. Charles, Order of the Day, 26 July 1809, KAFA, 1462; Hohenzollern's copy, 26 July 1809, KAFA, 1410.
49. 'Der letzte Akt', p. 160; *Darstellung des Feldzugs vom Jahr 1809. Von einem Augenzeugen*, n.p., 1811, pp. 177–8; Eduard Duller, *Erzherzog Carl von Oesterreich*, Vienna: Kaulfuß, 1847, pp. 713–14.
50. 'Welche Ursachen bewogen den österreichischen Feldherrn zu dem Waffenstillstand von Znaym und war er vortheilhaft für Oesterreichs Interesse?', initially published in 'Deutschland', 1809 and later in Pest: n.p., 1811, p. 39; and *Berichtigung über die letzten Ereignisse des Krieges zwischen Osterreich und Frankreich im Jahr 1809*, Frankfurt: n.p., 1810.
51. Hübner, *Denkwürdigkeiten*, pp. 900–3. This local history erroneously places Napoleon's visit on the night of 11/12 July, but he was still issuing orders from 'camp du Znaim' (Hödnitz) on 13 July. The whereabouts of Frau Tulipan's husband during these hours is unknown.
52. Marmont, *Mémoires*, vol. III, pp. 255–6.
53. Criste, *Liechtenstein*, p. 134.
54. Franz to Charles, 15 July 1809, MNL, P300 Carton 44.
55. Zichy to Franz, 15 July 1809, in Criste, *Liechtenstein*, p. 138. In contrast, officials as far away as Bern, Switzerland, had the armistice details that same day (18 July) as one of Napoleon's staff officers was speeding through to inform Eugène's wife in Milan of the news (Albert de Watteville, *Un Suisse Officier d'Ordonnance de Napoléon*, Lausanne: Rouge, 1951, p. 77).
56. Unless otherwise specified, the following paragraphs, including quotations, are drawn from Franz to Charles, 18, 19, 20 (two letters) and 23 July 1809, MNL, P300 Carton 44.
57. Metternich to Hudelist, 18 July 1809, in Criste, *Liechtenstein*, p. 135.
58. 'Kaiser Franz an die Tyroler', 29 May 1809, in Joseph von Hormayr, *Geschichte Andreas Hofer's*, Leipzig: Brockhaus, 1845, vol. I, p. 435. Emphasis in the original.
59. Rauchensteiner, *Kaiser Franz und Erzherzog Carl*, p. 109.

60. Charles to Franz, 23 July 1809 with Kaiser's 29 July marginalia, MNL, P300 Carton 18; facsimile in Criste, *Carl*, vol. III, pp. 276–7. Charles to Albert, 27 July 1809, in Criste, *Carl*, vol. III, pp. 499–501; Charles 'Beitrag', *Ausgewählte Schriften*, vol. VI, pp. 383–4.
61. Lindenau's after-action report, BayHStA, B445; Hauptarmee, Op. J. 1f, KAFA, 1381; 'Rückzug des abgeschnittenen 4. Jäger-Bataillons, im Jahre 1809', *Oesterreichische militärische Zeitschrift*, vol. IX, 1843, pp. 312–20.
62. Charles to Albert, 18 July 1809, in reference to the reports of earlier British landings on the German coast, in Criste, *Carl*, vol. III, p. 496. Problems of timing also dogged the Austrian envoy who was sent to London in an attempt to promote a British expedition to northern Germany: dispatched from Wolkersdorf on 22 June, he did not arrive in London until 26 July, see Intermezzo, 'The Other Theatres of War'.
63. For details of the action later in the war, see John H. Gill, 'A Poor Place to Fight a War: Franco-Italian Operations in the Tyrol 1809', in *Glory is Fleeting: New Scholarship on the Napoleonic Wars*, Andrew Bamford (ed.), forthcoming from Helion & Company.
64. Ferdinand to Franz, 16 July 1809, KAFA, 1462; VII Corps Operations Journal 40, KAFA, 1385. This paragraph is adapted from John H. Gill, 'Galician Gambles: Austrian Approaches to Russia at the Climax of the 1809 War', unpublished paper presented to the Consortium on the Revolutionary Era, 2011.
65. Instructions for Metternich, 14 August 1809, in *Nachgelassenen Papieren*, vol. III, pp. 313–14.
66. Caulaincourt to Napoleon, 28 May 1809, Mikhaïlowitch (ed.), *Les Relations Diplomatiques*, vol. III, pp. 332–3.
67. An anonymous contemporary diarist quoted in Wertheimer, *Geschichte Österreichs und Ungarns*, vol. II, p. 399.
68. Jean Baptiste Nompère de Champagny, *Souvenirs*, Geneva: Slatkine-Megariotis, 1975, p. 113.
69. Bubna was promoted from GM to FML on 10 September 1809; Liechtenstein was made a field marshal two days later.
70. Champagny, *Souvenirs*, p. 116; Jean Tulard, *Napoléon: Une Journée Particulière, 12 Octobre 1809*, Paris: Lattès, 1994.
71. Criste, *Liechtenstein*, pp. 147–8.
72. Metternich to Starhemberg, 29 October 1809, in Thürheim, *Starhemberg*, p. 237.
73. Gentz to Bubna, 5 October 1809, in Criste, *Liechtenstein*, p. 227; see also Wertheimer, *Geschichte Österreichs und Ungarns*, vol. II, p. 429.
74. Stadion to Metternich, 31 July 1809, NA, AC 2/62 C 10/6. Francis Loraine Petre wrote that 'they had thrown away, by the dismissal of the Archduke Charles, their best, perhaps their only general' (*Napoleon and the Archduke Charles*, London: John Lane, 1909, p. 407).
75. Wertheimer, *Geschichte Österreichs und Ungarns*, vol. II, p. 412.
76. Gentz discussion with Bubna, diary entry for 22 August 1809, *Tagebücher*, p. 126.
77. Franz to Liechtenstein, 12 September 1809, in Criste, *Liechtenstein*, p. 222.
78. Radetzky, 'Erinnerungen', p. 70; Viktor Bibl, *Radetzky: Soldat und Feldherr*, Vienna: Günther, 1955, pp. 100–3.

79. His brother, Friedrich Lothar, remained in Prague, ruing that the army's morale was not commensurate with its potential strength and the 'national will' (F. L. Stadion to Binder, 24 August 1809, NA, AC 2/61 C 10/7).
80. Joseph to Johann, 22 August and 20 September 1809, Domanovszky, ed., *Palatin Josephs Schriften*, vol. IV, pp. 112, 120.
81. Beer, *Zehn Jahre*, p. 430–50. Sickness figures from 'Früh-Rapport' summary for 5 September 1809, KAFA, 1389.
82. Bellegarde to Metternich, 22 August 1809, NA, AC 2/3 C 6/3.
83. Gentz discussions with Liechtenstein and Stadion, diary entry for 24 September 1809, *Tagebücher*, pp. 159–61. Just after the peace treaty, Gentz bitterly observed that 'those who do not know how to make war can make no claims on good peace agreeements' (letter to Freiherr Karl vom und zum Stein, 20 October 1809, in Erich Botzenhart, ed., *Freiherr vom Stein: Briefwechsel, Denkschriften und Aufzeichnungen*, Berlin: Heymann, 1932, vol. III, p. 187.
84. Gentz discussion with Stadion, diary entry for 28 September 1809, *Tagebücher*, p. 156.
85. Viktor Bibl, *Der Zerfall Österreichs: Kaiser Franz und seine Erbe*, Vienna: Rikola, 1922, pp. 180.
86. Wertheimer, *Geschichte Österreichs und Ungarns*, vol. II, pp. 389–96.
87. Joseph to Johann, 22 August 1809, Domanovszky, ed., *Palatin Josephs Schriften*, vol. IV, p. 112.
88. 'Situation du Armée d'Allemagne, compare au 15. Juin et 15. Juillet' and 'Situation de l'Armée au 1er Septembre 1809', SHD, 2C/520.
89. Bubna's 21 September 1809 report in Beer, *Zehn Jahre*, p. 442.
90. Caulaincourt to Napoleon, 16 April 1809, in Mikhaïlowitch (ed.), *Les Relations Diplomatiques*, vol. III, p. 211.
91. On this point, see the thorough analysis in Anton Chroust, *Geschichte des Grossherzogtums Würzburg*, Würzburg: Becker, 1932, pp. 320–2; and Dieter Schäfer, *Ferdinand von Österreich*, Graz: Styria, 1988, pp. 231–4; also Savary, *Mémoires*, vol. IV, pp. 235–6; and Charles W. Ingrao, *The Habsburg Monarchy 1618–1815*, Cambridge: Cambridge University Press, 2000, pp. 236–7.
92. Napoleon to Alexander, 10 October 1809, *CG*, no. 22,308, vol. IX, p. 1322.
93. As Paul W. Schroeder notes, the conditions imposed in 1809 were not as onerous as those inflicted on Prussia in 1807: *The Transformation of European Politics*, Oxford: Clarendon Press, 1994, p. 367. For these treaties, see Jules de Clerq, *Recueil des Traités de la France*, Paris: Amyot, 1864, vol. II, pp. 293–303, 318–21, 369–72.

Epilogue

1. Louis Bertrand Pierre Brun de Villeret, *Les Cahiers du Général Brun*, Paris: Plon, 1953, p. 91; Hohenzollern, 'Bermekungen Ueber die Schlachten von Wagram und Znaim', addendum to II Corps, Op. J. 15, 1 June 1810, KAFA, 1382; Baden Brigade journal, GLA 48/4287; Schaller, *Fragmente*, pp. 92–3.

2. 'Der letzte Akt', p. 158.
3. Thiers, *Histoire du Consulat*, vol. X, pp. 489.
4. Maurice Dumolin, *Précis d'Histoire Militaire: Révolution et Empire*, Paris: Barbere, 1913, p. 153.
5. Bornemann, *Napoleon bei Znaim*, p. 48.
6. Gueheneuc, 'Historique du 26e Léger'.
7. Christopher Duffy, *By Force of Arms*, Chicago: Emperor's Press, 2008, p. 396.
8. Gentz to Bubna, 8 October 1809, in August Fournier, 'Gentz und der Friede von Schönbrunn', *Deutsche Rundschau*, vol. XLIX, October-November-December 1886, p. 113.
8. Gaspard Gourgaud, *Sainte-Hélène: Journal Inédit de 1815 à 1818*, Paris: Flammarion, 1899, vol. II, p. 112.
10. On these issues (in addition to Chroust and Schäfer cited above), see his letters to Champagny of 19 August, 10, 15 and 21 September 1809, *CG*, nos. 21,847, 22,022, 22,088 and 22,129, vol. IX, pp. 1037–9, 1149–52, 1191–2, 1211–12.
11. Marie-Joseph Las Cases, *Journal of the Private Life and Conversations of the Emperor Napoleon at Saint Helena*, London: Colburn, 1823, vol. II, part 3, pp. 103–4; Barry Edward O'Meara, *Napoleon at St. Helena*, London: Bentley & Son, 1888, vol. II, p. 212; Gourgaud, *Sainte-Hélène*, vol. I, p. 202, and vol. II, p. 112. Interestingly, Austrian patriot Joseph von Hormayr asserted that Napoleon, for his own purposes, *should* have dismantled the Austrian empire: 'Napoleon's fall did not come about because he went too far, rather because he did not go far enough' (*Lebensbilder*, vol. I, p. 223).
12. Jean-Baptiste Nompère de Champagny, *Note sur un Article des Mémoires sur l'Intérieur du Palais Impérial, et sur la Conclusion de la Paix de Vienne en 1809*, Paris: Potey, 1827, p. 11.
13. Charles called the peace treaty 'a new step in Napoleon's rise' (Charles, 'Denkschrift', *Ausgewählte Schriften*, vol. VI, p. 348). See also Fournier, 'Gentz und der Friede von Schönbrunn', p. 104.
14. Édouard Driault, *Tilsit*, Paris: Alcan, 1917, p. 478.

Appendix 1
The Coalitions against France

The various alliances formed to oppose Revolutionary and Napoleonic France are generally known as 'coalitions' and the respective wars are thus frequently referred to as the 'War of the Third Coalition', etc. By this taxonomy, the 1809 war was the 'War of the Fifth Coalition'. The accompanying chart aims to assist the reader by providing a simplified outline of these conflicts, which is especially relevant to the Wars of the Third and Fourth Coalitions that had direct bearing on the Austrian decision to initiate hostilities in 1809. The 'Peninsular War' in Iberia (1808–14) and the Russian Campaign (1812) are not generally included among the listings of 'coalitions'.

Coalition	Years Active	Members	Key Neutrals	Major Battles
First Coalition	1792–97	Holy Roman Empire (incl. Austria), Great Britain, Prussia (to 1795), Spain (to 1795), Dutch Republic (to 1795), Portugal, Sardinia (to 1796), Naples, French royalists	N/A	General Bonaparte's First Italian Campaign
Second Coalition	1798–1802	Holy Roman Empire (incl. Austria), Great Britain, Russia (to 1799), Portugal, Tuscany, Ottoman Empire, Naples, Malta, French royalists	Prussia	Egypt, Marengo, Hohenlinden
Third Coalition	1803–5	Holy Roman Empire (incl. Austria), Great Britain, Russia, Naples/Sicily, Sweden	Prussia	Ulm, Trafalgar, Austerlitz
Fourth Coalition	1806–7	Prussia, Russia, Great Britain, Saxony (to Dec. 1806), Sweden, Sicily	Austria	Jena–Auerstedt, Eylau, Friedland
Fifth Coalition	1809	Austria, Great Britain, Spain, Naples, Sicily	Prussia	Abensberg/Eggmühl, Aspern-Essling, Wagram, Znaim
Sixth Coalition	1813–14	Russia, Prussia, Austria, Great Britain, Sweden, Spain, Portugal, Sicily, Sardinia, German states (from Oct. 1813), Netherlands (1814), Naples (1814)	N/A	Lützen & Bautzen, Dresden, Leipzig, Paris
Seventh Coalition	1815	Great Britain, Prussia, Austria, Russia, Sweden, Spain, Portugal, Sicily, Sardinia, German states, Netherlands, Tuscany, Switzerland	N/A	Waterloo

Appendix 2
Key Habsburg Personalities

Only those living in 1809 shown. Names in **bold** indicate those who played a significant part in the events described in this book.

Main branch: Habsburg-Lothringen (Habsburg-Lorraine)*

Franz I	1768–1835. Kaiser. (He had been 'Franz II' until 1806 when he abdicated as Holy Roman Emperor; he had adopted an Austrian imperial title in 1804 in anticipation of the end of the old *Reich*.)
Ferdinand	1769–1824. Grand Duke of Würzburg (thus a member of the Rheinbund).
Maria Anna	1770–1809. Archduchess.
Carl/Charles**	1771–1847. Generalissimus.
Joseph	1776–1847. Palatine of Hungary, Commander of Hungarian Insurrection.
Anton	1779–1835. Grand Master of the Teutonic Order.
Johann	1782–1859. Commander of the Army of Inner Austria.
Rainer	1783–1853. Archduke.
Ludwig	1784–1864. Commanded V Corps from April to early May.
Rudolph	1788–1831. Archduke.

Key Habsburg Personalities

Children of the Kaiser from his second marriage
(none from first, third or fourth)

Marie Louise	1791–1847. Future wife of Napoleon.
Ferdinand	1793–1875. Future Kaiser.
Caroline Josepha	1797–1826. Archduchess.
Maria Klementina	1798–1881. Archduchess.
Maria Karolina	1801–32. Archduchess.
Franz Karl	1802–78. Archduke.
Maria Anna	1804–58. Archduchess.

Cadet branch: Austria-Este (or Habsburg-Este)

Maria Beatrice	1750–1829. Mother of the following:
Maria Theresa	1773–1832. Archduchess.
Maria Leopoldina	1776–1848. Archduchess.
Franz	1779–1846. Archduke.
Ferdinand	1781–1850. Commander of VII Corps in Poland/Galicia.
Maximilian	1782–1863. Banished to Bukovina after failing to hold Vienna in May.
Karl Ambrosius	1785–1809. Primate of Hungary.
Maria Ludovika	1787–1816. Kaiserin, third wife of Kaiser Franz.

* Founded with the marriage of the eldest direct Habsburg descendant, Maria Theresa, to Franz Stephan of Lorraine in 1736 and assured its position on the thrones of the Holy Roman Empire and Austria through the War of the Austrian Succession (1740–8), the House of Habsburg-Lorraine was still a relatively recent creation in 1809. Kaiser Franz was Maria Theresa's grandson, so when Napoleon publicly referred to the ruling family as 'the House of Lorraine', he was questioning the legitimacy of the Kaiser's rule and signalling that the monarchy might be subject to dissolution. The members of the dynasty, of course, found such references both insulting and deeply threatening.

** Charles was adopted by Herzog Albert von Sachsen-Teschen and his wife, Maria Christine, moving with them to the Netherlands in 1791. He formed a close bond with the childless couple and his detailed letters to Albert are a key source for his private thoughts.

Appendix 3
Outline Chronology, July 1809

2 July	Metternich and Dodun exchanged.
	Berthier and Wimpffen correspond regarding prisoner exchange.
	Napoleon issues orders to cross onto the Marchfeld.
3 July	Metternich arrives at Wolkersdorf, has audience with Kaiser Franz.
4 July	Weißenwolff arrives at 5:00 a.m., meets Napoleon, detained in Vienna.
	French begin crossing onto Marchfeld at night under thunderstorm.
5 July	Battle of Wagram, first day.
6 July	Battle of Wagram, second day.
	Austrians initiate retreat; Franz moves to Ernstbrunn.
7 July	Engagement at Korneuburg.
	Rosenberg pursued to Mistelbach.
	Franz, Stadion, Metternich confer: decide to send Liechtenstein to Napoleon.
	Stadion submits resignation, Franz accepts.
	Franz moves to Hollabrunn.
	Napoleon moves to Wolkersdorf.
8 July	Engagement at Stockerau.
	Marmont turns left, occupies Mistelbach; Rosenberg reaches Laa.
	Franz and Charles meet twice, morning and afternoon.

Outline Chronology

	Franz orders Charles to prepare Liechtenstein mission.
	Franz moves to Znaim.
9 July	Engagement at Hollabrunn.
	Rearguard actions at Laa and Staatz/Neuburg.
	Marmont captures Laa, patrols towards Znaim; halted by drunkenness among troops.
	Rosenberg retreats north of the Thaya towards Muschau.
	Franz warns Charles of French advance on Znaim.
	Franz warns Charles of danger to Olmütz, and reports Rosenberg's alleged disorderly retreat.
	Franz departs Znaim for Mährisch-Budwitz in late afternoon/evening.
	Franz sends Charles letter from Znaim with Stadion's memo.
	Franz sends Charles brusque letter from Czaslau.
	Davout reaches Nikolsburg and Poysdorf, Grouchy storms Nikolsburg in the night.
	Napoleon orders Nansouty to Wilfersdorf.
10 July	Battle of Znaim, first day.
	Charles receives Franz's letter with Stadion memorandum.
	Austrians propose ceasefire at Znaim; Marmont rejects.
	Weißenwolff joins Hauptarmee at Znaim.
	Grouchy captures bridge over the Thaya at Unter-Wisternitz.
	Rosenberg retires towards Brünn.
	Rearguard engagements from Schöngrabern to Guntersdorf.
	Liechtenstein departs Znaim battlefield c. 2:00 p.m. to search for Napoleon.
	Napoleon orders Davout, Oudinot, Nansouty and the Guard to Znaim.
	Napoleon arrives in Laa.
	Franz continues through Czaslau towards Olmütz, accompanied by Metternich.
	Stadion remains in Mährisch-Budwitz.
11 July	Battle of Znaim, second day.
	Massena reaches Znaim battlefield.
	Charles receives Franz's brusque letter from Czaslau.
	Napoleon holds council of war.

French accept Austrian ceasefire offer; Berthier and Wimpffen meet.

Ceasefire agreed late afternoon.

Berthier and Wimpffen negotiate armistice in Rother Hof near Zuckerhandl.

Austrian II Corps, VI Corps and two grenadier brigades depart Znaim area during night.

Armistice signed late on night of 11/12 July, dated to 12 July.

12 July   Liechtenstein arrives at battlefield after midnight, meets Napoleon.

Remaining Austrians withdraw from Znaim.

Massena establishes headquarters in Znaim, Napoleon reviews part of 4th Corps.

Charles, Liechtenstein, Wimpffen meet Stadion in Mährisch-Budwitz.

Napoleon stops at Hödnitz mill.

Appendix 4
Headquarters Locations
6–12 July

	Austrian Hauptarmee	Kaiser Franz
Night 5/6 July	Wagram	Wolkersdorf
6 July	Wagram to Oberrohrbach	Wolkersdorf to Ernstbrunn
7 July	Oberrohrbach to Göllersdorf	Ernstbrunn to Hollabrunn
8 July	Göllersdorf to Guntersdorf	Hollabrunn to Znaim
9 July	Guntersdorf	Znaim to Czaslau
10 July	Brenditz/Znaim	en route to Hungary
11 July	Wolframitzkirchen	en route to Hungary
12 July	Mährisch-Budwitz	Olmütz (arrived Komorn late on 14 July)

	French Army of Germany, Emperor Napoleon	
Night 5/6 July	on the field near Raasdorf	
6 July	on the field near Raasdorf	
7 July	Wolkersdorf	(occupied mid-morning from the Raasdorf encampment)
8 July	Wolkersdorf	
9 July	Wolkersdorf	
10 July	Laa	
11 July	on the field at Znaim	
12 July	Hödnitz Mill	

Appendix 5
Orders of Battle

Introductory Note: Unit Strengths and Orders of Battle

Unit strengths. Uncovering formation organisations and calculating unit strengths is always a challenge. In the charts below, I have attempted to use archival records wherever possible, keeping in mind that even these have their own problems, such as officers who might submit false reports, simple transcription errors, delayed entries, etc. In many cases, however, I have had no recourse but to turn to secondary sources. These appendices thus represent best estimates of the forces available to each side at the indicated points in time.

I have using the following guidelines in composing the main text and in assembling these orders of battle:

General strength figures in the main text. In almost all cases, strength figures in the main text give numbers of infantry and cavalry only. If the figure includes other troops (artillery, train, etc.), I have tried to indicate this in the text or in an endnote. The idea is to give the number of muskets and sabres available by listing officers and men of infantry and cavalry units; I let the artillery's guns speak for that branch. For those who wish to do so, one may add approximately 80 to 100 men per battery as a rule of thumb.

Detailed strength figures in this appendix. All strength figures are based on the number of 'effectives' or 'present under arms' (*présens sous les armes, Summa der Dienstbaren, Ausrückenden, bleibt zum Dienst*, etc.), and thus do not include detached troops (often a substantial number), those in hospital, or prisoners – all of whom remained on the formal rolls of units in many countries until they returned to duty or were mustered

Orders of Battle

out of service. My aim here is to portray the number of soldiers actually available on the battlefield.

All figures agglomerate officers and men (including drummers, light infantry hornists, cavalry trumpeters, and so on). Some of these persons were considered 'non-combatants' in some armies. This can lead to minor discrepancies, but seldom any of a major order.

I did not calculate losses to march attrition or illness. Unless I had a source that gave a specific piece of data (such as several consecutive tables for a single unit – very rare), I therefore carried the old numbers forward and continued to use those until I had new information. This means that units may sometimes appear stronger than they actually were, but I felt it was better to give the available figures and allow readers to calculate march attrition, sickness rates, desertion, etc. according to their own formulae. Moreover, in most cases, I suspect that the *ratio of forces* on the battlefield (as opposed to actual raw numbers) would not be much affected by trying to guess attrition rates.

I did adjust figures for battle losses as well as the available information allowed. Znaim presents an especial challenge in assessing losses because both sides tended to aggregate losses of 4–12 July, so it is unusual to find casualties specific to Wagram, Znaim or the intervening rearguard engagements. Where a unit has had losses deducted (or where data are otherwise uncertain), I have used 'c.' (*circa*) to indicate the adjustment or where the information is approximate. I use a question mark (?) where the data are especially uncertain.

Cavalry units present a special problem as the number of horse casualties can far outnumber those among the troopers and their officers. The French light cavalry at Znaim is the greatest victim of this crucial variable as formal reports are so scarce for these units.

Likewise, the artillery available after Wagram can only be estimated. Both sides certainly suffered some damaged guns in the great battle and the French redistributed their pieces to some degree, while many Austrian batteries were separated from their assigned corps during the retreat (many of the II Corps guns, for instance, seem to have retreated with Rosenberg). The tables below thus carry forward the guns available on 5 July with the recognition that the numbers actually on the field at Znaim were likely less in many cases, especially on the Austrian side.

Casualty figures in the main text. I followed similar methods in calculating the casualty figures that appear in the main text. For example, the Austrian I Corps after-action report ('*Relation*') for Znaim does not include any casualty figures. However, most of the regimental histories give specific losses for the battle. The *Erbach* Infantry's history, unfortunately, does not. To arrive at an estimate for that regiment, I averaged the losses of the others to gain a general sense of casualties per company, treating *Kolowrat* as an outlier for its exceptionally heavy losses. This yielded a figure of 20–40 men per company. As the one-battalion *Erbach* took *Mittrowsky*'s place in the line, I used the figure for that regiment of 30–40 per company and multiplied those numbers by three because only three *Erbach* companies were seriously engaged; I therefore used a round figure of 100 as the estimate for the *Erbach* battalion's losses. A similar method was used for French losses. In this case, I started by developing what seemed plausible ratios of officer-to-ranker casualties based on known cases (such as the 5th Ligne and 26th Léger where there are good figures in regimental histories). I then took the officer casualties from Martinien's work, multiplied the number of officer losses by the likely number of other rank losses per officer (these ranged from 1:12 to 1:30 in gross numbers for the infantry and 1:10 for the heavy cavalry; I applied the higher end of the range in most cases), and seasoned the result with a dash of common sense. To avoid under-representing French casualties, in most cases I rounded up (generously).

Finally, note that additional research has allowed me to refine the material presented in *Thunder on the Danube* and in some cases to correct errors.

Abbreviations

btn	battalion	how	howitzer(s)
pdr	pounder (artillery calibre)	sqdn	squadron

OWW	Ober dem Wienerwald Landwehr
OMB	Ober dem Manhartsberg Landwehr
UWW	Unter dem Wienerwald Landwehr
UMB	Unter dem Manhartsberg Landwehr

Order of Battle A
The Battle of Wagram, 5–6 July 1809

Showing organisations (with number of battalions or squadrons) as of morning 6 July and strengths as of the morning of 5 July. In most cases it is impossible to differentiate losses taken on 5 July from casualties suffered over both days of the battle.

AUSTRIA[1]

Hauptarmee   *Archduke Charles*
Headquarters guard
    2nd Grenadier Company, *Kerpen* Infantry No. 49

I Corps   *GdK Bellegarde*

Attacking force

Advance Guard	*GM Stutterheim*	
2nd Jäger Battalion	1	664
4th *EH Carl* Legion (OTL Jannek)	1	1,200
Klenau Chevaulegers No. 5	2	*c.* 200
Support for the advance guard		
II/*Kolowrat* Infantry No. 36	1	*c.* 900
Klenau Chevaulegers No. 5	6	*c.* 600
Cavalry battery		4 × 6-pdr, 2 × how
Position battery		4 × 6-pdr, 2 × how

Main Body **FML Fresnel**

Brigade GM Henneberg
- Reuss-Plauen Infantry No. 17 3 3,516
- Kolowrat Infantry No. 36 (I, III) 2 c. 1,800
- Erzherzog Rainer Infantry No. 11 3 2,994
- Brigade battery   8 × 6-pdr

Brigade
- Anton Mittrowsky Infantry No. 10 2 2,421
- Erbach Infantry No. 42 2 2,908
- Brigade battery   8 × 6-pdr

Defensive position FML Dedovich
- Vogelsang Infantry No. 47 3 2,892

Brigade GM Clary
- Argenteau Infantry No. 35 3 3,382
- 1st Hradisch Landwehr (OTL Magny) 1 732
- Brigade battery   8 × 6-pdr

Artillery Reserve
- Two position batteries each 4 × 12-pdr, 2 × how
- Two position batteries each 4 × 6-pdr, 2 × how

Corps Totals
- Infantry 23,585
- Cavalry 801
- Artillery 8 × 12-pdr, 40 × 6-pdr, 12 × how

II Corps **FML Hohenzollern**

Division **FML Brady**

Brigade GM Paar
- Infantry Regt No. 25 (former Zedtwitz) 3 2,217
- 2nd Znaim Landwehr (Maj Sterzl) 1 801
- Froon Infantry No. 54 3 3,273
- 3rd Hradisch Landwehr (Maj Höger) 1 753
- Brigade battery   8 × 6-pdr

Brigade GM Buresch
- Zach Infantry No. 15 2 2,035
- 3rd Brünn Landwehr (Maj Ségur) 1 913
- Josef Colloredo Infantry No. 57 2 3,122

1st Brünn Landwehr (OTL Taafe)		1	750
Brigade battery			8 × 6-pdr
Position battery			4 × 6-pdr, 2 × how

Division	*FML Ulm*		
Brigade	*GM Altstern*		
Rohan Infantry No. 21		3	3,748
Brigade battery			8 × 6-pdr
Brigade	*GM Wied-Runkel*		
D'Aspre Infantry No. 18		3	3,001
Frelich Infantry Regiment No. 28		3	3,485
Brigade battery (?)			8 × 6-pdr
Position battery			4 × 6-pdr, 2 × how

Division	*FML Siegenthal*		
Brigade	*GM Ignaz Hardegg*		
8th Jäger Battalion		1	675
2nd *EH Carl* Legion (OTL Kinsky)		1	883
Vincent Chevaulegers No. 4		6	537

Artillery Reserve
Cavalry battery	4 × 6-pdr, 2 × how
Two position batteries	4 × 12-pdr, 2 × how each
Position battery	4 × 6-pdr, 2 × how

Corps Totals
Infantry	25,656
Cavalry	537
Artillery, train, staff, engineer personnel	2,640
Artillery	8 × 12-pdr, 48 × 6-pdr, 12 × how

III Corps — *FML Kolowrat*

Division	*GM Schneller*		
Brigade	Oberst Schmuttermayer		
Lobkowitz Jäger		4 companies	608
Schwarzenberg Uhlans No. 2		6	667
Cavalry battery			4 × 6-pdr, 2 × how
Brigade	Oberst Giffing		
Schröder Infantry No. 7		3	1,995

Wenzel Colloredo Infantry No. 56	3	2,765
Brigade battery		8 × 6-pdr

Brigade   *Oberst Wratislaw*

1st and 2nd Combined Prague Landwehr (Oberst Wratislaw)	1	746
1st Beraun Landwehr (Maj Wrtby)	1	576
2nd Beraun Landwehr (Maj Klebelsberg)	1	591
Brigade battery		8 × 3-pdr

Division   ***FML St Julien***

Brigade   *Oberst Chiesa*

Kaiser Infantry No. 1	2	1,736
Manfredini Infantry No. 12	3	2,662
Würzburg Infantry No. 23	2	872
Brigade battery		8 × 6-pdr

Brigade   *GM Biber*

Kaunitz Infantry No. 20	3	2,469
Württemberg Infantry No. 38	2	909
Brigade battery		8 × 6-pdr

Artillery Reserve

Two position batteries	4 × 12-pdr, 2 × how each
Position battery	4 × 6-pdr, 2 × how
Position battery	4 × 6-pdr, 2 × how

Corps Totals

Infantry	15,929
Cavalry	667
Artillery	8 × 12-pdr, 36 × 6-pdr, 8 × 3-pdr, 10 × how

IV Corps   ***FML Rosenberg***

Disposition for morning attack[2]

Advance guards for 1st and 2nd Columns
         FML Radetzky

1st Column   *GM Provenchères*

Erzherzog Carl Infantry No. 3	3	1,699
4th OMB Landwehr (Oberst Fölseis)	1	578
attached from 1st OMB Landwehr	1 company	123
1st *EH Carl* Legion (Maj Watterich)[3]	1	1,015
Erzherzog Ferdinand Hussars No. 3	4	c. 390

The Battle of Wagram

2nd Column   *Oberst Prinz Coburg (EH Ferdinand Hussars)*

Stain Infantry No. 50	3	1,652
4th UWW Landwehr (Maj Gilleis)	1	559
2nd Moravian Volunteers (Maj Vetter)	1	584
Erzherzog Ferdinand Hussars No. 3	4	c. 390

One pioneer company

1st Column   *FML Hohenlohe-Bartenstein*

Brigade   *GM Philipp Hessen-Homburg*

Hiller Infantry No. 2	3	2,717
Sztaray Infantry No. 33	3	2,101
Brigade battery		8 × 6-pdr

2nd Column   *FML Rohan*

Brigade   *Oberst Swinburne*

Erzherzog Ludwig Infantry No. 8	3	2,189
1st Iglau Landwehr (Maj Nesselrode)	1	877
Koburg Infantry No. 22	3	2,001
1st Znaim Landwehr (Maj Haugwitz)	1	829
Brigade battery		8 × 6-pdr

Brigade   *GM Mayer*

Deutschmeister Infantry No. 4	3	1,533
6th UWW Landwehr (Maj Hoyos)	1	683
Kerpen Infantry No. 49	3	1,460
5th UWW Landwehr (Maj Cavriani)	1	544
Brigade battery		8 × 6-pdr

3rd Column Advance Guard   *FML Nordmann*

Brigade   *GM Vécsey*

Hessen-Homburg Hussar Regiment No. 4	7¾	942
Cavalry battery		4 × 6-pdr, 2 × how

Brigade   *GM Fröhlich*

Stipsicz Hussars No. 10	4½	815
Primatial Insurrection Hussars	1½	c. 210
Cavalry battery		4 × 6-pdr, 2 × how

One pioneer company

3rd Column   *FML Nostitz*

Brigade   *GM Rothkirch*

EH Johann Dragoons No. 1	6	631

Riesch Dragoons No. 6	6	671
Cavalry battery		4 × 6-pdr, 2 × how
Brigade	**GM Wartensleben**	
Blankenstein Hussars No. 6	10	1,164
O'Reilly Chevaulegers No. 3	7	862
Cavalry battery		4 × 6-pdr, 2 × how

In reserve:

Brigade	**GM Riese**	
Bellegarde Infantry No. 44	3	1,344
2nd UWW Landwehr (Maj Steinsberg)	1	491
Chasteler Infantry No. 46	3	1,190
1st UWW Landwehr (Maj Richter)	1	633
Beaulieu Infantry No. 58 (I, III)	2	1,249
3rd UMB Landwehr (OTL Obergfell)	1	568
Brigade battery		8 × 6-pdr

Corps Totals

Infantry: 24,100 on 6 July
Cavalry: 4,600 on 6 July
Artillery: 8 × 12-pdr, 40 × 6-pdr, 12 × how plus whatever remained from the 28 guns and 8 how of the former Advance Guard.

Notes: The former Advance Guard (FML Nordmann) suffered heavy losses on 5 July and was absorbed by IV Corps that evening. IV Corps is the only one whose operations journal provides a gross estimate of troops for 6 July. Assignments of the following are not clear: 1st and 7th Jäger Battalions (remnants serving as a combined unit); Carneville Freikorps (73 infantry, 48 cavalry). The location of the remnants of the *Wallach-Illyria* Grenz Regiment No. 13 (combined into one battalion) on 6 July is also unclear; this battalion ended up with II Corps. II/*Beaulieu* detached early on 5 July to Marchegg.

VI Corps   *FML Klenau*
Disposition for morning attack[4]

Advance Guard	***FML Vincent***	
Brigade	**GM August Vécsey**	
Kienmayer Hussars No. 8	8	639
Warasdin-St Georg Grenz Regt No. 6	1	937

Brod Grenz Regiment No. 7 (remnants)	2 companies		326
Cavalry battery			4 × 6-pdr, 2 × how
Brigade	*GM Mariassy*		
1st Vienna Volunteers (Maj St Quentin)	1		575
2nd Vienna Vols (OTL Steigentesch)	1		567
4th UMB Landwehr (Maj Colloredo)	1		466

Division — *FML Hohenfeld*

Brigade	*GM Hoffmeister*		
Duka Infantry No. 39	3		1,737
Gyulai Infantry No. 60	3		2,194
Brigade battery			8 × 6-pdr
Brigade	*GM Adler*		
Klebek Infantry No. 14	2		1,180
1st OWW Landwehr (Maj Prachma)	1		640
Jordis Infantry No. 59	2⅓		1,110
1st Combined Upper Austrian (Innviertel) Landwehr (Maj Straka)	1		948
3rd *EH Carl* Legion (Maj Laugier)	1		792
Brigade battery			8 × 6-pdr

Division — *FML Kottulinsky*

Brigade	*GM Splenyi*		
Benjovszky Infantry No. 31 (II, III)	2		1,588
Splenyi Infantry No. 51	3		1,514
Brigade battery			8 × 6-pdr
3rd Vienna Volunteers (Maj Waldstein)	1		475
4th Vienna Volunteers (OTL Küffel)	1		221
3rd Moravian Volunteers (Maj Boxberg)	1		927
Brigade	*GM Wallmoden*		
Liechtenstein Hussars No. 7	8		767
Cavalry battery			4 × 6-pdr, 2 × how

Artillery Reserve
Three position batteries — 12 × 6-pdr, 6 × how

Corps Totals

Infantry	16,197
Cavalry	1,406
Artillery, train, staff, engineer personnel	1,987
Artillery	44 × 6-pdr, 10 × how

Notes: In the schematic for the day's attack, the corps' Operations Journal lists the *Warasdin-St Georg* Grenz as only one battalion, probably as it was so reduced; the schematic does not show the *Brod* Grenzer at all, it is assumed they were attached. The 2nd Vienna combined with 1st under Mariassy on 6 July.

Reserve Corps — GdK Liechtenstein

Cavalry Reserve

Division	**FML Friedrich Hessen-Homburg**		
Brigade	GM Roussel d'Hurbal		
Erzherzog Franz Cuirassiers No. 2		6	493
Herzog Albert Cuirassiers No. 3		6	541
Brigade	GM Lederer		
Kronprinz Ferdinand Cuirassiers No. 4		6	563
Hohenzollern Cuirassiers No. 8*		6	645
Brigade	GM Kroyher		
Kaiser Cuirassiers No. 1		4	302
Liechtenstein Cuirassiers No. 6		6	504
Division	**FML Schwarzenberg**		
Brigade	GM Theimern		
Rosenberg Chevaulegers No. 6		8	973
Knesevich Dragoons No. 3		6	639
Two cavalry batteries			4 × 6-pdr, 2 × how each
Insurrection	GM Kerekes		
Neutra Insurrection Hussars		6	802
Primatial Insurrection Hussars		4½	*c.* 560

Cavalry Totals

Cavalry	8,790
Artillery	6 × 6-pdr, 8 × how

Note: The *Hohenzollern* Cuirassiers (*) were detached to the left wing on 6 July and retreated towards Brünn in the evening. Two squadrons of *Kaiser* Cuirassiers guarding trains.

Grenadier Reserve

Division	**FML d'Aspre**		
Brigade	GM Merville		
Scharlach Grenadier Btn (31, 32, 51)		1	562
Scovaud Grenadier Btn (4, 49, 63)		1	503

Jambline Grenadier Btn (14, 45, 59)⁵	1	422
Brzezinski Grenadier Btn (24, 30, 41)	1	537
Brigade battery		8 × 6-pdr
Brigade	**GM Hammer**	
Kirchenbetter Grenadier Btn (34, 37, 48)	1	462
Bissingen Grenadier Btn (3, 50, 58)	1	633
Oklopsia Grenadier Btn (12, 20, 23)	1	571
Locher Grenadier Btn (8, 22, 60)	1	612
1st OMB Landwehr (Hptm Marchal)	1	464
Brigade battery		8 × 6-pdr
Division	**FML Prochaska**	
Brigade	**GM Murray**	
Frisch Grenadier Btn (10, 11, 47)	1	620
Georgy Grenadier Btn (17, 36, 42)	1	555
Portner Grenadier Btn (40, 44, 46)	1	727
Leiningen Grenadier Btn (25, 35, 54)	1	801
Brigade	**GM Steyrer**	
Hahn Grenadier Btn (2, 33, 39)	1	716
Hromada Grenadier Btn (1, 29, 38)	1	772
Legrand Grenadier Btn (9, 55, 56)	1	776
Demontant Grenadier Btn (7, 18, 21)	1	777
Berger Grenadier Btn (15, 28, 57)	1	723
Brigade battery		8 × 6-pdr

Grenadier Totals
Infantry	11,233
Artillery	24 × 6-pdr
Total Reserve Corps artillery, train, staff, engineer personnel	1,147

Note: The regiments composing each grenadier battalion are shown in parentheses. Thus Leiningen's Grenadier Battalion included the grenadier companies of the following regiments: former *Zedtwitz* No. 25, *EH Johann* No. 35 and *Froon* No. 54.

Hauptarmee Totals
Total infantry/cavalry	136,496, on 5 July
Guns	388

FRANCE

Army of Germany[6]   *Emperor Napoleon*

Attached to Imperial Headquarters
    Württemberg *Herzog Heinrich*

Chevaulegers	–	234
Württemberg I/*Camrer* Infantry	1	477
Company of Guides	–	120

Imperial Guard[7]

Division (Young Guard)   *GD Curial*

Brigade   *GB Rouget*

Tirailleur-Chasseurs	2	1,287
Tirailleur-Grenadiers	2	1,116

Brigade   *GB Dumoustier*

Fusilier-Chasseurs	2	1,120
Fusilier-Grenadiers	2	1,145
5th and 6th Foot Batteries		12 × 6-pdr

Division (Old Guard)   *GD Dorsenne*

Chasseurs *GB Gros*	2	1,452
Grenadiers *GB Michel*	2	1,203
1st and 2nd Foot Batteries		12 × 6-pdr

Cavalry   *GD Walther*

Polish Chevaulegers	4	414
Chasseurs-à-Cheval	4	1,046
Dragoons	4	976
Grenadiers-à-Cheval	4	1,001
Elite Gendarmes	2	266
1st–4th Horse Batteries		24 × 6-pdr

Artillery Reserve
3rd and 4th Foot Batteries		12 × 12-pdr

Guard Totals

Infantry	7,323
Cavalry	1,305
Artillery, train, engineer personnel	1,276
Artillery	48 × 6-pdr, 12 × 12-pdr

2nd Corps	**GD Oudinot**[8]		
1st Division	**GD Tharreau**		
1st Brigade	GB Conroux		
1st Light Demi-Brigade			
IV/6th Léger		1	585
IV/24th Léger		1	451
IV/25th Léger		1	552
3rd Light Demi-Brigade			
Tirailleurs Corses		1	528
IV/9th Léger		1	538
IV/27th Léger		1	612
2nd Brigade	GB Albert		
1st Line Demi-Brigade			
IV/8th Ligne		1	650
IV/24th Ligne		1	435
IV/45th Ligne		1	464
2nd Line Demi-Brigade			
IV/94th Ligne		1	650
IV/95th Ligne		1	537
IV/96th Ligne		1	481
3rd Brigade	GB Jarry		
3rd Line Demi-Brigade			
IV/54th Ligne		1	581
IV/63rd Ligne		1	428
4th Line Demi-Brigade			
IV/4th Ligne		1	518
IV/18th Ligne		1	567
Artillery		1 foot and 1 horse battery	
2nd Division	**GD Frère**		
1st Brigade	GB Coëhorn		
2nd Light Demi-Brigade			
IV/17th Léger		1	476
IV/28th Léger		1	504
4th Light Demi-Brigade			
IV/16th Léger		1	658
IV/26th Léger		1	539
Tirailleurs du Po		1	543

2nd Brigade	GB Razout		
5th Line Demi-Brigade			
IV/27th Ligne		1	633
IV/39th Ligne		1	458
6th Line Demi-Brigade			
IV/59th Ligne		1	535
IV/69th Ligne		1	634
IV/76th Ligne		1	480
3rd Brigade	GB Ficatier		
7th Line Demi-Brigade			
IV/40th Ligne		1	481
IV/88th Ligne		1	690
8th Line Demi-Brigade			
IV/64th Ligne		1	633
IV/100th Ligne		1	486
Artillery			1 foot and 1 horse battery
3rd Division	**GD Grandjean**		
1st Brigade	GB Marion		
10th Léger		3	1,846
2nd Brigade	GB Lorencez		
3rd Ligne		3	1,644
57th Ligne		3	1,572
3rd Brigade	GB Brun		
72nd Ligne		3	1,344
105th Ligne		3	1,452
Artillery			2 foot batteries, 1 horse battery
13th Demi-Brigade d'Elite (Portuguese Legion)			
	GB Carcome Lobo		
Infantry		3	1,422
Cavalry		2	229
Light Cavalry Brigade	GB Colbert		
9th Hussars		4	617
7th Chasseurs-à-Cheval		3	543
20th Chasseurs-à-Cheval		3	519
Attached			
Saxon *Prinz Johann* Chevaulegers		4	524
Corps Artillery			2 foot batteries

The Battle of Wagram

Corps Totals
- Infantry — 25,616
- Cavalry — 2,432
- Artillery, train, engineer personnel — 2,001
- Corps/divisional artillery — 4 × 12-pdr, 30 × 6-pdr, 14 × how
- Regimental artillery — 16 × 6-pdr

3rd Corps — Marshal Davout[9]

1st Division — GD Morand

1st Brigade	GB Guiot de Lacour		
13th Léger		3	1,965
17th Ligne		3	2,092
2nd Brigade	GB L'Huillier		
30th Ligne		3	2,053
61st Ligne		3	2,094
Artillery, train, engineer personnel			441

2nd Division — GD Friant

Brigade	GB Gilly		
15th Léger		3	1,822
33rd Ligne		3	1,717
Brigade	GB Barbanègre		
48th Ligne		3	1,937
Brigade	GB Grandeau		
108th Ligne		3	1,956
111th Ligne		3	1,878
Artillery, train, engineer personnel			423

3rd Division — GD Gudin

1st Brigade	GB Boyer		
7th Léger		3	2,329
2nd Brigade	GB Leclerc		
12th Ligne		3	1,795
21st Ligne		3	1,953
3rd Brigade	GB Duppelin		
25th Ligne		3	1,915
85th Ligne		3	2,130
Artillery, train, engineer personnel			392

4th Division	**GD Puthod**		
1st Brigade	*GB Girard*		
IV/17th Ligne		1	526
IV/7th Léger		1	280
IV/12th Ligne		1	465
IV/61st Ligne		1	546
IV/65th Ligne		1	275
2nd Brigade	*GB Desailly*		
IV/21st Ligne		1	632
IV/30th Ligne		1	577
IV/33rd Ligne		1	512
IV/85th Ligne		1	572
IV/111th Ligne		1	624
Artillery, train, engineer personnel			386

Light Cavalry Division	**GD Montbrun**		
Brigade	*GB Pajol*		
5th Hussars		4	684
11th Chasseurs-à-Cheval		4	674
12th Chasseurs-à-Cheval		4	718
Brigade	*GB Jacquinot*		
7th Hussars		4	567
1st Chasseurs-à-Cheval		4	325
2nd Chasseurs-à-Cheval		3	359

Corps Totals

Infantry	32,645
Cavalry	3,327
Artillery, train, engineer personnel	3,691
Corps/divisional artillery	8 × 12-pdr, 25 × 8-pdr, 18 × 4-pdr, 2 × 3-pdr (reserve park), 8 × how
Regimental artillery	16 each, 3-pdr and 6-pdr

Attached

1st Dragoon Division	**GD Grouchy (*GB Debroc*)**		
7th Dragoons		4	502
30th Dragoons		4	634
Italian *Queen's* Dragoons		4	477
Artillery and train personnel			133, 4 or 6 guns

2nd Dragoon Division	*GD Pully (GB Poinsot)*	
23rd Dragoons	3	502
28th Dragoons	3	241
29th Dragoons	3	392
Total attached cavalry		2,748
Total attached artillery/train personnel		133

4th Corps — *Marshal Massena*[10]

1st Division — *GD Legrand*

1st Brigade	*GB Friedrichs*	
26th Léger	3	1,630
18th Ligne	3	1,787
2nd (Baden) Brigade	*Oberst von Neuenstein*	
1st Baden Infantry *Großherzog*	1⅓	975
2nd Baden Infantry *Erbgroßherzog*	2	1,399
Jäger Battalion *Lingg*	1	463
Artillery, train, engineer personnel		493

2nd Division — *GD Carra St Cyr*

1st Brigade	*GB Cosson*	
24th Léger	3	1,741
2nd Brigade	*GB de Stabenrath*	
4th Ligne	3	1,964
46th Ligne	3	1,953
3rd (Hessian) Brigade	*GB Schiner* (French) and *GM von Nagel* (Hesse-Darmstadt)	
Leib-Garde Regiment	2	1,181
Leib-Garde Fusiliers	1	489
Leib Regiment	2	1,167
1st Leib Fusiliers	1	548
Artillery, train, engineer personnel		529

3rd Division — *GD Molitor*

1st Brigade	*GB Leguay*	
2nd Ligne	2	1,292
16th Ligne	3	1,399

2nd Brigade	*GB Viviès*		
37th Ligne		3	1,464
67th Ligne		2	1,184
Artillery, train, engineer personnel			346
4th Division	***GD Boudet***		
1st Brigade	*GB Grillot*		
3rd Léger		2	1,406
2nd Brigade	*GB Valory*		
56th Ligne		3	1,590
93rd Ligne		2	1,309
Artillery, train, engineer personnel			343

Light Cavalry

Division	***GD Lasalle***		
Brigade	*GB Piré*		
8th Hussars		3	500
16th Chasseurs-à-Cheval		3	441
Brigade	*GB Bruyère*		
13th Chasseurs-à-Cheval		3	485
24th Chasseurs-à-Cheval		2	288
Division	***GD Marulaz***		
3rd Chasseurs-à-Cheval		2	329
14th Chasseurs-à-Cheval		3	139
19th Chasseurs-à-Cheval		3	322
23rd Chasseurs-à-Cheval		3	324
Baden Light Dragoons		4	208
Hessian Chevaulegers		3	179

Corps Totals

Infantry	24,941
Cavalry	3,215
Artillery, train, engineer personnel	2,000
French corps/divisional artillery	8 × 12-pdr, 42 × 6-pdr, 11 × how
French regimental artillery	14 × 6-pdr, 3 × 3-pdr
Baden artillery	8 × 6-pdr, 4 × how
Hessian artillery	5 × 6-pdr, 1 × how

Notes: Four musketeer companies of II/1st Baden Infantry (544) guarding park and baggage.

9th Corps (Saxon) — Marshal Bernadotte[11]

Staff Battalion	1	470
Horse Artillery Battery		3 × 8-pdr, 1 × how

Advance Guard — **GM von Gutschmid**

Prinz Clemens Chevaulegers	4	462
Hussar Regiment	3	327
Herzog Albrecht Chevaulegers	1	147

1st Division — **GL von Zezschwitz**

1st Brigade — *GM von Hartitzsch*

Combined Leib Grenadier Guard Btn	1	513
2nd Grenadier Btn (Major von Bose)	1	529

2nd Infantry Brigade — *GM von Zeschau*

König Infantry Battalion	1	899
von Niesemeuschel Infantry Battalion	1	954
Combined Inf Btn (OTL von Klengel) (from I/*Dyherrn* and II/*von Oebschelwitz*)	1	805
1st Heavy Battery		4 × 8-pdr, 2 × how
1st Light Battery		4 × 8-pdr, 2 × how

2nd Division — **GL von Polenz**

1st Infantry Brigade — *GM von Lecoq*

Prinz Clemens Infantry Battalion	1	750
von Low Infantry Battalion	1	837
von Cerrini Infantry Battalion	1	876
2nd Schützen Btn (Major von Egidy)	1	623

2nd Infantry Brigade — *GM von Steindel*

Prinz Anton Infantry Battalion	1	893
Prinz Maximilian Infantry Battalion	1	896
Prinz Friedrich August Infantry Battalion	1	909

Cavalry Brigade — *GM von Feilitzsch*

Leib-Garde Cuirassiers	4	572
Gardes du Corps Regiment	2	284
Karabiniers Regiment	2	206
2nd Heavy Battery		4 × 8-pdr, 2 × how
2nd Light Battery		2 × 8-pdr, 2 × how

French Division   **GD Dupas**

1st Brigade   GB Gency
- 5th Léger   2   1,547

2nd Brigade   GB Veau
- 19th Ligne   3   2,197

Attached
- 1st Saxon Grenadier Btn (Major von Radeloff)   1   526
- 1st Saxon Schützen Btn (Major von Metzsch)   1   657

Artillery   12 guns

Corps Totals

Infantry (not including Staff Battalion)	14,411
Cavalry	1,998
Artillery, train, engineer personnel	1,965
Artillery	17 × 8-pdr, 9 × how (all Saxon), plus 12 French pieces

Army of Italy   **Viceroy Eugène**[12]

Right Wing   **GD MacDonald**

Division   **GD Lamarque**

1st Brigade   GB Huard
- 18th Léger (III, IV)   2   894
- 13th Ligne   3   1,880

2nd Brigade   GB Alméras
- 23rd Ligne (III, IV)   2   508
- 29th Ligne   3   1,994

Attached
- 92nd Ligne (I, IV)   2   c. 1,100

Total artillery, train, engineer personnel   328

Centre   **GD Grenier**

Division   **GB Moreau** (replacing wounded **GD Seras**)

1st Brigade   GB Moreau
- IV/35th Ligne   1   556
- 53rd Ligne   3   1,569

The Battle of Wagram

2nd Brigade	GB Roussel		
IV/42nd Ligne		1	435
106th Ligne		3	1,384
Attached			
112th Ligne		3	1,088
Total artillery, train, engineer personnel			363
Division	**GD Durutte**		
1st Brigade	(GB Valentin)[13]		
23rd Léger		3	1,246
62nd Ligne		4	1,796
2nd Brigade	GB Dessaix		
60th Ligne (III, IV)		2	494
102nd Ligne		3	1,675
Total artillery, train, engineer personnel			338

Royal Italian Guard

Cavalry	GB Viani		
Honour Guards		1	142
Dragoons		2	324
Infantry	GB Lecchi		
II/Royal Velites		1	576
Line Infantry of the Guard		2	753
Artillery and train personnel			172
Light Cavalry	GB Gérard (GD Sahuc wounded on 5th)		
6th Chasseurs-à-Cheval		4	415
8th Chasseurs-à-Cheval		4	634
9th Chasseurs-à-Cheval		3	384
IV/1st Italian Chasseurs Royal Italian[14]		1*	c. 120
With army headquarters: IV/24th Dragoons		1*	195
With artillery park: IV/Napoleon Dragoons		1*	68

Corps Totals

Infantry	17,948
Cavalry (*not including asterisked units)	1,899
Artillery, train, engineer personnel	613
Artillery	33 × 6-pdr, 10 × 3-pdr, 12 × how (plus in parks: 2 × 12-pdr, 3 × 3-pdr, 2 × how)[15]

Cavalry Reserve	**_Marshal Bessières_**[16]		
1st Heavy Cavalry Div	**GD Nansouty**		4,029
1st Brigade	*GB Defrance*		
1st Carabiniers		4	663
2nd Carabiniers		4	701
2nd Brigade	*GB Doumerc*		
2nd Cuirassiers		4	708
9th Cuirassiers		4	776
3rd Brigade	*GB St Germain*		
3rd Cuirassiers		4	592
12th Cuirassiers		4	589
2nd Heavy Cavalry Div	**GD St Sulpice**		2,070
1st Brigade	*GB Fiteau*		
1st Cuirassiers		4	485
5th Cuirassiers		4	503
2nd Brigade	*GB Guiton*		
10th Cuirassiers		4	543
11th Cuirassiers		4	539
3rd Heavy Cavalry Div	**GD Arrighi**		1,921
1st Brigade	*GB Reynaud*		
4th Cuirassiers		4	404
6th Cuirassiers		4	421
2nd Brigade	*GB Bordessoulle*		
7th Cuirassiers		4	503
8th Cuirassiers		4	593

Corps Totals
  Cavalry   8,020
  Artillery, train, engineer personnel   732
  Artillery   10 × 8-pdr, 10 × 4-pdr, 6 × how

Lobau Island	**GD Reynier**[17]		
Baden 3rd Infantry *Graf Hochberg*		2	1,197
Saxon 3rd Grenadier Btn (Maj von Hake)		1	448
Saxon 4th Grenadier Btn (Maj von Winkelmann)			
		1	496
Neufchâtel Battalion		1	460

The Battle of Wagram

IV/21st Léger	1	574
IV/103rd Ligne	1	510
Artillery		109 guns and mortars

Army of Germany Totals
Total infantry/cavalry	147,855, on 5 July
Guns	404

Troops/guns on Lobau not included.

French and Allied Reinforcements Arriving by Morning, 6 July

Army of Dalmatia — **GD Marmont**[18]

1st Division — **GD Claparède**

1st Brigade — *GB Plauzonne*
5th Ligne	2	1,345

2nd Brigade — *GB Bertrand*
79th Ligne	2	1,372
81st Ligne	2	1,089

2nd Division — **GD Clauzel**

1st Brigade — *GB Delzons*
8th Léger	2	1,203
23rd Ligne	2	1,527

2nd Brigade — *GB Bachelu*
11th Ligne	3	1,786

Light Cavalry
(8th Company/3rd Chasseurs, 3rd Company/24th Chasseurs)   259

Army of Dalmatia Totals
Infantry	8,322
Cavalry	259
Artillery, train, engineer personnel	721
Artillery	4 × 6-pdr, 4 × 3-pdr, 3 × how, 6 × 3-pdr mountain guns

Army of Italy

Division — **GD Broussier**
9th Ligne	3	1,648
84th Ligne	3	2,015

92nd Ligne (II and III)	2	1,280
Total artillery, train, engineer personnel		342
Artillery		8 × guns, 4 × how

Division — **GD Pachtod**

1st Brigade	GB Abbé		
8th Léger (III, IV)		2	1,062
1st Ligne		3	1,349
2nd Brigade	GB Pastol		
52nd Ligne		3	1,701
Total artillery, train, engineer personnel			226
Artillery			6 guns

2nd Bavarian Div — **GL von Wrede**[19]
From 7th Corps

1st Brigade	GM Minucci		
6th Light Battalion		1	569
3rd Infantry *Prinz Karl*		2	1,277
13th Infantry		2	1,157
2nd Brigade	GM Beckers		
6th Infantry *Herzog Wilhelm*		2	1,070
7th Infantry *Löwenstein*		2	1,388
Cavalry	GM Preysing		
2nd Chevaulegers *König*		4	474
3rd Chevaulegers *Leiningen*		4	513

Division Totals

Infantry	5,461
Cavalry	987
Artillery, train, engineer personnel	566
Artillery	4 × 12-pdr, 20 × 6-pdr, 12 × how
Total reinforcements	22,838 infantry, 1,246 cavalry, 71 guns

Army of Germany Totals

Total infantry/cavalry	171,939, on 6 July
Guns	475

Troops on Lobau Island not included, casualties not deducted.

The Battle of Wagram

Notes to Order of Battle A

1. Corps strengths and initial organisations taken from 'Früh-Rapports' of 27 June (I, III, IV, V) and 4 July (II, VI, Reserve), KAFA, *Operationsjournale der Hauptarmee und Korps*, 1389. These data were then adjusted for 6 July in accordance with corps and sub-unit after-action reports and operations journals where available. Names of Landwehr and volunteer commanders are included as other sources often use names rather than numbers as references.
2. IV Corps, Op. J. 22, KAFA, Kart. 1383.
3. Austrian reports at the time often spell his name 'Wadrich', but I have used the spelling from the memorial essay published by his family: 'Watterich'.
4. VI Corps, Op. J. 32, KAFA, Kart. 1384.
5. According to the regimental history (Grois, p. 237), Hauptmann Hieronimus Jambline assumed command of this battalion before Wagram, but Austrian reports still list it as Puteany through Znaim.
6. Note on artillery: number and distribution of guns/howitzers is unclear, complicated by the inclusion of regimental pieces in June. Numbers in this appendix are taken from corps 'Situations' (which give only corps totals, not distribution); from the 15 July 'Livret' (SHD, C2/676); or from Buat, vol. II, pp. 159–66.
7. Imperial Guard, 'Situation', 12 June, SHD, C2/505; guns from Litre, pp. 57–9. Note that the Guard's 12 June 'Situation' gives the Tirailleur-Grenadiers only one battalion (as reflected in the orders of battle in *Thunder on the Danube*, vol. III). However, the 'Situation' for 15 July (SHD, C2/505) and the 'Livret de Situation' for June (SHD, C2/675) list two battalions as shown here. In all cases, the strength is approximately the same.
8. 2nd Corps, 'Situation', 1 July, SHD, C2/506 (number of batteries from 15 July 'Situation').
9. 3rd Corps 'Situation', 1 July, SHD, C2/506; Jacquinot: Cavalry Reserve 'Situation Sommaire', 1 July, SHD, C2/510; Montbrun: 30 June report, SHD, C2/510; dragoons: Army of Italy, 'Situation Sommaire', 25 June, SHD, C2/509.
10. 4th Corps 'Situation', 1 July, SHD, C2/507; Baden: Lauriston report, 13 June, SHD, C2/510; Hessians: Lasalle, 30 June report, SHD C2/510; Lasalle: Cavalry Reserve, 'Situation Sommaire', 1 July, SHD, C2/510. Grillot's position as a brigade commander is my assumption (Fririon had become corps chief of staff).
11. 9th Corps report, 20 June, and 9th Corps 'Situation', 15 June, SHD, C2/508. Organisation reflects changes up to 5 July (Gill, *Eagles*, pp. 294, 526). Staff Battalion remained on the south bank with the baggage.
12. Army of Italy, 'Situation Sommaire', 25 June, SHD C2/509; artillery from Buat; *Historique du 112e Régiment*, p. 50.
13. Though still listed as brigade commander, Valentin had been badly wounded at Raab and likely was not at Wagram.
14. Presence of this squadron at Wagram is uncertain; it seems likely based on: Buat, vol. II, p. 163; and Jean-Pierre Perconte, *Les Chasseurs à Cheval Italiens 1800–1814*, Lyon:

Perconte, 2008, p. 190. However, all of the Army of Italy's official situation reports from 25 June through 1 August place it with Rusca's division.
15. Assumes three 6-pounders and one howitzer with Grouchy.
16. 'Situation Sommaire' 1 July, SHD, C2/510.
17. Detachment of IV/21st Léger based on regimental history and Martinien; and IV/103rd Ligne based on Martinien. Lobau artillery consisted of thirty 6-pounders, eighteen 12-pounders, eighteen 18-pounders, ten howitzers, and ten mortars. Napoleon ordered a reinforcement of nine 6-pounders, four 12-pounders, six 18-pounders, and eight mortars for a total of 113 pieces, but four of these (unspecified) did not arrive, leaving the number on hand at 109 (Buat, vol. II, pp. 130–3). Naulet (1809, p. 325), gives slightly higher figures: 32 × 18-pounders, 18 × 12-pounders, 39 × 6-pounders, 10 × howitzers, 22 × mortars.
18. Army of Dalmatia, 'Situation' 1 July, SHD, C2/509. Although Marmont (*Mémoires*, vol. III, p. 218) states he brought his artillery to 24 guns while in Laibach, figures from the 1 and 15 July 'Situations' are used here.
19. 7th Corps, 'Situation', 2 July, SHD, C2/507.

Order of Battle B
French Pursuit Forces
7–8 July 1809

As arrayed left–right/west–east

4th Corps   **Marshal Massena**

1st Division   **GD Legrand**   c. 5,300 infantry

1st Brigade	*GB Friedrichs*	
26th Léger		3
18th Ligne		3
2nd (Baden) Brigade	*Oberst von Neuenstein*	
1st Baden Infantry *Großherzog*		1⅓
2nd Baden Infantry *Erbgroßherzog*		2
Jäger Battalion *Lingg*		1

2nd Division   **GD Carra St Cyr**   c. 5,000 infantry

1st Brigade	*GB de Stabenrath*	
24th Léger		3
4th Ligne		3
46th Ligne		3
3rd (Hessian) Brigade	*GB Schiner* (French) and *GM von Nagel* (Hesse-Darmstadt)	
Leib-Garde Regiment		2
Leib-Garde Fusiliers		1
Leib Regiment		2
1st Leib Fusiliers		1

3rd Division   **GD Molitor**   c. 4,000 infantry

1st Brigade	*GB Leguay*	
2nd Ligne		2

16th Ligne	3	
2nd Brigade	*GB Viviès*	
37th Ligne	3	
67th Ligne	2	
4th Division	***GD Boudet***	*c.* 3,400 infantry
1st Brigade	*GB Grillot*	
3rd Léger	2	
2nd Brigade	*GB Valory*	
56th Ligne	3	
93rd Ligne	2	
Light Cavalry	*GB Bruyère*	*c.* 2,300 cavalry
Division	(formerly ***Lasalle***)	
Brigade	*GB Piré*	
8th Hussars	3	
16th Chasseurs-à-Cheval	3	
Brigade	*GB Bruyère*	
13th Chasseurs-à-Cheval	3	
24th Chasseurs-à-Cheval	2	
Division	(formerly ***Marulaz***)	
3rd Chasseurs-à-Cheval	2	
14th Chasseurs-à-Cheval	3	
19th Chasseurs-à-Cheval	3	
23rd Chasseurs-à-Cheval	3	
Baden Light Dragoons	4	
Hessian Chevaulegers	3	
2nd Heavy Cavalry Div	***GD St Sulpice***	*c.* 1,700–1,900 cavalry
1st Brigade	*GB Fiteau*	
1st Cuirassiers	4	*c.* 350
5th Cuirassiers	4	*c.* 480
2nd Brigade	*GB Guiton*	
10th Cuirassiers	4	*c.* 530
11th Cuirassiers	4	*c.* 530
Corps Totals		
Infantry	*c.* 17,700	
Cavalry	*c.* 4,200	

French Pursuit Forces

Artillery, train, engineer personnel	c. 3,410
French corps/divisional artillery	8 × 12-pdr, 42 × 6-pdr, 11 × how
French regimental artillery	3 × 6-pdr, 14 × 3-pdr
Baden artillery	8 × 6-pdr, 4 × how
Hessian artillery	5 × 6-pdr, 1 × how

Note: Four musketeer companies of II/1st Baden Infantry (540) guarding park and baggage.

1st Heavy Cavalry Div	**GD Nansouty**		2,469 cavalry
1st Brigade	*GB Defrance*		
1st Carabiniers		4	394
2nd Carabiniers		4	392
2nd Brigade	*GB Doumerc*		
2nd Cuirassiers		4	490
9th Cuirassiers		4	439
3rd Brigade	*GB St Germain*		
3rd Cuirassiers		4	411
12th Cuirassiers		4	343
Total artillery and train personnel			246
Attached from Army of Italy	*GB Gérard*		1,192 cavalry
6th Chasseurs-à-Cheval		4	490
8th Chasseurs-à-Cheval		4	470
9th Chasseurs-à-Cheval		3	232
IV/1st Italian Chasseurs Royal Italian*		1	c. 120]
Reconnaissance detachment	*Oberst Lindenau*		
3rd Bavarian Chevaulegers *Leiningen*		2	c. 250
From Oudinot's 2nd Corps			c. 1,400
Light Cavalry Brigade	*Col. Gauthrin* (of 9th Hussars)		
9th Hussars		4	
7th Chasseurs-à-Cheval		3	
20th Chasseurs-à-Cheval		3	
From Davout's command			
Light Cavalry Division	**GD Montbrun**		c. 3,000
Brigade	*GB Pajol*		
5th Hussars		4	
11th Chasseurs-à-Cheval		4	
12th Chasseurs-à-Cheval		4	

Brigade	GB Jacquinot	
7th Hussars	4	
1st Chasseurs-à-Cheval	4	
2nd Chasseurs-à-Cheval	3	
1st Dragoon Division	***GD Grouchy (GB Debroc)***	
7th Dragoons	4	
30th Dragoons	4	
Italian Queen's Dragoons	4	
		4 or 6 guns
2nd Dragoon Division	***GD Pully (GB Poinsot)***	
23rd Dragoons	3	
28th Dragoons	3	
29th Dragoons	3	
Total dragoons:		c. 2,500

* Presence of this squadron at Wagram is uncertain; it seems likely based on: Buat, vol. II, p. 163; and Jean-Pierre Perconte, *Les Chasseurs à Cheval Italiens 1800–1814*, Lyon: Perconte, 2008, p. 190; Zanoli, p. 98. However, all of the Army of Italy's official situation reports from 25 June through 1 August place it with Rusca's division.

Order of Battle C
Austrian IV Corps
10 July 1809

Commander   ***FML Rosenberg***

Rosenberg changed his order of battle daily, sometimes several times a day, during the retreat after Wagram. The following can only give a representative arrangement to illustrate how the corps was structured as hostilities came to a close and to suggest how the corps might have looked (minus whatever detachments he may have left to watch the Brünn highway) had it been called to join the Main Army at Znaim.

1st Division   ***FML Radetzky***

Brigade   *Maj Haugwitz* (of 1st Znaim Landwehr)

Erzherzog Ludwig Inf No. 8 & 1st Iglau Landwehr (Maj Nesselrode)		
	4	1,038
Koburg Infantry No. 22 & 1st Znaim Landwehr (Maj Haugwitz)		
	4	1,485
Brigade battery		8 × 6-pdr

Brigade   *Oberst Klopstein* (of *Deutchmeister* Infantry)

Deutschmeister Infantry No. 4	3	803
6th UWW Landwehr (Maj Hoyos)	1	253
Kerpen Infantry No. 49	3	809
5th UWW Landwehr (Maj Cavriani)	1	156

Rearguard   ***GM Provenchères***

Stain Infantry No. 50	3	640
4th UWW Landwehr (Maj Gilleis)	1	169
2nd Moravian Volunteers (Maj Vetter)	1	*c.* 460

Erzherzog Ferdinand Hussars No. 3	8	c. 370
Hessen-Homburg Hussars No. 4	6½	c. 220
Erzherzog Johann Dragoons No. 1	1	c. 80
Brigade battery		8 × 6-pdr

2nd Division — **FML Hohenlohe-Bartenstein**

Brigade — Oberst Torry (of Hiller Infantry)

Hiller Infantry No. 2	3	2,047
Sztaray Infantry No. 33	3	1,637
Brigade battery		8 × 6-pdr

Brigade — Oberst Fröauf (of Beaulieu Infantry)

Bellegarde Infantry No. 44	3	573
2nd UWW Landwehr (Maj Steinsberg)	1	c. 30?
Chasteler Infantry No. 46	3	406
1st UWW Landwehr (Maj Richter)	1	152
Beaulieu Infantry No. 58 (I, III)	2	361
3rd UMB Landwehr (OTL Obergfell)	1	93
O'Reilly Chevaulegers No. 3	3	c. 210
Brigade battery		8 × 6-pdr

Rearguard — **GM Fröhlich**

Erzherzog Carl Infantry No. 3	3	1,030
4th OMB Landwehr (Oberst Fölseis)	1	c. 70?
1st EH Carl Legion (Maj Watterich)	1	c. 300
1st and 7th Jägers (Maj Nesselrode)	remnants	c. 200?
Stipsicz Hussars No. 10	4½	c. 160
Primatial Insurrection Hussars	1½	c. 130
O'Reilly Chevaulegers No. 3	4	c. 280
Brigade battery		8 × 6-pdr

Corps Totals

Infantry	c. 12,700
Cavalry	c. 1,360?
Artillery	8 × 12-pdr, 40 × 6-pdr, 12 × how plus whatever remained from the 28 guns and 8 how of the former Advance Guard.

Notes: Organisational structure from IV Corps operations journals (Op. J. 22 and 24, KAFA, 1383). Most strength figures are from 7–10 July returns ('Früh-Rapport', 7–10 July 1809, KAFA, 1461). Units that were effectively destroyed at Wagram are not shown. Using two later reports ('Früh-Rapport' of 18 July and 'Ordre de Bataille und Standes Rapport', 23 July 1809, KAFA, 1462 and 1422), I have endeavoured to estimate strengths for units that had not submitted returns by 10 July; these are shown with a question mark, but are less reliable than those for the rest of the Hauptarmee. Artillery shown based on pre-Wagram 1 July returns (thus aggregated at corps level); many pieces were likely damaged and unavailable on 10 July.

The remainder of the *Stipsicz* Hussars, cut off during the withdrawal, had attached themselves to Archduke Johann's corps. The junior ranks of many brigade commanders led Rosenberg to request several additional *General-Majors* in his report to Charles on the evening of 9 July. II/*Beaulieu* had been detached before Wagram and did not rejoin until after the armistice.

Order of Battle D
Austrian V Corps
10 July 1809

Commander	*FML Reuss*		
Rearguard	*GM Klebelsberg*		
Gradiska Grenz Infantry No. 8		2	1,781
3rd Jäger Battalion		1	770
EH Carl Uhlans No. 3 (Oberst Heinrich von Hardegg)			
		7	c. 600
Blankenstein Hussars No. 6		6	c. 600
Brigade	*GM Neustädter*		
Reuss-Greitz Infantry No. 55		2	847
3rd Prerau Landwehr (Maj Bukovsky)		1	794
Czartoryski Infantry No. 9		3	1,390
4th Brünn Landwehr (Maj Hoffmann)		1	920
Brigade battery			8 × 6-pdr
Brigade	*Oberst Pflüger*		
Lindenau Infantry No. 29		3	2,402
Brigade battery			8 × 6-pdr
Detached on right flank for liaison with Schustekh			
Blankenstein Hussars No. 6 (Maj Teschenberg)			
		2	c. 200
Detached on left flank:			
5th Vienna Volunteers (Maj Salis)		1	414
Detached on left flank	*OTL Wilgenheim*		
4th Jäger Battalion		5 companies	c. 650
EH Carl Uhlans No. 3		1	c. 80

Corps Totals
Infantry		9,968
Cavalry		c. 1,480

Detached towards Maissau *FML Schustekh*

Liaison Detachment	*GM Anton von Hardegg*	
1st Moravian Volunteers (Maj Seyffert)	1	933
6th *EH Carl* Legion (Maj Czernin)	1	982
Levenehr Dragoons No. 3	1	45

Main Body
Infantry Regiment No. 40 (formerly *Josef Mittrowsky*)	3	2,006
5th *EH Carl* Legion (Maj Woracziczky)	1	826
2nd Combined Upper/Lower Austrian Landwehr (Maj Lichtenberg)	1	441
3rd Combined Upper/Lower Austrian Landwehr (Maj Fürstenberg)	1	535
Levenehr Dragoons No. 3	5	c. 230
Artillery		3 × 6-pdr, 8 × 3-pdr, 2 × how

Sources: V Corps, Op. J. 26 and 28, KAFA, Kart. 1383. The 'main body' included numerous detachments Schustekh had posted towards the Danube.

Order of Battle E
The Battle of Znaim
10–11 July 1809

Showing strengths as of 10 July and organisations as of afternoon 11 July.[1]

AUSTRIA[2]

Hauptarmee	***Archduke Charles***		
Headquarters guard			
2nd Grenadier Company, *Kerpen* Infantry No. 49			one company
Liaison Detachment	*GM Ignaz Hardegg*		
on left flank			
2nd Znaim Landwehr		1	c. 400?
Rosenberg Chevaulegers No. 6		2	c. 140
Schwarzenberg Uhlans No. 2		2	c. 140
I Corps	***GdK Bellegarde***		
'Forward element'			
Anton Mittrowsky Infantry No. 10		1	c. 650
Reuss-Plauen Infantry No. 17		1	c. 560
2nd Jäger Battalion		1	c. 350?
4th *EH Carl* Legion (Hptm Homme)		2 or 3 companies	c. 190
Klenau Chevaulegers No. 5		3	c. 240
First Line	***GM Henneberg***		
Brigade	*GM Henneberg*		
Reuss-Plauen Infantry No. 17		2	c. 1,120
Kolowrat Infantry No. 36		3	1,935

Brigade	Oberst Fabré (of Rainer Infantry)		
Erzherzog Rainer Infantry No. 11		3	1,657
Vogelsang Infantry No. 47		3	1,472

Second Line — **GM Clary**

Brigade	GM Clary		
Erbach Infantry No. 42		2	1,574
Brigade	Oberst Schäffer (of Argenteau Infantry)		
Argenteau Infantry No. 35		3	1,516
Klenau Chevaulegers No. 5		5	c. 400
In front of Brenditz:			
Anton Mittrowsky Infantry No. 10		1	c. 650

Corps Totals

Infantry	c. 11,674
Cavalry	c. 640
Artillery	8 × 12-pdr, 40 × 6-pdr, 12 × how

Note: Location of 1st Hradisch Landwehr Battalion (Oberstlt Magny; strength 223 men) (from *Anton Mittrowsky*) not clear – likely with one of the battalions or guarding trains.

II Corps — **FML Hohenzollern**

Division — **GM Buresch**

Brigade	Oberst Quallenberg (of former Zedtwitz Infantry)		
Infantry Regt No. 25 (former Zedtwitz)		3	1,038
Froon Infantry No. 54		3	1,970
3rd Hradisch Landwehr (Maj Höger)		1	c. 110?
Brigade	GM Buresch		
Zach Infantry No. 15		2	1,038
3rd Brünn Landwehr (Maj Ségur)		1	incl with regt
Josef Colloredo Infantry No. 57		3	c. 2,000?
1st Brünn Landwehr (OTL Taafe)		1	c. 300?

Division — **GM Wied-Runkel**

Brigade	GM Altstern		
Rohan Infantry No. 21		3	1,721
Brigade	GM Wied-Runkel		
d'Aspre Infantry No. 18		3	1,456
Frelich Infantry Regiment No. 28		3	1,335

Brigade

Wallach-Illyria Grenz Regiment No. 13	2	413
2nd *EH Carl* Legion (OTL Kinsky)	1	c. 600?
Vincent Chevaulegers No. 4	6	290

Other

The following seem to have been temporarily attached to II Corps

4th *EH Carl* Legion (Major Jannek)	3 or 4 companies	c. 370
Blankenstein Hussars No. 6	2	c. 120?

Corps Totals

Infantry	c. 12,351
Cavalry	290 and c. 120 hussars
Artillery	8 × 12-pdr, 48 × 6-pdr, 12 × how. Many of these seem to have withdrawn with Rosenberg; Hohenzollern reported that he only had 3 (unspecified) batteries on 10 July.

Notes: GM Ignaz Hardegg detached on far left beyond Winau with 2nd Znaim Landwehr and a division each of *Rosenberg* Chevaulegers and *Schwarzenberg* Uhlans to observe army's flank and make contact with Rosenberg. The assignment of the 4th *EH Carl* Legion companies and the *Blankenstein* Hussar squadrons is unclear. The strength of *Rohan* Infantry is that given in the 7–10 July Früh-Rapport, but Altstern claimed it only numbered some 800 men in his 9 July report.

III Corps   *FML Kolowrat*[3]

Division   **GM Schneller**

Brigade   *Oberst Schmuttermayer* (of *Schwarzenberg* Uhlans)

Lobkowitz Jäger	4 companies	653
Schwarzenberg Uhlans No. 2	4	c. 400

Brigade   *Oberst Giffling* (of *W. Colloredo* Infantry)

Schröder Infantry No. 7	3	2,258
Wenzel Colloredo Infantry No. 56	3	2,421

Brigade   *Oberst Wratislaw* (of *Prague Landwehr*)

1st and 2nd Combined Prague Landwehr (Oberst Wratislaw)	1	436
1st Beraun Landwehr (Maj Wrtby)	1	492

The Battle of Znaim

2nd Beraun Landwehr (Maj Klebelsberg)		1	473

Division — *FML St Julien*
Brigade — *Oberst Chiesa* (of Würzburg Infantry)

Kaiser Infantry No. 1	2	1,174
Manfredini Infantry No. 12	3	2,167
Würzburg Infantry No. 23	2	1,124

Brigade — *GM Biber*

Kaunitz Infantry No. 20	3	2,235
Württemberg Infantry No. 38	2	1,220

Corps Totals

Infantry	14,653
Cavalry	c. 400
Artillery (Wagram)	8 × 12-pdr, 36 × 6-pdr, 8 × 3-pdr, 10 × how

Note: Two squadrons of *Schwarzenberg* Uhlans were detached in Germany.

V Corps — *FML Reuss*[4]

Brigade — *GM Neustädter*

Reuss-Greitz Infantry No. 55	2	1,065
3rd Prerau Landwehr (Maj Bukovsky)	1	803
Czartoryski Infantry No. 9	3	1,844
4th Brünn Landwehr (Maj Hoffmann)	1	874
Brigade battery		8 × 6-pdr

Brigade — *Oberst Pflüger*

Lindenau Infantry No. 29	3	2,505
Gradiska Grenz Infantry No. 8	2	1,770
Brigade battery		8 × 6-pdr

At Pöltenberg

3rd Jäger Battalion	1	822

Right flank security along the Thaya

Blankenstein Hussars No. 6	2	c. 120

In reserve — *GM Klebelsberg*

5th Vienna Volunteers (Maj Salis)	1	392
EH Carl Uhlans No. 3	7	c. 660
Blankenstein Hussars No. 6	6	c. 360

Corps Totals

Infantry	10,075
Cavalry	c. 1,140
Artillery	32 × 6-pdr, 10 × how

Note: Reuss's artillery complement is poorly recorded. He seems to have had at least two 6-pdr brigade batteries and a cavalry battery, supported by up to three position batteries as shown here. Wilgenheim had been cut off with one squadron of Uhlans (c. 90–100) and 4th Jägers (c. 650). The *Blankenstein* Hussars had ten squadrons, two new ones having been formed during the war.

VI Corps — FML Klenau[5]
At Wolframitzkirchen

Division — FML Hohenfeld

Brigade — GM Hoffmeister

Duka Infantry No. 39	3	798
Gyulai Infantry No. 60	3	1,769

Brigade — GM Adler

Klebek Infantry No. 14	2	733
1st OWW Landwehr (Maj Prachma)	1	125
Jordis Infantry No. 59	2⅓	732
1st Combined Upper Austrian (Innviertel) Landwehr (Maj Straka)	1	533
3rd *EH Carl* Legion (Maj Lougier)	1	569

Division — FML Kottulinsky

Brigade — GM Splenyi

Benjovszky Infantry No. 31 (II, III)	2	818
Splenyi Infantry No. 51	3	743
3rd Vienna Volunteers (Maj Waldstein)	1	254
4th Vienna Volunteers (OTL Küffel)	1	89
3rd Moravian Volunteers (Maj Boxberg)	1	280

Division — FML Vincent

Brigade — GM August Vécsey

Kienmayer Hussars No. 8	4	488

Brigade — GM Mariássy

1st Vienna Volunteers (Maj St Quentin)	1	260
2nd Vienna Vols (OTL Steigentesch)	1	342

The Battle of Znaim

Liechtenstein Hussars No. 7	4	547
Brigade	**GM Peter Vécsey**	
Warasdin-St Georg Grenz Regt No. 6	2	432
Brod Grenz Regiment No. 7 (remnants)	2 companies	252

Corps Totals
Infantry	8,729
Cavalry	1,035
Atillery	40 × 6-pdr, 8 × 3-pdr, 8 × how

Note: The 4th UMB Landwehr (Maj Colloredo) had been destroyed at Wagram.

Reserve Corps   **FML Schwarzenberg**
GdK Liechtenstein absent

Cavalry Reserve   **FML Schwarzenberg**

Division   **FML Friedrich Hessen-Homburg**

Brigade	**GM Roussel d'Hurbal**		
Erzherzog Franz Cuirassiers No. 2	6		231
Herzog Albert Cuirassiers No. 3	6		291
Brigade	**GM Lederer**		
Kronprinz Ferdinand Cuirassiers No. 4	6		389
Hohenzollern Cuirassiers No. 8	6		210

Division   **FML Schwarzenberg**

Brigade	**GM Kroyher**		
Kaiser Cuirassiers No. 1	4		192
Liechtenstein Cuirassiers No. 6	6		351
Brigade	**GM Theimern**		
With Nostitz south of the Thaya on 10th			
Rosenberg Chevaulegers No. 6	6		c. 460
Knesevich Dragoons No. 3	6		471
Two cavalry batteries		4 × 6-pdr, 2 × how each	

Division   **FML Nostitz**

Brigade	**GM Rothkirch**		
North of the Thaya on 10th			
EH Johann Dragoons No. 1	6		365
Riesch Dragoons No. 6	6		461
Cavalry battery		4 × 6-pdr, 2 × how	

Insurrection Brigade GM *Kerekes*
    With Nostitz south of the Thaya on 10th
        Neutra Insurrection Hussars   6   715
        Primatial Insurrection Hussars   4½   346

Cavalry Reserve Totals
    Cavalry   *c.* 4,482
    Artillery   16 × 6-pdr, 8 × how

Note: Two squadrons of *Kaiser* Cuirassiers guarding trains.

Grenadier Reserve FML *Prochaska*[6]

Brigade   OTL *Scovaud* (replacing *Merville*)   1,423
    Scharlach Grenadier Btn (31, 32, 51)   1
    Scovaud Grenadier Btn (4, 49, 63)   1
    Jambline Grenadier Btn (14, 45, 59)   1
    Brzezinski Grenadier Btn (24, 30, 41)   1
    Brigade battery   8 × 6-pdr

Brigade   GM *Hammer*   2,270
    Kirchenbetter Grenadier Btn (34, 37, 48)   1
    Bissingen Grenadier Btn (3, 50, 58)   1
    Oklopsia Grenadier Btn (12, 20, 23)   1
    Locher Grenadier Btn (8, 22, 60)   1
    Brigade battery   8 × 6-pdr

Brigade   GM *Murray*   2,243
    Frisch Grenadier Btn (10, 11, 47)   1
    Georgy Grenadier Btn (17, 36, 42)   1
    Portner Grenadier Btn (40, 44, 46)   1
    Leiningen Grenadier Btn (25, 35, 54)   1

Brigade   GM *Steyrer*   3,329
    Hahn Grenadier Btn (2, 33, 39)   1
    Hromada Grenadier Btn (1, 29, 38)   1
    Legrand Grenadier Btn (9, 55, 56)   1
    Demontant Grenadier Btn (7, 18, 21)   1
    Berger Grenadier Btn (15, 28, 57)   1
    Brigade battery   8 × 6-pdr

Attached to Hammer's brigade
    1st OMB Landwehr (Hptm Marchal)   1   241

Grenadier Reserve Totals
  Infantry   9,506
  Artillery   24 × 6-pdr

Estimated forces available by midday, 11 July
  Total infantry   c. 67,418
  Total cavalry   c. 8,387

FRANCE

Army of Germany[7]   ***Emperor Napoleon***

As of 10 July

Army of Dalmatia	**GD Marmont**		
1st Division	***GD Claparède***		
1st Brigade	*GB Plauzonne*		
5th Ligne		2	1,345
2nd Brigade	*GB Bertrand*		
79th Ligne		2	1,372
81st Ligne		2	1,089
2nd Division	***GD Clauzel***		
1st Brigade	*GB Delzons*		
8th Léger		2	1,203
23rd Ligne		2	1,527
2nd Brigade	*GB Bachelu*		
11th Ligne		3	1,786
Light Cavalry (8th Company/3rd Chasseurs, 3rd Company/24th Chasseurs)			259
Total infantry		8,322	
Total cavalry		259	
Total artillery, train, engineer personnel		721	
Total artillery		4 × 6-pdr, 4 × 3-pdr, 3 × how, 6 × 3-pdr mountain guns	

Attached
2nd Bavarian Division   **GM von Minucci**
From 7th Corps   (at start in place of the wounded *Wrede*)

1st Brigade	GM Minucci		
6th Light Battalion		1	569
3rd Infantry *Prinz Karl*		2	1,277
13th Infantry		2	1,157
2nd Brigade	GM Beckers		
6th Infantry *Herzog Wilhelm*		2	1,070
7th Infantry *Löwenstein*		2	1,388
Cavalry	GM Preysing		
2nd Chevaulegers *König*		4	474
3rd Chevaulegers *Leiningen*		2	c. 250

Total Bavarian infantry	5,461
Total Bavarian cavalry	566
Total Bavarian artillery/train personnel	721

Attached
Light Cavalry Div   **GD Montbrun**[8]   c. 4,400

Brigade	GB Pajol	
5th Hussars		4
11th Chasseurs-à-Cheval		4
12th Chasseurs-à-Cheval		4
Brigade	GB Jacquinot	
7th Hussars		4
1st Chasseurs-à-Cheval		3
2nd Chasseurs-à-Cheval		3
Brigade	Col Gauthrin (9th Hussars)	
9th Hussars		4
7th Chasseurs-à-Cheval		3
20th Chasseurs-à-Cheval		3

Note: The 7th Chasseurs-à-Cheval, initially detached at Laa, apparently rejoined Marmont by the evening of 10 July.

Totals for Marmont's command (Army of Dalmatia and attachments)
Total infantry	13,783
Total cavalry	c. 5,000

The Battle of Znaim

Total artillery, train, engineer personnel   1,287
French corps/divisional artillery   8 × 12-pdr, 30 × 6-pdr, 7 × how

Arriving midday/early afternoon of 11 July

Imperial Guard

Cavalry	**GD Walther**	*c.* 3,500 cavalry
Polish Chevaulegers	4	
Chasseurs-à-Cheval	4	
Dragoons	4	
Grenadiers-à-Cheval	4	
Elite Gendarmes	2	

1st through 4th Horse Batteries (24 × 6-pdr)

Detachment of Baden Light Dragoons
    A detachment of 50 Baden Light Dragoons under Leutnant Franz Georg von Stern arrived on Marmont's side of the field on 11 July and joined Montbrun.[9]

4th Corps   **Marshal Massena**[10]

1st Division	**GD Legrand**	*c.* 5,000 infantry
1st Brigade	*GB Friedrichs*	
26th Léger	3	
18th Ligne	3	
2nd (Baden) Brigade	*Oberst von Neuenstein*	
1st Baden Infantry *Großherzog*	1⅓	
2nd Baden Infantry *Erbgroßherzog*	2	
Jäger Battalion *Lingg*	1	

2nd Division	**GD Carra St Cyr**	*c.* 5,000 infantry
1st Brigade	*GB de Stabenrath*	
24th Léger	3	
4th Ligne (Captain Jean Lanes)	3	
46th Ligne	3	
2nd (Hessian) Brigade	*GB Schiner/GM von Nagel*	
Leib-Garde Regiment	2	
Leib-Garde Fusiliers	1	
Leib Regiment	2	
1st Leib Fusiliers	1	

Light Cavalry   **GB Piré**

Division (formerly **Lasalle**)   c. 2,000 cavalry

Brigade   *GB Piré*
- 8th Hussars   3
- 16th Chasseurs-à-Cheval   3

Brigade   (former *Bruyère*)
- 13th Chasseurs-à-Cheval   3

Division (formerly **Marulaz**)
- 3rd Chasseurs-à-Cheval   2
- 14th Chasseurs-à-Cheval   3
- 19th Chasseurs-à-Cheval   3
- 23rd Chasseurs-à-Cheval   3

2nd Heavy Cavalry Div   **GD St Sulpice**   c. 1,700–1,900 cavalry

1st Brigade   *GB Fiteau*
- 1st Cuirassiers   4
- 5th Cuirassiers   4

2nd Brigade   *GB Guiton*
- 10th Cuirassiers   4
- 11th Cuirassiers   4

Corps Totals

Infantry	c. 10,000
Cavalry	c. 3,900
French corps/divisional artillery	8 × 12-pdr, c. 18 × 6-pdr, c. 4 × how
French regimental artillery:	c. 8–10 × regimental pieces
Baden artillery	8 × 6-pdr, 4 × how
Hessian artillery	5 × 6-pdr, 1 × how

Notes: 24th Chasseurs and most of the Baden Light Dragoons detached to Krems under Colonel Ameil. 5th Léger and 19th Ligne, formerly of Dupas's division, had not yet joined 4th Corps. Hessian Chevaulegers reorganising in the rear. It is not clear how many of Massena's guns accompanied the corps to Znaim.

Cavalry Reserve[11]

1st Heavy Cavalry Div	**GD Nansouty**		2,469 cavalry
1st Brigade	GB Defrance		
1st Carabiniers		4	394
2nd Carabiniers		4	392
2nd Brigade	GB Doumerc		
2nd Cuirassiers		4	490
9th Cuirassiers		4	439
3rd Brigade	GB St Germain		
3rd Cuirassiers		4	411
12th Cuirassiers		4	343
Total artillery and train personnel			246
3rd Heavy Cavalry Div	**GD Arrighi**		1,921 cavalry
1st Brigade	GB Reynaud		
4th Cuirassiers		4	404
6th Cuirassiers		4	421
2nd Brigade	GB Bordessoulle		
7th Cuirassiers		4	503
8th Cuirassiers		4	593
Total artillery and train personnel			235
Total artillery (both divisions)			6 × 8-pdr/4-pdr, 4 × how

Note: Marshal Bessières had been wounded at Wagram and was not present at Znaim.

Estimated forces available by midday, 11 July
Total infantry	c. 22,130
Total cavalry	c. 14,530

En route on 11 July (available on 12 July)

From 4th Corps

3rd Division	**GD Molitor**		c. 4,000 infantry
1st Brigade	GB Leguay		
2nd Ligne		2	
16th Ligne		3	
2nd Brigade	GB Viviès		
37th Ligne		3	
67th Ligne		2	
Divisional artillery			c. 6 × 6-pdr, c. 2 × how
Regimental artillery			?
Colonel Ameil			
23rd Chasseurs-à-Cheval		3	c. 200
Baden Light Dragoons		4	c. 150

Imperial Guard[12]

Division (Young Guard)	**GD Curial**		
Brigade	GB Rouget		
Tirailleur-Chasseurs		2	
Tirailleur-Grenadiers		2	
Brigade	GB Dumoustier		
Fusilier-Chasseurs		2	
Fusilier-Grenadiers		2	
5th and 6th Foot Batteries			12 × 6-pdr
Division (Old Guard)	**GD Dorsenne**		
Chasseurs		2	
Grenadiers		2	
1st and 2nd Foot Batteries			12 × 6-pdr
Artillery Reserve			
3rd and 4th Foot Batteries			12 × 12-pdr
Royal Italian Guard Infantry	GB Lecchi		
II/Royal Velites		1	576
Line Infantry of the Guard		2	753

Guard Totals
Infantry	c. 8,500
Artillery	24 × 6-pdr, 12 × 12-pdr

2nd Corps — GD Oudinot[13]

1st Division — GD Tharreau
1st Brigade	GB Conroux
2nd Brigade	GB Albert
3rd Brigade	GB Jarry
Artillery	1 foot and 1 horse battery

2nd Division — GD Dupas[14]
1st Brigade	GB Coëhorn
2nd Brigade	GB Razout
3rd Brigade	GB Ficatier
Artillery	1 foot and 1 horse battery

3rd Division — GD Grandjean
1st Brigade	GB Marion
2nd Brigade	GB Lorencez
3rd Brigade	GB Brun
Artillery	2 foot batteries and 1 horse battery

13th Demi-Brigade d'Elite (Portuguese Legion)
GB Carcome Lobo

Infantry	3
Cavalry	2
Corps artillery	2 foot batteries

Corps Totals
Infantry:	c. 18,000
Corps/divisional artillery	4 × 12-pdr, 30 × 6-pdr, 14 × how
Regimental artillery	16 × 6-pdr

3rd Corps **Marshal Davout**[15]

1st Division	**GD Morand**	c. 5,000
1st Brigade	GB Guiot de Lacour	
2nd Brigade	GB L'Huillier	
2nd Division	**GD Friant**	c. 8,500
1st Brigade	GB Gilly	
2nd Brigade	GB Barbanègre	
3rd Brigade	GB Grandeau	
3rd Division	**GD Gudin**	c. 7,700
1st Brigade	GB Boyer	
2nd Brigade	GB Leclerc	
3rd Brigade	GB Decouz	
4th Division	**GD Puthod**	c. 3,600
1st Brigade	GB Girard	
2nd Brigade	GB Desailly	

Corps Totals
  Infantry   c. 25,000
  Corps/divisional artillery   8 × 12-pdr, 25 × 8-pdr, 18 × 4-pdr,
                                          2 × 3-pdr (reserve park), 8 × how
  Regimental artillery   16 each 3-pdr and 6-pdr

Note: Grouchy's dragoon division detached along the Thaya between Muschau and Unter-Wisternitz with two battalions of 13th Léger and one battalion of 30th Ligne.

Notes to Order of Battle E

1. Note: the artillery components of both armies were in flux after Wagram. The situation was especially difficult on the Austrian side as units became intermingled or marched off in the wrong directions during the retreat. Much of Hohenzollern's artillery, for instance, seems to have headed off towards Brünn with Rosenberg. Additionally, it is not clear how many pieces on either side had been rendered unserviceable during the battle. The available archival material does not shed much light on this problem. What is listed here thus largely carries forward the information from 5 July with the assumption that percentage losses on both sides were likely similar and that any discrepancy in

The Battle of Znaim

losses would not be sufficiently great as to influence the outcome of combat. The key difference would remain how each side employed its artillery (i.e., not numbers): such as the Bavarian batteries above Klein-Tesswitz, the Austrian 12-pounder battery opposite Zuckerhandl and Massena's intelligent use of his guns in crossing the Thaya.

2. Drawn from official 'Relations', regimental histories, Heller (vol. II, pp. 264–6) and other accounts. Most strength figures are from 7–10 July returns ('Früh-Rapport', 7–10 July 1809, KAFA, 1461). Units that were effectively destroyed at Wagram are not shown. As noted earlier, I have used later official reports to estimate strengths for units that had not submitted strength returns by 10 July; these are shown with a question mark. Artillery shown based on pre-Wagram 1 July returns and is thus aggregated at corps level; many pieces were likely damaged and unavailable on 10–11 July.
3. Strength returns for III Corps are in some cases *higher* than before Wagram; this seems unlikely, but data is presented here with that caveat.
4. Structure from V Corps, 'Relation', 17 July, KAFA, 1462. Strengths do not show losses for 10 July.
5. The figure for *Gyulai* seems unusually high and may be an error of transcription.
6. Grenadier Corps, 'Relation', 17 July 1809, KAFA, 1462.
7. Artillery shown based on 1 July availabilities. The Bavarians and Marmont's Army of Dalmatia seem to have had their full complements of guns; for the others, however, some pieces were likely damaged or still en route on 11 July.
8. Montbrun's strength could have been as high as 4,600 or as low as 3,500 or so, depending on the number of horses lost on 5 and 6 July.
9. 'Tagebuch des Großherzoglich badischen Dragoner Regiments vom 1sten Juni bis 20ten Juli 1809', GLA, 48/4271.
10. Strength estimate based on comparison of 1 July and 15 July strengths (considering officer losses and actions 7–10 July).
11. 1st and 3rd Heavy Cavalry Division 'Situations' for 7 and 8 July, SHD, C2/93.
12. Imperial Guard, 'Situations', 12 June and 15 July, SHD, C2/505; guns from Litre, pp. 57–9.
13. 2nd Corps, 'Situations', 1 and 15 July, SHD, C2/506. See Wagram order of battle for organisational details.
14. Dupas was assigned to command this division, but he turned down the assignment, apparently for reasons of health. Nonetheless, he is listed in the 2nd Corps 'Situation' of 15 July.
15. 3rd Corps 'Situations', 1 and 15 July, SHD, C2/506. See Wagram order of battle for organisational details.

Appendix 6

The French Cuirassiers on 11 July

The depiction of the French cuirassier charge that defeated the *Leiningen* Grenadiers south of Znaim on 11 July relies on a number of personal memoirs and histories written by participants in the battle. All of these are useful and generally reliable as source material, but they do not agree on several key points. Unfortunately, we do not have after-action reports for St Sulpice or any of his subordinate units and the histories of the cuirassier regiments involved are weak on detail. The same applies to Carra St Cyr's division and its regiments. The narrative in the main text gives the most likely sequence of events and the most likely units involved based on my analysis in the absence of other primary-source material. There are, however, other plausible explanations and the following is offered to provide additional depth for interested readers.

Which French regiment led the successful charge? The usually reliable Markgraf Wilhelm of Baden says he took the order to charge to 'General Berckheim'. Berckheim was not yet a general at Znaim, but he was commanding the 1st Cuirassiers and was thus on the field south of the bridges. However, all of the other French sources (Pelet, Massena, Marbot, etc.) cite Colonel Lhéritier and his 10th Cuirassiers as the lead regiment. Although it seems almost certain that the 1st and 5th Regiments followed (again, there is no direct evidence of this, but it seems logical), there is little reason to doubt that the 10th was the first to charge.

Did the charging regiment use a ford or the bridges? Buat (vol. II, p. 363) and some Austrian sources state that the attacking cuirassier regiment (the 10th) crossed the Thaya using a ford near Oblass. While possible,

The French Cuirassiers on 11 July

this seems unlikely. Most French accounts and Markgraf Wilhelm state that the regiment charged across the bridges; Baden Leutnant de Beau also relates that he found himself badly injured when he fell wounded on the bridge and the attacking cavalry rode over him. It is possible that some accounts confuse the 11th Cuirassiers fording the river earlier in the action with the later charge over the bridges.

Did the cuirassiers strike the grenadiers head-on or hit them in the flank? Accounts differ on whether the cuirassiers rode straight at the grenadiers or somehow hit them in the left (east) flank and cut the battalion in two. The Massena memoir speaks of the cuirassiers striking the Austrian left and the V Corps after-action report provides a similar description with the added detail that the French attacked suddenly out of an alleyway to surprise the grenadiers. This is clearly related to whether the horsemen attacked over the bridges or used a ford; it is also related to the role, if any, played by the 11th Cuirassiers who were already across the Thaya when the grenadiers' counterattack began. I have portrayed the cavalry charge booming across the bridges, but it is possible that both stories are correct. The 10th Cuirassiers, doubtless followed by the 1st and 5th Regiments, most likely charged across the bridges. It seems reasonable, however, that the 11th would have tried to join the attack rather than remain useless bystanders. It is thus possible, perhaps probable, that the 11th Cuirassiers managed to slog their way out of the mud and attack through the alleys of Altschallersdorf even if only at a trot or walk, thereby creating the impression of the attack on the grenadiers' left and the battalion being cut in two. While this remains speculation barring new information, it would account for the various versions of the French cavalry charge that afternoon.

Appendix 7

Tactical Notes

The following are observations on the tactical behaviours of the two armies during the period of the retreat up to and including the Battle of Znaim that may be of interest to specialists. Rather than tuck them away in endnotes, they are aggregated here for the reader's convenience.

Austrian Orders of Battle

Rearguard forces at the tactical level. At both Korneuburg and Stockerau, Klenau used mixtures of troops from different regiments to hold key points rather than assigning these tasks to a single unit. At Stockerau on the 8th, for example, a detachment sent to a small wood was composed of the 1st Combined Upper Austrian Landwehr, one company each from *Benjovszky* and *Splenyi*, and the third ranks from *Klebek* and *Jordis* (Justus Knorz, *Geschichte des k. k. Infanterie-Regiments Erzherzog Rainer Nr. 59*, Salzburg: regimental, n.d., p. 249).

Corps structures. The Austrian corps during the retreat, especially IV and VI Corps, altered their orders of battle with bewildering regularity. In part this was the result of units becoming temporarily attached to other corps in the post-Wagram confusion, but most of the changes took place within the corps' original structures using their original or 'organic' regiments. Rosenberg shifted his order of battle almost every day, sometimes two or three times a day; and Klenau was likewise prone to repeated changes, leading FML Vincent to complain at one point that he was being left with almost no troops to command. All of this makes it very difficult to depict the Austrian order of battle at any one time on any one day with satisfactory accuracy.

Light brigades. Austrian commanders were especially loose with their light brigades. Where brigades of line infantry were usually kept together, the elements of the light brigades were routinely broken up and redistributed. The light troops of V Corps on 11 July provide an example with the Grenzer attached to Pflüger's brigade, the 3rd Jägers detached on the right and the cavalry in reserve.

French Guard cavalry. Contrary to what many might expect, the French repeatedly employed small detachments from the Guard Cavalry to help locate the Austrians after Wagram. At least one patrol from the Guard Dragoons crossed the Bisamberg, while elements of the Polish Chevaulegers scouted towards the army's right flank and beyond to the March River. Similarly, a squadron-sized detachment of the Polish Chevaulegers was sent to escort Napoleon's messenger to Marmont on 10 July.

French skirmish line. Gueheneuc recorded that his 26th Léger sent its voltigeur companies forward as skirmishers on 8 July north of Stockerau; when these ran out of ammunition, however, they were replaced by the regiment's three 4th Companies.

German allies as advance guards. French corps commanders consistently employed their German allied troops in demanding advance-guard roles. Massena relied on the Baden Jäger Battalion *Lingg* in conjunction with his French light horse throughout the pursuit; Marmont and Montbrun likewise used the Bavarian light cavalry in a similar capacity; and Napoleon personally selected Oberst von Lindenau and his Bavarian chevaulegers for an extended reconnaissance mission on the morning of 7 July. Given the importance and difficulty of these tasks, the praise the units received, and the simple fact they were not withdrawn and replaced by French troops, it is evident that the French commanders regarded these German units as both reliable and tactically competent. Though not stated in any of the primary sources, it is possible that the Germans were valued for their language abilities as well as their battlefield skills.

The earthworks at Znaim. There were three or four small earthworks (*Schanzen*) south of Znaim on 10 and 11 July. Their exact number and their locations are portrayed differently on different period maps (one Austrian set and one French in the Vienna Kriegsarchiv), but there seem to have been two above the Brünn highway east of Altschallersdorf, one east of the Iglau highway north of Altschallersdorf, and another west of the Iglau highway between Klosterbruck and Znaim. Their tactical utility was limited. They provided some cover for a few Austrian guns on 10 July and again on the morning of the 11th, and they made useful landmarks or helpfully visible objective points for tactical action. The *Gradiska* Grenzer, for example, reported capturing the earthwork west of the highway at least four times. Beyond that, the *Schanzen* do not figure prominently in accounts of the fighting. We have few details other than map depictions and minimal mentions in reports, but it seems none of them would have been large enough to accommodate more than two or perhaps four cannon. They were thus in no way comparable to field fortifications on battlefields such as Borodino. Their provenance and condition are also unclear. According to Prochaska's report, the works were already in place when his grenadiers arrived early on 10 July (and thus well before the arrival of V Corps that night), but Altstern does not mention them in his report. It seems unlikely that his men or the grenadiers would have had the time or resources to dig them, and neither formation claims to have done so. On the other hand, Brinner's excellent history of the Austrian pioneers mentions construction of several earthworks by the 5th and 6th Pioneer Divisions during the night of 10/11 July (vol. 1/2, pp. 91–2). In the absence of other information, all we can do is speculate that perhaps they dated from 1805, during the previous French advance into Moravia, and that the pioneers were thus improving previously existing works.

Bibliography

Abbreviations

AE	Archives des Affaires Étrangères, France
AN	Archives Nationales, France
BKA	Bayerisches Hauptstaatsarchiv, Kriegsarchiv, Bavaria
CdN	*Correspondance de Napoléon*, 1858–70
CG	*Correspondance Général*, 2004–18
FO	Foreign Office files, PRO/National Archives, United Kingdom
GLA	Generallandesarchiv, Baden-Württemberg
HHStA	Haus-, Hof- und Staatsarchiv, Austria
KAFA	Kriegsarchiv, Alte Feldakten, Austria
MNL	Magyar Nemzeti Levéltár, Hungary
NA	Národni Archiv, Czech Republic
Op. J.	Operations Journal of an Austrian formation
PRO	Public Record Office (now National Archives), United Kingdom
SHD	Service Historique de la Défense, France
WHStA	Württemberg Hauptstaatsarchiv, Germany

Note: I have used the American military term 'after-action report' for several Austrian and French phrases, most commonly 'Relation'.

Archival Material

Austria: Branches of the Oesterreichisches Staatsarchiv, Vienna:
  Haus-, Hof- und Staatsarchiv (HHStA).
  Kriegsarchiv (KA), primarily the 'alte Feldakten' (KAFA). The four-digit number after 'KAFA' in the notes indicates the carton (*Karton*) from which the material was drawn.
  Two detailed maps in the Kriegsarchiv have been very useful in this study: 'Plan Minute des Positions occupées par les deux armées près de Znaim lors de la

conclusion de l'Armistice', July 1809, KA KPS KS G I h, 1520; and 'Plan des Treffens bei Znaim am 10. und 11.7.1809', no date, KA KPS KS H IV a, 1284.

Czech Republic: Národni Archiv (NA), Prague

France:
Archives des Affaires Étrangères (AE), Paris.
Archives Nationales (AN), Paris.
Service Historique de la Défense (SHD), Archives de la Guerre et de l'Armée de Terre, Vincennes, Série GR C, Premier Empire, especially the files of 'Situations' and 'Correspondance de l'Armée'.

Germany:
Bayerisches Haupstaatsarchiv, Abt. IV/Kriegsarchiv (BKA), Munich.
Generallandesarchiv (GLA), Karlsruhe.
Württemberg Hauptstaatsarchiv (WHStA), Stuttgart.

Hungary: Magyar Nemzeti Levéltár (MNL), Budapest.

United Kingdom: Although now known as the National Archives, I have retained the abbreviation (PRO/FO) denoting Foreign Office files I consulted when this fine institution in Kew was called the Public Record Office.

Dictionaries and Encyclopedias

Hirtenfeld, Jaromir. *Der Militär-Maria-Theresien-Orden und seine Mitglieder,* Vienna: Staatsdruckerei, 1857

Kudrna, Leopold and Digby Smith. 'Biographical Dictionary of All the Austrian Generals during the French Revolutionary and Napoleonic Wars 1792–1815', www.napoleon-series.org

Martinien, Aristide. *Tableaux par Corps et par Batailles des Officiers Tués et Blessés pendant les Guerres de l'Empire (1805–1815),* Paris: Editions Militaires Européennes, 1984

Pigeard, Alain. *Les Etoiles de Napoléon,* Entremont-le-Vieux: Quatuor, 1996

——, *Les Campagnes Napoléoniennes,* Entremont-le-Vieux: Quator, 1998

Quintin, Danielle and Bernard. *Dictionnaire des Colonels de Napoléon,* Paris: SPM, 1996

Six, Georges. *Dictionnaire Biographique des Généraux & Amiraux Français de la Révolution et de l'Empire,* Paris: Manutention à Mayenne, 1989

Tulard, Jean. *Dictionnaire Napoléon,* Paris: Fayard, 1987

Wurzbach, Constant von. *Biographisches Lexikon des Kaiserthums Oesterreich,* Wien: Zamarski, 1856–91

Bibliography 451

Memoirs, Correspondence, Biographies

Ameil, Auguste Jean Joseph Gabriel. *Notes et Documents provenant des Archives du Général Baron Ameil*, Paris: Teissèdre, 1997 (originally published in the *Carnet de la Sabretache* in 1906–7)

'Anmerkungen über die im 8ten und 10ten Stück der europäischen Annalen Jahrgang 1810 enthaltene Darstellung der Schlachten auf dem Marchfelde', *Europäische Annalen*, vol. VIII, 1811

Angeli, Moriz Edlen von. *Erzherzog Carl von Oesterreich als Feldherr und Heeresorganisator*, Wien: Braumüller, 1897

Ardeche, Laurent de l'. *Réfutation des Mémoires du Maréchal Marmont*, Paris: Plon, 1857

Augustin-Thierry, A. *Masséna*, Paris: Albin Michel, 1947

Austrian official publications:

—— *Dienst-Reglement für die kaiserlich-königliche Infanterie*, Wien: k.u.k. Hof- und Staats-Druckerey, 1807–8

—— *Grundsätze der höheren Kriegskunst und Beyspeile ihrer zweckmässigen Anwendung für die Generale der Österreichischen Armee*, Vienna: Kaiserl. Königl. Hof- und Staatsdruckerey, 1808

—— *Schematismus der Kais. Königl. Armée auf das Jahr 1808*, Vienna: Graeffer, 1808

—— *Relation über die Schlacht bei Deutsch-Wagram auf dem Marchfelde am 5ten und 6ten July 1809, und die Gefechte, welche derselben bis zum Abschlusse des Waffenstillstandes am 12ten des nämlichen Monats folgten*, Pest, 1809

—— *Schematismus der Oesterreichisch-Kaiserlichen Armée für das Jahr 1810*, Vienna: Graeffer, 1810

Authentischer Bericht über die Schlacht bei Wagram am 5ten und 6ten July 1809: Von einem Augenzeugen, Hannover: Hahn, 1813

'Beiträge zur Geschichte des österreichischen Heerwesens 1809', *Oesterreichische Militärische Zeitschrift*, Band 3, 1869; also *Beiträge zur Geschichte des österreichischen Heerwesens*, Vienna: Seidel und Sohn, 1872

'Bemerkungen eines Officiers vom österreichischen Generalstabe zu der in Pesth, im Druck erschienenen Relation über die Schlacht bei Teutsch-Wagram', *Pallas*, vol. III, 1810

'Bemerkungen über den gegenwärtigen Feldzug', *Minerva*, June 1809

'Bericht eines Augenzeugen über die Schlacht bei Deutsch-Wagram', *Minerva*, vol. IV, 1809

Berichtigung über die letzten Ereignisse des Krieges zwischen Osterreich und Frankreich im Jahr 1809, Frankfurt: n.p., 1810

Berthezène, Pierre. *Souvenirs Militaires de la République et de l'Empire*, Paris: Dumaine, 1855

Bertrand, Henri Gatien. *Cahiers de Sainte-Hélène*, Paris: Flammarion, 1949

Bial, Jean-Pierre. *Souvenirs des Guerres de la Révolution et de l'Empire,* Paris: Pensée Latine, 1927
Bibl, Viktor. *Der Zerfall Oesterreichs: Kaiser Franz und seine Erbe,* Vienna: Rikola, 1922
——, *Radetzky: Soldat und Feldherr,* Wien: Günther, 1955
Bonnéry, Jean-Louis. *Ledru des Essarts: Un Grand Patriote Sarthois Méconnu,* Le Mans: Imprimerie Maine Libre, 1988
Botzenhart, Erich, ed. *Freiherr vom Stein: Briefwechsel, Denkschriften und Aufzeichnungen,* Berlin: Heymann, 1932
Boyeldieu, Louis Léger. 'Itinéraire et Notes Historiques du 4e Régiment de Ligne', published in Léon Charles Emile Auguste Loÿ, 'Le Général de Division Baron Boyeldieu', *Carnet de la Sabretache,* No. 260 (August 1914–May 1919)
Brandner, F. A. *Aus dem Tagebuch eines österreichischen Soldaten im Jahre 1809,* Lobau: J. Breyer, n.d
Bro, Louis. *Mémoires,* Paris: Plon, 1914
Brun, Louis Bertrand Pierre. *Les Cahiers du Général Brun,* Paris: Plon, 1953
[Bruyère, Jean Pierre Joseph] 'Notices Historiques et Topographiques sur les Marches et Combats des Troupes aux Ordres du Général Bruyère en 1809', *Carnet de la Sabretache,* 1909
Castellane, Espirit Victor Elisabeth Boniface de. *Journal du Maréchal de Castellane,* Paris: Plon, 1895
Castillon, Jean François Antoine Marie. 'Mémorial Militaire', *Carnet de la Sabretache,* 1902
Castex, Bernard Pierre. 'Quatre Lettres du Colonel Castex', *Carnet de la Sabretache,* 1903
Champagny, Jean Baptiste Nompère de. *Note sur un Article des Mémoires sur l'Intèrieur du Palais Impérial, et sur la Conclusion de la Paix de Vienne en 1809,* Paris: Potey, 1827
——, *Souvenirs,* Geneva: Slatkine-Megariotis, 1975
Chandler, David G. (ed.). *Napoleon's Marshals,* New York: Macmillan, 1987
Charles, Archduke of Austria. *Ausgewählte Schriften,* Wien: Braumüller, 1893–4
Chlapowski, Dezydery (Désiré). *Mémoires sur les Guerres de Napoléon 1806–1813,* Paris: Plon, 1908
Chevalier, Jean Michel. *Souvenirs des Guerres Napoléoniennes,* Paris: Hachette, 1970
Chroust, Anton. *Geschichte des Grossherzogtums Würzburg,* Würzburg: Becker, 1932
Coignet, Jean-Roche. *The Note-Books of Captain Coignet,* London: Greenhill, 1989
Constant Wairy, Louis. *Memoirs of Constant,* New York: Scribner's Sons, 1985
Coudreux, Alexander. *Lettres du Commandant Coudreux à Son Frère 1804–1815,* Gustave Schlumberger (ed.), Paris: Plon, 1908

Criste, Oskar. *Feldmarschall Johannes Fürst von Liechtenstein*, Wien: Seidel & Sohn, 1905
——, *Erzherzog Karl und die Armee*, vol. V of *Das Kriegsjahr 1809 in Einzeldarstellungen*, Emil von Woinovich and Alois Veltzé (eds.), Wein: Stern, 1906
——, *Erzherzog Carl von Oesterreich: Ein Lebensbild*, Wien: Braumüller, 1912
Damas, Roger de. *Mémoires*, Paris: Plon, 1912–14
'Darstellung der Schlachten auf dem Marchfelde', *Europäische Annalen*, vols. VII, VIII, X, 1810
Darstellung des Feldzugs vom Jahr 1809. Von einem Augenzeugen, n.p., 1811
Davout, Marshal Louis-Nicolas. *Correspondance de Maréchal Davout*, Charles de Mazade (ed.), Paris: Plon, 1885
'Der letzte Akt des französich–österreichischen Feldzugs im Jahre 1809', *Europäische Annalen*, vol. V, 1811
Duller, Eduard. *Erzherzog Carl von Oesterreich*, Vienna: Kaulfuß, 1847
Garnier, Auguste. *Notice sur le Général Delzons*, Paris: Belin, 1863
Genet, Alexandre, *Notice Nécrologique sur le Général de Stabenrath*, Paris: Christophe, 1858
Desboeufs, Marc. *Souvenirs du Capitaine Desboeufs*, Paris: Picard, 1901
Du Casse, Albert. *Mémoires et correspondance politique et militaire du Prince Eugène*, Paris: Lévy, 1858–60
Dumas, Count Mathieu. *Memoirs of His Own Time*, Philadelphia: Lea & Blanchard, 1839
Dumolin, Maurice. *Précis d'Histoire Militaire: Révolution et Empire*, Paris: Barrere, 1913
Dupuy, Victor. *Souvenirs Militaires*, Paris: Lévy, 1892
Eccardt, Balthasar. *Als badischer Militärmusiker in Napoleons Kriegen*, Mirielle Geering (ed.), Stuttgart: Kohlhammer, 2013
Ernouf, Alfred Auguste. *Maret Duc de Bassano*, Paris: Perrin, 1884
Espinchal, Hippolyte d'. *Souvenirs Militaires*, Paris: Ollendorf, 1901
Faré, Charles A. *Lettres d'un Jeune Officier a sa Mère*, Paris: Delgrave, 1889
Fezensac, Raymond-Aimery-Philippe-Joseph de Montesquiou. *Souvenirs Militaires de 1804 à 1814*, Paris: Dumaine, 1870
Fournier, Jean Baptiste. *Souvenirs*, Maurepas: La Vouivre, 2009
Frèche, Louis. *Mémoire de mes Campagnes (1803–1809)*, Fernand Beaucour (ed.), Levallois: Centre d'Études Napoléoniennes, 1994
Freller, Thomas. 'Adelskarriere in einer Umbruchszeit: Der Deutschordenskomtur von Virnsberg Graf Ferdinand Ernst Gabriel von Waldstein', *Jahrbuch für fränkische Landesforschung*, vol. 72, 2012
Friant, Jean François. *Vie Militaire du Lieutenant-Général Comte Friant*, Paris: Dentu, 1980

Gachot, Edouard. *1809 Napoléon en Allemagne*, Paris: Plon, 1913

Gallaher, John G. *The Iron Marshal*, Carbondale & Evansville: Southern Illinois University Press, 1976

Gassicourt, Charles Louis Cadet de. *Voyage en Autriche, en Moravie et en Bavière fait a la suite de l'Armée Française pendant la Campagne de 1809*, Paris: L'Huillier, 1818

Gentz, Friedrich von. *Tagebücher* (ed.). K. A. Varnhagen von Ense, Leipzig: Brockhaus, 1861

Girault, Philippe Réne. *Mes Campagnes sous la Révolution et l'Empire*, Paris: Le Sycomore, 1983

Godin, Jean-Baptiste.'Abrégé de mes Voyages Faits Pendant les Annés 1808-1809-1810-1811-1812 et 1813', *La Giberne*, IX/1, July 1907

Gougaud, Gaspard. *Sainte-Hélène: Journal Inédit de 1815 à 1818*, Paris: Flammarion, 1899

——, *Talks of Napoleon at St. Helena*, Elizabeth Wormeley Latimer, trans., Chicago: McClurg, 1904

Griois, Charles Pierre Lubin. *Mémoires du Général Griois*, Paris: Plon-Nourrit, 1909

Grueber, Karl Johann Ritter von. *Lebenserinnerungen eines Reiteroffiziers vor Hundert Jahren*,Wien: Seidel und Sohn, 1906

Guyot, Claude Etienne. *Carnets de Campagnes*, Jean Hugues de Font-Réaulx (ed.), Paris: Teissèdre, 1999

Hausmann, Cynthia Joy and John H. Gill (ed.). *A Soldier for Napoleon: The Campaigns of Franz Joseph Hausmann, 7th Bavarian infantry*, London: Greenhill, 1998

Henckens, J. L. *Mémoires*, La Haye: Nijhoff, 1910

Hertenberger, Helmut and Franz Wiltschek. *Erzherzog Karl: Der Sieger von Aspern*, Graz: Styria, 1983

Hormayr, Josef Freiherr. *Geschichte Andreas Hofer's*, Leipzig: Brockhaus, 1845

Jacquin, François-Joseph. *Carnet de Route d'un Grognard de la Révolution et de l'Empire*, Paris: Clavreuil, 1960

Johann, Archduke of Austria. *Erzherzog Johanns 'Feldzugserzählung' 1809*, Alois Veltzé (ed.), *Supplement zu den Mitteilungen des k. u. k. Kriegsarchivs*, Wien: Seidel & Sohn, 1909

Joseph, Archduke of Austria. *Joszef Nador Elete es Iratai*, Sandor Domanovszky (ed.), Budapest, 1929-44 (vols. I-III); *Palatin Josephs Schriften*, Budapest, 1991 (vol. IV)

'Journal über der Operation des kais. österreichischen Truppen-Corps unter dem Generalmajor von Am-Ende von 12ten bis 22ten July 1809 in Sachsen', *Europäische Annalen*, vol. VI, 1810

Kaufmann, Reinhard Franz. 'Die Schlacht bei Znaim veränderte die Landkarte Europas', *Zusammenfassung der Beiträge zum Napoleon Symposium 'Feldzug 1809'*, Vienna: Delta Druckproduktionen, 2009

Kenis, Wilhelmus. *Soldaten van Napoleon*, K. C. Peeters (ed.), Antwerp: de Vlijt, 1955

Kerchenawe, Hugo and Alois Veltzé. *Feldmarschall Karl Fürst zu Schwarzenberg*, Wien: Gerlach & Wiedling, 1913

Kircheisen, Friedrich M. *Gespräche Napoleons*, Stuttgart: Lutz, 1912

Koch, Jean Baptiste. *Mémoires d'André Massena*, Paris: Bonnot, 1967 (reprint of 1850 edition)

Kübeck von Kübau, Carl Friedrich Freiherr. *Tagebücher*, Wien: Gerold, 1909

Laborde, Alexandre de. *Précis Historique de la Guerre entre la France et l'Autriche en 1809*, Paris: Anselin et Pochard, 1823

[Larisch, Ferdinand von], 'Meine zweite Campagne (Aus dem Tagebuche eines Verstorbenen)', *Bautzener Nachrichten*, vols. 21–5, 1883

Larrey, Dominique Jean. *Mémoires de Chirugie Militaire et Campagnes de D. J. Larrey*, Paris: Smith, 1812

Las Cases, Emmanuel. *Journal of the Private Life and Conversations of the Emperor Napoleon at Saint Helena*, London: Colburn, 1823

Lejeune, Charles Henri. 'Souvenirs', *Carnet de la Sabretache*, September 1910

Lejeune, Louis-François. *Memoirs of Baron Lejeune*, Felling: Worley reprint, 1987

Ligne, Prince Charles Joseph de. *Fragments de l'Histoire de Ma Vie*, Félicien Leuridant (ed.), Paris: Plon, 1928

Lorencez, Guillaume de Latrille, Comte de. 'Etat Raisonné de Mes Services', *Le Carnet Historique & Littéraire*, X, 1901

Löwenstern, Vladimir Ivanovich Baron. *Mémoires du Général-Major Russe Baron de Löwenstern*, M. H. Weil (ed.), Paris: Fontemoing, 1903

Madroux, Ludwig von. 'August von Floret', *Archiv für Offiziere aller Waffen*, 2, 1846

Mändler, Friedrich. *Erinnerungen aus meinen Feldzügen*, Nürnberg: Lotzbeck, 1854

Marbot, Jean-Baptiste-Antoine-Marcelin. *Remarques Critiques sur l'Ouvrage de M. le Lieutenant-Général Rogniat, intitulé Considérations sur l'Art de la Guerre*, Paris: Anselin et Pochard, 1820

——, *The Memoirs of Baron de Marbot*, Arthur J. Butler (trans.), London: Longmans, Green, and Co., 1905

Marbotin, Pierre. 'Deux Lettres de 1809 du Lieutenant de Marbotin à sa Mère', *Carnet de la Sabretache*, 1909

'Marginalien zur Relation über die Schlacht bey Wagram: Eingesendet von einem Offizier des k. k. östreichischen Generalstabs', *Europäische Annalen*, vol. II, 1810

Marmont, Marshal Auguste-Frédéric-Louis Viesse de. *De l'Esprit des Institutions Militaires*, Paris: Librairie Militaire, 1845

——, *Mémoires du Maréchal Duc de Raguse de 1792 à 1832*, Paris: Perrotin, 1857

Marshall-Cornwall, James. *Marshal Massena,* London: Oxford University Press, 1965

Meier, Wilhelm. *Erinnerungen aus den Feldzügen 1806 bis 1815,* Karsruhe: Müller, 1854

Méneval, Napoléon Joseph Ernest Baron de. *Le Général Baron de Coëhorn: Un Bayard Alsacien,* Paris: Fischbacher, 1912

Metternich-Winneburg, Prince Clemens Lothar Wenzel von. *Aus Metternichs Nachgelassenen Papieren,* Vienna: Braumüller, 1880

Mikhaïlowitch, Grand Duke Nicolas (ed.). *Les Relations Diplomatiques de la Russie et de la France d'après les Rapports des Ambassadeurs d'Alexandre et de Napoléon,* St Petersburg, 1905

Mohr, Johann Friedrich. *Geschichte und Schicksale,* Nürnberg: Tümmelschen, 1830

Moisette, Jean. 'Le Général François-Nicolas Fririon', *Le Pays Lorrain,* vol. XXX, January 1938

Mortemart-Boisse, François Jérome Léonard. *Histoire, Voyages et Scènes Intimes,* Paris: Vimont, 1834

——, 'Préliminaires de la Campagne d'Autriche', *Napoléon: Journal Anecdotique et Biographique de l'Empire et de la Grande Armée,* vol. II, 1835

Napoléon I. *Correspondance de Napoléon Ier publiée par ordre de l'Empereur Napoléon III,* Paris: Imprimerie Impériale, 1858–70

——, *Correspondance Générale,* vols. VIII and IX, Paris: Fayard, 2011–13

Nicolas, César. *Une Famille de Sommiérois,* Nîmes: Revue du Midi, 1904

Noubel, Jean and Olivier Lapray, 'Le Général Marulaz et le 8e Hussards à Wagram', *Traditions,* no. 22, October 2018

O'Meara, Barry Edward. *Napoleon at St. Helena,* London: Bentley & Son, 1888

Ommen, Heinrich. *Die Kriegsführung des Erzherzogs Carl,* Vaduz: Kraus Reprints, 1965

Pahl, Johann Gottfried von. *Denkwürdigkeiten aus meinem Leben und aus meiner Zeit,* Tübingen, 1840

Pajol, Comte. *Pajol: Général en Chef,* Paris: Didot, 1874

Parquin, Charles Denis. *Souvenirs et Campagnes d'un Vieux Soldat de l'Empire,* A. Aubier (ed.), Paris: Berger-Levrault, 1903

Paulin, Jules Antoine. *Les Souvenirs du Général Baron Paulin,* Paris: Plon, 1895

Pelleport, Pierre. *Souvenirs Militares et Intimes du Général Vicomte de Pelleport,* Paris: Didier, 1857

Persan, Commandant Comte de. 'Le Général Comte Le Grand', *Carnet de la Sabretache,* 1908

Picard, Ernest, (ed.). *Préceptes et Jugements de Napoléon,* Paris: Berger-Levrault, 1913

Pouget, François Réné. *Souvenirs de Guerre du Général Baron Pouget,* Mme. de Boisdeffre (ed.), Paris: Plon, 1895

Radetzky, Josef von. 'Ein Memoire Radetzky's, das Heerwesen Oesterreichs beleuchtend, aus dem Jahre 1809', *Mittheilingen des k. k. Kriegsarchivs*, vol. VIII, 1884

——, 'Erinnerungen aus dem Leben des FM. Grafen Radetzky', *Mittheilingen des k. k. Kriegsarchivs*, new series I, 1887

Rapp, Jean. *Memoirs of General Count Rapp*, London: Colburn, 1823; Ken Trotman reprint, Cambridge, 1985

Rauchensteiner, Manfried. *Kaiser Franz und Erzherzog Karl*, Wien: Verlag für Geschichte und Politik, 1972

Regele, Oskar. *Feldmarschall Radetzky: Leben, Leistung, Erbe*, München: Herold, 1957

[Regnier, Ferdinand] 'Auszug aus dem Tagebuch eines k. bayerischen Stabsoffiziers', *Archiv für Offiziere aller Waffen*, II, 1844

Reichold, N. *Soldaten-Sohn und das Kriegsleben von 1805 bis 1815*, München, 1851

Robiquet, Paul. 'Le Général de Galbois 1778–1850', *Revue Historique*, vol. CXX, 1915

Roederer, Pierre Louis. *Oeuvres du Comte P. L. Roederer*, Paris: Firmin Didot Frères, 1854

Roguet, François. *Mémoires Militaires*, Paris: Dumaine, 1865

Rössler, Hellmuth. *Oesterreichs Kampf um Deutschlands Befreiung*, Hamburg: Hanseatische Verlagsanstalt, 1940

——, *Graf Johann Philipp Stadion: Napoleons deutscher Gegenspieler*, Wien: Herold, 1966

Rothenberg, Gunther E. 'The Case of Archduke Charles', Clarence B. Davis (ed.), *Proceedings of the Consortium on Revolutionary Europe 1983*, Athens, GA: Consortium on Revolutionary Europe, 1985

Rühle von Lilienstern, Johann Jacob Otto August. *Reise mit der Armee im Jahre 1809*, Rudolstadt: Hof- Buch- und Kunsthandlung, 1810

——, 'Gedanken über die beiden Schlachten auf dem Marchfelde bei Wien', *Pallas*, vol. XI, 1809

Russia, Ministerstvo Inostrannykh del. *Vneshniaia Politika Rossii XIX i nachala XX veka: dokumenti rossiiskogo Ministersva Inostrannykh del*, Moscow, 1965

Savary, Anne-Jean-Marie-René. *Mémoires du Duc de Rovigo*, Paris: Bossange, 1828

Schäfer, Dieter. *Ferdinand von Österreich*, Graz: Styria, 1988

Schaller, Christian. *Fragmente aus dem Feldzuge gegen Oestreich im Jahr 1809*, Augsburg: Bürglen, 1810

Schlossberger, August von, (ed.). *Politische und Militärische Correspondenz König Friedrichs von Württemberg mit Kaiser Napoleon I. 1805–1813*, Stuttgart: Kohlhammer, 1889

Schlotheim, Capitain von. *Berichte von den Schlachten auf dem Marchfelde bey Wien, Groß-Aspern und Deutsch-Wagram von einem Augenzeugen*, Gotha, 1809

Schnierer, Johann. *Aus der Franzosenzeit, Innviertler Volksbücher*, 4 and 5, Braunau: Stampfl, 1914

Ségur, Philippe-Paul. *Histoire et Mémoires*, Paris: Didot, 1873

Siemann, Wolfram. *Metternich: Strategist and Visionary*, Cambridge, Massachusetts: Harvard University Press, 2019

Skall, Johann Baptist. 'Feldzugsreise des Kaisers Franz I. von Oesterreich im Jahre 1809', Hauptmann Sommeregger (ed.), *Mitteilungen des K. und K. Kriegsarchivs*, Band 5, Wien, 1907

Smola, Karl Freiherr von. *Das Leben des Feldmarschalls Heinrich Grafen von Bellegarde*, Wien: Heubner, 1847

Szymanowski, Joseph. *Mémoires*, Paris: Lavauzelle, 1900

'Tagebuch eines bayerischen Artillerieoffiziers aus dem Jahre 1809', *Das Bayernland*, München, 1908

Tascher, Maurice de. *Journal de Campagne d'un Cousin de l'Imperatrice (1806–1813)*, Paris: Plon, 1933

Thielen, Maximilian Ritter von. *Erinnerungen aus dem Kriegerleben eines 82jährigen Veteranen der österreichischen Armee*, Wien: Braumüller, 1863

Thürheim, Andreas Joseph von. *Ludwig Fürst Starhemberg: eine Lebens-Skizze*, Graz: Styria, 1889

Triare, Paul. *Dominique Larrey*, Tours: Mame, 1902

'Ueber die Benutzung der in der Schlacht von Aspern erfochtenen Vortheile und über den Waffenstillstand von Znaym', *Pallas*, vol. IV, 1810

Varnhagen von Ense, Karl August. *Denkwürdigkeiten des eigenen Lebens*, Leipzig: Brockhaus, 1843

Vaudoncourt, Frédéric Guillaume de. *Histoire politique et militaire du Prince Eugène Napoléon*, Paris: Mongie, 1828

Veigl, Josef. 'Erinnerungen eines Veteranen aus dem Jahre 1809', *Oesterreichische militärische Zeitschrift*, II, 1860

Venturini, Karl. *Geschichte unserer Zeit*, Leipzig: Steinacker, 1811

Vergnes, J.-P. 'Le Lendemain de la Bataille de Wagram', *Revue de l'Empire*, vol. IV, 1845

Watteville, Albert de. *Un Suisse Officier d'Ordonnance de Napoléon*, Lausanne: Rouge, 1951

'Welche Ursachen bewogen den österreichischen Feldherrn zu dem Waffenstillstand von Znaym und war er vortheilhaft für Oesterreichs Interesse?', first published in 'Deutschland', 1809 and later in Pest: n.p., 1811

Wilhelm von Baden, Markgraf. *Denkwürdigkeiten des Markgrafen Wilhelm von Baden*, Karl Obser (ed.), Heidelberg: Winter, 1906

Würdinger, Josef. 'Das Leben des königl. bayerischen Generallieutenants Maxim. Grafen v. Preysing-Moos', *Verhandlungen des Historischen Vereins für Niederbayern*, Band 9, 1863

Bibliography

General Works

Several of these histories were written by participants in the campaign or other contemporaries.

Allmayer-Beck, Christoph and Erich Lessing, *Das Heer unter dem Doppeladler: Habsburgs Armeen 1718–1848*, Munich: Bertelsmann, 1981
'Die Armee Napoleon I. im Jahre 1809', *Mittheilungen des k. k. Kriegs-Archivs*, Wien, 1881
Arnold, James R. *Crisis on the Danube*, New York: Paragon House, 1990
——, *Napoleon Conquers Austria*, London: Arms and Armour, 1995
Balagny, Dominique E. P. *Campagne de l'Empereur Napoléon en Espagne (1808–1809)*, Paris: Berger-Levrault, 1902–7
Beer, Adolf. *Zehn Jahre österreichischer Politik 1801–1810*, Leipzig: Brockhaus, 1877
'Beiträge zur Geschichte des österreichischen Heerwesens', *Österreichische Militärische Zeitschrift*, vol. IX, no. 4, 1868
Béraud, Stéphane. *La Révolution Militaire Napoléonienne*, Paris: Giovangeli, 2007–13
Bezemerk, Ernst and Willibald Rosner (eds). *Vergangenheit und Gegenwart: Der Bezirk Hollabrunn und seine Gemeinden*, Hollabrunn, 1993
Binder von Krieglstein, Christian Freiherr. *Der Krieg Napoleons gegen Oesterreich 1809*, Maximilian Ritter von Hoen (ed.), Berlin: Voss, 1906
Bleibtreu, Carl. *Aspern und Wagram in neuer Beleuchtung*, Vienna, Seidel & Sohn, 1902
Blin, Arnaud. *Wagram*, Paris: Tallandier, 2010
Bonnal, Henry. *La Manœuvre de Landshut*, Paris: Chapelot, 1905
Bornemann, Karl. *Napoleon bei Znaim*, Geislingen/Steige: Verlag des Südmährischen Landschaftsrates, 1975
Bowden, Scotty and Charlie Tarbox. *Armies on the Danube 1809*, Arlington: Empire Games Press, 1980; revised and expanded edition, 1989
Bran, Friedrich Alexander. 'Fortgesetzte Bemerkungen über den gegenwärtigen Krieg', *Minerva*, July 1809
Buat, Edmond Alfonse Léon. *1809 De Ratisbonne à Znaïm*, Paris: Chapelot, 1909
Caemmerer, Rudolf von. *Die Entwicklung der strategischen Wissenschaft im 19. Jahrhundert*, Berlin: Baensch, 1904
Camon, Hubert. *La Manoeuvre de Wagram*, Paris: Berger-Levrault, 1926
——, *La Guerre Napoléonienne: Précis des Campagnes*, Paris: Teissèdre, 1999
Casareto, Marco. *L'Esercito Austriaco 1805/15: Fanteria*, Milan: Editrice Militare Italiana, 1987
Chandler, David G. *The Campaigns of Napoleon*, New York: Macmillan, 1966
Chroust, Anton. *Geschichte des Grossherzogtums Würzburg*, Würzburg: Becker, 1932

Clausewitz, Carl von. *Die Feldzüge von 1799 in Italien und der Schweiz*, Berlin: Dümmler, 1833
——, *On War*, (ed.). and trans. Michael Howard and Peter Paret, Princeton: Princeton University Press, 1984
Clercq, M. de. *Recueil des Traités de la France*, Paris: Amyot, 1864
Craig, Gordon A. 'Command and Staff Problems in the Austrian Army, 1740– 1866', in his *War, Politics, and Diplomacy*, New York: Praeger, 1966
Delbrück, Hans. *Erinnerungen, Aufsätze und Reden*, Berlin: Stilke, 1905
Demelitsch, Fedor von. *Metternichs auswärtige Politik*, Stuttgart: Cotta, 1898
'Der k. k. Feldmarschall-Lieutenant Graf Klenau im Gefechte bei Hollabrunn, 1809', *Österreichische Militärische Zeitschrift*, vol. VII/I, 1866
Driault, Edouard. *Tilsit*, Paris: Alcan, 1917
Duffy, Christopher. *The Army of Maria Theresa*, Doncaster: Terence Wise, 1990
——, *Instrument of War*, Chicago: Emperor's Press, 2000
——, *By Force of Arms*, Chicago: Emperor's Press, 2008
Dumolin, Maurice. *Précis d'Histoire Militaire: Révolution et Empire*, Paris: Barbere, 1913
Eggendorfer, Anton, (ed.). *Guntersdorf und Großnondorf: Die Geschichte der Marktgemeinde Guntersdorf*, Wien: Berger, 2008
Egger, Rainer. *Das Gefecht bei Hollabrunn und Schöngrabern 1805*, Vienna: Heeresgeschichtliches Museum, 1982
'Einige Bemerkungen über die Disposition zur Schlacht bei Wagram', *Zeitschrift für Kunst, Wissenschaft und Geschichte des Krieges*, vol. XVIII, 1830
Elting, John R. *Swords Around a Throne*, New York: The Free Press, 1988
Epstein, Robert M. *Napoleon's Last Victory and the Emergence of Modern War*, Lawrence: University of Kansas Press, 1994
Esdaile, Charles. *The Peninsular War*, London: Allen Lane, 2002
Esposito, Vincent J. and John R. Elting. *A Military History and Atlas of the Napoleonic Wars*, New York: Praeger, 1968
Eysturlid, Lee W. *The Formative Influences, Theories and Campaigns of Archduke Carl of Austria*, Westport: Greenwood, 2000
Fedorowicz, Wladyslaw de. *1809 Campagne de Pologne*, Paris: Plon, 1911
Fitzka, Karl.*Geschichte der Stadt Mistelbach*, Mistelbach: Stadtgemeinde, 1901
Fremont-Barnes, Gregory, (ed.). *Armies of the Napoleonic Wars*, Barnsley: Pen & Sword, 2011
Fournier, August. 'Oesterreichs Kriegsziele im Jahre 1809', *Beiträge zur neueren Geschichte Oesterreichs*, IV, December 1908
——, 'Gentz und der Friede von Schönbrunn', *Deutsche Rundschau*, vol. XLIX, October-November-December 1886
Fürnkranz, Rudolf. *Laa an der Thaya 1800–2000*, Gösling: Edition Weinviertel, 2009

Gaede, Udo. *Preussens Stellung zur Kriegsfrage im Jahre 1809*, Hannover: Hahn, 1897

[Gallina, Josef Freiherr von], 'Reglements und Instructionen für die Ausbildung der Truppe und ihrer Führer', *Österreichische militärische Zeitschrift*, Jahrgang 24, 1881

Garros, Louis. *Quel Roman que ma vie! Itinéraire de Napoléon Bonaparte*, Paris: Éditions de l'Encyclopédie Française, 1947; new edn with revisions by Jean Tulard published as *Itinéraire de Napoléon au Jour le Jour* in 1992 and re-issued in 1998

'Gedanken über die beiden Schlachten auf dem Marchfelde bei Wien', *Pallas*, Band 2, 1809

Gill, John H. *With Eagles to Glory: Napoleon and His German Allies in the 1809 Campaign*, London: Greenhill, 1992; revised paperback edition, 2018

——, *1809 Thunder on the Danube: Napoleon's Defeat of the Habsburgs*, London: Frontline, 2008–10; revised paperback edition, 2014

——, 'What Do They Intend? Austrian War Aims in 1809', The Consortium on Revolutionary Europe, *Selected Papers 1996*, Charles Crouch, Kyle O. Eidahl, and Donald D. Horward (eds), Tallahassee: Florida State University, 1996

——, 'The Strategic Setting in 1809: Intelligence and Operational Decisions on the Road to War', The Consortium on Revolutionary Europe, *Selected Papers 1997*, Kyle O. Eidahl, Donald D. Horward, and John Severn (eds), Tallahassee: Florida State University, 1997

——, 'From Wagram to Schönbrunn: War and Peace in 1809', The Consortium on Revolutionary Europe, *Selected Papers 1998*, Kyle O. Eidahl and Donald D. Horward (eds), Tallahassee: Florida State University, 1998

——, 'Impossible Numbers: Solving Rear Area Security Problems in 1809', The Consortium on Revolutionary Europe, *Selected Papers 2000*, Donald D. Horward, Michael F. Pavkovic, and John Severn (eds), Tallahassee: Florida State University, 2000. Note that the title given here is a misprint: it should read 'Imaginary Numbers' reflecting Napoleon's use of deception as a means of securing the army's rear areas.

——, 'I Fear Our Ruin is Very Near: Prussian Foreign Policy during the Franco-Austrian War of 1809', The Consortium on Revolutionary Europe, *Selected Papers 2002*, Bernard Cook, Susan V. Nicassio, Michael F. Pavkovic, and Karl A. Roider (eds), Tallahassee: Florida State University, 2002

——, 'Galician Gambles: Austrian Approaches to Russia at the Climax of the 1809 War', unpublished paper presented to the Consortium on the Revolutionary Era, 2011

——, 'Responding to Military Defeat: The Habsburg Case', unpublished paper presented to the Consortium in the Revolutionary Era, 2016

——, '1809: The Most Brilliant and Skillful Maneuvers', in Michael V. Leggiere (ed.), *Napoleon and the Operational Art of War*, Leiden: Brill, 2016

——, 'From Abensberg to Znaim: The Franco-Austrian War of 1809', in Bruno Colson and Alexander Mikaberidze (eds), *The Cambridge History of the Napoleonic Wars*, vol. II (forthcoming)

Groote, Wolfgang von, and Klaus-Jürgen Müller (eds). *Napoleon I. und das Militärwesen seiner Zeit*, Freiburg: Rombach, 1968

Hassel, Paul. *Geschichte der Preussischen Politik*, Leipzig: Hirzel, 1881

Heimatbuch des Bezirkes Hollabrunn, Hollabrunn, n.p., 1951

Heller von Hellwald, Friedrich Anton. *Der Feldzug des Jahres 1809 in Süddeutschland*, Wien: Gerold, 1864

Hertenberger, Helmut. 'Die Schlacht bei Wagram', dissertation, University of Vienna, 1950

Hirn, Josef. 'Das kaiserliche Handbillet aus Wolkersdorf (29. Mai 1809) für Tirol', *Beiträge zur neueren Geschichte Österreichs*, September 1906

Hoen, Maximilian Ritter von. *Wagram*, Wein: Stern, 1909

——, '1809. Ein Gedenkblatt zur Jahrhundertfeier des großen Krieges', *Streffleurs militärische Zeitschrift*, 1, January 1909

Hollins, David. *Austrian Auxiliary Troops 1792–1816*, London: Osprey, 1996

——, *Austrian Grenadiers and Infantry 1788–1816*, London: Osprey, 1998

Holtzheimer, Hans. 'Erzherzog Karl bei Wagram', dissertation, University of Berlin, 1904

[Hormayr, Josef Freiherr]. *Das Heer von Innerösterreich unter den Befehlen des Erzherzogs Johann im Kriege von 1809 in Italien, Tyrol und Ungarn*, Leipzig & Altenburg: Brockhaus, 1817

——, *Lebensbilder aus dem Befreiungskriege*, Jena: Frommann, 1841

Hübner, Anton. *Denkwürdigkeiten der königl. Stadt Znaim*, Znaim: Lenk, 1869

Just, Gustav. *Der Friede von Schönbrunn*, Wein: Stern, 1909

Klinkowström, Clemens von. *Aus der alten Registratur der Staatskanzlei*, Vienna: Braumüller, 1870

Király, Béla K. *East Central European Society and War in the Era of Revolutions, 1775–1856*, New York: Brooklyn College Press, 1984

Kohlhauser, Friedrich and Karl Müller, *Heimatmuseum der Stadt Laa a. d. Thaya und Umgebung*, Laa an der Thaya: Heimatmuseum, 1930

Kosáry, Domokos. *Napoléon et la Hongrie*, Budapest: Akademiai Kiado, 1979

Kraehe, Enno E. *Metternich's German Policy*, Princeton: Princeton University Press, 1963

Krenstetter, Josef. 'Die Folgen der Schlacht bei Wagram in militärischer Hinsicht', dissertation, University of Vienna, 1959

Krieg 1809, Vienna: Seidel & Sohn, 1907–10

Krieg gegen die Französische Revolution 1792–1797, Vienna: Seidel & Sohn, 1905

Krones, Franz. *Geschichte der Neuzeit Oesterreichs*, Berlin: Hofmann, 1879
Kwiatowski, Ernst von. 'Die Kämpfe bei Schöngrabern und Ober-Hollabrunn 1805, 1809', *Mittheilungen des K. K. Archivs für Nieder-Österreich*, I/4, 1908
Laborde, Alexandre de. *Précis Historique de la Guerre entre la France et l'Autriche en 1809*, Paris: Didot, 1822
Langsam, Walter C. *The Napoleonic Wars and German Nationalism in Austria*, New York: Columbia University Press, 1930
——, 'Count Stadion and Archduke Charles', *Journal of Central European Affairs*, vol. VI, no. 2, July 1946
Lanyi, Ladislas. 'Napoléon et les Hongrois', *Annales Historiques de la Révolution Française*, no. 141, October–December 1955
Ledru, Albert Gabriel Hubert. *Montbrun 1809*, Paris: Fournier, 1913
Lefebvre, Armand and Eduard Lefebvre de Béhaine. *Histoire des Cabinets de l'Europe pendant le Consulat et l'Empire*, Paris: Amyot, 1867–8
Lentz, Thierry. *Napoléon et la Conquête de l'Europe*, Paris: Fayard, 2001
Liechtenstern, Joseph Marx Freyherrn von. *Handbuch der neuesten Geographie des Österreichischen Kaiserstaates*, Vienna: Bauer, 1817
Lipscombe, Nick. *The Peninsular War Atlas*, revised edition, Oxford: Osprey, 2014
Martens, Fedor. *Recueil des Traités et Conventions conclus par la Russie avec les Puissances Etrangères*, St. Petersburg, 1876–1908
Mayerhoffer von Vedropolje, Eberhard. *Oesterreichs Krieg mit Napoleon I*, Wien: Seidel & Sohn, 1904
Molières, Michel. *Napoléon en Autriche: La Campagne de 1809: Les Opérations du 24 Avril au 12 Juillet*, Paris: Le Livre Chez Vous, 2004
Mowat, R. B. *The Diplomacy of Napoleon*, London: Arnold, 1924
Münchow-Pohl, Bernd von. *Zwischen Reform und Krieg: Untersuchungen zur Bewusstseinlage in Preussen 1809–1812*, Göttingen: Vandenhoeck & Ruprecht, 1987
Naulet, Frédéric. *Wagram*, Paris: Economica 2009
Nipperdey, Thomas. *Deutsche Geschichte 1800–1866*, Munich: Beck 1983
Ommen, Heinrich. *Die Kriegsführung des Erzherzogs Carl*, Berlin, 1900
Oncken, Wilhelm. *Oesterreich und Preussen im Befreiungskriege*, Berlin: Grote, 1879
Ouvrard, Robert. *1809: Les Français à Vienne*, Paris: Nouveau Monde, 2009
——, 'La Campagne de 1809', *Gloire & Empire*, No. 26, 2009
[Pahl, Johann Gottfried von, writing under the pseudonym 'Alethinos'] *Der Krieg in Deutschland im Jahre 1809 und dessen Resultate politisch und militärisch betrachtet*, Munich: Lentner, 1810
Pascal, Adrien. *Les Bulletins de la Grande Armée*, Paris: Prieur, 1844
Pawlowski, Bronislaw. *Historja Wojny Polsko-Austrajackiej 1809 Roku*, Warsaw, 1935
Pelet, Jean-Jacques. *Mémoires sur la guerre de 1809 en Allemagne*, Paris: Roret, 1824–6

[Petit]. *Histoire des Campagnes de l'Empereur Napoléon dans la Bavière et l'Autriche en 1805, dans la Prusse et la Pologne en 1806 et 1807, dans la Bavière et l'Autriche en 1809*, Paris: Piquet, 1843

Petre, Francis Loraine. *Napoleon and the Archduke Charles*, London: John Lane, 1909

Petritsch, Ernst D. 'Österreich und der Fürstenkongreß', in Rudolf Benl (ed.), *Der Erfurter Fürstenkongreß 1808*, Erfurt: Stadtarchiv Erfurt, 2008

Pigeard, Alain. *Les Étoiles de Napoléon*, Paris: Quatuor, 1996

——, 'L'Artillerie Régimentaire sous le Premier Empire', *Tradition*, no. 154, March 2000

Pleyer, Karl. 'Zwei Berichte über Schöngrabern im Jahr 1809', *Unsere Heimat*, vol. XXX, 8/10, 1959

Rauchensteiner, Manfried. *Die Schlacht bei Deutsch Wagram am 5. und 6. Juli 1809*, Militärhistorische Schriftenreihe 36, Wien: Bundesverlag, 1977

Renémont, C. de [pseudonym for General Auguste Clément Gérome] *Campagne de 1809*, Paris: Charles-Lavauzelle, 1903

Reschounig, Friedrich. 'Das Jahr 1809 im Urtheile der Zeitgenossen', dissertation, University of Vienna, 1939

Rothenberg, Gunther E. *The Military Border in Croatia 1740–1881*, Chicago: University of Chicago Press, 1966

——, *The Army of Francis Joseph*, West Lafayette: Purdue University Press, 1976

——, *Napoleon's Great Adversaries: The Archduke Charles and the Austrian Army 1792–1814*, Bloomington: Indian University Press, 1982

——, *The Emperor's Last Victory: Napoleon and the Battle of Wagram*, London: Weidenfeld & Nicolson, 2004

R. [Rothenburg], F. R. von. *Die Waffentaten der Oesterreicher im Jahre 1809*, Vienna: Hirschfeld, 1838

Rumi, Karl Georg. *Geographisch-statistisches Wörterbuch des östereichischen Kaiserstaates*, Vienna: Doll, 1809

Saski, Charles. *Campagne de 1809 en Allemagne et en Autriche*, Paris: Berger-Levrault, 1899–1902

Schimmer, Karl August. *Die Französichen Invasionen in Oesterreich und die Franzosen in Wien in den Jahren 1805 und 1809*, Vienna: Dirnböck, 1846

Schloßberger, August von. 'Aus der Zeit des französisch–österreichischen Krieges im Jahre 1809', *Besondere Beilage des Staats-Anzeigers für Württemberg*, 13 July 1887

Schneidawind, Franz J. A. *Carl, Erzherzog von Oesterreich*, Bamberg: Literarisch-artistisches Institut, 1840

——, *Der Krieg Oersterreich's gegen Frankreich, dessen Alliirte und den Rheinbund im Jahre 1809*, Schaffhausen: Hurter, 1842

Schroeder, Paul W. *The Transformation of European Politics*, Oxford: Clarendon Press, 1994

Ségur, Philippe Paul Comte de. *Histoires et Mémoires*, Paris: Didot, 1873

Sorel, Albert. *L'Europe et la Révolution Française*, Paris: Plon, 1904

Steiner, Herta. 'Das Urteil Napoleons I. über Oesterreich', dissertation, University of Vienna, 1946

Stern, Alfred. *Abhandlungen und Aktenstücke zur Geschichte der preussischen Reformzeit 1807–1815*, Leipzig: Duncker & Humblot, 1885

Strobl, Ad. *Aspern und Wagram*, Vienna: Seidel & Sohn, 1897

[Stutterheim, Karl Freiherr von] *La Guerre de l'An 1809 entre l'Autriche et la France*, Wien: Strauss, 1811

Thiers, Adolphe. *Histoire du Consulat et de l'Empire*, Paris: Paulin, 1845–69

Thiry, Jean. *Wagram*, Paris, Berger-Levrault, 1966

Tranie, Jean and Juan Carlos Carmigniani. *Napoléon et l'Autriche – La Campagne de 1809*, Paris: Copernic, 1979

[Traux, Ludwig de] 'Bermerkungen über die im 2ten und 3ten Stück der europäische Annalen enthaltenen Marginalien zur Relation über die Schlacht bei Wagram', *Europäische Annalen*, vol. V, 1810

Tulard, Jean. *Napoléon: Une Journée Particulière, 12 Octobre 1809*, Paris: Lattès, 1994

U., J. A. *Der Feldzug Frankreichs und seiner Verbündeten gegen Oesterreich im Jahre 1809*, Meissen: Goedsche, 1810

Valentini, Georg Freiherr von. *Versuch einer Geschichte des Feldzugs von 1809 an der Donau*, 2nd edition, Berlin: Nikolai, 1818

Vandal, Albert. *Napoléon et Alexandre Ier*, Paris: Plon, 1918

Vann, James Allen. 'Habsburg Policy and the Austrian War of 1809', *Central European History*, VII, 4 (December 1974)

Vignolle, Martin. 'Historique de la Campagne de 1809 (Armée d'Italie)', *Revue Militaire*, no. 16, July 1900. This published account is incomplete; for the full version, see his 'Armée d'Italie: Journal Historique de la Campagne de 1809', AG, *Manuscrits*, MR 734

Wagner, Walter. *Von Austerlitz bis Königgrätz: Österreichische Kampftaktik im Spiegel der Reglements 1805–1864*, Osnabrück: Biblio-Verlag, 1978

Welden, Ludwig Freiherr von. *Der Krieg von 1809 zwischen Oesterreich und Frankreich von Anfang Mai bis zum Friedensschlusse*, Vienna: Gerold, 1872

Wertheimer, Eduard. *Geschichte Oesterreichs und Ungarns im ersten Jahrzehnt des 19. Jahrhunderts*, Leipzig: Duncker & Humblot, 1890

——, 'Zur Geschichte Wiens im Jahre 1809', *Archiv für österreichische Geschichte*, 47, 1889

Wisnar, Julius. 'Die Schlacht bei Znaim im Jahre 1809', *Jahresbericht des k. k. Gymnasiums in Znaim für das Schuljahr 1909 1910*, Znaim: Lenk, 1910

Wolf, Franz. *Schöngrabern im Wandel der Zeiten*, Schöngrabern: self-published, 1995

Yorck von Wartenburg, Maximilian Count. *Napoleon as a General*, Carlisle: U.S. Army War College, 1983

Zehetbauer, Ernst. *Landwehr gegen Napoleon: Oesterreichs erste Miliz und der Nationalkrieg von 1809*, Wien: öbv & hpt, 1999

Zitterhofer, Karl. *Streffleurs Militärische Zeitschrift 1808–1908*, Vienna, 1908

Zschokke, Heinrich. *Der Krieg Oesterreichs gegen Frankreich und den rheinischen Bund im Jahre 1809*, Aarau: Remigius, 1810

Zwiedineck-Südenhorst, Hans von. *Erzherzog Johann von Oesterreich im Feldzuge von 1809*, Graz: Styria, 1892

Austrian Unit Histories: Infantry

Amon von Treuenfest, Gustav Ritter. *Geschichte des k. k. Infanterie-Regiments Nr. 20*, Wien: Mayer, 1878

——, *Geschichte des Kaiserlich Königlich Infanterie-Regiments Hoch und Deutschmeister*, Wien: 1879

——, *Geschichte des k. k. Infanterie-Regiments Nr. 47*, Wien: Mayer, 1882

——, *Geschichte des k. k. Infanterie-Regimentes Nr. 50*, Vienna: Mayer, 1882

——, 'Die Fahne des k. k. 2. böhmischen Legions-Bataillons Erzherzog Carl', *Oesterreichische militärische Zeitschrift*, III, 1883

——, *Geschichte des k. u. k. Infanterie-Regimentes Nr. 46*, Vienna: regimental, 1890

——, *Geschichte des kaiserl. und königl. Kärnthnerischen Infanterie-Regiments Feldmarschall Graf von Khevenhüller Nr. 7*, Wien: St. Norbertus, 1891

Auspitz, Leopold. *Das Infanterie-Regiment Freiherr von Hess Nr. 49*, Teschen: Prochaska, 1889

Baxa, Jakob. *Geschichte des k. u. k. Feldjägerbataillons No. 8 1808–1918*, Klagenfurt: Kameradschaftsbundes ehemaliger Achterjäger, 1974

Beran, Julius. *Die Geschichte des k. und k. Infanterie-Regiments Freiherr von Merkl Nr. 55*, Wien: regimental, 1899

Bichmann, Wilhelm. *Chronik des k. k. Infanterie-Regiments Nr. 62*, Wien: Mayer, 1880

Blazekovics, Karl von and Julius Pössl. *Geschichte des k. u. k. Infanterie-Regiments Nr. 31*, regimental, 1909

Branko, Franz von. *Geschichte des k. k. Infanterie-Regimentes Nr. 44*, Wien: kaiserlich-königlich Hof- und Staatsdruckerei, 1875

Ebhardt, Ferdinand. *Geschichte des k. k. 33. Infanterie-Regiments*, Ung. Weisskirchen: Wunder, 1888

Faust, Fr. *Geschichte des k. k. Infanterie-Regiments von Plüschau, nun Prinz Leopold beider Sicilien*, Wien, 1841

Geschichte des k. k. Infanterie-Regimentes Oskar II. Friedrich No. 10, Vienna: regimental, 1888

Geschichte des k. und k. Infanterieregiments Markgraf von Baden No. 23, Budapest: regimental, 1911

Geschichte des k. k. 25. Infanterie-Regiments, Prag: regimental, 1875

Geschichte des kaiserlichen und königlichen Infanterie-Regimentes Freiherr von Mollinary Nr. 38, Budapest: regimental, 1892

Geschichte des k. und k. Infanterie-Regiments Erzherzog Ludwig Salvator Nr. 58, Vienna: regimental, 1904

Grois, Victor. *Geschichte des k. k. Infanterie-Regiments Nr. 14,* Linz: Feichtinger, 1876

Hermannsthal, Friedrich von. *Geschichte des Tyroler Feld- und Land-, später 46. Linien-Infanterie-Regiments,* Krakau: Czas., 1859

'Historische Darstellung des Antheils, welchen das 5te Wiener Frey-Bataillon an dem Feldzuge des Jahres 1809 genommen hat', *Neue militärische Zeitschrift,* vol. III, 1811

Hödl, Rudolf von. *Geschichte des k. und k. Infanterieregimentes Nr. 29,* Temesvár: regimental, 1906

Janota, Robert. *Geschichte des k. und k. Infanterie-Regimentes Graf Daun Nr. 56,* Teschen: Prochaska, 1889

Johann, Erzherzog von Oesterreich. *Geschichte des K. K. Linien-Infanterie-Regiments Erzherzog Wilhelm No. 12,* Vienna: Seidel & Sohn, 1877

Kandelsdorfer, Karl. *Geschichte des K. und K. Feld-Jäger-Bataillons Nr. 7,* Bruck an der Mur: battalion, 1896

——, *Geschichte des k. u. k. Feld-Jäger-Bataillons Nr. 3,* Vienna: Vergani, 1899

Kirchthaler, Ludwig. *Geschichte des k. k. Infanterie-Regiments Nr. 2,* Vienna: n.p., 1895

Knorz, Justus. *Geschichte des k. k. Infanterie-Regiments Erzherzog Rainer Nr. 59,* Salzburg: regimental, n.d

Maendl, Maximilian. *Geschichte des k. und k. Infanterie-Regiments Nr. 51,* Klausenburg: regimental, 1899

May, Josef. *Geschichte des kaiserlich und königlich Infanterie-Regimentes No. 35,* Pilsen: Maasch, 1901

Mayer, Ferdinand. *Geschichte des k. k. Infanterie-Regimentes Nr. 39,* Vienna: kaiserlichen-königlichen Hof- und Staatsdruckerei, 1875

Nahlik, Johann Edlen von. *Geschichte des kais. kön. 55. Infanterie-Regimentes,* Brünn: Winiker, 1863

Netoliczka, August. *Geschichte des k. k. 9. Infanterie-Regiments,* Comorn: Siegler, 1866

Neuwirth, Victor Ritter von. *Geschichte des K. u. K. Infanterie-Regimentes Alt-Starhemberg Nr. 54,* Olmütz: Hölzel, 1894

Oesterreichische militärische Zeitschrift:

—— Waida, Vinzenz. 'Geschichte des 21. Linien-Infanterieregiments Prinz Victor Rohan (dermalen Albert Graf Giulay) im Feldzug 1809', vol. IX, 1819

—— 'Geschichte des k. k. 49. Linien-Infanterie-Regiments Baron Kerpen in den Feldzügen von 1809, 1813, 1814 und 1815', vol. X, 1821. This is a published version (with some redaction) of the regimental history that Johann O'Brien wrote in 1818 (O'Brien's manuscript in the Austrian Kriegsarchiv).

—— 'Geschichte des kaiserlichen-österreichischen 7. Linien-Infanterie-Regiments Grossherzog Toskano', no. 8, 1824

—— 'Episoden aus der Geschichte des k. k. 49. Infanterie-Regiments Baron Hess', no. 7, 1861

—— 'Rückzug des abgeschnittenen 4. Jäger-Bataillons, im Jahre 1809', vol. IX, 1843

Padewieth, Mansuet. *Geschichte des kaiserl. königl. 18. Linien-Infanterie-Regimentes*, Wien: Hof- und Staatsdruckerei, 1859

Pillersdorf, Albert Freiherr. *Das 57. Infanterie-Regiment*, Wien: Sommer, 1857

Pizzighelli, Cajetan. *Geschichte des k. k. Infanterie-Regimentes Kaiser Franz Josef No. 1*, Troppau: regimental, 1881

Posselt, Oskar. *Geschichte des k. und k. Infanterieregiments Ritter v. Pino Nr. 40*, Rzeszow: Gerold, 1913

Rona, Ludwig. *Geschichte des k. u. k. Infanterie-Regimentes Adolf Grossherzog von Luxemburg, Herzog zu Nassau Nr. 15*, Prague: Bellmann, 1901

Schmedes, Emil. *Geschichte des k. k. 28. Infanterie-Regimentes*, Wien: Seidel & Sohn, 1878

Schweigerd, C. A. *Geschichte des k. und k. Linien-Infanterie-Regimentes No. 8*, Wien: Wallishauser, 1857

Seeliger, Emil. *Geschichte des kaiserlichen und königlichen Infanterie-Regiments Nr. 32*, Budapest, 1900

Sittig, Heinrich. *Geschichte des k. u. k. Feldjäger-Bataillons Nr. 1*, Reichelberg: Stiepel, 1908

Stanka, Julius. *Geschichte des K. und K. Infanterie-Regimentes Erzherzog Carl Nr. 3*, Wien: regimental, 1894

Sypniewski, Alfred Ritter von. *Geschichte des k. und k. Infanterie-Regimentes Feldmarschall Carl Joseph Graf Clerfayt de Croix*, Jaroslau: regimental, 1894

Uhlig, Gottfried. *Militärische Erinnerungen vom Jahre 1701 bis 1838 mit besonderer Berücksichtigung des aus den Divisionen des 35., 36. und 42. Linien-Infanterie-Regiments bestehenden Grenadier-Bataillons John*, Prague: Thabor, 1839

Virtsolog, Coloman Rupprecht von. *Geschichte des k. k. 60. Linien-Infanterie-Regimentes*, Wien: k. k. Hof- und Staatsdruckerei, 1871

Watterich, F. C. *Das Denkmal der Erzherzog Carl-Legion im Südost der Staatsbahn*, Prague: Medau, 1846

Wrede, Alphons Freiherr von. *Geschichte der K. und K. Wehrmacht*, Vienna: Seidel & Sohn, 1898

Austrian Unit Histories: Cavalry and Other

Amon von Treuenfest, Gustav Ritter. *Geschichte des k. k. Huszaren-Regimentes Alexander Freiherr v. Koller Nr. 8*, Wien: Mayer, 1880

——, *Geschichte des k. k. Dragoner-Regimentes Feldmarschall Alfred Fürst zu Windisch-Graetz Nr. 14*, Wien: Brzewzowsky, 1886

——, *Geschichte des kaiserl. und königl. Husaren-Regimentes Nr. 10*, Vienna: regimental, 1892

——, *Geschichte des k. und k. Bukowina'schen Dragoner-Regimentes Nr. 9*, Vienna: regimental, 1892

——, *Geschichte des k. u. k. Husaren-Regiments Nr. 4*, Wien: regimental, 1903

Brinner, Wilhelm. *Geschichte des k. k. Pionnier-Regimentes*, Vienna: Seidel & Sohn, 1878

Dedekind, Franz. *Geschichte des k. k. Kaiser Franz Joseph I. Dragoner-Regimentes Nr. 11*, Vienna: regimental, 1879

Dolleczek, Anton. *Geschichte der Oesterreichischen Artillerie*, Vienna: Kreisel & Gröger, 1887

Geschichte des k. und k. Dragoner-Regiments Graf Paar Nr. 2, Olmütz, 1895

Jedina, Karl Anton Ritter von. *Geschichte des kaiserlich königlich österreichischen ersten Uhlanen-Regimentes*, Vienna: Schmid, 1845

Kielmansegg, Oswald Graf. *Schwarzenberg Uhlanen 1790–1887*, Tarnow, 1887

Komers, E. *Geschichte des vierten Cuirassier-Regiments*, Pressburg: Schmid, 1843

Oesterreichische militärische Zeitschrift:

—— 'Das Wirken des k. k. Husaren-Regiments Baron Blankenstein Nr. 6 (jetzt König von Würtemberg) im Feldzuge 1809', vol. V, 1846

—— 'Kriegsszenen aus der Geschichte des k. k. Uhlanen-Regiments Erzherzog Karl Nr. 3', vol. VI, 1846

—— 'Kriegsszenen aus der Geschichte des k. k. Husaren-Regiments Nr. 10', vol. VI, 1846

—— 'Kriegsszenen aus der Geschichte des k. k. Husaren-Regiments Fürst Reuß Nr. 7', vol. VII, 1846

Ow, Josef Baron. *Geschichte des kaiserl. königl. Erzherzog Ferdinand dritten Husaren-Regiments*, Sarvos Patak: regimental, 1843

Pizzighelli, Cajetan. *Geschichte des k. u. k. Husaren-Regimentes Wilhelm II. Deutscher Kaiser und König von Preussen Nr. 7*, Vienna: regimental, 1896

——, *Geschichte des k. u. k. Husaren-Regimentes Wilhelm II. König von Württemberg Nr. 6*, Rzeszów: regimental, 1897

——, *Geschichte des k. und k. Dragoner-Regimentes Kaiser Ferdinand Nr. 4*, Wiener Neustadt: regimental, 1902

———, *Geschichte des K. und K. Dragoner-Regimentes Johannes Josef Fürst von und zu Liechtenstein Nr. 10*, Vienna: regimental, 1903

———, *Geschichte des k. u. k. Dragoner-Regimentes Friedrich August, König von Sachsen Nr. 3*, Vienna, 1925

Riedl von Riedenau, Erich Freiherr. *Geschichte des k. und k. Uhlanen-Regimentes Erzherzog Karl Nr. 3*, Vienna: Hof- und Staatsdruckerei, 1901

Schwarzbach, Moriz. *Gedenkblätter aus der Geschichte des k. k. 3. Dragoner-Regimentes*, Vienna: Hof- und Staatsdruckerei, 1868

Semek, Major. 'Die Artillerie im Jahre 1809', *Mittheilungen des K. und K. Kriegsarchivs*, vol. III, 1904

Strack, J. *Geschichte des Sechsten Dragoner-Regimentes*, Vienna: kaiserlich-königlich Hof- und Staatsdruckerei, 1856

Strobl von Ravelsberg, Ferdinand. *Geschichte des k. und k. 12. Dragoner-Regiments*, Vienna: regimental, 1890

Tomaschek, Eduard Freiherr von. *Geschichte des k. k. Dragoner-Regiments No. 8*, Vienna: Hof- und Staatsdruckerei, 1889

Thürheim, Andreas Graf. *Geschichte des k. k. achten Uhlanen-Regimentes*, Vienna: Hof- und Staatsdruckerei, 1860

———, *Die Reiter-Regimenter der k. k. österreichischen Armee*, Vienna: Geitler, 1866

Wrede, Alfons Freiherr von. *Geschichte des K. u. K. mährischen Dragoner-Regimentes Albrecht Prinz von Preussen*, Brunn: Rohrer, 1906

French Unit Histories: Infantry

Ceccaty, M. de. *Le 23me d'Infanterie: Historique*, manuscript, SHD, n.d

Chaperon, Clément Louis. *Historique du 46e Régiment d'Infanterie*, Paris: Charles-Lavauzelle, 1894

Clerc, Léon Jean Baptiste. *Historique du 79e Régiment d'Infanterie*, Paris: Berger-Levrault, 1896

Demiau, Henri. *Historique du 5e Régiment d'Infanterie*, Caen: Brulfert, 1890

Faivre d'Arcier, Charles Sébastien and Auguste Henri Roye. *Historique du 37e Régiment d'Infanterie*, Paris: Delagrave, 1895

Grémillet, Paul. *Un Régiment pendant Deux Siècles*, Paris, 1899

Gueheneuc, Charles Louis Joseph Olivier. 'Historique du 26e Léger pendant la Campagne de 1809', manuscript, SHD, August 1810

Historique du 99e Régiment d'Infanterie de Ligne, manuscript, SHD, 1889

Jacquinot, Lieutenant and Capitaine Limal. *Historique du 4e Régiment d'Infanterie*, Auxerre: np, 1904

Labouche, Jean Henri Éliacin. *Historique du 18e Régiment d'Infanterie de Ligne*, Pau: Garet, 1891

Noret, Chef de Bataillon. *Historique du 2e Régiment d'Infanterie de Ligne*, manuscript, SHD, 1875

Pitot, Georges Edmond. *Historique du 83e Régiment d'Infanterie,* Toulouse: Privat, 1891
Poitevin, Maurice Alexandre. *Historique du 16e Régiment d'Infanterie,* Paris: Baudoin, 1888
67e Régiment d'Infanterie: *Historique du Corps,* manuscript, SHD, 1891
Vassal, Bonaventure Marie Joseph. *Historique du 11e Régiment d'Infanterie,* Montauban: Forestié, 1900

French Unit Histories: Cavalry and Other

Albert, A. *Manuscrit des Carabiniers, Le,* Paris: Bruno Sepulchre, 1989
Allenou, Capitaine. *Historique du 7eme Régiment de Dragons,* manuscript, SHD, 1890
Amonville, Marie François Josep Raoul d'. *Le 8e Cuirassiers,* Paris: Lahure, 1892
Aubier, Achille. *Un Régiment de Cavalerie Légère,* Paris: Berger-Levrault, 1888
Bonie, A. *Historique du 3e Régiment de Chasseurs,* manuscript, SHD, 1875–6
Bouchard, Stéphane. *Historique du 28e Régiment de Dragons,* Paris: Berger-Levrault, 1893
Brye, P. de. *Historique du 6e Régiment de Cuirassiers,* np, 1839
Canonge, Alphone Henri. *Historique du 3e Régiment de Chasseurs,* Abbeville: Retaux, 1879
Castillon de Saint-Victor, Marie Emilien de. *Historique du 5e Régiment de Hussards,* Paris: Lobert/Person, 1889
Chavane, J. *Histoire du 11e Cuirassiers,* Paris: Charavay, 1889
Chevillotte, Lieutenant. *Historique du 16eme Chasseurs à Cheval,* manuscript, SHD, 1887
Cosse-Brissac, René de. *Historique du 7e Régiment de Dragons,* Paris: Leroy, 1909
Desgraves, P. *Historique du 13e Régiment de Chasseurs,* Béziers: Bouineau, 1891
Dezaunay, Capitaine. *Historique du 1er Régiment de Cuirassiers,* Angers: Lachèse & Dolbeau, 1889
Diamant-Berger, Marcel. *Le 19e de Chasseurs à Cheval,* Paris: Courtot, 1933
Dupuy, Raoul. *Historique du 12e Chasseurs de 1788 à 1891,* Paris: Person, 1891
Fontenaille, H. de. *Histoire Militaire: 5eme de Cuirassiers,* manuscript, SHD, 1890
Gay de Vernon, François Simon Marle Jules. *Historique du 2e Régt de Chasseurs à Cheval,* Paris: Dumaine, 1865
Hache, Édouard. *Historique du 23e Régiment de Dragons,* Paris: Hachette, 1890
Histoire du 1er Régiment de Cuirassiers, Angers: Lachese & Dolbeau, 1889
Histoire Militaire: 5eme de Cuirassiers, manuscript, SHD, n.d
Historique du 7e Régiment de Chasseurs, Valence: Céas, 1891 (virtually the same as Capitaine Stoffels, *Historique du 7e Régiment de Chasseurs,* manuscript, SHD, 1890)
Historique du 19e Chasseurs à Cheval, manuscript, SHD, 1878

Historique du 10e Régiment de Cuirassiers, manuscript, SHD, 1892
Ivry, Ogier d'. *Historique du 9e Régiment de Hussards,* Valence: Céas, 1891
Juzancourt, Georges Guimet de. *Historique du 7e Régiment de Cuirassiers,* Paris: Berger-Levrault, 1887
——, *Historique du 10e Régiment de Cuirassiers,* Paris: Berger-Levrault, 1893
Lamotte, Charles H. P. P. *Historique du 8e Régiment de Hussards,* Valence: Ceas, 1891
Lemoine de Margon, Gabriel Marie Joseph René. *Historique du 11e Régiment de Chasseurs,* Vesoul: Bon, 1896
Lepage, Paul and Pierre Parrot. *Historique du 19e Régiment de Chasseurs,* Lille: Danel, 1893
Litre, Emile François. *Les Régiments d'Artillerie à Pied de la Garde, le Régiment Monté de la Garde et le 23e Régiment d'Artillerie,* Paris: Plon, 1895
Longin, Anatole Henri Emile. *Historique du 14e Régiment de Chasseurs,* Paris: Person, 1907
Louvat, Edmond Charles Constant. *Historique du 7eme Hussards,* Paris: Pairault, 1889
Martimprey, Charles Marie Auguste. *Historique du 9e Régiment de Cuirassiers,* Paris: Berger-Levrault, 1888
Massoni, Gérard Antoine. *Histoire d'un Régiment de Cavalerie Légère: Le 5e Hussards de 1783 à 1815,* Paris: Archives & Culture, 2007
Maumené, Charles Gustave Vincent. *Historique du 3e Régiment de Cuirassiers,* Paris: Boussod, Valadon et Cie, 1893
Moulins-Rochefort, L. *Histoire du 4e Régiment de Cuirassiers,* Paris: Lahure, 1897
Oré, Delphin Charles. *1er Régiment de Chasseurs,* Chateaudun: Laussedat, 1903
Place, R. de. *Historique du 12e Cuirassiers,* Paris: Lahure, 1889
Ponton d'Amécourt, Lieutenant. *Historique du 29e Régiment de Dragons,* manuscript, SHD, 1891
Quinemont, Commandant de. *Historique du 2e Régiment de Chasseurs à Cheval,* manuscript, SHD, 1888
Rembowski, Alexandre. *Sources Documentaires concernant l'Histoire du Régiment des Chevau-légers de la Garde Napoléon I,* Warsaw: Rubieszweski and Wrotnowski, 1899
Rothwiller, Baron Antoine Ernst. *Histoire du Deuxième Régiment de Cuirassiers,* Paris: Plon, 1877
Rouel, Charles. *Historique du 13e Régiment de Chasseurs à Cheval,* manuscript, SHD, 1872

Baden & Hessian Unit Histories

Barsewisch, Theophil von. *Geschichte des Grossherzoglich Badischen Leib-Grenadier-Regiments 1803–1870,* Karlsruhe: Müller, 1893

Beck, Fritz, Karl von Hahn and Heinrich von Hahn. *Geschichte des Grossherzoglichen Artilleriekorps 1. Grossherzoglich Hessischen Feldartillerie-Regiments Nr. 25 und seiner Stämme*, Berlin: Mittler & Sohn, 1912

Bigge, Wilhelm. *Geschichte des Infanterie-Regiments Kaiser Wilhelm (2. Grossherzoglich Hessisches) Nr. 116*, Berlin: Mittler & Sohn, 1903

Bray-Steinburg, Wilhelm von. *Geschichte des 1. Badischen Leib-Dragoner-Regiments Nr. 20 und dessen Stammregiments des Badischen Dragoner-Regiments von Freystedt von 1803 bis zur Gegenwart*, Berlin: Mittler & Sohn, 1909

Caspary, Ernst. *Geschichte des dritten Grossherzoglich Hessischen Infanterie-Regiments (Leib-Regiments) Nr. 117*, Darmstadt: Lange, 1877

'Feldzug der 2ten Division 4ten Armeecorps der Armee von Teutschland im Jahr 1809', *Pallas*, 1810

Ferber, Alexander. *Geschichte des 1. Badischen Feldartillerie-Regiments Nr. 14*, Karlsruhe: Müller, 1906

Kattrein, Ludwig. *Ein Jahrhundert deutscher Truppengeschichte dargestellt an derjenigen des Grossh. Hessischen Kontingents 1806–1906*, Darmstadt: Schlapp, 1907

Keim, August. *Geschichte des Infanterie-Leibregiments Grossherzogin (3. Grossherzogl. Hessisches) Nr. 117*, Berlin: Bath, 1903

Klingelhöffer, Friedrich. *Geschichte des 2. Grossherzoglich Hessischen Infanterie-Regiments (Grossherzog) Nr. 116*, Berlin: Mittler & Sohn, 1888

Rau, Ferdinand. *Geschichte des 1. Badischen Leib-Dragoner Regiments Nr. 20 und dessen Stamm-Regiments von Freystedt von 1803 bis zur Gegenwart*, Berlin: Mittler & Sohn, 1878

Röder von Diersburg, Carl Christian Freiherr von. *Geschichte des 1. Grossherzoglich Hessischen Infanterie- (Leibgarde-) Regiments Nr. 115*, Fritz Beck (ed.), Berlin: Mittler & Sohn, 1899

Sauzey, Camille. *Le Contingent Badois*, Paris: Terana, 1987

——, *Les Soldats de Hesse et de Nassau*, Paris: Terana, 1988

Söllner, Gerhard. *Für Badens Ehre: Die Geschichte der Badischen Armee*, Karlsruhe: Info Verlagsgesellschaft, 1995-2001

Theilnahme der Grossherz. Hess. Truppen an dem Kriege zwischen Oestreich und Frankreich im Jahre 1809, Darmstadt: Auw, 1850 (written in October 1809)

Wenz zu Niederlahnstein, Rolf von, Heinrich Hentz and Otto Abt. *Dreihundert Jahre Leibgarde Regiment (1. grossherzoglich Hessisches) Nr. 115*, Darmstadt: Kichler, 1929

Zech, Karl von and Friedrich von Porbeck. *Geschichte der Badischen Truppen 1809 im Feldzug der Französischen Hauptarmee gegen Oesterreich*, Rudolf von Freydorf (ed.), Heidelberg: Winter, 1909

Zimmermann, Karl von. *Geschichte des 1. Grossherzoglich Hessischen Dragoner-Regiments (Garde-Dragoner-Regiments) Nr. 23.*, Darmstadt: Bergsträsser, 1878

Bavarian Unit Histories

Auvera, Alfred. *Geschichte des Kgl. Bayer. 7. Infanterie-Regiments Prinz Leopold von Bayern*, Bayreuth: Ellwanger, 1898

Buxbaum, Emil. *Das königlich Bayerische 3. Chevaulegers-Regiment 'Herzog Maximilian' 1724 bis 1884*, München: Oldenbourg, 1884

Fabrice, Friedrich von. *Das Königlich Bayerischen 6. Infanterie-Regiment Kaiser Wilhelm, König von Preussen*, München: Oldenbourg, 1896

Grosch, Feodor, Eduard Hagen and Albert Schenk. *Geschichte des K. B. 12. Infanterie-Regiments Prinz Arnulf und seiner Stammabteilungen*, München, 1914

H., M. *Kurze Darstellung der Geschichte des Königlich Bayerischen 4. Chevaulegers-Regiments 'König' von 1744 bis zur Gegenwart*, Berlin: Mittler & Sohn, 1895

Heinze, Emil. *Geschichte des Kgl. Bayer. 6. Chevaulegers-Regiments 'Prinz Albrecht von Preussen'*, Leipzig: Klinkhardt, 1898

Leyh, Max. *Die Feldzüge des Königlich Bayerischen Heeres unter Max I. Joseph von 1805 bis 1815*, volume VI/2 of *Geschichte des Bayerischen Heeres*, München: Schick, 1935

Sauzey, Camille. *Nos Alliés des Bavarois*, Paris: Terana, 1988

Schubert, Franz und Hans Vara. *Geschichte des K. B. 13. Infanterie-Regiments*, München: Lindauer, 1906

Sichlern, Oskar von. *Geschichte des königlich bayerischen 5. Chevaulegers-Regiments 'Prinz Otto'*, München: regimental, 1876

'Skizzen einer Geschichte des 11ten k. baierischen Linien-Infanterie-Regiments', *Kriegs-Schriften, herausgegeben von baierischen Offizieren*, vol. I, Munich, 1820

Ulrich, Maximilian. *Die Königs-Chevaulagers*, Vienna: Hölzl, 1892

Völderndorff und Waradein, Freiherr von (ed.). *Kriegsgeschichte von Bayern unter König Maximilian Joseph I.*, München, 1826

Wolf, Gustav. *Der Eilmarsch Wrede's von Linz bis Wagram*, Innsbruck: Wagner, 1909

Xylander, Rudolf Ritter von. *Geschichte des 1. Feldartillerie-Regiments Prinz-Regent Luitpold*, Berlin: Mittler & Sohn, 1909

Zoellner, Eugen. *Geschichte des K. B. 11. Infanterie-Regiments 'von der Tann' 1805–1905*, München: Lindauer, 1905

Newspapers and Journals

Europäische Annalen, 1809–11
Gazette Nationale ou Moniteur Universel, 1809
Journal de l'Empire, 1809
Wiener Zeitung, 1809

Index

'→' indicates a promotion during 1809

Albert, Herzog von Sachsen-Teschen: 13, 15, 16, 89, 106, 145, 146, 299, 305, 307, 308
Alexander I, Tsar: xx, 5, 15, 22, 27, 29, 36, 84, 91, 140, 286, 316, 322, 330
Altstern, GM Johann Ritter Allmeyer von: 132, 133, 136–7, 146, 147, 155, 158, 159–60, 163, 170, 179–80, 187, 188, 209, 235
Ameil, Colonel Auguste Jean Joseph Gabriel: 127, 147
Andréossy, GD Antoine: 27, 87, 101, 309
Arrighi de Casanova, GD Jean Toussaint: 57, 98, 104, 111, 139, 147, 159, 178, 231–2, 245, 254, 276, 288
Aspern (Aspern-Essling), Battle of: 39, 41, 52, 57, 58, 63, 64, 66, 72, 79–80, 85, 88–90, 96, 98, 111, 173, 265, 197, 331
Austerlitz, Battle of (1805): 2, 4, 14, 34, 62, 100, 284, 294, 327, 329, 331, 333
Austrian military formations:
  I Corps (*see also* Bellegarde): 25, 45, 78, 88, 95–9, 108, 111, 116, 119, 125, 132, 165, 195, 198–9, 203–11, 225–7, 243, 254–60, 270–2, 279, 283
  II Corps (*see also* Hohenzollern): 25, 45, 67, 69, 78, 88, 95–9, 108, 111, 118–19, 125, 129, 132, 133, 136, 146, 177, 195, 201, 203–11, 212, 225–7, 243, 254–8, 283, 297
  III Corps (*see also* Kolowrat): 45, 70, 78, 88, 95–9, 108, 111, 116, 125, 165, 195, 205–11, 225–7, 243, 248, 254–60, 283
  IV Corps (*see also* Rosenberg): 25, 45, 78, 88, 95–9, 106, 108–9, 111, 121–2, 124, 132, 133–7, 155–60, 177, 226, 232, 236–8, 325
  V Corps (*see also* Reuss): 45, 69, 78, 88, 95–9, 108, 109, 111, 116, 125, 130, 132, 149–50, 164–5, 199, 206–10, 211–19, 225–7, 243–53, 254–8, 260–9, 273–6, 279, 283, 308, 310
  VI Corps (*see also* Klenau): 45, 69, 78, 88, 95–9, 108, 111, 116, 118, 119, 125, 129, 150–4, 164–5, 171, 195, 206–11, 225–7, 243, 254–7, 283, 297
  VII Corps (*see also* Ferdinand): 26, 45, 83, 175, 313
  VIII Corps (*see also* Chasteler): 24, 45, 68, 81
  IX Corps (*see also* Ignaz Gyulai): 24, 45, 81–2, 85, 93, 174, 309, 315
  Reserve Corps (Cavalry and Grenadiers): 38–9, 42, 45, 78, 88, 95–9, 108, 111, 116, 125, 130, 132, 162, 164, 187–203, 205–11, 225–7, 243,

245, 254–60, 262–8, 273–6, 279, 280, 283, 296, 297, 326, 329
Army of Inner Austria (*see also* Johann): 24, 45, 68, 81, 95, 102, 175, 309
Hungarian Insurrection: 10, 37, 39, 74, 76, 81, 93, 148, 156, 174, 189, 201–2, 206, 210, 309, 319, 330
Landwehr: 7, 37, 38–9, 74–6, 82, 85, 88, 109, 120, 132, 133, 169, 174, 244, 300; specific battalions: 107–8, 117, 118, 170, 203, 226, 236, 237, 247
Vienna Volunteers: 39, 42, 11, 117, 152, 162, 214, 216–17, 227, 247–8, 253, 268–9

Baden troops: xxii, 51, 54–5, 59, 79, 111, 117–18, 127–9, 152–5, 212, 213–18, 221, 245, 246–53, 260, 263–68, 273, 279, 308, 325
Baraguey d'Hilliers, GD Louis: 87, 93, 113–14, 147, 148–9, 175, 179, 296, 309, 315
Bavarian troops:
  1st Division: 60, 93, 179, 309
  2nd Division: 55, 60, 87, 103, 111, 191–204, 257–61, 310, 325
  3rd Division: 60, 93, 309, 310
Bellegarde, GdK Heinrich Graf: 25, 45, 67, 68, 69, 88, 164, 198, 205, 208, 226–7, 258–9, 270–3, 308, 319
Bernadotte, Marshal Jean-Baptiste: 18, 44, 97, 139, 149
Berthier, Marshal Alexander: xvii, 31, 33, 54, 69, 77, 86, 101, 113–14, 118, 123–4, 139, 148, 158, 162, 227, 229–30, 232–3, 242, 243, 283–5, 292–3, 300, 302–3, 308, 313, 333
Bianchi, GM → FML Friedrich Baron: 147, 175, 296, 304, 313

Boudet, GD Jean: 87, 96, 98, 147, 149–50, 178, 217, 239, 296
British raids on German coast: 22, 91, 173–4, 311, 312
Brunswick, Duke of, raid in Germany: 311, 312
Bruyère, GB → GD Jean Pierre Joseph: 103, 111, 116–17, 127, 129, 151, 155, 162, 214, 293
Bubna, GM → FML Ferdinand Graf von Littitz: 316–18, 321

Carra Saint Cyr, GD Claude 55–6, 96, 98, 147, 149–50, 178, 215–17, 245, 264, 273, 329
Champagny, Jean-Baptiste de Nompère de: 27, 314–17, 333–4
Charles, FM Archduke: 4–5, 7, 35, 37–9, 45, 60–3, 65, 67, 68, 74, 81, 88, 111, 114, 115, 126, 127, 128, 131, 132–3, 135–7, 142, 147, 148, 154, 158, 160, 163, 169–70, 171, 173, 174, 179–80, 187, 194, 219, 220, 229, 230, 231, 232, 238, 243, 247, 277, 318, 219, 323, 324, 327; battlefield actions & decisions: 69–71, 80, 97–106, 109, 198, 209–10, 225–8, 239, 243, 245, 248, 254–5, 261–2, 291, 326, 328, 329; strategy and operational planning: 21, 23–5, 42, 72–3, 78–9, 90–1, 93, 102, 103, 122, 124–5, 163–5; cordon defence: 46, 121, 131, 136, 146, 168, 248, 325; defensive 'positions': 102, 122, 126, 137, 142–3, 146, 168, 182, 185–6, 243, 280, 325; letter to Napoleon: 76–7, 81; letters to Herzog Albert: 13, 89–90, 106, 145, 299, 305, 307; relations with Franz: xxi, 14–15, 90–1, 122–3, 144–6, 163–8, 219, 298–302, 304–7; relations with Stadion and court: 11–13, 23, 75–8, 83, 85–6, 88–90, 92–3; views of Austrian forces: 19, 23,

39–41, 43, 46, 106–7, 123, 130, 208, 218, 244; views of French forces: 50, 52, 64, 243; views on Russia: 26, 74, 84, 91–2, 175; views on ceasefire/peace negotiations: xx, 100–7, 172, 186, 209–10, 219, 283–6, 295–8, 311, 317, 331; resignation: 290, 307–8
Chasteler, FML Jean Marquis de: 45, 68, 72, 81–2, 85, 93, 95, 174, 286, 298, 309, 315
civilian experiences: 220–5
Claparède, GD Michel Marie: 58, 195, 279
Clauzel, GD Bertrand: 58, 195, 228, 258

Dalmatia: 2, 24, 31, 32, 45, 65, 68, 80–2, 85, 176, 294, 303, 311–13
Davout, Marshal Louis Nicholas: 18, 29, 44, 69–70, 77, 96–9, 111, 114, 125, 139–42, 147, 158–9, 161, 171, 193, 228–34, 236, 242, 244, 254, 257, 272, 288, 292–3, 326

Eugène de Beauharnais, Viceroy of Italy: 30, 44, 72, 81–2, 111, 113, 114, 139, 147–9, 179, 296, 309, 313, 315

Ferdinand d'Este, GdK Archduke: 3, 11, 26, 45, 68, 83–4, 91–2, 122, 135–6, 175, 313–14
Ferdinand von Habsburg, Großherzog of Würzburg:, 322, 333
Francken, Baden Oberstleutant Karl von: 111, 117, 151, 153, 252, 267
Franz I, Kaiser of Austria: xxi, 2–3, 7, 13, 15, 33, 45, 90, 109, 147, 160, 220, 296; and peace negotiations: 86, 100, 143–5, 239, 285–7, 316, 318, 320–2, 332; and Napoleon: 15, 17, 28, 29, 34, 172, 284, 293, 322, 333; relations with Charles: 14, 75–6, 122, 163, 165–8, 239, 298–308; and Russia: 84, 91–2, 286
French military formations:
Army of Dalmatia (*see also* Marmont): 32, 44, 53, 57–60, 87, 99, 110, 123–4, 199, 327
Army of Italy: 30, 32, 44, 58, 64, 87, 96, 97, 98, 99, 103, 111, 125, 139, 147, 178, 255, 309
Imperial Guard: 32, 44, 48, 52, 87, 96, 97, 98, 104, 110, 111, 125, 140, 146, 147, 171, 178, 231, 242, 253, 257, 291, 326; Guard cavalry: 53, 57, 229–30, 233, 239, 245, 254, 278, 288
2nd Corps (*see also* Oudinot): 32, 44, 48, 53, 57, 80, 87, 96, 97, 98, 110, 113, 124, 291
3rd Corps (*see also* Davout): 31, 44, 48, 70, 87, 96, 97, 98, 158–9, 230, 231–3, 237, 255, 291
4th Corps (*see also* Massena): 32, 44, 48, 53–6, 96–9, 103, 116, 129, 150, 159, 178, 211, 217, 230, 246, 288
7th Corps (*see also* Lefebvre): 32, 44, 52, 59, 69, 87, 309
8th Corps (*see also* Vandamme): 32, 44, 52, 69, 87, 147, 179, 309
9th Corps (*see also* Bernadotte): 32, 44, 87, 96, 97, 98, 149
10th Corps (*see also* Jérôme): 32, 44, 52, 93, 315
1st Heavy Cavalry Division (*see also* Nansouty): 44, 56, 117, 231, 245, 254
2nd Heavy Cavalry Division (*see also* St Sulpice): 44, 57, 257
3rd Heavy Cavalry Division (*see also* Arrighi): 44, 57, 104, 231, 257
Fresnel, FML Johann Carl Hennequin Graf von: 227, 259, 270–1
Friedrich Wilhelm III, King of Prussia: 22, 24, 64, 320

Galbois, Captain Nicolas Marie Mauthurin: 101, 162

Gérard, GB François Joseph: 98, 117, 128, 141, 178

Germany, Austrian diversionary operations in: 72, 75, 82–3, 89, 91–3, 173, 294, 311

Great Britain: 6, 20, 27–8, 30, 31, 73, 293, 308; Austria seeks as ally: 19, 22–6, 63, 91, 173–4, 287, 294; landing in Holland (Walcheren): 174, 311, 312

Grouchy, GD Emmanuel: 96, 98, 104, 111, 120, 147, 158–9, 189, 232, 235, 236–8, 296, 315

Grünne, FML Philipp Graf: 12, 46, 75, 167, 299, 308

Gyulai, FML Albert: 45

Gyulai, FML Ignaz: 45, 85, 93, 95, 122, 174, 286, 294, 298, 300, 309, 313, 315

Hardegg, GM Johann Anton Graf: 131, 177–8, 239, 296, 310

Hardegg, Oberst Johann Heinrich Graf: 214–19, 247

Hardegg, GM Johann Ignaz Graf: 131–2, 226

Hessian troops: xxii, 51, 55, 59, 128–9, 213, 218, 244, 252, 267, 270, 275, 279

Hiller, FML → FZM Johann Freiherr von: 45, 78

Hohenlohe-Waldenburg-Bartenstein, FML Ludwig Fürst: 158, 235, 238

Hohenzollern-Hechingen, FML → GdK Friedrich Xaver Fürst zu: 45, 88, 109, 118–19, 130, 132–3, 134, 136–7, 142, 159–60, 164, 169, 177, 208–10, 289, 324, 329

Hollabrunn, Engagement at (9 July): 149–55

Italy: 2–3, 9, 12, 18, 20–1, 24–6, 30, 31, 45, 57, 61, 65, 72, 73–6, 80–2, 85, 89, 176, 294

Jérôme Bonaparte, King of Westphalia: 33, 44, 52, 311

Johann, GdK Archduke: 13, 24, 45, 62, 68, 72, 75, 77, 81–2, 93, 95, 98, 102–5, 143, 145, 147, 174–5, 238; expanded command post-Wagram: 122, 136, 174, 298, 304–5, 309, 313, 315; as a concern for Napoleon post-Wagram: 105, 114, 125, 148–9, 170–1, 327

Joseph, FM Archduke, Palatine of Hungary: 81–2, 93, 114, 122, 298, 304, 309, 315, 319, 320–1

Klebelsberg, GM Johann Nepomuk Joseph Graf von: 211–15, 218–19

Klenau, FML Johann Graf: 130–1, 137, 143, 146, 150–5, 162, 163, 164, 169, 171, 211, 226

Kolowrat-Krakowsky, FZM → FM Karl Graf: 25, 45, 69, 88, 164, 165, 205–7, 226, 256

Korneuburg, Engagement at (7 July): 108, 111, 116–18, 119, 122

Lannes, Marshal Jean: 48, 80, 87, 293

Lasalle, GD Antoine Charles: 87, 96, 98, 103, 293

Legrand, GD Claude Juste Alexander: 55, 96, 98, 117, 127–8, 147, 149–53, 171, 178, 213–17, 245, 246–53, 261–9, 273–7, 281, 328, 329

Lefebvre, Marshal François: 44, 59, 87, 139, 179, 296, 309

Leiningen-Westerburg, Oberstlt August Graf zu: 38, 200, 262–7, 274, 279, 329

Liechtenstein, GdK → FM Johannes Fürst von: 42, 45, 88, 108, 125, 130, 143–5, 161–2, 166–7, 186–7, 188, 211, 219, 227, 239–40, 243, 272, 273, 284–6, 298–9, 302, 304–6, 308, 316–18, 321, 332–4

Lindenau, Bavarian Oberst Friedrich von: 116, 124, 127–9, 155, 178, 308–10

MacDonald, GD → Marshal Etienne Jacques: 96–9, 112

Maret, Hughes Bernard: 292, 317, 322–3

Maria Ludovika, Kaiserin: 3, 10, 13, 26, 77

Marie Louise, Archduchess: xxi, 322–3

Marmont, GD → Marshal Auguste: 32, 44, 57–60, 72, 82, 87, 96, 98, 99, 104, 110, 111, 134, 141–2, 147, 155–61, 168–9, 171–2, 176, 178, 185, 189–211, 216–17, 223, 227–9, 238–9, 246, 247, 250–1, 254–61, 270–3, 277, 280, 289, 310, 313, 325–9; correspondence with Napoleon & Berthier: 123–5, 137–9, 190, 196, 230–5, 242–4; correspondence with Davout: 141–2, 158–9, 229; elevation to marshal: xxi, 303–4

Marulaz, GD Jacob François: 98, 103, 104

Massena, Marshal André: 32, 44, 53–6, 61, 74, 78, 87, 96–9, 103, 111, 116–18, 127–9, 140–2, 147, 150–5, 168, 169, 171–2, 178, 182, 185, 211–19, 220, 222–3, 239, 242, 244–70, 273–7, 279, 282, 288, 291, 302, 326, 328–9; correspondence with Napoleon & Berthier: 114, 118, 123, 125, 137–9, 229–30; injury: 95, 128, 265–6; role in communications with Austrians: 162–3; liaison with Marmont: 193, 196, 211, 231

Maximilian d'Este, FML Archduke: 3, 176

Mayer von Heldensfeld, GM → FML Anton: 21, 24, 62

Mecséry de Tsoor, Oberst Carl Johann Baron: 133, 146, 209

Metternich, Clemens von: xxi, 9, 18–19, 28, 100, 143–5, 166, 285–7, 305, 314–19, 322, 332

Minucci, GM Franz Freiherr von: 103, 116, 191–204, 221, 260–1, 310

Molitor, GD Gabriel: 87, 96, 98, 147, 149–50, 217, 239, 246, 257, 326

Montbrun, GD Louis Pierre: 87, 96, 98, 104, 114, 120–1, 124, 160, 189–97, 205–8, 227–8, 245, 254–60, 283, 292

Nansouty, GD Etienne Marie Antoine Champion, Comte de: 44, 56–7, 96, 98, 117, 141–2, 146, 147, 178, 230–1, 233, 245, 254

Napoleon: 1–2, 6, 8, 30, 44, 47, 48, 52, 53–6, 59–60, 67, 69, 81–3, 91–3, 105, 117, 127, 146, 148, 173, 224, 239, 277, 288, 296, 297, 302–4, 306, 307, 308, 311, 312, 313, 323; views of Austria: 27–8, 31, 162, 71, 85; command and leadership: 50, 58, 63–5, 112–13, 143, 190, 203–4, 233–6, 253–4, 260; strategy and operations: 31–2, 71–4, 78–80, 86–90, 123–5, 137, 142, 169, 170–1, 176, 179, 229–33, 242–3, 253–60, 270–3, 280, 316–17; peace and negotiations: 86, 100–1, 143–5, 161–3, 186–7, 210, 219, 227–8, 240, 283–6, 290–3, 299, 302, 314–17, 320, 334; and Russia: xx, 15–17, 22, 27–9, 84–5, 122, 139–40, 175, 292, 300, 314–16, 330; Wagram: 94–100, 111, 114–15; war aims: 1, 33–4, 86, 172, 293–5, 301, 321–2, 332–3; assassination attempt:

317; Austrian views of: 3–5, 7, 8–11, 15, 18–20, 29, 35, 37, 46, 50, 61, 75, 76–7, 86, 88, 90, 143, 166–8, 244, 253, 262, 289, 297–8, 305, 318, 324, 332

Nostitz-Reineck, FML Johann: 96, 98, 189, 195, 201, 206, 210, 225, 226

Oudinot, GD → Marshal Nicholas Charles: 31, 32, 44, 49, 53, 87, 96–9, 104, 111, 112–15, 120, 125, 140, 142, 146, 147, 171, 178, 229–30, 233–4, 239, 254, 257, 272–3, 290, 326

Pelet, Captain → Chef de Bataillon Jean-Jacques: 219, 261, 292

Pergen mission: 86, 100

Piré, GB Hippolyte Comte de: 214, 217, 231, 245, 246, 249, 297

Poland (Duchy of Warsaw) and Polish troops: xx, 3, 9, 18, 20, 24, 26–7, 32, 44, 45, 65, 73, 81, 83–5, 90, 92, 122, 140, 175–6, 287, 313–14, 316, 323, 330

Pressburg, Treaty of (1805): 2, 20, 82, 89, 294, 333

Preysing, GM Maximilian Graf von: 156, 189, 200–1, 203

Prochaska, GM → FML Johann von: 62, 78, 189, 192, 195, 201–4

Prussia: 2–3, 6, 18, 20, 22, 24, 26, 27, 89, 91, 145, 320

Pully, GD Charles Joseph: 96, 98, 104, 111, 139

Raab, Battle of: 81–2

Radetzky, GM → FML Josef von: 109, 111, 120–1, 134, 146, 155–7, 160, 235, 238; as chief of staff: 319–20; post-war analyses: 23, 46, 289, 322

Rainer, FZM Archduke: 86

Rapp, GD Jean: 317

Reuss-Plauen, FML → FZM Heinrich XV Fürst zu: 88, 95, 130, 164–5, 177, 208, 210–19, 226–9, 244–53, 255, 261–70, 273–9, 308, 329

Reynier, GD Jean: 96, 98, 113, 147, 149, 309

Rosenberg-Orsini, FML Franz Seraph Fürst von: 25, 45, 88, 103, 119, 138, 141, 155–60, 172, 209, 226, 232, 235, 236–9, 296, 304; blamed for poor performance: 106, 135, 163, 167, 299; confusion concerning retreat orders: 108–9, 120–2, 124, 133–7, 143, 146, 155, 158, 163, 169, 177, 325

Rouyer, GD Marie François: 44

Royal Marines (British): 174, 312

Royal Navy (British): 30, 174, 176

Rusca, GD Jean: 93, 147, 174, 309, 315

Russia: xx, 2–3, 5, 6, 15, 17, 22, 28, 29, 33, 64, 74, 84, 176, 292, 316, 319, 322–3; Russian corps in Galicia: 24, 26–7, 31, 36, 72, 75, 83–5, 90–3, 109, 175, 287, 301, 314, 315, 330–1; Russian officers with Napoleon: 139–40, 268

Salis-Zizers, Major Rudolph Graf: 216–17, 248, 268–9

St Sulpice, GD Raymond Gaspard de Bonardi, Comte de: 57, 98, 103, 111, 117, 127, 129, 151, 171, 245, 246, 257

Saxon troops (incl. 9th Corps): 32, 44, 52, 87, 95, 96–9, 103, 104, 111, 125, 147, 149, 309, 313

Schill, Major Ferdinand von, raid: 82, 312

Schneller, GM Andreas von: 164, 177, 179–80, 185–95, 203, 204

Schöngrabern, Engagement at (10 July): 211–19

Schustekh, FML Emanuel Freiherr von: 93, 95, 122, 131, 146, 147, 150, 152, 169, 177–9, 211, 239, 296, 310, 315, 325

Schwarzenberg, FML → GdK Carl Fürst zu: 188, 211, 226, 259–60, 323

Somariva, FML Hannibal Graf: 88, 93, 95, 131, 178, 296, 310, 315

Spain/Iberian Peninsula: 6–11, 15, 17–20, 25, 27–30, 32, 33, 47–8, 53, 56, 63, 76, 293, 320, 322, 324

Staatz/Neuburg, Engagement at (9 July): 155–8

Stabenrath, GB Jean Marie Eléonor Léopold de: 56, 264–5, 267, 279

Stadion, Friedrich Lothar von: 20–1, 33, 45, 75, 77, 78

Stadion, Johann Philipp Graf: 3, 15, 24–6, 45, 73, 81, 82, 85–6, 319, 331; search for allies: 17–18, 22, 91–3, 173, 311, 330; peace negotiations: 143–5, 165–8, 285–7, 295; relations with Charles: 5, 9, 11–13, 62, 75–8, 88–9, 166–7, 211–12, 297, 305, 318; relations with Franz: 13–14, 18, 90, 165–6, 320; views of Napoleon: 4, 7–10, 19, 29; war aims: 20–2, 23, 33, 34

Stockerau, Engagement at (8 July): 125–9

Stoichevich, GM → FML Andreas von: 45

Stutterheim, GM Carl von: 73

Stutterheim, GM Joseph von, mission to Russians: 91–2

Tilsit, Treaties of (1807): 2–3, 5–6, 286

Tyrol: 2, 22, 24, 45, 59–60, 72, 73, 81–2, 85, 87, 89, 93, 176, 179, 286–7, 300–1, 306, 310, 313, 315, 321

Vandamme, GD Dominique René: 44, 87, 95, 113, 147–8, 179, 309

Vorarlberg: 2, 72, 176, 287, 306, 313

Wagram, Battle of: xxi, xx, xxiv, 1, 39, 42, 52, 58–60, 63–5, 66, 75, 77, 78, 82, 87, 88, 94–100, 111, 121, 122, 124, 125, 128, 133, 139–40, 144, 147, 149, 162, 168, 170–2, 174–5, 188, 218, 221, 247, 256, 266, 270, 274, 276, 278, 281, 286, 291, 293, 297, 300, 305, 308, 324–6, 330, 334; Napoleon's desire to equate with Austerlitz: 64, 100, 112, 294, 327, 333; town: 51, 93, 103, 114

Walcheren expedition: 174, 311, 312

Waldstein, Graf Ferdinand Ernst von: 91, 174

Warsaw, Duchy of: *see* Poland

Weißenwolff, GM → FML Nikolaus Ungnad Graf: 100–1, 162–3, 187, 219

Westphalian troops (10th Corps): 32, 44, 52, 93, 311, 312, 315

Wilgenheim, Oberstleutnant → Oberst Ludwig: 153–4, 212, 217, 308–10

Wimpffen, Oberst → GM Maximilian Freiherr von: 62, 78, 84, 92, 101, 130, 188, 283–6, 289–90, 293, 295, 308, 313, 319, 333

Wrede, GL Carl Philipp Freiherr von: 60, 96, 98, 103, 310

Württemberg troops: 32, 44, 51–2, 87, 95, 123, 147, 169, 179, 222, 309, 310

Gazetteer

Numbers indicate the maps on which the various places appear. In some cases, the map only includes an arrow pointing towards the location, not the location itself. Modern/alternate names are given here in parentheses.

Abensberg: 2
Aderklaa: 5, 6, 7
Adige River (Etsch): 2, 3, 4, 22
Altschallersdorf (Starý Šaldorf): 14, 15, 16, 19
Amberg: 2, 21
Antwerp: 2, 21
Asparn an der Zaya: 8
Aspern and Essling: 3, 5, 6, 7, 8
Auersthal: 5, 6, 7
Austerlitz (Slavkov u Brna): 2, 18

Bamberg: 22
Baumersdorf (Parbasdorf): 5, 6
Bayreuth: 1, 2, 3, 4, 22
Berlin: 1, 2, 3, 4, 22
Bisamberg: 5, 6, 7, 8
Bockfließ: 5, 6, 7, 8, 10
Bohemia: 1, 2, 3, 4, 5, 6, 20, 22
Brenditz (Přímětice): 8, 13, 14, 15, 16, 19
Bruck an der Leitha: 10
Bruck an der Mur: 22

Brünn (Brno): 1, 2, 3, 4, 7, 8, 10, 13, 18, 20, 22
Brunswick (Braunschweig): 2, 3, 4, 21, 22
Budweis (Budejovice): 20
Burghausen: 1, 3
Burgholz (Purkrábka): 13, 14, 15, 16, 19

Carinthia: 22
Carniola: 22
Croatia: 22
Cuxhaven: 21
Czaslau (Čáslav): 1, 20

Dalmatia: 2
Danube (Donau, Duna) River: 1, 2, 3, 4, 5, 6, 7, 8, 10, 20
Danzig (Gdansk): 1
Donau-Graben: 7
Donauwörth: 2, 3
Dörflitz: 13, 14
Drasenhofen: 8, 18
Dresden: 1, 2, 3, 4, 22
Dunajec River: 1, 4, 22
Dürnholz (Drnholec): 8, 18
Dürnkrut: 7, 8, 10, 20

Ebelsberg: 1, 3, 20
Ebersdorf/Vienna: see Kaiser Ebersdorf

Gazetteer

Edelspitz (Sedlošovice): 13, 14, 15, 16, 19
Eggmühl: 2
Ehrendorf (now Ernsdorf): 12
Eichenbrunn: 8, 12
Eisgrub: 18
Elbe River: 1, 2, 3, 4, 21
Emmersdorf: 20
Enzersdorf: *see* Groß-Enzersdorf
Enzersdorf im Thale: 8
Enzersfeld: 5, 6, 7
Erdberg (Hrádek): 8, 10, 13
Erfurt: 1, 4, 21, 22
Ernstbrunn: 8, 10
Ernstbrunner Wald: 8
Essling: 5, 6, 7

Feldsberg (Valtice): 8, 18, 20
Fischamend: 10, 20
Fiume (Rijeka): 2, 3, 4, 22
Floridsdorf (am Spitz): 5, 6, 7
Frain (Vranov ad Dyjí): 22
Frainersdorf (Vranovská Ves): 13, 20

Galicia: 1, 2, 3, 4, 22
Gaweinstal (Gaunersdorf in 1809): 7, 8
Gerasdorf: 5, 6, 7
Gettsdorf: 8, 11, 20
Gföhl: 20
Gnadendorf: 8, 12
Göding (Hodinin): 8, 10, 20
Göllersbach: 8, 9, 11
Göllersdorf: 8, 10, 11, 20
Göpfitz: 20
Göttweig: 10, 20
Grafenwörth: 20
Granitzbach (Gránický potok): 13, 14, 15, 16, 19
Graz: 2, 3, 4, 22
Grein: 20
Groß-Engersdorf: 5, 6
Groß-Enzersdorf: 5, 6

Groß-Schweinbarth: 7, 8
Großmugl: 8
Groß-Niemschitz (Velké Němčice): 18
Großrußbach: 7, 8
Großstelzendorf: 8, 11
Grund: 8, 17
Guntersdorf: 8, 10, 17, 20

Hadres: 8
Halberstadt: 21
Hanover (Hannover): 2, 3, 4, 21, 22
Harmannsdorf: 7
Hatzenbach: 8, 9
Haugsdorf: 8
Hausen: 2
Herzogbirnbaum: 8
Hochleithen (Hoheleithen in 1809): 7, 8
Hödnitz (Hodonice): 8, 13
Hollabrunn (Ober-Hollabrunn in 1809): 8, 10, 11, 17, 20
Hörersdorf: 8, 12
Horn: 10, 20

Iglau (Jihlava): 1, 2, 10, 13, 14, 15, 16, 20
Immendorf: 8, 17
Inn River: 1, 2, 3, 4, 22
Innsbruck: 2, 3
Irritz (Jiřice u Miroslavi): 18
Isar River: 2, 4, 22
Istria: 2, 3, 22

Jaispitz (Jevišovice): 13
Jedlersdorf: 5, 6, 7, 12
Jedlersee: 5, 6, 7
Jesuitenhof: 14, 15, 16, 19
Jetzlsdorf: 8, 10, 12, 13, 14, 17
Joslowitz (Jaroslavice): 8, 13

Kaiser Ebersdorf: 10
Kallendorf (Chvalovice): 8, 13
Kammersdorf: 8

Klagenfurt: 3, 4, 22
Klein-Tajax (Dyjákovičky): 8, 13
Klein-Tesswitz (Dobšice): 10, 13, 14, 15, 16, 19
Klosterbruck (Louka): 14, 15, 16, 19
Komorn (Komárom): 1, 2, 4, 22
Königsbrunn: 5, 6, 7
Korneuburg: 7, 8, 10
Krakow: 1, 2, 3, 4, 18, 20, 22
Krems: 1, 8, 10, 20
Kreuzenstein Heights: 7, 8
Kühberg (Kraví Hora): 14, 15, 16, 19
Kukrowitz (Kuchařovice): 8, 13, 14, 15, 16, 19
Kukrowitzerbach (Dobšický potok): 14, 15, 16, 19

Laa an der Thaya: 8, 10, 12, 13, 14, 18, 19, 20
Lake Balaton: 4, 22
Landshut: 2
Langenzersdorf: 7, 8
Lech River: 2, 3, 4
Leipzig: 21
Leitomischl (Litomyšl): 20
Leitzersdorf: 8, 9
Leoben: 22
Leopoldau: 5, 6, 7
Leska: 13, 14, 15, 16, 19
Linz: 1, 3, 20
Lobau: 5, 6, 7

Mährisch-Budwitz (Moravské Budějovice): 20
Mailberg: 8
Maissau: 8, 10, 20
March (Morava, Morva) River: 1, 10, 20
Marchfeld: 5, 6
Marchegg: 10, 20
Mariahilf (Nová Ves): 8, 18
Markgrafneusiedl: 5, 6

Medritz (Modřice): 18
Melk: 20
Menitz (Měnín): 18
Mistelbach: 8, 10, 20
Moravia: 1, 2, 3, 4, 20, 22
Mramotitz (Mramotice): 13, 14, 15, 16, 19
Mühlfraun (Milfron, now Dyje): 13, 14, 15, 16, 19
Munich: 1, 2, 3, 4, 22
Muschau (Musov): 8, 10, 18

Naschetitz (Načeratice): 8, 13, 14, 15, 16, 19
Neuaigen: 8, 20
Neudorf: 8, 12, 18
Neuschallersdorf (Nový Šaldorf): 13, 14, 15, 16, 19
Niederfellabrunn: 8
Niederrußbach: 8, 9
Nikolsburg (Mikulov): 8, 10, 12, 18, 20
Nuremberg: 1, 2, 3, 4, 22

Oberfellabrunn: 8, 11
Obermallebarn: 8
Oberrohrbach: 7, 8
Ober-Siebenbrunn: 5, 6
Oberstinkenbrunn: 8, 17
Oblass (Oblekovice): 13, 14, 15, 16, 19
Ödenburg (Sopron): 1, 10
Oelper: 21
Olmütz (Olomouc): 1, 2, 3, 4, 18, 20, 22

Passau: 1, 2, 3, 4
Pelzwald (Palice): 14, 15, 16, 19
Pirawarth: 7, 8
Plenkowitzer Mühlbach (Plenkovický potok): 13, 14, 15, 16, 19
Pohrlitz (Pohořelice): 18
Pöltenberg (Hradiště): 13, 14, 15, 16, 19
Porrau: 8, 11

Gazetteer

Poysdorf: 8, 10, 12, 18
Prague (Praha): 1, 2, 3, 4, 20, 22
Prerau (Nový Přerov): 8, 18
Pressburg (Bratislava): 1, 2, 3, 4, 20, 22
Pulkau (town): 20
Pulkau Stream: 8, 10
Pumlitz (Bohumilice): 13, 14, 15, 16, 19

Raab (Györ): 1, 2, 3, 4, 22
Raasdorf: 5, 6, 7
Regensburg: 1, 2, 3, 4, 22
Retz: 13, 20
Rother Hof (Zuckerhandlhof): 14, 15, 16, 19
Rückersdorf: 7, 8
Ruhhof: 8, 12, 18
Rußbach: 5, 6, 7, 8

Sachsenburg: 4, 22
Sacile: 2
Salzburg: 1, 22
Scheletau (Želetava): 1, 22
Schloß Sinzendorf: 8
Schönau (Šanov): 8, 10
Schönborn/Schloß Schönborn: 8
Schönbrunn: 10
Schöngrabern: 8, 10, 17, 20
Schrems: 20
Schrick: 8, 10
Seebarn: 7
Seefeld: 8, 12
Semmering Pass: 10, 22
Sexenberg (Načeratický kopec): 14
Siebenhirten: 8, 12
Sierndorf: 8, 9
Sitzendorf: 8, 11, 20
Spielberg: 18
Staatz: 10, 12, 18
Stadtler Arm: 5, 6
Stammersdorf: 5, 6, 7
Stampfen: 10, 20, 22

Steinamanger (Szombathely): 22
Stetten: 7, 8
Stockerau: 7, 8, 9, 10, 20
Stralsund: 21
Straubing: 1, 2
Strebersdorf: 5, 6, 7
Süßenbrunn: 5, 6, 7
Suttenbrunn: 17
Szent Gróth (Zalaszentgrót): 4, 22

Tabor Bridge: 7
Teschen (Ces Tesin): 1
Tasswitz (Tasovice): 8, 13
Teugn: 2
Thaya (Dyje) River: 1, 8, 10, 12, 13, 14, 15, 16 18, 19, 20
Tief Maispitz (Hluboké Mašůvky): 13, 14, 15, 16, 19
Totis (Tata): 1
Tracht (Strachotín): 8, 18
Traun River: 1
Trebitsch (Třebíč): 20
Tresdorf: 7
Trieste: 2, 3, 4, 22
Tyrol: 2, 3, 4, 22

Ulm: 3, 4
Ungarisch Altenburg (Magyarovar): 10
Untergrub: 8
Unter-Wisternitz (Dolni Vestonice): 8, 10, 18
Urban (Vrbovec): 8, 13, 14, 15, 16, 19

Vienna: 1, 2, 3, 4, 7, 10, 20, 22
Villach: 4, 22
Vistula River: 1, 2, 3, 4, 22
Vorarlberg: 2, 3, 4, 22

Wagram: 2, 4, 5, 6, 7, 8, 10
Walcheren: 2, 21
Waltrowitz (Valtrovice): 8, 13

Warsaw: 1, 2, 3, 4, 22
Weser River: 21
Weistätten (Pasohlávky): 8, 18
Weyerburg: 8
Wildendürnbach: 8, 12, 18
Wilfersdorf: 8, 10
Winau (Únanov): 8, 13, 14, 15, 16, 19
Windpassinger Graben: 17
Wisloka River: 1, 4, 22
Wolframitzkirchen (Olbramkostel): 13, 14, 15, 16, 19, 20

Wolkersdorf: 7, 8, 10

Zlabern: 12
Zlabings (Slavonice): 20
Znaim (Znojmo): 1, 2, 3, 4, 8, 10, 12, 13, 14, 15, 16, 18, 19, 20, 22
Zuckerhandl (Suchohrdly): 8, 13, 14, 15, 16, 19
Zwettl: 20